CITY ON THE OCEAN SEA
LA ROCHELLE, 1530-1650

# STUDIES
# IN MEDIEVAL AND
# REFORMATION THOUGHT

EDITED BY

HEIKO A. OBERMAN, Tucson, Arizona

VOLUME LXIV

KEVIN C. ROBBINS

CITY ON THE OCEAN SEA
LA ROCHELLE, 1530-1650

# CITY ON THE OCEAN SEA
# LA ROCHELLE, 1530-1650

## URBAN SOCIETY, RELIGION, AND POLITICS ON
## THE FRENCH ATLANTIC FRONTIER

BY

KEVIN C. ROBBINS

TUTA SUB AEGIDE PALLAS · 1683 ·

## BRILL
### LEIDEN · NEW YORK · KÖLN
1997

This book is printed on acid-free paper.

**Library of Congress Cataloging-in-Publication Data**

Robbins, Kevin C.
   City on the ocean sea  :  La Rochelle, 1530–1650  :  urban society,
religion, and politics on the French Atlantic frontier  /  Kevin C.
Robbins.
        p.   cm. — (Studies in medieval and Reformation thought, ISSN
0585-6914  ; v. 64)
   Includes bibliographical references and index.
   ISBN 9004108807 (cloth : alk. paper)
   1. La Rochelle (France)—History.   2. Religion and politics–
–France—La Rochelle.   3. France—Politics and government—16th
century—Religious aspects.   4. Sea stories.   5. Reformation–
–France—La Rochelle.   6. Anti-Catholicism—France—La Rochelle.
I. Title.   II. Series.
DC801.L43R63    1997
944'.64—dc21                                     97–24830
                                                      CIP

**Die Deutsche Bibliothek - CIP-Einheitsaufnahme**

**Robbins, Kevin C.:**
City on the ocean sea  :  La Rochelle, 1530–1650  :  urban society,
religion, and politics on the French atlantic frontier  /  by Kevin C.
Robbins. – Leiden ; New York ; Köln : Brill, 1997
  (Studies in medieval and reformation thought ; Vol. 64)
  ISBN 90–04–10880–7

ISSN   0585-6914
ISBN   90 04 10880 7

PRINTED IN THE NETHERLANDS

*This book is respectfully dedicated to the
teachers with whom I began to learn the
history of France:*

*Raymond Kierstead
Robert Forster
Orest Ranum*

# CONTENTS

# ACKNOWLEDGMENTS

The interpretation of La Rochelle's history offered here is grounded upon a mass of local archival material I could only consult through the generosity of patrons whose support enabled me to live and work in France for long periods of time. I would like to thank my country's Department of Education for awarding me a Jacob Javits Fellowship that paid for my graduate education and for extended research travel abroad. Through a Chateaubriand Fellowship, the French Ministry of Culture gave me a living in La Rochelle for which I will always be grateful. Subsequent grants from the Office of Faculty Development at Indiana University Purdue University Indianapolis, from the Indiana University Center on Philanthropy, from the West European Studies program at Indiana University Bloomington, and from the Office of Overseas Study in Bloomington allowed me to return to France at will. Funds provided by the Department of History at IUPUI also afforded me access to national and international conferences where I have shared my research work widely and improved it through many peer critiques. I thank my colleagues in these organizations for their liberating help and encouragement.

In France I am deeply obligated to a host of scholars, archivists, librarians, reading room attendants, book dealers, and friends. My special thanks are due to Mlle. Françoise Giteau, formerly the Chief Conservator of the Departmental Archives of the Charente-Maritime, and to her very able successor, Mon. Pascal Even. With the aid of their kindly staff, they enabled me to read and copy a vast quantity of documents forming the gist of this book. At La Rochelle's Bibliothèque Municipale, the Bibliothèquaires Adjoints, Mlle. Anne Rocher and Mlle. Pascalle Vignau, repeatedly aided me in gaining access to rare manuscripts and books. Their kindness and devotion to their *métier* made my work in their company a delight.

While in La Rochelle, I benefitted from the assistance of Mon. Marcel Delafosse, the dean of local historians, who directed me toward caches of archival material I might never have found on my own. I thank him for his expert assistance. Father Bernard Coutant always shared with me his thorough knowledge of La Rochelle's architectural history and happily guided me through the intricate vocabularies of its craftsmen. Mon. and Mme. Pierre Hubert were the kindest of landlords in La Rochelle. These thanks are poor recompense for their exemplary hospitality.

The making of this book was greatly aided by several of my professional colleagues. I must thank first Mlle. Pauline Arseneault, *Chargé de Recherche* with the Canadian Embassy in Paris, for her meticulous assistance in locating and microfilming testamentary documents in La Rochelle. Mr. William Stuckey, Director of the Computer Aided Research Laboratory at IUPUI cheerfully assisted me in creating computerized databases for the systematic analysis of Protestant and Catholic testaments from La Rochelle. Mr. Kevin Mickey, Head Cartographer in IUPUI's Laboratory for Applied Spatial Information Research, created the maps and graphs illustrating my conception of La Rochelle's history.

I owe more debts of gratitude to my colleagues who benefited me with their critiques of this text and its earlier drafts. In particular, I would like to thank Professor James Farr for reading through the entire work and saving me from numerous errors and passages of bad prose. Professor William Beik also deserves my thanks for improvements he suggested in various parts of this manuscript. My thanks also to Professors James Farr and John Contreni, editors of *French Historical Studies*, and to Professor Richard Bonney, editor of *French History*, for their permission to reprint here portions of text which previously appeared in articles published in the journals under their direction. Professor Heiko Oberman, senior editor for the series *Studies in Medieval and Reformation Thought*, has, from the outset, been a most gracious and encouraging collaborator. May he find here my sincere thanks for his assistance in making this book. The anonymous reviewers retained by Professor Oberman for the evaluation of my draft text also made excellent and precise recommendations for its improvement. I thank them also for their conscientious and helpful review of my work. Mr. Theo Joppe, Acquisitions Editor at Royal Brill Publishers in Leiden, greatly facilitated the production of this volume. I thank him for his courtesy.

I wish also to acknowledge here the research assistance my wife, Melissa S. Brown, has provided to me throughout the composition of this text, especially her aid in patiently transcribing by hand fragile documents from La Rochelle. Beyond this, words can not sound my gratitude for her magnanimous help while La Rochelle has been one of the poles of our life together.   Finally, I would like to thank Professors Raymond Kierstead, Robert Forster, and Orest Ranum for their kind and insightful direction of my studies in the French past. Through their masterly writings, teaching, friendship, and joie de vivre they have imparted to me their regard for history as a *science humaine*. This gift has long sustained and continues to inspire my own work. For that, this book is theirs. Its remaining errors are mine alone.

# LIST OF FIGURES

# LIST OF TABLES

# ABBREVIATIONS

## Archives

| | |
|---|---|
| AAE | Archives des Affaires Etrangères, Quai d'Orsay, Paris. |
| ADCM | Archives Départementales de la Charente-Maritime, La Rochelle. |
| AMLR | Archives Municipales de La Rochelle. |
| AN | Archives Nationales, Paris. |
| BMLR | Bibliothèque Municipale de La Rochelle. |
| BN | Bibliothèque Nationale, Paris. |
| BPG | Bibliothèque Publique, Geneva. |

## Printed Works

| | |
|---|---|
| AHSA | *Archives historiques de la Saintonge et Aunis.* |
| BHL | *Bulletin historique et litteraire.* |
| BSHPF | *Bulletin de la Société de l'histoire du protestantisme français.* |

# INTRODUCTION

Between 1530 and 1650 no city in France led a more tumultuous life than La Rochelle. However, few modern historians have examined this history in detail. At the outset of this period, François I, distrustful of French municipal liberties, tried to abrogate the city's ancient civic constitution by destroying its old town council. The Rochelais tenaciously opposed this project and, in a feat unmatched elsewhere, ultimately succeeded in reestablishing their historic, potent communal institutions at full strength. At a time when most French cities were losing their capacity of self-governance, La Rochelle regained and reinforced this important political advantage. The following chapters examine how the Rochelais achieved this coup and the consequences of their stalwart devotion to civic freedoms.

Guarded by privileged agencies of communal police, La Rochelle developed into one of the freest, self-governing towns of the kingdom, a marine commune in which ambitious residents long combated one another for the control of powerful civic offices. Possessed of massive fortifications, a heavily armed citizen militia, and a huge arsenal of deadly artillery, La Rochelle not only deterred coastal aggression by France's inveterate enemies of the era, Spain and England, but also mustered sufficient raw force to challenge French monarchs successfully when their policies of statecraft abridged the prerogatives townspeople took for granted. This book will examine closely the imbricated political struggles of La Rochelle's early modern history.

In the mid-sixteenth century, a majority of La Rochelle's citizens joined the Calvinist Reformation, turning their town into a center of political and religious dissent. In an epic siege battle, the future Henry III tried to annihilate the rebel city in 1573. Rochelais defenders expertly parried hundreds of assaults from the largest royal army ever marshaled during the French Wars of Religion and won for themselves not only a favorable armistice, but also new civic privileges reinforcing the city's independence. Measuring the impact of this triumph on the mentalities and subsequent politics of the Rochelais is another of my objectives.

In a municipal political environment largely free of royal interference and charged by growing religious tensions between local Protestants, leading citizens from all social strata violently contended for the control of influential civic offices. The formation of a tight ruling oligarchy comprised of wealthy Calvinist merchants exacerbated the complaints of unenfranchised Protestant members of the bourgeoisie. In 1614, these dissidents, with the help of La Rochelle's bellicose citizen militia and sympathetic artisans, perpetrated a rare and highly successful bourgeois urban rebellion, completely shattering the old civic oligarchy and sharply curtailing the public authority of Calvinist pastors closely allied to the old regime. Over several chapters, I will examine the social origins and political repercussions of this unknown uprising, showing how the interparochial clientage networks of middle ranking merchants contributed to its success. This investigation adds to our knowledge about the varieties of successful insurrectionary behavior in early modern France.

During the next fifteen years (1614-1628), rochelais civic institutions progressively fell under the control of elected middle class citizens and workingmen firmly committed to communal independence and congregational direction of church affairs. This cadre of uncompromising civic leaders led La Rochelle into ever more violent confrontations with a Bourbon monarchy determined to police the French west country more effectively. In 1628, this opposition led to a second catastrophic siege of La Rochelle during which disciplined royal forces under the command of Cardinal Richelieu starved the Rochelais into submission. At least 15,000 trapped citizens died.

In the aftermath of this hecatomb, royal agents with the aid of local Catholics took over rochelais civic institutions and forcibly converted them into agencies of the Counter-Reformation. This transformation radically altered the ethos and operation of communal government. Working in an environment free from the meddling of intermediary parliamentary institutions, Louis XIII could endow La Rochelle with the regulatory bodies most in keeping with his own vision of proper royal statecraft. The crown here favored very antique solutions to the pressing problems of civic administration. The logistics of implementing these policies forms another primary subject of my analysis, enlarging current understandings of relations between city, church, and state in early modern France.

Despite the drama and importance of these interconnected events, their details and the lives of the citizens who made them happen remain almost entirely unknown. The aim of this book is to rectify this neglectful situation by providing a comprehensive social history of the urban community addressing the contemporary political and religious upheavals it experienced. Primary archival sources from several rich depots in La Rochelle and Paris anchor this analysis amidst the daily realities of rochelais life.

This history proceeds from the ground up. Despite pioneering French efforts in the field of environmental history dating back to Montesquieu, no previous chroniclers of La Rochelle, ancient or modern, have investigated how the city's exceptional location on a dangerously exposed littoral shaped the mentalities of residents and the polity they formed.

Sited directly on the sea, an element commonly terrifying to early modern Europeans including the Rochelais, La Rochelle sat on a poorly governed oceanic frontier surrounded by a swampy, malarial, and thickly forested back country. Townspeople considered the inhabitants of this hinterland to be savages whose aberrant behaviors displayed all the malevolent effects of a brutalizing environment. Punitive rochelais expeditionary forces ventured into this riparian wilderness to hunt down native pirates and to kill the more vicious terrestrial outlaws who continually gathered there. A rochelais obsession with the defense of civilizing urban institutions grew out of the citizenry's acute sense of isolation amid a hostile landscape. The effects of this frontier civic identity on early modern rochelais politics and diplomacy will be examined throughout this text.

Exposed to a gamut of ambient hazards, west country coastal residents, urban and rural, developed an elaborate spiritualism amalgamating cautionary folktales about sea monsters, protective magical charms of pagan derivation, and a practical, barely orthodox Christianity invoked to save believers from immediate, visible and invisible harms. Natives regarded all clergymen warily, considering them to be powerful, cunning magicians capable of some good and more evil. An enduring fear of clerics as saboteurs of male sexual potency gripped all strata of town and country society in the French west. Catholic churchmen scattered very thinly across this inhospitable landscape labored vainly to inculcate among the laity even the most rudimentary notions of theological Christianity.

The French Reformation easily took root among a populace little devoted to the exponents of Catholic dogma. However, after local onset of the *Réforme*, Calvinist ministers found their own authority increasingly compromised by a perdurable west country anticlericalism and further limited by town dwellers' strong congregationalist sympathies. The development of Protestantism in La Rochelle is marked by ever sharper and more violent confrontations between these antagonists. My history of La Rochelle, for the first time, examines these battles in detail, bringing into clearer light the internal sociopolitical dynamics of a French Protestant municipality. A prosopography of the rochelais pastorate complements this investigation, showing not only how ministers rapidly assimilated themselves into the highest, most exclusive ranks of urban society, but also how the training and predication of local clerics increasingly diverged from Genevan models of Calvinist indoctrination. Sources in La Rochelle reveal much about relations between clergy and laity in a dissenting town, a subject still infrequently addressed in social histories of the Reformation.

To track these religious contests deep within rochelais society, I rely on the voluminous, surviving original vital statistics of the city's Protestant community, civic legal records, and a multivariate database of information gleaned from over 1,000 wills redacted by Protestants and Catholics residing in the city between 1550 and 1650. This database, unique in the annals of rochelais history, records socioeconomic factors defining a testator's status and the amounts and beneficiaries of all posthumous charitable gifts made by testators. Analysis of this information over time allows one to gauge the fidelity of ordinary benefactors toward fundamental church teachings about philanthropy and the degree to which philanthropists from differing confessions and social strata financially supported a variety of church-related institutions.

Individually and in aggregate, these documents reveal progressive social fragmentation within La Rochelle's Protestant churches, broad public irreverence toward Calvinist disciplinary bodies, much lower rates of charitable giving among rochelais Protestants than are to be found in other French Reformed communities of the era, and a growing unwillingness among Protestant townspeople to offer local ministers material support of any kind through testamentary gifts. From these perspectives, La Rochelle's Calvinist community, long regarded as a well-disciplined, doctrinally homogeneous urban church, appears riven by social, economic, and political tensions, cleavages ultimately fatal to the city's independence and detrimental to the alliance of social forces upon which the security of French Protestantism depended. This history of La Rochelle works, in part, to offer one localized explanation of what may be termed the failure of the French Reformation.

Girded by thick fortifications, La Rochelle was a compact town marked by extremely high intramural population densities. The topography and sociology of rochelais neighborhoods warrant and receive special attention in this history of the place. They formed essential contexts for the political and religious battles urban residents joined. I am particularly intrigued by the intra- and interparochial sociabilities and clientage networks developed over time by dissident members of La Rochelle's bourgeoisie. By mapping these human relations in urban space, I have tried to show how they modulated popular protest movements directed against civic and religious authorities. The built environment of the city is here construed as a vital actor literally and figuratively shaping its combative history.

Intricate webs of family connections bound together rochelais political actors, undergirding the successive regimes of early modern communal government they directed. Ties of real and fictive kinship persistently informed civic affairs, shaping the values and functions of municipal administration. At key points in this work, I reconstruct these alliances to show the enduring familial context of urban politics. From this analysis, it becomes clear that bourgeois families in La Rochelle also long acted as catalysts and moderators of violent protest movements directed against established civic and church officials. Over several chapters, I explore the various roles family members took in these cabals animating an urban polity.

An active port city, La Rochelle sheltered a flourishing community of merchants whose wealth became another bulwark of the city's privileges and political influence. Commercial successes afforded the citizenry a cosmopolitan culture through which rare commodities, alien publications, and novel opinions circulated with little interference. La Rochelle became an important center of the book trade in western France. Enterprising local printers turned out hundreds of publications appealing to the eclectic reading habits of highly literate town dwellers. A cadre of resident aliens, mainly bilingual Scotch Presbyterians, funneled bizarre, apocalyptic works from the Atlantic Reformations into the local print trade. Many of these books and pamphlets first disseminated in La Rochelle outraged city pastors and censorious higher officials of the French Reformed Church. These long-neglected texts and the now forgotten scandals they raised can recall for us the peculiar heterodoxy of La Rochelle's intellectual environment. Where appropriate in my analysis, I have attempted to restore these publications and the angry controversies they inspired to the flux of rochelais religious dissent and cultural politics.

As a singularly privileged municipality largely emancipated from the tutelage of parlements and ecclesiastical overlords, La Rochelle developed an array of powerful civic judicial institutions. I have employed the surviving daily records of these tribunals to evoke the litigious atmosphere of La Rochelle and the prevailing conceptions of justice held by its inhabitants. Both before and after the great siege of 1628, a municipal magistracy functioned in La Rochelle, first under Protestant domination and then under Catholic control. A comparison of the day-to-day case loads and legal opinions of these courts operating under different confessional regimes provides a novel urban institutional view of the Counter-Reformation's impact on the dispensation of civic justice broadly affecting the lives of all citizens. I have undertaken this task in order to demonstrate not only the legal ramifications of epochal religious changes, but also the great utility of massive civic judicial records for exposing the mechanics of urban power politics in early modern European towns especially subject to the Reformations.

La Rochelle became a demonstration site of the French Counter-Reformation. Innumerable books, pamphlets, mediocre epic poems, and songs celebrated Louis XIII's victory in 1628 over a rebellious Protestant town. Grand celebrations of this costly triumph still obscure the more mundane methods by which the formerly independent La Rochelle came under royal and Catholic control. This important segment of La Rochelle's existence, directly tangent to the development of monarchical statecraft in early seventeenth-century France, remains the least studied era in the city's history. The concluding chapters of this book, in part, rectify this imbalance of scholarly attention.

After 1628, sources in La Rochelle and Paris proliferate on the reincorporation of the city into the Bourbon realm and the Catholic faith. The archaic nature of this process, heavily dependent on the most traditional agencies of provincial government in post-feudal France, is striking to the modern observer. From a body of heretofore neglected documentation including the family archives of the dukes de Saint-Simon, the diaries of rochelais observers, the case books of Catholic municipal magistrates, and the registers of town notaries, I can provide the first comprehensive history of La Rochelle's pacification and Catholic confessionalization after 1628. As will become clear, while royal lieutenants attempted to remake the city from the ground up, permanently altering fundamental urban topographies of power, they also showed real solicitude for some ancient civic institutions deemed essential for effective projection of monarchical authority. This case study of kingly rule over a recalcitrant frontier town develops new evidence by which to measure, in less than absolute terms, the governing capacity of the French crown in early modern times.

To promote clarity of exposition in this narrative about deeply interconnected social, political, religious, and cultural affairs, the chapters that follow are arranged roughly in chronological order covering the period from 1530 to 1650. However, Chapters 3 and 7, based upon previously unexamined serial sources from rochelais archives, adopt broader temporal spans and thematic foci, moving backward and forward in time to evoke vital trends in the development of Protestant religious institutions and civic judicial bodies significantly influencing rochelais society and politics over decades. This expository structure, eschewing prolix simultaneous discussion of complex, intertwined political, religious, and cultural movements in every chapter, strikes me as more congruent with the primary sources grounding this study and more comprehensible to readers unfamiliar with La Rochelle's convoluted early modern history. Ample cross-references between discrete segments of my arguments should help the reader to retain a holistic view of the rochelais urban community over this period of its history. To the fullest extent permitted by the archives at my disposal, I have tried to reconstruct the most eventful era in the life of one important French town.

CHAPTER ONE

# A CITY IN A LANDSCAPE OF ISLANDS AND FRONTIERS

> Ville infortunée combien endures tu de traverses... que de maux as
> tu souffert parmy les tormentes? Il semble à voir que le ciel n'ait
> des foudres que pour te faire escrouler dans la terre, que la mer
> n'eust des tempestes que pour t'abimer et que la terre n'aye pas de
> force pour te soustenir. De tous cotez on te poursuit, le Ciel, l'Air,
> la Mer, la Terre ne cherchent que ta ruyne, tous les elements sont
> bandez contre toi, il n'y a rien qu'il ne te soit contraire.
>
> *Les meditations d'un avocat de La Rochelle,* 1622

Since the advent of the *Annales* school, many French historians,
particularly experts on rural societies, have shown special regard
for environmental history and for the impact of landforms and
crop cultivation methods on the mentalities of rural dwellers.
Attention to such subjects is much less common among the historians of early modern French towns. Judging by the brief attention they give to extramural landscapes, one might wrongly
conclude that the city was a world apart where its citizens' comportments were little influenced by external topographies of place
and power.

To the contrary, I would argue that most early modern French
urbanites, some as recent immigrants to town, many as rural land-
holders, others as frequent travellers, and those serving as suburban legal officials, possessed a strong, impressionable consciousness of extramural territory vital in shaping their experiences and
expectations of civic life. Recent histories of early modern French
coastal communities, urban and rural, have shown that littoral
inhabitants developed strong sensitivities and antipathies to their
physical surroundings.[1] Living on the continental margins in close

---

[1] See for examples, Alain Cabantous, *Le ciel dans la mer: Christianisme et civilisation maritime, XVIe-XIXe siècle,* (Paris, 1990), especially Chapter III, "L'Océan
redoutable;" *idem., Les côtes barbares: Pilleurs d'épaves et sociétés littorales en France,*
(Paris, 1993); and Alain Corbin, *The Lure of the Sea,* (Cambridge, Mass., 1994),
especially Chapter 1.

proximity to the sea, an unpredictable element even in the best of times, was no easy predicament.

The various segments of this chapter work to situate La Rochelle and its residents amidst the ecosystems, demographics, and economies of the French mid-Atlantic coast. My intent here is to show the impress of these factors on the mentalities and comportments of the Rochelais. This analysis seeks to uncover the distinctive folkways of urbanites and to ground these practices amidst their concentric regional and civic identities.

## 1. *Unsettling Neighbors*

Along the French Atlantic frontier, La Rochelle is the only major, ancient town to be sited directly on the sea. Its weathered ramparts overlook a shallow crescent bay churned out of the continental landmass by swift ocean currents passing around and between the adjacent islands of Ré and Oléron. Through narrow straits (*pertuis*), found only in this French maritime environment, the Atlantic runs upon a constantly changing shore. For centuries, the term "coastline" has poorly described the littoral north and south of La Rochelle. Here, miles of tidal marine marshes, salt pans fed by ocean sluices, shifting mud flats, creeping dunes, fresh water bogs, and polders laced with a bewildering array of drainage channels prevent any fixed demarcation between land and sea. Seven meandering rivers and hundreds of creeks irrigate this region, sustaining the Breton fens, the vast Poitevin marshes, and the trackless mires of the lower Charentais. La Rochelle has long sat at the center of an aqueous and forbidding landscape. (Figure 1 displays the early modern geography of the French mid-Atlantic coast around La Rochelle).

This is a stormy seaboard, vulnerable to fierce south-south-westerly gales from September to June. In the turbid estuaries of local rivers, sandbars rapidly coalesce and dissolve, compounding the hazards of coastal navigation. In the sixteenth and seventeenth centuries, many small ports of the region silted up and vanished; the sea raged in and submerged others. Royal surveyors continually ranked surrounding waters among the most treacherous in the kingdom. Early modern historians of the region described in cautionary detail the rocks, bights, shoals, and rapid currents so hazardous to local shipping.[2] But the dangers mariners of the old regime confronted here also included brazen Spanish, French, and English pirates as well as shore communities notorious for cold expertise in pillaging shipwrecks and their hapless survivors.[3] In the argot of local sailors, "to be on (or near) the coast" (être à la côte), meant a dangerous situation not a fortuitous landfall.[4]

Prolonged flooding is still common in the regional wetlands and can become calamitous when heavy spring rains coincide with rising, wind-driven tides. Even the warmest weather will not completely dry the ubiquitous marshes. Formerly, with summer's heat came clouds of disease-bearing mosquitoes. In September 1704, Michel Bégon, intendant for La Rochelle and its hinterland, noted "the very frequent double and triple fevers" afflicting the coastal population. Malaria was endemic to these shores until the 1880's.[5] Such ambient hazards resound in the local folklore, a bestiary of marauding sea monsters, storm creatures, sirens, delirious night stalkers, and water goblins poised to drown unwary children in muddy rivers, ponds, and wells.[6] The wildness of the environment around La Rochelle gained legendary status well before the

---

[2] Lancelot du Voisin de La Popelinière, *Histoire de France*, (Paris, 1581), 480-481. Having travelled extensively in the French west country, La Popelinière knew well the ubiquitous dangers there confronting natives and travellers on land and sea.

[3] Contemporaries identified the French mid-Atlantic coast and the waters around the Arvert peninsula in particular as extremely hazardous zones of navigation where wrecked ships and crews could expect no mercy from native pillagers who descended ruthlessly on every disaster scene. See Cabantous, *Les côtes barbares*, 30-45.

[4] For the various admonitory and pejorative meanings of this phrase in the lexicon of west country sailors see Paul Sébillot, *Légendes, croyances et superstitions de la mer*, 1, "La mer et le rivage," (Paris, 1886), 213. "To be all washed up" is one possible English equivalent of the meaning conveyed by the French locution.

[5] See the letter of Michel Bégon dated 14 September 1704 included in a selection of his administrative correspondence, AHSA, 44 (1935): 61-73. Bégon noted the "fièvres double tierce...très fréquentes" among residents of La Rochelle's *généralité* under his supervision. Later Imperial *préfets* and hardy travellers to the shore also remarked on the endemic diseases ravaging coastal and island populations of the region. These afflictions included severe fevers ("fièvres quartes"), pulmonary inflammations, pleurisy, and dysentery, see François Julien-Labruyère, *Paysans charentais. Histoire des campagnes d'Aunis, Saintonge et bas Angoumois*, 2 vols. (La Rochelle, 1982), 1: 184-185 and 2: 28-29.

[6] For a representative sample of local folktales from the provinces of Aunis and Saintonge around La Rochelle see Dominique Jacquin and Philippe Jacquin, *Récits et contes populaires d'Aunis et Saintonge*, (Paris, 1979).

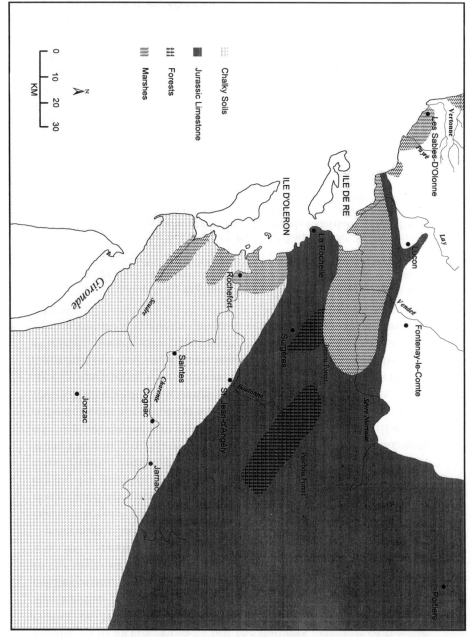

Figure 1. Early Modern Geography of the French Mid-Atlantic Coast

sixteenth century. A sweep of the horizon from atop the city's early modern battlements would have revealed the roiling waters of the Atlantic on one side and a damp, ominous, sparsely populated back country on the other. These proximate, disturbing environments profoundly shaped the urban society, politics, and culture of La Rochelle.

A land of numerous natural obstacles, the French mid-Atlantic littoral in the vicinity of La Rochelle has long supported many distinctive, small zones of human habitation. In his territorial survey of the seventeenth-century Catholic bishopric established in La Rochelle, Louis Pérouas delineated at least thirteen separate *pays* within the borders of this narrow coastal diocese covering only about 120 kilometers from north to south.[7]

During the early modern era, the islands of Ré and Oléron, although lying close inshore just off La Rochelle's harbor, sheltered populations with customs and privileges significantly different from mainland communities. Beginning in the late twelfth century, absentee island noblemen, anxious to populate their wind-swept fiefs, renounced exercise of many seigneurial prerogatives or converted them into simple cash payments to attract new settlers. Once emancipated from aristocratic justice, hunting rights, and tolls on commerce, the inhabitants of Ré capitalized on their island's strategic importance during prolonged Anglo-French military conflict to gain new freedoms of self-government and self-defense from contending, distant overlords. During the Hundred Years' War, islanders, led by a small elite of merchants and non-noble landowners, managed to obtain even greater communal and commercial freedoms from French and English monarchs competing to buy local allies.[8] This process culminated in 1408 when the French king Charles VI perpetually exempted the *Rétais* from all "aides, subsidies, and other *tailles* and subventions whatsoever."[9]

Writing two hundred ninety years later, the intendant Bégon noted that these unusual and enduring liberties entitled the île de Ré to the status of a foreign country ("pays étranger") and

[7] Louis Pérouas, *Le diocèse de La Rochelle de 1648 à 1724*, (Paris, 1964), 75-126.

[8] Privileges bestowed on the islanders by Charles VI are described in Louis-Etienne Arcère, *Histoire de la ville de La Rochelle et du pays d'Aunis*, 2 vols. (La Rochelle, 1756-57; reprint, Marseille, 1975), 1: 64-65.

[9] *Ibid.*, 64.

confirmed popular perceptions of its alien nature.[10] Sixteenth-
century native chroniclers of the west country, like La Popelinière,
described the islanders as "the most tumultuous, insolent, and
impassioned" inhabitants of the region. They were individuals by
nature "very turbulent" and long set free from the ordinary bonds
of deference and subordination to superiors.[11] They clung to
wind-scarred fields dubbed "the deserts of hell" by outsiders.
These detached westerners, most preoccupied with unremitting
labor in the salt pans and vineyards of local notables, brusquely
referred to the kingdom of France as "the continent."[12]

Although one mid-seventeenth-century intendant of Rochefort,
Colbert de Terron, classified the island of Oléron as "more
French" than Ré, mainlanders had long viewed the place as peculiar.[13] Endowed with privileges from the kings of France and
England dating back to the twelfth century, the inhabitants of
Oléron also gained perpetual exemption from royal *tailles*, special
levies, ballasting charges, and taxes on maritime commerce.[14] The
eighteenth-century royal cartographer, Claude Masse, based in La
Rochelle, was intrigued by the exceptional island women: robust,
stubborn, industrious, profane, superb swimmers, and skilled at
handling all kinds of boats. For Masse, these women, compared
to their worldlier, seafaring menfolk, possessed a nature "more
brutal" and more exemplary of the punishing insular environment.[15]

A nineteenth-century subprefect for the region of Oléron was
impressed by the islanders' dogged resourcefulness in utilizing
seaweed to enrich the sandy soils of their fields. Gathering the
nutritive kelp was an ancient and arduous task. Entire villages
would usually collect the precious fertilizer nocturnally at the
height of winter storms when violent tides ripped many plants

---

[10] A complete reprint of Michel Bégon's "Mémoire sur la généralité de La
Rochelle" (1698-99) appears in AHSA 2 (1875): 9-174. For Bégon's observations
of the île de Ré see 53-54.

[11] La Popelinière, *Histoire de France*, 425.

[12] Pierre Rézeau, *Dictionnaire du français régional de Poitou-Charentes et de Vendée*,
(Paris, 1990), s.v. "continent."

[13] For Colbert de Terron's opinions about the foreignness of west country
natives see Pérouas, *Le diocèse de La Rochelle*, 108 and n. 2.

[14] Arcère, *Histoire de La Rochelle*, 1: 83.

[15] Masse's observations about the female inhabitants of Oléron are quoted by
Julien-Labruyère, *Paysans charentais*, 1: 488-489.

from the seabed and scattered them on shore. The subprefect noted that these inclement expeditions caused "innumerable maladies" among the weathered croppers, significantly reducing their life spans. Night harvests regularly became even more dangerous when villagers from different island communities attacked one another with rakes, oars, and boat hooks in bloody disputes over the richest kelping grounds.[16]

Even local place names confirmed popular perceptions of Oléron's remove from civilization. For centuries terrestrial maps and navigational charts labeled the island's northwestern tip "the point at the end of the world" (*le point du but du monde*).[17] The islands and their human complement long stood apart; they were the close yet perturbing neighbors of diverse communities on the continental shore including the townspeople of La Rochelle. Rochelais bids for military supremacy over the irreverent islanders recurrently shaped the geopolitics of the region.

Along the coast near La Rochelle, adjacent broad river estuaries divide up the terrain, creating numerous isolated ecosystems and human settlements. East of Oléron and south of La Rochelle, the heavily wooded Arvert peninsula lies between the gaping mouths of the Gironde and Seudre rivers.[18] With dangerous waters on three sides, groundings and shipwrecks frequently occurred here in early modern times. On shore, thick stands of pine trees concealed a diversity of wildlife, including wolves, until the middle of the nineteenth century. Confronted by a landscape unsuitable for intensive farming, inhabitants of the peninsula in the sixteenth and seventeenth centuries struggled to gain livelihoods legally from lumbering, boat building, working salt pans, fishing, and crewing on merchant ships based in the larger ports

---

[16] In 1692, for example, armed confrontations between laborers seeking seaweed became so severe on the islands and coasts around La Rochelle that the admiralty court based in Marennes tried with little success to regulate these harvests through promulgation of ordinances assigning collection days and quotas to local villages, Julien-Labruyère, *Paysans charentais*, 1: 195-196 and n. 32.

[17] See, for example, the engraved map entitled "Carte du Pays d'Aulnis" (dated 1756) reproduced in Arcère, *Histoire de la ville de La Rochelle*, 1.

[18] Since medieval times natives in the provinces of Aunis and Saintonge have customarily referred to the Gironde as "the sea." In the mid-nineteenth century a national oceanographic expedition confronted by the Seudre's vast, convoluted estuary could not accurately classify it as riverine, defining it instead as an arm of the sea subject to the state's maritime regulations, see Julien-Labruyère, *Paysans charentais*, 1: 479-481.

of the region. Locals frequently resorted to piracy as a supplement to their meager incomes. According to the Reformed churchman and west country traveller, Théodore de Bèze (1519-1605), the strange population of the côte d'Arvert comprised the hardiest of seafarers, "nearly savages and lacking in any humanity."[19]

The Rochelais, desirous of protecting their own commercial shipping and pirate ventures, occasionally mounted punitive campaigns to hunt down bands of corsairs operating out of the Seudre estuary. In the running battles that ensued neither side gave quarter. During one such rochelais foray in 1619, city forces attacked a renegade vessel operating out of the Seudre channel. In a daylong firefight on land and sea, the pirate captain was shot dead and most of his crew captured. The captain's corpse was returned to La Rochelle, salted, and stored in the city's charity hospital while the entire gang was tried for a host of capital offenses by the local royal presidial court. After sentences of death had been duly meted out, the captain's lifeless, dehydrated body was broken on the wheel. Six of his crewmen died together under the hammer blows of rochelais executioners.

For centuries, shipowners in La Rochelle favored the peninsular town of La Tremblade as a recruitment zone for skilled captains and able seamen willing to risk the many dangers of transoceanic voyages. The toughness and irascibility of residents became proverbial up and down the coast. They earned this combative reputation as the inhabitants of a marshy and forested territory, doubly uninviting to outsiders and bleak in the estimation of infrequent visitors. At the end of the seventeenth century, dilapidated local churches had no bells to summon parishioners nor even crucifixes to impress upon them the most rudimentary symbols of Christianity. Religious indoctrination remained haphazard on the Arvert peninsula throughout the nineteenth century, with Easter communicants rarely amounting to more than 15% of the

---

[19] Théodore de Bèze, *Histoire ecclésiastique des églises réformées au royaume de France*, 3 vols., ed. G. Baum and E. Cunitz (Paris, 1883-1889), 1: 103. Calvin's chief lieutenant found the natives on the Arvert headlands to be "presque sauvages et sans aucune humanité." Bèze attributed their Protestant sympathies to the unorthodox preachings of defrocked priests who sought refuge in this malgoverned wilderness.

local population.[20] Low population densities, dispersed settlements, difficulties of inland travel, and absentee landlords of the first, second, and third estates, attenuated the development of effective governing institutions and contributed to the uncivilized reputation of this frontier throughout the sixteenth and seventeenth centuries.

Further up the coast, the twisting Charente river enters the sea through a broad mouth. Wetlands formed here are nearly contiguous with those plenished by the Seudre to the south. The intendant Bégon considered this muddy landscape to be among the most insalubrious of the entire region with a "malignant air" caused by prevailing sea breezes blowing over marshes flooded or stagnant much of the year.[21] The worn, stone *lanternes des morts*, tall funerary obelisks dominating the central squares and cemeteries of local villages, signaled the heavy human toll exacted by this punishing, diseased environment.[22]

Prior to the costly development of Rochefort as a royal naval arsenal in the latter seventeenth and eighteenth centuries, the scattered population of this area lived in small hamlets and villages situated atop isolated hillocks rising a mere eight to ten meters above the surrounding marshes. These terrestrial islands of population long remained detached from regional circuits of communication and police. The only local town, the old medieval salt port of Brouage, waged an ultimately losing battle against the silting up of its harbor and suffocated along with its commerce before the end of the seventeenth century. Consumers throughout Europe prized salt from the local pans for its purity. This lucrative trade enriched absentee landowners, above all merchants in regional centers like La Rochelle, whose stiff sharecropping agreements with salt harvesters (*sauniers*) kept many local laborers teetering on the brink of insolvency, starvation, and rebel-

---

[20] Julien-Labruyère, *Paysans charentais*, 2: 267. For the frequent condemnations of this region's deeply irreligious character voiced by mid-nineteenth-century clerics, see Judith Devlin, *The Superstitious Mind: French Peasants and the Supernatural in the Nineteenth Century*, (New Haven, 1987), 2-3.

[21] Bégon, "Mémoire sur la généralité," 49-50.

[22] On the history, architecture, and unique west country emplacement of *lanternes des morts* see Edmond-Réné Labande, ed., *Histoire du Poitou, du Limousin et des pays charentais: Vendée, Aunis, Saintonge, Angoumois*, (Toulouse, 1976), 171-173 and illustration XIII facing page 160.

lion.[23] Underemployment and indigence drove many of these rural inhabitants to crime which, when combined with immemorial local resistance to all royal efforts at taxing salt, gave the territory a notorious reputation for lawlessness especially troubling to the Rochelais.[24]

The marshes of the lower Charente estuary extend northward along the coast over a distance of sixteen kilometers, petering out against a slight rise of jurassic limestone. This crest of terra firma marks the southern boundary of La Rochelle's immediate hinterland (*banlieue*). The city and its environs occupy the western tip of a spur of calcareous earth extending seaward over one hundred kilometers from its origin in the rolling hills of Poitou. As it approaches the sea near La Rochelle, this finger of stony land narrows to a width of only twenty kilometers. The name "La Rochelle" (*Rupella* in Latin), meaning "little rock," derives from the town's location atop one of the few bits of solid ground anywhere in the vicinity.

In sharp contrast to adjacent marshes, the comparatively well drained soil of the thin, rocky plain will support intensive agriculture, particularly the cultivation of vines and, to a lesser extent, cereals. Since ancient times, the arable and passable terrains of this narrow corridor have enabled tenuous links to form between coastal communities, the continental interior, and the wider Atlantic world. A Gallo-Roman roadway traversed this strip of land, connecting the deeper provincial town of Poitiers to the sea. One

---

[23] Julien-Labruyère, *Paysans charentais*, 1: 76 and 2: 326, details the sharecropping agreements contributing to a proletarianization of agricultural laborers harvesting west country sea salt. According to him, these contracts and their rigid enforcement by salt pan owners in the courts of regional capitals greatly contributed to the formation of "un type original de civilisation d'agriculteurs-prolétaires de la mer" in close proximity to La Rochelle.

[24] Sixteenth-century pilgrims passing through the French west country on the route to St. Jean de Compostella understood the notorious insecurity of the region. To gird themselves for this dangerous passage they sang together:

Quand nous fûmes en Saintonge
Le meilleur pays du monde
Mais il y a de méchantes gens
Ils s'en vont sur les passages
Pour nous voler notre argent.

These ancient lyrics evoke the ambient hazards of the countryside around La Rochelle. For further documentation of these dangers see Jean-Noel Luc, ed., *La Charente-Maritime, L'Aunis et la Saintonge des origines à nos jours*, (Saint-Jean-d'Angély, 1981), 206.

of La Rochelle's first municipal charters (from Eleanor of Aquitaine in 1199) exempted townsmen from ordinary tolls and taxes on viticulture, enabling them to sell their locally produced wine advantageously throughout Europe.[25] The development of La Rochelle's port from the twelfth century onward funneled more commercial traffic across the plain, aligning the market centers of a small regional economy.

The tributaries of several rivers eroded the flanks of the low, limestone plateau approaching La Rochelle. This process resulted in subtle but ethnographically significant variations in elevation. Compared to settlements on the plain, pre-modern villages nestled in stream valleys, twenty to forty meters below the surrounding countryside, had very different microclimates, different mixes of crops and farm animals, and different economic orientations toward riparian networks of commerce and communication flowing away from the flatter high ground. High rates of endogamy among villagers inhabiting plain and valley reinforced these differences, creating proximate yet distinct communities.

Throughout the early modern era, thick stands of trees cut across the plain leading to La Rochelle. These woodlands, now almost entirely vanished, sustained populations ominously set apart from the towns and farming villages of the open country. The woods gave work to itinerant bands of loggers, charcoal burners, and distillers. The forests became the base camps of highwaymen and a terror to travellers and pilgrims.[26] In December 1613, François d'Epagnac, a royal captain for the provinces of Angoumois and Aunis around La Rochelle, pleaded with the crown for six more archers to add to his regional police force totalling only sixteen men. D'Epagnac noted that his bailiwick was enormous and covered with "several dense forests, great copses, and thickets to which many vagabonds and fugitives have retired who daily menace highway traffic and commerce." D'Epagnac claimed to have bravely led his little squad of gendarmes into the

---

[25] On the early development of La Rochelle's wine trade see Etienne Trocmé and Marcel Delafosse, *Le commerce rochelais de la fin du XVe siècle au début du XVIIe*, (Paris, 1952), 74-85 and 104-114.

[26] On the distinct culture of early modern French forest dwellers, a culture inscrutable and threatening to outsiders see Tina Jolas and Françoise Zonabend, "Gens du finage, gens du bois," *Annales E.S.C.*, 28 (1973): 285-305. On the role of forests and forest dwellers as malevolent characters in French folklore see Philippe Barrier, *Le forêt légendaire*, (Paris, 1991).

deep forests in hopes of arresting the bandits. But these shows of force were futile since he had been compelled "to retreat at great peril to his life by the large numbers of armed vagabonds and thieves."[27] Indifferent to d'Epagnac's request, the crown allowed him wages for an extra three men. Despite this reinforcement, the permanent local forces of royal police were grossly inadequate for effective surveillance or control of the region.

The eastern border of La Rochelle's *banlieue* was fixed at the edge of the dense Benon forest. The city, its laws, and privileges stopped at the tree line. Here began a world alien and menacing to townspeople.[28] Despite receiving much of their wood for heating, domestic construction, and ship building from Benon forest, inhabitants of La Rochelle avoided the place, never travelling its woodland paths alone, unarmed or after dark. Further east, the *pelebois*, a low ridge of red earth covered with chestnut trees, interrupted the plain leading to La Rochelle. This forest's place name referred to its impoverished inhabitants who managed a bare subsistence stripping (*peler* in French) the trees of every useful or marketable arboreal product.[29] Poachers of timber and wildlife long roamed these coastal woods, contemptuous of the regulations and threats of prosecution issued by the nominal secular and ecclesiastical overlords of the territory. Poor, irreverent, and threatening forest dwellers hovered at the fringes of La Rochelle's fortified urban space. Townspeople called them "wolves."[30]

To the north, La Rochelle's planar *banlieue* ended abruptly at the Poitevin marshes. Covering more than 600 square kilometers in early modern times, these bogs were nourished and divided by three serpentine rivers: the Lay, Vendée, and Sèvre-Niortaise. Sinuous river tributaries and rudimentary drainage canals made this "natural Venice" a patchwork of waterways and tiny arable

---

[27] AN, Conseil d'état et des finances, registre E 42b, fol. 321. In 1609, the royal *sénéchal* for Saintonge also informed the king's bureaucracy in Paris of the many notable crimes rendering police of local highways virtually impossible, see AAE, Mémoires et Documents, France, 1475, fols. 4r-v.

[28] The deep, mutual, and persistent suspicions opposing urban officialdom and frontier forest dwellers in the early modern French Pyrenees have been sensitively analyzed by Peter Sahlins, *Forest Rites: The War of the Demoiselles in Nineteenth-Century France*, (Cambridge, Mass., 1994), 1-60.

[29] Rézeau, *Dictionnaire du français régional de Poitou-Charentes*, s.v. "pèlebois"

[30] See Robert Colle, *Saintonge mystérieuse, Aunis insolite*, (La Rochelle, 1976), 76. Such traditional locutions had their origins in medieval times.

plots barely sufficient for agriculture. Transport over any distance was invariably water-borne. No earthen roads penetrated this humid region. The local patois conjoined road and water, here streams became "routes d'eau."[31]

An ever shifting population of subsistence farmers, drovers, fisherfolk, and manual laborers inhabited the Poitevin marshes. These hardy souls eked out a living from a land stingy in food, building material, and fuel. They frequently dwelled in reed huts warmed by smoldering and malodorous fires of dried cow dung. Outsiders, like the Rochelais, spoke suspiciously and derisively of these "hutters" (*huttiers*) living rudely amidst an inhospitable landscape.[32]

Swamp dwellers, *maraîchins* or *marouins* as they called themselves, were equally contemptuous of the aliens on terra firma, referring to plainsmen as "damnions," "damned men."[33] As these invectives suggest, intermarriages between the two groups were extremely rare. The swampers' elaborate patois, differing markedly from standard French and other regional dialects, further limited communication with outsiders.[34] On La Rochelle's northern border, proximate but deeply antagonistic communities faced one another.

A *tour d'horizon* from atop La Rochelle's old walls reveals an early modern town surrounded by challenging landforms and their disparate, provocative inhabitants. Near La Rochelle and its *banlieue*, the Atlantic frontier accommodated heterogeneous human settlements distinguished by a multiplicity of dialects, customs,

---

[31] Rézeau, *Dictionnaire du français régional de Poitou-Charentes*, s.v. "route d'eau."

[32] One mid-nineteenth-century glossary of regional expressions noted that "huttier" referred to "a curious race" of men "who live outside of any social order in the marshes of the Sèvre," see L. Favre, *Glossaire du Poitou de la Saintonge et de l'Aunis*, (Niort, 1867), 193.

[33] Rézeau, *Dictionnaire du français régional de Poitou-Charentes*, s.v. "damnions." This expression utilized by marsh dwellers with reference to most outsiders was common in early modern times and would have been considered especially offensive by members of Reformed congregations deeply implanted in regional towns like La Rochelle after 1550. No neighboring Calvinist could easily accept the derisive title "damned."

[34] The isolation of tightly knit marsh communities and the slow diffusion of public schooling in the region kept the patois of the *marais poitevin* vibrant until the beginning of the twentieth century. Its decline was not precipitous until the 1950's, see Pierre Gachignard, *Dictionnaire du patois du marais poitevin*, (Marseille, 1983).

measures, and crafts.[35] The city's encircling walls defended a forward post of urban civilization against potential enemies, foreign
or domestic, far or near, approaching from any quarter of the
compass. Proximate marshes and forests separated the city from
major terrestrial axes of commerce, communication, and police.
With no navigable river passing through town, La Rochelle also
lacked an easy natural passage into the continental interior.

The sea provided the Rochelais with the highways they lacked
on land. By the mid-sixteenth century, city merchants profited
from trade on a global scale, pursuing commercial ventures on
the Iberian peninsula, in all the English Channel ports, throughout the Baltic, and across the Atlantic to the Caribbean and Newfoundland.[36] The port's role as a transshipment point between
northern and southern Europe brought vessels from many nations
to its quays.

However, the liberating effect of the high seas on local mentalities should not be overemphasized. The rochelais commercial
fleet remained a comparatively small one. Townsmen's cargos frequently came and went in vessels flying foreign flags and crewed
by total strangers. Nearly all of the largest and swiftest boats owned
by Rochelais during the early modern era had been constructed
in distant dock yards. No great shipbuilding industry ever developed in the city. Local naval carpenters stuck to traditional methods of fabrication, turning out small craft equipped in rudimentary fashion.[37] City merchants, although often apprenticed to
foreign businessmen while young, tended to become much more
sedentary by early middle age, staying in La Rochelle to hold prestigious, powerful offices in municipal government and to ad-

---

[35] In a region like the French west country, where formerly every seigneurie
had its own system of weights and measures, a long absence of standardization
in these matters could be expected. In fact, even long after the introduction of
the metric system, the French west remained parcelled up into hundreds of
zones defined by wildly differing units of calculation in area and volume. A term
like "journal," widely used to size landholdings, did not signify a uniform quantity of property throughout its range of use. Within a radius of fifty kilometers
around La Rochelle, local communities employed no less than twelve different
reckonings of the space denoted by a "journal." See Julien-Labruyère, *Paysans
charentais*, 1: 154–156.

[36] Trocmé and Delafosse, *Le commerce rochelais*, 146–171.

[37] On the modest dimensions of the rochelais shipbuilding industry and on
the unremarkable quality of its products see Trocmé and Delafosse, *Le commerce
rochelais*, 15–16.

minister their extensive rural estates on a daily basis. The city's notarial archives are full of the elaborate contracts by which home-bound rochelais merchants employed ship captains and passing commercial travellers to act as surrogate trading partners in distant locales. These contracts are notable for the minute instructions they contain and the alternative commercial strategies steadfast rochelais traders concocted for their deputies to handle unpredictable business opportunities at great distances from the city.[38]

Not all citizens in La Rochelle lived or profited by the economic activity of the harbor. In the early modern era, Europeans still commonly regarded the sea as the eery, shameful dregs of God's punishing flood.[39] Great bodies of unfathomable water provoked men more quickly to fear than to adventure. The overwhelming presence of the open ocean around La Rochelle could never entirely eradicate, and may actually have reinforced, its residents' sense of isolation amid a hostile environment.[40] Judging by surviving notarial records in La Rochelle, the two leading causes compelling townspeople to prepare a last will and testament were imminent death and taking ship for a sea voyage. Leaving the French Atlantic shore was a risky business the Rochelais specialized in hiring others to perform. The dangers on land and sea were numberless and real.[41]

---

[38] For examples of such contracts see ADCM 3 E 174, 4 April 1601, 3 E 203, fol. 122v, and 3 E 216 (1610), fols. 16r, 36r, and 49v. Trocmé and Delafosse, *Le commerce rochelais*, 151-155, note how rarely native rochelais merchants ventured abroad to prospect new markets. They more often relied upon factors in the towns of the Low Countries and northern Spain. Non-native settlers in La Rochelle, especially Basque shippers, nearly monopolized the Biscay trade, accomplishing this in part through more frequent personal displacements toward their homeland.

[39] Corbin, *Lure of the Sea*, 1-18. Corbin here describes in masterly detail how profound fears of the sea, the "territoire du vide," gripped early modern Europeans. For coastal populations, proximity to the ocean and its meteorological disturbances continually reinforced popular apprehensions of this primordial element.

[40] Jean Delumeau, *La peur en occident*, (Paris, 1978), see in particular Chapter 1, "Omniprésence de la peur," subsection 1, "Mer variable où toute crainte abonde," 31-42. This sense of isolation may have been even more acute among Protestant coastal dwellers than among their Catholic neighbors since the sea, in an early modern cosmology, was a potent reminder of God's ire over the ubiquity of human sin, the ever-spreading stain that also preoccupied most Calvinists.

[41] In La Rochelle's notarial archives one catches glimpses of how city elders worried over educating their children about the sea's dangers. To cite but one

Many Rochelais living in the sixteenth and seventeenth centuries professed a deep wariness of their natural surroundings.
The proximity of the sea could not have been reassuring for citizens who shared the contemporary belief that the end of the
world would commence with oceanic inundations of the earth.
Popular rhymes and folk sayings of the French mid-Atlantic coast
foretell the sea's raging destruction of local towns.[42] La Rochelle's
municipal council reorganized the administration and finance of
the city's charity hospitals in 1516 with the hope that these measures would not only aid the poor, but also encourage God's "protection of the city from the continual danger she faces without
support or aid, something she merits above all other towns in
France."[43] In 1530, members of the town council opposed a popular initiative to raise the legal age at which councilmen's children could succeed them in office from eighteen to twenty-five.
Among their contrary arguments, municipal officials pointed out
that local fathers rarely lived to see their sons at twenty-five
because the "gross and infected air" of the marine region led to
the frequent premature death of family members.[44]

Contemporaries agreed in defining the air and environment of
La Rochelle as "gross," "foul," "unmerciful," and "dangerous."[45]
These descriptions strengthened popular fears about the atmos-
pheric hazards presented by deep bays and sheltered ports, the
exact topographical elements shaping La Rochelle's ecology. Such
locales turned malevolent even in calm weather because the
absence of winds concentrated the noxious effluvia of stagnant
waters.[46] At the time, natural philosophers considered the Atlantic

example, in November 1601 Simon Papin, the patriarch of a local mercantile
family, used a loan of 9,000 *livres* to set up his twenty-one-year-old son, Jean, in
business. Among the multiple clauses in the notarized contract establishing this
family firm, Simon Papin stipulated that his eager junior partner could never
commit any merchandise to a sea voyage without his father's explicit approval.
See ADCM, 3 E 210, fols. 127v-128r. Even young men on the verge of emancipation still needed paternal instruction about marine hazards.

[42] Sébillot, *Légendes de la mer*, 1: 303-304.

[43] These measures were taken "afin que Dieu préserve cette ville du contin-
uel danger ou elle est pour n'avoir aucun support et appui, combien qu'elle le
mérite sur toutes les villes de France." Cited in Léopold Delayant, *Histoire des
Rochelais*, 2 vols., (La Rochelle, 1870), 1: 146.

[44] *Ibid.*, 160.

[45] See Arcère, *Histoire de La Rochelle*, 1: 593-94, and Note XIV.

[46] On the toxic emanations early modern Europeans commonly attributed to

littoral nearest La Rochelle to be the French seacoast most toxic to human physiologies.[47] Jacques Merlin, a leading Calvinist pastor and diarist in La Rochelle from 1589 to 1620, assiduously recorded the tempests, earthquakes, and "pestiferous fogs" besetting the community. He attributed the frequent bad weather enveloping the city to "malign aerial spirits" haunting the region.[48]

In 1591, La Rochelle's foremost Calvinist printer published a treatise on a particularly insidious form of black magic widely feared in town. The probable author of this text, Louis Hesnard, a Protestant minister working temporarily in La Rochelle, admitted the reality of this charm practiced locally by minions of the devil including clergymen. Hesnard argued that such sorcery, rendering newly married grooms impotent, should also serve to remind the Rochelais of the many "enemies" and "dangers" continually surrounding them and assailing even their most intimate unions.[49] In June 1619, La Rochelle's mayor mobilized the city militia after receiving warnings that evil magicians were preparing to attack the city with "aerial enchantments" to poison citizens and destroy civic arsenals.[50]

Pastor Merlin took special care to describe in his diary the

---

arms of the sea, especially in clement weather, see Alain Corbin, *The Foul and the Fragrant*, (Cambridge, Mass.: 1986), 13. Early modern French natural scientists believed that the proximity of sea and swamp produced the most insalubrious of all landscapes: "even worse were the ravages caused by emanations from waterlogged soil...the saline lands exuded a gas that was unfit for respiration...the subsoil of ponds exuded the worst stench..." See Corbin, *Foul and Fragrant*, 21-24.

[47] Judging by the environmental opinions of pre-modern Frenchmen Alain Corbin has dredged up, no part of the French Atlantic coast was considered more dangerous than the bogs around La Rochelle: "The most deadly swamps were those like the abandoned salt marsh of the Charente coast, where fresh and salt water mingled," Corbin, *Foul and Fragrant*, 34.

[48] Jacques Merlin, "Diaire ou recueil des choses plus mémorables qui se sont passées en ceste ville," BMLR, MS 161, fols. 407r-408v. Merlin here describes the "brouée empestée" afflicting the entire government of Aunis. For the reference to evil aerial spirits see fol. 276r.

[49] See the *Traité de l'enchantement qu'on appelle vulgairement le nouement de l'Esguillette*, (La Rochelle, 1591), BN, Rés. D2.13667, 83. For more detailed analysis of this treatise, its author, and the tensions within rochelais society revealed by this publication, see my article "Magical Emasculation, Popular Anticlericalism, and the Limits of the Reformation in the French West Country, Circa 1590," forthcoming in the *Journal of Social History.*

[50] Merlin, "Diaire," fol. 539v.

crimes for which frightening human residents of La Rochelle's *banlieue* were condemned and executed by city magistrates.[51] Another rochelais diarist among these officers, Joseph Guillaudeau, *avocat* before the city's presidial court from 1584 to 1645, also regularly noted the youth and precociously vicious acts of criminals brought in from the wilds of the *banlieue*.[52] Animal predators from the rochelais back country also long posed a danger to town dwellers. On occasion, wolves infiltrated the city through its sewers. In 1572, a band of city meat cutters surrounded and hacked to death one such stealthy visitor who had come up through the sewers in the central market place.[53]

The intendant Bégon, based in La Rochelle, found urban residents in 1698 to be "very polite," but chastised inhabitants of the city's hinterland for living in "great debauchery" (*grand libertinage*). Bégon despaired of moral improvement in the rochelais backcountry, "there being no province in Christendom where there are so few charitable people as in this one."[54] Catholic missionaries, working La Rochelle's *banlieue* with logistical support from revitalized local bishoprics in the mid-eighteenth century, dejectedly concurred with Bégon's earlier assessment. They recurrently described the residents of hamlets near La Rochelle as "tough," "selfish," "irreligious," and "intractable."[55] For generations, the citizenry's perceptions of harsh and threatening worlds beyond the town walls shaped the form and ethos of rochelais governing institutions.

Throughout the early modern era, La Rochelle developed as a heavily defended, maritime municipality. City fathers invoked divine assistance and aggressively sought royal privileges to make their community an impregnable entrepot protected against the multiple dangers of a marine frontier. Feeling threatened and test-

---

[51] *Ibid.*, fols. 541r-542r.

[52] Joseph Guillaudeau, "Journal de ce qui c'est passé à La Rochelle, depuis 1584 jusqu'à 1643," published as "Diaire de Joseph Guillaudeau, Sieur de Beaupréau," AHSA 38 (1908): 1-422. For examples of Guillaudeau's remarks on criminals from the rochelais hinterland see 37 and 51-52.

[53] Delayant, *Histoire des Rochelais*, 1: 249.

[54] Bégon, "Mémoire sur la généralité," 28, 39, and 40.

[55] P.-F. Hacquet, *Mémoire des missions des Montfortains dans l'ouest (1740-1779)*, ed. L. Pérouas, (Fontenay-le-Comte, 1964), 25, 30, 46, 63 reports on extended missionary visits to villages of Saint-Christophe, 1743; Angoulins-sur-Mer, 1745; Aytré, 1751; and Aigrefeuille-d'Aunis, 1757; the first three of these places sit within a radius of five kilometers from La Rochelle.

ed by this environment, townspeople construed their city and themselves as isolated civilizing agents especially worthy of their superiors' protection.

## 2. *Local Topographies of Power*

Unlike many provincial cities of old regime France, La Rochelle in the mid-sixteenth century was not directly subject to potent, resident ecclesiastical, seigneurial, or parliamentary authorities. Much to the benefit of local notables, the city stood peripheral to the jurisdictions of several institutions contending ineptly to govern the French west country. No bishopric or cathedral chapter existed in La Rochelle before 1648. Until that date, the city and its environs lay at the malgoverned interstices of three minor sees: Saintes, Luçon, and Maillezais. (Figure 2 displays the early modern borders of the provinces and bishoprics surrounding La Rochelle). The bishops installed at Saintes, sixty-five kilometers southeast of La Rochelle, held titular responsibility for overseeing the spiritual welfare of the Rochelais. For centuries prior to 1550, prelates in Saintes lacked the funds and the manpower to fulfill this obligation. From the first decade of the fourteenth century, the Rochelais had challenged the right of bishops at Saintes to collect a *dîme* from the town and its surrounding parishes. A compromise brokered by Charles V in 1377 reduced the bishop's pretensions from one-tenth to one-one-hundredth of local harvests in exchange for a lump sum payment from the residents of La Rochelle's government.[56] Pope Clement VII ratified this balance of fiscal power in 1382. The subtraction of the Rochelais from ecclesiastical supervision continued when the town council (*corps de ville*) decreed in 1401 that no churchman could join its ranks and when Pope Alexander VI (pontificate 1492-1503) denied any ecclesiastic the right to bring legal suit against a citizen of La Rochelle in a tribunal outside the city.[57]

Absentee bishops and their incompetent local subordinates also weakened episcopal influence over La Rochelle. In 1504, for example, the *archiprêtre* of La Rochelle, chief lieutenant of the

---

[56] Delayant, *Histoire des Rochelais*, 1: 111.
[57] *Ibid.*, 145.

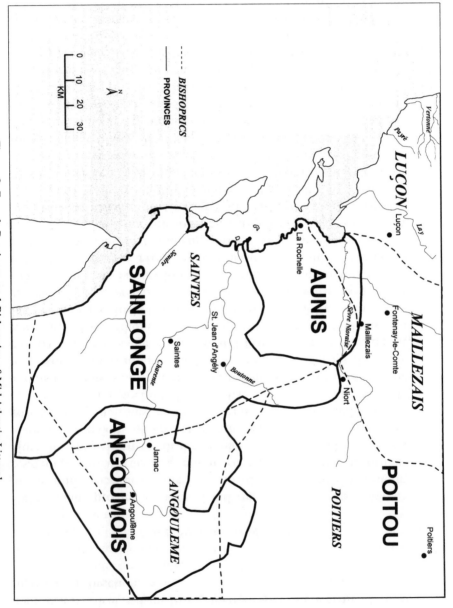

Figure 2. French Provinces and Bishoprics of Mid-Atlantic Littoral

bishop of Saintes, was a nine-year-old child.[58] A lack of major
abbeys in or near the city also deprived regional prelates of local
pedagogical bases. Episcopal agents rarely made inspection tours
through parishes on the margins of the diocese in pre-Tridentine
times. Dwindling numbers of regular and secular Catholic churchmen in La Rochelle before 1550 further attenuated the bishop's
influence over the eccentric urban parishes.[59]

The small, modestly endowed bishoprics of Luçon and Maillezais had been carved out of the diocese of Poitiers in 1317. The
episcopal seat of Luçon, a bourg with fewer than 3,000 inhabitants in 1608, stood thirty-four kilometers due north of La
Rochelle, across the intervening and frequently impassable Poitevin marshes.[60] Generations of non-resident bishops had left the
cathedral dilapidated and the episcopal palace uninhabitable.
Long-standing disputes between foreign bishops, the clergy of the
cathedral chapter, and small country abbeys with autonomous control over appointments to many parish benefices in the diocese
undermined local church discipline. Fractious Catholic orders
here could exert no real influence on La Rochelle before or after
1550.

The same could be said for the bishopric erected in the hamlet of Maillezais, surrounded by wetlands forty kilometers northeast of La Rochelle. With a small and diminishing population in
the sixteenth and seventeenth centuries, this locale could not
maintain any active center of Catholic instruction.[61] Low population densities in the adjoining marshes required uncommonly
large parishes to assemble enough communicants for ordinary
church services. The size of these church districts and the forbidding terrain over which they sprawled rendered parochial government haphazard. Under these conditions, the clerics of Maillezais could barely instruct their own community, let alone extend
their influence towards distant La Rochelle.

No permanent, resident aristocracy could be found in early

---

[58] Labande, *Histoire du Poitou, Limousin, pays charentais*, 225.

[59] Pérouas, *Le diocèse de La Rochelle*, 127-144.

[60] On Luçon and its diocese see L. Lacroix, *Richelieu à Luçon*, (Paris, 1890),
73.

[61] The village of Maillezais approached its nadir in 1707 when the total population dwindled to less than 900 souls. See Pérouas, *Le diocèse de La Rochelle*,
110 and n. 2.

modern La Rochelle. No quarter of noble or *parlementaire* town houses dominated the city's built environment. Representatives of old seigneurial families in the region, d'Aubigné, Chabot de Jarnac, d'Escoubleau, Rohan, Soubise, and La Trémouille, occasionally visited the mercantile port town but never established a lasting, physical presence there. The Wars of Religion would exceptionally bring many Protestant grandees through La Rochelle, but their impermanent lodgings within the city always varied.

In the absence of powerful, fixed representatives from the first or second estates, commoners active in civic administration largely controlled local police. La Rochelle owed its fundamental right of communal self-government (*droit de commune*) to a privilege probably awarded by the English king Henry II (ruled 1154-1189) in the late twelfth century. A municipal charter specifying the form and function of town government had been drafted by 1199, the earliest year in which a recorded mayor is known for the community and the year in which Eleanor of Aquitaine acknowledged the town council's corporate identity.[62] The town's first charters clearly defined the governors and governed within rochelais society, placing a mayor and town council of 100 members at the head of a commune divided into a bourgeoisie and ordinary inhabitants.

La Rochelle's town council (*corps de ville*) handled most tasks of municipal administration. Seventy-six *pairs*, twelve *conseillers*, and twelve *échevins*, all ranked in order of seniority, comprised this body. Members of this council served for life. Although early civic charters stipulated that new *pairs* be recruited from among the bourgeoisie and that *conseillers* and *échevins* be chosen from among the *pairs*, cooptation became the mode of replacement in both groups. During the fifteenth and sixteenth centuries, the practice of "resignation" became increasingly condoned, whereby each town council member could transfer his office to a successor, usually a son or other close kinsman, provided that the new councilman met minimum residency and age requirements. As

---

[62] The institutions of town government in La Rochelle were modelled on the civic administration of Rouen. See A. Giry, *Les établissements de Rouen*, (Paris, 1885), 60-64. Giry contends that La Rochelle's charter was conferred between 1169 and 1199 by either Henry II or Richard I. Prior historians of the city date the charter to 1199 and identify Eleanor of Aquitaine as its donor. See Arcère, *Histoire de la ville de La Rochelle*, 1: 193-195.

will be shown in Chapter 2, by the mid-sixteenth century, a small number of wealthy, densely intermarried, Protestant, mercantile families monopolized the available town council offices.

The membership of the *corps de ville* selected from within itself the mayor of La Rochelle in a procedure initially controlled by that body and the royal *sénéchal* of Saintonge or his lieutenant. Each year, on the first Sunday after Easter, the *échevins*, *conseillers*, and *pairs* met in the Church of St. Barthélémy and elected three candidates, each voter casting a ballot inscribed with the names of three fellow councilmen he felt were qualified for the job. The three men who received the most votes, usually senior *échevins* with considerable experience of civic administration, went before the king's lieutenant or his deputy who chose one of the three to be mayor for the coming year. The candidate with the highest number of votes typically won the mayoralty, with the first run-ner-up named as vice-mayor. La Rochelle's mayor held the title of "captain of the city," kept the keys to all town gates, had charge of the city's seal, presided over the mayor's court of justice, and commanded the city's militia companies made up of all townsmen with the status of *bourgeois-juré de commune*. In Chapter 2, the mechanics of this electoral process and the governing responsi-bilities of its participants will be examined in detail.

La Rochelle's early charters empowered the town council to rule over a community hierarchically divided between "bour-geoisie" and "inhabitants." Ordinary residents of the city were referred to as "habitans." These individuals held no special rights guaranteed by municipal charters and were under the legal juris-diction of the king's *prévôt*, the lowest ranking royal official in the city. The town council conferred the distinction of "bourgeois" on Rochelais who had lived in the city for a year and a day, who maintained a residence there (*feu et lieu* in the parlance of the day), who swore an oath of fidelity to municipal ordinances (hence the additional title of "juré de commune"), who enrolled themselves on the list of citizens contributing to the costs of town government, and who committed themselves to personal service and gifts in defense of communal security. In a prospering mer-cantile community like La Rochelle, large numbers of men from the middle and lower middle strata of urban society could attain these qualifications. A *bourgeois-juré de commune* could partake in the privileges of the city, could have his legal cases exclusively

tried in the first instance before the mayor's court, and gained
admittance to the group of citizens with a monopoly over intramural retail trade. Wholesale and retail merchants, shopkeepers,
and skilled artisans predominated among the bourgeoisie of La
Rochelle. These men also formed the backbone of the heavily
armed and well-drilled civic militia, a force with an approximate
maximum strength of 2,000 citizens by the mid-sixteenth century.

Additional liberties conferred by Philip Augustus (1200) and
Philip III (1278) gave sworn members of the urban commune
sweeping exemptions from *tailles, aides,* and customs duties.
Privileges from Jean II and Edward III in 1360 invested the may-
or and town council of La Rochelle with primary civil and criminal justice over all sworn citizens and the territory of the city's
*banlieue.* The mayor's court exclusively exercised these legal powers. An annual assembly of *conseillers* and *échevins* selected members of the town council to serve as the magistrates of this court
under the presidency of the mayor. All town councilmen met
together to choose the senior judge of the tribunal. A charter
from Charles V in January 1373 fixed the boundaries of La
Rochelle's *banlieue* and reaffirmed the town's legal dominion
there.[63] (Figure 3 shows the boundaries of La Rochelle's *banlieue*
and its emplacement within the surrounding province of Aunis).
A citizen of La Rochelle regularly served as the *bailli* of the district outside the walls, supervising the extramural administration
of the law in conjunction with personnel of the mayor's court.

By a second edict of January 1373, Charles V incorporated La
Rochelle and its *banlieue* within the new province of Aunis
detached from the *sénéchaussée* of Saintonge. The province now
fell under the control of a royal governor established in La
Rochelle who became the ranking local representative of the king
responsible for the annual selection of the mayor. The governor's
entourage included a *lieutenant, procureur,* and *avocat du roi*
charged with the formation of a royal court of law (*cour du gouvernement*) covering all of Aunis and based in La Rochelle.[64]

---

[63] On the royal privileges conferring this jurisdiction on the Rochelais see
Arcère, *Histoire de la ville de La Rochelle,* 1: 195; Jean-Noel Luc, *La Charente-Maritime,* 179-80; and Marcel Delafosse, ed., *Histoire de La Rochelle,* (Toulouse, 1985),
25-27.

[64] Arcère, *Histoire de la ville de La Rochelle,* 1: 261, identifies this court as a "tribunal des appellations pour les causes de ce nouveau gouveneement."

Townsmen with legal training scrambled to fill available posts in the governor's court. Embedded institutions of communal and royal justice provoked recurrent jurisdictional disputes between local magistrates. As will be shown in Chapter 2, such institutional conflicts animated urban politics throughout the early modern era and kept the agents of municipal government in fighting trim at a time when many other French towns became dominated by royal judicial officials.

Appeals from these new urban courts went directly to the Parlement of Paris (400 kilometers away), denying the closer Parlement of Bordeaux any legal power over La Rochelle or its environs. The capacity of alien magistrates to meddle in the judicial affairs of the port or the surrounding province of Aunis was further restricted by the distinct customary law of La Rochelle redacted and acknowledged by royal commissioners in 1514 and 1559. Multiple customary law codes divided up the French west country reinforcing cultural distinctions between proximate human settlements.[65]

Verdicts of the Paris Parlement (in 1278 and 1283) and subsequent edicts from royal judicial inspectors (1315-16) had confirmed La Rochelle's *droit de commune* and limited the potential of the king's *sénéchaux* or their lieutenants to interfere in the administration of the city or its immediate hinterland. Since the early fourteenth century, local viceroys, before entering la Rochelle, had to swear an oath of allegiance to all of the town's accumulated liberties. These political constraints transferred to the royal governors for Aunis established in La Rochelle in 1373. At the same date, a large, secure intramural accommodation for the king's men-at-arms vanished with the demolition of the derelict royal château looming over the northwest quadrant of the city. The crown's loss was La Rochelle's gain since the stones from the old château went to extend and strengthen the town's walls. By letters patent of May, 1465, Louis XI confirmed the right of La Rochelle's town council to select independently all candidates for municipal offices "with no regard for any orders, entreaties, or requests made on the subject by the king or others."[66] Such exten-

---

[65] Jean Yver, *Essai de géographie coutumière*, (Paris, 1966), 125-131.

[66] Amos Barbot, "Histoire de La Rochelle," ed. Denys d'Aussy, AHSA, 14 (1886): 1-516; 17 (1889): 1-373; and 18 (1890): 1-226. For Barbot's commentary on this key rochelais civic privilege see AHSA, 14 (1886): 355.

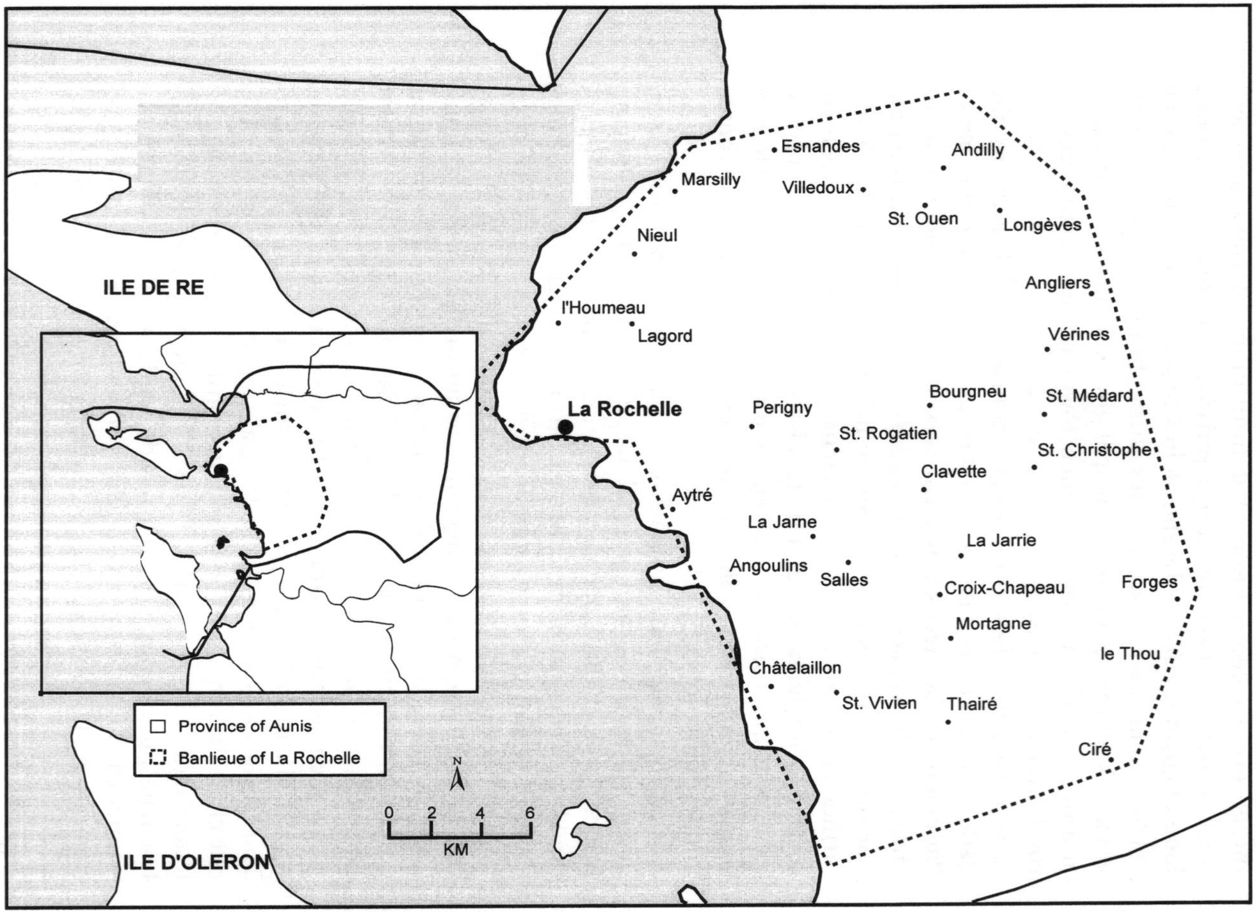

Figure 3. Province of Aunis and *Banlieue* of La Rochelle

CHAPTER ONE

sive franchises long protected communal administration against subservience to the crown.

These early and enduring rochelais privileges gave city fathers uncommon liberties in economic and political affairs while also extending to them real responsibilities for police of the region. The province of Aunis, covering about 1,600 square kilometers, and the *banlieue* of La Rochelle, with thirty-eight parishes occupying a surface area of approximately 750 square kilometers became double, concentric buffer zones identified by townsmen with the vital interests and safety of their urban community. Throughout the early modern period, privileged Rochelais struggled to bring these territories under fiscal, judicial, and military control beneficial to their *bonne ville*.

Townsmen's extensive rights of commerce and justice discouraged the emplacement of noble estates anchored by a fortified château within a terrestrial radius of forty kilometers around La Rochelle. As Figure 4 illustrates, far fewer fourteenth-, fifteenth-, and sixteenth-century châteaux existed in the vicinity of La Rochelle than within the orbits of such adjacent provincial towns as Luçon, Fontenay-le-Comte, Niort, and Saintes. The absence of such noble refuges along a stretch of coast long vulnerable to attack in part accounts for the many subterranean hideouts and stoutly fortified churches in the region, distinctive features of the built environment in the provinces of Aunis and Saintonge.[67] The strong architecture of rochelais town government can also be attributed to the scarcity of focused authority in the region.

From the early fourteenth century onward, wealthier townsmen bought up unfortified noble estates near La Rochelle. These real estate investors took advantage of a privilege conferred on rochelais citizens by Philip IV in 1312 exempting them from pay-

---

[67] From the time of Julius Caesar's Gallic campaigns until the late seventeenth century, the western French provinces of Aunis and Saintonge contained thousands of rough hewn stone shelters below ground where natives could seek refuge from Roman invaders, Norse marauders, and warring bands of religious fanatics. These local hideouts, popularly referred to as "trous de lapin" ("rabbit holes"), still number in the hundreds and reach a density of more than one per square kilometer on the Arvert peninsula below La Rochelle and in the south central reaches of Saintonge. Partisans in the Wars of Religion and in local seventeenth-century rebellions regularly made use of these lairs. The ubiquitous "rabbit holes" and the heavily fortified coastal churches of the region are among the most striking physical embodiments of the area's long history of insecurity. See Julien-Labruyère, *Paysans charentais*, 2: 15-19.

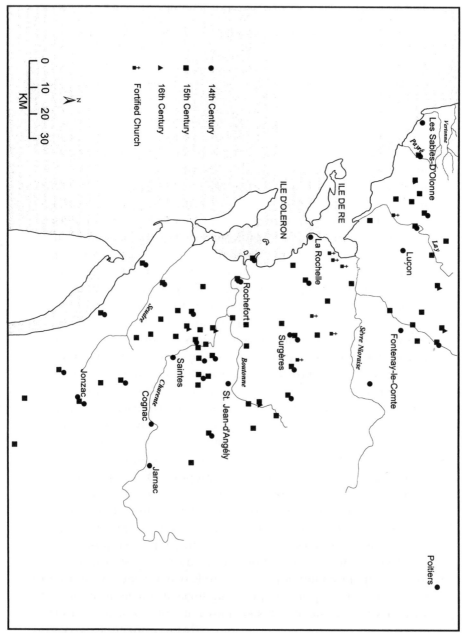

Figure 4. Fortified Châteaux of the French Atlantic Frontier

ing any feudal levies on noble properties they might acquire.[68] Members of La Rochelle's governing elite owned extensive tracts of land outside the city. By 1588, for example, at least 70% of La Rochelle's senior town councilmen (*échevins* and *conseilliers*) identified themselves with the honorific "sieur" followed by a place name in the *banlieue* signifying ownership of a noble estate.[69] However, this ennoblement never dissuaded rochelais citizens from the practice of commerce. Town councilmen who accumulated honors and encumbering civic offices long remained active in the maritime trade and wholesale businesses upon which their wealth depended. Townsmen who became landed notables trafficked expertly in the agricultural produce of their holdings.

Non-resident seigneurs also found the Rochelais difficult to command since another royal privilege granted first by Philip IV in 1312 and reconfirmed by Louis XI in 1472, exempted townsmen from military service under the *ban et arrière ban* of the western provinces. The Rochelais also attempted to subtract able-bodied residents of the town's *banlieue* from the ranks of external military forces. In 1557, the mayor and town council reorganized the municipal militia, invoking civic privileges to assert that residents of the *banlieue* had to enroll themselves in this new force and to fight under rochelais command against all enemies designated by the city's governors.[70] The crown frequently assented to these expressions of municipal authority because of its heavy reliance on the wealthy and well-armed Rochelais for effective defense of the seacoast. This topography of power enabled La Rochelle to become the quintessentially bourgeois *chef-lieu* of the French Atlantic frontier, a town capable of tenaciously opposing royal, ecclesiastical, and seigneurial influence within its precincts.

### 3. *Problematic Relations Between Town and Country*

Over time, a complex economic and cultural symbiosis formed between La Rochelle and segments of its *banlieue*. The active port

---

[68] BMLR, "Manuscrit Baudouin," (an early modern chronicle of the city's history) MSS 45/46, fols. 217 and 335.

[69] See the lists of civic officeholders for the years 1574-1622 preserved in BMLR, MS 97.

[70] Barbot, "Histoire de La Rochelle," AHSA 14 (1886): 118.

became a consumer of and natural transshipment point for bulky
agricultural commodities like salt and wine produced abundantly
in nearby marine marshes and on the limestone soils of the adjacent plain. The inhabitants of the rochelais backcountry, approximately 20,000 souls circa 1600, the majority manual laborers,
could also rely on the town and its more prosperous residents as
sources of employment, diverse imported commodities, crafted
goods of all kinds, loans, and stockpiled cereals in times of subsistence crises.[71] However, the manifold commercial privileges
amassed by citizens of La Rochelle gave this rank of the town's
populace a commanding role in the local, suburban economy.
These advantages combined with an imbalance of coercive armed
might between urban and rural dwellers on the Atlantic littoral
made for a troubled relationship of town and country in which
latent animosities could flare at any point of contact.

Winegrowing, the most ancient and locally preeminent ritual
of husbandry, associated the residents of town and countryside.
Beginning in 1172, sea traders in La Rochelle acquired franchises from northern European rulers allowing them to stock and sell
prized French west country wines in port towns from the Channel
to the Baltic. Numerous opportunities to profit in the European
wine trade encouraged the acquisition and expansion of local
vineyards by entrepreneurs large and small based in La Rochelle.
For urban merchants, innkeepers, and artisans possessed of ready
cash and confronted by few opportunities for secure investment,
purchasing plots of vines became a comparatively safe and remunerative placement of their surplus income.[72] By 1315, the resulting development of wine production had made vine tending a
dangerous monoculture within a radius of twenty kilometers
around La Rochelle.[73] Local vintners profitably relied on a grape

---

[71] Pérouas, *Le diocèse de La Rochelle*, 104.

[72] The diversity of rochelais social groups involved in the ownership and
exploitation of local vineyards is detailed in Julien-Labruyère, *Paysans charentais*,
1: 374-381 and in Trocmé and Delafosse, *Le commerce rochelais*, 105-114.

[73] See Etienne Trocmé, "La Rochelle de 1560 à 1628. Tableau d'une société
réformée du temps de guerres de religion," (Bachelor's thesis, Faculté libre de
théologie protestante, Paris, 1950), 9-11. Trocmé reckons that by 1500 vines covered three-quarters of the arable land in La Rochelle's *banlieue*. Julien-Labruyère,
*Paysans charentais*, 348-352, cites a variety of indices confirming the heavy, early
modern implantation of vines around La Rochelle. In the early fourteenth century, rochelais city councillors lamented that a proliferation of vineyards over an

varietal known as the *folle blanche* ("crazy white") for its prodigal growth on the well-drained soils of La Rochelle's arable hinterland.

The proliferation of vines first in the immediate vicinity of La Rochelle and then along cart tracks linking the port to adjacent market towns deprived these communities of ready access to vital grain supplies. Verdant vineyards provoked chronic shortages of cereals in the region. Fearful of intramural and extramural bread riots in times of dearth, rochelais civic officials maintained unusually strict surveillance over the local grain trade. City merchants regularly purchased wheat flour at the markets of Luçon, Marans, Fontenay-le-Comte, Niort, Saint-Maixent, Parthenay, and Saint-Jean-d'Angély, towns up to one hundred kilometers from La Rochelle.[74] The rochelais town council continually feuded with the officers of inland bourgs and the farmers of local tolls whom it accused of seeking to profit unscrupulously from the city's heavy dependence on grain provided by outsiders.

Shortfalls in the local grain supply could be made up by seaborne shipments brought in from as far away as Poland. Such deliveries became essential and nervously awaited by the Rochelais when catastrophic crop failures entirely shut down the west country trade in cereals, a recurrent predicament for urban consumers in the sixteenth and seventeenth centuries.[75] In times of famine, the mayor prohibited grain exports from the region and confiscated supplies horded by speculators in town and country.[76] All grains brought into the city were distributed through a single, municipally supervised wholesale grain market (*minage*).[77] Here,

---

area of five leagues in all directions meant that no nearby fields could be found for pasturage of brood mares generating horsepower for local farming and chivalric levies.

[74] Trocmé and Delafosse, *Le commerce rochelais*, 116, also note that few flour mills could be found in early modern La Rochelle. This is another aspect of the urban environment marking the absence of an adequate local grain supply.

[75] According to Trocmé and Delafosse, *Le commerce rochelais*, 181, especially bad harvests around La Rochelle occurred in the years 1515, 1582, 1587, 1590, 1594, 1596, 1598, and 1613. For much of its history the city rarely escaped a disastrous harvest at least once every five years. During such times of want, urban prices for basic foodstuffs could easily quintuple.

[76] Julien-Labruyère, *Paysans charentais*, 2: 63.

[77] The city's *droit de minage* amounted to a tax of between five and twelve percent on the total value of each local grain transaction depending on the type and quantity of the cereals exchanged. The *corps de ville* gained this lucrative franchise as a privilege from Philip III (ruled 1270-1285). See Julien-Labruyère, *Paysans charentais*, 2: 63.

a civic official recorded current market prices and collected the city's *droit de minage,* a tax in kind on all bushels changing hands. Using this information, the mayor and town sergeants performed spot checks on retail bread prices and punished bakers unfairly pushing up the price of a loaf. Local diarists, like pastor Merlin, also obsessively recorded grain prices in La Rochelle, inveighing against the "avaricieux usuriers" who speculated in grain to drive up prices especially in the lean months preceding an uncertain harvest.[78]

Around La Rochelle, owners typically exploited their vineyards directly, eschewing rental of their plots or restrictive contractual agreements with sharecroppers. Property owners employed salaried *vignerons* from villages of the *banlieue* to perform the strenuous, year-round cultivation of the vines necessary to maintain peak production. This practice contributed to the formation of a rural proletariat in the vicinity of La Rochelle incapable of growing its own subsistence and precariously reliant on cash wages for buying the necessities of life. Harvest failures and rising prices could make this a deadly predicament, heightening tensions between town and country populations.[79]

For the future Reformed city, a hinterland populated disproportionately by poor vineyard workers would become very troubling. As Mack Holt has incisively demonstrated for the region of Dijon and elsewhere, *vignerons* remained stubbornly attached to Catholicism and largely impervious to the French Reformation.[80] Although we possess no comprehensive history of the *Réforme* in La Rochelle's backcountry, local studies show that Protestant communities were very unevenly distributed over its area. Most Calvinist congregations established themselves in the market towns and larger villages of the region.[81] Over large expanses of vine-

---

[78] Merlin, "Diaire," fol. 367r.

[79] Trocmé and Delafosse, *Le commerce rochelais,* 105, note the general lack of industry and wide underemployment of labor in the rochelais hinterland during the early modern era. Julien-Labruyère, *Paysans charentais,* 2: 185-187, identifies the city's early modern acculturation of this region as a process leading inexorably to the proletarianization of its population.

[80] Mack Holt, "Wine, Community, and Reformation in Sixteenth-Century Burgundy," *Past and Present,* 138 (1993): 58-93.

[81] Pérouas, *Le diocèse de La Rochelle,* 130-131; see also Jean-Noel Luc, *La Charente-Maritime,* 196-197 and Figure 115 on page 197, for a mapping of Calvinist congregations established in Aunis and Saintonge before 1660.

yard territory proximate to La Rochelle, no Calvinist churches would develop at all and scarcely any members of the laboring population would rally to the new faith.[82] When the Reformation took hold among the citizens of La Rochelle, the hostility of the city's surrounding environment became spiritual as well as physical.

Vines could also usually be found on local estates where polyculture and lease holdings prevailed. Here, however, land rents drawn up between urban proprietors and rural laborers normally reserved all the grapes to the owner while requiring the tenant to maintain the vines as a necessary condition of the contract and with no additional salary or benefit. The ubiquity of such agreements so clearly favorable to townsmen has led François Julien-Labruyère, the foremost historian of this rural world, to describe the region as a rochelais plantation, subject to "thorough colonial exploitation."[83] Although this comparison may be anachronistically extreme, early modern peasant rebellions in the district directed against privileged outsiders and fueled by popular grievances over land tenure do suggest that a fundamental hostility born of dependence warped relations between laborers of the rochelais backcountry and consumers within the heavily fortified city. Splintering religious allegiances in the mid-sixteenth century only aggravated this situation.

The control of rochelais citizens over the local wine trade increased in 1461 when Louis XI conceded to the town council the right to collect and employ a formerly royal tax of 12.5% on all retail wine sales within the city and its *banlieue*. The council farmed out the lucrative receipts of this toll and empowered the *fermier*, usually a resident of La Rochelle, to inspect and mark all wine barrels offered for sale within the city's government. The *fermier* increased his profits by auctioning off subleases of his farm parish by parish in town and country. Citizens of La Rochelle, with ready credit or capital to expend, predominated in this regional cadre of excise men.[84] Abuses in the attribution and

---

[82] Pérouas, *Le diocèse de La Rochelle*, 131-139

[83] Julien-Labruyère, *Paysans charentais*, 2: 77 and 115.

[84] The best sources of information on the operation of the wine tax farms in early modern La Rochelle are the record books of the city's mayoral court, the body that supervised the bidding for and conferral of these franchises. See AMLR, E Suppl. 281 (FF 5), E Suppl. 282 (FF 6), E Suppl. 286 (FF 9), E Suppl.

administration of the wine retail tax farm provoked popular protests against the system in the 1520's. City sergeants arrested wine merchants in La Rochelle who refused to pay the tax. The captives commenced legal challenges to the levy and the slow pace of litigation envenomed urban politics throughout the decade.[85]

New commercial advantages townspeople secured from French monarchs aggravated popular dissatisfaction with regulation of the wine trade. By letters patent of November 1551, Henry II obliged leading Rochelais with an order compelling the proprietors of local cabarets to sell from Pentecost to the end of September only wine produced on estates in the *banlieue* owned by citizens of the city.[86] Between 1577 and 1581, the *corps de ville* attempted to consolidate a highly favorable rochelais hegemony over the local wine trade when it issued a series of decrees stipulating that a councilman appointed annually would now inventory and tax all foreign wine shipments arriving by land or sea. The ensemble of these measures caused wine smuggling to flourish in and around La Rochelle. The town council rapidly became embroiled in long disputes with rural wine makers, non-resident wine merchants, and rochelais wine dealers over clandestine provisioning, tax frauds, and the subornation of municipal inspectors. The mechanics of the regional wine markets (official and black) destabilized relations between town and country communities.

Salt, like wine, became a staple of the local agricultural economy. Although salt pans attracted less bourgeois investment that did vineyards, citizens of La Rochelle actively participated in this trade as property owners, middlemen, and bulk exporters exempt from royal salt taxes. Rochelais proprietors of salt pans were more willing to enter into sharecropping agreements with rural laborers, but at a rate that always reserved at least two-thirds of the fruits (and profits) to the land owner.[87] For no more than a third

---

287 (FF 10), and E Suppl. 288 (FF 12), deliberations of the *Cour de la mairie*, 1600-1605 and 1617-1620.

[85] Barbot, "Histoire de La Rochelle," AHSA, 14 (1886): 489-490.

[86] Trocmé and Delafosse, *Le commerce rochelais*, 108. Coming well after most of the perishable new wine from the last harvest had been sold, the spring and summer period of monopoly sales by bourgeois vineyard owners guaranteed these men the highest possible annual prices for their product to the consternation of poorer consumers.

[87] Pérouas, *Le diocèse de La Rochelle*, 107, notes that on the île de Ré around

of the harvest, *sauniers* committed themselves to arduous, year-round upkeep of the pans, dikes, and sluices essential for salt production. These tasks became particularly onerous on low-lying coastal tracts during the damp, stormy winter months.

As renters, *sauniers* also found little adequate space in this landscape to tend gardens or fields of food crops. Chronic and often severe grain shortages afflicted these districts, contributing to a steady exodus of impoverished rural laborers toward the docks and workshops of Atlantic port towns like La Rochelle. City magistrates struggled to police urban populations regularly swelled by large numbers of starving migrants. This flow of manpower matched the transit of regional salt production through rochelais warehouses and onto foreign bound merchant vessels. The city siphoned off salt stocks from the estuary of the Seudre, the islands of Ré and Oléron, and the valley of the Charente to supply northern European states and the Newfoundland fishing fleets. Profits from these enterprises accumulated in the coffers of city merchants, reinforcing the economic domination of La Rochelle over its hinterland. Laborers in the saline marshes, where salt production far exceeded consumption, resentfully complied with the demands of urban dealers prospecting vital distant markets for the spice.[88]

La Rochelle's dual performance as a consumer and as an exporter of diverse commodities created material needs the dependent regional economy became organized to supply. Besides wine, grain, and salt, a variety of finished products flowed into La Rochelle from the countryside. Within the adjacent provinces of Aunis and Saintonge, country bourgs and hamlets developed artisanal specialties designed to satisfy the urban marketplace. Charcoal for rochelais stoves and forges came in from the woodsmen of Benon forest and the *pelebois*. Coopers working in settlements on the tree line and just outside La Rochelle's city limits

---

1660 less than one percent of salt harvesters (*sauniers*) owned the property they worked. According to Julien-Labruyère, *Paysans charentais*, 1: 76, many of the common sharecropping contracts between *sauniers* and their employers gave the laborer rights to only one-quarter of the salt collected.

[88] As Pérouas, *Le diocèse de La Rochelle*, 107, argues, on the island of Ré and in the rochelias *banlieue*, workers in the salt pans "se trouvaient de plus assujetti aux marchands par le caractère aléatoire de leur industrie." Trocmé and Delafosse, *Le commerce rochelais*, 114-115, also emphasize the near servitude of *sauniers* to urban wholesalers under the local regime of salt production.

supplied barrels. Quarrymen and lime burners extracted urban building materials from promontories of the bedrock beneath villages of the rochelais plain.

These specialized and localized crafts supplied a preeminent civic, consumer economy inimical to the proliferation of employments among rural workers. The comparative economic underdevelopment and political subservience of La Rochelle's hinterland gave country residents enduring grievances against more prosperous and apprehensive city dwellers.[89]

## 4. *Dimensions of the Townscape*

La Rochelle absorbed rural products and refugees. A steady stream of immigrants swelled the ranks of inhabitants and increased urban population densities. Within a thick circuit of walls, the surface area of La Rochelle in 1550 extended barely one kilometer north to south and no more than 700 meters east to west. Within the walls, the habitable precincts of the city varied little in size between 1215 and 1615, covering at most approximately 500,000 square meters (50 hectares or about 124 acres).[90] (Figure 5 displays a plan of streets and neighborhoods in early modern La Rochelle). Reckoning by these dimensions, one architectural historian has aptly likened La Rochelle to the compactly built bastide towns of Aquitaine.[91]

Little is known about the number of citizens occupying this urban space in the mid-sixteenth century. The demographic history of the city has only been investigated sporadically. This lacuna is explained in part by the absence of pre-modern tax rolls or

---

[89] Julien-Labruyère, *Paysans charentais*, 2: 185-187, identifies a "mentalité d'enfermement" as characteristic of residents within the rochelais backcountry. This strikes me as an apt description of westerners' comportments also applicable to the townspeople of the region, urbanites proudly defending a civic way of life popularly regarded as threatened by local peasants and jealous outsiders.

[90] See Trocmé and Delafosse, *Le commerce rochelais*, 2; and Thierry Veillot, *La ville blanche*, (La Rochelle, 1992), 87 and 100.

[91] Veillot, *La ville blanche*, 87. This comparison is appropriate because, like the bastides, La Rochelle was situated on an uncertain frontier where Anglo-French military conflict long traumatized human settlements. The city's massive walls, erected and maintained by generations of town councilmen, best testify to how acutely leading citizens felt the "continual danger" they believed the isolated city faced.

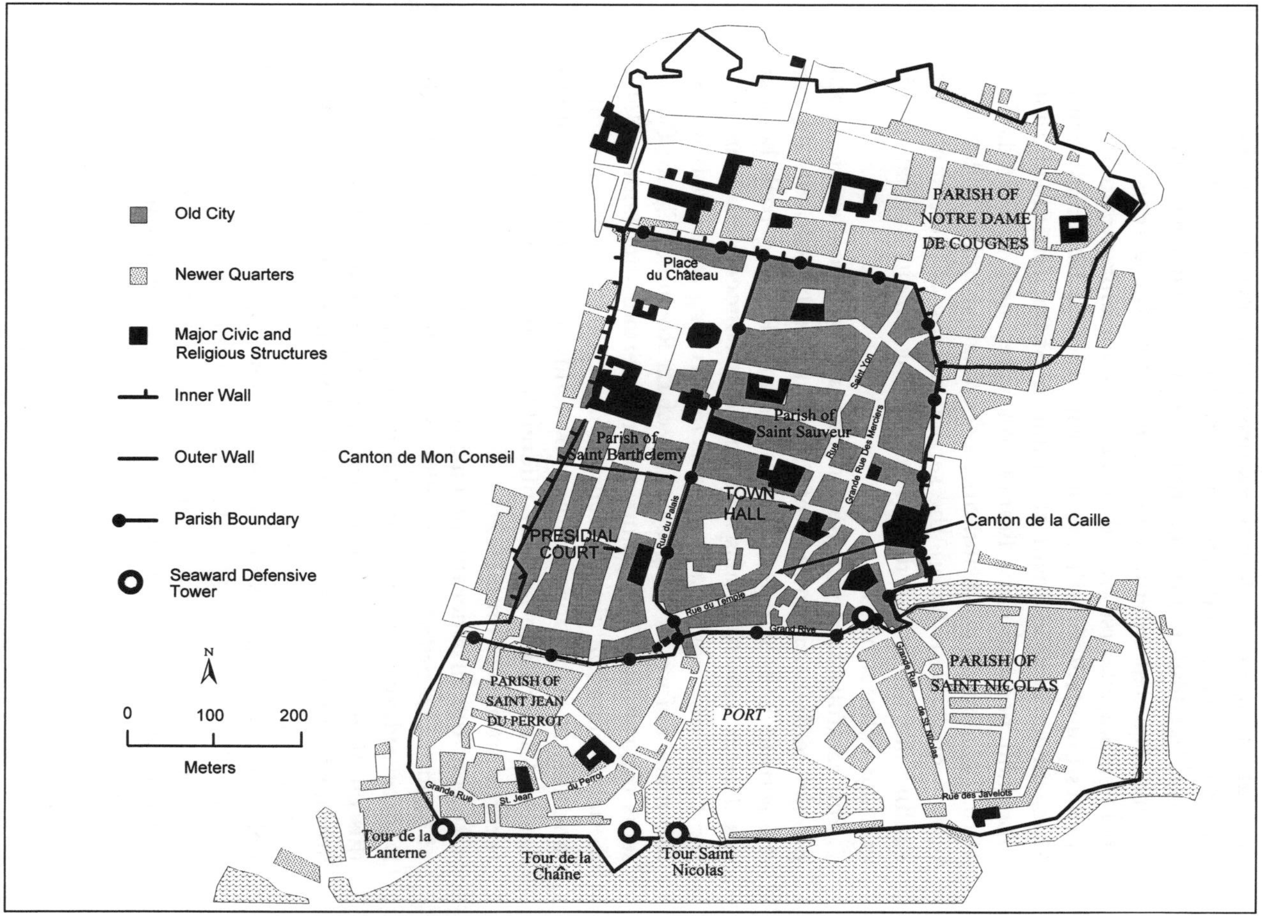

Figure 5. Plan of Early Modern La Rochelle

censuses from which a total population estimate could be easily derived. However, we do possess reasonably complete registers of Calvinist baptisms and marriages covering the period from 1561 to 1684. In addition, local Catholic baptisms, marriages, and burials are recorded intermittently after 1598. These registers have been employed first by Louis Pérouas to approximate La Rochelle's population in the period from 1610 to 1685 and then by Philip Benedict to estimate the number of Rochelais in the total Protestant population of France from the same starting date of 1610.[92] Neither of these authors have evaluated La Rochelle's population movements before the second decade of the seventeenth century nor within the deeper context of the city's social, political, and cultural history.

The carefully kept Calvinist baptismal registers allow us to approximate the total number of Protestants in La Rochelle during the second half of the sixteenth century. Pushing back beyond the date at which Pérouas and Benedict commenced their studies, I have inventoried all baptisms in surviving registers from the five main Reformed congregations of La Rochelle. Figure 6 presents the results of this count over the period from January 1564 to December 1627. Not all records for all congregations are simultaneously available for each year over this time span. Total numbers of Calvinist baptisms are offered for those years in which the records are most complete.

During the first decade of La Rochelle's *Réforme*, the number of baptisms recorded among adherents of the new religion steadily increased, reaching high peaks in the years 1574 to 1577. From this pinnacle, surviving recorded baptisms decline and fluctuate around the level of 700 per year until the late 1620's. New natality peaks occurred in 1586, 1588, 1610, and 1621. La Rochelle's Reformed community sustained a high level of fecundity no doubt bolstered by births attributable to Protestant immigrants settling in the principal Calvinist refuge of the French west country.

To convert numbers of baptisms into rough estimates of urban population levels, let us assume that the local Protestant birthrate fell between thirty-five and forty per thousand. This assumption

---

[92] See Louis Pérouas, "Sur la démographie rochelaise," *Annales E.S.C.*, 16 (1961): 1131-1140 and Philip Benedict, *The Huguenot Population of France, 1600-1685: The Demographic Fate and Customs of a Religious Minority*, Transactions of the American Philosophical Society, Vol. 81, pt. 5 (Philadelphia, 1991), 132.

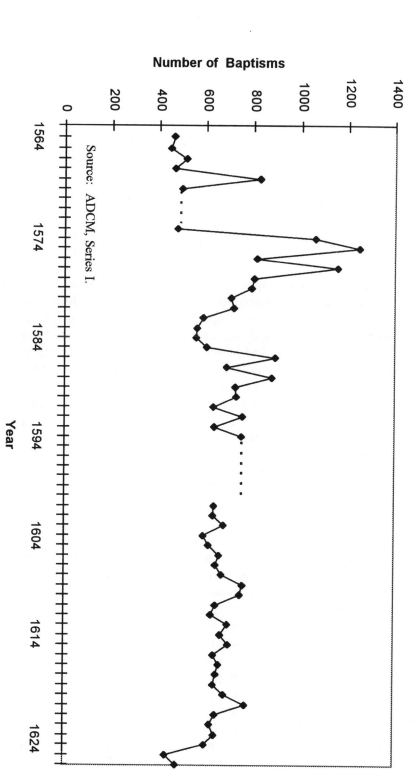

Figure 6. Annual Baptisms in Main Calvinist Congregations of La Rochelle, 1564-1627

is justified by Benedict's determination of a birthrate among rochelais Calvinists at forty per thousand in the decade 1610-1619.[93] It is also supported by Alain Croix's exhaustive study of sixteenth- and seventeenth-century birthrates in the neighboring towns of Brittany where he finds citizens reproducing at rates falling between thirty and forty per thousand.[94] Using these rates, we can estimate that the Protestant population of La Rochelle in 1564 probably ranged between 11,500 and 13,200, rising to between 20,400 and 23,300 a decade later when La Rochelle was flooded with refugees from the Religious Wars.[95] This scale accords with Pérouas' estimation of 18,000 Protestants in La Rochelle circa 1610.[96] To this number Pérouas adds an estimate of 5,000 Catholics to arrive at a total urban population in the early seventeenth century of 22,000 to 23,000 souls. Assuming that the rochelais Catholic community in the mid-sixteenth century was also about one-third the size of the Protestant citizenry (a reasonable supposition given the large number of notarized documents for the era dealing with the affairs of Catholics), "Papists" would have amounted to between 3,800 and 4,300 at this time. Total urban population circa 1560 would then have fallen between 15,300 and 17,500 souls.

Combining measures of urban topography and demography, we can conclude that in the mid-sixteenth century at least 15,300 Rochelais packed into the city's small quarters, yielding population densities of no less than 300 people per hectare, a rate nearly one thousand times greater than the population density per hectare of the city's *banlieue*.[97] By the first decade of the seventeenth century, a total population approaching 22,000 or more would have pushed urban population densities up toward 500 peo-

---

[93] Benedict, *Huguenot Population*, 52-55.

[94] Alain Croix, *La Bretagne aux 16e et 17e siècles*, 2 vols., (Paris, 1981), 1: 144-147 and Table 18.

[95] Use of estimated birthrates combined with the inability of baptism lists to account for population growth due to immigration means that all figures for total Protestant population in La Rochelle are subject to significant margins of error and may underrepresent actual population levels at the time.

[96] Pérouas, "Sur la démographie rochelaise," 1132.

[97] Pérouas calculates population densities in La Rochelle's rural hinterland (circa 1648) at approximately twenty-five to twenty-nine residents per square kilometer. This figure yields a rate of .25 to .29 inhabitants per hectare, see *Le diocèse de La Rochelle*, 101-103. Rural population densities would not have been appreciably greater in the mid-sixteenth century and may have been even lower.

ple per hectare, severely compounding demographic pressures and problems of alimentation within rochelais neighborhoods.[98]

High urban population densities could not be relieved by the development of habitable faubourgs outside the old town walls. The proximity of the sea and marshy land on three sides kept building outside the walls to a minimum. What few structures that did go up were repeatedly demolished during the Wars of Religion when the town council ordered their destruction as part of prudent protection against sieges. For example, prior to the 1572 encirclement of the city by royal troops, civic demolition brigades levelled every structure within cannon range of the outer defenses.

La Rochelle sits at the sheltered end of a bay partially shielded from the forces of the open sea by the large, sandy islands of Ré and Oléron. This superb natural harbor and the sturdy stone quays of La Rochelle's inner port accommodated ships from many nations. Capable of sheltering the largest royal Atlantic fleets, La Rochelle also served as a strategically sited frontier naval base covering sea lanes in the Bay of Biscay vital to the navies and maritime commerce of Spain and England. La Rochelle's locale merited heavy fortification against attack from any quarter. Successive English and French kings had liberally endowed the city with special privileges empowering the *corps de ville* to erect, maintain, and upgrade the most sophisticated and thickest defenses of any town in western France.[99]

By 1612, the city walls, eight to twelve feet in breadth, had attained a perimeter of more than 3,100 meters (10,170 feet). Twelve great towers and over twenty crenelated bastions anchored these formidable defenses. Before the end of the sixteenth century, La Rochelle's ramparts bristled with over 175 cannons of all calibers comprising the civic artillery. Gunners fed their weapons from volatile city magazines holding tons of powder and shot.[100]

---

[98] Pérouas, "Sur la démographie rochelaise," 1132 and Veillot, *La ville blanche,* 100. To take but one comparative example, average urban population density in late nineteenth-century Liverpool, one of the fastest growing British provincial cities, only reached about 230 residents per hectare.

[99] For details on the variety of municipal privileges obtained by the Rochelais for upkeep of city defenses see Delayant, *Histoire des Rochelais,* 120 and 147, on royal grants of 1442 and 1480.

[100] Arcère, *Histoire de la ville de La Rochelle,* 1: 321-322 and 419. In 1544, an accidental explosion in one such municipal ordnance warehouse devastated La

Nightly, the town watch, composed of men from the rochelais bourgeoisie, hauled up a massive, iron link chain between the tour Saint Nicolas (1382) and the tour de la Chaîne (1390), closing the seaway to the inner port that ran between the towers.

Behind its stout fortifications, La Rochelle divided itself into five parishes: Saint Jean du Perrot in the southwest fronting on the inner harbor; Saint Nicolas to the southeast also on the port; Saint Barthélémy covering the west center and northwestern sections of town; Saint Sauveur in the center east; and Notre Dame de Cougnes in the northeast. The parishes of Notre Dame, St. Sauveur, and St. Barthélémy formed the oldest inhabited parts of town and had shared a common defensive wall since the early thirteenth century. The old faubourgs of St. Jean du Perrot and St. Nicolas initially developed outside of the earliest fortifications and did not become securely enclosed within municipal defenses until the last quarter of the fourteenth century. Even after this larger protective circuit closed, the quarters of Perrot and Nicolas remained separated from the center of town by remnants of the original walls and the drainage ditches beneath them. Although numerous foot bridges spanned these gaps, a disjuncture between the port neighborhoods and the city center endured and, as we will see, profoundly affected urban politics over time.

Inside its walls, La Rochelle was a densely built town. Its principal streets, running north-south, were long, narrow, and gently curved, denying pedestrians dominant vistas and magnifying the height of the tall, closely packed, white stone houses fronting along each side. East-west transversals were similarly configured, up to 200 meters in length, cramped, untrue, and frequently disappearing into closed courts and cul-de-sacs. Only one big, open square existed in early modern La Rochelle. In the northwest quadrant of town, the parvis of the demolished royal château served as the *place d'armes* (or *place du château*). Throughout La Rochelle, streets meeting at irregular angles produced oddly shaped intersections referred to as "cantons" by natives. These intersections served as small squares and favored venues for official proclamations and neighborly socializing.

Although the concentrations of rich and poor varied from

---

Rochelle's port neighborhood of St. Jean du Perrot, killing forty and injuring hundreds.

parish to parish, rigid spatial segregation of townspeople by socioeconomic status did not exist in La Rochelle. Some wealthy magistrates and merchants shared parishes with poorer artisans and seamen. This distribution of citizens created the potential for a variety of politically important solidarities to form in and between neighboring status groups.

Although no comprehensive early modern municipal tax records exist to give this dispersion statistical precision, a comparison over time of annual and average house rental costs in the five parishes gives a rough indication of their relative social heterogeneity and wealth (see Table 1).[101]

*Table 1*
Annual and Average House Rental Costs by Parish
(1550–1620)

*Rent (in livres)*

| Parish | Rentals | 0-49 | 50-99 | 100-149 | 150+ | Ave. |
|--------|---------|------|-------|---------|------|------|
| Barthélémy | 14 | 1 | 4 | 1 | 8 | 172 |
| Cougnes | 56 | 28 | 19 | 2 | 7 | 63 |
| Nicolas | 25 | 13 | 6 | 4 | 2 | 73 |
| Perrot | 28 | 11 | 2 | 7 | 8 | 117 |
| Sauveur | 54 | 6 | 17 | 13 | 18 | 123 |

Adjoining the port and separated from La Rochelle's inner precincts by a small stream, the parish of St. Jean du Perrot accommodated merchants, artisans, shipwrights, stevedores, and a large transient population of mariners. Warehouses fronted on the port and bakers' ovens dotted the neighborhood, feeding locals and supplying passing ships with biscuit. Notarized residential rental contracts for the parish show wide variation in prices paid for shelter and in the composition of households established here. On 1 November 1599, two sailors and their wives took a house together for fifty-four *livres* a year.[102] Pierre de Bois, a merchant in

---

[101] This table is derived from notarized house rental contracts preserved in the voluminous archives of La Rochelle's notaries, ADCM, Series 3 E, *Notaires.*

[102] ADCM, 3 E 2043, fols. 178v-179r. Mariners comprised at least thirty percent of Perrot's entire population.

the neighborhood, agreed to pay his landlord 120 *livres* in annual rent for a house in February 1605.[103] In 1611, rooms could be
found in the quarter for as little as twenty-four *livres* per year.
Perrot long attracted a socially and economically mixed population.

The main street in this neighborhood was the curving rue du
Perrot over which loomed the thirty-meter gothic lighthouse spire
of the tour de la Lanterne (1468), the round stone bastion bul-
warking the quarter's seaward defenses. Rue du Perrot was lined
with wineshops, skittle-pin yards, *jeux de paume*, and numerous
auberges: "The Pewter Plate," "The Moor's Castle," and "The City
of Plymouth," where local residents and seamen passing through
could find a drink, a meal, a wager, or more illicit pleasures. The
volume of such business was evidently high. On 18 September
1576, Michel Esprinchard, an *échevin* on the town council, rented a house and adjoining *jeu de paume* he owned in Perrot's main
street to a master *paumier* for the huge sum of 400 *livres* a year.
The contract states that the *paumier*, Antoine de Pré, could not
sign his name. Although considerably lower in social status than
his noble landlord, de Pré was apparently counting on a high volume of sporting customers to meet his expensive rent.[104] The
auberges in Perrot counted among the more than thirty hostel-
leries to be found in the city. The parishes of St. Nicolas and St.
Barthélémy also had heavy concentrations of rooming houses.[105]
In threatening times of war, religious strife, or social conflict over
municipal politics, the inns, yards, and public spaces of Perrot
made room for popular assemblies. As we shall see, the unruly
denizens of Perrot were important actors shaping the economy,
religion, and politics of La Rochelle.

The parish of Saint Nicolas also fronted on the port and sheltered a diverse population of sailors, artisans, and travelling merchants who frequented the inns located around the central rue
Saint Nicolas. Evidence from notarial archives indicates that properties fetching high and low rents coexisted in the neighborhood,
attracting merchants in search of moderately priced homes, prop-

---

[103] ADCM, 3 E 2158, fol. 121v.

[104] ADCM, 3 E 152, fols. 598r-v.

[105] See the lists of innkeepers swearing to uphold municipal ordinances regulating their trade, AMLR, E Suppl. 278, fols. 2-41 and 175-218 and E Suppl.
279, fols. 1, 4, 21 and 66.

erties to let, and cheap warehouse space.[106] During the 1590's, Jacques Javalleau ran his international trading business from a compound of family residences and warehouses clustered around the homonymic rue des Javelots in Nicolas parish. In the late sixteenth century, Jean Imbert, a rochelais merchant with regional shipping interests, took a house in Nicolas and then married the daughter of Isaac du Querny, a prosperous neighboring businessman who traded in dried fish, grain, naval stores, and paper. With his widowed mother-in-law, Imbert petitioned the town council for a building permit to redo in stone the wooden facade of a jointly occupied house in rue St. Nicolas.[107] Successful neighborhood merchants spent conspicuously on home improvements to embellish a commercial quarter without the impressive edifices of the city center. Boat builders, ship chandlers, and rope makers also inhabited St. Nicolas, making it a major site of marine manufacturing and trade in the city. The raffish and enterprising inhabitants of districts peripheral to La Rochelle's port formed neighborhoods distinct from the inner precincts of town.

North and east of the port, the parish of Saint Sauveur encompassed the houses and shops of many rochelais merchants profiting from regional and transoceanic trade. At the canton de la Caille, the town's major commercial streets intersected in a tiny square. The rue du Temple ran westward from the canton leading to one of the largest municipal food markets. The rue du Port came up to the canton from the official customs weigh station (*poids le roi*) on the harbor. On the opposite side of the canton, this street continued as the rue Saint Yon, where richer wholesale merchant families had their town houses. The rue des Gentilshommes ran north of the canton, passed behind the fortified *hotel de ville* (town hall), and connected to the long grande rue des Merciers. Here, prosperous merchants with global connections lived in high stone houses distinguished by carved facades dis-

---

[106] In 1577, for example, Jean Assailly, *marchand et bourgeois* of La Rochelle, took a house in rue de la Sardinerie for 100 *livres* a year, ADCM, 3 E 153, fols. 12r-14v. He established his family in the neighborhood and by 1610 was renting out rooms in a house in the rue St. Nicolas to foreign merchants for twenty-three *livres* per annum, ADCM 3 E 216, fol. 91v.

[107] For Imbert's ties to the parish of St. Nicolas and details on his business ventures see ADCM, 3 E 206 11 March 1610, and 3 E 208, fols. 6r and 56r. See also BMLR, MS 763, fols. 2r-v.

playing classically ordered columns, caryatides, and friezes. Like many of La Rochelle's principal streets, the grande rue des Merciers was arcaded along both sides, allowing sheltered access to the artisans' boutiques set back from the pavement at the street level of each residence. A shoemaker on the ground floor with a modest clientele in the quarter might live and work beneath an upstairs family with business interests on three continents.

Rent in St. Sauveur varied but tended to be higher than in St. Nicolas or Perrot. In 1572, a wealthy merchant paid out 475 *livres* annual rental for a house in the rue du Temple owned by a member of La Rochelle's town council. Buying a home in the neighborhood required a major capital investment. In 1567, the sale price of a large house adjoining the town hall was 3,000 *livres*, a sum easily surpassing the yearly landed income of many minor French noblemen, especially in the neighborhood of La Rochelle. In the early seventeenth century, wealthier residents of St. Sauveur were aiding the duc de Sully in his reform of royal finances by establishing *rentes* through him with the crown and pledging their houses in the quarter as collateral to cover interest-bearing government loans exceeding 5,000 *livres*. The value of the houses at this time must have approximated the total amount of the state loans.[108] As the Reformation gained strength in La Rochelle, large private homes on the fringes of the St. Sauveur quarter served as the first meeting sites for local adherents of the new religion.

To the north and west of the port, the old parish of Saint Barthélémy was chiefly inhabited by foreign merchants and wealthier local *gens de justice*. Near the harbor, in rue Chef de Ville, congregated Dutch, Flemish, and German merchants with commercial operations in La Rochelle. In their honor, Rochelais called the main street intersection in the vicinity the "canton des Flamands." This canton could be closed off with chain barriers forming an open air commodities market from whence a babel of languages echoed down the arcaded street fronts.

The rue du Palais ran northward from the canton des Flamands. At the street's center point stood buildings housing the royal governor's court of justice. In 1552, Henry II elevated this tribunal

---

[108] Loan agreements between rochelais merchants and the duc de Sully can be found throughout the registers of Masset, notary of La Rochelle, see ADCM, 3 E 2160-2162.

to the rank of a presidial court to speed the local administration of the king's justice and to fight religious heresy in the region. Up the street from the courts, houses of magistrates, lawyers, and town council members clustered around the canton de Mon Conseil named for the many royal proclamations, municipal ordinances, and court decisions cried out here, printed up, and then affixed to the walls of surrounding structures. Although houses could be found in the neighborhood that rented for as little as thirty to forty *livres* per year, surviving notarized rental contracts indicate that annual rents over 150 *livres* were typical and that rents over 200 *livres* not uncommon.[109] Relatively high housing costs, a heavy contingent of resident magistrates, the absence of food markets, and fewer artisanal boutiques than elsewhere in the city made St. Barthélémy a less overtly commercial neighborhood which many Rochelais identified with the city's governing elite. The proximity of the *place du château*, prime venue for civic pageantry, *feux de joie*, public executions, and the reception of distinguished visitors, reinforced the notoriety of the quarter.

The parish of Notre Dame de Cougnes occupied the northeast quadrant of La Rochelle. Lower house rental costs here coupled with the presence of smelly slaughterhouses, tanneries, and dye works mark Cougnes as primarily an artisanal district housing a few mercantile families active in food processing and leather supply. For example, two generations of the Georget family operated a large tannery in the quarter, processing hides from as far away as Ireland and negotiating with Dutch merchants and shippers for the delivery of beaten copper cauldrons and other well-tooled business equipment.[110] The Georget family house and outbuildings in the rue Cardouan were worth approximately 4,500 *livres* in 1598.[111] Around the corner, Mathurin Georget, the family patriarch, was renting a small house to a cooper in 1585 for only twelve *livres* a year.

In daylight hours, streams of local merchants, visiting traders, wagoners, and day laborers passed through the neighborhood, entering and exiting the nearby town gate (*porte de Cougnes*) on the main road to the inland communities of Marans, Niort, and

---

[109] For examples of house rental contracts of between thirty and forty *livres* here see ADCM, 3 E 147, fols. 387v-388v and 3 E 2038, fols. 72r-v.
[110] ADCM, 3 E 199, fol. 266v.
[111] See ADCM, 3 E 199, fol. 266v and 3 E 2162, fols. 13v-14r.

Surgères. This traffic supported several large auberges in rue du
Minage adjoining the municipal granaries where the noisy off-
loading of cereal shipments contributed to the street life of the
quarter.

Within its neighborhoods, La Rochelle supported a heterogeneous population and economy divided into more than twenty
municipally sanctioned corporations of professional men, artisans,
and laborers. The absence of comprehensive civic tax rolls or censuses makes it difficult to analyze and subdivide the rochelais population exactly. However, disparate notarial papers and municipal
documents allow us to estimate orders of magnitude for specific
groups of urban residents.

The precise proportion of mariners in La Rochelle's population at any given moment cannot be determined given the ebb
and flow of people this livelihood generated. Shipping contracts
and crew manifests drawn from the registers of one rochelais
notary, David Bion, regularly employed by ship captains between
1585 and 1600, show that, by 1600, La Rochelle was home port
for about thirty ships each having crews numbering between five
and thirty-five men.[112] In 1599, for Newfoundland fishing expeditions alone, the Rochelais amassed a varied fleet of twenty-one
local vessels. In 1614, twenty-four ships gathered along the littoral
set sail on a similar venture. The most well informed economic
historians of La Rochelle estimate that by 1622 at least 150 vessels capable of taking to the high seas regularly operated out of
the city's harbor.[113]

A conservative estimate of the number of local sailors inhabiting the city in the mid-sixteenth century would be about 750. To
approximate the size of the laboring population earning a living
at work on the waterfront, one would have to multiply the figure
for local sailors by a factor of five or six to account for the lighter-
men, stevedores, warehousemen, and dock yard repair crews that
serviced ships and cargos. Rochelais living directly off the port
probably amounted to between a fifth and a quarter of the city's
entire population (above 15,000 in 1560) with the parishes of
Perrot and Nicolas housing the largest portion of these workers.

---

[112] ADCM, 3 E 186-201. See also Trocmé and Delafosse, *Le commerce rochelais*,
103.

[113] Trocmé and Delafosse, *Le commerce rochelais*, 103.

The number of laborers around the port, when added to the population of semi-skilled urban workers in other fields, probably ensured that the total proportion of common laborers in La Rochelle's population exceeded the level of a third regularly counted in other early modern French towns.

The port's workforce, it should be remembered, contained mostly self-employed laborers operating outside of all traditional guild regulations. These masterless men, unaccustomed to the deferential etiquette of the workshop, formed a volatile and irreverent cohort engaged in the city's economic, political, and religious affairs. Their concentration in the neighborhoods of Perrot and Saint Nicolas often made these quarters epicenters of popular protest in early modern times.

For the period 1588-1605, lists survive of rochelais masters in a number of different trades who went before the mayor's court annually to swear allegiance to their respective guild bylaws.[114] Table 2 gives the average number of masters in specific trades who participated in these ceremonies. Since testimonial lists are lacking for other major urban trades active in La Rochelle (like carpenters, masons, and tanners), the total number of master artisans in early modern La Rochelle was undoubtedly much higher. Extrapolating from the testimonial lists, Etienne Trocmé posits a rochelais community of at least 500 masters. Adding estimates of journeymen and apprentices to this figure, Trocmé proposes that the minimum number of townsmen employed in skilled trades was between 1,500 and 2,000 during this period.[115]

Master artisans who kept a shop and held the coveted honorific of "bourgeois" could be found in all sectors of the city with higher concentrations in the parishes of St. Nicolas and Cougnes. As religious tensions increased in La Rochelle during the second half of the sixteenth century destabilizing municipal governance, members of the town's ruling elite became more suspicious and censorious of the many *gens mécaniques* dwelling there. The etiology of this conflict will be tracked in subsequent chapters.

The number of merchants large and small operating in La Rochelle also can only be estimated. Trocmé notes that fifty

---

[114] See AMLR, E Suppl. 278, fols. 2-41 and 175-218; E Suppl. 279, fols. 1, 4, 21, and 66; E Suppl. 281 (FF 5), fols. 132r-134v; and E Suppl. 284 (FF 8), fol. 120r.

[115] Trocmé, "La Rochelle de 1560 à 1628," 109.

*Table 2*
Average Number of Masters Swearing Allegiance to Guild Statutes
in La Rochelle's Mayoral Court, 1588-1605

| Trade | Number |
|-------|--------|
| Blacksmiths | 12 |
| Butchers | 38 |
| Cloth Weavers | 25 |
| Coopers | 15 |
| Fullers | 10 |
| Gunsmiths | 15 |
| Innkeepers | 35 |
| Jewellers | 9 |
| Cutlers | 10 |
| Locksmiths | 10 |
| Pastry Cooks | 10 |
| Pewterers | 8 |
| Shoemakers | 40 |
| Sword Makers | 10 |
| Tailors | 60 |
| *Total* | 307 |

notable "marchands et bourgeois" annually elected the judge and councillors for the rochelais merchants' tribunal (established in 1565).[116] In mid November 1614, assembled members of La Rochelle's bourgeoisie in each parish elected representatives responsible for demanding greater political rights from the town council. While the radical nature of these conclaves no doubt kept some bourgeois at home, eighty attended the meeting in the parish of Perrot, fifty in St. Nicolas, 128 in St. Sauveur, 121 in St. Barthélémy, and 109 in Cougnes.[117] Although bourgeois of different occupations turned out, the reunions were well-attended by the headmen of merchant families. In St. Nicolas, for example, nineteen of the fifty attendees were certainly merchants. In Perrot, thirty-seven of the eighty who came were merchants. In St. Sauveur, fifty-nine out of 128 present can be positively identified as merchants. In Cougnes, twenty-nine merchants showed up

---

[116] Trocmé, "La Rochelle de 1560 à 1628," 109. See also BMLR, MSS 45-46, fols. 969-970.
[117] ADCM, 3 E 2161, fols. 152r-155v.

for the meeting and in St. Barthélémy nineteen of those present were running commercial enterprises. Of the 408 disgruntled bourgeois who attended the assemblies, 134 (33%) were definitely merchants, several of whom took a leading role in the deliberations. If merchants constituted about one-third of all bourgeois in La Rochelle (a reasonable assumption in a port town), we can use Trocmé's estimate of at least 500 artisan bourgeois to posit at a minimum a total bourgeois community of approximately 750 with merchants accounting for one-third of that number and possibly more by the early seventeenth century.

Similar in size was the community of *gens de justice* who served as judges and filled subordinate positions in the royal courts and regional tribunals sitting in La Rochelle. In 1552, the *siège présidial* (successor to the old *cour du gouvernement*) included a president, lieutenants general and criminal, lieutenants particular serving as assessors civil and criminal, a king's attorney, a king's prosecutor, and thirteen councillors.[118] By 1611, the number of councillors was up to twenty and the court now operated with two *avocats du roi* and an *enquêteur*. Forty-two *avocats* and twenty-six *procureurs* had the right to plead before the *présidial* in 1611.[119] Fourteen other judges headed smaller tribunals in the city, eight *élus* prosecuted cases arising from administration of the *taille*, and fifteen notaries aided in the preparation of legal documents and depositions. By 1621, members of the legal profession in La Rochelle could field an entire company of the municipal militia or approximately 250 men.

Among La Rochelle's inhabitants, several booksellers had opened shop by 1550. Barthélémy Berton, a major regional printer of Protestant texts, began working in La Rochelle in 1563.[120] In 1540, François I accorded the Rochelais a privilege to establish a college for young scholars with an endowment of 600 *livres* drawn from city revenues. By the 1570's, a Protestant school of

---

[118] Arcère, *Histoire de la ville de La Rochelle*, 2: 539, "Matricule des Officiers du présidial."

[119] ADCM, B 1340, fols. 219r-v.

[120] On printing and bookselling in early modern La Rochelle, see Louis Audiat, *Essai sur l'imprimerie en Saintonge et Aunis*, (Pons, 1879); Louis Desgraves, "L'Introduction de l'imprimerie dans le Sud-Ouest de la France jusqu'à la fin du XVIe siècle," in M.-A Arnould, ed., *Villes d'imprimerie et moulins à papier du XIVe au XVIe siècle*, (Brussels, 1976), 39-80; and E. Droz, *L'Imprimerie à La Rochelle*, Vol. 1: *Barthélémy Berton, 1563-1573*, (Geneva, 1960).

theology under the patronage of the municipality had begun to train aspirants to the Calvinist clergy. Town revenues paid for faculty positions in Greek, Hebrew, and Latin. Foreign merchants with no French easily found rochelais traders capable of speaking English, Dutch, German, Italian, or Spanish who could help them conduct business negotiations and understand final contracts drafted in French by local notaries.[121] Amidst lectures in learned tongues and polyglot business dealings, a visitor to La Rochelle could also hear the patois of Aunis spoken in the markets, between householders and their servants, and occasionally even during deliberations of the town council. In the mid-sixteenth century, La Rochelle's proximity to busy coastal shipping routes, heterogeneous, enterprising populace, quasi-independent civic government, regional administrative institutions, and expanding schools made it the most important center of unfettered urban civilization on the French Atlantic coast between Nantes and Bordeaux.

La Rochelle's city fathers held no illusions about the geopolitical hazards threatening their frontier seaport. The elaborate catalogue of La Rochelle's municipal privileges testifies to natives' resolve over generations to endow their city with the commercial, judicial, and military advantages essential for durable communal self-government. Dangerously exposed to the inscrutable sea, vulnerable to the navies of Europe's most bellicose maritime powers (Spain, Holland, and Britain), surrounded by lawless territory, and packed with fractious inhabitants, La Rochelle became a mercantile fortress whose leading citizens in all social strata contended with one another for direction of potent civic institutions. Subsequent chapters will explore the early modern dimensions of these struggles.

---

[121] See for examples, ADCM, 3 E 150, fols. 134r-v; 3 E 198, fol. 76r; and 3 E 2160, fol. 85r.

# CHAPTER TWO

# AN INTRODUCTION TO THE POWER POLITICS OF SIXTEENTH-CENTURY LA ROCHELLE

## 1. *The Powers and Prerogatives of Municipal Government*

Over the century from 1550 to 1650, La Rochelle was an important venue of the institutional and confessional conflicts shaping early modern France. Here, royal servants confronted municipal officials. Oligarchic town councilmen struggled with unenfranchised groups of citizens over the control of civic government. A Reformed laity with strong congregational sympathies tested and diminished the authority of a Calvinist pastorate and consistory. These oppositions were simultaneous and imbricated. Their intensity increased when militant Protestants and Catholics turned La Rochelle into a theater of the French Religious Wars. The ensemble of these antagonisms resulted in a thorough politicization of La Rochelle's early modern populace. A long succession of violent internal and external challenges to the community's repose drew more and more Rochelais from all ranks of urban society into the fray of town politics and habituated them to this engagement. Intramural clashes between armed factions contending to dominate municipal government, religious riots, and extramural assaults by royal armies against a rebel town combined to force dramatic alterations in the number and social origins of rochelais political actors.

Before entering into a history of these transformations, it is essential to discuss the fundamental agencies of town government and the stresses they underwent in the three decades before 1550. This exposition will show the mechanics of civic administration in La Rochelle, the dynamics of the city's troubled relationship with the French crown, and the resurgence of powerful communal government on the eve of the rochelais Reformation. Examining the situation of the town's leading citizens within urban neighborhoods and institutions after 1550 will clarify the topography and sociology of politics in early modern La Rochelle.

Successive generations of rochelais city fathers responded to the challenges of coastal urban government by stubbornly pursuing one key strategy: accumulation of municipal privileges empowering the community to administer itself under the sovereignty of English or French kings. The objective here, it should be remembered, was not La Rochelle's complete emancipation from royal authority, but rather a mutually advantageous symbiosis with monarchy. This respectful union, structured by the protocol of privileges the town would willingly pay for and only the king could grant, became an early paradigm of rochelais politics and diplomacy. La Rochelle quickly achieved the status of a *bonne ville* and this enduring distinction reflects the ambition of the town's wary governing elite to establish a special relationship with the French crown. Municipal officials construed such an entente as a bulwark of the city's defenses against the hazards they faced on a marine frontier.

The history and vocabulary of La Rochelle's many royal privileges attest to the long, statutory compact linking monarchy and municipality. As early as 1224, Louis VIII had promised the Rochelais that their city would never be separated from the crown of France. Jean II (ruled 1350-1364) conferred extensive commercial liberties on the mayor, bourgeoisie, and inhabitants of La Rochelle in recompense for "the agreeable services and loyal obedience they have invariably and inimitably rendered to us."[1] Charles V (ruled 1364-1380) fixed the dimensions of La Rochelle's *banlieue* and invested municipal officers with legal jurisdiction over the territory as a reward for "the willing and immense services offered to our predecessors and to us by our beloved and loyal subjects, the city fathers and residents of our La Rochelle."[2] Royal favor acknowledge the city's aid in the difficult task of policing the French west country. For generations, upon their election, the mayors of La Rochelle swore to uphold everywhere the fidelity

---

[1] For histories and citations of La Rochelle's many municipal privileges see Louis-Etienne Arcère, *Histoire de la ville de La Rochelle et du pays d'Aunis*, 2 vols. (La Rochelle, 1756; reprint, Marseille, 1975), 1: 260-263, 278-280 and 573. See also Jean-Noel Luc, *La Charente-Maritime, l'Aunis et la Saintonge des origines à nos jours*, (Saint-Jean-d'Angély, 1981), 179-181. Several critical royal fiscal and commercial privileges of the fourteenth century underlying La Rochelle's civic independence are collected in dossiers now conserved at the Archives Nationales in Paris, see AN, JJ 85, fol. 57 and JJ 89, fol. 171v.

[2] Arcère, *Histoire de la ville de La Rochelle*, 1: 577.

(*féaulté*) due to French kings and to dispense justice equitably as agents of monarchical legal authority.[3] These duties extended the purview of municipal officials far beyond the city walls.

To conserve these empowering and enriching responsibilities, town governors were prepared to pay dearly. Impecunious French kings expected the *corps de ville* in La Rochelle to equip at its own expense warships for royal naval forces operating intermittently in the Atlantic. In 1465, Louis XI demanded an additional cash subsidy from the Rochelais in return for confirmation of their privileges. The monarch received a lump sum payment of 4,000 *écus*. Two years later the town council sent an additional "gift" of 4,250 *livres* to the king for maintenance of civic privileges.[4] In 1495, city envoys managed to convince Charles VIII that his demand for two fully equipped warships from the Rochelais to be delivered in two months was unfeasible. The emissaries offered 6,000 *livres* instead, in part to dissuade Charles from his project of installing a permanent royal squadron in the rival west country port of Brouage.[5] Although not legally bound to do so, the Rochelais paid out 2,400 *livres* in 1538 to aid in subsidizing the wages of infantry troops serving François I. Only eleven other French towns paid as much or more to meet this contribution expected by the crown.[6] When necessary, La Rochelle's town council deeply tapped the city's mercantile wealth, enabling it to remain active in a political economy linking French monarchs and their *bonnes villes*. Tensions between the partners in this alliance of convenience were not uncommon and tended to multiply as royal fiscal demands increased in French towns.

The central institution of municipal government in La Rochelle was the town council or *corps de ville*. Originating in the twelfth century, this corporate body exercised powers of police recurrently confirmed and enlarged by successive French kings. By the early sixteenth century, the town council had developed into a

---

[3] *Ibid.*, 590. Jean de Conan, mayor of La Rochelle in 1516, erected a chapel shortly after his election where daily prayers were to be said for the king and city. See Léopold Delayant, *Histoire des Rochelais*, 2 vols. (La Rochelle, 1870), 1: 151, and M. Dupont, *Histoire de La Rochelle*, (La Rochelle, 1830), 69.

[4] Arcère, *Histoire de la ville de La Rochelle*, 1: 278-79.

[5] Delayant, *Histoire des Rochelais*, 1: 141-142.

[6] See Bernard Chevallier, *Les bonnes villes de France du XIVe au XVIe siècle*, (Paris, 1982), 40, and R. Chartier, G. Chaussinand-Nogaret, *et. al.*, *Histoire de la France urbaine*, vol. 3, *La ville classique*, (Paris, 1981), 24-25.

multitiered political institution served by a subordinate bureaucracy of clerks, assessors, inspectors, and sergeants reaching into
every neighborhood of town.

Compilations of ancient privileges and civic ordinances made
by local historians in the sixteenth and seventeenth centuries
detail the structure of municipal government in La Rochelle. The
civic administration included a mayor elected annually and a town
council composed of seventy-six *pairs*, twelve *échevins*, and twelve
*conseillers*, all of whom served for life. *Pairs* were subordinate to
*échevins* and *conseillers*. The *échevins* and *conseillers* shared the same
status but bore different civic duties and alternated offices from
year to year. *Echevins* and *conseillers* who had previously served as
*pairs* retained the lower office upon their elevation to higher rank.
All grades of councilmen were ranked by seniority and special deference was shown to the eldest members in each division.

Yearly, on the first Sunday after Easter, all town councilmen met
in the Church of St. Barthélémy after high mass to elect new candidates for mayor. The three candidates with the highest vote
totals then went before La Rochelle's royal governor who chose
one of the three to be mayor. The candidate who had received
the highest number of votes in mayoral balloting was normally
chosen to be mayor. The first runner-up became the vice-mayor
or *co-élu*.

The new mayor swore an oath to guard the city for the king
and to dispense municipal justice equitably. After swearing a second oath to protect all civic privileges, the mayor was installed in
the chair of honor at the head of the great council table. The
mayor, as "capitaine de la ville," was commander of the 2,000-man
municipal militia, took personal charge of the keys to all city gates,
and supervised the town watch. His captaincy of armed forces
made La Rochelle's chief executive a potential ally or rival of royal governors charged with mustering troops for defense of the
region against invasion and sedition. An ancient civic custom
required mayors at the end of their term of office to donate a
cannon of large calibre to the arsenal of municipal artillery. This
rite reinforced the mayor's identification with the armed forces
protecting the city. The heavy guns donated were frequently
named to commemorate either the benefactor or a notable event
that had occurred during his term of service. Fulfillment of this
official obligation by generations of departing mayors gave La

Rochelle one of the largest collections of civic artillery among all the towns of France. In part, rochelais civic authorities ritually responded to a threatening external environment by amassing a great communal arsenal of modern weaponry meant to intimidate outsiders and annihilate aggressors.

Municipal ordinances imposed stiff penalties on citizens who refused to obey the mayor's commands or who otherwise insulted him. The bell of the town hall tolled lugubriously to signal a mayor's demise. For the interment of a deceased mayor, civic officials proclaimed a day of public mourning, suspended all commerce in the port city, and called out the citizenry to witness a solemn funeral procession bearing the body on a final patrol of the community.

The mayor, the twelve *échevins*, and the twelve *conseillers* comprised the ruling elite of La Rochelle. Mayors were normally selected from among the *échevins* and *conseillers*. *Echevins* and *conseillers* benefitted from special civic privileges for themselves and their families. From 1300, the sons of *échevins* and *conseillers* were given preference for the offices and honors of the commune. The sons of *échevins* had the first right to replace any *échevin* or *conseiller* dying in office. In 1373, the French king Charles V ennobled *échevins*, *conseillers*, and their descendants. Between 1437 and 1509, additional municipal ordinances gave the sons of *échevins*, *conseillers*, and *pairs* first preference in succession to their fathers' offices. By the early sixteenth century, the practice of "resignation" was openly condoned whereby each member of the *corps de ville* could transfer his office to a son or kinsman so long as the new officeholder met a minimum age requirement of eighteen. This practice made La Rochelle's town council an oligarchy effectively closed to humbler citizens. Old council bylaws limiting the number of family members serving at one time became moribund.

A week after the mayoral election, *échevins* and *conseillers* assembled to choose three candidates from the *corps de ville* to compete for each of several important posts in town government. These positions included the municipal treasurer, secretary of the town council, city attorney, city engineer, the controller of expenditures for civic improvements, and the captains commanding the three great towers guarding La Rochelle's harbor. The new mayor chose one of the three candidates to fill each post for one year. The *échevins* also annually selected members of the town council to serve as magistrates on the mayor's court. This tribunal, delegated by the mayor to render justice in his name, was comprised of a senior judge and four assistant justices (*co-adjuteurs*). By royal letters patent given in the fourteenth century, the mayor's court exercised civil and criminal jurisdiction in the first instance over all sworn members of the rochelais commune, their families, and the inhabitants of the city's *banlieue*. Jurisdictional disputes between the mayor's tribunal and local royal courts of law under the governor's supervision were frequent and integral to rochelais urban politics.

Every three years, the *échevins* and *conseillers* selected three candidates from the *corps de ville* to compete for each of nine local offices requiring a triennial term of service for maximum efficiency in the maintenance of public order. These three-year appointments, also made by the mayor, included the governorships of La Rochelle's four public hospitals, four offices of municipal police inspector (*procureurs de police*), and the command of the city's large arsenal.[7] A mayor would thus ascend to a powerful position of civic influence and patronage from whence he would have the chance of advancing kinsmen and supporters on the town council to positions of real authority within the urban community. With such considerable prerogatives at stake, competitions among town councilmen for the mayor's office grew fierce.

Annually, the *pairs*, *conseillers*, and *échevins* meeting together selected outright the senior judge of the mayor's court, twelve town sergeants for enforcement of municipal ordinances, twelve *halberdiers* serving as the mayor's honor guard, the five town gate keepers, the marshal of the night watch, skilled cannoneers for the city's many artillery batteries, and the town council's attorney accredited to plead before the presidial court.[8] All members of the town council were equally responsible for selecting the captains and lieutenants of La Rochelle's eight militia companies. These vital posts of municipal military command normally went to *échevins* and senior *pairs*. During the sixteenth century, annual tours of duty replaced life appointments to these positions.

---

[7] BMLR, MS 40, "Du corps et college de la maison de la ville de La Rochelle," fols. 106r-107v.

[8] *Ibid.*, fol. 108r.

Although officered by senior town councilmen, the rank and file of La Rochelle's militia units comprised all members of the bourgeoisie occupying a single street or network of interconnected streets. Neighborhoods throughout the city contributed armed forces for communal defense. Citizen-soldiers in the militia, while sharing bourgeois status, held a wide variety of artisanal, mercantile, and professional occupations.

The entire town council also received and reviewed all petitions prepared by residents of the city for membership in La Rochelle's bourgeoisie. The council set admission standards to this privileged segment of the citizenry and collected the enrollment fees required from successful candidates. Manipulation of these requirements by the *corps de ville* was a sore point between city councilmen, bourgeois without access to civic offices, and aspirants to the bourgeoisie in the sixteenth and early seventeenth centuries. Rochelais outside the *corps de ville* made increasingly strident allegations against town councilmen for favoritism and misconduct in the conferral of bourgeois status. Growing animosities like these contributed to the destabilization of traditional communal government in the latter sixteenth century

A profile of civic institutions in La Rochelle shows that the town council controlled the distribution of multiple offices placing its functionaries in every urban neighborhood. However, as subsequent chapters will demonstrate, this presence did not cower local critics of the council, its policies, and its operation.

Once the mayor's court convened each year, one of its chief duties was to farm out by auction municipal rights to collect a wide variety of tolls and taxes in the city and region. Farms on civic taxes for sale included the right to collect one-eighth of the value of all wine sold at retail in the city and its *banlieue*, a small tax on all wine exported from La Rochelle, the *droit d'aulnage* imposed on all retail sales of cloth in the city, landing duties on all cereals, salt, coal, and oils entering the port, charges on tiles, slates, and bricks delivered, brokerage fees on every sale of horses and mules made in town, imposts on hides imported for tanning, and entry tolls collected at the five main gates of the city.[9]

---

[9] Minute books of the mayor's court record bidding sessions and prices paid for the tax farms. See AMLR, MSS E Suppl. 280 (FF4), fols. 50r-53v, E Suppl. 281 (FF5). fols. 16v-24v, and E suppl. 282 (FF 6), fols. 17r-18v. The *huitième* on wine

Bidding for these tax farms always became intensely competitive and the city annually collected large sums from the auction. Proceeds from these sales contributed greatly to a total municipal income of between 10,000 and 15,000 *livres* per year in the 1530's. Town budgets grew in size over the century as maritime commerce expanded and civic tax revenue from mercantile activity increased.[10] In 1580, for example, selling the *huitième* on retail wine sales alone earned the city more than 9,000 *livres*.[11] By 1598, the city was obtaining 15,600 *livres* annually from farming out the *huitième*. During the 1590's, the tax farm on horse trading regularly went for more than 1,000 *livres* annually. The *droit d'aulnage* was bringing in 1,400 *livres* to city coffers by 1618.[12] The proceeds from the sale of civic tax farms added to income produced by urban and rural rental properties owned by the *corps de ville*, enrollment fees from new members of the bourgeoisie, and the collection of fines for infringements of municipal ordinances gave La Rochelle's town council an income in the latter sixteenth century in excess of 20,000 *livres* per annum. This carefully administered cash flow, although subject to fluctuations in trade cycles, provided strong, reliable financial backing for the town council's participation in local, regional, and national politics throughout the early modern era.

The mayor's court was also the venue for settling all disputes between guild officers and guild members as well as the tribunal for enforcing shopkeepers' adherence to municipal orders stipulating standard weights and measures for the fabrication and sale of foodstuffs. The mayor's court waged a ceaseless campaign against bakers cheating their customers by selling light loaves or bad bread made from adulterated flour.[13] Townspeople who repudiated their debts, polluted the streets, violated municipal building codes, or kept unauthorized farm animals in their homes could also be called to account in the mayor's court.

---

was assessed on tavern owners who could pay off the *fermier* in one lump sum based on previous and projected annual sales. The owner of the *huitième* regularly subdivided his farm, auctioning off the right to collect the tax intramurally and extramurally parish by parish. See also Etienne Trocmé and Marcel Delafosse, *Le commerce rochelais de la fin du XVe siècle au début du XVIIe*, (Paris, 1952), 23-44.

[10] Delayant, *Histoire des Rochelais*, 160.

[11] AMLR, E Suppl. 280 (FF 4), fol. 53r.

[12] *Ibid.*, fols. 258r-261v. See also BMLR, MS 763, fol. 8v and MS 160, fol. 18v.

[13] AMLR, E Suppl. 281 (FF 5), fols. 2r-v. BMLR, MS 155, "Registre de la cour de la mairie," (Nov. 1569-Sept. 1573), fol. 1v.

The executive, legislative, and judicial powers vested in the *corps de ville* and its subsidiary agencies left no town dweller immune to the regulatory authority of municipal government. Decisions made by town councilmen set standards of public and private behavior, policing the ordinary and extraordinary events of each citizen's life. Whether buying bread or going bankrupt, a resident of La Rochelle acted under the purview of the town council. Members of the *corps de ville*, were directly responsible for the financial administration of La Rochelle, dispensing justice in the city, keeping the peace, supervising military defense, and guarding the elaborate privileges perpetuating semi-autonomous civic administration. Daily performance of the tasks civic officeholding entailed and closed competitions to fill town posts gave municipal officials ample opportunities to entrench themselves and their kin in the institutions of rochelais government. The tax exemptions, commercial privileges, and prestige civic offices conferred induced elite family members to keep a firm grip on the positions they held in town government. The scope of the town council's prerogatives made it the center of local politics.

## 2. *Formative Conflicts between City and Crown*

Ill-omens in the French west country marked the beginning of François I's reign. Disastrous crop failures from 1513 to 1515 produced widespread food shortages, tripling the cost of flour in La Rochelle. With famine looming, La Rochelle's mayor authorized the capture of passing grain vessels and the forced sale of their cargos on the town docks at prices far below market value.[14] These desperate measures could not forestall mass starvation in the region. Severe outbreaks of the plague accompanied this dearth and impeded replanting of the fields, prolonging the local subsistence crisis. Maritime commerce was also interrupted and La Rochelle's economy shrivelled. To escape contagion, most members of the town council fled the city, leaving the urban community directionless. To shore up communal government, the mayor was forced to order all fugitive town councilmen back to the

---

[14] Arcère, *Histoire de la ville de La Rochelle,* 1: 308 and Dupont, *Histoire de La Rochelle,* 69.

city under threat of losing their offices. Repeated summonses barely yielded a quorum of councilmen sufficient for the administration of civic affairs. Emergency measures to bolster the finances and administration of the city's four hospitals, filled with the dead and dying, were the first order of business.[15] Uncommonly severe storms aggravated these adversities. Floods inundated coastal villages making refugees of their inhabitants. Hurricane gales uprooted trees and tore out vines, destroying in a moment decades of agricultural labor.

Suffering from these blows to the local economy, the Rochelais were ill-prepared and unwilling to meet increased royal demands for cash subsidies to fund French armies campaigning in northern Italy. In 1516, François I summarily demanded an inspection of municipal account books and used the information he obtained to justify a special levy of 3,000 *livres* on La Rochelle to aid the king in reconquering the duchy of Milan. As was customary, upon ascending to the throne, François I had reconfirmed the privileges of La Rochelle. The king's letters of approval had been duly registered by the Parlement of Paris, but final confirmation of the city's all-important liberties was deferred when the *Chambre des Comptes* initiated a review of La Rochelle's numerous fiscal immunities. François I's demand for funds came while confirmation of town privileges lay in abeyance and may have been calculated as a pressure tactic forcing the Rochelais to pay up in hopes that their "gift" would secure royal guarantees of a favorable outcome in the *Chambre*.

To test his subjects further, François had ordered the Rochelais to receive his new governor of Aunis and Guyenne, de Lautrec, with pageantry befitting the monarch himself.[16] Civic officials promptly organized the commanded reception but included a symbolic snub of the king's deputy. De Lautrec was met outside the city by an opulent procession of local notables who, with the accompaniment of musicians, conveyed him to his intramural lodgings. Although de Lautrec, like all previous royal governors, swore before entering town not to infringe La Rochelle's privileges, at no point during the welcoming ceremonies did anyone offer the city's keys to him as was customary.[17] With the status of

---

[15] Delayant, *Histoire des Rochelais*, 1: 146.
[16] Dupont, *Histoire de La Rochelle*, 67.
[17] Dupont, *Histoire de La Rochelle*, 67; and Delayant, *Histoire des Rochelais*, 1: 144.

their civic liberties uncertain, La Rochelle's leading citizens were unwilling to demonstrate their usual degree of deference toward outside authorities and pointedly refused the ritual gift of their keys to the king's representative.

Citing adverse climatic and economic conditions in the west country, La Rochelle's town council then refused to pay the 1516 imposition François I had deemed appropriate. A token, one-time gift of 1,000 *livres* was offered instead as the largest possible contribution the city could make to royal military ventures outside the kingdom. With reluctance and recriminations, the king accepted this sum. Piqued by this diminution in respect paid to him and to his representatives by the Rochelais, François I harbored a lingering animosity toward the city and its representatives.[18]

The *Chambre des Comptes* did not finish its review of La Rochelle's privileges until February 1519. Fiscal officers based in Paris endorsed most of the Rochelais' immunities from commercial duties; however, the Chamber narrowly defined the provenance of goods and the types of citizens eligible for exemptions. Henceforward, only wines and merchandise produced within the government of Aunis could be traded by city merchants free of certain tolls and taxes. The Chamber further stipulated that only Rochelais holding the status of bourgeois could rightly claim these advantages.[19] Ordinary citizens (*habitans*) did not qualify. The town council appealed this decision to the Parlement of Paris but the Chamber refused to recognize the Parlement's competence in this financial matter. Rochelais envoys, kept in Paris at considerable expense to the town council, contested the Chamber's ruling before a special commission named by the king to investigate the dispute. Royal commissioners upheld the Chamber's strict application of La Rochelle's fiscal privileges.

This bureaucratic wrangling had two serious local repercussions. First, ordinary residents of the city now obligated to pay additional taxes blamed the town council for not protecting them from new charges threatening their livelihood in difficult economic times. This anger translated into a loss of popular respect for the *corps de ville* and heightened tensions between the various

---

[18] Dupont, *Histoire de La Rochelle*, 70.
[19] Delayant, *Histoire des Rochelais*, 1: 154-155.

strata of rochelais society. Second, members of the bourgeoisie read the Chamber's verdict as an official sanction of their claim to exemption from the municipal excise of 12.5% on all retail wine sales in the town and government of La Rochelle. Several prominent bourgeois refused to pay the impost, threatening the market value of the municipal tax farm profitably established on the levy by town councilmen. The mayor promptly arrested the recalcitrant tax payers who appealed their imprisonment to the Parisian Parlement. The mayor and town council lost the appeal for having violated municipal judicial procedures in the rush to jail the protestors. Yet, neither side rested content with this verdict. Subsequent litigation stoked reciprocal distrust between the various ranks of townspeople.

Simultaneously, the *corps de ville* had to fend off an opportunistic attack on the city's exemption from the *taille* mounted by the *élus* of Saintonge. The town council tenaciously opposed this bid to levy more taxes on La Rochelle, a move by outsiders in blatant contravention of civic privileges. Rochelais representatives ultimately managed to obtain royal confirmations of the city's immunity in return for an annual exemption fee of 3,000 *livres*.[20]

The defeat of a French royal army and capture of François I by Imperial forces at the pitched battle of Pavia (24 February 1525) cast La Rochelle into more troubled times. The rivalry fought out between François I and Charles V had interrupted profitable rochelais commerce with Spain and Flanders, weakening the city's economy. Now, the regent, Louise of Savoy, as part of her hastily conceived plan to strengthen the realm's frontier defenses during the king's captivity, ordered Charles Chabot, Baron de Jarnac, royal governor of La Rochelle, Aunis, and Saintonge, to move from his family estates and take up residence at his urban post.[21] The citizenry of La Rochelle suspiciously regarded the presence of this magnate and his auxiliary troops as another threat to the city's welfare.

---

[20] *Ibid.*, 1: 156; and Amos Barbot, "Histoire de La Rochelle," ed. Denys d'Aussy, AHSA 14 (1886): 1-516; 17 (1889): 1-373; and 18 (1890): 1-226. See in particular 14 (1886): 493. Louise of Savoy, inclined to conciliation by the exigencies of her regency, finally granted royal endorsement of La Rochelle's full exemption from the *taille* in 1525.

[21] Delayant, *Histoire des Rochelais*, 1: 156; Arcère, *Histoire de la ville de La Rochelle*, 1: 309.

Under the terms of the treaty of Madrid (14 January 1526), François I was freed from Spanish captivity in exchange for his renunciation of all claims on Italian territory, the cession of Burgundy to Charles V, and the transfer of François' two eldest sons into Spanish custody as hostages to ensure French fulfillment of the pact. François I agreed to these terms and returned to France in April 1526. In August 1529, the Madrid compact was revised allowing the French to pay a ransom of two million gold *écus* for return of the king's sons rather than conceding Burgundy to the Habsburgs.

Rochelais discomfort with a small royal garrison was superseded by more dangerous popular consternation when it was learned that the town had been assigned a 10,000 *livre* contribution to the ransom fund for the safe return of the French princes.[22] Restive members of La Rochelle's bourgeoisie, alarmed at the prospect of further extraordinary charges imposed locally by the town council, used the ransom assessment as a pretext to foment dissent and attack the town council's entire recent management of civic affairs.

Merchants opposing the *huitième* tax on retail wine sales took the lead in organizing a challenge to the town council's authority. Local attorneys attached to the royal governor's court of justice, ineligible for town council membership and covetous of greater influence in civic affairs, grew sympathetic to this protest. A few disaffected members of the *corps de ville*, losers in contests for the accumulation of subaltern municipal offices, also backed the dissidents in hopes that their protest would lead to changes in the personnel of town government.[23] This coalition of rochelais notables formed a council and appointed two *syndics*, the *marchands-bourgeois* Georges Corru and Yves Testard, to demand from civic officials repeal of new taxes and expansion in the number of citizens eligible to join the *corps de ville*.[24]

To pressure their adversaries, Corru, Testard, and their confederates staged a show of force in streets throughout the city, shouting "liberté et exemption" to rally support. The dissidents

---

[22] Delayant, *Histoire des Rochelais*, 1: 156. Dupont, *Histoire de La Rochelle*, 73, puts the contribution imposed on the Rochelais at 12,000 *livres*.

[23] Delayant, *Histoire des Rochelais*, 1: 156.

[24] Barbot, "Histoire de La Rochelle," 499. See also Dupont, *Histoire de La Rochelle*, 74.

drew a crowd of over 700 "simples artisans et gens mécaniques" whom they encouraged to come along and challenge the council to reduce taxes and enlarge the municipal political franchise.[25] In a misguided effort to overawe his opponents, the mayor paraded out in the company of his bodyguards bearing civic banners and insignia. The crowd met the mayor's party with insults and a hail of paving stones, forcing it to beat a humiliating retreat.[26]

The following day, the town council adopted a more conciliatory strategy to pacify the restive members of the citizenry. The *corps de ville* decreed that the town's 10,000 *livre* contribution to the king's ransom payment would not be levied solely on the sworn members of the rochelais commune, but rather on all townsmen according to their ability to pay. A mayoral proclamation accompanied this decree banning all tumultuous assemblies and threatening the use of the civic militia against troublemakers. For the apportionment and collection of the ransom money, the town council appointed committees of assessors from among prominent residents in each intramural parish. To co-opt one of their most intransigent critics, the town councilmen selected the bourgeois *syndic* Georges Corru to serve as a ransom assessor in the mercantile quarter of Saint Sauveur.[27] This plan backfired when Corru refused to carry out his duties, claiming that rich town councilmen were still not willing to bear a part of the ransom charge proportionate to their actual wealth. Alarmed at the lengthening delay in collection of the rochelais contribution, the *corps de ville* agreed that its 100 members would pay half of the city's ransom charge if Corru and his fellow protestors would return to work. This concession produced a tentative accord.

However, once the monies had been raised, bourgeois assessors, again led by Corru and Testard, refused to hand over their collections to the town council's treasurer. Obstreperous assessors alleged that the *corps de ville* was insolvent, demanded to see the municipal treasury account books, and insisted that Corru and Testard be deputized to give the city's entire ransom payment directly to the king while soliciting from him additional local tax

---

[25] Barbot, "Histoire de La Rochelle," 499. Arcère, writing long after the fact, asserts that the crowd was composed of "vils plebeiens," Arcère, *Histoire de la ville de La Rochelle*, 1: 310.

[26] Delayant, *Histoire des Rochelais*, 1: 157; Dupont, *Histoire de La Rochelle*, 74.

[27] Delayant, *Histoire de La Rochelle*, 1: 157; Dupont, *Histoire de La Rochelle*, 75.

exemptions for the loyal rochelais bourgeoisie.[28] Ransom assessors in the parish of St. Sauveur backed Corru and refused to entrust the town council with over 4,000 *livres* collected from this commercial quarter, home to many of La Rochelle's most prosperous merchants. The magnitude of this sum, approximating 50% of the city's total ransom assessment and equalling 80% of the payment the town council assigned to citizens outside its ranks, shows the large number of wealthy residents in the St. Sauveur neighborhood and the importance of this district in the rochelais political economy of the early sixteenth century.

Town council members adamantly refused to meet the protestors' new demands and threatened the contentious assessors with imprisonment if their collections were not immediately turned over to the council's treasurer. Using militia forces, the mayor arrested Corru, Testard, and their closest followers. Partisans of the assessors still at liberty coursed through the streets stirring up a crowd for an assault on the town hall's jail to free the detainees. Men in the street now also called for pillaging the homes of town councilmen. This agitation was met by the mayor and a troop of over 500 bourgeois militiamen determined to prevent any popular attacks on private property. A large proportion of militiamen disavowed the reckless tactics of the protestors and closed ranks behind the town's governing elite. Bourgeois members of the militia companies constituted a vital intermediary group in town politics whose support was crucial for the successful challenge or defense of established municipal authorities. The protestors' detention continued. The St. Sauveur collection committee relented and turned over its receipts. The town council finally transferred the city's ransom payment to the crown while preparing to try Corru for sedition in the mayor's court.

At a time when the Valois dynasty and the integrity of the French realm were equally threatened, wrangling between rochelais citizens over municipal politics delayed the city's material response to a royal command for help. Throughout the provinces of Aunis and Saintonge, François I's urgent appeal to his nobles and good towns for ransom contributions produced extremely disappointing results. Besides the tardy payment from La Rochelle, many nobles in Saintonge flatly refused to give up the ten per-

---

[28] Delayant, *Histoire des Rochelais*, 1: 157-158.

cent of their annual income demanded by the crown. The second estate offered a small lump sum payment of 6,000 *livres* instead. François I was deeply offended by the insubordinate behavior of his west country vassals. On 27 December 1529, the king wrote to Charles Chabot de Jarnac, governor of the region, expressing his incredulity and consternation at the parsimony of the local aristocracy. The king found his nobles' tepid offering "very strange" and noted that "one could not be too amazed" at their willful disregard of their duty. The aristocrats' stinginess gave François "a perfect understanding of what little love and affection they bear to me and my sons who are the children of the country."[29] The king ordered Jarnac to assemble the Saintongeais nobility, to employ royal notaries to list all who fulfilled the extraordinary levy, and to prepare a roster of those who refused to pay so that later they might be punished for their "ingratitude."

Alerted to the sovereign's anger at disobedient westerners, Charles Chabot de Jarnac schemed to extract maximum personal benefit from this discord. To keep François I well apprised of unruly subjects in La Rochelle and environs, Jarnac relied on two influential contacts within the king's entourage: his brother, Philippe Chabot, seigneur of Brion, governor of Burgundy, and Admiral of France, one of François' closest confidants; and Anne de Pisseleu, duchess d'Etampes, a favorite royal mistress and head of an eminent court faction. Through these channels, Jarnac induced the crown to intervene more forcefully in rochelais civic affairs.

In 1530, Guillaume de Vieilleseigle, lieutenant to the *sénéchal* of Poitou based in Niort, was deputized to investigate long-standing allegations that town councilmen in La Rochelle were resigning their offices in favor of kinsmen too young to serve effectively. The lieutenant managed to broker a compromise between the town council and its bourgeois critics setting the minimum age for council officers at twenty-one.

Vieilleseigle was followed by another royal envoy, Jean de Langeac, bishop of Avranches, whose primary charge was to judge

---

[29] See the letter from François I to Jarnac dated 27 December 1529, BMLR, MS 2667/2. The king found the response of his west country nobility "si très estrange qu'il ne seroit possible de plus." François avowed that by this neglect "ilz me donnent bien parfaite cognoissance du peu d'amour et affection qu'ilz ont envers moy et mesdits enfants, qui sont les enfans de la chose publicque."

definitively whether members of the rochelais bourgeoisie were exempt from paying the *huitième* tax on retail wine sales. Langeac was also empowered by the crown to adjudicate three other disputes between the town council and the citizenry. These involved continuing popular allegations that councilmen were mismanaging municipal finances, that illegal sales of minor civic offices had been committed, and that the admission of local royal jurists to town council seats made it impossible for opponents of the *corps de ville* to obtain a fair hearing of their grievances before the king's magistrates in La Rochelle.[30] Before rendering his verdicts, the bishop received delegations from each side and took depositions from the representatives. Advocates for the bourgeoisie were preponderantly merchants from several urban neighborhoods but also included one man, Jean Grenot, identified as a "conseiller," perhaps a member of the city's legal confraternity, and Guillaume Chapron, a man whose kinsmen can be subsequently associated with commanding and repairing merchant ships in the port district of St. Jean du Perrot.[31]

Langeac's rulings in April 1530 generally favored the town council while increasing incrementally royal supervision of its operations. The visiting bishop struck down all of the bourgeoisie's claims to new tax exemptions. Langeac admonished the dissidents that it was illegal for them to form councils and appoint *syndics* in opposition to the governing authority of the *corps de ville*. He ordered disaffected members of the bourgeoisie to cease all of their protests, abandon their law suits, and accommodate themselves to the mayor's command. However, Langeac did find other complaints against the town council justified. He cancelled the alienations of certain *rentes* previously sold by the town council, revoked the sale of several bureaucratic posts, and decreed that henceforward the lieutenant, king's prosecutor, and king's attorney of the governor's court would be ineligible for service on La Rochelle's town council. To mollify the protestors, Langeac further ordered the town council to keep accurate records of all meetings and required the council's financial officers to provide the royal governor with annual accounts of all municipal business transactions for verification.

---

[30] Delayant, *Histoire des Rochelais*, 1: 159-160; Dupont, *Histoire de La Rochelle*, 76.
[31] Barbot, "Histoire de La Rochelle," 510.

The ensemble of these measures reinforced the police powers of the town council while subjecting councilmen to a little more surveillance by agents of the crown. Separation of senior royal magistrates from the town council conserved the sovereign's role as an arbiter of civic affairs while confirming municipal officials' essential competency to administer the urban polity in the king's name. Such careful delineations of political responsibility, requiring the consolidation rather than the suppression of old governing institutions, were typical gestures of power made by renaissance princes like François I. The rigor of the monarch's corrective intervention in subordinate agencies of government was usually calculated and proportionate to any dysfunctions alleged or revealed in the operation of these corporative bodies.

Langeac's transient intervention in rochelais affairs calmed but did not end long disputes between unenfranchised members of the citizenry and the oligarchic town council. The bishop's injunctions left co-optation intact as the primary mode of councilmen's recruitment and did not reprove the factional infighting characteristic of council politics and frustrating to outsiders. Touring royal inspectors never challenged the mayor's police powers, exercised through his captaincy of the communal militia and dispensation of justice in the mayor's court. This stasis was vexing to Charles Chabot de Jarnac, who had counted on the presence of the king's men to reduce the town council's prerogatives and enhance his own stature as the strong man of the region.

Jarnac grew angrier about an unresolved contest with the mayor over which man could rightfully claim the title "captain of the city." He complained to the king that town councilmen and the principal bourgeois of the city showed him an insulting lack of deference.[32] After Langeac's departure, Jarnac advised the crown in a series of dispatches that factions continued to battle within the town council, limiting its effective government of a vulnerable frontier region.[33] Continued financial mismanagement by

---

[32] Delayant, *Histoire des Rochelais*, 1: 162-63.

[33] Speaking of the rochelais town council, Jarnac advised the crown, "Le pouvoir, trop divisé pour être fort a besoin d'être concentrer dans un seule main, et le coprs de ville, composé de cent échevins, conseillers et pairs, presente une trop grande divergence d'opinions pour qu'il y ait jamais dans le conseil cette homogenéité de pensée et cette unité d'action qui seules peuvent lui donner de la force et de la stabilité," cited in M.D. Massiou, *Histoire politique, civile et religieuse de la Saintonge et de l'Aunis*, 6 vols. (Paris, 1836-1838), 3: 427-428.

town councilmen, he alleged, left no monies for the necessary upkeep of La Rochelle's defenses. Jarnac even went so far as to suggest that the city's long history of commercial contacts with Spaniards might undercut townsmen's traditional loyalty to the French crown and promote their connivance with Spanish raiders.[34] Jarnac recommended a major restructuring of La Rochelle's municipal government to cope with supposedly imminent threats to state security. He proposed the reduction of the town council to a more efficient and less factionalized body of twenty members and presented himself as a worthy candidate for royal investiture as perpetual mayor of the city.

Jarnac's dire but unwarranted alarm signals were well-timed, reaching Paris in 1534-35 just as François I prepared to resume hostilities against his old Habsburg rival Charles V. François' biographer, R.J. Knecht, has noted that at this moment the French court was "gripped by a war fever" incited by a bellicose, anti-Habsburg palace faction led by admiral Philippe Chabot, elder brother of Jarnac.[35] The admiral, who became François' chief minister in the summer of 1535, conveyed to the king his brother's warnings from La Rochelle. The king's mistress, the duchess d'Etampes, an ally of the Chabot brothers, amplified the bad news from the west country and endorsed Jarnac's proposed solutions to allegedly recurrent problems of police in his seaboard fife.[36] The contemporaneous sortie of a Spanish war fleet from Barcelona and a succession of Spanish naval victories in the Mediterranean called for a heightened state of readiness in all French coastal defenses.

Before setting out to supervise his army's field operations against Imperial forces in Piedmont, François I wished to strengthen the frontier redoubts of his kingdom, especially in regions like Saintonge and Aunis proximate to future adversaries and populated by notables of uncertain allegiance to the French crown. Now, European power politics, French court intrigues, and François I's long-standing distrust of west country vassals came into an extraordinary conjuncture unfavorable to the old regime of La Rochelle's town government. By letters patent issued in July

---

[34] Arcère, *Histoire de la ville de La Rochelle,* 1: 310-311; Delayant, *Histoire des Rochelais,* 1: 163.

[35] R.J. Knecht, *Francis I,* (Cambridge, 1984), 274 and 276.

[36] Massiou, *Histoire politique,* 3: 428; Dupont, *Histoire de La Rochelle,* 77.

1535, François I adopted Jarnac's recommendations for the emergency "reform" of rochelais civic institutions. The king dissolved the 100-member town council and substituted for it an advisory body of twenty *échevins*. Jarnac received permission to name the first twenty holders of these offices. In subsequent years, annual balloting by parishioners in the city would replace half the members of this new council. The king annulled the 1535 mayoral election and made the mayor's office a purely appointive post. Henceforward, the mayoralty was to be "perpetual," held by a royal designate for an indefinite term at the king's pleasure. The king named Charles Chabot de Jarnac as the first "perpetual mayor" of La Rochelle. Jarnac also gained the right to select a vice mayor (*sous-maire*) from among the *échevins* to assist him or rule in his name should his duties as royal governor of the region take him out of La Rochelle.[37]

The new town council's parochial election procedures outlined in the king's decree were unusual. Two weeks before the end of the year, vestrymen in the five parishes of the city were to inform their congregations at high mass that all male parishioners were to assemble on the following Sunday. At this reunion, the parishioners were to elect ten of their number who would, in turn, choose two *échevins* to represent the neighborhood on the new town council. Before proceeding to their choice, the ten electors in each parish were required to swear an oath that they would only select men of ability and good repute in the quarter to become *échevins*. These minor qualifications allowed merchants and artisans of middling rank to compete for office, men of humbler social rank than the patricians of the old town council. The perpetual mayor was obligated to accept the candidates advanced by the electors.

The new constitution of town government satisfied bourgeois demands for broader citizen participation in municipal affairs. Two levels of annual balloting for *échevins* reversed a trend toward oligarchy in town government. The possibility of re-electing *échevins* also permitted the formation of experienced and reliable urban magistrates. This system reconfigured but did not abandon

---

[37] For details on the new institutions of civic government created by François I, see Delayant, *Histoire des Rochelais*, 1: 163; Dupont, *Histoire de La Rochelle*, 76-77; and Barbot, "Histoire de La Rochelle," AHSA 17 (1889): 4-6.

a ruling partnership between monarchy and municipality that accorded to each distinctive responsibilities. The example of La Rochelle suggests that the king's propensity toward authoritarianism was tempered by an abiding respect for intermediate organizations of government vital to the ancient political arrangement of his realm. However, the potential advantages of the new governing regime to ordinary rochelais citizens were entirely occluded by the imperious and threatening behavior of Jarnac who brought the entire system into disrepute.

Finally invested with the local authority he had long craved, Jarnac set out to humble his former adversaries within municipal government. For his first *sous-maire* Jarnac chose Jean Foucaut, one of the few members of the old *corps de ville* who in 1529 broke ranks and sided with unenfranchised merchants protesting the town council's policies. Jarnac's advancement of this renegade was a snub to more senior and collegial municipal officers who had resisted both the bourgeoisie's bid for participation in town government and Jarnac's efforts to influence civic administration. Jarnac attempted to curry favor with the rochelais bourgeoisie by tapping Foucaut, Yves Testard, and other leaders of past bourgeois political agitation to serve with him in a revamped town government. Such stratagems won Jarnac only a limited number of local supporters who were increasingly vilified by displaced former town councillors and more humble defenders of the old communal governing regime.

Jarnac's coup, described by one early historian of La Rochelle as "the greatest wound and affliction that could ever strike the repose and liberty of the city," inspired opposition from its beginning by a coalition of forces including officers of the old town council, influential members of the bourgeoisie, and leaders of the city's artisans.[38] Jarnac compounded his unpopularity by not reproving the dissolute behavior of troops in his employ and by confiscating many minor offices in the civic bureaucracy. Inspiring popular outrage, Jarnac turned these sequestered offices over to servants in his own household.[39] Contravening the bylaws of La Rochelle's bourgeoisie and guild organizations, Jarnac allowed men in his retinue, who were not sworn members of the com-

---

[38] Barbot, "Histoire de La Rochelle," AHSA 14 (1886): 6.
[39] Delayant, *Histoire des Rochelais*, 1: 166.

mune, to open wineshops and other businesses in town. The new
perpetual mayor took a cut of the profits from these enterprises
in return for special licenses to operate.[40]

Within days of Jarnac's ascension to power, he was forced to
rely on brutal intimidation tactics to secure the citizenry's grudging obedience. Selection of Foucaut as vice-mayor incited widespread public complaints. Troops under Jarnac's command over-
reacted and lynched one merchant who outspokenly criticized the
appointment. With the assistance of Jarnac's gendarmes, Foucaut
erected two gallows outside of his house to cower opponents of
the new regime.[41] A crowd of townspeople, operating under cover of darkness, soon smashed these symbols of oppression. Fearing
for his personal safety, Jarnac obtained permission from the crown
to employ another thirty bodyguards whose wages would be drawn
from the income of the rochelais commune.[42] Such unprecedented impositions galvanized local opposition to Jarnac's government.

To challenge the perpetual mayor's haughty rule, former town
councilmen and their erstwhile bourgeois opponents made common cause. The opposition hired two royal notaries to draw up
and circulate a petition of complaint addressed to the king. This
document asserted that the new regime was violating the city's
ancient privileges, was detrimental to all segments of the city's
economy and hence to the welfare of the kingdom, and, contrary
to all expectations, imperiled rather than improved urban
defense. The petition was carried secretly from neighborhood to
neighborhood, gaining endorsements from more than 400 prominent citizens, including 174 *marchands et bourgeois*, 185 *bourgeois et
habitans*, and 122 local clergymen.[43]

By 1538, parish elections of new town councilmen and sustained
popular opposition to the perpetual mayor's regime made conciliatory modifications in Jarnac's government inevitable. After

---

[40] Dupont, *Histoire de La Rochelle*, 77. These criminal rackets greatly angered
the city's merchants and ordinary consumers now forced to deal with businessmen contemptuous of municipal ordinances and communal mores.

[41] *Ibid.*, 78.

[42] Delayant, *Histoire des Rochelais*, 1: 166-167.

[43] BMLR, MS 152, *Recueil.* See in particular the "Enqueste pour l'élection
annuale du maire de La Rochelle," 16 February 1536. On the creation and circulation of this petition see also Barbot, "Histoire de La Rochelle," AHSA 17
(1889): 8; and Delayant, *Histoire des Rochelais*, 1: 166.

selecting Yves Testard as his *sous-maire* in 1537, Jarnac was forced to abandon his policy of picking his lieutenants from among inveterate opponents of the old town council. Parochial elections now yielded a body of *échevins* dominated by prominent Rochelais with prior experience on the old town council. Jarnac could not avoid selecting esteemed members of the former town council to serve as vice-mayors. Between 1538 and 1548, a total of nine men became *sous-maire*, two of the nine holding the office twice. The six who can be identified by name had all occupied senior posts in the old *corps de ville*. Olivier Lequeux (*sous-maire* in 1542 and 1548) and Jean Clerbaut (*sous-maire* in 1543) had both been mayor of La Rochelle before the reduction of the old town council. Jarnac had to countenance the aid of reputable Rochelais in maintaining a semblance of effective civic administration. With their assistance, Jarnac remained the nominal ruler of the city.

Under the leadership of experienced officers from the city's old political regime, the new *échevins* worked concertedly to diminish Jarnac's powers over the municipality. Their efforts were rewarded in 1538 when, upon petition, the crown confirmed the old civic privilege stipulating that all merchants opening a retail shop in La Rochelle had to be "residents, sworn members of the commune, and contributors to the finances of the city."[44] Considering renewal of the privilege to be an official rebuff of Jarnac's profiteering, the *échevins* moved to shut down the shops of the cronies Jarnac had peremptorily licensed to trade in the city. The prospect of greater fiscal authority for Jarnac evaporated in 1539 when town councilmen managed to convince the king that a new emergency levy of 6,000 *livres* on the community to be raised by the royal governor could never be met by an overburdened communal treasury and an impoverished citizenry. The crown cancelled the forced loan. The *échevins* also hedged Jarnac's police powers by successfully defending the right of the city's gatekeepers to hold all keys to their portals during daylight hours. A squad of civic militiamen retained sole authority to transport the keys to Jarnac at nightfall.

The *modus vivendi* struck by Jarnac and pugnacious town councilmen nearly degenerated into civil war under the stresses of the 1541 regional salt tax rebellion. This violent unrest stemmed from

[44] Barbot, "Histoire de La Rochelle," AHSA, 17 (1889): 8.

the crown's plan to consolidate a variety of differing regional
levies on salt into one uniform *gabelle* throughout the kingdom to
be collected at the site of production. In the major salt-produc-
ing regions of Angoumois, Aunis, and Saintonge, where previously
salt taxes had been among the lowest in the kingdom, this innovative scheme outraged the *sauniers* and threatened the profits of
many rochelais entrepreneurs who owned salt pans. Inhabitants
of the salt marshes feared that their principal livelihood would
now be taxed away by the infamous *gabeleurs*.[45] Royal commissioners sent into the west country to enforce the new legislation
met fierce armed resistance.[46] Locals ambushed, tortured, and dismembered several of the hated tax officials. Around La Rochelle,
royal agents identified the communities of Marennes, Oléron, and
Saint-Jean-d'Angély as active centers of rebellion. The king's conciliatory reduction of the new tax in April 1542 did not mollify
the protestors. Bands of rebels numbering in the thousands and
equipped with artillery looted from town arsenals threw up a military cordon around the salt marshes preventing the royal commissioners from entering. François I was forced to call up the *ban
et arrière ban* of Poitou to counter this resistance.[47]

At La Rochelle, Jarnac endeavored to use the rebellion as a
means to enlarge his own powers. He sent a steady stream of communiqués to Paris advising the king that the uprising had reached
terrifying ("effrayante") proportions and requesting the increase
of troops under his command to deal with the insurgents.[48]
Jarnac's capacity to gain the king's ear and support of his proposals was improved in February 1541 when his son, Guy Chabot
de Jarnac, married Louise de Pisseleu, sister of the duchess
d'Etampes. This match established a direct familial connection
between the Chabots and the king's most influential mistress.

On 6 August 1542, Jarnac received royal orders to strengthen
his garrison at La Rochelle and to exile any rebel sympathizers
he found in the city. Simultaneously, the king wrote to the
rochelais town council informing it of his military preparations in
the west country and charging it to obey Jarnac's orders sup-

---

[45] Massiou, *Histoire politique*, 3: 434-435.
[46] Delayant, *Histoire des Rochelais*, 1: 169.
[47] Knecht, *Francis I*, 385-387; Massiou, *Histoire politique*, 3: 435.
[48] See Massiou, *Histoire politique*, 3: 436; Dupont, *Histoire de La Rochelle*, 79-80;
and Arcère, *Histoire de la ville de La Rochelle*, 1: 311.

porting this endeavor. A detachment of 300 mercenaries from the company of the duc d'Orléans, another ally of the duchess d'Etampes, was dispatched to La Rochelle. Jarnac caused this force to be admitted within the walls and quartered in the artisanal neighborhood of St. Nicolas outside the oldest and wealthiest precincts of the city.[49] These troops were an undisciplined lot who repaid the citizenry's suspicion of them with insults, larcenies, and physical assaults. On the evening of 30 August, a group of the foreign soldiers confronted the squad of municipal militiamen charged with carrying the keys for all town gates back to the *hôtel de ville*. The soldiers drew their weapons and demanded that the keys be turned over to them. The militiamen refused and a battle broke out.[50] The noise of shots brought a crowd of citizens to the militiamen's aid and the soldiers were forced to flee into private homes, leaving several comrades dead in the street. The crowd pursued the fugitives and melées flared throughout the city. Many were wounded on both sides and several more combattants died before darkness halted the conflict. Militiamen had captured several of the marauding soldiers including the captain-ensign of the company. The prisoners were marched under guard to Jarnac's residence. The perpetual mayor promised a swift court martial for the aggressors and this pact calmed the crowd for the night.

With the occupying forces dispersed and diminished in both numbers and leadership, the citizenry decided to press its advantage and attempt to expel the entire contingent of foreign troops. Jarnac awakened to find his house surrounded by armed militiamen. His parley with representatives of the commune devolved into a shouting match during which emissaries from both sides were roughed up. To avoid further bloodshed, Jarnac transferred the prisoners in his house over to a delegation of militiamen, who led the captive mercenaries to the town hall's jail. Jarnac then ordered the soldiers remaining at liberty to quit the city immediately. The municipal militia accorded Jarnac bodyguards while his own troops marched out and finally freed its captives to be rid of all the alien soldiers.[51] Jarnac himself retired to his local

---

[49] Massiou, *Histoire politique*, 3: 436-437.
[50] Delayant, *Histoire des Rochelais*, 1: 170; Dupont, *Histoire de La Rochelle*, 81-82.
[51] Delayant, *Histoire des Rochelais*, 1: 171.

estates on 5 September, sending a special envoy to the king with an account of the recent riots depicting the Rochelais as seditious rebels entirely at fault for the bloodshed.[52]

Jarnac's inflammatory messages, seconded in the king's company by admiral Chabot and the duchess d'Etampes, resolved François I to make a punitive tour of the west country, stopping at Cognac, Angoulême, and La Rochelle. He ordered that preparations be made at La Rochelle for trial of the rebellious salt harvesters and condemnation of the townsmen responsible for the riots against Jarnac. Deputies from La Rochelle sent to appease the king were refused access to him or to his council. Royal servants insinuated that exemplary punishment awaited the city. City ambassadors communicated these warnings back to La Rochelle where frightened notables organized communal prayer services imploring God to inspire the king with clemency.[53]

Protected by an advance guard of 200 infantry under the command of Gaspard de Saulx-Tavannes, Jarnac re-entered La Rochelle riding at the head of fifty mounted men-at-arms.[54] These forces proceeded to disarm the citizenry, to impose a curfew on the city, and to round up rebels from the salt marshes for trial. Royal heralds arrived summoning the *sous-maire* and prominent opponents of Jarnac within the bourgeoisie to appear before the forthcoming tribunal of the king. By royal command, the Rochelais were denied the right to greet the king upon his arrival. Welcoming fanfares, artillery salutes, and the peal of church bells were all expressly forbidden. Such somber dispositions caused further alarm among the citizenry.

On 30 December 1541, proceeded by a pitiful group of rebellious *sauniers* in chains, François I entered an anxious, silent city. To heighten the suspense of his mission, François spent the first full day in town attending mass and inspecting communal fortifications. Sovereign judgment of the rebels from town and country was set for 1 January 1543, forty-eight hours after the king's arrival. During this interval, the *sous-maire* Olivier Lequeux, a mayor of La Rochelle under the old regime of civic government, worked diligently behind the scenes to engineer a settlement of

---

[52] Massiou, *Histoire politique*, 3: 438.
[53] Arcère, *Histoire de la ville de La Rochelle*, 1: 313-314.
[54] Massiou, *Histoire politique*, 3: 439.

the cases favorable to all parties involved.[55] Speaking before the king's council, Lequeux managed to convince his audience that the Rochelais' fidelity to the crown was undiminished and that their battles against Jarnac were less of a crime and more a fault of their zeal in defense of communal privileges. Such a fault, Lequeux adroitly argued, could be expiated in conformity with French law by a sizeable fine payable to the crown. Lequeux promptly added that leading citizens were prepared to construe this indemnity as a gift to the crown for repair of the city walls so interesting to the king.[56] In exchange for this payment, Lequeux requested a royal pardon for all those on trial. The old mayor's proposition was encouraged and favorably received by Montholon, the keeper of the seals, and Raymond, the king's *avocat général*. Lequeux immediately assembled the *échevins* of La Rochelle and they settled on an offering of 40,000 *livres* to the king. Shuttling back to the royal council, Lequeux proffered this amount and Raymond accepted the deal on behalf of the king.[57] Both sides agreed that the solemn legal ceremonies scheduled for the next day would proceed as planned; but, to those in the know, the outcome of these theatrics was assured, royal clemency was bought and would prevail.

At the appointed hour on 1 January 1543, the sovereign's tribunal convened. The king and his retinue were impressively arrayed. François I sat on a dais several feet off the ground. On his right stood the dukes of Vendôme and Orléans backed by princes of high rank. On the king's left were the cardinals of Tournon, Lorraine, and Ferrara. Members of the royal council stood

---

[55] Delayant, *Histoire des Rochelais*, 1: 174; Arcère, *Histoire de la ville de La Rochelle*, 1: 315-316.

[56] Arcère, *Histoire de la ville de La Rochelle*, 1: 316; Delayant, *Histoire des Rochelais*, 1: 74.

[57] This pact was later augmented by a settlement between the crown and fractious salt marsh owners in Guyenne and Saintonge whereby they would obtain the king's pardon for rebellion in return for the transfer of 15,000 *muids* of salt to royal warehouses in Rouen; see Knecht, *Francis I*, 388. Knecht points to the salt exchange as proof that François I's magnanimity to west country rebels in 1542-43 was not unconditional or disinterested. Although Knecht makes no reference to it, the 40,000 *livre* payment to the king from La Rochelle strongly reinforces this interpretation of the events, further indicating the prevalence of pragmatism over theory in Valois statecraft. Rochelais payment of a fine exonerating the salt harvesters also conveniently scotched any further royal investigation of the extent to which urbanites had fomented dissent in the marshes.

behind the throne and Montholon sat at his master's feet. The prisoners stood on the floor below the great personages of state. A jurist from the Parlement of Bordeaux made the first address to the king, speaking on behalf of the captured salt harvesters. The advocate implored the king to pardon them for their crimes and restore to them their confiscated salt pans without which they could not survive. At this point, the captives all fell to their knees and cried "Miséricorde!" in unison. Etienne Noyau, a lieutenant in the governor's court, represented the rebellious citizens of La Rochelle. Noyau begged the king to consider the long fidelity of the Rochelais to French monarchs, their spirited defense of commune and region, and their many commercial exploits beneficial to the economic welfare of the realm. He concluded by requesting royal forgiveness of townsmen's disobedient acts.[58]

The king began his reply by emphasizing the gravity of the crimes the prisoners had committed at a moment when the monarch was defending his dominions against the Spanish. For this treachery they all deserved a penalty of death and forfeiture of all property. However, noting the sincerity of the captives' repentance, François admitted that his duty as their prince could only be fulfilled by a grant of pardon. François stated he did not wish to treat the misbehavior of his subjects with brutal tactics like those used by the emperor to rule over his misfortunate peoples. The king additionally allowed the Rochelais to recover the keys to their city, their municipal artillery, and all other public and private arsenals previously confiscated by royal officers. Jarnac was ordered to evacuate his troops from town.[59] At the end of the king's speech, the city's church bells and cannon rang out signaling La Rochelle's return to the monarch's favor. The next day, amid public festivities, François announced his imminent departure to defend a distant corner of the kingdom. He charged the Rochelais to care for the defense of their own vulnerable frontier and expressed his confidence in their ability to do so. François I left La Rochelle assuring its inhabitants that they had won back his heart. Several senior royal advisors remained behind to arrange collection of the citizenry's 40,000 *livre* gift. Four months

---

[58] Arcère, *Histoire de la ville de La Rochelle*, 1: 317-318.
[59] Arcère, *Histoire de la ville de La Rochelle*, 1: 318; Dupont, *Histoire de La Rochelle*, 86.

later, the king suspended the imposition of a uniform gabelle throughout France.

The king's performance in La Rochelle was intended to impress witnesses with the august powers of the monarch. However, examined more closely, François I's visit to La Rochelle, the diplomatic manoeuvres it engendered, and the outcome of the entire royal tour reveal the practical mechanics and limits of Valois government. In this case, the exemplary punishment of obstreperous subjects inhabiting a strategic coastal town was not cost effective. It was preferable for the king to excuse their disobedience, extract maximum financial gratification from the misunderstanding while avoiding the appearance of extortion, and to preserve intact the privileged position of towns like La Rochelle as valued associates in defense of the realm. This was a political calculus well understood by the principal agent of compromise, the wily Olivier Lequeux, a former mayor of La Rochelle with long experience of civic affairs in the west country. The rapprochement he engineered between city and king allowed each to save face and restored an essential balance of power between local royal officers and representatives of the commune. The noble Jarnac's capacity to rule over La Rochelle waned after the intercession of the king.

From 1543 until François I's death in March 1547, relations between La Rochelle and the crown were more cooperative. When Spanish naval forces threatened a descent on the French Atlantic coast in 1543, several thousand heavily armed members of La Rochelle's bourgeois militia, "les defenseurs naturels du pays" according to the historian Dupont, marched out, fortified the beaches, and dissuaded the enemy from attempting a landing. The crown also exercised restraint in levying extraordinary taxes on the walled towns of Aunis to pay for emergency coastal defense. Upon remonstrance from La Rochelle's governing council, the king reduced the city's required contribution to this fund by more than half.[60] A politics of compromise rather than confrontation reassociated king and *bonne ville* in the last years of François I's reign.

---

[60] La Rochelle's charge for seaboard protection dropped from 28,900 *livres* to 13,200 *livres* with the difference being assessed on other walled towns in the region, Delayant, *Histoire des Rochelais*, 1: 178.

The ascension of Henry II put an end to Jarnac's perpetual mayoralty in La Rochelle. The new king swept all of Jarnac's most powerful patrons at court from their positions of influence. Anne de Pisseleu was stripped of the precious gifts showered upon her by the late king and banished to one of her few remaining country houses.[61] Admiral Philippe Chabot, brother to Jarnac and a principal confederate in Anne's court faction, also fell precipitously from grace. The admiral's repute disappeared when his arch-rival, the Constable Anne de Montmorency, one of the new king's closest confidants, became president of the reconstituted royal council and commander of all French armed forces.[62] Immediately after François I's death, the Chabot family's prestige at Henry's court diminished further through the outcome of a famous duel arising from the factionalism of the preceding reign.

During the last years of François' rule, a rumor, circulated at court by the party of the dauphin Henry, insinuated that Guy Chabot de Jarnac, brother-in-law to Anne de Pisseleu and son of the governor of La Rochelle, was guilty of incestuous relations with his stepmother. Guy Chabot initiated a law suit for defamation before the Parlement of Bordeaux against François de La Châtaigneraie, one of the dauphin's closest friends, and then challenged the man to formal combat to redeem his honor. The king intervened to prevent this battle at the urging of the duchess d'Etampes who feared that her young kinsman would be no match for his battle-hardened opponent. Less than a month after Henry's ascension, both of the aggrieved parties petitioned the new king for permission to fight. The royal council assented and scheduled the confrontation before the entire court on 10 July 1547.

In the dramatic showdown, Guy Chabot unexpectedly landed the first blow, a swift rapier thrust to the back of La Châtaigneraie's knee that cut down the man whom all in attendance regarded as the king's champion. Empowered by the rules of dueling to decide his wounded adversary's fate, Chabot offered La Châtaigneraie's life to the king, requesting the monarch to declare his honor restored. Affronted by the outcome, Henry II first hesitated to respond. Prompted by his sister and the Constable Mont-

---

[61] Frederic Baumgartner, *Henry II, King of France 1547-1559*, (Durham, North Carolina, 1988), 43.

[62] Baumgartner, *Henry II*, 35 and 46.

morency to be gracious, the new king announced Chabot de Jarnac as the victor and took La Châtaigneraie under his protection. However, Henry did not—as was customary—declare to the winner "You are a man of honor." Chabot prudently retired from the field while his defeated rival, realizing his disgrace, tore off his bandages and promptly bled to death.[63]

Henry II mitigated his retribution so as not to appear unduly vindictive. Guy Chabot de Jarnac was permitted to continue in royal service as a provincial military commander and would later return to the west country as a new menace to the Rochelais. Chabot's father, in a weakened position at La Rochelle, was not so fortunate. Alert to the reconfigurations of power at court, the *échevins* of La Rochelle appealed to the new king for an end to the perpetual mayoralty. In time for Henry II's coronation, four delegates from the old town council were dispatched to present the young monarch with a petition signed by more than 200 citizens requesting the complete restoration of the old 100-member *corps de ville*.[64]

The lobbying of distinguished rochelais envoys met with some success when the king confirmed all of the city's commercial privileges and fiscal exemptions in January 1548. Encouraged by this royal favor, city ambassadors pressed their demands for removal of Jarnac and re-establishment of the old town council, cleverly emphasizing improvements in the military preparedness and police of their community that were bound to result from a return to a tried and true system of municipal government. To counter Jarnac's vehement protests, the ambassadors informed the king by letter that the twenty *échevins* permitted under the new civic regime were insufficient to handle the multiple duties ensuring good town government. They advised Henry that the election of new *échevins* by parish councils should be scrapped because "in three city parishes these are only artisans, paupers, seamen, and day laborers ill-bred and unaccustomed to the discipline and administration of a Republic. When elected they miss council meetings because they cannot afford to leave the work that feeds them. When they do show up, they are usually late and are only interested in laws that favorably affect their own line of work.

---

[63] *Ibid.*, 60-61.
[64] Barbot, "Histoire de La Rochelle," AHSA, 17 (1889): 58.

Nothing important ever gets done."[65] These petitions reached
Henry after the Chabots' eclipse as courtiers and gave the king a
sound pretext for further withdrawal of royal favor from the family. Such arguments may also have appealed to the dutiful Henry
II whose contemporaneous visits to great cities in southeastern
France brought him into immediate contact with the urban institutions of government and finance so essential for the projection
of his authority and the increase of his treasury.[66] Unfettering La
Rochelle from Jarnac's costly rule through armed force also complemented Henry's policy of encouraging mercantile activity and
attracting foreign merchants to French entrepots.[67]

By letters patent issued at Dijon on 11 July 1548, Henry II abolished the *mairie perpétuelle* at La Rochelle and reinstated the 100
members of the old *corps de ville* with all of their ancient rights
and privileges. Municipal elections and administration now
returned to the preeminent control of the town council. Communal fortifications garrisoned by royal troops were evacuated and
turned over to rochelais militiamen. Charles Chabot de Jarnac got
orders to leave the city. The crown later pensioned him off at
municipal expense.[68]

After thirteen years in abeyance, La Rochelle's ancient town
council recovered its full authority in local politics. Such a renewal is very rare in the annals of French urban history and attests
to the tenacity with which leading Rochelais resisted a novel system of municipal government that courtiers induced the king to
establish. La Rochelle's experience illustrates how the shifting fortunes of court factions could correlate with French civic affairs in
the mid-sixteenth century, confronting town dwellers with centrally mandated changes in communal government but also with
opportunities to oppose the implementation or consolidation of
such innovations. La Rochelle's tumultuous political history in the

---

[65] BMLR, MS 81, "Titres de la ville de La Rochelle," fols. 153r-154r.
Neighborhoods singled out for patrician scorn were St. Jean du Perrot, St. Nicolas,
and Notre Dame de Cougnes. Political tensions between these districts and the
wealthier parishes of St. Barthélémy and St. Sauveur would grow over time and
ultimately lead to violent struggles for control of town government between the
residents of these quarters.

[66] Baumgartner, *Henry II*, 71-72.

[67] *Ibid.*, 76.

[68] Arcère, *Histoire de la ville de La Rochelle*, 1: 322; Delayant, *Histoire des Rochelais*,
1: 180-181.

1530's and 1540's also indicates that the era was not one of inexorable progress toward the complete subordination of French municipalities to the political designs of French monarchs. The transition in rulership from François I to Henry II brought with it a clear reversal of the elder's attempt to condense rochelais town government. The city reached the midpoint of the century and the eve of the French Reformation with its ancient constitution intact and fully operational.

### 3. *The Resurgence of Urban Political Infighting*

The reestablishment of the 100-member *corps de ville* vivified urban politics in La Rochelle. An indigenous governing elite reasserted itself as its members resumed jockeying for positions of advantage in civic administration. The first surviving, nearly complete roster of town council members dates from 1558 and can be used to show the spatial concentration of La Rochelle's restored governors within the urban environment. On the date of the 1558 mayoral election, ninety-eight town councilmen were present.[69] A variety of contemporary notarized documents, including real estate transactions, marriage contracts, and wills, permit location of the principal residences for fifty-one of the these ninety-eight councilmen. As the map in Figure 7 shows, the vast majority of these town councilmen lived in the central parishes of the city. High concentrations of civic magistrates were to be found in streets adjacent to the *hôtel de ville* and along the main arterials of the St. Sauveur and St. Barthélémy parishes. By comparison, very few towncouncilmen inhabited the parishes of St. Jean du Perrot, St. Nicolas, or Notre Dame de Cougnes, neighborhoods peripheral to the old city center.

Other documents confirm this distribution of municipal officers. In 1556, for example, eighty-one prominent residents of the Perrot quarter contracted with an attorney to oppose construction of a royal citadel in the parish. This list of neighborhood notables includes only three town councilmen.[70] These three may have been the harbor district's only representatives in the *corps de*

---

[69] BMLR, MS 97, fol. 5.
[70] ADCM, 3 E 138 (12 Jan. 1556).

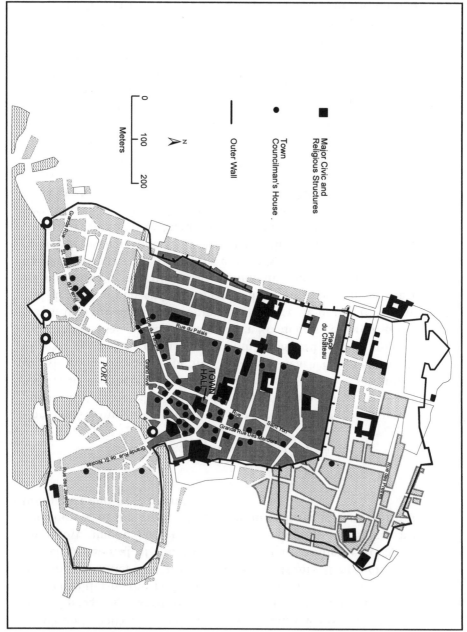

Figure 7. Location of Town Councilmen's Houses Circa 1558

*ville.* La Rochelle's excentric artisanal and manufacturing districts were very weakly represented in the restored town council at mid-century.

Even long after the onset of La Rochelle's Reformation in the later 1550's, these same neighborhoods also did not contain any Calvinist church structures. All Reformed congregations became concentrated within the old city. Comparatively isolated from urban institutions of political and religious control, the residents of La Rochelle's waterfront and laboring precincts were rarely as tractable as the ruling patriciate desired. However, this configuration of civic authority was not immutable and subsequent chapters will trace alterations in the balance of political power between rochelais neighborhoods.

The first major feud between town councilmen post-dating reestablishment of the old *corps de ville* well illustrates the sociology of urban politics in La Rochelle at mid-century. The root of contention lay in the local inconsistency of recent royal edicts pertaining to municipal government. Rochelais active in town politics questioned whether Henry II's edict of October 1547, banning all royal officials from holding any post in French municipal councils, was applicable to the newly reconstituted *corps de ville* in La Rochelle. If it were, nine prominent royal jurists now sitting on the refurbished town council would be compelled to relinquish their civic offices and to pay heavy fines to the crown and city. Led by two members of the *corps de ville*, Andre Morisson and Guillaume Guy, nine ambitious citizens without connections to the king's bureaucracy brought suit against the royal officials, demanded their removal from office, temporarily deposed the king's men, and took their places on the *corps de ville*.[71] On the surface, this conflict appears to be a typical struggle between local corporate governing elites competing for jurisdictional turf and the coveted privileges of office. But underneath the impersonal collision of public institutions, family feuds and family interests envenomed and propelled legal combat.

Litigation over the nine seats on the *corps de ville* began in 1550 when André Morisson and Guillaume Guy, fellow merchants serving as *pairs* on the *corps de ville*, surprised the confraternity with letters they had obtained from the king mandating immediate

---

[71] Barbot, "Histoire de La Rochelle," AHSA, 17 (1889): 72.

local enforcement of the 1547 edict against royal officers sitting
on town councils.[72] The initiative of Guy and Morisson cannot be
ascribed to their altruistic determination to see the king's law
enforced. On the contrary, both men were bidding to put kinsmen on the town council and Morisson had a score to settle for
a relative. Thanks to the royal letters obtained by Guy and
Morisson, nine men gained access to the town council replacing
the royal officers ruled ineligible to serve. Among the nine incoming members were Jacques Coulon and Pierre Regnault. Coulon
was André Morisson's nephew. Regnault was Morisson's father-in-
law.[73] The injunction Morisson and Guy obtained from the king
drove nine men from office. Among those deposed was Francois
Joubert, *avocat du roi*, the brother-in-law of Jacques de Nagères, a
ranking member of the *corps de ville*. Jacques de Nagères was a
sworn enemy of André Morisson. Morisson's own brother-in-law,
Jacques Regnault, had bought up de Nagères' debts and, exasperated by his refusal to pay, was now suing him for the recovery
of a large sum.[74] In driving de Nagères' kinsman Joubert from
office, Morisson publicly humiliated both families with a blow calculated to demonstrate his own political clout and to bring further pressure to bear on a recalcitrant debtor owing a large sum
of money to a relative.

Guillaume Guy, a member of one of La Rochelle's most prominent political families, also had a personal stake in rearranging
the *corps de ville*.[75] Putting Pierre Regnault on the town council

---

[72] *Ibid.*, 72-74. Barbot notes that André Morisson was among a group of fifteen
Rochelais elected by the *corps* as *pairs* on 21 March 1550 to fill vacancies that had
occurred in that body due to deaths of former members during the thirteen years
La Rochelle was governed by a life mayor and a town council of twenty. The
junior status of Morisson in 1550 would amply justify Barbot's remark that his
legal challenge to other members of the *corps* came as a great surprise to fellow
councilmen with more seniority in office.

[73] André Morisson is identified as Jacques Coulon's uncle in a legal opinion
dated 12 May 1554 handed down by Louis Seigne, *sénéchal* of Poitou. A manuscript copy of this document is contained in BMLR, MS 81, fol. 165r. The same
source lists Pierre Regnault as a "parent et allié" of André Morisson. Morisson's
wife was Pierrette Regnauld, daughter of Pierre, see the wedding contract of
Morisson's daughter Collette, BMLR, MS 235, fols. 505r-507v. In 1572, the children of André Morisson and Pierrette Regnault: Jean, Andrée, and Collette, each
inherited a one-third share in half the estate of their maternal grandparents,
Pierre Regnauld and his wife Jeanne Guyet, see ADCM, 3 E 2151, 7 June 1572.

[74] BMLR, MS 81, fol. 165r.

[75] Besides Guillaume Guy, *pair* in 1550 and *échevin* by 1558, at least four

would mean another kinsman to the Guys also occupied high civic office. Pierre Regnault's wife was Jeanne Guyet. Her kinsman was Pierre Guyet, husband to Anne Guy.[76] Pierre Regnault's access to municipal office would thus not only expand the political contacts of the Guys and solidify their ties to the Guyet clan, but also reinforce their alliance with the Morissons, with whom they were already prepared to work for mutual political benefit. Construction and defense of such intricate networks of interrelated place holders were fundamental features of familial civic politics in La Rochelle at the midpoint of the sixteenth century.

The nine displaced royal jurists mounted a vigorous counterattack against the assault of Guy and Morisson. The family ties that bound together the city's legal confraternity sustained this riposte. François Joubert, *avocat du roi*, could call on his brother-in-law, Jacques de Nagères for help. De Nagères, who became mayor of La Rochelle in 1552, lent the prestige of his name and office to the dogged appeals of the 1547 edict filed by the nine jurists before the *Conseil Privé* of the king. René Jouanneau, the king's judge and lieutenant of the port, a former *pair*, could also rely on his family's prominence and his personal connections in the neighborhood of St. Sauveur to vouch for his utility to the crown as an influential standing member of the *corps de ville*. Jouanneau's brother, Jean, was a well-placed *fabriqueur* of the parish Church of St. Sauveur.[77]

René Jouanneau and two close colleagues, Hughes Pontard and Gilles Bretinault, all displaced from the *corps*, were partially compensated for their loss of office and encouraged to press their appeals by Louis d'Estissac, the king's own lieutenant in the city and government of La Rochelle. D'Estissac appointed Jouanneau and Pontard to be judges and Bretinault to be a councillor on

---

other members of the Guy family can be traced to the *corps de ville*: Claude Guy, member of the old *corps* and mayor in 1549; Jean Guy, a high ranking *échevin* by 1558; Michel Guy, brother of Jean, also a senior *échevin* and mayor in 1557; and Pierre Guy, *co-élu* for mayor in 1554. Contemporaneous occupation of such senior positions implies long presence in the *corps*, good family connections, and similar ages for Guillaume, Jean, Michel, and Pierre. Baptismal records from the early 1560's suggest that Pierre Guy was closely related to Jean and Michel and was probably their cousin, if not their brother.

[76] See ADCM, 3 E 2151 for dispensation of the estate of Pierre Regnault and Jeanne Guyet. See ADCM, I 1, fol. 18v for the close relations between Pierre Guyet and the Guy family.

[77] ADCM, 3 E 131, 29 June 1550.

the new presidal court established in La Rochelle in 1552. These appointments came while their appeals to be reinstated on the *corps de ville* continued.[78]

With the backing of d'Estissac and other prominent Rochelais, the jurists' appeal for reinstatement finally triumphed in 1553. Nearly seven years after the legal dispute broke out, the king reversed himself, stated that he never meant for his edict of 1547 to apply in La Rochelle, deposed the allies of Guy and Morisson, and readmitted the nine *gens de justice* to their offices on the town council.[79] The king stipulated that henceforward the total number of royal jurists on the *corps* could not exceed sixteen: eight *pairs* and eight *échevins*. This decision stymied the king's original intention to curtail the local political affiliations of his officers that might divide their loyalties and impede their obedient execution of his commands.

The king's personal representative in La Rochelle, d'Estissac, evidently disagreed with his sovereign's original policy and worked to prevent its imposition. D'Estissac's lobbying to keep royal jurists on the *corps de ville* thwarted the king's intent but may have stemmed from d'Estissac's own well-informed assessment of the political benefits to be gained by maintaining even a potentially disaffected royal "presence" in the *corps*, undoubtedly the most powerful local force keeping the peace in the region. The king depended upon such organized bodies to govern his vast realm effectively. Keeping his *gens de justice* on the town council gave him at least the possibility of favorably influencing its deliberations and decisions while keeping tabs on the family rivalries that animated the politics of that institution. Doing without the fraternization of royal magistrates and municipal governing elites was an impractical, autocratic luxury d'Estissac knew his prince could ill afford. The continued presence of royal magistrates on the *corps* kept lines of communication open between the council and the courts while favoring the inter-marriage of families serving each.[80]

---

[78] For the appointments made to the presidial see Barbot, "Histoire de La Rochelle," AHSA 17 (1889): 84. According to Barbot, d'Estissac was convinced that royal jurists were absolutely necessary on the *corps de ville* in order to handle expeditiously the voluminous legal affairs of the city. D'Estissac harangued the town council to readmit royal officers and was instrumental in nullifying on appeal the letters obtained by Guy and Morisson, see Barbot, 84-86.

[79] *Ibid.*, 91-92.

[80] One representative example of inter-marriages between judicial families and

Such alliances expanded and further complicated the familial politics of the city, creating personal attachments capable of expe-
diting or blocking efficient conduct of municipal and royal affairs.

In an effort to manage better the familial politics inherent in
a local system of government highly resistent to external reform,
rochelais town councilmen tightened the rules governing the
transmission of municipal office. In a resolution of 15 April 1558,
they forbade resignations of office by sitting members of the *corps*
in favor of anyone not native to the city and without permanent
residence there.[81] They took this action "so that we may better
know and fully comprehend the parentage ( *la parenté*), the character, the condition, and the ability of those who henceforward
present themselves to hold office."[82] Parentage, the quality and
extent of a man's family ties, took precedence over everything else
in evaluating the suitability of an individual to hold office. In
effect, for the astute and watchful councilmen of La Rochelle,
there were no individuals aspiring to hold municipal office, only
family members whose obligations, connections, and ambitions as
kinsmen were the truest measure of their political mettle.

The importance of family ties in the protracted legal battle over
seating on the reconstituted *corps de ville* was by no means extraordinary. Comparison of town council personnel lists, notarized
marriage contracts, baptismal registers, testaments, and court
papers for the period 1558-1565 shows that the *corps de ville* of La
Rochelle was largely comprised of townsmen from densely interrelated families. For example, of the twenty-four *échevins* serving
in 1558, eleven were related by blood or marriage. In addition,
thirteen *échevins* were kinsmen to *pairs* serving below them on the
town council. François Joubert, *avocat du roi*, who regained his
seat as an *échevin* in 1553 and served in that capacity until 1573,
was the brother-in-law of Jacques de Nagères, *échevin* and mayor
in 1550.[83] Claude d'Angliers, *échevin* in 1558, was a *parent* to

---

families of the *corps de ville* is the household formed in the 1550's by *noble homme*
Mathurin Tarquais, *avocat*, and Pierrette Thevenin, kinswoman of several municipal office holders. The daughters of Tarquais and Thevenin: Catherine, Silvie,
and Françoise, all married members of the *corps*, see ADCM, 3 E 147, fols. 421r-
427v.

[81] BMLR, MS 81, fol. 167r.

[82] *Ibid.*, fol. 167r. The town councillors took their action, "...afin que l'on puisse
mieux cognoistre et entendre la parenté, les qualités, conditions, et facultés de
ceux qui cy-après se presenteront pour être reçus auxdits états."

[83] *Ibid.*, fol. 165v.

Hughes Pontard, *échevin* in 1558, and to Hughes' son, François, mayor in 1568.[84]

Several *échevins* had their sons-in-law serving as *pairs*. Jean Salbert, *sieur* de Villiars, a *pair* in 1558, was the son-in-law of Pierre Boisseau, an *échevin*.[85] Boisseau, through his wife Catherine du Jardin, was also a *parent* of Pierre du Jardin, a *pair* in 1558. The typical density of family connections between town council members is illustrated in another brief genealogical history. Pierre de Mirande, a *pair*, whose brother Jean was an *échevin* in 1550, was married to Marie du Perat, whose father, Jean, *sieur* de Fief Coultrait, was an *échevin* in 1558.[86] When Sara, the daughter of Pierre de Mirande and Marie du Perat, was born in 1563, her godfather was Jean Guy, another *échevin*.[87]

Figure 8 presents a partial schematic reconstruction of kin networks organized around the brothers Raoullet du Jau I and Jean du Jau, their children, and their in-laws from the politically active Salbert and Thevenin families. In this example, matrimonial ties, parentage, step-parentage, godparentage, trusteeship, and legal guardianship overlap and reinforce one another, weaving together the private lives and political interests of three great rochelais town council families. Contacts of this complexity were very common between members of the city's ruling elite.[88]

The complex family alliances attaching du Jaus to Thevenins and Salberts had tactical political significance. In 1558, the threat of a rumored English invasion prompted quick action by the *corps de ville*. A special civil defense council was hurriedly named to oversee refurbishment of the city's walls and armories. Raoullet du Jau I, Pierre Salbert, and Pierre Thevenin, all *échevins*, worked closely and smoothly together on the council summoning members of the bourgeoisie back to town from their rural estates, organizing neighborhood repair crews for the fortifications, negotiating for emergency powers with the king's lieutenant general

---

[84] See Barbot, "Histoire de La Rochelle," AHSA 17 (1889): 255. See also BMLR, MS 153, fol. 4r.

[85] Barbot, "Histoire de La Rochelle," AHSA 17 (1889): 162. See also BMLR, MS 219, cahier 38, fols. 40v-41r.

[86] ADCM, 3 E 132, 4 Nov. 1550.

[87] ADCM, I 1, fol. 43r.

[88] Sources for Figure 8 include ADCM, 3 E 144, fols. 133v-134v, 3 E 2148, 31 March 1565, and 3 E 2159, fol. 91r; ADCM, I 1, fols. 43r, 16v, and 85v; I 5, fols. 2r and 39r; and I 6, fol. 27r.

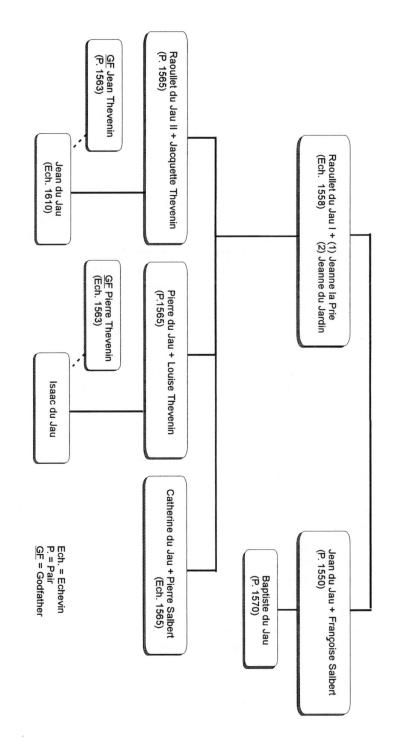

Figure 8. Kin Networks of Raoullet du Jau and Jean du Jau

d'Estissac, and rapidly augmenting city revenues to defray the cost of military preparedness.[89]

Dense family alliances common among La Rochelle's *échevins* were also the norm among the *pairs* of the town council. Of the seventy-six *pairs* serving in 1558, at least 46 (60%) were related by consanguinity or affinity to other members of the *corps de ville*. The Barbier brothers, Joseph and Zacherie, were both *pairs*. Through Joseph's wife, Anne Guyton, both men were brothers-in-law to Jean and Yves Guyton, two other brothers on the town council.[90] Numerous other enduring alliances can be documented between families long represented on the *corps de ville*.

Not only was endogamy high amongst families on the *corps*, the choice of godparents for newborns of town council members was usually made from the extended family and fellow members of the *corps*, social groups whose dimensions tended to coincide. The first surviving volume of the Protestant baptismal registers for La Rochelle runs from 26 January 1562 to 27 December 1566.[91] It records the baptism of forty-nine infants born to fathers serving on the *corps*. In twenty-two cases, one or both of the godparents share the surnames of the parents and can be considered immediate relatives. In twenty-seven cases, the godparents have surnames differing from the biological parents suggesting more distant affinity. In twenty-four of the twenty-seven cases where surnames differ, one (or both) of the godparents bears the name of another family long represented in the *corps de ville*. An examination of Protestant baptismal registers in La Rochelle reveals the workings of a sociopolitical system in which the practices of civic office and the protocols of extended family life were deeply enmeshed.

Further evidence of family interests at work to shape the political culture of La Rochelle can be found in the long-neglected and voluminous transcripts of legal proceedings before the presidial court (also referred to as the *cour du gouvernement* or *siège présidial*) of La Rochelle. Among the earliest existent records of this tribunal are a folio-sized, 285-page manuscript register of cases heard and decisions rendered between 23 February 1565 and

---

[89] Barbot, "Histoire de La Rochelle," AHSA 17 (1889): 137.
[90] ADCM, 3 E 154, fol. 51r.
[91] ADCM, I 1, fols. 1r-86v.

14 January 1566.[92] In addition, the *Bibliothèque Municipale* of La Rochelle also holds fifteen manuscript *cahiers* in which depositions were recorded and copies made of documents pertaining to cases heard before the court in 1565.[93]

The main register of the court for 1565 lists 850 major decisions rendered (not counting frequent opinions to postpone hearings for procedural reasons or to allow plaintiffs to amass further evidence). The *cahiers* contain information on 783 separate *procès* which, given that only fifteen of the original forty-nine *cahiers* exist, may amount to only about a third of all cases on the docket for the year 1565. The 783 cases for which the *cahiers* provide detailed information concerning the matter at issue can be classified in seven categories (see Table 3).

As one might expect in a port town home to many merchants, the local royal court handled numerous cases arising out of contracts broken, bankruptcies, and personal loans past due. While these matters accounted for a third of all known litigation in 1565, disputes over the distribution, administration, and care of family assets and family members were, collectively, the second leading cause of law suits preserved in the archives. This genre of contention was more common than disputes arising over real estate transactions or the privileges of office holding. Cases included Olivier Rondeau's bid to regain property previously alienated by his father through a *retrait lignager* proceeding—a move that was opposed by the presumable beneficiaries of the alienation, Rondeau's sisters, Leonor and Catherine and their husbands, Jean Pierres and Jean Berne, *échevins*. The court authorized Olivier to recover the property.[94] Raoullet du Jau II, Pierre du Jau, their

---

[92] BMLR, MS 222, "Registre de la cour du gouvernement de La Rochelle."

[93] BMLR, MSS 212, 213, 219, 220, and 221. The *registre* and the *cahiers* are complementary documents. Marginal notes in the register of court actions refer by number to the *cahiers* in which the claims of litigants were recorded. At least forty-nine *cahiers* were filled for cases brought before the *présidial* in 1565. Of this number, fifteen remain: *cahiers* XIX to XXV (15 Dec. 1564 - 2 April 1565) and *cahiers* XXXIII to XL (14 May - 15 Nov. 1565). Several *cahiers* cover the same chronological period and attest to the great volume of litigation ordinarily before La Rochelle's *siège présidial.*

[94] BMLR, MS 212, *cahier* 20, fols. 22v-23v. A *retrait lignager* agreement allowed an individual to alienate family property to a third party to obtain immediate income with the provision that members of the family would have a preemptory right to reacquire the property should the new owner decide to sell. Use of *retrait lignager* was common in La Rochelle, especially among city families possessing numerous urban and rural properties available for sale or rent.

*Table 3*

Presidial Court Cases by Type in 1565

| Type | Number | Percentage |
| --- | --- | --- |
| Commerce<br>Bankruptcy<br>Unrecovered Debt | 270 | 34.5 |
| Inheritance Disputes<br>Family Patrimony<br>*Retrait Lignager*<br>Guardianship | 185 | 23.6 |
| Real Estate | 134 | 17.1 |
| Appeals | 118 | 15.0 |
| Office Holding<br>Office Privileges | 27 | 3.5 |
| Miscellaneous Property | 20 | 2.6 |
| Other | 28 | 3.7 |
| Totals | 783 | 100.0% |

brother-in-law Pierre Salbert, and their cousin by marriage, Jacques Dennebault, all dissatisfied with the inheritance their late kinsman Jean du Jau settled on his son Baptiste, jointly filed an appeal of a prior court decision upholding the bequest. The court demanded that the plaintifs produce additional evidence to justify their new appeal.[95] Isabeau du Jardin, widow of Raoullet du Jau I, and her new husband Pierre Thevenin, acting as tutors and conservators of her minor children and heirs, sought repayment of a debt outstanding since 1548 that now belonged to the estate of her late husband she held in trust for his descendants. The debtors were ordered to pay up.[96]

The cases cited above are a small but representative sample of presidial decisions affecting households in the year 1565. Notable in the court's work are deep respect for testamentary decisions of fathers, opinions that favor transmission of paternal property to

---

[95] BMLR, MS 212, *cahier* 22, fols. 163v-64r.
[96] *Ibid.*, *cahier* 22, fols. 177r-178v.

male lineal descendants, a care for limiting the claims of daughters, wives, and widows on family wealth, and general approbation of legal provisions for wards made by male kinsmen, under the aegis of paternal authority, with or without the consent of their charges, male or female. The resolution of such cases in accord with paternal wishes and parental care was a heavy responsibility of the presidial court that intimately familiarized opposing attorneys and magistrates with the structure and interests of rochelais families. In 1565, a quarter or more of the court's time was devoted to the delicate task of ordering family affairs and cooling the tempers of feuding in-laws. This undertaking made the dispensation of royal justice in a public court an important regulator of the obligations and animosities kinship could create. The vocabulary of royal justice was often one of parentage, patrimony, and birthright that wove legal decision making into the fabric of family life while reinforcing the authority of menfolk in the community.

The local custom of *insinuations* reinforced the role of the presidial court as a frequent arbiter of familial disputes. Townspeople regularly had the texts of marriage contracts, inheritance agreements between spouses, guardianship provisions, and wills registered before the presidial and copied into special rolls the court maintained.[97] This readily accessible official archive of family papers was an essential resource for the attorneys of litigious relatives who went before the tribunal. Moreover, the volume and diversity of documents registered with the court show the willingness of the Rochelais to make that institution the confidant and guarantor for fateful decisions they made about the rules of family life. The magistrates' own extensive family connections occasionally impeded the settlement of disputes when judges removed themselves from cases involving close relatives or faced appeals by litigants claiming that a magistrate's failure to recuse himself from a prior case involving kin had made an impartial hearing impossible.

The legal archives of La Rochelle reveal the importance of domestic politics in the day-to-day operation of the city's highest court. When coupled with lists of municipal officeholders and

---

[97] See "Insinuations de la cour du gouvernement de la ville de La Rochelle," BMLR, MSS 235, 236, 237, 238, 239, and 240.

demographic data, these documents portray an urban society in
which calculations of affinity and consanguinity clearly influenced
the conduct of municipal government, the dispensation of justice,
and the establishment of contractual obligations between citizens.
Such habits of mind and demeanor were only to be expected in
a community where no hard and fast distinctions, no bureaucratic
maxims, civil-service examinations, or homilies on the sanctity of
the small, conjugal family allowed the realms of public and private life to be neatly disentangled.

In their form, content, and conservation, documents of the era
show a different world in which ties of blood and marriage bound
together family members and the governing institutions they occupied and obeyed. When lifted from the realm of the picayune and
restored to the context of urban politics, genealogical facts provide a human foundation for understanding the structure, operation, and ethos of municipal government. Diarists among the
attorneys and town councilmen of early modern La Rochelle who
dutifully filled their journals with news of local engagements, weddings, births, and christenings did so not solely to relieve the tedi-
um of provincial office. They appreciated such information as a
running commentary on urban society and politics too vital to
ignore.

The collection of such intelligence became even more essential
with the restoration of La Rochelle's ancient *corps de ville* in 1548.
Once again, local citizens became real actors in the city's power
politics. Participants in this struggle for meaningful public authority had to keep close tabs on the formation of family cliques and
intrigues underlying alliances between municipal governors. The
resurgent town council brooked no outside interference in the
prerogatives of civic administration and resumed its efforts to
police the wild frontier region under its surveillance. Civic officials maintained their wary attitude toward the king and his west
country agents. Royal lieutenants and *sénéchaux* in the region saw
their capacity to influence urban affairs diminish after 1548. La
Rochelle entered the early years of the French Reformation as a
rejuvenated, quasi-independent municipality whose litigious civic
leaders bore the heavy and practical responsibilities of defending
public order. Their own intra- and interfamily feuds complicated
performance of these duties, heightening local apprehensions of
misrule and the destructive capacity of human foibles. This was
the state of La Rochelle when the French Reformation began.

# CHAPTER THREE

# NO CITY ON A HILL:
# THE ROCHELAIS REFORMATION,
# CIRCA 1550–CIRCA 1620

Save me O God;
for the waters are come into my soul.
I sink in deep mire where there is no standing:
I am come into deep waters where the floods
overflow me. (Psalm 69:1-2).

By terrible things in righteousness wilth thou
answer us, O God of our salvation; who art
the confidence of all the ends of the earth,
and of them that are far off upon the sea:
Which by His strength setteth fast the mountains
being girded with power: Which stilleth the noise of
the seas, the noise of their waves,
and the tumult of the people. (Psalm 67:5-7).

Despite La Rochelle's reputation as a great bastion of Calvinism in France, the course of the city's Reformation over time has never been studied in detail. What few histories of rochelais religious life we do possess have not dispelled enduring myths about the orthodoxy, unity, and discipline of this Reformed community. Without comprehensive analysis of indigenous religious practices, based upon empirical archival research, little of substance can be learned about the dynamics of La Rochelle's Reformation and the changing roles of various urban social groups within this movement. In lieu of common generalizations about La Rochelle's stolid Protestantism, this chapter offers concerted histories of the geopolitical factors, clergymen, congregations, ordinary believers, and local printers all interacting to drive one town's religious transformations over three-quarters of a century.

My intent here is not merely to chart La Rochelle's progress from one faith to another, but rather to evoke the succession of

controversies occurring before and after a majority of the Rochelais adapted themselves to new modes of religious devotion. This
chapter addresses the variety of motives which may have prompted different segments of the urban population to participate in
this conversion. Massed archival evidence reveals La Rochelle to
have been a persistently heterodox religious community, an isolated coastal town ideally sited for harboring heretics offensive to
Rome and Geneva. Successive generations of the city's quarrelsome, superstitious Reformed clergy grew apart from distant Swiss
centers of Calvinist indoctrination and chafed at the refusal of
townspeople, patrician and plebeian, to heed their teachings. The
increasing material and political identification of La Rochelle's
Calvinist pastors with the wealthy merchant oligarchs controlling
the city council estranged the clergymen from the unenfranchised
mass of the urban population. This antagonism would ultimately
lead to harsh popular censure of Reformed ministers and the near
total collapse of their public authority during the first two decades
of the seventeenth century.

Rochelais printers, with close ties to other worlds of Protestant
dispute in England, Scotland, and the Netherlands, kept their
town well-supplied with polemical and explicitly apocalyptic literature fueling religious dissent. Reformed congregations within La
Rochelle differed significantly in size and membership over time.
Trends manifest in the sociology of these assemblies indicate
declining cohesion between congregants of differing social status.
An analysis of contemporaneous Calvinist testamentary behavior,
evoking the personal religious commitments of individual congregants as indicated in their last wills, shows the Rochelais to
have been much less charitable, on average, than other French
Reformed townspeople, more selective in their philanthropy over
time, far less supportive of Calvinist clergymen over time, and
apparently less susceptible to instruction in these matters by their
ministers.

The mosaic of old La Rochelle, assembled from surviving archival pieces, shows an extraordinary French provincial town
inhabited by a fractious citizenry. Here, the Reformation enlarged
and compounded the struggles of residents to fashion an exemplary municipality: secure, just, enviable among men, and pleas-
ing to God. The result was an urban community never wholly

devoted to the new faith and frequently at odds with other bodies of French Protestants.[1]

### 1. *The Weakness of Catholic Culture and the Origins of the Reformation in the French West Country*

The strange coast of western France was long renowned as a breeding ground of prophets, clairvoyants, and *fous de dieu* possessing miraculous powers. This was a landscape fit for hermits. In 1379, the French king Charles V, in great need of spiritual guidance, sought out the famous Guillemette, a young woman from the wilderness of La Rochelle widely believed to converse with God. The king brought her to Paris, housed her at court, and took her counsel regularly.[2] Contemporaneously, the visionary Rochelaise named Catherine travelled across France in company with a Franciscan friar, drawing crowds with wonderful tales of her celestial revelations.[3] During the 1490's, passion plays and public burlesques, in which biblical figures, pagan deities, and fairy folk cavorted together on stages in the center of La Rochelle's largest square, celebrated popular religious devotions in the city.[4] During the early decades of the sixteenth century, local lay and ecclesiastical authorities had to contend with itinerant preachers sermonizing freely and with naked religious fanatics running through the streets announcing arrival of the final judgment.

The police of Catholic doctrine was impossible amidst the tran-

---

[1] Georges Serr is among the very few earlier historians of the French west country and of the Wars of Religion to have recognized the distinctive, heterodox religiosity of the Rochelais. As he once concluded, "La Rochelle never held a normal place within the Reformed party of France." See Serr, "Henri de Rohan. Son rôle dans le parti protestant, 1617-1622," in *Divers aspects de la Réforme aux XVIe et XVIIe siècles*, (Paris, 1975), 289-622, here at 573.

[2] Louis-Etienne Arcère, *Histoire de la ville de La Rochelle et du pays d'Aunis*, 2 vols. (La Rochelle, 1756; reprint Marseille, 1975), 1: 261-262. Léopold Delayant, *Histoire des Rochelais*, 2 vols. (La Rochelle, 1870), 1: 97-98, also notes an "exaltation mystique" popularly associated in late medieval times with the region and residents of La Rochelle.

[3] Arcère, *Histoire de la ville de La Rochelle*, 1: 262.

[4] M.D. Massiou, *Histoire politique, civile, et religieuse de la Saintonge et de l'Aunis*, 6 vols. (Paris, 1836-38), 3: 404-405. Arcère, *Histoire de la ville de La Rochelle*, 1: 293, notes the "tournure burlesque" of these popular entertainments.

sient population of La Rochelle's port. Enduring popular allegiance to ancient folkways and widespread beliefs about the malefic powers of clerics further compromised church discipline in
town and countryside. Throughout the provinces of Aunis and
Saintonge, the laity treated Catholic clergy reservedly, not only as
potent intermediaries with heaven, but also as potentially dangerous sorcerers, easily capable of sickening farm animals, infesting fields with moles, and causing hailstorms.[5] From at least as
early as the 1540's up through the mid-nineteenth century, local
Catholic wedding ceremonies, urban and rural, contained salvif-
ic gestures for bride and groom specifically intended to counter-
act priestly hexes cursing the fiancé with impotence and the
future household with rancor.[6] Even local Calvinist ministers were
not above similar popular suspicion of connivance with the devil. In 1591, the leading Protestant printer in La Rochelle issued
a book chastising Reformed congregants for avoiding local church
weddings because of their persistent fears about the secret curses of pastors.[7] However, the author of this screed, a visiting Cal-

---

[5] J. L.-M. Noguès, *Les moeurs d'autrefois en Saintonge et Aunis*, (Saintes, 1891),
125 and 128-130. Among the Saintongeais peasantry, the association of curés with
threatening storms produced the phrase "priests' shanks" to describe the rays of
sunlight penetrating between thick, lowering cloud banks.

[6] *Ibid.*, 7 and n. 1. Such protective gestures certainly antedated the onset of
the Reformation locally. Some natives of the region, including learned magistrates and municipal officials, sought to minimize the dangers of a priest's witchcraft by marrying secretly in churches far outside their own communities where
such clerical curses were less likely. Locals particularly feared the "noueries de
l'aiguillette," charms by which priests rendered grooms impotent. To avoid such
lacerating wounds, worried couples announced and celebrated betrothals far away
from church structures, choosing instead rural estates, fields, copses, and farm
buildings for the sites of their engagements. See A.D. de la Fontenelle de
Vaudoré, ed., *Journal de Guillaume et de Michel Le Riche, avocats du roi à Saint-Maixent
de 1534 à 1586*, (Saint-Maixent, 1846; reprint Geneva, 1971), 209-210. In 1574,
Michel Le Riche's son, a highly educated Catholic jurist, and his bride celebrated their marriage ("avoient fait les épousailles") two days before their church ceremony for fear of priestly spells hexing the groom's procreative powers. On popular apprehensions over "noueurs de l'aiguillette" among the clergy in the region
of sixteenth-century Montpellier, another epicenter of the French Reformation,
see *Félix et Thomas Platter à Montpellier 1552-1559—1595-1599. Notes de voyage de
deux étudiants Balois*, (Montpellier, 1892), 376-377.

[7] See the *Traité de l'enchantement qu'on appelle vulgairement le nouement de l'esguillette en la celebration des marriages en l'eglise reformée et des remedes à l'encontre pour
le soulagement des fideles*, (La Rochelle: H. Haultin, 1591), BN Rés. D2.13667, 4.
The author of this piece, the visiting pastor Louis Hesnard, dedicated it to the
ministers and elders of the rochelais Calvinist church. Although this tract may

vinist minister, did admit that even Reformed congregations (and by implication their clergy) could be surreptitiously invaded by evil magicians, requiring congregants' exemplary performance of all Calvinist devotions as a sure remedy against emasculating enchantment.[8]

Inveterate popular wariness of Catholic clerics was strengthened by their avaricious and dissolute behavior in a region poorly supervised by senior prelates. Since the early fourteenth century, residents of La Rochelle and neighboring communities had combated mounting priestly financial demands through collective refusals to pay the *dîmes* assessed by the church. The islands of Ré and Oléron, the Arvert peninsula, and the *banlieue* of La Rochelle were all subject to *dîmes* imposed by distant abbeys or absentee churchmen. Between 1310 and 1405, vineyard workers in La Rochelle's hinterland proclaimed their immunity to a *dîme* demanded by the bishop of Saintes.[9] Local congregants used legal action to oppose an effort by the curé of Bignay, southeast of La Rochelle, to raise his *dîme* in 1421.[10] When a band of highwaymen later took over the curé's church, the parishioners simply set fire to the structure, happy to be rid of a common lair for robbers.

The scandalous misconduct of local clerics encouraged the laity's irreverence toward them. Records of disciplinary cases prosecuted in the *officialité*, or ecclesiastical court of the bishopric of Saintes, from 1545 to 1552 reveal that rochelais priests were rebuked for insolence toward parishioners, neglect of parochial duties, and the consecration of bigamous marriages arranged between spouses allowed to wed without proper examination.[11] In 1546, it was discovered that over the prior four years nuns at the local convent of Sainte Claire had quit their cloister without prop-

---

have been conceived as an inducement for Catholics to convert, its publication almost two generations after the inception of the rochelais Reformation suggests the tenacity of such popular beliefs about evil clerics and shows an effort by Calvinist authorities to condemn these ineradicable superstitions as impediments to thorough reform.

[8] *Ibid.*, 80-81.

[9] Arcère, *Histoire de la ville de La Rochelle*, 1: 265-266. François Julien-Labruyère, *Paysans charentais. Histoire des campagnes d'Aunis, Saintonge, et bas Angoumois*, 2 vols. (La Rochelle, 1982), 2: 130.

[10] Julien-Labruyère, *Paysans charentais*, 2: 130.

[11] BMLR, MS 241, *registre* of the *officialité* of La Rochelle, July 1545-December 1552. See also Delayant, *Histoire des Rochelais* 1: 193-194.

er authorization, conducted sacrilegious love affairs, and even married.[12]

At a material level, the Reformation's outbreak along the French mid-Atlantic coast can be appreciated as a cataclysmic phase in an ancient struggle pitting ecclesiastical overlords against resolute parishioners. In the west country, lay communities jealously guarded their hard-won sustenance by legal stratagems and inveterate reliance on the artifices of an ancient folk magic attuned to the rudeness of the local environment. Accumulating instances of clerical turpitude during the early sixteenth century only sapped the suasive powers of the parish clergy, leaving ordinary congregants more receptive to the innovative preaching of disaffected churchmen. On a spiritual plane, the message of salvation circulated by the Reformation's avatars in western France (including Jean Calvin himself at Poitiers and Angoulême in 1534) may have had a special emotional and theological appeal to natives of the region.

For centuries it has been argued that the maritime, cosmopolitan culture of La Rochelle predisposed its residents to welcome foreign ideas and question those verities sacrosanct to inlanders. Writing in 1756, Arcère attributed the Reformation's local success to a rochelais taste for novelty in all things.[13] Massiou (1836), contrasted the slow diffusion of the Reformed religion south of the Charente river with its quick triumph in La Rochelle and along the coast of Saintonge, areas where "un peuple navigateur" readily accepted religious innovations.[14] More recently, Alain Cabantous has emphasized the commercial incentives which may have prompted rochelais merchants to embrace the Protestantism of their main business partners in England and the Low Countries.[15]

The traffics, human and material, licit and illicit, of sea ports do keep them continually (and dangerously) open to a wide, external world of ideas. These entrepots for exotic goods also channel distribution of alien books and opinions potentially subversive of public order and religious discipline. La Rochelle's mar-

---

[12] Arcère, *Histoire de la ville de La Rochelle.* 1: 328.

[13] *Ibid.*, 326.

[14] Massiou, *Histoire politique*, 4: 6-7.

[15] Alain Cabantous, *Le ciel dans la mer. Christianisme et civilisation maritime XVIe –XIXe siècle*, (Paris, 1990), 250.

itime culture should not be discounted as a contributing factor to the local proliferation of unorthodox religious attitudes. However, La Rochelle's status as a port town by itself is insufficient to explain the Reformation's attractiveness to the majority of citizens who ultimately converted, a number far exceeding the total of all inhabitants directly or indirectly involved in the operations of the harbor.

And here one must also acknowledge the research findings of Judith Meyer first incorporated in her 1977 doctoral dissertation and published quite recently.[16] Meticulously investigating rochelais economic conditions contemporaneous with the onset of the Reformation, Meyer finds no signs whatsoever of any dramatic fluctuations which might have prompted materially threatened or newly disadvantaged segments of the population to embrace a novel religion.[17] Noting the various socioeconomic ranks of rochelais converts to Calvinism and their diverse political opinions, Meyer also contends that the local Reformation cannot be attributed to the agitation of a specific social group nor to the agency of a single political faction.[18]

Rejecting specific material or political triggers of the rochelais *Réforme*, Meyer emphasizes that citizens' "strong sense of lay independence from ecclesiastical authority" and "their commitment to...civic independence" were crucial local catalysts of Protes-

---

[16] See Judith Pugh Meyer, "Reformation in La Rochelle, Religious Change, Social Stability, and Political Crisis 1500-1568," (Ph.D. diss. University of Iowa, 1977), recently published with minor revisions as *Reformation in La Rochelle: Tradition and Change in Early Modern Europe 1500-1568*, Travaux d'Humanisme et Renaissance, No. 298, (Geneva, 1996).

[17] See Meyer, *Reformation in La Rochelle*, 69-70. "The absence of serious social and economic dislocation among a significant part of the Rochelais population offers no obvious causal explanation for the Reformation. The shifts in Rochelais religious beliefs and practices brought about by the Reformation can be hardly explained by widespread social or economic dislocation."

[18] *Ibid.*, 141-142. Meyer's discoveries about the Reformation in La Rochelle challenge the local applicability of older explanations regarding the genesis of French Protestantism put forth by Henry Heller and David Rosenberg, historians who emphasize the preponderance of increasingly disadvantaged journeymen and poorer craftsmen among converts to Calvinism in French textile centers like Amiens. See Heller, *The Conquest of Poverty: The Calvinist Revolt in Sixteenth-Century France*, (Leiden, 1986), especially 234; and Rosenberg, "Social Experience and Religious Choice, A Case Study: The Protestant Weavers and Woolcombers of Amiens in the Sixteenth Century," (Ph.D. diss., Yale University, 1978), especially 74-75.

tantism.[19] While I do not disagree with these conclusions, I seek to know more about rochelais beliefs, sacred and profane, than Meyer can reveal. If, as she implies, the mentalities of townspeople essentially impelled religious change, I want to know more about the values, convictions, and fears shaping their dissent.

Along this tack, Denis Crouzet has argued that French believers were attracted to Calvinism because, by establishing an ineffable God and subtracting miracles from daily life, the new doctrine "disenchanted" the world, offering Christians a serene, irenic alternative to the anguished, apocalyptic, and terrifying eschatology of baroque Catholicism.[20] However, Crouzet's thesis is predicated upon two fundamental assumptions unjustified for the French west country. First, in a region where the simplest rites of Catholicism were impeded by poor church attendance and a listless priesthood, it cannot be safely argued that Catholic proselytizers successfully communicated their dire warnings of perdition to the laity. Second, simply because Jean Calvin never offered extensive commentaries on the apocalyptic books of the Bible (an isolated fact central to Crouzet's thesis), it is dubious to claim that his followers scattered throughout the deep provinces of France derived a solace from their new devotions that overwhelmed and discouraged acute reflection on the miseries of daily life, the ubiquity of malevolent spirits, the mystery of final judgment, and the uncertainties of the hereafter.[21]

---

[19] Meyer, *Reformation in La Rochelle*, 141-143.

[20] D. Crouzet, *Les guerriers de Dieu*, 2 vols. (Paris, 1990), 1: 144-153 and 525-527. According to Crouzet, "...le propre du Calvinisme est de proposer une foi qui rétrécit, racourcit le sacré à la seule Révélation, le retirant du monde et de l'homme pour plus le laisser subsister que dans le Livre...la théologie calvinienne est une théologie de l'apaisement et de la sérénité...la construction dogmatique calvinienne permet de briser l'encerclement obsessionel que le prophétisme d'angoisse, qui gravite autour de la religion ancienne, avait progressivement faconné ou actualisé." Tracking the course of only one, fiery Catholic preacher across southwestern France, Crouzet claims "le cas de la Guyenne validerait mon hypothèse selon laquelle l'essor de la Réforme est lié en France à la diffusion d'une grande angoisse eschatologique." Such claims cannot be safely advanced on such flimsy evidence and are surely overblown.

[21] Crouzet, *Les guerriers*, 1: 146-147. Crouzet's thesis is further contradicted by recent investigations of Calvinist attitudes toward the supernatural in early modern Europe revealing a preoccupation among Reformed polemicists with specters, devils, witches, and the place of such monsters within God's creation. See for example Stuart Clark, "Protestant Demonology: Sin, Superstition, and Society (c. 1520–c. 1630)," in Bengt Ankarloo and G. Henningsen, eds., *Early Modern European Witchcraft: Centers and Peripheries*, (Oxford, 1990), 45-81.

Evidence from La Rochelle suggests that Reformed ministers and their congregants long manifested a taste for apocalyptic religious discourse, a fascination with the black spirit realm, and a tremendous fear of the natural world where the forces of good and evil did conspicuous battle. Such habits were especially characteristic of early modern populations dwelling in close proximity to the sea, a chaotic and menacing element whose overwhelming floods it was popularly believed would commence the final judgment.[22] If rochelais Calvinists were not amenable to a disenchantment of the world, what drew them so strongly to the new faith? The answer I believe lies more in how Calvinism appealed to the practical and spiritual sides of French westerners, how it sacralized human perseverance, and how it made fortitude the most Christian of virtues.

The enemies of French Calvinists frequently rebuked them for pride (*orgueil*). Crouzet argues that Calvinists invited this reproach when they displayed a serene conviction of personal salvation based upon intimations of election manifest in their daily lives.[23] Here, Crouzet perpetuates a fundamental misunderstanding of Reformed comportment. Calvin and his adherents constantly emphasized the inscrutable nature of God's grace and denied any signals of this unmerited gift in the worldly lives of the elect.[24] The pride of the Rochelais brethren did not devolve essentially from their supreme confidence of election and impending salvation. The mysteries of Calvinist belief and the vicissitudes of life in a frontier town precluded such certainties.

Rather, I would argue, the conceit for which contemporaries chided the Rochelais stemmed from their embrace of a Reformed faith celebrating the resolute strength of believers, an ordinary, utilitarian virtue of townspeople who found themselves surround-

---

[22] See Alain Cabantous, "Espace maritime et mentalités religieuses en France aux XVIIe et XVIIIe siècles," *Mentalities/Mentalités*, 1 (1982): 4-12.

[23] Crouzet, *Les guerriers*, 1: 148-149.

[24] See Jean Calvin *Institutes of the Christian Religion*, ed. John T. McNeill, 2 vols. (Philadelphia, 1960), especially Book III, Chapter 23, Articles 11-14, 2: 959-64. Note also McNeill's emphasis in his Introduction on Calvin's regard for "the high and incomprehensible mystery" of predestination. According to McNeill, "[t]he fruits of election are in no respect visible in any outward advantage or prosperity enjoyed in this life, where impiety prospers and the pious are forced to bear a cross," 1: lix. Even an individual's slightest speculation on the election or reprobation of his or her soul was considered as surrender to damnable Satanic temptations by Calvin and his followers.

ed by a threatening wilderness of biblical proportions. For the Rochelais and their neighbors perched on the dangerous margins of land and sea, allegiance to the Reformation was a gesture of self-respect, self-assertion, and emancipation from a Catholic cosmology presided over by a distant, vengeful, unhelpful God. Here, the priesthood of all believers recognized and complemented the citizenry's collective responsibility for the defense of civic culture. The Christian stoicism Calvinism championed easily aligned with and sanctified the steely self-reliance demanded of isolated town dwellers by their environment. The quick embrace of Protestantism by Rochelais responsible for the sustenance, government, police, and military protection of the city supports this conclusion.

Moreover, in a town distinguished by its citizenry's long fight for exceptional self-government guaranteed by numerous royal privileges, the Reformation offered the Rochelais an opportunity to align their civic and ecclesiastical communities. Through driving out the agents of Catholicism, townspeople could finally remove from the urban polity an internal threat to its integrity posed by the divided loyalties of resident clergy ultimately answerable to the bishop of Rome.

One needs only to traverse the Psalms, those human calls for a loving Savior's worldly aid that cadenced rochelais spiritual life from the 1550's onward, to appreciate the attractiveness of an heroic, Reformed Christianity for frontier townsfolk inured to battling the elements, seaborne marauders, unruly peasants, and indifferent, hexing Catholic clerics.[25] This new faith, like the old, did not supplant more ancient popular magic, but more advantageously coexisted with it, renewing believers' conviction of a vital link between human agency and divine protection.[26] Here,

---

[25] Considering the religious practices of the early modern French, Robin Briggs emphasizes how important local perceptions of communal vulnerabilities were in shaping the spiritual allegiances of believers. The protective attributes of a creed were crucial to its appeal and rendered confessional orthodoxies subject to popular amalgamation with older, defensive magics. According to Briggs, "...local religion was relatively economical, discarding outworn saints as new favorites emerged, and allowing practices to wax and wane in response to particular needs...[r]eligion remained for virtually everyone the experience of powerful affective practices and symbols, which included rituals of protection and sanctification." See Briggs, *Communities of Belief*, (Oxford, 1989), 390-91 and 394.

[26] "I waited patiently for the Lord, and He inclined unto me and heard my cry. He brought me up also out of a horrible pit, out of the miry clay, and set

Calvinism may have been widely perceived as a more supernaturally (or supranaturally) efficacious creed and thus a worthy addition to the arsenal of incantations and privileges coastal town dwellers already employed to preserve and distinguish themselves.[27]

The possibility of such an appropriation of Calvinism by French westerners is supported by the findings of historians like Robert Muchembled, who notes that early modern French populations possessed religious attitudes amalgamating Christian and neo-pagan rituals primarily because believers sought consoling benefits and worldly, "concrete results" from their devotions.[28] The durability of such belief systems, especially in the French west country, has been shown by Judith Devlin. She sees sustained popular regard for the practical rewards and psychological benefits of confessional identification among nineteenth-century French countryfolk indifferent to the canonical aspects of official reli-

---

my feet upon a rock and established my goings," Psalm 40: 1-2. The very name "La Rochelle," derived from the Latin "rupella" for "little rock," contained within it an evocation of God's favor to the city and its inhabitants. Consider also the message of God's salutary dominion over the unruly forces of nature, especially the sea, celebrated in Psalms 1, 24, 33, and 60. Calvin, too, celebrated this natural aspect of God's majesty, "With what clear manifestations his might draws us to contemplate him! Unless perchance it be unknown to us in whose power it lies to sustain this infinite mass of heaven and earth by his Word...to compel the sea, which by its height seems to threaten the earth with continual destruction, to hang as if in mid-air; sometimes to arouse it in a dreadful way with the tumultuous force of winds; sometimes with waves quieted, to make it calm again!," *Institutes of the Christian Religion*, Book I, Chapter V, Article 6, (McNeill edition) 1: 59. Such oceanic passages could not have failed to attract and hold the attention of the Rochelais.

[27] Jean Calvin unequivocally declared, "Nature is God" and "nature is the order prescribed by God." "When dense clouds darken the sky, and a violent Tempest arises, because a gloomy mist is cast over our eyes, thunder strikes our ears and all our senses are benumbed with fright, everything seems to us to be confused and mixed up; but all the while a constant quiet and serenity remain in heaven. So we must infer that, while the disturbances of the world deprive us of judgment, God out of the pure light of his justice and wisdom, tempers and directs these very movements in the best-conceived order to a right end." See *Institutes of the Christian Religion*, Book I, Chapter V, Article 5 and Chapter 18, Article 1, (McNeill edition) 1: 58 and 211. Such declamations could only have been regarded with the greatest interest and relief by coastal residents like the Rochelais who continually worried over their exposure and vulnerability to the violent forces of nature.

[28] See Robert Muchembled, *Sorcières, justice et société aux 16e et 17e siècles*, (Paris, 1987), especially Chapter 1, "Sorcellerie, culture populaire, et christianisme," 33-59.

gion.[29] As long as they were confronted by pressing ambient dangers, French townspeople retained the deeper folkways of their rural neighbors, modifying their church creeds accordingly.

For the literate townspeople of a marine outpost, Jean Calvin's celebration of God's majesty over threatening primordial elements like the sea would undoubtedly have been attractive. The reformer's assurances that faithful readers of scripture could become adept at discerning a divine orderliness in nature's apparent maelstrom offered the Rochelais empowerment as individual interpreters of God's word who no longer needed to fear their environment or their Catholic priests so intimately. Such emancipation, at once corporeal and emotional, infused the Rochelais with pride and relief, complementing their long, successful accretion of municipal privileges exempting them from the usual vexations French citizens suffered at the hands of aristocrats and kings. A synergy of spiritual and political liberation underlies the rochelais Reformation.

However, urbanites' selective incorporation of Protestant teachings within a reordered vocabulary of satisfying religious practice prevented the triumph of orthodox Calvinism in La Rochelle. The laity's stubbornly utilitarian beliefs about religion's role in remedying immediate problems impeded diffusion of clerical opinions on providence, sin, and salvation.

A number of the earliest French martyrs for the Reformed religion were natives of La Rochelle and its region. Their biographies indicate that townspeople from all social ranks adopted and expounded heretical religious opinions. In 1526, *maître* Guillaume Joubert, a law student in Paris and son of a royal attorney in La Rochelle, received a death sentence from the Parlement of Paris for blaspheming God and mocking Parisians' devotion to their

---

[29] See Judith Devlin, *The Superstitious Mind: French Peasants and the Supernatural in the Nineteenth Century,* (New Haven, 1987), 20-21 and 101. Devlin surmises that for most French peasants of the era "official religion seems to have been seen more as a practical than as a spiritual affair." Similarly, "[t]he very adaptability of the magical rites of which witchcraft formed a part suggests that we should see them not so much as a kind of theory but more as a vocabulary. In rural France in the nineteenth century, magic furnished people with a way of expressing and sometimes of overcoming disorienting feelings, of satisfying their dreams: as practiced, it was a psychological technique with social rather than scientific overtones." The heterodox spiritualities of the early modern Rochelais comprise an earlier vocabulary of the kind Devlin describes. It formed out of and addressed the collective anxieties of the citizenry.

patron saint, Geneviève.[30] Parisian magistrates supervising the 1539 sovereign judicial sessions (*grands jours*) at Angers noted with alarm that "in the city of La Rochelle and its government there are numerous heretics holding and professing scandalous blasphemies and supporting many heretical propositions against the holy Catholic faith and ecclesiastical doctrine...today this is the foremost region where heretical blasphemies propagate."[31]

In 1544, three such rochelais miscreants died for their sacrilegious crimes. In Paris, Pierre de la Vallée went to the stake for "execrable blasphemies." Charles Anthoyne burned to death before the Church of Notre Dame de Cougnes in La Rochelle for "blasphemies against the holy sacrament of communion, the honor and reverence of saints, and the constitution and traditions of our holy mother church." Marie Gaborite, a chambermaid employed in La Rochelle who attacked a Franciscan monk for not preaching the word of God, was condemned to death by the Parisian Parlement for uttering "scandalous, erroneous, and blasphemous propositions contrary to the honor of God and the sacrament of communion."[32]

In succeeding months, new heresy prosecutions targeted Rochelais from all social strata: day laborers, millers, bakers, armorers, book sellers, merchants, and town councilmen.[33] The transcripts of these trials show conclusively the wide influence of Protestant ideas and the growing organization of Calvinist believers within clandestine networks of worship. The mockery of saints and their alleged intercessory powers was a very common transgression of rochelais heretics. While such an attitude was a hallmark of Protestant controversy everywhere in Europe, its special

---

[30] Although Joubert's father used all his influence in a desperate attempt to save his son, it was unavailing. The notoriety of the condemned man's offenses made his judgement swift and harsh. See Nathanael Weiss, "Choix de documents inédits sur la Réforme à La Rochelle et en Ré," BHL, 44 (1895): 443-508, in particular 443-445.

[31] *Ibid.*, 445-446. This quotation is drawn from transcripts of the Angers legal proceedings, AN, X2a 89. "Il y a en la ville de La Rochelle et gouvernement audit lieu plusieurs hérétiques tenans propos et proferans plusieurs propositions hérétiques contre la saincte foy Catholique et doctrine ecclesiastique...c'est un pais pour le jourd'huy auquel plus pullullent lesd. blasphemes hérétiques."

[32] *Ibid.*, 449.

[33] *Ibid.*, 451-458. The crimes prosecuted included an attack on a Corpus Christi day parade by a townsman hurling excrement on the participants and besmearing the sacred objects they carried.

attraction for religious dissidents in western France also suggests that their quest for greater assurance of supremely powerful divine protection against the myriad travails of their worldly predicament drove them to become schismatics.

Viewed from Parisian courtrooms, the French mid-Atlantic littoral appeared beset by an intractable disorder. Magistrates of the Paris Parlement decried "la division qui de present règne audict pais."[34] The crown's acquiescence to the reestablishment of the fractious 100-member rochelais town council in 1548 and the coincident retirement of the king's local strongman, Charles Chabot de Jarnac, limited local diffusion of royal authority. The establishment of a new presidial court at La Rochelle in 1552 can be read as a belated but determined effort by the monarchy to combat proliferating heresy in a region where traditional agents of kingly police became impotent through their own defections to the Calvinist cause. The edict by which Henry II constituted *cours presidiaux* throughout France accorded these tribunals special jurisdiction over crimes such as heresy requiring rapid punishment.[35]

The presidial court of La Rochelle only briefly took up the task of repressing religious dissent. In May 1552, it meted out harsh sentences to three rochelais bourgeois convicted of "le crime d'hérésie, erreurs et fausse doctrine et dogmatisation." Two of the accused burned at the stake.[36] Shortly thereafter, Claude d'Angliers, lieutenant general of the presidial court, who directed the executions, embraced the Calvinist faith. Presidial cases against heretics dwindled.

In the rochelais hinterland, notable seigneurial families, including the Jarnacs, also converted to Calvinism. In 1553, Jean Chabot de Jarnac, brother to the king's former local agent and abbé of the Benedictine monastery in Saint-Jean-d'Angély, personally insti-

---

[34] Weiss, "Choix de documents," 454, sentence of Oct. 1545, AN, X2a 99.

[35] Jean Declareuil, *Histoire generale du droit français*, (Paris, 1925), 599. See also E. Laurin, "Essai sur les presidiaux," *Nouvelle revue historique du droit français et etranger*, 19 (1895): 355-407 and 739-799; 20 (1896): 47-104 and 273-329, especially 20: 72.

[36] BMLR, MS 150, fols. 4-5. Arcère, *Histoire de la ville de La Rochelle*, 1: 328-329. Delayant, *Histoire des Rochelais*, 1: 192-93. According to their indictment, each man had mocked the Virgin Mary and denied the beneficent intermediary powers of saints.

gated the mass conversion of his monks to Protestantism.[37] Defections from the Catholic church by formerly powerful aristocrats should not solely be attributed to genuine crises of conscience or the desire to trade terrestrial for celestial protectors. In the case of western seigneurs in general and the Jarnacs in particular, their wavering devotion to the Valois dynasty, further undercut by recurrent withdrawals of royal favor, gave them ample political reasons to quit the king's church. In the west country, a breakdown of tenuous police networks extending from Paris facilitated the propagation of heretical religious beliefs.

Contemporaneous royal efforts to fortify French Atlantic towns against anticipated English raids aggravated sociopolitical tensions in coastal communities. In 1555-56, this friction ignited major public disturbances in La Rochelle where residents of the city's poorer neighborhoods banded together in armed opposition to crown projects. Baron Louis d'Estissac, new royal governor of Aunis and La Rochelle, attempted to quarter troops under his command in La Rochelle. Natives identified the alien soldiers as a likely garrison for a new citadel to be built at the city's expense in the port district of Perrot. D'Estissac promptly ordered his men to begin demolition of over 100 civilian structures on the site of the proposed fortification. Armed residents of the port quarter, seconded by the town council, rioted and drove off d'Estissac's men. Intense lobbying by town councilmen at court got the controversial building project suspended. Feisty householders in Perrot still coordinated a neighborhood watch to prevent resumption of citadel construction.[38] Accustomed by this victory to organized agitation in civic affairs, residents of the Perrot quarter would take commanding roles in subsequent movements for religious and political reform in La Rochelle.

## 2. The Calvinist Clergy of La Rochelle

Against this background of religious schism, weakening royal police, and popular political action, a Calvinist church developed in La Rochelle between 1557 and 1559. Charles de Clermont,

---

[37] Massiou, Histoire politique, 4: 29.
[38] Barbot, "Histoire de La Rochelle," AHSA 17 (1889): 118.

called "La Fontaine," one of many itinerant preachers in the region, founded a Reformed congregation of fifty souls who met clandestinely at night in the cellars of rochelais houses.[39] Pierre Richer became the first resident pastor of this church. Richer was a former Carmelite monk and doctor of theology who had trained for his ministry under Jean Calvin in Geneva.[40] Richer became instrumental in organizing the first consistory, or church governing board in La Rochelle. Founded on 17 November 1558, the consistory (*consistoire* in French) included the presiding minister, four elders (*anciens*), two deacons (*diacres*), a secretary, and treasurer.[41] By Christmas 1558, the number of *anciens* had increased to eight.

Before August 1560, another Genevan trained pastor, Ambroise Faget, had established himself in La Rochelle. Faget was a firebrand whose zealous preaching and tireless church building quickly expanded the local congregation.[42] Early converts to the new church included numerous senior *échevins* of the town council. By November 1561, rapid growth of the rochelais congregation, fueled by many adherents among the city's leading families, prompted Faget to write to the Genevan company of pastors requesting two more ministers immediately and reporting that most of La Rochelle's governing authorities were now Reformed church members.

In La Rochelle, the rally of numerous town councilmen to Calvinism parallels quick adoption of Lutheranism by many

---

[39] Contemporaneously, Protestant preaching attracted vast crowds to outdoor services in the *banlieue* of La Rochelle. D'Estissac, royal governor for La Rochelle and Aunis, reported to the king on a Sunday assembly of more than 2,000 people to hear a preacher of "très mauvaise réputation" visitng Aulnay in 1559, BN, Manuscrits Français, 15872: 48, (letter of 23 March 1559).

[40] BMLR, MS 150, 6. See also Robert Kingdon, *Geneva and the Coming of the Wars of Religion in France 1555-1563*, (Geneva, 1956), 10. Richer was a veteran of the abortive attempt to found a French Calvinist colony in Brazil. He made the perilous Atlantic crossing twice, returning to France in 1557.

[41] BMLR, MS 150, 9. According to the earliest *Discipline* of French Calvinist churches (1559), "the elders and deacons are the senate of the church where ministers preside...elders will assemble the faithful and report scandals and similar things to the consistory...Deacons will visit the poor, the imprisoned, and the sick, passing from house to house to catechize." See the text reprinted in J. Pannier, *Les origines de la confession de foi et la discipline des églises reformées de France*, (Paris, 1936), 164-167.

[42] BMLR, MS 150, 10-11. See also Eugène Haag and Emile Haag, *La France protestante*, 2nd ed., 6 vols. (Paris, 1877-1888), 6: 362-363.

German city fathers in the 1520's and 1530's. These processes can, in part, be explained by deep congruities between Protestant dogma and civic magistrates' practical experience of municipal government. This was a task constantly reminding them of their fellow citizens' rash, self-centered, and immoral behaviors compounding the insecurities of urban life. As Gerald Strauss has argued in the case of Nuremberg, city councillors' early allegiance to Protestantism was facilitated by the doctrine's emphasis on human depravity and the necessity of curbing the individual's willful propensity to do evil. In the daily conduct of town government and administration of municipal justice, city magistrates constantly witnessed such sinfulness and battled against it. Lutheranism, like Calvinism, gave a new aura of sanctity to these disciplinary pursuits.[43] As the diaries and public pronouncements of rochelais patricians make clear, they, too, were struck by the viciousness of those they tried to rule and were inveterately skeptical of others' devotion to the security of the urban commune. For town councilmen, embracing Calvinism was thus a dutiful religious and political act, harmonizing these spheres of human travail and guarding the town against persistent internal and external threats.

From 1559 onward, baptismal registers for the brethren of La Rochelle began to be kept by the elders. By 1563, the burgeoning Calvinist congregation in La Rochelle had four pastors trained

---

[43] Gerald Strauss, "Protestant Dogma and City Government: The Case of Nuremberg," *Past and Present*, 36 (1967): 38-58. Regarding town councilmen and their beliefs, Strauss notes: "Suspicion defined their world, the real world of palpable human deeds that confronted them every day in the Council Chamber. It was...a petty world of trivial derelictions, requiring constant admonition, censure, punishment, above all unremitting vigilance...And on this point their practical wisdom coincided with the salient element of the Lutheran creed as it was being presented to them...the line of contact where Lutheran theology touched the councillors' real world experience was its fundamental theme of human depravity and willful dereliction, because this illuminated much that had formerly been unexplained, and offered a theory where formerly no one had even asked a question...For this doctrine with its suspicion of human motives and its negation of the natural instincts was the theological counterpart of what municipal politicians assumed...about the individual and what they asked of him as citizen: denial of the self-seeking drives of his natural proclivities, and submission to a larger purpose and greater power than his own. Neither in religion nor in politics could the natural man be justified," (52 and 54-55). Given the ambient hazards of their environment, Rochelais magistrates experienced the same anxieties and made the same demands on their subjects as did contemporary German city fathers.

in Geneva: Richer, Faget, Nicolas Folion, and Odet de Nort.

Very little attention has been given to the socioeconomic status of rochelais ministers, nor have their relations with the laity over time been explored in any detail.[44] Despite the abundance of original archival material bearing on the lives of these clergymen, most historians of La Rochelle have ignored these sources. No detailed measure has ever been made of the ministers' socioeconomic stature in the community and, consequently, no assessments offered of how their social networks influenced the course of the Reformation in La Rochelle.

Judging by the documents they filed with local notaries and left in the Protestant *état civil*, La Rochelle's pastors were quickly incorporated into the community's narrow governing elite. Foreigners were normally excluded from this prestigious social circle; its admission of the first pastors, all immigrants or refugees from elsewhere, underscores a strong, early commitment to the Reformation among La Rochelle's most powerful citizens.

In March 1564, a son was born to the wife of Calvinist minister Nicolas Folion, a resident of La Rochelle for less than two years. The boy was carried to the baptismal font of the Reformed congregation by his godfather, Raoullet du Jau, a senior *échevin* of the city council.[45] The boy's godmother was Leonor Rondeau, wife to the king's *lieutenant général* in La Rochelle's presidial court.[46] A month later, pastor Odet de Nort, a native of Agen, resident in La Rochelle for barely a year, married a local woman. His bride was Judith Chauvin, daughter of the late *noblehomme* and *maître* Jean Chauvin, in life the ranking *avocat* of La Rochelle's presidial court. Witnesses to the wedding contract included Hughes Pontard, *procureur du roi* of the court, a future mayor of La Rochelle, *noblehomme* Pierre Bouchet, another attorney of the royal tribunal, and Louis Gargoulleau, an *échevin*.[47] The parties

---

[44] For brief biographies of rochelais ministers see E. Trocmé, "L'Eglise reformée de La Rochelle," BHL, 99 (1952): 133-199, especially 152-172.

[45] ADCM, I 1 (Protestant *état civil*) fol. 40r. Du Jau, a member of one of the city's most distinguished, politically active families, was among the earliest patrician supporters of the Reformed church. He had been serving as an elder for the congregation since 1560.

[46] Rondeau and her husband, *maître* Jean Pierres, also a *conseiller du roi*, were both members of prominent rochelais robe families and early converts to Calvinism.

[47] N. Weiss, "Documents: Odet de Nort, pasteur de La Rochelle," BHL, 36 (1887): 15-24.

involved, all Calvinists, settled on a marriage contract giving pastor de Nort a rich dowry of 2,000 *livres*, a sum equivalent to the wedding gifts commonly exchanged at the time by the city's wealthiest native families.[48] The new couple's first child, a daughter, was presented for baptism in 1566 by her godfather, *sieur* Jean Manigault, a *pair* of the town council and elder of the consistory.[49]

Between 1564 and his death in 1593, pastor de Nort obliged his patrons by serving as the godfather for at least eight patrician children including the daughters of two *échevins*, a *pair*, a former mayor, and the president in the *élection* of Aunis.[50] After de Nort's death, the town council compelled the late minister's widow to make a major cash contribution to an extraordinary municipal levy because her "grandes richesses" were common knowledge in town.[51]

De Nort's colleagues in the early rochelais pastorate, Pierre Richer and Noel Magnan, also established ties of fictive kinship with the city's leading families. Between August 1564 and February 1565, Magnan became the godfather of three children all born to senior members of the *corps de ville*, including a former mayor.[52] During the summer of 1568, pastor Richer and *demoiselle* Pierrette Buisseau, daughter of a former mayor, became the godparents of a child born to the town councilman Pierre Mignonneau.[53] Among his other services to the rochelais patriciate, pastor Richer also witnessed the last wills and testaments of notable converts to Calvinism.[54]

Succeeding generations of Calvinist clergymen in La Rochelle developed equally intimate connections with noted members of the city's patriciate. The pastor Jacques Merlin, who arrived in La Rochelle in November 1589, quickly ingratiated himself with local

---

[48] De Nort's status as the son of an *échevin* in Agen may have qualified him for such treatment. However, rochelais patricians very rarely intermarried with the governing families of other west country towns.

[49] ADCM, I 1, fol. 72r.

[50] ADCM, I 1, fols. 48r and 85r; I 3, fol. 9v; I 6, fol. 53r; I 7, fol. 18v; I 14, fol. 76v; and I 16, fols. 83v and 102r.

[51] Jacques Merlin, "Diaire ou recueil des choses plus mémorables qui se sont passées en ceste ville," BMLR, MS 161, fols. 356v-57r (May 1593).

[52] ADCM, I 1, fol. 46r and I 3, fols. 14r and 16v.

[53] ADCM, I 5, fol. 43r (26 July 1568).

[54] See, for example, Richer's signature as witness to the will of the *pair* Simon Thevenin, one of the earliest and most influential partisans of religious reform on the town council, BMLR, MS 235, fol. 248r.

notables. In 1592, Merlin married Elisabeth Rivette, the sister of two lawyers accredited to the presidial court.[55] Between 1595 and 1610, this couple produced seven children. The godparents of the Merlin siblings included the president of the local *élection*, the *lieutenant criminel* of the presidal court, and an *échevin* of the town council.[56] Over the same period, Merlin became the godfather of children born to a prosecutor of the presidial and to the *lieutenant civil* of the tribunal.[57]

Merlin's colleagues in the pastorate entered into similar privileged relationships. In 1596, *pasteur* Samuel Loumeau married the daughter of a *pair* on the town council. The Calvinist pastor Gedeon Dumetz de Montmartin, preaching in La Rochelle from 1605 to 1608, married Elisabeth Mignonneau, widow to a former mayor and blood relation to another mayor and a city attorney.[58]

The intersection of pastorate and patriciate in La Rochelle became complete in 1613 when Jean-Pierre Salbert joined the Calvinist clergy of the city. Salbert, the son of an *échevin*, descended from a long lineage of mayors and town councilmen. This new minister moved easily in the most rarified circles of rochelais society. When he married in April 1615, Salbert collected over 6,000 *livres* in dowry cash and landed estates from his in-laws led by his mother-in-law, wife to the senior prosecutor of the royal presidial court.[59]

Calvin frequently exhorted his apostles to develop close relations with notable French families. In La Rochelle, Reformed clergymen followed this advice all too well, identifying themselves almost exclusively with the powerful oligarchs running city government.[60] The rapid religious conversion of La Rochelle's ruling elite coupled with the town's early emergence as a safe haven for Protestants soon enabled ministers to work openly. Thus they could become more selective in their social contacts than pastors living semi-clandestine existences in regions with heavy Catholic

---

[55] See the printed excerpts from Merlin's *livre de raison, Diaire ou journal du ministre Merlin*, ed. A. Crottet, (Geneva, 1855), 65.

[56] *Ibid.*, 64-65. See also ADCM, I 18, fol. 93v and I 23, fol. 2v.

[57] ADCM, I 17, fol. 20v (5 January 1591); I 19, fol. 40v; and I 20, fol. 97v.

[58] See ADCM, 3 E 197, fols. 327r-v and ADCM, I 19, 94r.

[59] ADCM, 3 E 2161 (1615), fols. 30r-31v.

[60] All surviving baptismal registers in the Protestant *état civil* show that rochelais pastors never served as a godfather to any child born outside the highest ranks of urban society.

majorities. Fugitive pastors, per force, had to rely on a wider variety of parishioners for support. However, the rochelais pastors' elite family contacts and social attachments separated them from the mass of the urban population and made the clergy as a whole a likely target of popular attack in the event of socioeconomic or sociopolitical tensions between patricians and plebeians that transcended their common religious affiliation. As will become clear, such tensions severely factionalized rochelais society after 1600 with dire consequences for the prestige and power of Protestant ministers.

Before 1600, Rochelais pastors clearly benefitted materially from their extensive contacts with the city's leading families. In their wills, notable citizens left substantial gifts of cash and real estate to local Calvinist ministers. The wives of town councillors and presidial court officers gave generously, regularly leaving pious bequests of one hundred *livres* or more to city pastors.[61] Patrician patrons also housed ministers advantageously. Jacques Merlin lived rent free in a town house belonging to *maître* Jean Cabry, the king's attorney before the rochelais presidial court. Merlin supplemented his small family income by subletting rooms on the upper floors of the large structure and pocketing rent paid by the tenants.[62] Through such copious patrician favors, rochelais Calvinist clerics were able to establish and distinguish themselves within the urban community.

Having incomes and estates to protect, local Reformed churchmen reacted violently to the municipality's rare efforts at taxing them to meet extraordinary expenses. When Henry IV requested an emergency levy of 50,000 *livres* from the Rochelais in 1591, city fathers contemplated including all ministers in the collection.[63] The pastors first responded by claiming complete exemption founded on precedents in scripture. They proceeded to plead poverty and, finding this excuse unavailing, finally argued that they could not submit to municipal taxation without prior

---

[61] See for examples the testament of Marie Moullinier, wife to a *conseiller* of the presidial, ADCM, 3 E 2034, fols. 75r-76r; the testament of Marie Debrie, wife of the *pair* Pierre Guillemin, ADCM, 3 E 202, fols. 108v-110r; and the last will of Marguerite Guyton, kinswoman to numerous municipal officials, ADCM, 3 E 193 (4 March 1592).

[62] ADCM, 3 E 2158 (1605) fol. 216r, sublet agreement between pastor Merlin and *maître* Etienne Regnault, a royal sergeant posted to La Rochelle.

[63] Merlin, "Diaire," fols. 370r-71r.

approval from a national synod of French Reformed churches.
From his pulpit, pastor de Nort vehemently denounced ministerial taxation and ultimately dissuaded town councilmen from
implementing the plan. This success could hardly have endeared
the Calvinist clergy to ordinary citizens who now had to shoulder
a heavier fiscal burden imposed by the crown. The clerics' assertion of binding regulation only from within the higher synodal
bureaucracy of the church would also have abraded their fellow
citizens who strongly believed in the right of all local congregants
to participate in policy making for church governance. This
rochelais congregationalism long shaped local religious and political affairs.

While successive generations of Protestant pastors in La
Rochelle shared in the patronage of notable urban families, their
religious schooling and ministerial careers differed considerably.
During the first twenty years of its existence (1558-1578), the
Reformed community in La Rochelle was firmly under the control of clergymen trained in the Genevan church and prepared
to enforce its discipline of the faithful. Between 1558 and 1572,
five of the six ministers active in La Rochelle had lived and studied in Geneva for varying lengths of time.

Pastor Odet de Nort (ministry 1563-1593), a highly learned the-
ologian and eloquent preacher known by friend and foe alike as
"the pope of La Rochelle," exhorted the local congregation to
Calvinist orthodoxy. In 1575, Noel Magnan, the only minister in
the first generation of rochelais Protestant clergymen whose theological training cannot be traced to Switzerland, lost his office
when the local consistory deposed him for holding heretical views
on the nature of the Trinity and the sanctification of Jesus.[64]
Magnan's dismissal in 1575 and the death in 1580 of Pierre Richer,
founding pastor of the city's Reformed congregation, marked a
turning point in the personnel history of the rochelais church.
During the last two decades of the sixteenth century, the long
tenures of the ministers who established La Rochelle's Calvinist
church ended. The 1580's and 1590's can be seen as a period of
transition and upheaval during which many new ministers arrived

---

[64] Magnan's censure and removal were endorsed by Genevan church authorities. Records of Magnan's erroneous opinions and their refutation are still conserved in the public library of Geneva, BPG, MS 197aa, Carton 2.

in La Rochelle but few ended up staying or surviving for very long. The predominance of Genevan-trained ministers in the local church polity ended at this time and never returned. Between 1584 and 1600, fourteen ministers worked in La Rochelle. Of this number, only four continued into the seventeenth century. Of the ten who died or departed, seven were present in La Rochelle for comparatively brief periods ranging from only three to eight years.

High turnover among the rochelais pastors can be attributed to several causes including ill health, premature death, financial ruin, refugee status, personality conflicts, and political differences. Jerôme Petit (ministry 1586-1591) died before reaching middle age.[65] Isaac Guyneau (ministry 1592-94) contracted dysentery and also died very young. Pastor Louis Hesnard (in La Rochelle 1584-1591) became a refugee at the time of the Ligue wars. He accepted a visiting position in La Rochelle's church but took the consistory's renewal of a search for a permanent minister as a sign of official displeasure with his performance. He left La Rochelle and refused to return under any circumstances. The church of La Rochelle was censured by the 1594 French Calvinist national synod for attempting to use secular legal constraints in an effort to force Hesnard's return.[66]

Jean-Baptiste Rotan (ministry 1592-1596) was a doctor of Protestant theology trained in Heidelberg who held Genevan citizenship. Rotan was uncomfortable in La Rochelle and became embroiled in controversies over church doctrine and governance with lay members of the *consistoire*. In a futile effort to quell this dissent, the provincial synod of Saintonge transferred Rotan to a pastorate in Castres. Although members of the local presidial court joined with senior clergymen in petitioning national synods of the French Reformed Church to order Rotan's maintenance in La Rochelle, national synodal officials noted that no similar requests came from civic magistrates in La Rochelle. Local animosities generated by the dispute over Rotan's suitability for the rochelais ministry became so great that two national synods sent special envoys to La Rochelle with specific instructions to resolve

---

[65] Merlin, "Diaire," fols. 419r-441v, "Divers mémoires concernans l'église."

[66] See John Quick, *Synodicon in Gallia Reformata: or the Acts, Decisions, Decrees, and Canons of Those Famous National Councils of the Reformed Churches in France*, 2 vols. (London, 1692), 1: 167.

the bitter local feuding over ecclesiastical appointments.[67] Such
embassies failed to contain growing popular dissatisfaction with
church government in the city.

A majority of Rotan's successors in the rochelais pastorate of
the seventeenth century did not have Genevan theological training nor any personal contacts in Swiss Reformed municipalities.
Although the period after 1596 saw far greater stability in the
tenure of rochelais ministers, anchored by the pastorate of Jacques
Merlin (1589-1620), M.A. in divinity, Oxford 1588, clergymen with
direct life experience of the Genevan mother church became a
distinct minority among local clerics. Jacques Merlin's own family history probably left him ambivalent toward the Calvinist culture of Geneva. Merlin's grandfather, Jean-Raymond Merlin, had
once been a distinguished pastor and professor of Hebrew in
Geneva. Incensed by the Genevan magistracy's efforts to direct
churchmen's relief work during a severe plague epidemic, Merlin
delivered a blistering public sermon denouncing the "pure tyran-
ny" of city fathers over the church, rebuking them for undue meddling in religious affairs. Civic councillors expressed their displeasure with this polemical sermon to the consistory. At a special
assembly of that body presided over by Théodore de Bèze, church
pastors and elders found Jean-Raymond Merlin guilty of insubordination. Merlin got orders to make a public apology for his outburst and to swear support for the consensual policy making of
the church leadership. Upon his flat refusal to make these acts
of contrition, Merlin was summarily dismissed from the Genevan
company of pastors and disgraced.[68] Although Jean-Raymond
Merlin's son, the pastor Pierre Merlin, developed more congenial
ties to the Genevan church, Pierre's son, Jacques Merlin, in his
education and friendships, shared his grandfather's disengage-
ment from Swiss Protestant communities.

Among Jacques Merlin's colleagues in La Rochelle were Louis
Le Cercler (ministry 1602-1627) who learned for the church in

---

[67] *Ibid.*, 186 and 201. In 1598, the synod of Montpellier recommended that its
emissaries to the Rochelais employ "the most powerful and cogent arguments to
persuade them unto peace." Doctrinal disputes within La Rochelle's Calvinist
church became recurrent national scandals deeply troubling to other French
Protestants.

[68] See Robert Kingdon, *Geneva and the Consolidation of the French Protestant
Movement 1564-1572*, (Madison, 1967), 19-23; and Haag and Haag, *La France protestante*, 1st ed., 10 vols. (Paris, 1846-1858), article "Merlin," 6: 385-387.

La Rochelle and Leiden; Daniel Gorré (ministry 1604-1615) who also trained in theology in Leiden; and Samuel Loumeau (ministry 1594-1629) whose ample and intimate correspondence with Protestant churchmen in England, Holland, and Saumur shows his strong attachment to the Reformed communities of the Atlantic world.[69] Another vital rochelais contact with the northern European Reformations at this time was provided by the Scottish merchant adventurer, Protestant propagandist, and Calvinist pastor at La Châtaigneraie, George Thomson. Thomson worked with rochelais printers to produce early French editions of Scottish presbyterian and apocalyptic works including one of the first French versions of John Napier's *Plaine Discovery of the Whole Revelation of Saint John.*[70] This elaborately prophetic and bellicose Protestant text contrasts sharply with the disdainful attitude of Calvin and his more doctrinaire followers toward eschatological numerology.[71] John Rose, a Scotsman serving as regent of La Rochelle's Protestant college after 1590, and his countryman, Duncam, hired by the municipality as a professor of theology in 1607, both contributed to the Scotch cast of the rochelais Reformation in the seventeenth century.[72]

The printing houses of La Rochelle utilized by Thomson and his colleagues now began to supplant Swiss booksellers as the primary suppliers of Protestant Bibles and polemical works to religious dissidents of the French west country. The rochelais bookshop of the Haultin family produced fourteen editions of the New Testament in French, four in Latin, and two complete French Bibles between 1577 and 1616. This business boomed when the national synod of the French Reformed churches meeting at Saumur in 1596 authorized the Haultins to print French Bibles and Psalms in quantities and at prices unavailable from Geneva.

---

[69] For a sample of Loumeau's letters to and from English correspondents, see Georges Musset, ed., "Documents sur la Réforme en Saintonge et Aunis XVIe et XVIIe siècles," AHSA, 15 (1888): 25-145.

[70] Thomson's French translation, *Ouverture des secretes de l'Apocalypse*, augmented by his own annotations and "quatre harmonies sur l'Apocalypse," was published in La Rochelle in 1603 and reprinted with the translator's supervision in 1604. See Louis Desgraves, *L'Imprimerie à La Rochelle*, Vol. 2: *Les Haultin, 1571-1623*, (Geneva, 1960), xxvii.

[71] Robert Clouse, "John Napier and Apocalyptic Thought," *Sixteenth Century Journal*, 5 (1974): 101-114.

[72] Merlin, "Diaire," fols. 133v-34r.

This license was unsuccessfully challenged by the city council, pastors, and professors of Geneva all anxious to protect their royalty income and editorial control over sacred texts.[73] Before the end of the sixteenth century, La Rochelle's Calvinist congregations no longer depended on the Genevan church for religious instruction and had familiarized themselves with the disputes of Protestants throughout northern Europe.

### 3. The Calvinist Consistory of La Rochelle

The history of La Rochelle's Calvinist consistory is far harder to reconstruct than the lives of the ministers who dominated it. Nearly total loss of the consistory's records means that any institutional history must be fashioned from the private papers of Rochelais active on or subject to the *consistoire*.[74] Although fragmentary, these materials render an image of the consistory as a church governing body quickly staffed through restrictive election procedures by the members of La Rochelle's ruling elite. Wealthy ministers working in concert with zealous patricians in the consistory's executive offices firmly controlled the body for most of its existence. Under their leadership, the consistory tried to regulate the public and private lives of all Reformed residents and Protestant visitors.

This mission became especially complicated because in relevant aspects of public affairs like poor relief, the town council adamantly refused to cede any direction to the consistory. So we find town councilmen sitting on the consistory and even appropriating the proceeds of church fund raising for poor relief but giving neither ministers nor congregants any decisive influence over distribution of the monies involved. This curious ambivalence to the governance of churchmen on the part of most city councillors seems

---

[73] Desgraves, *Les Haultin*, xxii-xxv. Quick, *Synodicon*, 181 and 238.

[74] Without records of the consistory's weekly deliberations and disciplinary activities, it is now impossible to judge the full impact of this religious body on the police of the community. A comparative analysis of consistorial deliberations in other French provincial towns is given in J. Estebe and B. Vogler, "La genèse d'une société protestante: étude comparée de quelques registres consistoriaux Languedociens et Palatins vers 1600," *Annales E.S.C.*, 31 (1976): 362-388. See also Solange Bertheau, "Le consistoire dans les églises réformées du moyen-Poitou au XVIIe siècle," BSHPF, 116 (1970): 332-359 and 513-549.

characteristic of the Rochelais as a whole. As evidence from the diaries of observant citizens suggests, town residents continually violated the *consistoire's* prescriptions and, in matters where their personal honor was at stake, often spurned the *consistoire* for its inability to redress their grievances satisfactorily. The Rochelais never enthusiastically embraced all features of the *Réforme;* they selectively appropriated its precepts, using them to complement, not to supplant the old institutions and folkways sustaining urban society. They fashioned a distinctive "patois" of protective rituals deemed effective against the ambient hazards frontier townspeople acutely sensed.

Established in 1558 with a staff of eight, the *consistoire* of La Rochelle had more than tripled in size to at least twenty-seven officers by 1561.[75] Methods of personnel recruitment for the organization remain obscure. Nearly complete loss of all internal consistory records prevents close analysis of its politics. However, an early and enduring preponderance of patricians on the consistory assured heavy, but not exclusive representation of La Rochelle's governing elite among new members. External evidence does show that several members of the consistory who served long terms of office were kinsmen and confidants of local ministers.

Rochelais diarists, including the pastor Jacques Merlin and the consistory member Joseph Guillaudeau, frequently comment on the operations of the consistory but never refer to any regular changes in its membership mandated by statute or tradition. Remarking on his own consistory service, Joseph Guillaudeau states that he was "admitted" to the office of elder in June 1617 with the assistance of a minister.[76] This vocabulary suggests that the election of consistory members was by cooptation, a process in which ministers were influential. In La Rochelle, it is clear, terms of service on the consistory were not annual, as in other French Reformed communities, nor were these posts reserved only for officeholders in town government. By contrast, in Calvin's Geneva, only city magistrates staffed the *consistoire.*

Elders (*anciens*) on the rochelais consistory had responsibility for supervising the spiritual life of Calvinists within specific urban

---

[75] BMLR, MS 150, 11.

[76] See "Diaire de Joseph Guillaudeau, Sieur de Beaupréau," AHSA 38 (1908): 1-422. For Guillaudeau's admission to the consistory see 150.

neighborhoods. They visited households, encouraged church attendance, reported moral lapses of the faithful, and mediated their disputes. Elders kept a sharp eye out for violations of the sabbath, immodest dress, dancing, swearing, gaming, carousing, and sexual misconduct. They denounced such malefactors to the *consistoire* which then summoned sinners to appear before it. Depending on the severity of the transgression, the consistory's punishments ranged from verbal admonitions to deprivation of a place at the communion table. Sentences imposed on the wayward included public acknowledgements of turpitude and avowals of repentance at morning church services. Although often threatened, excommunication of transgressors was very rarely carried out, seriously weakening the ultimate disciplinary powers of the consistory. Deacons (*diacres*) on the consistory also had neighborhood assignments wherein they handled church finances and tried to superintend the charitable works of congregants.

The earliest roster of *anciens* and *diacres* (1561) reveals a plurality of patrician family men occupying these key posts of church administration.[77] Of the twenty-seven officers of the *consistoire* listed in 1561, at least seventeen (63 percent) can be positively identified as members of old town council families or of lineages monopolizing access to urban judicial posts.[78] All deacons managing church funds between January 1561 and December 1566 held high rank in the town council. Although consistory appointments were not made for life, elders and deacons commonly served long, continuous terms in office. This practice perpetuated patrician influence within the disciplinary body.[79]

For decades, presiding minsters with multiple ties of real and fictive kinship to subordinate officers shaped the deliberations of the consistory. In the 1560's pastor Odet de Nort could count at

---

[77] BMLR, MS 150, 11.

[78] ADCM, I 1-2; BMLR, MS 97, 5-6. The social composition of consistories in other French Calvinist towns was significantly more diverse than in La Rochelle, see Estebe and Vogler, "Genèse d'une société protestante," 363.

[79] The consistory of La Rochelle did not follow the example of the Reformed church in Nîmes where *anciens* at least were limited to annual terms of office. See R. Mentzer, "*Disciplina nervus ecclesiae.* The Calvinist Reform of Morals at Nîmes," *Sixteenth Century Journal,* 18 (1987): 89-115. Estebe and Vogler show that elsewhere in Languedoc terms of service on consistories were at most annual, "Genèse d'une société protestante," 364. The organization of La Rochelle's *consistoire* was thus different from most forms of Calvinist church government in other French and Swiss Reformed cities.

least three *anciens* among his closest friends and kinsmen. Between 1589 and 1620, pastor Jacques Merlin drew support on the *consistoire* from the elders *sieur* Jean Chalmot, president of the local *élection* and godfather to Merlin's son, and *maître* Isaac Rivette, a presidial court jurist and Merlin's brother-in-law. Such potent combinations were a fixture on the consistory and rendered it vulnerable to factionalization. The influence of these elite subgroups within the consistory was not fully balanced by the service of less notable citizens as *anciens* and *diacres* until late in the sixteenth century.[80] Even then, vacant consistory offices normally went to comparatively wealthy townsmen: successful wholesale merchants, apothecaries, and royal notaries. Petty shopkeepers, skilled artisans, and workingmen never gained admittance to the Reformed church's highest internal offices of administration and police. These staffing patterns also suggest that cooptation may have been the preferred method of personnel recruitment within the rochelais consistory just as cooptation determined the membership of the town council.

The preponderance of notable Rochelais on the consistory did not facilitate its difficult task of disciplining the fluid, heterodox, and polyglot human traffic of a port town. A list of offenses censured by the *consistoire* in 1562-63 includes drunkenness, swearing, gaming during church services, pimping, prostitution, and wife beating.[81] While endeavoring to police these vices of individual comportment, the consistory also tried to enforce higher standards of economic behavior promoting the general welfare of the community. When several "notables marchands" shipped grain out of the city at a time of local subsistence crisis, the *consistoire* condemned the action and ordered the perpetrators to make a public apology and then freely distribute flour to the poor.[82] The wealthy grain dealers complied. However, such acceptance by guilty bourgeois of the consistory's sanctions was more than offset by the contumacy of a broader public lamented

---

[80] Although Etienne Trocmé rightly emphasizes how hard it is to ascertain the social status of consistory members, his suppositions that most were of middling rank and selected for religious zeal rather than family connections or political sympathies strike me as ill-founded. The small evidence he cites to support these claims comes only from late seventeenth-century sources. See Trocmé, "Eglise réformée," 181-182.

[81] BMLR, MS 150, fols. 11-12 and 32.

[82] *Ibid.*, fol. 19.

by local pastors and recorded by early historians of the city.[83]

The consistory's efforts to suppress popular revelries and mockeries of authority (lay or ecclesiastical) were far less successful. In May 1563, the consistory summoned before it twenty-two townsmen for having committed a great "public insolence." The outrage occurred just before Pentecost, the date of one of the four annual public communion services required of all Reformed church members and the day after which only wine produced on the estates of wealthier citizens could be sold at retail in the city until the next grape harvest. The accused had boisterously paraded through the streets, carrying aloft a banquet table covered with bread and meat atop which one of their confederates gorged himself and drank to the health of every passerby with the last cheap wine to be had.[84] This derisive bacchanal, appropriating the instruments of the Lord's supper to salute the cupidity of city fathers, scandalized church officials. Even worse, before the full consistory, half of the irreverent celebrants refused to repent their actions or accept any punishment whatsoever. Church discipline failed entirely when the mayor personally intervened and excused all of the drunken jesters, dismissing them from testimony in the presence of the consistory.

More adherents to the Reformed church over time did not improve the consistory's limited police powers. As Calvinist converts and refugees flooded into the city, town councilmen enacted a series of ordinances reiterating their exclusive control over the administration of local poor relief and the governance of civic charity hospitals. In 1554, by a statue "perpetual and irrevocable," the *corps de ville* declared that only poor laws debated in its chambers, duly adopted, and written into its official minute books were valid and enforceable.[85] Funds for poor relief amassed by the deacons from church poor box collections and the pious bequests of deceased Calvinists were also subject to disbursement under the orders of municipal officials.

By 1588, the town council had tightened its surveillance over all poor townspeople by appointing two "recteurs des pauvres" in

---

[83] On these "refractaires aux ordonnances des ministres," see, for example, Arcère, *Histoire de la ville de La Rochelle*, 1: 343.
[84] BMLR, MS 150, fol. 20.
[85] BMLR, MSS 45/46, fol. 937.

each of the five old urban parishes. The work of the *recteurs* was augmented by neighborhood militiamen holding annual commissions from the mayor to make weekly inspection tours of their quarters ascertaining the number and religion of householders, servants, and foreign visitors as well as keeping an eye out for "gamesters, swearers, blasphemers, and residents of bad repute."[86]

An apparent absence of friction between town council and consistory over poor relief administration should not be taken as proof of a lasting entente uniting the two bodies in godly town government. We have already seen one mayor intervene to stop religious disciplinary action by the *consistoire*. In earlier years, town councilmen intent on maintaining public order at all costs complained about intemperate sermons given by the first pastors in La Rochelle, clerics who were inattentive to the licentiousness they stirred among their humbler followers.[87] Additional evidence from the sixteenth and seventeenth centuries suggests that enduring rivalries over police powers and personal animosities between municipal officials, royal jurists, and prominent churchmen prevented the town council, city courts, and the consistory from always governing the city in concert.

The traditional, irreverent pranks perpetrated at carnival time by members of La Rochelle's legal confraternity, the *bazoche*, uniting the clerks and subaltern officers of local tribunals, mocked in ribald fashion the inability of Calvinist churchmen to police community morals effectively. These incidents suggest that relations between urban judicial and religious institutions were occasionally competitive and inimical. Such discord among powerful agencies of social control undermined thorough enforcement of Reformed doctrine in La Rochelle and enabled religious heterodoxy to flourish in the city.

---

[86] The mayor used preprinted commissions for the empowerment of these civil servants. See the exemplar preserved in BMLR, MS 308, fol. 22r. These municipal inspectors were instituted to "maintain public order and citizens' devotion to their duties." This purview overlapped with that of the consistory and indicates that the town council was unwilling to cede its jurisdiction over the citizenry's moral offenses or rely solely on church agents as municipal policemen. This legislation also suggests that, in the estimation of town councilmen, the consistory was not capable of policing a port town effectively.

[87] As noted by the rochelais patrician and town councilman Amos Barbot, some sermons preached by local ministers caused ordinary residents of the city to commit "diverses licences." Remark quoted in Arcère, *Histoire de la ville de La Rochelle*, 1: 345.

A bizarre appellate case brought before La Rochelle's presidial court in February 1578, carnival time, well illustrates how the
Rochelais lived their Reformation.[88] They never merely acquiesced to the dictates of Calvinist clerics, but rather selectively
appropriated elements of their moral discourse, incorporating
them within older modes of popular, communal government insu-
lated from, if not antithetical to, the designs of churchmen.

The plaintiffs in the appeal were two sisters, Catherine and
Pierrette Bondrone, who, in a law suit apparently first brought
before the king's *juge prévôt* in La Rochelle, accused Jean Chantre
and several confederates of impersonating magistrates, arresting
them without due cause, falsely imprisoning them, and outra-
geously insulting them and their husbands. The sisters denounced
Chantre under his current guise as "king of the bazoche" and
identified his companions as members of his "court."

Chantre had been elected to his "throne" due to his populari-
ty and seniority among the secretaries, archivists, and copyists of
the various law courts operating in La Rochelle. The entourage
of the *roi de bazoche* included other notable scribes who were
responsible for supervising the training, conduct, and welfare of
the confraternity's membership. The "king" and "court" also traditionally exercised minor judicial powers themselves, imposing
fines, brief jail sentences, and other legal settlements in cases
involving confraternity members. These dignitaries also served as
the confraternity's sovereign representatives at all carnival festivities and claimed a special role in urban police at this time of public revelry. Despite these disciplinary pretensions, confraternities
of the *bazoche* throughout France were renowned for their rowdi-
ness and the dissolute behavior of officers, especially in the
months leading up to the great *fête* of the *bazoche* held annually
on May 1.

Before the *prévôt*, the Bondrone sisters had sought Chantre's
condemnation for the alleged assault, official denial that a
"bazoche king" possessed any real police powers, and a formal
apology for the many insults they had received from Chantre and
his cohorts. Chantre had rebutted his accusers by claiming that,
although they were married to a royal sergeant and a municipal
courier, the sisters were simply prostitutes whom he and his

---

[88] ADCM, B 1338, Registre Cour du gouvernement, fols. 46r-49r.

"court" had caught flagrantly plying their trade and corrupting the morals of young clerks during Mardi gras. Citing the inspirational example of the Israelites, who had successfully stamped out such vice, Chantre, describing himself as a "virtuous, Christian king of the bazoche," explained that he and his men had only tried to punish two of the many "femmes abandonnées" infesting La Rochelle.[89] Asserting his jurisdiction over the events of carnival, the *bazoche* king closed his initial defense by stating that his police action was legitimate and only proportionate to the Bondrone sisters' shameless misconduct. Apparently, the *juge prévôt* agreed and dismissed the charges against Chantre and his helpers.

The Bondrones then appealed this contrary decision to the presidial court. Here, their advocate grandiloquently demanded higher legal action since Chantre's outrageous acts were committed in La Rochelle, "a city which pretends to have a stronger Reformation than many other towns in France."[90] The sisters' lawyer further insisted on their propriety and noted that by their marriages they had "risen to the level of respectable women." This advocate's peroration concluded with a demand for reversal of the original verdict and condemnation of the *bazoche* king and his supporters. Presidial magistrates quashed the *prévôt's* decision and found Chantre and his henchmen guilty of grossly disturbing the peace. The court imposed fines but postponed final sentencing until a later date. I have not found any further documents pertaining to the ultimate disposition of the case in the early, fragmentary records of La Rochelle's presidial court.

The case of the *bazoche* king is an extraordinary one for several reasons. First, if accepted as a real legal procedure, it shows that even twenty years after the inception of La Rochelle's *Réforme*, traditional carnival pranksters continued to be raucously active despite strong Calvinist opposition to such ancient coteries of misrule. Secondly, carnivalesque actors like the *roi de bazoche* now cleverly manipulated a biblical lexicon of crime and punishment in hopes of explaining and legitimating their Mardi gras exploits. Ordinary townsmen appropriated the biblical fundamentalism of learned Calvinist preachers while trying to conserve and protect

---

[89] *Ibid.*, fols. 47r-v.

[90] "Une ville ou l'on pretend avoir plus grande Reformation qu'en plusieurs autres de la France," *ibid.*, fol. 46v.

their own right of participation in communal police through the normative games of carnival. Churchmen undoubtedly blanched at seeing holy scripture put to such a profane use but could not eradicate such behavior through the sanctions of the consistory. Finally, the contradictory verdicts of minor and major royal courts in the trials of the *bazoche* king bespeak the poor coordination of urban tribunals and their inability (or unwillingness) to suppress ruder forms of popular justice.

However, another reading of this curious case may be warranted. Upon closer examination, the registered text of the Bondrones' appellate trial is unusually detailed and colorful. In stark contrast to the prosaic and abbreviated records typical of most presidial cases tried at other times of the year, this transcript of a case adjudicated just after Mardi gras contains elaborate references to the skills of attorneys for the prosecution and defense, pointed commentary on the Bondrone sisters' ascension to higher social status through marriage, digressive exculpatory speeches by Chantre, and seemingly extraneous remarks on La Rochelle's supposedly exemplary Reformation. There is an acerbic, comic air to this legal document, a burlesque tone suggesting to me that the entire proceeding it relates was not a "real" censure of *bazoche* revelry at all, but rather a final, densely theatrical act of carnival in which numerous members of the city's legal confraternity took mirthful parts. As such, it cleverly accomplished the broadly satirical intent typical of *bazoche* tricks.[91]

First, this "trial" may have rehearsed a real charivari conducted by Chantre and his men against the *arriviste* Bondrone sisters. Perhaps they actually were former whores who had married above their station, possibly through snaring much older, sinecured husbands. The "kings" and "courts" annually formed within French corporations of labor like the *bazoche* everywhere claimed the right, especially during carnival time, to reprove such matrimonial disorder.[92]

---

[91] *Bazoche* confraternity members throughout France were renowned for regularly conducting hilarious mock trials, ostensibly to train brothers in the arts of court reporting. These "trials" usually involved concocted, convoluted tales of seduction, rape, attempted sodomy, and other sexual imbroglios wherein the Bazochians used gross exaggerations, double entendres, and non sequiturs to vie with one another in elaborate feats of verbal invention.

[92] On the cultural history of carnival in France and on the carnival rites of French artisanal and professional corporations see Martine Grinberg, "Carnival

Second, Chantre's elaborate defense used scripture itself to poke fun at the local Calvinist clergy's inability to correct La Rochelle's many wayward citizens. The presidial court bureaucracy, with a collective snicker, officially recorded that La Rochelle was a town where, as yet, one could only pretend to have a vigorous Reformation. Hereby, the city's legal fraternity derisively served notice on rival Reformed church authorities that local court personnel retained the potent right to act formally and informally in defense of old communal values. Furthermore, the satirical testimony of a "defendant" like Chantre made it clear that pastors had no monopoly on the interpretation of holy writ nor on police action inspired by scripture. Through the normative jests of carnival, the *bazoche* repeatedly staked its claim to a role in shaping the city's moral economy.

And third, the uproarious trial of the *bazoche* king brought a fitting legal end to Chantre's "reign," deflecting criticism of his misrule by civic authorities operating outside the judicial company. By their complicity in the post-carnival condemnation of the *bazoche* "king," rochelais judges obliged their essential subordinate personnel by allowing them to retain control over the scripting and rhythm of confraternal celebrations. Soon the time would come to select a new *roi de bazoche*. In this way, the city's legal community defended the integrity of an immemorial festive cycle that began and ended with carnival. In La Rochelle, Calvinist pastors could decry but not easily check popular participation in these ill-disciplined celebrations of dubious religious orthodoxy. Try as they might, city clerics could not standardize the local argot of word and gesture used to express popular mores and communal concerns.

Church officials' moral suasion also had no lasting effect when a Protestant mayor of La Rochelle repeatedly lapsed into religious heresy and used his office to patronize a radical, itinerant holy man billing himself as "the second Jeremiah." Trouble began when the wealthy merchant-banker and *échevin* Paul Yvon returned to La Rochelle from Paris in 1612. He sought out ministers to dispute with them, affirming, among other things, that all men were saved, that hell did not exist, and that the Bible was made up of

---

et société urbaine XIVe-XVIe siècles: le royaume dans la ville," *Ethnologie Française*, 4 (1974): 215-245.

stories never intended by God to be understood literally.[93] Between 1612 and 1616, rochelais clergy, convinced that Yvon was insane, used a recurrent threat of suspension from communion only to dissuade him from publicizing his views. This *modus vivendi* ended when Yvon won election as mayor in 1616 and began declaiming his opinions to townspeople of every description.

Already alarmed at growing popular confusion over religious orthodoxy, rochelais ministers were horrified to discover that the city's captain now denied the divinity of Christ and the existence of the damned. Yet, the consistory did not proceed to any sharper sanction of the mayor, again threatening only his suspension from communion, but backing down when Yvon admitted that he was perhaps being led astray by "demons." In the interim, Yvon offered asylum to the defrocked pastor La Nagerie, now a vagabond prophet of God. In streets and public squares throughout La Rochelle, La Nagerie preached an apocalyptic message of impending doom for the city unless ordinary residents, true agents of the divine, purged the town of ministers and magistrates who were hostile toward a popular religious revival.[94]

Confronted by La Nagerie's radical congregationalism, local clergy petitioned the mayor to exile the rabble rouser. Yvon flatly refused but, at the urging of fellow town councilmen, relented and agreed to sequester La Nagerie in a city tower. The "second Jeremiah" continued his lamentations from this perch. Finally, worried magistrates arranged La Nagerie's exit by ship and burned his private papers while the consistory vainly attempted to confiscate the seditious writings the new Jeremiah had distributed throughout the city.[95] The *consistoire's* running battle with Paul Yvon would last another decade until the ex-mayor abjured Calvinism altogether in 1627. Throughout this period, Yvon benefitted from the support of the *corps de ville*.

Enduring patrician disregard for the complaints of churchmen fostered an environment in which more humble townsfolk could challenge the consistory's authority and in which no strong popular confidence could develop in the consistory as a trustworthy

---

[93] Merlin, "Diaire," fols. 450r-451v.

[94] *Ibid.*, fols. 491r-497r.

[95] *Ibid.*, fols. 460v-472v. One measure of churchmen's desperation to round up La Nagerie's tracts is the extraordinary punishment of immediate excommunication they decreed for anyone retaining or circulating the suspect manuscripts.

defender of a citizen's honor or the moral values by which reputation was defined. The consistory's habit of compromising with
dissidents who merely agreed not to publicize their heretical
beliefs undercut its capability to deter irreverence. In 1590, the
Reformed church in La Rochelle was troubled by the notorious
Brochard brothers, advocates of polygamy, one of whom had managed to find work as a regent of the city's *collège*.[96] Ordered by
the consistory to renounce multiple marriages and subscribe to
all the articles of French Calvinist church discipline, both men
refused, only to be warned that church officials would not prosecute them any further so long as they did not teach their errors
to anyone. When the Brochards flagrantly broke this compact, the
ministers attacked their doctrines in a series of sermons calling
on civil authorities to exile both men from the city.

The Brochards fought back, bringing suit in La Rochelle's presidial court against the entire consistory, claiming that church officials were unfairly denying them their freedom to participate in
the rites of the Reformed community.[97] The Brochards requested the court to summon pastors and elders and to order them to
answer the brothers' complaints. To pastor Merlin's great consternation, the presidial agreed to hear the case and summoned
churchmen to appear and testify.[98] Pastors and elders quickly
agreed that no one would respond to the menacing subpoena, to
do so would admit that church officers were subject to lay courts
and that such bodies were competent to adjudicate ecclesiastical
disagreements and discipline. Finding such concessions unthink-
able, the consistory threatened the presidial judges, all Calvinists,
with every punishment in the Reformed canon including excommunication.

Abandoning these empty threats, the senior pastors de Nort and

---

[96] The 1594 national synod meeting in Montauban put out an all points bulletin warning the brethren about Isaac and Moyse B[r]ouchard, "who wander up
and down sowing false doctrines...the elder of them is a little dapper fellow, red
face and beard, roving eye; the younger is much the same, but blackish beard,
pale and sad, and roving eyes as his brother," Quick, *Synodicon*, 172. That one of
the Brochards gained affiliation with La Rochelle's *collège* despite its close ties to
the city's Calvinist clergy is not too surprising given the fact that commentators
like pastor Merlin were still complaining about great disorder in the administration and teaching of the school as late as 1596, Merlin, "Diaire," fols. 357v-358r.

[97] Merlin, "Diaire," fols. 425r-427r.

[98] *Ibid.*, fol. 426r. Merlin confided to his journal that the consistory found this
legal affront "fort remarquable" and "fort estrange."

Merlin also began pragmatic negotiations with the king's attorney and presidial officers in an effort to convince them of the Brochards' manifold doctrinal errors. Church envoys encountered strong opposition from advocates for the Brochards among presidial attorneys of middling bureaucratic rank. This standoff was only resolved when the mayor personally ordered the Brochards to leave town in 1591.[99]

While the Brochard affair festered, outraged citizens challenged the consistory's autonomous operations on another legal front. The wife of a rochelais master surgeon had been embroiled in a noisy quarrel with a neighbor woman during which her adversary publicly called her a "whore" (*putain*).[100] Alerted to this trouble, the *consistoire* called the feuding women before it to reconcile them and prevent further scandal. Attended by her husband, the aggrieved woman listened as her opponent confessed to the consistory that she had indeed cried "putain" several times during the altercation. Hearing this admission, the husband, named La Mousche, stormed out before any reconciliation could be effected in direct contravention of the consistory's operating procedures during such cases.

The fuming spouse went directly to the presidial court and swore out a complaint against his wife's enemy seeking full satisfaction for the injury through the secular tribunal. The surgeon asserted that consistory officers had all heard the defamer's admission and should be called to testify by the presidial as corroborating witnesses for the prosecution. The presidial's lieutenant duly summoned the entire *consistoire* to give evidence before the court. Churchmen refused, arguing that confessions before the consistory were confidential and that if ministers or elders were compelled to reveal such information in civil law suits placing penitents in double jeopardy no persons would ever admit their transgressions before them.

Swayed by this logic, the lieutenant hesitated to issue new subpoenas. Undeterred, the enraged La Mousche went on to obtain an injunction from the Parlement of Paris ordering the presidial

---

[99] *Ibid.*, fols. 426r-427v. The Brochard incident occurred during the period of highest turnover in the offices of the rochelais pastorate suggesting that heretical tendencies among the laity flourished in the absence of firm ministerial service.

[100] *Ibid.*, fols. 427v-428r.

to proceed with the investigation and to call consistory members as witnesses. Unable to quash the injunction, Calvinist officials upped the pressure on the surgeon, calling him a deranged troublemaker, chastising him for disturbing his own church, and threatening him with complete ostracism from his congregation.[101] Ultimately, La Mousche compromised, agreeing to drop his presidial case so long as the consistory imposed exemplary punishment of his choice on his wife's attacker. Local clerics complied while immediately drafting a new regulation for all French Calvinist churches stipulating that congregants who embroiled consistories in civil law suits would be subject to escalating ecclesiastical punishments up to excommunication. Pastor Merlin proudly noted that representatives of La Rochelle at the 1594 national synod in Montauban succeeded in getting this provision adopted as an integral part of the French Reformed Church's written discipline.[102]

The legal stratagems of the Brochards and Monsieur La Mousche show that La Rochelle's Calvinist church exercised no hegemony over urban politics at either the macro or micro level. Although capable of wresting acts of contrition from avaricious grain dealers and even a former *ancien* guilty of dancing at a wedding reception, the local consistory, inclined to temporize with sinners, exercised little effective disciplinary power over the middle and lower ranks of rochelais society. Pastor Merlin's private diary is a long testament to this impotence. Not once in thirty-one years did Merlin record an excommunication from the Reformed church of La Rochelle.[103] By contrast, his daily journal

---

[101] *Ibid.*, fols. 428v-429r. La Mousche's failure to discipline his wife, allowing her to quarrel with neighbors, was another transgression of Calvinist discipline of which he was undoubtedly reminded by the consistory's defensive members.

[102] *Ibid.*, fol. 429r-v. See also Quick, *Synodicon*, 159, Synod of Montauban, Chapter III, paragraph 9. Quick, 162, documents related concerns expressed by the synodal delegation from Saintonge.

[103] The reluctance of rochelais church officials to resort to excommunication as a means of disciplining the faithful matched consistorial behavior in other French Reformed communities. Clerics and lay church authorities preferred, if at all possible, to arrange the sinner's reconciliation with the brethren. This policy worked to conserve the number of church members but gave incorrigible congregants many opportunities to persist in irreverent, disruptive, and immoral behavior. See Raymond Mentzer, "Marking the Taboo: Excommunication in French Reformed Churches," in R. Mentzer, ed., *Sin and the Calvinists: Morals Control and the Consistory in the Reformed Tradition*, (Kirksville, Mo., 1994), 97-128.

is full of personal laments over the impetuous, irreverent, and incorrigible behavior of La Rochelle's artisans and laborers, groups whose behavior he likened to "a raging sea."[104]

The *consistoire* was a new agency of police struggling to assert itself within a thickly regulated urban environment dominated by more ancient institutions of social control whose officers jealously guarded their turf. Protestant natives and even transient visitors clearly perceived these power arrangements and tried to manipulate them for private advantage, motivated not only by a desire for personal gain, but also by an abiding belief that a novel church was not fully capable of maintaining the fundamental protocols of neighborliness and citizenship upon which orderly civic life depended. The disputatious Rochelais confronted local and national Calvinist bodies with continual challenges to their authority, testing the limits of ecclesiastical discipline and provoking its modification at various levels of the church hierarchy. An early surfeit of patricians on the *consistoire* did not guarantee its preeminence in municipal police. Their service to the church only further enmeshed it in the dynamics of urban power politics, adding a new religious dimension to the contentions of townspeople.

### 4. *The Calvinist Congregations of La Rochelle*

Although many members of La Rochelle's governing elite quickly converted to Calvinism, the best evidence now available indicates that these leading citizens did not impose the Reformation on the lower orders of urban society. Rochelais from all social groups commonly made willful conversions to the new faith. Unfortunately, extensive Calvinist baptismal registers and conversion lists rarely give the occupation of congregants, thus a precise socioeconomic profile of the brethren over time is impossible. The complete absence of fiscal records for La Rochelle also makes correlations between citizens' relative wealth and the timing of their religious conversion impracticable.

Using painstaking comparisons between baptismal registers and diverse notarial records, Judith Meyer has sketched trends in

---

[104] Merlin, "Diaire," fols. 152v-153r, 184r-186v, 232v-233r, and 378r-380v.

Rochelais' adherence to the Reformed church over the period 1559-1566.[105] She concludes that Protestantism's appeal cut broadly across social and occupational divisions. Skilled artisans, merchants, civic officials, and local royal officers became most strongly attracted to Calvinism, although no occupational group was entirely unrepresented in the ranks of early converts. Various types of merchants accounted for about 44% of the early rochelais Calvinists in Meyer's sample. Among artisans, coopers, tailors, and bakers accepted the new faith in large numbers. But seamen, wagoners, and agricultural laborers could also be counted, albeit in smaller numbers, among the first generation of rochelais Calvinists.

These findings are more amply borne out by my own analysis of 881 testaments drawn up by Protestant Rochelais. For the sampling period 1561-1581, 45% of all Protestant wills I have found were redacted by merchants. Artisans of various trades, highly skilled and skilled, produced 33% of the total, with municipal officials, town councilmen, and presidial court officers contributing 15%. Producing 7% of all Protestant wills recovered for the period, sailors and unskilled laborers apparently formed the smallest occupational cohort in the local Reformed community.[106] Calvinist indoctrination was probably least advanced among these groups, justifying in part pastors' later censures of their unorthodox religious behaviors.

As the Protestant baptismal statistics discussed in Chapter 1 make clear, the Calvinist church in La Rochelle grew rapidly after 1558. Within a decade of its founding, more than 1,000 new members joined the congregation annually, counting births to Calvinist families and adult conversions. Elders keeping vital statistics on the

---

[105] Meyer, *Reformation in La Rochelle*, 105-113. See, in particular, Table 8, 106-108. Meyer's small sample of rochelais Protestants identified by occupation (n=402) can give only the most approximate impression of recruitment to the new church in a town with a total contemporary population of more than 15,000.

[106] Alain Cabantous has documented the great difficulties Catholic clerics faced in their efforts at confessionalizing seamen in the ports of western France. It seems clear that Calvinist ministers in La Rochelle fared little better at bringing mariners into the fold of Reformed Christians. As noted by Cabantous, sailors' cosmologies incorporated a wide variety of tenaciously held magical, pagan, and Christian beliefs oriented around the protection of ships and crews against the many hazards of navigation. See Cabantous, *Le ciel dans la mer*, 123-171 and 249-304.

rochelais faithful carefully recorded all souls inducted into the church.

Comparison of surviving admission rosters and baptismal registers shows how Protestant recruitment expanded through town residents' family connections and social networks. While an adult's desertion of Catholicism may have been prompted by a deeply personal crisis of conscience, admission to La Rochelle's Calvinist church was never a solitary or merely private event. Adult admission lists show that inhabitants of the city joined the new church *en masse* and frequently in the company of their closest relatives and neighbors. Admission lists maintained by three of the five Calvinist congregations established in La Rochelle show that between 1573 and 1582 up to thirty new adult members could be admitted to the church in a single day.[107]

For the thirty-three years between 1573 and 1605 during which serial admission rosters are available for these three Reformed congregations, combined adult admissions peaked at more than 400 per annum in 1574 and then declined, fluctuating around 150 per year until the end of the sixteenth century (see Figure 9). This pattern reflects an unprecedented boost in Calvinist recruitment, due in part to La Rochelle's successful resistance to a royal siege in 1572-73, followed by a return to less dramatic levels of growth in Reformed congregations. Subsequent moderation in the flow of Protestant refugees toward La Rochelle and the emigration of local Catholics contributed to the decline in new church admissions and conversions among adults.[108]

---

[107] Reliable admission lists exist for the three rochelais Calvinist congregations which met in the *salle* Gargoulleau, a large hall owned by an early patrician convert to the new faith; in the old Catholic Church of St. Marguerite; and in the municipal assembly hall named the *salle* St. Michel. Admissions statistics at my disposal do not account for all adults newly enrolled in the church because no rosters survive for the Calvinist congregation of St. Yon, the largest Reformed church in La Rochelle. All statistics presented here should thus be considered as representative but not definitive indices of adult admissions to rochelais churches. For admissions during the decade from 1572 to 1582, see ADCM I 7 (Admissions), fols. 1r-6v, and I 12 (Admissions), fols. 2r-28v.

[108] Statistics presented in Figure 9 should not be read as indicative of a general decline in the size or strength of La Rochelle's Protestant community. These figures are contemporary with high peaks in total Calvinist baptisms within the city (1575, 1577, and 1586) which were succeeded by less spectacular but comparatively stable annual baptism counts in all local Reformed congregations. Since detailed adult admission lists are not available for all rochelais Reformed congregations, no firm conclusions can be reached about the role of immigration in

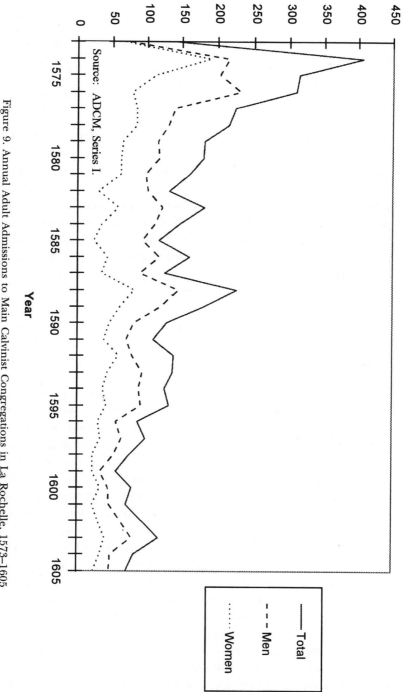

Figure 9. Annual Adult Admissions to Main Calvinist Congregations in La Rochelle, 1573–1605

Figure 9 makes it clear that for the period under study adult males joined La Rochelle's Protestant congregations in significantly higher numbers than adult females (3,264 men vs. 1,738 women between 1573 and 1605). These totals may simply result from the fact that more men than women were migrants in early modern times and that the various trades plied in a seaport would make it a more attractive settlement for men than women. However, they also suggest that among adult converts to these congregations at this time men were more likely than women to abandon Catholicism.

Men's greater freedom to participate in hazardous and unrelentingly stressful commercial, judicial, and political affairs animating public life in a port town may have heightened their desire for mitigation of these inescapable tensions through congregational fellowship in accord with the more egalitarian, fraternal, and irenic theology of Calvinism.[109] In La Rochelle, the complexity of its risky maritime economy, the ubiquity of neighborhood associations like the militia companies in which masculine prestige was continually at stake, and the intensity of municipal politics—still free from deadening royal control, placed male residents in many emotionally challenging predicaments. The dysfunction of local Catholic institutions, notorious before the *Réforme*, may have induced some townsmen to embrace new, heretical modes of collective religious behavior in part as a means to diminish the psychic toll of merciless contention in urban public life on a threatening oceanic frontier. This process may also help to explain why skilled artisans, merchants, and municipal officials—the men most engaged in the challenging political economy of a maritime *bonne ville*—joined Protestant congregations in large numbers.

Regardless of their personal motives for seeking membership in rochelais Reformed congregations, men and women frequently joined in the company of siblings, spouses, and other relatives.

building up the local church nor about the efficacy of Calvinist proselytizing in the city or region.

[109] See Ronald Weissman, *Ritual Brotherhood in Renaissance Florence*, (New York, 1980), 26-41. The essentially agonistic character of male social relations in the Italian Renaissance commercial center of Florence has been brilliantly evoked by Weissman. He explains the proliferation of new Florentine lay charitable confraternities as an outgrowth of male citizens' quest for fellowship unencumbered by the scheming and competitiveness of urban business and politics.

In December 1572, for example, the brothers Jean and Josue Morisseau gained admittance to the assembly meeting in the *salle* Gargoulleau.[110] In 1573-74, at least four pairs of siblings, comprising brothers together, sisters together, and brothers and sisters together, joined the church simultaneously.

Scrutiny of induction lists and baptismal registers shows that aspirants to congregation membership frequently baptized their children as Calvinists before their own entrance into the Reformed church had been formally accomplished.[111] Other established Calvinists facilitated the church admission of friends and relatives by selecting them to serve as godparents at the christening of their newborns before the surrogate parents had been fully admitted to membership in the congregation.[112] Engaging prospective converts or immigrants by stages in the life of the church deliberately familiarized them with the creed and ritual of the new faith. Such strategies of recruitment also tested the sincerity of newcomers' religious convictions and employed the obligations of real and fictive kinship to consolidate and expand church membership.

These various types of "chain migration" into the rochelais Calvinist church helped to convert the bulk of the city's population and indicate that the local Reformation was a hybrid, combining elements of the *ratsreformation* and *volksreformation* archetypes observable in German Reformed cities of the early modern era.[113] In La Rochelle, Calvinism was neither primarily imposed upon the citizenry by coercive actions of the municipal governing elite nor established solely through popular agitation. Magistrates and ordinary citizens entered into a dynamic, occasionally troubled alliance promoting imperfect Protestant confessiona-

---

[110] ADCM, I 7, Admissions, fol. 2r.

[111] See, for examples, the case of Jean Rousseau whose daughter, Suzanne, was baptized on 10 June 1575, six months before her father's admission to the church was recorded; and the case of François Torterue whose daughter, Jehanne, was baptized on 18 August 1575 before his own official admission to the church which came on 7 April 1576. ADCM, I 8, fol. 120v; I 9, fol. 4r; and I 12 (Admissions), fols. 7r and 9r.

[112] ADCM, I 7 (Admissions), fol. 3r and I 8, fols. 3r and 5r. The church induction of Marie Dourneau was recorded on 7 September 1573, three months after she served as godmother of a son born to an established member of that body. Three months before her own admission to La Rochelle's Calvinist church, Marie Riffault served as the godmother for a daughter born to Jean Aubin, member of a rochelais family with a long prior attachment to the Calvinist church.

[113] On the sociopolitical status of Calvinism's staunchest proponents in German

lization of the city after 1558. The new faith meshed easily with municipal officials' rigorous ethos of watchful civic government and provided the bourgeoisie with a flattering creed and accommodating institutions to buffer the anxieties of city life. For some humbler residents at the bottom of one of the most privileged urban social hierarchies in France, Calvinism, with its levelling dogma of common human sinfulness and scriptural empowerment of the laity, offered new means to organize collectively and demand due respect from the entrenched elites vying for control of communal affairs.

La Rochelle's burgeoning Calvinist population was divided into several separate congregations identifiable by the town buildings in which they met. In May of 1561, half of the *salle* St. Michel, an old municipal meeting hall within the city walls, was fitted with pews and transformed into a Reformed church.[114] Two months later, the town councilman Louis Gargoulleau gave local Calvinists use of a larger hall and tennis court belonging to him in the northern part of the city.

Still in need of meeting space, the consistory petitioned the mayor and town council to allow Calvinist meetings in alternation with Catholic services at two of La Rochelle's inner city parish churches. Civic officials authorized the alternation of cults. However, this ecumenical understanding soon died away. Bursts of iconoclasm from rochelais Protestants after 1562 demolished most of the city's old Catholic churches.

Feeling increasingly unwelcome in a reforming town, all members of the regular and secular Catholic clergy quit La Rochelle in 1568. This departure freed up a former Augustinian refectory for the use of Calvinist congregations. The dining hall, located on the rue St. Yon, became the *salle* St. Yon, accommodating the city's largest Calvinist congregation. Within La Rochelle's Calvinist meeting halls, the furniture of the cult varied little. The rooms were dominated by the pastor's pulpit and a raised "parquet" on

---

and Netherlandish cities see the various articles of Heinz Schilling collected in his *Civic Calvinism in Northwestern Germany and the Netherlands*, (Kirksville, Mo., 1991) and in his *Religion, Political Culture and the Emergence of Early Modern Society*, (Leiden, 1992). Schilling's detection of a *hofcalvinisimus* imposed on congregants from above by noble adherents to the new faith does not exist in the rochelais urban world of the sixteenth and seventeenth centuries.

[114] Meschinet de Richmond, "Anciennes églises et lieux de culte des reformés à La Rochelle," BHL, 44 (1895): 364-383.

which seating was arranged for members of the consistory. At St. Yon and later in the *grand temple*, a "banc du magistrat" was installed where the mayor and senior town councilmen could sit apart when attending church services. However, these were the only reserved seats. No other pews were ever exclusively assigned to any individuals either by custom, rental or sale. No gradations of wealth or status were allowed physically to divide or rank most assembled congregants.

By 1577, space constraints at the makeshift meeting halls prompted the consistory to undertake construction of an entirely new Reformed church on a prominent site within La Rochelle's largest square, the place du Château. The town council leased this building plot to the consistory. No private donor among the brethren stepped forward to purchase the property outright. The consistory commissioned plans for a *grand temple*, an imposing stone structure capable of seating more than 3,000 worshipers. However, sufficient construction funding could not be raised among local Calvinists and this ambitious building project stalled even before the foundation was completed. Only when the lack of Protestant meeting space in La Rochelle became acute in 1600 did work recommence on the great temple. Superintended by a committee of patrician church members, construction of the new temple ended successfully in 1603. Yet, the desultory building history of La Rochelle's great Protestant temple evokes not a community of zealous converts devoting all available resources to finance church expansion, but rather a more parsimonious and disunited urban congregation, unwilling to make major collective expenditures for a godly house before such steps became absolutely necessary.

Over decades, all sites for Calvinist worship in La Rochelle were concentrated within the oldest, central precincts of the city. No Reformed churches were based in the peripheral urban quarters of Perrot, St. Nicolas, or Notre Dame de Cougnes. This spatial concentration of Protestant meeting houses may be partially attributable to a lack of suitably large structures and vacant building space in the outlying urban neighborhoods. But the unwillingness of most Protestant congregants to subsidize physical expansion of church properties also restricted local sites of worship.

However, the actions of a few rochelais patricians decisively

influenced emplacement of La Rochelle's main Calvinist churches. In the case of the *salle* Gargoulleau, the *salle* St. Michel, and
the new temple, wealthy oligarchs of the town council, acting individually or corporately, determined the exact location of these
new congregations. In so doing, they clearly favored their own
quarters.

The pattern of Calvinist church distribution in La Rochelle
reveals another disparity between the inner and outer precincts
of the city. Calvinist residents of the port districts and the artisanal quarter of Notre Dame continually had to leave familiar surroundings and enter other urban wards to attend religious services. The physical structures of La Rochelle's Calvinist church
were all rooted in the old central parishes of the city, areas popularly identified with the wealthier merchants and powerful governing officials of the community. For nearly the entire span of
the local Reformation, three *quartiers* in La Rochelle, inhabited
by the bulk of the city's laboring population, were left without
any churches inculcating the new faith and institutionalizing
Calvinism's ascendancy at the neighborhood level. The confined
siting of new religious authorities worked against thorough Calvinist evangelization of the entire urban population.

The private residences of La Rochelle's Calvinist pastors also
tended to cluster in the old central parishes of the city adjacent
to the homes of their patrician kinsmen and patrons. At this level of human geography, the pastors were also unable to establish
personal social contacts and networks of influence among the
merchants and working people living in the densely populated
neighborhoods of Perrot, St. Nicolas, and Cougnes. In a small
town, where neighborhoods and neighborhood attachments were
correspondingly small and tightly concentrated, the pastors' physical estrangement from the little vicinages of many congregants
diminished their capacity to discipline the flock of new Calvinists.
Under these conditions, the orthodoxy of Calvinist devotions in
La Rochelle could never be guaranteed.

Tensions between the core and periphery of La Rochelle's
Calvinist church dramatically manifested themselves at an outdoor
reenactment of the Lord's supper staged in May 1562 at a curious urban venue. Although officers of the consistory anticipated
a huge turnout of the citizenry, prompted in part by popular agitation over the recent massacre of Protestants at Vassy, they did

not locate the ceremony in La Rochelle's largest open square, the place du Château in the northwest sector of the old town. Instead, Protestant leaders erected tables and strung tenting in the much smaller place du Foin, a square of the Perrot quarter intervening between the head of the district's main street and an arched entry-way leading to the inner city. Perhaps members of the centrally based consistory sought to reach out toward angry Protestants living near the port. Whatever their design, church elders quickly regretted the ritual site selected.

A crowd estimated at between 7,000 and 8,000 strong clogged the square and all of its approaches.[115] All day long, groups of communicants in succession sat down and broke bread together, listening to pastors extoll defense of the faith. In late afternoon, the emotions of celebrants packed together exploded. A detachment of 300 artisans and common people, all Calvinists from the city's poorer, peripheral quarters, surged out of the square and attacked every Catholic church in town, destroying altars, desecrating patrician tombs, smashing statues, and setting interior fixtures ablaze.[116] By nightfall, most of La Rochelle's old parish churches lay in ruins.

The next day, Calvinist clerics and members of the *consistoire*, although at least partially responsible for inciting this campaign of destruction, went before the Protestant royal governor of La Rochelle and condemned the iconoclasts. Church officials disavowed any intent to stir up the lower orders and blamed uncontrollable poor men for the trouble. The church hierarchy abetted the efforts of town sergeants to track down and arrest those who had led the assaults. Two men were jailed by La Rochelle's Calvinist mayor but withheld from trial for fear of greater popular tumult. The captives were then granted a royal pardon and released.

La Rochelle's Reformation intensified with an outburst of popular violence frightening to Calvinist church leaders who could not control it. Agitation directed against Catholic structures

---

[115] Barbot, "Histoire de La Rochelle," AHSA 17 (1889): 170-72. Meschinet de Richmond, "Eglises et lieux du culte," 368.

[116] Writing in the early seventeenth century, the rochelais historian Amos Barbot identified the main perpetrators of this vandalism as "artisans et commung du peuple" and "menu peuple," see Barbot's "Histoire de La Rochelle," AHSA 17 (1889): 170-71.

welled up and overflowed in the urban neighborhoods home to
large numbers of working men and women without direct access
to Reformed church institutions. While many of the iconoclasts
undoubtedly sympathized with ministerial preachings, their
destructive furor surpassed the pastorate's direction.

The events of May 1562 were not isolated occurrences in La
Rochelle's religious history. Peace accords punctuating the Wars
of Religion regularly included provisions for the reestablishment
of Catholic services in majority Protestant towns like La Rochelle.
Although rochelais town councilmen and Calvinist churchmen felt
obliged to honor these treaties, popular opposition to reestablishment of the mass impeded local enforcement of their terms.[117]
While town councillors and officers of the consistory negotiated
with royal envoys during the summer of 1599 to establish the Edict
of Nantes in La Rochelle, ordinary citizens again took the law into
their own hands in hopes of preventing the return of Catholic
services warranted by the accord.

On the day the edict was published in La Rochelle, (4 August
1599), a delegation of Calvinist elders backed by the mayor's
armed guards began transferring church property out of the *salle*
St. Marguerite destined for reconversion to Catholic use. Before
the work could be accomplished, the building was invaded by a
large number of Calvinist women and children accompanied by
several groups of young artisans and servants.[118] This force began
to shatter all the church windows, break apart the pulpit, and tear
up the wooden galleries of the interior. The mayor himself quickly showed up and ordered the Protestant vandals to disperse. They
ignored the magistrate's command, cursed him freely, and threatened to murder anyone who attempted to stop the demolition in
progress.

The town beadles then seized a valet in the employ of pastor
Samuel Loumeau whom they accused of striking the first blow
against the church fixtures. A general melée ensued during which
the insurgents rescued the servingman and beat off the forces of
order. Here, again, members of the city's ruling elite were pow-
erless to regulate popular violence targeting Catholic property for

---

[117] Reintroductions of the mass at La Rochelle in 1571, 1576, and 1577 met
with popular protests that sharply curtailed Catholic churchgoing and the liberties of priests. See BMLR, MS 165, *pièces* 26 and 44.

[118] Merlin, "Diaire," fol. 332r.

destruction. The leading role taken by a minister's own servant in this illegal action also suggests possible factionalization within the pastorate itself. Some Calvinist churchmen, determined to thwart accommodation with Catholics, may have encouraged their own household subordinates to sabotage implementation of peace treaties acceptable to other pastors. Such splintering among Reformed church authorities would have further weakened rochelais municipal police and ecclesiastical discipline.

Serial demographic evidence from within La Rochelle's Calvinist churches suggests a slow withdrawal from congregational life over the period 1575-1625 by wealthier members of the community. However, these vital statistics from the Calvinist *état civil* need to be used with caution. Although Protestant ministers and elders were careful to record the names of all people baptized, admitted, married or buried in the church, the notation of additional valuable information such as the title, occupation, and literacy of participants was haphazard, depending on the whim of the scribe recording the event. Thus, for most rochelais congregations, detailed analysis and comparisons of members' socioeconomic status over time are unfeasible. The exceptions here include the large Church of St. Yon, where standards of record keeping from 1574 to 1625 were higher and regular enough to permit more comprehensive investigation of the congregation's sociology, and the new *grand temple* where, from 1604 to 1620, records are more informative than usual.

At St. Yon, church secretaries attentively noted the honorifics of parishioners and regularly recorded whether participants in and witnesses to church ceremonies could sign their own names. Similar data are available for the new temple. The secretaries' habits of record keeping allow at least partial reconstruction of these churches' social complexion over time and the degree to which townspeople of particular ranks participated in the life of each congregation. Table 4 shows the raw numbers of parents baptizing children at St. Yon each year who were identified by certain honorifics denoting social status. Table 5 presents these numbers as percentages of all baptisms recorded at St. Yon in each sample year. Table 6 shows the raw numbers of godparents, identified by similar honorifics, who witnessed baptisms at St. Yon and the number of godparents who were incapable of signing their names to the baptismal registers. Table 7 expresses these num-

*Table 4*

Recorded Social Rank of Parents Baptizing Children
at Protestant Congregation of St. Yon
(1574-1625)
(Raw Numbers)

*Social Ranks*

| Year | Sieur Noble Homme Gentilhomme | Demoiselle Honnête Femme | Honnête Homme Maître Ministre | Total Baptisms |
|------|------|------|------|------|
| 1574 | 11 | 10 | 16 | 775 |
| 1575 | 19 | 20 | 21 | 915 |
| 1577 | 9 | 9 | 14 | 873 |
| 1579 | 4 | 5 | 13 | 677 |
| 1581 | 6 | 8 | 10 | 600 |
| 1583 | 6 | 9 | 14 | 433 |
| 1585 | 9 | 9 | 17 | 493 |
| 1587 | 12 | 17 | 15 | 537 |
| 1589 | 6 | 8 | 10 | 572 |
| 1591 | 6 | 8 | 9 | 508 |
| 1593 | 1 | 6 | 12 | 518 |
| 1601 | 3 | 6 | 15 | 545 |
| 1603 | 1 | 7 | 16 | 427 |
| 1605 | 3 | 7 | 9 | 261 |
| 1607 | 1 | 7 | 13 | 296 |
| 1609 | 2 | 12 | 11 | 350 |
| 1611 | 4 | 11 | 7 | 345 |
| 1613 | 4 | 10 | 17 | 489 |
| 1615 | 5 | 3 | 7 | 530 |
| 1617 | 3 | 2 | 6 | 554 |
| 1619 | 8 | 9 | 13 | 518 |
| 1620 | 2 | 4 | 9 | 537 |
| 1621 | 5 | 4 | 13 | 568 |
| 1623 | 4 | 4 | 7 | 480 |
| 1625 | 1 | 4 | 4 | 519 |

*Table 5*

Recorded Social Rank of Parents Baptizing Children
at Protestant Congregation of St. Yon
(1574-1625)
(As Percentages of All Baptisms Performed in Sample Year)

*Social Ranks*

| Year | Sieur Noblehomme Gentilhomme | Demoiselle Honnête Femme | Honnête Homme Maître Ministre | Total % |
|------|------|------|------|------|
| 1574 | 1.4 | 1.2 | 2.0 | 4.6 |
| 1575 | 2.0 | 2.1 | 2.2 | 6.3 |
| 1577 | 1.0 | 1.0 | 1.6 | 3.6 |
| 1579 | .5 | .7 | 1.9 | 3.1 |
| 1581 | 1.0 | 1.3 | 1.6 | 3.9 |
| 1583 | 1.3 | 2.0 | 3.2 | 6.5 |
| 1585 | 1.8 | 1.8 | 3.4 | 7.0 |
| 1587 | 2.2 | 3.1 | 2.7 | 8.0 |
| 1589 | 1.0 | 1.3 | 1.7 | 4.0 |
| 1591 | 1.1 | 1.5 | 1.7 | 4.3 |
| 1593 | .1 | 1.1 | 2.3 | 3.5 |
| 1601 | .5 | 1.1 | 2.7 | 4.3 |
| 1603 | .2 | 1.6 | 3.7 | 5.5 |
| 1605 | 1.1 | 2.6 | 3.4 | 7.1 |
| 1607 | .3 | 2.3 | 4.3 | 6.9 |
| 1609 | .5 | 3.4 | 3.1 | 7.0 |
| 1611 | 1.1 | 3.1 | 2.6 | 6.8 |
| 1613 | 2.2 | 2.0 | 3.4 | 7.6 |
| 1615 | .9 | .5 | 1.3 | 2.7 |
| 1617 | .5 | .5 | 1.0 | 2.0 |
| 1619 | 1.5 | 1.7 | 2.5 | 5.7 |
| 1620 | .3 | .7 | 1.6 | 2.6 |
| 1621 | .8 | .7 | 2.2 | 3.7 |
| 1623 | .8 | .8 | 1.4 | 3.0 |
| 1625 | .2 | .7 | .7 | 1.6 |

*Table 6*

Recorded Social Rank and Illiteracy of Godparents Attending
Baptisms at Protestant Congregation of St. Yon
(1574-1625)
(Raw Numbers)

*Social Ranks*

| Year | Sieur Noblehomme Gentilhomme | Demoiselle Honnête Femme | Honnête Homme Maître Minister | Unable to Sign |
|------|------|------|------|------|
| 1574 | 33 | 15 | 16 | N/A |
| 1575 | 51 | 67 | 55 | N/A |
| 1577 | 19 | 27 | 46 | N/A |
| 1579 | 12 | 17 | 34 | 9 |
| 1581 | 14 | 25 | 48 | 3 |
| 1583 | 14 | 16 | 42 | N/A |
| 1585 | 14 | 13 | 47 | 6 |
| 1587 | 17 | 23 | 33 | 6 |
| 1589 | 18 | 22 | 26 | 40 |
| 1591 | 8 | 20 | 44 | 15 |
| 1593 | 8 | 20 | 42 | 37 |
| 1601 | 10 | 25 | 54 | 27 |
| 1603 | 7 | 24 | 50 | 21 |
| 1605 | 6 | 23 | 34 | 23 |
| 1607 | 13 | 21 | 36 | 29 |
| 1609 | 10 | 24 | 50 | 16 |
| 1611 | 16 | 33 | 36 | 30 |
| 1613 | 15 | 29 | 45 | 33 |
| 1615 | 16 | 21 | 34 | 29 |
| 1617 | 14 | 19 | 37 | 51 |
| 1619 | 29 | 32 | 54 | 68 |
| 1620 | 17 | 26 | 51 | 36 |
| 1621 | 24 | 22 | 46 | 78 |
| 1623 | 9 | 14 | 30 | 46 |
| 1625 | 8 | 13 | 22 | 49 |

*Table 7*

Recorded Social Rank and Illiteracy of Godparents Attending
Baptisms at Protestant Congregation of St. Yon
(1574-1625)
(As Percentages of All Baptisms Performed in Sample Year)

*Social Ranks*

| Year | Sieur Noblehomme Gentilhomme | Demoiselle Honnête Femme | Honnête Homme Maître Minister | Unable to Sign |
|---|---|---|---|---|
| 1574 | 4.2 | 1.9 | 5.1 | N/A |
| 1575 | 5.6 | 7.3 | 6.0 | N/A |
| 1577 | 2.1 | 3.0 | 5.2 | N/A |
| 1579 | 1.8 | 2.5 | 5.0 | 1.3 |
| 1581 | 2.3 | 4.1 | 8.0 | .5 |
| 1583 | 3.2 | 3.6 | 9.7 | N/A |
| 1585 | 2.8 | 2.6 | 9.5 | 1.2 |
| 1587 | 3.1 | 4.3 | 6.1 | 1.1 |
| 1589 | 3.1 | 3.8 | 4.5 | 7.0 |
| 1591 | 1.5 | 3.9 | 8.6 | 3.0 |
| 1593 | 1.5 | 3.8 | 8.1 | 7.1 |
| 1601 | 1.8 | 4.6 | 9.9 | 5.0 |
| 1603 | 1.6 | 5.6 | 11.7 | 5.0 |
| 1605 | 2.2 | 8.3 | 13.0 | 8.8 |
| 1607 | 4.3 | 7.0 | 12.1 | 9.8 |
| 1609 | 2.8 | 6.8 | 14.2 | 4.6 |
| 1611 | 4.6 | 9.5 | 10.4 | 8.7 |
| 1613 | 3.0 | 5.9 | 9.2 | 6.7 |
| 1615 | 3.0 | 3.9 | 6.4 | 5.5 |
| 1617 | 2.5 | 3.4 | 6.6 | 9.2 |
| 1619 | 5.6 | 6.1 | 10.4 | 13.1 |
| 1620 | 3.1 | 4.8 | 9.4 | 6.7 |
| 1621 | 4.2 | 3.8 | 8.0 | 13.7 |
| 1623 | 1.8 | 2.9 | 6.2 | 9.5 |
| 1625 | 1.5 | 2.5 | 4.2 | 9.4 |

bers as percentages of all baptisms conducted in the congregation during each sample year. Since it is probable that church
scribes did not systematically identify all congregants by the honorifics they may have deserved, the data presented here should
only be considered as an approximate rather than an exact measure of demographic trends within the congregation.

Given these caveats, what do the numbers suggest? First, among
parents baptizing children at St. Yon, the numbers of fathers
addressed as "Noblehomme," "Gentilhomme" or "Ecuyer" declined after 1587. A similar decline, more pronounced after 1613,
is noticeable for mothers of newborns saluted as "Demoiselle" or
"Honnête Femme." The numbers of fathers titled "Honorable
Homme," "Ministre" or "Maître" fluctuated in a narrower band
but also dropped off after 1613. Parents from all of these social
ranks were involved in approximately 8 percent of all baptisms
recorded at St. Yon in 1587. This figure falls to less than 3 percent in 1615 and to less than 2 percent in 1625. Wealthier and
more privileged Rochelais were apparently less active in the life
of the congregation of St. Yon over time while the participation
of townspeople of middling rank held steadier.

Among godparents witnessing baptisms at St. Yon, male notables of high rank declined from fifty-one in 1575 to less than twenty per annum in all but two of the succeeding twenty-three sample years. In five of these years, fewer than ten godfathers came
from the highest social ranks. The numbers of godmothers listed
as "Demoiselle" or "Honnête Femme" also declined from a high
of sixty-seven in 1575 toward lows of thirteen per annum in 1585
and again in 1625. The numbers of godfathers identified as "Honnête Homme," "Ministre" or "Maître" fluctuated, but in a higher
range and participated in a larger proportion of baptisms over
time than did congregants of more elevated social status.

Over time, it seems that fewer congregants chose godparents
from the highest, literate ranks of the urban population. This
trend is confirmed by data on the literacy of godparents at St.
Yon, the characteristic of parishioners most reliably recorded from
1585 to 1625. The numbers of illiterate godparents selected by
congregants rose, reaching peaks in the sample years after 1613.
In 1620, for example, approximately 14 percent of all baptisms
in the congregation involved at least one godparent incapable of
signing his or her name to the registry. By contrast, in 1591, only

about 3 percent of baptisms in the congregation had involved an illiterate witness. Rising illiteracy rates for godparents correspond with declining rates of service as godparents for more notable and typically more literate townspeople. These complementary sets of statistics indicate a shift in the social composition of the St. Yon congregation. Although the majority of church members remained of middling social rank and literate, citizens of higher social status became less active in the congregation while townsfolk of more humble means and lower literacy rates became more active. One implication of these figures is a slow but growing estrangement between congregants of higher social prestige and those of middling or lower status.

The generally declining congregational presence of more distinguished townspeople and an influx of ordinary citizens after 1613 may have come about as direct results of the 1614 political rebellion by rochelais bourgeois that broke the power of the city's old ruling elite. As will be shown in Chapter 5, the congregation of St. Yon was dominated by the rebel merchants who perpetrated the successful overthrow of La Rochelle's old governing regime. Municipal political tensions may have aggravated a dissolution of vertical social attachments between the various ranks of the urban population gathered in the congregation of St. Yon.

Less complete demographic data from the new church housed in the *grand temple* suggest an even more unstable congregation also afflicted by the withdrawal of citizens from higher social ranks. The great new stone church ensconced within La Rochelle's largest square apparently opened with a flourish in late 1603. In the first full year of operation (1604), 544 baptisms were performed at the new structure involving at least forty-one parents identified with the honorifics at the level of "Honnête Femme" and "Honnête Homme" or above. Among godparents, at least eighty distinguished citizens including eight pastors, were singled out as present at christenings. However, in the very next sample year (1606), all of these numbers fell by 50 percent or more. Total baptisms dropped to only 247 in 1606 and continued to fall thereafter, slipping to 143 in 1620.

After 1604, far fewer notable parents were listed in the birth register, and declines also occurred in the numbers of godparents listed as "Demoiselle" and "Honorable Homme." Again, these figures reached new lows after 1614. Despite reductions in the absolute numbers of distinguished citizens serving as godparents, the totals for godparents listed as illiterate also declined at *temple neuf*, from sixty-eight in 1604 to thirteen in 1620. This trend suggests that changes in the congregation's sociology resulted in a more stable base of literate parishioners and a proportionally greater loss of poorer, less literate witnesses.

Although ostensibly constructed to ease overcrowding in other rochelais Calvinist churches, it does not appear from church records that the new *grand temple* attracted or held a large number of faithful congregants. Townspeople flocked to the impressive new church upon its opening for all types of services in 1603-04, but this enthusiasm apparently died away quickly. Were many Rochelais only drawn by the novelty of the grand edifice, quickly returning to their usual places of worship? Baptisms at St. Yon, for example, did fall unusually by 166 births between 1603 and 1605 but steadily recovered thereafter, reaching new peaks above 500 per annum while baptisms continued to decline at *temple neuf*.

Perhaps the new temple's location on the city's main parade ground in a corner of its most prestigious neighborhood dissuaded ordinary citizens from prolonged membership while growing sociopolitical tensions within the city reduced the congregational activity of more distinguished townspeople who could pursue their devotions on their rural estates and at proximate Calvinist churches established in the city's *banlieue*. Although endowed with a more majestic church structure, the congregation of *temple neuf* was evidently much smaller than that at St. Yon. La Rochelle's new temple, opened at great expense in 1603, served only very briefly as a rallying point for the city's increasingly divided Calvinists.

### 5. Disinheriting the Pastorate: Calvinist Testamentary Practices in La Rochelle, Circa 1561–Circa 1650

The fractious character of La Rochelle's Reformed inhabitants is further revealed by long-term analysis of their testamentary practices. Few studies have examined in aggregate the wills of French Protestants redacted before the eighteenth century.[119] In La

---

[119] Thorough statistical analyses of testamentary behavior among French

Rochelle, despite extensive early modern notarial archives including hundreds of Calvinist testaments, no systematic research has ever been undertaken on this important body of evidence relating how religious values shaped the behavior of individual congregants. For the period from 1561 to 1649 I have assembled a sample of 1,004 Protestant and Catholic wills redacted by residents of La Rochelle. Protestant wills total 881, Catholic 123. The vast majority of these documents were drawn up before 1628. Considered in their entirety, Protestant wills show that La Rochelle's Calvinists were significantly less charitable than the Reformed inhabitants of seventeenth-century Lyon and Nîmes, the only other towns where Protestant testamentary charity has been examined in detail.[120] Wilma J. Pugh found that between 1600 and 1699, on average, 87.4 percent of wills redacted by Protestant Lyonnais and 90 percent of wills drawn up by Calvinist Nîmois contained charitable bequests.[121] My analysis shows that on average, over the nine decades from 1561 to 1649, only 61.5 percent of wills filed by rochelais Protestants contained charitable bequests. Over the first seven decades during which will sample sizes are largest, percentages of Calvinist testaments containing philanthropic gifts range from a low of 27.5 percent of all wills found in 1570-79 to a high of 75.8 percent of all wills discovered in 1590-99 (see Table 8). However, this higher level of charitable giving was never sustained. The percentage of testaments containing charitable bequests fell to 56.3 percent of all wills in 1600-09 and rose to only 62.5 percent of all wills in 1620-29, arguably the decade in which the rochelais Reformed church was most in need of financial support from its local membership.

---

Protestants are very rare. For the best available study of the topic including ample citations to earlier relevant literature see Wilma J. Pugh "Catholics, Protestants, and Testamentary Charity in Seventeenth-Century Lyon and Nîmes," *French Historical Studies* 11 (1980): 479-504. On the implications of Protestant charitable practices for French civil governments see E. Haag, "Le protestantisme, en favorisant le développement de la charité civile, a-t-il été contraire à la charité religieuse?" BHSPF 1 (1853), 213-214. No studies of French Protestant testamentary charity rival in scope the now classic histories focusing on posthumous Catholic philanthropy and its cultural implications. See for examples Michel Vovelle, *Piété baroque et déchristianisation en Provence au XVIIIe siècle: les attitudes devant la mort d'après les clauses des testaments*, (Paris, 1973), and Pierre Chaunu *La mort à Paris: XVIe, XVIIe, XVIIIe siècles* (Paris, 1978).

[120] Pugh, "Catholics, Protestants, and Testamentary Charity," 482-488.

[121] *Ibid.*, 483-484, "Table 1" and "Figure 1."

*Table 8*

Percentages of All Rochelais Protestant Wills Containing
Charitable Bequests by Decade and Gender
(1561-1649)

| Decade | Total Number Male Female | | With Charity M F | | % Charitable M F | | Total % with Charity |
|--------|------|--------|----|----|------|------|--------|
| 1561-69 | 26 | 22 | 8 | 7 | 30.7 | 31.8 | 31.2 |
| 1570-79 | 38 | 31 | 10 | 9 | 26.3 | 29.0 | 27.5 |
| 1580-89 | 58 | 72 | 34 | 48 | 58.6 | 66.6 | 63.0 |
| 1590-99 | 56 | 64 | 39 | 52 | 69.6 | 81.2 | 75.8 |
| 1600-09 | 44 | 59 | 20 | 38 | 45.4 | 64.4 | 56.3 |
| 1610-19 | 74 | 109 | 57 | 70 | 77.0 | 64.2 | 69.3 |
| 1620-29 | 77 | 126 | 50 | 77 | 64.9 | 61.1 | 62.5 |
| 1630-39 | 2 | 11 | 2 | 9 | 100.0 | 81.8 | 84.6 |
| 1640-49 | 6 | 6 | 5 | 5 | 83.3 | 83.3 | 83.3 |

For the first decade (1600-09) during which the testaments of
Calvinists in La Rochelle can be directly compared to Pugh's data
on the Reformed communities of Lyon and Nîmes, we find that
Protestant Rochelais were the least charitable of all. Over these
ten years, only 56.3 percent of all Calvinist wills redacted in La
Rochelle contained charitable bequests whereas 72 percent of
Reformed testaments in Nîmes and 100 percent of such documents in Lyon included such gifts.[122] Pugh attributes consistently high rates of Protestant testamentary benefactions in Lyon and
Nîmes to the Reformed church's effective inculcation of charitable habits as an article of faith among the laity.[123] Evidence from
La Rochelle indicates that local Calvinist church authorities were
far less successful overall in this process of indoctrination, confronting a seaport population less tractable and less philanthropic than French inland Reformed communities.

When rates of posthumous Protestant charity in La Rochelle
are correlated with the social status of testators, it appears that
well-born citizens were more charitable and more observant of

---

[122] *Ibid.*, 484 and "Figure 1."
[123] *Ibid.*, 499.

church teaching than humbler residents. Average charitable bequest rates as a percentage of all wills recovered fall steeply as one descends the urban social hierarchy (see Table 9).

Members of La Rochelle's governing elite, closely associated personally and politically with Calvinist clergymen, were particularly generous in their bequests to the new church and its officers. Patrician women married to town councilmen regularly left large legacies to the ministers and to the poor of the Reformed community, playing a critical role in the financial support and institutionalization of Calvinism in an urban milieu.

The bulk of Protestant wills I have found comes from members of families established by the merchants and artisans who dominated La Rochelle's maritime economy. Among these segments of the urban population, rates of charitable benefactions were lower than among testators from the households of town councilmen, presidial court officers, and local attorneys. Although highly skilled artisans and their families frequently made provisions for testamentary charity, philanthropic wills were much less common among ordinary skilled craftsmen. The artisanal community as a whole made will gifts with about half the frequency of the most philanthropic citizens. Sailors and day laborers showed the lowest rates of testamentary charity I have discovered.

Rates of charitable giving within status groups occupying the middle and lower echelons of La Rochelle's social hierarchy are also far below those recorded by Pugh for comparable ranks of citizens in Lyon and Nîmes. Among the Protestant Nîmois for example, all strata of the citizenry made charitable wills at rates exceeding 78.5%. In La Rochelle, only Calvinist nobles and the families of town councilmen managed to file charitable wills at a comparable rate. All other rochelais status groups fall far below levels of philanthropy observed in other French Protestant towns.

Here, again, it is evident that for the Rochelais, engagement in the life of the Reformed church, allegiance to its precepts, and financial sacrifice for its support were heavily dependent on one's social status. Placed in this context, the complaints of local ministers over the unruliness of ordinary townspeople manifest clerical disgust with a laity largely ambivalent toward endorsement and endowment of the Reformed church hierarchy.

Shifting from comparative analysis of the percentages of wills containing charitable bequests made by various Reformed social

*Table 9*

Percentages of Protestant Wills Redacted in La Rochelle
Containing Charitable Gifts by Social Status of Testators
(1561-1649)

| Social Group | % Charitable Wills |
|---|---|
| Nobles and High Civic Officials[1]: | 85.7 |
| Royal Magistrates and Lawyers: | 75.6 |
| Merchants (Wholesale and Retail): | 69.5 |
| Ministers, Notaries, Physicians, and Minor Civic Officials: | 61.8 |
| Artisans | |
|    Highly Skilled[2]: | 69.6 |
|    Skilled[3]: | 41.5 |
|    Total: | 46.8 |
| Sailors: | 40.6 |
| Day Laborers (Urban and Rural): | 36.4 |
| Average: | 61.0 |

[1] Includes members of the town council (*corps de ville*).
[2] Includes *joailliers, armuriers,* and *fourbisseurs d'armes.*
[3] Includes *charpentiers, tailleurs, chapeliers,* etc.

groups to scrutiny of actual cash flows involved reveals not only
the small proportion of Protestant family wealth transferred by
will for charitable purposes, but also changes in the philanthropic
priorities of Calvinist testators over time. To evaluate Calvinist
charitable practices in La Rochelle between 1561 and 1649, I have
recorded the number and cash value of all testamentary gifts
made directly to the poor (in contravention of strict Calvinist doctrine that discouraged such legacies), to the poor box of the
Reformed church (under the control of lay deacons), to seminarians aspiring to the ministry, to the ministers themselves, and
to the municipal hospitals adhering to Calvinist dogma but administered by town councilmen. These were the five most common
recipients of Calvinist benefactions in La Rochelle.

Although in no will known to me does the testator state openly his or her exact motivations for making a specific kind of charitable donation, nonetheless the immediate consequences of a
particular type of gift were undoubtedly clear to a giver and from

these we can discern some objectives that may have impelled benefactors to donate money in one of the five typical ways listed
above. Gifts directly to the poor circumvented ecclesiastical administration entirely, a practice condemned by the written *Discipline* of French Calvinist congregations which sought to establish
the church's administration through its deacons over all forms of
poor relief.[124] Thus a gift of this kind constituted a blatant dis-
avowal by the donor of the Reformed church's philanthropic policy. The traditional nature of these direct alms to the poor, sug-
gestive of Papist "good works" redounding to the salvation of the
giver, also made them highly suspect to Calvinist clerics.

Gifts to the Calvinist poor box placed private resources in the
hands of church deacons for charitable purposes. Since deacons
were predominantly recruited from amongst La Rochelle's mercantile and governing elites, supplying the poor box was a philanthropic practice empowering lay church officials of higher
social status. Such gifts also reinforced the laity's administrative
role within the Reformed community, complementing but also
counterbalancing the authority of ministers. Such donations were
in accord with Calvinist church discipline but also enabled donors
to show their support for more democratic precepts of ecclesiastical administration charging ordinary brethren with tasks preserving congregational life.

Will gifts made directly to the ministers channeled funds to the
most prominent spiritual guides of the faithful, manifesting a
donor's high regard for the importance and material comfort of
these learned preachers. Bequests in aid of students studying for
the ministry at La Rochelle's *collège* or elsewhere built up the
church from below, encouraging expansion of the pastorate
through training of native sons and multiplying voices of authority within the Reformed community. These donations could make
clear a giver's appreciation for the thorough theological training
championed by Protestantism but might also signal the testator's
dissatisfaction with the current generation of pastors supervising

---

[124] For a modern transcript of the French Protestant *confession de foi* accompanied by historical and bibliographical essays, see Jacques Pannier, *Les origines
de la confession de foi et la discipline des églises réformées de France,* (Paris, 1936). For
analysis of each credo comprising the *confession* within the context of Biblical literature and earlier Protestant theology see Roger Mehl, *Explication de la confession de foi de La Rochelle,* (Paris, 1959). Article 22 of the original *confession* gave
*diacres* (deacons) responsibility for care of the poor among Calvinist congregants.

church life. Gifts to hospitals indicated a donor's special regard for the weakest members of the urban congregation and his or her willingness to entrust civic officials, who controlled the administration of these institutions, with the ultimate dispensation of one's pious bequests.

What were the dimensions of Calvinist testamentary charity in La Rochelle? To gauge the relative importance of this activity, I also recorded the cash value explicitly stated of all bequests listed in the wills I located. Legacies to immediate relatives, passing on the family patrimony, greatly predominated in wills composed by all social groups of both confessions. For example, the total amount of all cash, investments, outstanding loans, material goods, and real estate explicitly valued and transferred by Protestant testators to other family members through the wills I have recovered came to 523,634 *livres*.[125] In the 540 rochelais Calvinist wills I found containing charitable bequests to one or more of the five most common recipients, the total cash value of these gifts was 30,831 *livres*. Thus testamentary charity among Reformed townspeople represented about 5.6 percent of the stated cash value of all testamentary bequests they made over the period investigated. By contrast, in the much smaller sample of rochelais Catholic wills (n=123), charitable gifts amounted to about 9.3 percent of the stated cash value of all testamentary bequests the "Papists" made over the same period.

Table 10 shows the cash amounts of Calvinist testamentary charity given directly to the poor, to the church poor box, to Reformed seminarians, to the pastors, and to the public hospitals over the nine decades from 1561 to 1649. This table also indicates what percentage of all charitable funding per decade went to each of the five most common beneficiaries.

Posthumous Protestant philanthropy peaked in the 1590's when over 8,000 *livres* went to needy individuals and institutions. This level of giving was not sustained, slipping to approximately 5,000 *livres* per decade between 1600 and 1629. After the great siege of 1628, Calvinist will gifts declined precipitously. Although during the 1570's 41.5 percent of all recorded donations went directly to

---

[125] This amount should be considered as the bare minimum value of all will gifts made by Calvinists since in many testaments the exact cash amount of the household wealth being transferred is not given.

*Table 10*

Protestant Testamentary Bequests to Primary Beneficiaries in La Rochelle
(1561-1649)
(Expressed in *Livres* and as Percentages of All Bequests in Sample Periods)

| Decade | DP | % | PB | % | SA | % | MA | % | HOS | % | Total |
|---|---|---|---|---|---|---|---|---|---|---|---|
| 1561-69 | 0 | 0 | 572.5 | 98.6 | 0 | 0 | 8.0 | 1.4 | 0 | 0 | 580.5 |
| 1570-79 | 657.5 | 41.5 | 778.0 | 49.0 | 0 | 0 | 150.0 | 9.5 | 0 | 0 | 1585.5 |
| 1580-89 | 130.0 | 4.1 | 2222.0 | 70.3 | 0 | 0 | 798.0 | 25.3 | 10.0 | 0.3 | 3160.0 |
| 1590-99 | 74.0 | 0.9 | 4586.0 | 57.2 | 1000.0 | 12.5 | 2238.0 | 27.9 | 120.0 | 1.5 | 8018.0 |
| 1600-09 | 120.0 | 2.7 | 2084.5 | 46.6 | 399.0 | 8.9 | 1858.0 | 41.5 | 15.0 | 0.3 | 4476.5 |
| 1610-19 | 184.0 | 3.1 | 3475.0 | 58.3 | 1031.0 | 17.3 | 1210.0 | 20.3 | 64.0 | 1.0 | 5964.0 |
| 1620-29 | 6.0 | 0.1 | 3229.0 | 71.5 | 430.0 | 9.5 | 395.0 | 8.7 | 459.5 | 10.2 | 4519.5 |
| 1630-39 | 0 | 0 | 810.0 | 45.9 | 300.0 | 17.0 | 655.0 | 37.1 | 0 | 0 | 1765.0 |
| 1640-49 | 30 | 3.9 | 510.0 | 66.9 | 30.0 | 3.9 | 192.0 | 25.3 | 0 | 0 | 762.0 |

Abbreviations:  DP = Direct to Poor. PB = Poor Box. SA = Seminarian Aid. MA = Minister Aid. HOS = Hospital Support.

the poor, this was an aberration probably due to the flood of Protestant refugees entering La Rochelle after the St. Bartholomew's Day Massacre and to the large numbers of refugees caught in the city during the abortive royal siege of 1572-73. In general, rochelais Calvinists adhered to church teaching and eschewed cash gifts directly to the poor. The amount of such gifts expressed as a percentage of all charitable donations per decade declines steadily, hovering around 4 percent or below from the 1580's onward. However, an irreducible faction of all Calvinist donors in La Rochelle did choose to contravene church policy and put alms directly into the hands of beggars. Bequests to the Reformed poor box also fluctuate over time but never drop below 45 percent of the total value of all donations per decade. Many givers consistently supported this congregational response to the ubiquity of the poor.

The most striking alteration in Protestant charitable behavior is the steep drop of 80 percent in the level of testamentary gifts made to local pastors between 1600 and 1629. Over these thirty years, Calvinist ministers went from being highly favored recipients of the laity's benefactions to being denied any lay bequests at all in the years 1610, 1615, 1618, and 1622. As will be shown in Chapters 5 and 6, this later period was a time of severe political and religious factionalization in La Rochelle resulting in the overthrow of oligarchical town government and in popular repudiation of ordained church leaders.  For the decade 1600-09,

41.5 percent of the value of all Protestant testamentary charity went directly to the ministers. Between 1610 and 1619 this figure dropped to 20.3 percent and for 1620-29 fell again to only 8.7 percent of the value of all Calvinist donations. These sharp reductions are not a statistical fluke attributable to smaller or declining sample sizes of wills in the decades examined. The total number of wills recovered for the period 1600-29 actually rises and then holds steady. Nor can this decline be safely attributed to public perceptions of more stable incomes for pastors guaranteed by the monarchy in the Edict of Nantes. State subsidies for French ministers after 1598 long went unpaid and pastors complained bitterly of this neglect.

It appears that public disaffection with La Rochelle's Calvinist pastors, notably articulated in the 1614 rebellion of the rochelais bourgeoisie against civic and religious authorities, also manifested itself through the citizenry's steady reductions in testamentary financial support for the Reformed clergy. Here, I believe we can observe townspeople of varying socioeconomic status using their philanthropic options to express their disapproval of ministers perceived as inimical to the common interests of their flocks. Under these conditions, will-making assumes personal, familial, and political significance allowing men and women, through entirely discretionary acts of benevolence, to assert their convictions about which public and private institutions within the urban polity are worthiest of sustained financial support.

Note that the decline in giving to Reformed clergymen is accompanied by a small rise in alms given directly to the poor, another snub to Calvinist teaching, by more donations to Protestant seminarians, and by greater funding of city hospitals. Such strategies of caring all reduce the pool of donations subject to direct control by ministers, bolster lay church administrators' discretionary budgets, reinforce civic officials' control of poor relief, and provide for the training of a new generation of pastors to replace the old. Although its exact cause can not be pinpointed, this precipitous drop in charitable donations to La Rochelle's Calvinist clergy suggests a commensurate fall in Reformed testators' respect for and care of their ministers. Significant numbers of Protestant benefactors in La Rochelle disinherited their pastors after 1600.

Considered in their entirety, serial data on the demographics and philanthropy of La Rochelle's Calvinist community show it to have been far from monolithic in social composition or religious practice. To the contrary, the rochelais Reformed church included several, distinctive congregations wherein the canons of church teaching were followed with varying degrees of obedience by the laity. These congregations were equally vulnerable to urban sociopolitical tensions opposing governors and governed. The exacerbation of such conflicts especially after 1600, in which certain churches became focal points of popular protests against oligarchical civic administration, was accompanied by a loss of social cohesion within the congregations and changes in the charitable giving of ordinary Calvinists. These developments show that a dynamic balance of power operated between Calvinist clerics, lay elders, and humble congregants. A bustling port town had a Reformed church no less active, enmeshed in citizen's competitive struggles for political, commercial, and religious advantages.

### 6. Printing and Religious Politics in La Rochelle

The activities of Protestant printers working in La Rochelle also contributed to the agitation and factionalization of literate Calvinists. A census of all books published in southwestern France during the sixteenth century shows at least 363 separate titles produced in La Rochelle after printing began there in 1563.[126] Within five years of the Reformation's outbreak in La Rochelle, the zealous Calvinist bookman Barthélémy Berton had set up shop.[127] Berton quickly ingratiated himself among the wealthy rochelais merchants and judicial officers forming the socioeconomic elite of the city's Reformed community. Berton quickly won the financial backing of several respected Calvinist merchants, who pro-

---

[126] Louis Desgraves, "Introduction de l'imprimerie dans le sud-ouest de la France jusqu'à la fin du XVIe siècle," in M.-A. Arnould, ed., Villes d'imprimerie et moulins à papier du XIVe au XVIe siècle, (Brussels, 1976). Although rochelais printers produced fewer books than their confrères in the neighboring university town of Poitiers (587 titles), they circulated nearly as many as were issued in Bordeaux (366 titles) where printing had been introduced more than thirty years earlier. La Rochelle quickly became an important center of the French west country book trade.

[127] E. Droz, L'Imprimerie à La Rochelle, vol. 1, Barthélémy Berton 1563-1573, (Geneva, 1960).

vided cash and supplies to operate a printing shop with up to six employees. The patrons retained the right to order the publication of books they liked and to stipulate the size of press runs.[128]

With Berton laboring under these conditions set by notable rochelais Protestants, it is not surprising that his initial publications included psalters, New Testaments, and simple Calvinist catechisms in a variety of formats and price ranges. He produced popular titles in press runs of up to 1,500 copies. The important evangelical role of Berton's enterprise was reinforced when he later turned to the mass production of cheap pamphlets defending the new faith and its adherents in combative terms.

Berton's catalogue of publications reflects both his clients' avidity for Protestant works and his own, hard-headed indifference to the copyright claims made by competing Genevan printers over key Calvinist texts. Berton first profited by producing an edition of Théodore de Bèze's Psalms done in verse.[129] Then, in 1565, Berton published Jean Calvin's *Quarante sept sermons sur les huict derniers chapitres des propheties de Daniel.* When news of this marketing reached Geneva, both the company of pastors and the deacons of the city's consistory denounced Berton for unscrupulously violating Genevan printers' supposedly exclusive rights to publish the great reformer's books. Even worse, by pirating the works of Bèze and Calvin, Berton cheated the Genevan consistory out of the production royalties the authors had assigned for poor relief in the Swiss city. Foreign animosities raised by the stratagems of Berton contributed to the estrangement of La Rochelle's Calvinist community from the mother church in Geneva.

Berton's Protestant beliefs and opportunistic business sense exposed his west country readers to one of the most spectacular constitutional crises of the nascent French Reformed Church. What subsequently became known as the "Morély affair" exploded in 1562 with the publication of Jean Morély's *Traicté de la discipline et police chrestienne.*[130] Morély advocated a radical congrega-

---

[128] The contracts are reproduced in *ibid.*, 16-18 and 25-26.

[129] *Ibid.*, 46-52.

[130] The most recent and comprehensive analysis of this text is given in Philippe Denis and Jean Rott, *Jean Morély et l'utopie d'une démocratie dans l'église* (Geneva, 1993). See also R. Kingdon, *Geneva and the Consolidation of the French Protestant Movement*, Chapter 3, "Arguments over French Reformed Church Organization," 37-148, especially 43-81 setting out Morély's arguments and their official refutation by the Parisian pastor Chandieu.

tionalism in the administration and police of the Reformed church. Taking as his model the consensual governance of the early Christian church by the apostles, Morély argued that the only way to reestablish the "rights of the people" in ecclesiastical affairs was to abolish all clerical, consistorial, synodal, and secular direction of French Protestant religious practices. Every important decision shaping Christian worship, including ministerial appointments, doctrinal formulations, and the punishment of sinners, must be adjudicated by the entire membership of each congregation voting together. Jean Calvin and the theocrats of Geneva anathematized Morély's endorsements of greater democracy in the discipline of the Reformed church. The Genevan consistory not only excommunicated Morély as "a schismatic and addict of controversy," but also immediately retained a Parisian pastor, Antoine de la Roche Chandieu, to produce a massive refutation of Morély's impudent plan.[131]

Chandieu's manuscript, personally corrected by Jean Calvin, was first published in 1566 by the great Calvinist bookman of Geneva, Henri Estienne.[132] The first edition printed in France came shortly thereafter from Barthélémy Berton in La Rochelle. Berton's local readership was thus quickly exposed to Chandieu's extensive citations and criticisms of Morély's theories and biblical exegesis. With few if any copies of Morély's own book circulating, Chandieu's refutation was the only readily available source of information about strikingly democratic alternatives to the hierarchical structure of the French Calvinist Church. In La Rochelle, a town already marked by outbursts of popular iconoclasm and widespread lay disrespect for ministerial authority, Morély's convictions—even if transmitted through Chandieu's rebuttal—probably piqued the interest of some readers. Indeed, pastor Pierre Merlin (father of Jacques Merlin, the future beleaguered minister of La Rochelle) warned Chandieu in a letter dated 2 April 1566, that among ordinary French people ideas like those of

---

[131] E. Droz, "Autour de l'affaire Morély, La Roche Chandieu et Barthélémy Berton," *Bibliothèque de l'humanisme et renaissance*, 22 (1960): 570-577. See also Philippe Denis, "Penser la démocratie au XVIe siècle, Morély, Aristote et la réforme de la Réforme," BSHPF, 137 (1991): 369-386.

[132] Antoine de la Roche Chandieu, *La confirmation de la discipline ecclésiastique observée es églises réformées du royaume de France*, (Geneva, 1566).

Morély were "fort plausible et populaire."[133] As Pierre Merlin's son would subsequently learn to his chagrin, insurrectionary members of La Rochelle's bourgeoisie, backed by artisans and laborers, were fully capable of censuring Calvinist ministers and demanding greater congregational control over local church affairs as part of their violent, successful reform of municipal politics in 1614.

Philippe Denis has recently argued that the Morély affair convulsed the French Reformed Church for at least a decade after 1562.[134] Earlier, Robert Kingdon described the development of a "congregational faction" led by Morély within French Protestantism, a party sustained by sympathetic nobles like Odet de Coligny (a power broker with numerous contacts in the French west country) and capable of winning over the entire memberships of numerous Reformed churches in the Ile-de-France.[135] However, according to Kingdon, Genevan authorities and their partisans were unrelenting in their attacks on the Morély group, and this assault, coupled with the depredations of the St. Bartholomew's Day Massacre, was sufficient to discredit and disperse the democratically inclined clique. While in France the Morély affair was essentially over by 1572, Kingdon finds echoes of this quarrel long resounding in the development of Calvinist churches elsewhere, especially in the Netherlands, England, and Scotland where advocates of episcopal, presbyterial, and congregational church polity bitterly clashed throughout the early modern era.[136]

But here it should be noted that rochelais entrepreneurs, who made these same countries the focal points of their commercial ventures, who regularly apprenticed their sons to foreign business contacts in these places, and who frequently received Dutch, English, and Scotch travelling Protestant merchants in their own homes, were more exposed to these continuing debates on Reformed church government than any other bourgeois commu-

---

[133] See the complete text of Peirre Merlin's letter to Chandieu reproduced in Droz, "Autour de l'affaire," 572-574. Pierre Merlin's impressions of the French populace were drawn from his extensive travels in France which took him throughout the west country and to La Rochelle.

[134] Denis, "Penser la démocratie."

[135] Kingdon, *Geneva and the Consolidation of French Protestant Movement*, 90.

[136] *Ibid.*, 122-137.

nity in France. After 1568, the Rochelais also became notorious for sheltering and resupplying corsairs crewed by Dutch Calvinists in open rebellion against the king of Spain.[137] The contentious history of La Rochelle's own Reformed church after 1572 is, in part, attributable to this process of acculturation through which many of its constituents learned about alternative congregational models of ecclesiastical government originally French in derivation.

The hardening of consistorial government within many French Calvinist churches does not seem to have been a fixture of religious life in La Rochelle. Here, pastors occasionally had their sermons interrupted by disputatious or distracted congregants.[138] Ultimately, lay believers pushed their demands for a voice in ecclesiastical affairs so far that local ministers nearly quit the city *en masse* in 1614 to protest the disrespectful affronts they suffered from rebellious citizens. As will be shown in subsequent chapters, the rochelais instigators of this challenge may well be counted among the last and most determined French exponents of more democratic church polities Morély first championed fifty years earlier.

Between 1576 and 1589, another rochelais printer, Jean Portau, produced works advocating, among other things, popular rebellion against tyrants and mystical, prophetic interpretations of the book of Genesis. Among the latter publications, Giacomo Brocardo's *Mystica et prophetica libri Genesis interpretatio* (1580) outraged the rochelais Reformed minister Odet de Nort, who publicly preached against the sale and reading of this highly unorthodox text. De Nort convinced the 1581 synod of French Reformed churches meeting in La Rochelle to censure Brocardo's visionary pronouncements. The synod condemned the book as "fraught with impieties and horrible profanations of the Sacred Scriptures, and pernicious errors in matters of revelation and prophecy."[139] Not to be deterred from a *succés de scandale*, Portau merely ripped

---

[137] Delayant, *Histoire des Rochelais*, 1: 229.

[138] See Merlin, "Diaire," fols. 34r-35r (26 October 1608), on the "insolences" directed at him by a congregant during his sermon at the new temple. In June 1599, Merlin had noted with anger that street commotion as ordinary as a child crying could induce most of the St. Yon congregation to quit the church in the middle of his sermon, leaving him almost alone inside, *ibid.*, fol. 368v.

[139] Quick, *Synodicon*, 1: 138.

out the first four pages of his copies on hand, inserted new title
pages with a different type face, and proceeded to sell out his
stock to avid buyers in and around La Rochelle.[140]

The circulation of books and pamphlets in La Rochelle
increased after 1570 when another printer, Pierre Haultin, opened
a shop in the city. Haultin and his heirs dominated rochelais printing and type-founding for the next fifty years. During his own
nineteen years of activity in La Rochelle (1570-1588), Pierre
Haultin produced at least eighty-six volumes. Haultin's nephew,
Jerôme Haultin, carried on the business between 1588 and 1600,
adding another 124 titles to the rochelais bibliography.[141] Protestant religious works in French, including Bibles, New Testaments, and psalters, comprised the bulk of the Haultins' production.[142]

Successive editions of such pious works did not insulate Haultin
nor his heirs from condemnation by church officials for the production of less canonical works. Pierre Haultin's three volume
folio edition of Lancelot du Voisin de La Popelinière's *Histoire de
France* (1581) got both men into serious trouble with powerful
Swiss and French defenders of the Reformed church. The gift
copy of his text La Popelinière sent to Théodore de Bèze in
Geneva only elicited the churchman's revulsion. Bèze sharply
attacked La Popelinière for a lack of due reverence toward
Reformed doctrine and for his scholarly refrain from celebrating
the virtues of notable Protestants. Influential French Calvinists
denounced La Popelinière to Henry of Navarre, then protector
of all French Reformed churches. Henry wrote to La Rochelle's
town council demanding that exemplary punishment be meted
out to La Popelinière and his printer Haultin.[143] The town council demurred.

---

[140] E. Droz, *L'Imprimerie à La Rochelle*, vol. 3, *La veuve Berton et Jean Portau 1573-1589*, (Geneva, 1960), 70-73.

[141] See Louis Desgraves, *L'Imprimerie à La Rochelle*, 2, *Les Haultin 1571-1623*, (Geneva, 1960).

[142] For example, between 1572 and 1613, the Haultins produced twenty-two editions of the psalter and fourteen separate French editions of the New Testament. About 90 percent of the texts issued by the Haultins were in French, Desgraves, *Les Haultin*, xxi-xxiii.

[143] *Ibid.*, xix, and xxix-xxx. La Popelinière and Haultin were allied not only by business connections but also through ties of fictive kinship. La Popelinière was the godfather of Haultin's daughter Marie.

The local minister, Odet de Nort, then took the lead in hounding both men for acts of contrition expiating their alleged calumnies of French Calvinists. To up the pressure, de Nort secured condemnation of La Popelinière's book by the 1581 national synod meeting in La Rochelle. The assembled churchmen examined the text and concluded that "in many places the author speaks exceedingly irreverently and irreligiously of divine things, and that it is a heap of idle, vain, and profane matters, full of falsehoods, lies, and calumnies to the great prejudice of God's glorious power, to the disadvantage and dishonor of holy doctrine and Reformed religion, to the defamation of divers godly persons living and dead."[144] The synod declared La Popelinière unfit for communion until he personally atoned for his faults and prepared an expurgated version of his history.

Under this barrage of criticism, La Popelinière capitulated, accepting the synod's guidance in rewriting his text. A copy of the first volume of La Popelinière's *Histoire* "corrected" by de Nort and other synod participants is preserved in La Rochelle's municipal library. Offensive passages have been crossed out (they remain legible) and corrections by the censors neatly hand-written into the margins.[145] Sixteenth-century books displaying such cuts and emendations imposed by official Calvinist censors are great bibliographic rarities.

From the expurgated copy kept in La Rochelle, it is clear that de Nort and his colleagues were determined to suppress only one specific argument developed in the text. La Popelinière's assertion that the freedom of the laity to debate Protestant church doctrine constituted a salutary, driving force of the Reformation was systematically effaced by his critics. Recurrent positive references to Protestant "schismatics," to "the opinionated faithful," to "the controversial Christian faith," and to the "good zeal" and "opinions" of humble believers were all expunged or reworded by senior church officials.[146] The censors entirely removed La

---

[144] Quick, *Synodicon*, 1: 138. The book condemnations de Nort engineered at the 1581 national synod in La Rochelle accompanied the assembly's sad acknowledgement that "there is a notorious contempt of religion in all places, yea also in our religious meetings." To correct this failing, the synod ordered all French Calvinists always to bring their prayer books and psalters to church.

[145] See La Popelinière, *Histoire de la France*, vol. 1 (La Rochelle: Haultin, 1581), BMLR, Rés. 40 A.

[146] *Ibid.*, 1r, 2r, 7r-v, 8r, and 9v for examples.

Popelinière's observation that doctrinal and political conflicts between high French Catholic prelates and Protestant nobles had loosened the police of society, greatly encouraging licentious religious speculations among "the people and, above all, the ordinary residents of cities."[147]

Pastor de Nort was instrumental in censoring the condemned text. The modifications he commanded in the 1581 rochelais edition of La Popelinière's *Histoire de France* reflect local churchmen's great discomfort with the circulation of unorthodox religious opinions inside their own congregations. All of La Popelinière's historical precedents illuminating and potentially legitimating divergent popular interpretations of Calvinist doctrine and ecclesiastical government were removed in a vain effort by ranking clerics to reassert their monopoly over biblical exegesis and church discipline. The amplitude of this scandal was commensurate with de Nort's own fears about the irreverent, speculative powers of his fellow citizens, rich, middling, and poor.

Read in the context of endemic rochelais political and religious dissent, even the vocabulary of popular Calvinist works that passed clerical censorship possessed the potential to encourage new public challenges toward the authority of the Reformed church hierarchy. In 1581, Pierre Haultin also published the first rochelais edition of Philippe de Mornay's *Traicté de l'église*, a refutation of Catholic religious rites and a defense of Calvinism as the only true form of Christian worship.[148]

In a chapter describing ministers' legitimate duties in the reformation of the Christian religion, Mornay employs civic terminology likening the true church to a besieged town wherein every resident, no matter how humble, has the right to participate in the common defense and denounce internal weaknesses. According to Mornay, this right to be heard extends even to "the most vile and contemptible" inhabitants of the city/church.[149] Among

---

[147] *Ibid.*, 13r. La Popelinière's critics evidently spent far more time excising passages like these than they did rectifying the author's occasional statements about the moral lapses of Calvinist ministers or the frequency with which great men, ancient and modern, had the good fortune to die while making passionate love to their mistresses; see 141r, 173r, and 229r.

[148] Louis Desgraves, *Les Haultin*, 27. See also Desgraves' article, "Aspects des controverses entre catholiques et protestants dans le Sud-ouest, entre 1580 et 1630," *Annales du Midi* (1964): 153-187, especially 162 and n. 23.

[149] Philippe de Mornay, *Traicté de l'église*, (London, 1579), 257, "Quand donc

the "combourgeois" and "concitoyens" who Mornay believed embody city or church, consultation over how best to achieve collective welfare is essential. The architects of the early Christian church clearly recognized this verity, Mornay emphasizes, when they predicated the final ordination of ministers upon the consent of all the people within the congregation.[150] While no partisan of the democratic schismatic Morély, Mornay unequivocally calls upon all humble congregants to assert their concerns about the health of their church.

Couched in these terms, Mornay's ostensible subject, "the legitimate vocation of ministers to restore the church," cannot be construed so narrowly. His similes and metaphors empower both clergy and laity to take active roles in defense of the true church as they respectively conceive it. Such authorizations would have been particularly encouraging to the *combourgeois* and *concitoyens* of La Rochelle who had not only direct experience of what life in a city under siege was like, but who also had long shown a solicitude for congregational church government and a willingness to dispute the powers of ministers outside and inside the *église*. The Haultins, highly successful in judging the literary tastes of their urban clientele, printed multiple editions of Mornay's *Traicté*. In thousands of exemplars, this book gave ordinary, literate Rochelais further license to engage themselves decisively in the reform of church and state.

The Haultins' printshop also became a main conduit by which the texts and ideas emerging from foreign Reformations reached La Rochelle. Jerôme Haultin's successor Camille Hartmann brought out the first French west country edition of John Napier's *A Plaine Discovery of the Whole Revelation of Saint John*.[151] One of the most influential prophets of Scottish church reform, Napier employed a complex numerology to foretell the accelerating decline and eventual destruction of the Roman Catholic church.[152] To share his Protestant revelations with the widest pos-

---

nous serions les plus viles et contemptibles de l'église, nous meritons d'être ouys."

[150] "Finalement par le consentement de tout le peuple, on leur donne l'imposition des mains, les authorisant de prescher...Que le Ministre de l'église soit ordonné par l'Election du clergé, et par le consentement du peuple," *ibid.*, 263.

[151] The English text was translated as *Ouverture des secrets de l'Apocalypse ou revelation de S. Jean*, (La Rochelle, 1603).

[152] See Clouse, "John Napier and Apocalyptic Thought," 110-114.

sible audience, Napier composed his text in the simplest English
for which he apologized in the book's dedication to James I.
Hartmann's equally accessible French version was prepared by the
Scotch-born Calvinist pastor George Thomson who was minister-
ing to the Reformed congregation at La Châtaigneraie in the
Vendée.

While Napier's apocalyptic text undoubtedly appealed to the
Rochelais' penchant for divination and speculation on the religious significance of ominous natural forces like the sea, the wording of its French translation also explicitly established parallels
between the social composition of cities and the constitution of
a heavenly church. Such modes of argument would certainly have
attracted and flattered the attention of town dwellers. In Thomson's French, Napier describes the elect as "ceux de l'église glori-
fiée, qui en sont les bourgeois et habitans."[153] According to
Napier, the faithful are the householders of heaven, the "bourgeois de la joyeuse demeur de la vie eternelle."[154] In La Rochelle,
the dissemination of analogies celebrating the citizenship of the
saved contributed to the culture of an urban Reformed church,
a culture in which the putative sanctity of ordinary burghers
assembled in their congregations counterbalanced the moral
authority of the deacons, elders, and ministers comprising the
higher ranks of the visible church.

Recurrently censured by regional and national bodies of Calvinist clerics for producing unorthodox publications, Protestant
printers in La Rochelle operated in a very uneasy alliance with
Reformed churchmen. With immediate access to a literate audience endowed with eclectic reading habits and possessing sufficient disposable commercial income to afford printed works of
all kinds, rochelais booksellers flaunted the strictures officious
Genevans, meddling local clerics, and distant French royal officials tried to impose on the publishing trade. The mechanics of
this art provided fellow members of La Rochelle's third estate with
a steady supply of arguments by which to justify their faith and
question its rightful manifestations. This process of acculturation
was only intermittently directed, at best, by ordained ministers who had to steel themselves against the often irreverent

---

[153] Napier, *Ouverture*, 380.
[154] *Ibid.*, 386.

and usually challenging opinions of their restive congregants.

As reviewed here, the history of La Rochelle's Reformation reveals an Atlantic port town whose inhabitants looked ambivalently at the strictures Calvinism attempted to impose on private behavior and public affairs. An enduring popular anticlericalism, rooted in fears of priestly black magic, made ordinary town dwellers wary of the dictates and alleged prerogatives of Reformed clerics. The fractious politics of the city, a vibrant urban calendar of mocking corporative festivals, and the citizenry's litigious habits all impeded orthodox Protestant confessionaliztion of the populace. The pronounced congregational sympathies of the Rochelais, endorsed in both the testamentary practices of the citizenry and in numerous pamphlets and treatises published and read in town, also became a bulwark against clerical control over popular devotions. Such identities were strongly reinforced by the neighborhood militia companies that enrolled homeowners throughout the city and formed the backbone of the city's collective defense.

As will be shown in subsequent chapters, the social influence of La Rochelle's pastorate was decisively broken when prominent merchants and militia company members, disgruntled at the pretensions of municipal oligarchs and Calvinist pastors, successfully employed brute armed force to enter town government and push the clerics out of public affairs. The police of daily life Calvinist ministers and consistories struggled to achieve in continental Reformed communities seems to have been permanently beyond the grasp of churchmen in La Rochelle. This made La Rochelle an ever more peculiar adherent to the cause of French Protestantism and no doubt sapped the cohesion of Reformed communities in France, in part explaining the persistent minority status of Calvinists within the Bourbon realm.

Outlandish, suspicious, skeptical, and quarrelsome Rochelais repeatedly challenged local church administration and the operations of synodal ecclesiastical government at the regional and national levels. The following analysis of the city's tumultuous internal politics confirms the citizenry's many disruptive powers.

# CHAPTER FOUR

# THE COURSE OF URBAN POLITICS IN LA ROCHELLE AND THE CONSOLIDATION OF A CALVINIST GOVERNING OLIGARCHY, CIRCA 1560–CIRCA 1610

## 1. *Introduction*

The peculiar development of La Rochelle's Reformation, a movement ineluctably factionalizing the urban community while embroiling the town as a whole in the most violent conflicts of contemporary French statecraft, made local politics increasingly controversial and perilous after 1560. Although a large majority of the city's inhabitants accepted Calvinism, they did so with differing conceptions of what Calvinism meant and with varying degrees of discipline. A quickly consolidated Calvinist oligarchy controlling the town council and subordinate municipal offices successfully defended the city against Catholic counter-attacks. Threats of external aggression transiently unified a normally fractious urban community. But the frequent oscillations between belligerence and truce characteristic of the French Religious Wars left the rochelais body politic unsettled. Murderous infighting continually afflicted members of La Rochelle's Reformed governing elite who competed ruthlessly for power and preferment. These internecine political battles compounded religious conflicts within the urban population and greatly alarmed the few remaining agents of the crown who struggled fruitlessly to preserve royal authority in La Rochelle and its region. Reweaving the history of these deeply interconnected events clarifies not only the neglected, long-term institutional history of La Rochelle, but also the multiple effects of the French Religious Wars on one early modern urban community at the center of that bloody cataclysm.

Confronted by the new necessity of maintaining diplomatic relations with other troubled French Reformed communities and with scheming Protestant grandees whose faithfulness could never be trusted, La Rochelle's Calvinist town council entered a period when it could not formulate policy and govern with the independence it would have preferred. Inconsistencies in its diplomacy, by turns bellicose and conciliatory toward external powers, increased the number of its local critics and gave them new occasions on which to demand sweeping changes in the personnel and structure of civic administration. Having repeatedly placed their city in imminent danger of armed aggression from outside, La Rochelle's town councillors often found themselves compelled to appoint special emergency committees of neighborhood leaders charged with organizing effective communal defense. These committees regularly included townsmen otherwise ineligible to serve in municipal offices.

At moments of extreme risk, the town council also convened general assemblies of all residents, primarily to exhort popular acceptance of the council's latest decisions. Nonetheless, during the tumultuous decades of the French Wars of Religion, the greater frequency of such assemblies gave even the most humble Rochelais unprecedented opportunities to participate directly in the politics and defense of their community. The citizenry's growing engagement in civic affairs coincided with the monopolization of municipal officeholding by the city's narrow Protestant ruling oligarchy. These contemporaneous, antithetical developments heightened tensions between governors and governed, priming the city for violent, revolutionary changes in its old political system. By the early seventeenth century, the French crown threatened La Rochelle with destruction because the town had become a double epicenter of religious schism and innovative communal government.

## 2. Conversions in Civic Rulership

The pace of Reformation accelerated in La Rochelle due to the city's isolation from organs of Catholic indoctrination, because of its residents' obdurate anticlericalism, and through the rapid conversion of influential patrician families to the new faith. The course of local religious reform could not be definitively arrested through royal intervention because crown envoys rarely visited the city for more than a few weeks at a time and because the principal indigenous noble servants of the monarchy, like the Jarnacs, also became Calvinists. By 1560, many of La Rochelle's senior town councilmen actively supported evangelization of the west country, employing their own homes and urban properties to shelter Reformed church services. The royal governor of La Rochelle and its region, Guy Chabot de Jarnac, appointed in January 1559, only gained admission to the city in 1561 after town councillors had assured themselves that his conversion to Calvinism was genuine.[1] Although he labored cautiously to uphold royal policies and chastised the Rochelais for disobedience, Jarnac nonetheless obliged his new hosts by authorizing an expansion of public Calvinist religious services.[2]

A growing number of converts among city councillors did not produce a municipal government sympathetic toward Protestant extremists nor ready to excuse violations of town law committed by zealous Calvinists. Civic officials did not censure popular diatribes against Catholic church personnel, heated criticism that induced a majority of priests, monks, and nuns to quit La Rochelle in 1561. However, that same year, city fathers swiftly and severely punished a band of sailors who robbed and murdered one of the few remaining "Papist" clerics. The perpetrators had their right hands chopped off by the town executioner and were then summarily hanged in the city square closest to the scene of the crime.[3]

Despite mounting provocations by Catholic partisans, neither Jarnac nor the *corps de ville* in La Rochelle as yet prepared to abandon a calculated neutrality in the nascent religious conflict or to give up protestations of fidelity to the crown. Beginning in 1562, a succession of destabilizing events eroded and finally broke this common resolve. The massacre of Protestants at Vassy in March 1562 greatly alarmed the Rochelais and convinced the town council only weeks later to elect the first avowedly Calvinist mayor, Jean Pineau. Contemporaries remarked that Pineau was the first chief executive carried into office primarily because of his forthright and public practice of Calvinism.[4]

---

[1] BMLR, MS 2667/2, pièce 1. See also Amos Barbot, "Histoire de La Rochelle," AHSA 17 (1889): 164.

[2] Louis-Etienne Arcère, *Histoire de la ville de La Rochelle et du pays d'Aunis*, 2 vols., (La Rochelle, 1756; reprint Marseille, 1975), 1: 337-338. Jarnac consistently facilitated Calvinist church services by entrusting the consistory with the use and maintenance of abandoned Catholic religious structures.

[3] Barbot, "Histoire de La Rochelle," AHSA 17 (1889): 165.

[4] *Ibid.*, 169. Pineau was also strongly backed by his brother, Guillaume, an *échevin* and notable member of the oldest Calvinist congregation in the city.

In a contemporaneous letter to Catherine de Medici, Jarnac recommended an immediate reinforcement of royal gendarmes in La Rochelle and a prudent expansion of religious liberties to cool local tempers. Jarnac assured the regent that the bulk of the urban population was composed of "gens de bien, bons serviteurs de la couronne."[5] However, the city also contained "a number of willful rogues from all nations" who might be dissuaded from even greater follies by more regular Calvinist churchgoing. No reinforcement of royal troops occurred.

The consolidation of a Protestant party around the prince Louis de Condé further complicated the tasks of government in La Rochelle. Condé invited the Reformed churches of Saintonge and Aunis to back his defense of the faith on a national scale with arms, munitions, troops, and cash. In April 1562, the rochelais pastor Ambroise Faget secured a subsidy for the rebel prince from La Rochelle's consistory.[6] Jarnac, backed by a majority of the town council, strongly opposed these preludes to sedition and used his influence to silence Faget and banish him temporarily from the city. It is within the context of this discord between lay and ecclesiastical leaders that the first serious outbreak of popular iconoclasm occurred in La Rochelle on 31 May 1562. Mayor Pineau and governor Jarnac jointly condemned the sack of parish churches by crowds of poorer citizens. Their unfeigned opprobrium derived from a common interpretation of this vandalism as a popular rebuke of their own refusal to support Condé's militancy. At the very least, the well-known religious allegiances of Pineau and Jarnac induced the vandals to act with expectations of impunity.[7]

---

[5] BMLR, MS 2935/11, letter of Jarnac to Catherine de Medici dated 2 March 1562. Jarnac warned the queen that "la ville est garnye de toutes nations de gens barbares qui n'ont cognoissance que de leur particulière volonté et pour les contenir et empescher qu'ils facent les folz vous ne trouverez maulvays, Madame...qui n'y auroit meilleur que de leur donner liberté de l'Evangile et qu'ilz lussent des presches..." Here begins Jarnac's long running commentary to the crown about the "fools" and "follies" gathered in La Rochelle. His dispatches reinforced the general reputation of the west country as a politically unstable and psychically destabilizing environment.

[6] See Arcère, *Histoire de la ville de La Rochelle*, 1: 336-337, and R.M. Kingdon, *Geneva and the Coming of the Wars of Religion in France 1555-1563*, (Geneva, 1956), 109-110.

[7] Arcère, *Histoire de la ville de La Rochelle*, 1: 337. Condé interpreted this outbreak of violence as a clear signal of popular support for his cause in La Rochelle

The Calvinist beliefs of La Rochelle's captains brought them more insistent requests for logistical support and alliance from imprudent Protestant notables. Count François de La Rochefoucauld, a kinsman of Condé and one of his most influential loyalists in the west country, sent numerous embassies to La Rochelle urging town governors to back the prince's party. Jarnac refused outright and the *corps de ville* replied by sending two deputies directly to the king charged with disavowing any rochelais interest in joining the radical Protestant resistance.

La Rochefoucauld's agents then conspired with several disaffected citizens to organize a coup d'etat that would remove the existing town government and install a new regime devoted to Condé. The moderate *échevin* Jean Nicholas learned of this intrigue only hours before its scheduled perpetration on 26 September 1562. He immediately ordered a changing of the town watch at all gates and brought out the city artillery. Informed of these alarms, Jarnac opened his own arsenals and armed the citizens loyal to him. Confronted by forewarned opponents, La Rochefoucauld and his rochelais partisans drew back from their attack and attempted to parley with the city's defenders. In no mood to negotiate, Jarnac opened fire with his cannons and drove off the Reformed conspirators.

News of this abortive cabal prompted the duc de Montpensier, commanding Catholic forces for the king in Guyenne, to demand a reception in La Rochelle for the purpose of inspecting and verifying the city's defenses. To allay local fears about his intentions, Montpensier promised to enter the city with only the forty cavaliers comprising his personal suite. However, this was a ruse. Making common cause with Jarnac, who remained deeply offended by the near success of La Rochefoucauld's complot, Montpensier ordered several hundred of his soldiers to disguise themselves as ordinary travellers and enter La Rochelle in small groups through different city gates. By the evening of 26 October 1562, the duke's troops within the walls easily outnumbered the rochelais militia. In a bloodless operation the next morning, these forces succeeded in escorting an entire regiment of Montpensier's army into the city. The duke thereby achieved complete military supremacy in town.

---

and promptly redoubled his efforts to win over uncommitted civic leaders. See Léopold Delayant, *Histoire des Rochelais*, 2 vols., (La Rochelle, 1870), 1: 206.

Jarnac's connivance in this plot ultimately proved fatal to his credibility among the Rochelais. Menaced by threats of assassination, he quit the city on 3 November and returned to his rural estates. Meanwhile, Montpensier issued a series of decrees mortifying to his unwilling hosts. The duke banned public and private Calvinist services. He exiled all pastors from La Rochelle and reestablished the Catholic church. Protestant iconoclasts were ordered to make full restitution for any damages previously done. All citizens got orders to participate in Catholic rites. Insubordination would be punishable by death. In contravention of La Rochelle's municipal privileges, Montpensier deposed mayor Pineau for allegedly showing favoritism toward Calvinist extremists. This was the most sweeping attack to date on La Rochelle's Protestant community and civic constitution. These exactions only strengthened residents' commitment to the new faith and their resolve to dislodge Montpensier by any practical means. Moderate political figures now began to ally themselves with Reformed agitators for fear of watching royalist strongmen dismantle the city's highly privileged municipal government.[8]

For the moment, armed citizen resistance to Montpensier was potentially too catastrophic to contemplate. Bribery was employed instead. Residents swiftly raised an indemnity of 10,000 *livres* and turned it over to the duke. With cash in hand to pay his troops and amuse himself, Montpensier fulfilled the bargain and quit La Rochelle on 15 November 1562. To guard the city for the king, he left behind a garrison of 1,200 soldiers occupying the massive seaward towers in the port district of Perrot.

The Rochelais now turned their attention to placating and expelling this smaller force. They got help in this endeavor from an unexpected quarter. In late November, an envoy at court returned to La Rochelle with royal letters authorizing recall of all ministers except Faget, reappointing Jarnac as sole military governor of the city, and stipulating that no inhabitants should be

---

[8] To overawe the angry Rochelais, Montpensier let it be known that he contemplated razing La Rochelle's walls. Although this plan was countermanded by more senior and more prudent royal commanders in the west, irreparable damage had already been done to support for the crown in La Rochelle. See Arcère, *Histoire de la ville de La Rochelle*, 1: 340, and M. Massiou, *Histoire politique, civile et religieuse de la Saintonge et de l'Aunis*, 6 vols., (Paris, 1836-1838), 4: 83.

troubled in any way on account of their religion.[9] For added leverage, town councillors offered Montpensier's lieutenant 1,200 *livres*
to pay off his men and leave town. When the outsider dallied in
order to up the price of his withdrawal and Jarnac refused to
intervene, city fathers risked the use of force. On 27 December
1562, at a moment when the senior garrison officers were
patrolling away from the port, the town watch backed by armed
householders seized gates and towers cutting off the commanders
from the bulk of their men. Firefights broke out at several points
leaving two Rochelais dead and many wounded. The garrison
remained divided. Under continuous sniper attack, the Catholic
captains bolted from the city. Leaderless, inadequately supplied,
and facing a hostile, well-armed citizenry, the Catholic troops
caught in the towers negotiated a safe conduct out of town and
abandoned La Rochelle during the first week of February 1563.
This victory charged residents' morale and emboldened Calvinist
evangelists.

Profiting from city fathers' diminished vigilance in the wake of
the garrison's departure, another of La Rochefoucauld's provo-
cateurs, captain Chesnet, attempted a new Protestant takeover of
La Rochelle on 8 February. Abetted by sympathetic residents in
the popular dockside quarter of Perrot, Chesnet managed to land
thirty heavily armed followers within the port. Joining up with several hundred rochelais supporters assembled at a tennis court and
tavern in Perrot, these soldiers stormed into the old city, shouting "Vive l'Evangile!" Moment by moment, more armed citizens
rallied to their battle cry.

Caught totally by surprise, royal judges of the presidial court
and many town councillors including Jean Nicholas, the *échevin*
who thwarted the last Protestant coup attempt, were immediately arrested. The acting mayor, the Calvinist Guillaume Pineau,
eluded capture and hid out for several hours in a stable. Awaiting
mounted reinforcements from outside, Chesnet took the bulk of
his force toward the St. Nicolas gate and squandered precious
time trying unsuccessfully to break it down. In the interim, sev-

---

[9] Delayant, *Histoire des Rochelais*, 1: 209. These moves were precursors of the
Peace of Amboise which ended the First War of Religion in March 1563. This
treaty guaranteed freedom of conscience and religious expression to French
Calvinists.

eral of Chesnet's notable prisoners managed to escape, arm themselves, and reassemble under the leadership of Pineau.

Taking to the streets and calling out "Vive l'Evangile, Vive le Roi, et Vive le Maire!," Pineau's battalion caught Chesnet and his men as they tried to regain the port. At the mayor's summons to surrender, most of the insurgents' local supporters fell back, laid down their weapons, or went over to Pineau's side. A brief exchange of musket shots scattered Chesnet's last loyalists into adjoining buildings where they were surrounded and forced to capitulate. The latest Protestant coup attempt collapsed in a matter of hours.[10]

At the behest of Count Charles de Burie, lieutenant general for the king in Aunis and Guyenne, Chesnet and his co-conspirators were tried for treason in La Rochelle. Among the accused were several Rochelais including a jeweller, a shoemaker, a stevedore, and other workingmen from port neighborhoods.[11] Seven of the defendants including natives of La Rochelle received guilty verdicts and death sentences. They suffered public dismemberment and had their heads staked up on the city gate they had tried to violate. A detachment of Burie's troops exiled the pastor Nicolas Folion, widely suspected of abetting Chesnet's assault. No protests by city residents interrupted or impeded these legal proceedings.

Although the socioeconomic status of those tried cannot be assumed to typify all of Chesnet's enthusiastic supporters, it appears that some skilled artisans and laborers, especially in the Perrot quarter, were quickly attracted to the cause of militant Protestantism. Many of their social superiors throughout La Rochelle regarded this zealotry with enduring ambivalence and questioned whether its motives were more political than religious.

Montpensier's exactions followed by Chesnet's nearly successful attack on municipal authorities combined to polarize rochelais politics. Three wary factions hotly contested the spring 1563 mayoral election. The city's remaining Catholics and their few co-religionists on the town council desperately sought moderation in

---

[10] See Arcère, *Histoire de la ville de La Rochelle*, 1: 341; Barbot, "Histoire de La Rochelle," AHSA 17 (1889): 194-96; and Delayant, *Histoire des Rochelais*, 1: 210-211. The king was so impressed with Guillaume Pineau's rally against the coup attempt that he conferred on the loyal mayor the office and fees of a *maître d'hôtel* in the royal household.

[11] Barbot, "Histoire de La Rochelle," AHSA 17 (1889): 196.

civic affairs without courting material ruin or physical extermi-
nation. Cautious Protestants, hoping to reconcile freedom of conscience and submission to the king while conserving civic privileges, formed another block known as the "politiques et royaux."
Prominent Catholics maintained clandestine contacts with this
group. These parties were individually and collectively opposed
by the "zelés," a hardcore Calvinist faction demanding pure advancement of the Reformation regardless of the cost in lives or
treasure. For mayor in 1563, the *zelés* backed their most prominent adherent, *maître* Jean Pierres, lieutenant civil and criminal
on La Rochelle's presidial court. Pierres was favored by the
*échevins* Raoullet du Jau and Pierre Thevenin, whose intermarried
families were pillars of the local Calvinist church. Pierres could
also count on the support of determined Calvinists occupying several subordinate presidial court offices. By 1563, zealous Protestants held key posts inside every powerful institution shaping
rochelais politics. Under these conditions, the infighting of religious factions was aggravated by bureaucratic turf battles and the
pettier squabbles of status-hungry officeholders in a provincial
town.

Still controlling a majority of votes on the town council, the
*politiques* with Catholic help managed in primary balloting to produce a slate of three finalists for mayor that did not include Jean
Pierres. Among the finalists, the *échevins* Jean Nicholas and Guillaume Pineau had already shown themselves inhospitable to
Protestant militancy. The third finalist, the *échevin* Michel Guy, was
also serving simultaneously as the collector of the royal *taille* for
the government of La Rochelle. Guy's mayoral bid had the support of prominent Catholics in town. Knowing that Guy stood the
best chance of being elected, the *zelés* vigorously opposed his candidacy on the grounds of a conflict of interest. They alleged that
Guy's current financial duties, involving verification of local tax
rolls, were incompatible with service as the city's chief executive.
Adjudication of this dispute was deferred to the Parlement of
Paris.

Before the distant court could render a verdict, Guy was duly
elected mayor the week after Easter and quickly sworn into office
by Amateur Blandin, the senior jurist on the presidial court. Blandin was a staunch royalist slow to abandon Catholicism. His later
conversion to Calvinism was equivocal and many townspeople long

regarded him as a crypto-Catholic.[12] By August 1563, Blandin was serving as Jarnac's principal lieutenant in La Rochelle.[13] This delegation of authority further discredited the city's royal governor among citizens determined to defend La Rochelle's Reformed congregations.

To challenge Guy's election, partisans of Jean Pierres claimed that official discrimination directed against their leader was the surest sign of Pierres' fitness for the mayor's office. They persuaded the second highest ranking member of the presidial, a committed Calvinist, to proclaim Pierres the rightful mayor of La Rochelle at least until Guy's eligibility for the post could be legally determined. For several weeks two antagonistic mayors asserted exclusive authority over the city, producing what one contemporary called an "extreme confusion" in civic affairs.[14] Raucous protests organized by each side paralyzed deliberations of the town council. To reiterate the scriptural dimensions of these hostilities, literate followers of the *politiques* and *zelés* inscribed their house fronts with Bible verses purportedly justifying their opposing political positions. Blunt threats and counter-threats publicly exchanged between the adversaries propagated their factions within every stratum of urban society. Finally, the arrival of royal letters patent establishing Michel Guy as lawful mayor compelled Pierres to withdraw his claim on the job, averting a hotter civil conflict between the opposing camps.

Anxious to deny the Rochelais new pretexts for dissension, Charles IX stipulated that Michel Guy was to hold the mayoralty until royal assent was given for resumption of annual elections. Moderate town councillors barely tolerated crown tampering with the machinery of local politics.[15] As Guy's tenure lengthened to

---

[12] Despite early and sincere conversions to Calvinism by many of his kin, Amateur Blandin shifted confession several times. His first documented presence at a Calvinist rite, the baptism of a niece, postdates his endorsement of Michel Guy by ten months. See ADCM, I 1, fol. 38v, 6 February 1564. On Blandin's persistent Catholic sympathies see Delayant, *Histoire des Rochelais*, 1: 212.

[13] See BMLR, MS 2935/14.

[14] Barbot, "Histoire de La Rochelle," AHSA 17 (1889): 202-203. See also Delayant, *Histoire des Rochelais*, 1: 212.

[15] In May 1564, Jarnac reported to the king that large delegations of town councilmen were pressing him to obtain from the crown a declaration stipulating exactly when regular mayoral elections would resume. See BMLR, MS 2935/15, letter of Jarnac to Charles IX and Catherine de Medici dated 16 May 1564.

three years (1563-1565), militants complained ever more bitterly about the degradation of civic institutions permitted by a majority of councillors lacking strong political and religious convictions. Restive town councilmen belonging to or sympathetic with the *zelés* demanded that Guy make all documents generated by his regime available for public inspection. His refusal to do so was met by boycotts of council meetings designed to deny Guy a working quorum. Letters patent forthcoming from the crown authorized decisions on council business by a bare majority of any councillors present.[16] This manoeuvre only incited more complaints about the debasement of municipal government by royal agents and traitorous natives.

To counter charges of gross irresponsibility, mayor Guy took the initiative in reorganizing and rearming La Rochelle's militia. Guy also ordered local royal fiscal officers to visit their Parisian superiors carrying with them reports on improved service under Guy's direction. The mayor used these communications to request additional tax exemptions for the residents of La Rochelle. In September 1564, Jarnac rebuked Guy for these endeavors, claiming that they intruded on his own authority as the king's governor and might provoke the crown to seize all municipal revenues (estimated at 50,000 *livres* per year) for the purpose of erecting a citadel and housing a permanent royal garrison in the city.[17] As news of this ominous reprimand circulated in town, Guy's credibility as a competent defender of his town and his church eroded more rapidly.

Popular animus toward hazardous expedients in civic government threatening local religious freedoms grew through the conjuncture of two events beyond the control of city councillors. On 4 August 1564 Charles IX promulgated the Edict of Roussillon sharply curtailing rights of worship and assembly previously accorded to French Protestants by the Peace of Amboise ending the First War of Religion.[18] By this gesture, the crown appeared

---

[16] Barbot, "Histoire de La Rochelle," AHSA 17 (1889): 204-06.

[17] BMLR, MS 2935/16, letter of Jarnac to Michel Guy, 2 September 1564. The emplacement of such a garrison would not only outrage the Rochelais, but also force Jarnac to share local administrative authority with a new cadre of royal servants, an outcome unfavorable to all parties currently trying to manage the city.

[18] Arcère, *Histoire de la ville de La Rochelle*, 1: 344-45. On the political and religious machinations resulting in the Roussillon declaration, see R.M. Kingdon, *Geneva and the Consolidation of the French Protestant Movement*, (Geneva, 1967), 157-

to countenance and encourage growing Catholic disregard for the stipulations of the peace treaty protecting Reformed congregations. This reversal of toleration coincided with Odet de Nort's establishment as a new pastor in La Rochelle's growing Calvinist church. Lauded as "a great servant of God and an incomparable preacher," de Nort employed his eloquence to denounce the crown's perfidy in violating prior peace accords.[19] La Rochelle's other Genevan-trained ministers joined their voices to this chorus of complaint, exhorting their congregants to oppose implementation of new royal edicts and to recognize the king and his minions as inveterate enemies of the faithful.[20]

Rumors of impending sedition orchestrated by the pastors prompted Jarnac to urge the king's inspection of La Rochelle during his great *tour de France*. A royal descent on the city occurred in September 1565. From the outset, things went badly for the Rochelais. Leading the king's advance guard, the constable Anne de Montmorency confiscated all of the city's artillery pieces and removed them from the walls for security reasons. Montmorency cancelled local plans for celebratory vollies of firearms to greet the sovereign. Approaching town, Charles IX broke with tradition and refused formally to confirm La Rochelle's municipal privileges as a condition of his admission. When pressed by the mayor to acknowledge these civic rights, the monarch curtly replied, "You be my loyal servants and I will be your good king."[21]

Multiple avowals of fidelity to the crown worked into the welcoming ceremonies did not dispel royal suspicions of the citizenry's disloyalty. Goaded by Jarnac's unfavorable reports, Charles

---

162. This edict expressly forbid local or national synods of the French Reformed Church and specifically enjoined French Protestants from raising money through such regional assemblies of churchmen.

[19] Barbot, "Histoire de La Rochelle," AHSA 17 (1889): 211.

[20] According to Barbot, "par le mouvement desquels pasteurs...les habitans prenoient diverses licences et y en avoit qui médisoient et invectivoient du Roi, de la Reine, et du conseil et se portoient d'empêcher ladite execution des déclarations faites sur ledit édit," cited in Arcère, *Histoire de la ville de La Rochelle*, 1: 345.

[21] Delayant, *Histoire des Rochelais*, 1: 216. Riding before his sovereign in the entry procession, Montmorency was the first to spy the ribbon of blue silk city councilmen customarily drew across the open town gate through which kings would pass. Visiting monarchs traditionally stopped at this symbolic barrier and swore to uphold La Rochelle's privileges before proceeding into the city. Montmorency sliced the cordon in half with his sword, advising chagrined natives that such customs were now obsolete.

IX issued a series of decrees shortly after his arrival intended to repress Protestant dissent in La Rochelle. The king ordered that the *corps de ville* be reduced in size from one hundred to twenty-four members. Jarnac's prerogative to choose the winning candidate for mayor from three finalists selected by town councilmen was reiterated. All city cannons were to be turned over to governor Jarnac, who was to sequester these weapons in La Rochelle's great towers. The king commanded all residents to obey Jarnac's orders promptly. To remove Jarnac's most tenacious Reformed critics, the king gave pastor Nicolas Folion forty-eight hours to leave town and exiled indefinitely seven other citizens including such militant Protestants as Jean Pierres, lieutenant general of the presidial, and the *échevins* Jean Morrison and Pierre Thevenin. All public Calvinist church services were suspended for the duration of the king's visit. This attempt to decapitate the leadership of the *zelés* only produced greater public sympathy for the movement and its native avatars.[22] The monarch's evident hostility toward the Reformed religion and toward La Rochelle's ancient civic constitution convinced many residents that local pastors had been justified in advocating armed resistance against the crown.

Protestant worship resumed in La Rochelle immediately after the departure of king and court in late September 1565. Although Jarnac remained in the city, threats against his life became so numerous that he rarely ventured out of his house unless accompanied by at least twenty mounted bodyguards. Increasingly fearful of personal harm and abandonment by his superiors, Jarnac sent a stream of dispatches to court warning the king against any reductions in the local *gendarmerie*. He begged the queen regent to make good on her promises of augmented funding for his garrison expenses and threatened withdrawal to his country manors if relaxations were made in earlier royal edicts policing the city. By December 1565, Jarnac no longer spoke of a rochelais population comprised largely of "gens de bien." Now he found himself surrounded by "ces méchants" with whom there were dwindling chances of reconciliation.[23] Jarnac's predicament came about because the king to whom he answered now attacked the

---

[22] BMLR, MSS 45/46, 966. Delayant, *Histoire des Rochelais*, 1: 217-218.
[23] BMLR, MS 2667/2, letter of Jarnac to Charles IX and Catherine de Medici, 27 December 1565.

city's ancient constitution and nascent Reformed church simultaneously.

Guy Chabot de Jarnac's fear of eclipse at court stemmed in part from his own father's inconstant support by François I and Henry II. Moreover, like his progenitor, Jarnac had to confront the vexing ability of the Rochelais to achieve by dogged petitions or opportune bribery what they could not gain through brute force. Within days of the king's exit from La Rochelle, city fathers began a concerted lobbying campaign to recover their old system of town government and their exiled compatriots. They extolled the sagacity of Charles' father who restored the one hundred-member city council in 1548. To a king with a nearly empty treasury, they pointed out the debilitating costs and inefficient police of Jarnac's garrison. A restored town council would dutifully, even gladly superintend urban defense and pay its costs. Current and former town councillors finally drew up a solemn declaration of their submission to royal authority and renewed their pledges to guard La Rochelle only for the king.

To Charles, assurances of fidelity now mattered less than promises of economy in royal expenditure. On 1 January 1566, the king sent Jarnac a blunt communiqué. Effective immediately, Jarnac was to disband ("licencier") the fifty musketeers comprising his garrison and bodyguard. The soldiers' pay was to be stopped at once and the crown would not remunerate them for any services rendered between January 1 and the date on which news of their irrevocable termination reached La Rochelle. Jarnac himself got orders to evacuate the city and turn over all towers, arsenals, and artillery to the mayor. All one hundred members of the old town council were reestablished in their offices and all exiles (again except pastor Folion) were free to return. The king ordered Jarnac to execute these commands "without delay or difficulty."[24]

His majesty's wishes were not obeyed. For months, Jarnac petitioned the king and queen mother, seeking maintenance of his

---

[24] BMLR, MS 2935/25, Charles IX to Jarnac, 1 January 1566. See also BMLR, MSS 45/46, 966. It is highly probable that successful overtures to the king made by prominent Rochelais were accompanied by promises of substantial cash "gifts" should Charles grant the requests for Jarnac's removal. However, I have found no evidence in La Rochelle or Paris that such transactions occurred. Given the charged French environment of politics and religion in 1566, both parties to such a bargain would have taken great pains to conceal it.

office through dire warnings about sedition brewing in La Rochelle. On 19 January 1566, he exclaimed to Charles, "you should remember, Sire, THE GREAT REBELLIONS, ERRORS, AND FAULTS THAT THE ROCHELAIS HAVE COMMITTED AGAINST FRENCH KINGS FOR OVER ONE HUNDRED YEARS."[25] Two weeks later, Jarnac sought backing in his suit from the Count de Chaulnes, urging his patron at court to see the folly in diminution of royal police at La Rochelle. Dissolving his authority, Jarnac predicted, would give a free hand to "a community of rebels so crazed and seditious that over a century they have committed a dozen acts warranting revocation of their privileges, confiscation of all municipal income, imposition of a citadel, and execution for at least twenty leading citizens."[26] While voicing these protests, Jarnac refused to abandon city towers under his control. The beleaguered governor reluctantly quit La Rochelle only after the king's lieutenant general from Poitiers read the royal evacuation order to his face in March 1566. Jarnac sulked at his château. He vowed to rectify "this wrong and shame done to an old soldier who has loyally served no less than three French kings."[27] Jarnac's evident disdain for Charles' behavior coupled with his persistent demands to the crown for reimbursement of his unpaid garrison expenses guaranteed that his appeals fell on deaf ears in Paris.

From his rural exile, Jarnac tried unavailingly to warn his correspondents at court that the preliminary balloting for the 1566 mayoral election in La Rochelle had been fixed by his chief opponents on the town council. The strategy of these "thieves," ("larrons"), Jarnac alleged, was to protect their ill-gotten political influence by engineering the election of his former deputy, Amateur Blandin, a man whose long service as a royal magistrate and whose reputation as a religious moderate made him outwardly appealing to the crown, but whose local unpopularity would always force him to compromise with his scheming electors in order to get

---

[25] BMLR, MS 2667/2, Jarnac to Charles IX, 19 January 1566. Capitalization in the original.
[26] BMLR, MS 2935/19, Jarnac to the first Count de Chaulnes, 31 January 1566. Jarnac castigated "une communauté si folle, sédicieuse et rebelle, que...depuis cent ans ilz ont faict une douzaine d'actes dignes de perdre leurs privilèges, oster leurs deniers commungs, leur fare une cytadelle et à une vingtaine des principaux la teste tranchée..."
[27] BMLR, MS 2935/20, Jarnac to Anne de Montmorency, 3 March 1566.

anything accomplished in town government.[28] Jarnac also reminded the king that his earlier edicts forbidding royal judges from
becoming mayors disqualified Blandin for command of La
Rochelle.

Ignoring all of Jarnac's admonitions, Charles IX promptly
ordered Blandin's confirmation as mayor. The king's determination to advance Blandin, despite previous injunctions prohibiting
the move and despite the objections of a formerly trusted royal
governor, suggests that the crown may have been fulfilling its part
of a tacit bargain struck earlier with rochelais city councilmen, a
deal of which Jarnac, as the principal victim, was wholly ignorant.
It is conceivable that city fathers (besides offering cash bribes)
promised the crown immediate election of a moderate as mayor
in exchange for the reestablishment of the one hundred-member
town council and for the dismissal of Jarnac. Blandin's curious
ascension to the mayoralty could thus be explained as a doubly
calculated risk promoted by town councilmen confident of his
weakness and by royalists expecting to aggrandize a new ally situated atop the municipal bureaucracy.

Blandin's first, unexpectedly bold official actions confirm his
ambition to make La Rochelle abide by the king's law and, in the
process, to enhance the authority of royal magistrates like himself at the expense of the town council. The new mayor moved
quickly to enforce the contemporaneous (1566) Edict of Moulins
by which Charles IX denied municipal tribunals the right to adjudicate civil cases, reserving these for royal courts. Such a reorganization of the law could only provoke alarm in a Protestant town
like La Rochelle endowed with a potent civic tribunal staffed primarily by Calvinists employing the court to defend the sanctity of
communal self-government. As the *assesseur* and *lieutenant particulier* of the king's presidial court in La Rochelle, Blandin would
augment his own judicial prerogatives (and income) by upholding the new edict. Selfishly breaking ranks with his fellow town
councillors, Blandin exposed himself to mounting criticism inside

---

[28] BMLR, MS 2667/2, Jarnac to Louis de Saint Gelays, 5 April 1566. In the
spring of 1566, Amateur Blandin's son, Jean, was the object of popular criticism
in La Rochelle for maintaining regular contacts with Guy Chabot de Jarnac outside the city. These protests may have been orchestrated by opponents of Blandin
and Jarnac seeking further reductions in the influence of royalists within the
urban community, Barbot, "Histoire de La Rochelle," AHSA 17 (1889): 232.

and outside the *corps de ville.* Blandin's defection generated strong opposition led by intermarried, staunchly Calvinist town councilmen and presidial magistrates fearful of innovations in communal justice diminishing the legal rank of Protestants.

Blandin's shocking bid for greater judicial authority turned even moderate Calvinists on the town council against him. Influential patrician families conspired to stymie proposed changes in the municipal system of justice. Blandin's scheme precipitated a temporary and crucial rapprochement between *politiques* and *zelés* on the *corps de ville,* as councillors of varying religious opinions united against a common enemy.[29] City fathers resolved to exclude Blandin from all electioneering prior to the next mayoral race. His chances of installing a loyal successor evaporated. Watching local politics spin out of Blandin's control, Jarnac warned the king that his copious favors to the Rochelais only reduced their respect for the crown and induced more leading citizens to behave recklessly. According to Jarnac, it was not religious fanaticism but exceptional civic liberties that fueled rochelais dissent.[30]

With the collapse of Amateur Blandin's administration, the 1567 mayoral race became an open contest as moderates and militants on the town council cast about to find an electable candidate. The troubles caused by Blandin, a seasoned veteran of local political infighting, augured against his replacement by a similarly experienced public figure. Blandin's frightening attack on communal institutions from inside civic government, apparently abetted by the crown, prompted militant electors to seek out a devotedly Calvinist candidate amenable to direction from their block.

Preliminary balloting yielded one aspirant capable of garnering votes from every camp: François Pontard, a twenty-seven-year-old *pair* whose recently deceased father had been a fervent builder of the first Calvinist congregation in the city and had long served as the *procureur du roi* on the local presidial court.[31] Through his family's personal and professional contacts, the younger Pontard was closely allied to Claude d'Angliers, president of the presidial

---

[29] Barbot, "Histoire de La Rochelle," AHSA 17 (1889): 236.

[30] BMLR, MS 2935/22, Jarnac to Charles IX and Catherine de Medici, 24 August 1566. To the king, Jarnac wrote, "Votre Majesté a faict faire tant de grâces et faveurs aux Rochelais que ceulx qui estoient sages sont devenus foulx."

[31] Barbot, "Histoire de La Rochelle," AHSA 17 (1889): 211.

and a fierce opponent of Amateur Blandin, and to Jean Pierres, the presidial officer leading the zelé faction in town politics.[32] In addition, François Pontard adroitly curried favor with governor Jarnac, invoking the close ties Pontard's father had maintained with Jarnac's predecessors and promising to perpetuate a family tradition of cordial relations with royal lieutenants in the west country. By such overtures, François Pontard engineered his own election as mayor in the spring of 1567. Capitalizing on new political alliances spawned in the wake of Blandin's escapade, Pontard managed to gain office while keeping his own ambitions well camouflaged under a thick web of auspicious family ties.

### 3. Town Politics Embroiled in Calvinist Dissent

Pontard's ascension to the mayoralty coincided with the end of Charles IX's policy of toleration toward Protestant critics of the monarchy. The resumption of civil war in the fall of 1568 brought renewed fighting to the French west country. Orléans was captured by rebel Calvinist forces on 28 September. Both religious camps now struggled to win control of strategic provincial towns. To counterbalance Protestant strength in the west, the crown ordered Jarnac to raise troops immediately and reoccupy La Rochelle. Charles commanded the town council to receive Jarnac and imposed an emergency levy of 3,000 livres on the community to defray costs for the reinstallation of the garrison. City fathers hesitated to obey. Unwilling to thwart the king's wishes all by themselves, they assembled the city's bourgeoisie and solicited its advice. Popular sentiment largely opposed reception of foreign troops. The insubordinate citizenry grew in size upon discovery that Amateur Blandin, chief advocate of compliance with crown policy, had abjured Calvinism several days earlier. Public fears of a Catholic fifth column inside the city mounted rapidly, inspired by the uncertain results of fighting on distant battle fronts.

Young, impetuous mayor Pontard seized this opportunity to throw off the tutelage of his elders and assert himself in defense

---

[32] Ibid., 255. Barbot refers to François Pontard as a "parent" of Claude d'Angliers. François Pontard's father had also served as the godfather of a son born to Jean Pierres in July 1563. See ADCM, I 1, fol. 3r.

of La Rochelle's Reformed community. Long importuned by his noble cousin, the *sieur* Jean de Sainte-Hermine (one of Condé's lieutenants), to join forces with the rebel prince, Pontard resolved to achieve this alliance by violent means. This course of action was dictated not simply by religious fervor, but also by patrician alarm over the imposition of a royal garrison and possible internal subversion of civic institutions.

In the early morning hours of 9 January 1568, Pontard led a contingent of armed supporters into the streets of La Rochelle, crying "To Arms!" Backed primarily by adherents of the *zelés*, Pontard rallied a force sufficient to occupy all of the city's main strong points. Accompanied by pastor Odet de Nort and *maître* Jean Pierres of the presidial, Pontard made the rounds of the city on horseback, deploying cannons from municipal arsenals to intimidate any potential adversaries. As the ranks of Pontard's faction swelled, rumors flew about a Catholic assault on the city and a plot to liquidate all Protestant residents. Coup commanders now stood back while their excited partisans surged into the remaining Catholic parish churches and ransacked them. Angry crowds confiscated ecclesiastical plate for the Protestant war chest. Twenty-seven priests were rounded up by mobs and driven into tower dungeons. Pontard's heavily armed captains targeted the homes of Catholic residents, sending more prisoners into dank confinement. At Pontard's demand, several moderately Protestant town councilmen were also hunted down and summarily arrested.[33]

Under cover of this violent confusion, antagonistic officeholders squared off against one another to settle old professional disputes permanently. The bailiff of the presidial court was publicly

---

[33] Barbot, *ibid.*, 270, gives the most complete list of captives taken during Pontard's coup. The notable Protestants imprisoned included the town counsellors Jean, Michel, and Pierre Guy (all presumably tainted by Michel's willing service as the king's appointed mayor of La Rochelle between 1563 and 1565); the *pair* Jacques du Lyon, who initially refused to give Pontard control of seaward towers under his watch; and the *échevins* Joseph Barbier, Zacherie Barbier, and Joseph l'Evesque whom Pontard accused of Catholic sympathies but whose real fault may simply have been their long status as challengers against several of Pontard's main supporters for control of disputed civic offices. Like most violent episodes in La Rochelle's history, the 1568 coup was animated by concurrent religious and political feuding between prominent townsmen, fights only occasionally in phase with power struggles at the regional or national level.

challenged and killed by a jealous colleague who falsely accused the victim of armed resistance against the providential coup.[34] Pontard's exploit caused further bloodshed when Protestant radicals massacred all of the captive priests. The executioners hurled the clerics' mutilated bodies into the sea from atop the city's gothic lantern tower. In this highly symbolic gesture, rochelais militants purged their community of spiritual enemies, consigning their polluted bodies to the ocean's foul dregs.

To consolidate his control of the city and its diplomacy, Pontard established a special advisory body of eleven town councilmen drawn primarily from the ranks of the zelés. Led by Jean Pierres and including at least one elder of the Reformed church, this Protestant junta authorized Pontard to disobey royal orders and refuse acceptance of Jarnac's garrison.[35] A week later, La Rochelle's entire town council, acknowledging a fait accompli, delegated to Pontard and his closest advisors discretionary use of the city's income and weaponry. The mayor immediately sent for Sainte-Hermine who arrived in La Rochelle on 23 January 1568 carrying letters from Condé establishing him as military governor of the city.[36]

Pontard arrested outspoken patricians opposed to this appointment. Purged of this opposition, the corps de ville ratified Sainte-Hermine's commission but firmly rejected a proposal to make him the next mayor of the city. Although Sainte-Hermine gained admittance into the bourgeoisie of La Rochelle, town councillors by secret ballot refused three times to give him a seat as a pair,

---

[34] Ibid., 272.

[35] Delayant, Histoire des Rochelais, 1: 223-24. Besides Pontard and Pierres, members of the emergency council included the échevins Guillaume Choisy, Jean Morrison, and Jean and Pierre Salbert, and the pairs Pierre Bouchet, Jacques Cochon, Pierre Gentils, Jean de la Haize, and Claude Huet. Bouchet and de la Haize were both attorneys accredited to the presidial. Cochon was one of the first elders of La Rochelle's Calvinist consistory. La Haize's brother was also serving at the time as an elder on the consistory. The Salbert brothers belonged to one of the most prominent Calvinist patrician families in La Rochelle. Besides his long involvement in the Reformed church, Jean Pierres was also connected by ties of fictive kinship to the radical pastor Nicholas Folion. Pierres' wife, Leonor Rondeau was the godmother of Folion's son, Tobias, baptised in March 1564. See ADCM, I 1, fol. 40r.

[36] On Sainte-Hermine and rochelais political machinations involving him see René Pétiet, "Un oublié, Jean de Sainte-Hermine gouverneur de La Rochelle," BSHPF, 59 (1910): 20-51.

the indispensable qualification for ascension to higher civic office.[37]

Although he was the virtual dictator of rochelais armed forces, Pontard made no effort to challenge or overturn Sainte-Hermine's successive electoral defeats. Even after delivering his city into Condé's camp, Pontard respected the undiminished voting authority of his fellow town councillors to insulate municipal government from undue influence by outsiders. Rochelais city fathers could never accept subservience to the rule of external magnates. This disdain had been and would long continue to be the organizing principle of civic politics, much to the consternation of great French nobles, Protestant and Catholic. While the Second War of Religion raged, La Rochelle's patricians approved only protective association with Condé's cause, never undying allegiance to his commands. As Pontard's chief local apologist asserted, the 1568 coup was necessary to assure freedom of conscience in La Rochelle, to protect the city against the intrigues of foreigners, and to aid Condé in defending "the liberties and civic privileges of the French people."[38]

The crown could mount no serious military challenge to the new regime in La Rochelle. Both the king and the royal captain Blaise de Monluc fruitlessly petitioned west country towns for the loan of troops, armaments, and cash without which no assault could be made against the Rochelais. Rebuffed everywhere, the old warrior Monluc refused to participate any longer in a campaign he labeled "a mockery and a farce."[39] Pontard and his confidants consolidated their government of La Rochelle.

To subsidize military preparations, Sainte-Hermine authorized seizure of all income from royal domains and excise taxes amassed in the region. By forced loans extracted from Catholic residents

---

[37] In special town council elections held in the spring of 1568 to fill three vacant seats among the *pairs*, Sainte-Hermine came dead last in each round of balloting, never receiving more that twenty-two votes out of one hundred cast. The council placed native-born Rochelais in each available position. See Barbot, "Histoire de La Rochelle," AHSA 17 (1889): 276; and Pétiet, "Un oublié," 49-50.

[38] Jean de la Haize, *Discours bref et veritable de ce qui s'est passé en la ville et gouvernement de La Rochelle depuis l'an mil cinq cent soixante sept jusque en l'année 1568*, 2nd edition, (La Rochelle, 1575), fol. B iiii, BMLR, Rés. 208c. This pamphlet originally appeared in 1568. See E. Droz, *L'Imprimerie à La Rochelle*, vol. 1, *Bartélémy Berton 1563-1573*, (Geneva, 1960), 60-63.

[39] Blaise de Monluc, *Commentaires 1521-1576*, (Paris: 1964), 623-628. City fathers

and Iberian merchants in La Rochelle new fortifications were built. Tombstones within the old parish Church of St. Sauveur were torn up and thrown into the defenses. Through impressment, labor gangs from the *banlieue* were brought in to level all structures outside the walls including Catholic churches and chapels. Internal dissent against the new regime was quelled by additional arrests of outspoken opponents. Jean Blandin, son of the apostate Amateur Blandin, an *échevin* popularly reviled for his denunciations of Pontard's coup, soon died mysteriously while in custody. Poisoning by agents of the junta was widely suspected.[40] To keep La Rochelle on a war footing, Pontard and Sainte-Hermine conspired to delay as long as possible official proclamation of the Peace of Longjumeau (3 March 1568) temporarily interrupting the Religious Wars.

Over the next three years, members of Pontard's faction managed to retain control of the mayor's office with at least the tacit support of most voting town councilmen. In 1568, all three of the finalists balloted for mayor, Pierre Bouchon, Jacques Cochon, and Jean Salbert, stood among Pontard's closest confidants. As the most senior royal officer actually serving in La Rochelle, Jean Pierres selected his brother-in-law, Jean Salbert, to be mayor in 1568. In 1569, Pontard, who was now first *échevin* of the city, engineered Salbert's renomination as a finalist for the mayoralty. Pierres again obliged by choosing his kinsman for mayor.[41] Guillaume Choisy, mayor of La Rochelle in 1570, had been a founding member of Pontard's eleven-man private council. These civic

---

in Bordeaux, Nantes, and Toulouse all refused to answer Monluc's calls for help. Pressed by the king to take La Rochelle, Monluc replied that in the present circumstances "only God could work such a miracle."

[40] Arcère, *Histoire de la ville de La Rochelle*, 1: 371; Barbot, "Histoire de La Rochelle," AHSA 17 (1889): 323.

[41] The young Henry de Navarre entreated rochelais municipal officials to reelect Salbert, a magistrate respected by most citizens and acceptable to great Protestant nobles. Although contrary to the tradition of a single term for each mayor, Salbert's consecutive mandates were not without precedent in the city's history. Henry scrupulously informed the Rochelais by letter that his preference for Salbert should not be construed in any way as an infringement of the city's privileges. The future king suggested that if the *corps de ville* duly participated in Salbert's reelection, no transgression of civic liberties could be imputed. "Il me semble que quand ladite continuation procédera de vous-même, et sera par vous faite, il ne sera fait breche à aucun de vos privileges..." Navarre promised to be a life-long "exact observateur" of all rochelais immunities. See Arcère, *Histoire de la ville de La Rochelle*, 1: 377-378.

leaders faced not only the exigencies of renewed civil war, but also the vexing presence of quarrelsome Protestant grandees in La Rochelle. The city was unaccustomed to the installation of aristocrats and the haughty manner of refugee nobles exacerbated urbanites' distrust of titled foreigners.

At the outbreak of the Third War of Religion, the Rochelais concluded a formal treaty of alliance with the Prince de Condé. As the principal conditions of their engagement, town negotiators demanded that Condé swear to maintain all of La Rochelle's privileges inviolate and to guarantee that all future military governors of the city would be Protestants.[42] In exchange for these promises, the Rochelais swore to obey Condé's orders and to join unreservedly in his armed defense of the French Reformed Church. However, the conclusion of this entente did not long prevent estrangement of the contracting parties over the direction and finance of their mutual cause. La Rochelle's wealthiest inhabitants balked at contributing to a forced loan of 120,000 *livres* demanded by bellicose Protestant nobles. When they drove down the city's contribution to 80,000 *livres*, even this smaller sum could not be raised, although confiscations of property were imposed on absent Catholics and Protestants tepid in their support for the cause. Humbler residents publicly accused mayor Salbert and senior Calvinist town councillors of lightening their own families' loan assessments and shifting the onus of military charges onto the poorer bulk of the citizenry.[43] Salbert and his cronies also profited from rigged sales of cargos captured by rochelais corsairs preying on coastal shipping with licenses obtained from Protestant

---

[42] *Ibid.*, 368 and marginal note XXXIII for quotations from the text of this treaty.

[43] *Ibid.*, 373-374; see also Delayant, *Histoire des Rochelais*, 1: 231. Contemporaries agreed that an imposition of 120,00 *livres* was far beyond the means of the Rochelais. Political infighting and economic rivalries made the revised fund raising goal equally unrealistic. Misquoting a secondary source, David Parker wrongly asserts that Protestant grandees, led by the Queen of Navarre, managed to extract the incredible sum of 800,000 *livres* from the Rochelais. See Parker, *La Rochelle and the French Monarchy*, (London, 1980), 97 and n. 4. See also Charles Dartigue, "Henri de Navarre dans l'Aunis et la Saintonge (1568-1577)," BSHPF, 100 (1951), 45-63, in particular 48. Disappointing cash flow from French Reformed towns, especially after the defeat and death of Condé at Jarnac (13 March 1569), in part prompted Jeanne d'Albret to hock her jewels and mortgage her domains to fund Calvinist armed forces in the field. In June of 1569, advisors to the Prince of Navarre complained of the "longeur et dilation" involved in obtaining funds for the Protestant cause from west country towns.

commanders. Abusing expedients offered to them in time of war, rochelais patricians raised the ire of ordinary citizens and fanned their desire for a louder voice in town government.

The comportment of great Calvinist personages residing temporarily in La Rochelle seriously disrupted the ordinary operations of ancient civic institutions. Jeanne d'Albret, the Queen of Navarre, and her council sought refuge and a new base of operations in La Rochelle between September 1568 and March 1572. During this period, the queen, exploiting her reputation as a patroness of the Reformed church, personally intervened in mayoral electioneering to advance her own protégés on the *corps de ville*. In 1571, d'Albret used promises of lucrative provisioning contracts and cash bribes to form a block of town councilmen backing the mayoral bid of her confidant, the *échevin* Jean Blandin. Blandin's victory over his fellow *échevins* Jacques Henry and Pierre Salbert broke the hold of the zealous Pontard faction on the mayor's office.[44]

The queen's council then acted even more peremptorily in its decrees infringing on the fiscal and judicial prerogatives of town government. Municipal customs authorities lost the right to levy duties and port fees on vessels serving the queen's household. Lawsuits involving royal agents and townspeople commenced in local courts were summarily evoked before the queen's council contrary to standard urban legal procedures. The royal council endorsed orders issued by the princes of Navarre and Condé prohibiting any subordinate city tribunals from adjudicating disputes generated by imposition of forced loans or confiscations of property required in defense of the Protestant cause.[45] The council commanded town beadles to imprison members of La Rochelle's bourgeoisie it condemned on criminal charges, defendants whose rights normally included trials in the first instance exclusively before civic magistrates.

By requiring rochelais merchants to buy passports for their cargos exiting the port, the council of Navarre practiced a hugely

---

[44] Barbot, "Histoire de La Rochelle," AHSA 18 (1890): 1, notes that the outcome of the 1571 mayoral election was decided "principallement par le mouvement et volonté de ladite reine de Navarre." Jacques Henry had been the clear winner in town council balloting for mayor.

[45] See "Le conseil de la Reine de Navarre à La Rochelle, ordonnances et délibérations inédites 1569-70," in BSHPF, 3 (1855): 123-137.

unpopular form of taxation on trade in violation of the city's commercial privileges. Smuggling, already common, intensified to beat the hated levy. Even sailors in town complained bitterly that orders from the royal council requiring them to serve on Protestant privateers lost them regular wages and business contacts with local shippers more dependent on their manpower. Rochelais from every stratum of urban society chafed under the demands of alien aristocrats. The dictates of visiting Protestant notables, whether manifest in d'Albret's council or in the proceedings of the contemporaneous national synod of French Reformed churches (La Rochelle, 1571), did not necessarily compel the respect or obedience of the Rochelais. Townspeople greeted with relief the successive departures of Condé, Coligny, and d'Albret necessitated by military and diplomatic manoeuvres for the Protestant cause.

Although by terms of the Peace of Saint Germain (August 1570), La Rochelle became one of four urban safe zones for French Calvinists, town coucillors remained distrustful of the crown, refusing all orders from the king to admit the city's new royal governor, Armand Gontaut de Biron. Once news of the St. Bartholomew's Day massacre hit the west country, La Rochelle returned almost instantly to a war footing. Calvinist refugees streamed into the city from all directions at once. By September 1572, more that fifty fugitive ministers had sought asylum within the walls.

To repulse an anticipated royal attack, town councilmen thoroughly reorganized the municipal militia. All able-bodied householders were numbered off and mustered into nine new companies. Six companies were commanded by senior town councilmen and two were led by prominent bourgeois, a departure from the traditional monopoly over militia commands enjoyed by *échevins*. The ninth unit, under the personal direction of the mayor, was comprised of la Rochelle's leading municipal and judicial officeholders. The new militia captains, members of established native families, were all Calvinists but of moderate disposition. None had been prominent supporters of Pontard or the *zelé* faction. A new squadron of rochelais cavalry, officered by refugee nobles, swept the *banlieue*, driving vast quantities of grain and livestock into municipal stores. These raids were also meant to harass royal forces gathering in a base camp at Brouage thirty kilometers to the south. Reasserting their autonomy, the Rochelais prepared to defend their community without the aid of princely armies on which they knew they could not and should not depend.

In the face of a mounting external military threat, civic leaders strived to enhance the citizenry's internal cohesion and morale. The new mayor, Jacques Henry, convened a special war council comprised of representatives from the *corps de ville*, from the bourgeoisie, and from the growing pool of refugees in the city.[46] Civic officials charged this body with selecting efficiently among alternative strategies of defense and with providing various ranks of the citizenry a forum for consensual policy making. The bourgeoisie jumped at the chance to participate more fully in municipal affairs, initially sending a delegation equivalent in size to the group of eight town councillors proposed for the new war committee. Patricians unhappy with this equality remonstrated and the council finally empanelled included five *échevins*, three *pairs*, four bourgeois, and three notable refugees. Calvinist clergymen received invitations to address the war council when expedient but gained no permanent seats on the committee. War council members included Claude Huet, Jean Pierres, and Jean Salbert, stalwart members of the old Pontard faction. These representatives were balanced by less zealous councillors employed as royal magistrates and wholesale merchants. All members of the war committee backed armed defense of city and church. They obtained emergency police powers from the town council and received permission to participate in deliberations of the full *corps de ville*.[47]

The war council quickly exercised its protective authority by arresting two town councillors and three bourgeois accused of openly favoring the royalist cause. The *échevin* Jean Nicholas, still tainted by his decisive action thwarting Chesnet's radical coup a

---

[46] Like his predecessor, Jean Blandin, Jacques Henry was a moderate Protestant. Henry was not on the best of terms with Reformed churchmen in La Rochelle. In 1565, the Calvinist consistory censured Henry for having fathered an illegitimate child. This indiscretion by no means tarnished his political career or repute among his patrician peers. In unorthodox La Rochelle, such disregard of the church's teaching may have even heightened Henry's notoriety. See ADCM, I 1, fol. 51v.

[47] Barbot, "Histoire de La Rochelle," AHSA, 18 (1890): 41. Delayant, *Histoire des Rochelais*, 1: 250-251. As a block, presidial jurists inclined to moderation in political and religious affairs. In 1572, several magistrates on this tribunal retired to their rural estates rather than continue to serve in a municipality increasingly contemptuous of the king's orders.

decade earlier, was rounded up along with the *pair* Jean Colin, a man disgruntled to the point of treason by his failure to win election as a captain of one of La Rochelle's seaward towers. The bourgeois François du Jau, receiver of municipal customs duties, was relieved of his office and jailed when he refused to authorize use of funds under his control for bonuses paid to merchants importing large quantities of war materiel. Advocates of accommodation with the crown continued to disquiet the community. The war council, with popular backing from the city's militia companies, managed to isolate and suppress unsympathetic patricians.

Accompanied by fervent public prayers for deliverance and massed psalm singing, preparations for a siege intensified. New, enlarged subcommittees of the municipal war council formed to handle military operations, city finances, and urban police. Members of La Rochelle's bourgeoisie excluded from the town council itself served on each of these vital supervisory bodies. Town sergeants drove the homeless and the derelict ("les bouches inutiles") out of the city in order to conserve supplies. Unwelcome Catholics fled into exile. Some urban notables, like the *pair* Jacques du Lyon, who advocated obedience to the king, left La Rochelle to join the royal army preparing an assault on their own home town. As the king's forces drew up outside the walls, rochelais ministers harangued their congregations, trying to stiffen public opposition against any negotiated settlement endangering Protestant rights of worship already attained. Betrayal of city and betrayal of church became conjoined, making devotion to civic independence a Calvinist virtue of almost sacramental importance.[48]

### 4. *The Siege of 1573 and Its Effects on Urban Politics*

Royal siegeworks closed around La Rochelle in January 1573. The grim battle of attrition waged here became the principal campaign of the Fourth War of Religion in which the French crown attempted to eradicate urban centers of religious and political dis-

---

[48] On the process by which "civisme" became a "valeur calviniste" for the Rochelais see Pascal Rambeaud, "La Rochelle de 1568 à 1576, la part du politique et du religion," BSHPF, 138 (1992): 391-99, here at 396.

sent. Against royal forces ultimately numbering at least 18,000, the Rochelais fought furiously.[49]

No chivalric rules of armed encounter governed this bloody conflict. In skirmishes outside the walls, the Rochelais, employing superior knowledge of local terrain, sprang deadly ambushes on the king's men. Under pursuit, native soldiers melted away into the swamps and salt pans of the marine landscape where outsiders easily became disoriented, lost, and then drowned. Assaults against the city walls were repulsed under blistering fire from 175 cannons of all calibers primed in municipal arsenals. City women took an active role in communal defense casting cauldrons of boiling pitch and tar into the midst of storming royal troops. Female residents also courageously ventured outside the walls to strip dead enemies of arms and equipment.

Mines imprecisely detonated by crown sappers only tore up earth under the walls enabling a better defense. Aggravated by damp weather, diseases and desertions greatly thinned the ranks of the assailants, making military conquest of La Rochelle increas-

---

[49] Although Charles IX promised the duc d'Anjou, his brother and west country commander, 40,000 troops and sixty siege cannons for the reduction of La Rochelle, it is extremely doubtful that a force of this size ever mustered before the city. Simultaneous military campaigns in western, southern, and central France stretched the king's irregular armed forces to the limit and made it unlikely that Charles could have kept his promise. French kings normally spent very little on artillery and during the Wars of Religion the monarchy was lucky to field even forty serviceable cannons at any one time. Before the encirclement of La Rochelle, Biron, royal governor for the town and region, disposed of no more than 4,000 troops in the west country. At the beginning of the siege, soldiers under the personal command of Henry duc d'Anjou (the future Henry III) numbered about 6,000 (5,000 infantry and 1,000 cavalrymen). In March 1573, the siege army grew by about 2,000 men from the regiment of the weary Catholic paladin Monluc. Thus a wavering force of approximately 12,000 royal soldiers probably carried on the bulk of the fighting. D'Anjou did receive about 6,000 Swiss reinforcements in late May 1573 but this was only weeks before conclusion of an armistice very favorable to the Rochelais. Given the consistently poor battlefield results obtained by the king's army encamped before La Rochelle, it is clear that it possessed neither the full strength nor the skilled leadership requisite to capture a heavily fortified town protected by a far superior stock of modern artillery. The Rochelais held their own despite being outnumbered at least five to one. See Arcère, *Histoire de la ville de La Rochelle*, 1: 432 (on Biron's contingent) and 458 (on d'Anjou's army and Montluc's contributions in manpower). On the insuperable financial, logistical, and operational problems compromising the military effectiveness of royal armies during the Wars of Religion see James B. Wood, *The Army of the King: Warfare, Soldiers, and Society During the Wars of Religion in France*, (Cambridge, 1996).

ingly unlikely. The sight of gallant courtiers like the duc d'Aumale blown in two or disemboweled by rochelais cannonades further undercut the morale of the king's army. The casualty rate among royal commanders reached 73% as the inept encirclement dragged on.[50]

Inside the besieged city, stockpiles of food, fuel, and ammunition diminished more rapidly than anticipated. Public unease over dwindling sustenance induced some townsmen who considered warfare against the king abhorrent to propose peace negotiations on honorable terms with envoys of the siege army. Pacific overtures from the crown, anxious to staunch heavy spending for more pointless carnage, encouraged the growth of a peace party among the Rochelais. Prominent members of this splinter group included Claude d'Angliers, presiding judge of the royal presidial court, the *échevins* Claude Huet and François Pajault, four *pairs*, and several attorneys serving the presidial.

The noble captain, François de La Noue, among the most experienced Protestant army officers in La Rochelle, now also sought to avoid prolonged fighting against royal forces. These notables backed tentative negotiations for an armistice with the king, raising the ire of fellow patricians and ordinary townsfolk.

Fearful of causing popular rebellion by deciding for peace unilaterally, a divided city council recurrently called large public assemblies to query the will of the people.[51] Councillors backing armed struggle undoubtedly hoped that these consultations would stifle the peace party.

In noisy town meetings, refugee ministers with no other safe haven but La Rochelle spoke up often, denouncing plans for peace, reminding auditors that unity in struggle with other embattled Protestant communities was essential, and rehearsing tales of atrocities committed by royal troops after earlier truces had been concluded. These arguments swayed public opinion. Members of

---

[50] See James B. Wood, "The Royal Army During the Early Wars of Religion, 1559-1576," in Mack P. Holt, ed., *Society and Institutions in Early Modern France*, (Athens, Georgia, 1991), 1-35.

[51] Emergency town meetings in which patricians, ministers, householders, ordinary residents, and refugees all participated occurred regularly during the months of the siege. Major debates took place on 18 January 1573, on 4 and 26 February, and on 3 and 13 March. On the content of popular debates during the siege see Arcère, *Histoire de la ville de La Rochelle*, 1: 456-57 and 468-69; and Delayant, *Histoire des Rochelais*, 1: 267-68.

La Rochelle's consistory and municipal militia swore to keep fighting. By popular acclaim, face to face negotiations with royal emissaries were prohibited and any written peace proposals from the town's war council made contingent upon approval by assemblies of the entire community. Frustrated by these constraints on his command and humiliated by a real slap in the face from a dissident minister, La Noue quit La Rochelle on 11 March 1573. His flight only strengthened popular contempt for alien nobles. Refusing to bridle his own peace proposals, judge d'Angliers found himself confined to house arrest and his property sequestered by the town council.

Adherents of the peace party still at liberty now petitioned the *corps de ville* for permission to leave town. Worried that such an exodus might break civic morale and spark more defections, bellicose town councillors imprisoned all the suppliants including six of their own colleagues.[52]

To bolster the fighting spirit of all civic military units, the fifty-seven Calvinist ministers now in La Rochelle volunteered for non-combattant duty in the ranks. Under the command of the new mayor, Jean Morrison, a veteran of Pontard's staunch Calvinist faction, the city militia withstood all subsequent royalist assaults, inflicting heavy casualties on the attackers. Stymied before La Rochelle and watching his repute as a warrior ebb away like the tides, the duc d'Anjou resolved to abandon the conflict. His additional responsibilities as the newly elected King of Poland also induced him to break off a pointless, unflattering campaign against the impregnable city.

A peace accord between monarchy and municipality, on terms highly favorable to the Rochelais, was finally reached in late June 1573. The pact, debated and approved in another general assembly of townspeople, guaranteed all rights of Protestant worship in La Rochelle, exempted the city in perpetuity from a royal garrison, and fully pardoned all inhabitants for any acts of rebellion committed during the entire conflict. The treaty reconfirmed all

---

[52] Barbot, "Histoire de La Rochelle," AHSA 18 (1890): 154-156. The *échevin* Claude Huet was the most prominent advocate of peace jailed. On the targets of this dragnet see Delayant, *Histoire des Rochelais*, 1: 282-83. Advocates of a truce managed to obtain more than 300 signatures from backers of their peace petition. Civic officials also arrested most of these supporters of negotiations during the last days of the siege.

existing civic privileges and made installation of a new royal governor in La Rochelle contingent upon disbandment and departure of all crown troops from the region. A final popular assembly in La Rochelle selected the local notables who would serve as hostages to the king assuring fulfillment of the pact. La Rochelle emerged from seven months of hard fighting with a Calvinist church intact and a municipal constitution reinvigorated through successful armed defense by a proud citizenry.

Peppered with royalist cannon shot, urban defenses had withstood multiple attacks. Over 800 refugees and 500 townspeople died in the fighting. Losses in the king's camp from combat and disease were much worse. It has been estimated that between a third and a half of all forces commanded by d'Anjou perished, perhaps as many as 10,000 men.[53] The first siege of La Rochelle broke the bulk of the king's army in the west and further reduced royal authority over the city. Prosecution of the urban war effort was largely directed by town council members who acted free from tutelage by Calvinist nobles. Town councillors' frequent recourse to public assemblies as the ultimate sanction of combat strategies politically empowered many citizens heretofore excluded from the management of civic affairs. Ordinary residents, now battle hardened, would not relinquish their newly won prerogative to intervene in momentous decisions affecting town government.

In the unsettled political environment left by the siege, unscrupulous town councilmen took the opportunity to aggrandize their

---

[53] With no exact numbering of royal units' total strength while at La Rochelle, all contemporary estimates of losses in the siege army should not be accepted at face value. Relying mainly on the memoirs of noble officers in the king's employ, Arcère quotes a figure of 22,000 dead among the attackers. Arcère dismisses as incredible other, earlier reports of as many as 40,000 men lost on the king's side. See Arcère, *Histoire de la ville de La Rochelle*, 1: 530 and marginal note XXXVII. Arcère's own casualty count seems predicated on the belief that a 40,000 man royal army did indeed assemble before La Rochelle. Given intractable problems of recruitment, desertions, and logistics at the time, the much smaller size of armies normally involved in the French Wars of Religion, and reasonably accurate counts of troop strength possessed by Biron and d'Anjou, I do not think that many more than 18,000 royal soldiers made it to the siege. Upwards of half this number may have perished. Widely varying but higher contemporary accounts of royal casualties suggest that both the level of violence attained in the fighting and the number of dead staggered observers. These suppositions are justified by James Wood's thorough documentation of very high casualty rates among the officer corps of the royal army assembled at La Rochelle. See Wood, "The Royal Army During the Early Wars of Religion," 26-29 and Table 8, subsection B.

own influence and to settle old vendettas against rivals for power. An opponent's record of wartime behavior, especially if unseemly, might now be used against him in battles for control of the *corps de ville*. Debilitating popular condemnation of any civic leader could be more readily obtained from a citizenry poised for political assemblies. Rumors of conspiracies preoccupied the Rochelais. Patricians plausibly accused of conniving with outsiders to betray the town faced death. Guilt was easily assumed before proven.

On 10 December 1573, pastor Odet de Nort, spokesman for a group of zealous Protestants, made public a letter in his possession that contained news of a plot purportedly hatched by the queen mother to take La Rochelle by surprise. Catherine de Medici instructed the royal governor Biron to conspire with several mercenary officers previously employed by the town whose allegiance was now again for sale. The letter insinuated that these hirelings already had secret contacts with disgruntled townsmen prepared to abet the royal coup. The letter was unsigned but bore at the bottom the symbol of a human heart pierced by a dagger.

Broadcasting news of the nefarious faction they called the "coeur navré" ("transpierced heart"), de Nort and his followers convinced rochelais militia officers to arrest the unemployed captains and to interrogate them by torture until they identified their urban cohorts. Acting mayor Jacques Henry, who as chief executive had led La Rochelle into the last siege and who was now back in office after the untimely death of his successor, permitted the captures to be made. Henry further ordered that the prisoners be put to the question. Under torture and perhaps only to placate their tormentors, the suspects named several prominent town councilmen as their co-conspirators.

The mayor immediately issued arrest orders against the kindred *échevins* Guillaume Guy and Claude Huet and against the *pair* Jacques du Lyon. Surrounded on his rural estate, du Lyon died in combat with the arresting officers. Guy went quietly to jail and, threatened with torture, denounced his uncle Huet as privy to the plot. Huet fled to the town hall, protesting his innocence to the assembled city council. Huet asserted that his persecution was being orchestrated by his vindictive political enemies Jacques Henry and Jean Salbert. Henry was the rochelais commander-in-chief against the king's siege army when Huet began lobbying for peace with the crown. Salbert was an ally of Huet on Pontard's war council who also felt betrayed when Huet joined the peace party during the last siege.[54] In fact, all of the prominent town councillors denounced, du Lyon, Guy, and Huet had previously manifested opposition toward policies of confrontation with the crown. Du Lyon had fought with the king's army against La Rochelle; Huet had petitioned to leave the city during the siege; and his kinsman Guy was also suspected of pro-royalist sympathies.[55]

To his peers, Huet vigorously denied the existence of any conspiracy. He maintained that all the accusations against him and his co-defendants had been concocted by political opponents seeking to purge the city council of moderates. From outside the town hall, groups of citizens whipped up by the ministers interrupted Huet's self-defense with shouts for his immediate execution. Unwilling to condemn a potentially innocent man yet greatly fearing popular unrest, the *corps de ville* ordered more evidence gathered. On his way to house arrest, Huet narrowly escaped being stabbed to death by an enraged artisan known as a protégé of mayor Henry.

Meanwhile, to satisfy demands from the city militia's rank and file for swift justice against the plotters, the presidial court proceeded to reinterrogate and try the mercenary captains. The jurists themselves came under heavy public pressure to convict, receiving numerous threats of assassination should they show any lenience toward the defendants. Under torture, all the captains again confessed the existence of a conspiracy. They were quickly

---

[54] Huet was also convinced that he was being calumnied by other town councillors incensed by his prior support for creation of a commercial tribunal staffed by city merchants. This court, operational since 1565, did cut into the judicial prerogatives of the *corps de ville* and some councilmen may have wished to see Huet die for this affront to civic authority. In short, Huet was a councilman vulnerable because his enemies were numerous and capable of opportunely working together to kill him.

[55] Du Lyon's warring against his own home town was probably considered unforgivable by many of his peers. Du Lyon's close *amitié* with the apostate Amateur Blandin contributed to his precipitous downfall. See Barbot, "Histoire de La Rochelle," AHSA 18 (1890): 199. Guillaume Guy was also tainted by his blood relation to Michel Guy, the former mayor who had opposed Pontard's 1568 coup and the subsequent emplacement of Sainte-Hermine as Condé's military governor for the city.

judged, found guilty, condemned to death, and executed to general rejoicing in La Rochelle's largest square.

Guillaume Guy, subjected to renewed torture, desperately affirmed every leading question put to him. He, too, was sentenced, by the presidial to death.[56] As Guy approached the executioner's block, Claude Huet, calling out from the expectant crowd, beseeched Guy to speak the real truth before dying. To a hushed audience, Guy avowed that all his confessions and denunciations of others were false, products of his inability to endure the physical anguish of torture. Damning himself to hell, Guy asked God to pardon all of his sins except bearing false witness against Huet. As the executioner's sword flashed, Guy was still imploring Huet to forgive him. Satiated with this bloodletting, neither rochelais patricians nor plebeians demanded further prosecutions. Claude Huet kept his head and his office as *échevin*. He died two years later, never having regained his former stature in civic affairs.

The reality and true scope of the *coeur navré* plot can not be ascertained from the surviving contradictory testimony of suspected conspirators. In the short run, Henry and Salbert did achieve violent removal of personal adversaries on the town council, victims also hated by other members of La Rochelle's governing elite. However, over the medium- and long-term, one can detect no lasting radicalization of city politics attributable to prosecution of the alleged traitors. Just the opposite, greater moderation, is visible in the subsequent conduct of town government.

Patricians revolted by the maltreatment of du Lyon, Guy, and Huet mitigated their support for over-zealous peers and opted to back more scrupulous politicians. At the close of his special term as acting mayor, Jacques Henry left office and did not secure succession by any personal protégé. Guillaume Texier became the new mayor of La Rochelle in 1574. No adherent of the *zelés*, Texier kept the reckless military adventurer Montgomery out of La Rochelle and further refused to grant licenses for piracy to Protestant corsairs operating from the port. Intent on rebuilding

---

[56] Guy's long-standing opposition to the remunerative service of presidial court justices on La Rochelle's town council surely won him no friends among the judges who tried him. By steering the alleged conspirators' trial to the presidial, Salbert and his followers may well have succeeded in maximizing the probability that some of their political opponents would be liquidated.

their trade networks, rochelais merchants strongly seconded
Texier's irenic policies. Businessmen serving on the town council
made resolutions inviting foreign merchants, even Catholics, to
recommence trading in La Rochelle. They also undertook to guarantee the personal safety of any Papist visitors. Upon the death
of Charles IX (30 May 1574), Calvinist civic leaders accepted a
renewable truce with the crown, anticipating more favorable treatment from the new king Henry III.[57]

Although La Rochelle again mobilized for armed conflict with
the crown during the Fifth War of Religion (1575-76), fighting in
the west country was limited to minor skirmishes in most of which
rochelais combatants were either absent or took no leading role.
Protestant nobles covetous of new war loans raised from emergency taxes on port traffic found the *corps de ville* inalterably
opposed to their schemes and left town empty handed. Local
*marchands-bourgeois* had threatened a commerce strike shutting
down the harbor and strangling all regional shipments of war
materiel if the detested noblemen's levies were imposed.

Rochelais engagement with bellicose Protestants lessened as
local advocates of the cause became divided over who could best
lead the party. Pastor de Nort backed the Catholic duc d'Alençon,
whom many in the Reformed community considered an untrust-
worthy opportunist. Pastor Magnan openly broke with his colleague and supported Prince Henry, scion of the Condé family.
Envoys of Alençon got a cold reception from the town council
and the mayor steadfastly refused to accept any of the grandee's
dictates regarding police of the city or finance of Protestant
forces. The agents of Prince Henry de Condé were treated with
equal caution.

Leery of all overtures from warring rebel nobles and fearful
that their quarrels might reignite internal dissensions, the Protestant inhabitants of La Rochelle decided to steel themselves against
new fighting through a collective declaration of communal solidarity. At a general assembly held on 29 September 1575, most
city residents publicly swore allegiance to a compact of ten articles intended to protect the city against factionalization and insu-

---

[57] Catherine de Medici's offer of a monthly 36,000 *livre* subsidy to La Rochelle
in return for a cessation of hostilities probably was the deciding factor impelling
rochelais magistrates to accept the pact.

late it from further meddling by the great lords of state. Adherents of this protocol committed themselves to defend:

> the honor, well-being, and advancement of this city against all those of whatever condition or quality they are or may be, even our fathers, mothers, brothers, wives, and children, who would ever despicably attempt to alter or overthrow the present state of God's church planted among us and the form of our town government, especially the city council, all municipal privileges, statutes, and ordinances, and the ranks, powers, and responsibilities of town magistrates.[58]

The oath conjoined the security of city and church, reiterating the civic Calvinism characteristic of the Rochelais.

Parties to the new accord also agreed to protect all the privileges of La Rochelle's bourgeoisie and to denounce immediately common enemies threatening the franchises enjoyed by any segment of the urban population. Senior town magistrates additionally swore to render justice equitably to all citizens and to inform them prudently about all decisions affecting the peace and prosperity of the city. Governors promised to respect and receive all envoys from their subordinates so long as the governed showed due veneration for existing civic institutions. The pact prohibited citizens from making specious accusations of treason against one another and empanelled a special inspectorate comprised of the mayor and three *échevins* to determine quickly whether any charges of sedition had merit.[59] Subscribers finally promised to await patiently a more general peace in the kingdom from God, but also resolved to fight in legitimate self-defense, if necessary.

Through the ceremonial union of 1575, the Rochelais closed ranks under the threat of external trouble while acknowledging the reciprocal obligations between all urban social strata holding the community together. Such commemorations gave townspeople of every description a clearer understanding of their essential political rights.

Royal acknowledgement of rochelais circumspection came in the Peace of Beaulieu (6 May 1576) ending the current phase of hostilities. In this truce accord, all of La Rochelle's civic privileges were reconfirmed by the Henry III who reiterated an earlier promise of no garrison for the town and added a new pledge that the city would now be forever spared a resident royal governor.

---

[58] BMLR, MSS 45/46, fols. 1021-1025.
[59] *Ibid.*, fols. 1022-23.

The *sénéchal* of Poitou based in Poitiers would henceforward serve
as an absentee viceroy. These concessions made La Rochelle the
largest town in France liberated from all direct surveillance by the
king's gendarmes.

Jealous of their enhanced freedoms, town councillors displayed
growing aversion to the reception of powerful outsiders regardless of their religious affiliation. In June 1576, Henry de Navarre
requested permission to visit La Rochelle. The *corps de ville* stipulated that he might be welcome so long as he accepted stringent
preliminary conditions. He could approach La Rochelle with only
the smallest possible retinue, the keys to the city would not be
offered to him, and he could under no circumstances claim to be
the city's governor. The future Henry IV complied and was accorded a short stay of six days. Briefly thereafter, the duc d'Alençon
petitioned for a visit and received a curt refusal from the city
council. Touring the west country in November 1576, the young
prince Henry de Condé also desired to parley with La Rochelle's
independent governors. They demanded that the prince first
swear allegiance to all municipal privileges, enter town without
military escort, promise no assembly of noble followers in the city,
and renounce all claims to be governor of the community. Dis-
simulating his consternation, Condé agreed. From his pulpit, pastor de Nort chided civic leaders for their haughty and presump-
tuous treatment of former allies. Despite ministerial rebukes, city
fathers persevered in their distrust of outsiders.

Condé returned to La Rochelle in quest of funds to pay for
imminent resumption of military activity against the crown. The
Sixth War of Religion broke out in January 1577. The Rochelais
were reluctant to jeopardize their political and economic recovery through hasty allegiance with battling nobles. To Condé's exas-
peration, civic leaders demanded numerous guarantees of their
autonomy before accepting a temporary alliance with him. They
expected the prince to uphold all town privileges, to refrain from
any involvement in municipal government, to impose no war taxes on citizens' commerce, to raise no other special levies in town,
to give the local admiralty court veto power over commissions
issued to privateers, and to acknowledge the city council's preeminent right to recruit its own military forces throughout the
province of Aunis.[60]

---

[60] Arcère, *Histoire de la ville de La Rochelle*, 2: 32.

Desperate for logistical support, Condé could only agree to these humiliating constraints. However, the prince immediately schemed to obtain a new chief executive in La Rochelle more sympathetic to his cause. This was a grave strategic error playing into the hands of townsmen long convinced that great aristocrats sought the destruction of La Rochelle's civic constitution.

According to the contemporary witness and historian La Popelinière, by spring 1577 Condé had become "so marvelously irritated" by obstreperous Rochelais that he attempted to sway the mayoral election that year in favor of his local partisan, the *échevin* Louis Gargoulleau.[61] Rumors circulated by the prince's adversaries on the *corps de ville* identified Gargoulleau as a pawn of Reformed nobles seeking to abridge municipal freedoms. Although this may not have been Condé's real intent, popular opinion turned quickly against Gargoulleau's candidacy and he was easily defeated in preliminary balloting for mayor. Councilmen too closely affiliated with alien aristocrats now risked rapid political eclipse. Incensed by this new snub from "men of vile and abject condition," Condé lamented that God had not spared him the dishonorable necessity of courting townspeople. He castigated his vexing allies who now "thought themselves kings and wished like sovereigns to command princes."[62]

Relations between the two camps continued to deteriorate and reached a new nadir in early 1578 when La Rochelle's consistory banned Condé from the communion table for acts of piracy he authorized after the conclusion of the Peace of Bergerac ending the Sixth War of Religion. When Condé appealed this banishment to the ninth national synod of French Reformed churches meeting in St. Foy, members of the consistory testified that "the whole church and city of La Rochelle were greatly scandalized" by Condé's "unlawful practices." His illegitimate acts of war defamed all the Rochelais as "violators of the public peace of the kingdom." The consistory disciplined the prince to protect the honor of a Christian community.[63] The ninth synod denied Condé's

---

[61] See La Popelinière, *Histoire de France* (Paris, 1581), 1114. La Popelinière describes Condé as "merveillement esmeu" by his opponents among native Rochelais.

[62] *Ibid.*, 1114. See also Arcère, *Histoire de la ville de La Rochelle*, 2: 34-35.

[63] Quick, *Synodicon*, 1: 122-23. The ninth synod commended "the zeal and good affection of the church and consistory of La Rochelle, especially in opposing itself against scandalous sins."

appeal, ruling that church officials in La Rochelle "had not acted beyond the line of their duty." It admonished Condé to cease
his sinful behavior and reconcile himself with the local congregation. To promote this goal, the synod rescinded his deprivation
of communion.

These accumulating recriminations between Huguenots of the
second and third estates show that Calvinism, a new creed susceptible to many democratic interpretations, coexisted poorly with
the discriminatory etiquette of neo-feudal French society. At La
Rochelle, such confrontations strengthened the repute of urban
magistrates opposed to entangling alliances with irreverent
nobles. From the civic Calvinism championed by rochelais patricians, politically ambitious members of the bourgeoisie derived
the legitimating precept that within a Christian polity accidents
of birth should not solely determine who rules. Putting this principle into practice embattled rochelais politics for another forty
years.

## 5. *The Contours of La Rochelle's Calvinist Ruling Oligarchy*

While tracking the dramatic factional struggles and siege warfare
animating rochelais history, one can easily overlook more prosaic developments shaping the fundamental structure of town politics. Among the most important of these sociopolitical mechanisms is the consolidation of a narrow oligarchy monopolizing
access to the offices of the city council. This exclusive process continued throughout the sixteenth century despite murderous patrician infighting because the removal of any one overly ambitious
or hated town councillor never entailed the complete disgrace of
his officeholding relations. The politically active kinsmen of a
marked man were not deprived of their civic offices and purged
individuals were often succeeded in their posts by members of
their own nuclear households. Clans battled for preeminence in
municipal government but it was only the individuals within them
who risked complete degradation or death for political misdeeds.
Reconstructing these basic mechanisms of urban politics is an
essential prelude to understanding why rochelais patricians and
members of the bourgeoisie came to battle one another for control of town government after 1600. This analysis shows the deep

imbrication of family affairs and civic affairs in early modern La Rochelle.

Over time, substantial percentages of *échevins* and *pairs* owed their office to bonds of consanguinity and affinity linking them to politically active forbearers. The interplay of family interests and municipal governing institutions was a constant feature of La Rochelle's history throughout the early modern period. Comparison of town councilmen's career paths over time reveals the importance of a councillor's family stature in the perpetuation and enlargement of his political responsibilities.

Long-term analysis of families in town politics is possible thanks to several complementary documents. The first is the "Matricule selon la réception des pairs au corps de ville et de ceux qui les ont premièrement possedés" drawn up in 1627 by Pierre Mervault, a scrupulous antiquarian particularly interested in the political and diplomatic history of his city.[64] This *matricule* lists the occupants of all one hundred seats on the *corps de ville* in 1627 and then names every holder of each council office reaching as far back as 1550. Every member of the 1627 council was listed because *échevins* (who almost uniformly began their political careers as *pairs*) kept their post as *pair* throughout their tenure on the town council. Their official title was "*pair* and *échevin*." When an *échevin* died or resigned, both his offices (as *pair* and *échevin*) fell vacant. Dual vacancies were usually filled simultaneously by the *échevin*'s successor. If the successor was previously a *pair*, a new *pair* also had to be appointed. Double openings of this kind complicated successions and gave retiring magistrates and their families special opportunities to put kinsmen in their places. Using Mervault's *matricule*, one can connect chains of successors to each council office stretching back over several generations of town councilmen.

Information contained in the *matricule* can be corroborated and augmented by lists of all town councilmen serving in certain years

---

[64] BMLR, MS 95, "Collections historiques concernant la ville de La Rochelle par Pierre Mervault." The *matricule* covers fols. 51r-64v. In the early seventeenth century, Mervault was among the most well-informed historians of La Rochelle. In addition to historical works based upon his own archival research in the city's treasury of municipal charters and privileges, Mervault also kept a journal during the siege of 1627-28 which remains one of the best sources of information about daily events in the surrounded city, see BMLR, MSS 3244-3246.

compiled from archival sources by other local *érudits* during the
seventeenth and eighteenth centuries.[65] These official lists (also
known as *matricules*) can be further checked and verified by con-
sulting the private diaries of rochelais town councilmen and jurists
who frequently recorded the deaths of fellow magistrates and the
disposition of their offices by testament.[66]

The names and occasional kinship ties listed in the various
*matricules* and diaries can be further checked against contemporary notarized wedding contracts and testaments, baptismal registers, and court papers in an effort to determine the exact family relationships between successive holders of the same municipal
office. I have attempted this for all successions to the office of
*échevin* between 1575 and 1605 and for all transfers of the office
of *pair* recorded by Mervault up to 1627. In total, I have sought
to ascertain the family connections of 618 councilmen involved
in 448 separate transfers of office. Biographical data on these men
reveal that, at the very least, 316 (51%) were relatives by blood
or marriage. This figure should be taken as a bare minimum of
kinfolk on the town council because lacunae in the documentary
record make any prosopography of rochelais town councilmen
necessarily incomplete.

In terms of age, experience, and political influence, *échevins*
were senior members of La Rochelle's municipal government.
Service as an *échevin* conferred hereditary nobility upon the officeholder. This distinction was a vital factor keeping transfers of
office within families. However, the post of *échevin* did not auto-
matically pass lineally from father to son. *Echevins* had to stipulate their successors and all evidence suggests that they did so very
carefully.

Of the forty-nine successions to the office of *échevin* recorded

---

[65] These lists for the years 1558, 1570-71, 1573-79, 1581, 1583-89, 1591, 1593-
97, 1599-1605, 1618, and 1622, are now collected in one manuscript volume, see
BMLR, MS 97, "Matricules des échevins, pairs et conseillers." Other documents
pertaining to La Rochelle's town council, including original minutes of town
council meetings, confirm the accuracy of the lists in MS 97. Manuscript 97 is
particularly useful for information on transfers of office by *échevins*. Beginning
with the year 1575, regular references are made to such transfers. The period
1575-1605 furnishes the raw data on transfers of municipal office by *échevins* I will
analyze below.

[66] See, for examples, the diary of Jacques Merlin, BMLR, MS 161, the journal
of Pierre Brunneau, BMLR, MS 50, the diary of Jean Bergier and the diary of
Pierre Guillaudeau bound together in BMLR, MS 80.

between 1575 and 1605, thirty-five (71.4%) involved relatives by blood or marriage. In fourteen transfers (28.6% of all cases), no family relationship between officeholder and successor could be established. Six of the fourteen apparently extra-familial transfers involved seats declared vacant by the town council after an officer died without male heirs or intestate. A total of seventy-two individuals were involved in the forty-nine transfers studied. Fifty-three of these men (73.6%) were related. Nineteen (26.4%) cannot be identified as kinsmen. For the thirty-five transfers involving kinsmen, Table 11 shows the type and frequency of family ties connecting officeholders to the relatives who succeeded them.[67]

*Table 11*

Type and Frequency of Family Ties Between
Echevins and Successors 1575–1605

| *Transfer of Office of Echevin from:* | *Cases* | *Percentage* |
|---|---|---|
| Father to Son | 15 | 42.7 |
| Brother to Brother (or Half-Brother) | 3 | 8.6 |
| Uncle to Nephew | 3 | 8.6 |
| Cousin to Cousin | 1 | 2.9 |
| Father-in-law to Son-in-law | 5 | 14.3 |
| Son-in-law to Father-in-law | 1 | 2.9 |
| Brother-in-law to Brother-in-law | 2 | 5.7 |
| Cousin by marriage to Cousin by marriage | 5 | 14.3 |
| *Totals* | 35 | 100.0 |

Recruitment of *échevins* tended to run in families. The nobility the office conferred was an important status distinction best kept and embellished by transmission of the office among closely related kinsmen. The high percentage of sons who succeeded their fathers as *échevins* attests to the incorporation of powerful civic offices in the private patrimonies of notable rochelais families. When successions from father to son are added to transfers

---

[67] BMLR, MS 97 is the principal source for Table 11. Family connections when not listed in MS 97 have been ascertained through consultation of notarial *registres* (ADCM, series 3 E), baptismal records (ADCM, series I), and court papers (ADCM, series B and BMLR, MSS 211-213 and 217-221).

between brothers, slightly more than 50% of all office conveyances took place between immediate family members. However, transfers along more distant lines of consanguinity and affinity also regularly occurred. The conjugal family did not become the exclusive unit through which resignations and legacies of municipal offices were made. Sons-in-law, brothers-in-law, and cousins by marriage were all potential successors to *échevins* leaving office.

Sons and sons-in-law became clearly favored conservators of *échevin* offices achieved by their forbearers. In 1585, Pierre Salbert I, a veteran of Pontard's radical faction now on his deathbed, transferred his office of *échevin* to his son Pierre II, a *pair*. Pierre I's post as *pair* went to his second son Jean I.[68] In 1586, Pierre Salbert II also died, leaving his offices to his brother, Jean I. Jean I, who could not hold two offices of *pair* at once, gave one to his cousin, Jean Salbert II. When Jean Salbert II died in 1597, his son, Jean Salbert III, succeeded to his offices. Under the regime of dual officeholding, deaths in the patrician male line of Salberts on the town council did not diminish the family's presence on the *corps de ville* but gave surviving Salbert kinsmen vital opportunities to multiply the offices they held continuously at the center of town government.

Over time, offices on the town council could also "drift" through extended families. Alexander de Harender succeeded his father, Pierre, as a *pair* and *échevin* in 1578. After serving on the town council for twenty-four years, Alexander resigned his offices in January 1602. Harender transferred his post as *échevin* to Jean Berne, his cousin by marriage, formerly a *pair*.[69] Harender's office of *pair* went to another kinsman, Michel Esprinchard, a cousin of Jean Berne. The Harender and Esprinchard families had been closely allied for years. By 1578, Pierre de Harender had made Michel Esprinchard I guardian of his children and trustee of his estate.[70] Thus, when Alexander de Harender resigned his office of *pair* in 1602, he did so in favor of the man (Michel Esprinchard II) whose father had looked after Harender for years. This series of transfers ensured that a seat as *pair* and a seat as *échevin* remained under the control of three allied families (Berne, Harender, and Esprinchard) for more than forty years.

---

[68] BMLR, MS 97, fols. 33r-v.

[69] *Ibid.*, fol. 88r.

[70] ADCM, B 1338, fols. 33r-34v.

In 1600 and 1603, Mathurin Regnault and Jean de Mirande each transferred a position as *échevin* to a brother-in-law. Archival sources show the importance of brothers-in-law in the daily social and economic life of La Rochelle. Evidently, strong bonds of trust and respect could form between brothers-in-law. In 1565, for example, Raoullet and Pierre du Jau were working together with their brother-in-law, Pierre Salbert, on a variety of commercial enterprises. Contemporaneously, all three men were making common cause in a series of law suits intended to win a mutually beneficial distribution of family property tied up in disputed legacies from forebears.[71]

Brothers-in-law were also prominent negotiators for and witnesses to wedding contracts drawn up between notable rochelais families. A sister's favorable marriage could extend a brother's fraternal bonds out beyond his immediate family. Arranging and cultivating such confraternities could have beneficial social, economic, and political consequences for both families involved. Within these alliances, patrician women served as essential linchpins holding together intermarried clans and extensive familial political networks.

Family connections could also be exploited by officeholders who transferred their charge temporarily to one kinsman who was to hold the position in trust only until a closer relative of the outgoing magistrate could take over the office. For example, in 1575, Claude Huet gave his place as *échevin* to his son Jean. On 6 May 1597, two days before his death, Jean Huet left his office to Guillaume Guybert, a cousin by marriage. On 3 July 1597, Guybert stepped aside and gave the office to Estienne Huet, the half-brother of Jean Huet.[72] Guybert's two-month tenure kept the family office occupied, gave outsiders no pretext to claim it vacant, and gave Estienne Huet time enough to settle his legal affairs in Paris before returning to La Rochelle to represent his family on the town council. Such combinations of intra- and interfamilial resignations for the conservation of municipal offices were common amongst the kinsmen of La Rochelle's governing elite.

The sustained importance of family interests as regulators of *échevin* recruitment after 1548 imparted great stability and conti-

---

[71] BMLR, MS 221, *cahier* 31, fols. 373v-374r.
[72] BMLR, MS 97, fol. 72r.

nuity to the highest levels of rochelais town government. For example, eleven of the twenty-four *échevins* holding office in 1625 bore exactly the same surnames as *échevins* serving in 1585.[73] Another five *échevins* in 1625 can be identified as in-laws of *échevins* serving in 1585. Two-thirds of the *échevins* in 1625 could claim for their families at least forty years of active service on the *corps de ville*.

The enduring political presence of key families furnishing *échevins* year after year ensured a steady supply of well-married, well-connected, and politically experienced magistrates at the pinnacle of municipal administration. This group of townsmen was no mere body of placeholders. It comprised men of proven financial acumen, religious conviction, diplomatic skill, political cleverness, and military prowess. Between 1530 and 1628, *échevins* negotiated with kings, furnished large amounts of capital to royal financiers, fought with pirates in hand-to-hand combat, tried to police one of the largest Calvinist communities in France, organized a civic militia, and coordinated their fellow citizens' stubborn and triumphant resistance against one of the fiercest sieges ever waged by a French monarch during the Wars of Religion. At crucial moments, particularly in response to outside threats, La Rochelle's *échevins* displayed a political cohesiveness that facilitated collective action in defense of an urban commonwealth. The social and religious homogeneity of this group could at times mitigate the divisiveness of its members' persistent conflicts over civic offices. A dense matrix of kinship ties, weaving together the honor and fortune of the extended families represented among the *échevins*, occasionally facilitated a unity of political purpose among normally ambitious and competitive urban magistrates.

Offices of *pair* in La Rochelle's municipal government did not confer hereditary nobility on their holders, making successions more complicated and problematic. However, rochelais families contrived over generations to retain control of offices of *pair* in their possession. Mervault's 1627 *matricule* lists a total of 399 successions to offices of *pair* between 1550 and 1627. Since there were one hundred offices of *pair* in La Rochelle, this implies that, on average, each office changed hands roughly four times during this period. *Paris* tended to serve long terms of office easily mea-

---

[73] Compare BMLR, MS 765, fols. 5r-v and BMLR, MS 97, fols. 33r-v.

sured in decades. Of the 399 office transfers involving *pairs,* at the very least 149 took place between kinsmen. Circumstantial evidence indicates that in another six cases the officeholder and his successor were related. At a minimum, 37% of all successions to the office of *pair* involved close relations by blood or marriage. A total of 546 men took part in these transactions. I have been able to determine that 263 (48%) of these individuals got their office from a relative, gave it to a relative, or both. For the 149 known cases of kin transfer, Table 12 shows the type and frequency of family ties connecting *pairs* to their successors.[74]

*Table 12*

Type and Frequency of Family Ties Between Pairs and Successors, Circa 1550–Circa 1627

| Transfer of Office of Pair from: | Cases | Percentage |
|---|---|---|
| Grandfather to Grandson | 1 | .7 |
| Father to Son | 86 | 57.7 |
| Stepfather to Stepson | 5 | 3.4 |
| Brother to Brother | 14 | 9.4 |
| Uncle to Nephew | 15 | 10.1 |
| Cousin to Cousin | 4 | 2.7 |
| Father-in-law to Son-in-law | 6 | 4.0 |
| Brother-in-law to Brother-in-law | 12 | 8.0 |
| Cousin by marriage to Cousin by marriage | 6 | 4.0 |
| *Totals* | 149 | 100.0 |

Among *pairs,* approximately 70% of office exchanges involving known relatives occurred between immediate family members (father to son, stepfather to stepson, or brother to brother). Office transfers were made to more distant relatives but, in this sample, to a lesser extent than among *échevins.* Since I was unable to determine whether family connections played a role in 245 other successions to the office of *pair,* it can not be inferred that the distances and frequencies of transfers found in my sample hold for the ensemble of successions to the office of *pair* over the period of Mervault's *matricule.*

However, the data I have gathered certainly suggest that fami-

---

[74] BMLR, MS 97 is the main source for information displayed in Table 12.

ly ties played an important role in the recruitment of new *pairs*
and that lineal descendants were heavily favored successors to
offices previously held by family members. Increasingly loud
protests of the domination of family cliques in the recruitment of
*pairs* and *échevins*, voiced in the early seventeenth century by
rochelais bourgeois excluded from officeholding, make it safe to
assume that intra- and interfamily successions did not appreciably decline over the period and quite probably increased.[75]

A variety of factors could account for the preponderance of
transfers between immediate family members serving as *pairs*.
Since a place as *pair* was the indispensable asset assuring a family's political representation and chances for political advancement
in the *corps de ville*, keeping a post of *pair* within a tightly-knit and
highly trustworthy group of immediate family members may have
been deemed essential by officeholders. The tendency of brothers, cousins, uncles, and nephews to hold offices of *pair* simultaneously indicates that each branch and generation of politically
active clans was well-represented in civic government and appreciated this pattern of placeholding as a guarantee that no distinguished city family could suddenly be deprived of all access to the
town council. Because of dual successions, where men already
serving as *pairs* simultaneously took over offices of *pair* and *échevin*
belonging to a kinsman, the number of relatives (263) involved
in transfers was less than twice the number of those exchanges
(148). The structure of La Rochelle's town council, the prevalence
of succession by resignation, and the practice of dual office transfers combined to reinforce the familial quality of the institution.

Despite the high instance of father-son office transfers, a variety of other succession patterns can be uncovered that persistently
kept offices of *pair* under the control of one family or a group of
intermarried families. For example, before 1558, Jean Clerbault
I, mayor of La Rochelle in 1535 and 1543, gave his office of *pair*
to his nephew, Jean Clerbault II.[76] In 1573, Jean Clerbault II
resigned his office in favor of his brother-in-law, Macé Thevenin.

---

[75] See for example, the *Brève déclaration* of the unenfranchised bourgeoisie
against the practice of office resignation among town councilmen, BMLR, Rés.
897c. This 1614 manifesto denounced both the increasingly common family
intrigues and blatant use of bribery evident in the formation of city governments
between 1605 and 1614.

[76] BMLR, MS 95, fol. 51r.

In 1591, Thevenin turned the office over to his son Jean, who went on to become mayor of La Rochelle in 1598. *Pairs*, like *échevins*, became adept at using bonds of blood and marriage as a means to conserve, to perpetuate, and to enlarge their family's political power. Examples drawn from the various *matricules* show that not only siblings, nephews, and cousins could be counted on to advance a family's political clout, but also a wider circle of in-laws could be engaged, if necessary, in the same endeavor. This phenomenon, integral to the social and political history of La Rochelle, underscores the necessity of reformulating the history of the early modern family in France to accommodate and illuminate more fully the extended family's crucial role in the government and police of urban society.

The various lists of magistrates I have consulted permit one to follow and compare the careers of individual town councilmen in La Rochelle. Long-term analysis of councilmen's service records reveals a variety of career tracks the length and notoriety of which depended on the extent and quality of an officeholder's family connections. Some men served for years on the town council, moved up in rank, and steadily expanded the scope of their responsibilities. Others gained more modest posts, enjoyed no upward mobility, and never succeeded at accumulating the broad experience in municipal government possessed by the well-married and wealthy men who dominated the senior positions of La Rochelle's civic administration before 1614.

Amidst the mass of names, titles, and dates stored in the archives of La Rochelle, the careers of certain town councilmen stand out because of their length and the exceptional regulatory authority each man exercised over the affairs of his fellow citizens.

By the early 1560's, Jean Barbot, *sieur* du Troilgras, was a *pair* in good standing on the *corps de ville*. In 1566, Barbot was appointed by his peers to the onerous job of city treasurer. Four years later, Barbot served a stint as commander of the tour de Garrot, a strong point in La Rochelle's outer defenses.[77] In 1572, Barbot held an office of judge on the merchants' tribunal. In 1580, he was collecting rents in cash and kind as the agent for properties

---

[77] BMLR, MS 97, fols. 3r and 151r. See also Barbot, "Histoire de La Rochelle," AHSA 17 (1889): 230.

in the parish of Perrot owned by the ancient *commanderie* of the
Knights Templar located in the quarter. In 1577, Barbot made
first runner-up in the election for mayor and became first vice-
mayor as was customary. When the winning mayor died in office,
Barbot served out the late mayor's term and became an *échevin*
in the process.[78] Barbot continued to serve his city as an *échevin*
and experienced *coadjuteur* on the mayor's court until his death
in 1594. Barbot's eldest sons, Jean and Pierre, succeeded to his
posts as *échevin* and *pair*.[79]

Jean Blandin, *sieur* des Herbiers, was a *pair* on the *corps de ville*
by 1558. His brother and cousin were both distinguished members of that body. Jean Blandin became city treasurer in 1561 and
captain of the tour St. Nicolas in 1570. He was nominated again
for treasurer in 1571 and ran for mayor in 1572. He made *échevin*
in 1573, mayor in 1579, and subsequently served as senior judge
on the mayor's court.[80] Blandin was also the godfather to the
eldest son of André Rousseau, a fellow *pair*. When Blandin quit
the *corps de ville* in 1603, he turned his offices over to his son,
Isaac.

Jacques Guyton, *sieur* de la Vallade, belonged to one of La
Rochelle's most notable families. Guyton's father was mayor of the
city in 1575. Guyton's brother, Jean, was also a distinguished member of the town council, serving as mayor in 1587 and assuming
command of a municipal militia company in 1598.[81] Jacques
Guyton, aged 28, joined the town council as a *pair* in 1573, succeeding to an office previously held by two kinsmen, Jean Nicolas
and Jean Bonier.[82] In 1584, Guyton got the office of *échevin* held
by Michel Esprinchard I. Guyton became vice-mayor in 1585, may-
or in 1586, and a militia company commander in 1598. In 1603,
after thirty years of service, Guyton resigned his post as *échevin* in
favor of his nephew, Jacques Mignonneau.

The brief official biographies above familiarize us with the

---

[78] BMLR, MS 97, fol. 19r.

[79] *Ibid.*, fols. 61r and 111r.

[80] *Ibid.*, see the lists of office holders for the years cited.

[81] *Ibid.*, see the lists of officeholders for the years cited. For information on
militia company captains and their service obligations, see BMLR, MSS 61/62,
"Annales de La Rochelle," fols. 319r-320v.

[82] BMLR, MS 95, fol. 54r. The Bonier, Guyton, and Nicolas families were linked
by old ties of marriage and godparentage, see, for examples, ADCM, I 1, fols. 33r
and 34r.

career paths of three notable rochelais town councilmen. Comparison of their service records with more personal data gleaned from wedding contracts, baptismal registers, wills, court papers, and notarized business contracts reveals common attributes that helped. these men rise fast and far in La Rochelle's town council. The chief political asset these men shared was a large family including other politically active forebears and contemporaries. Numerous successful members of the *corps de ville* not only inherited the posts of kinsmen, but also could call upon relatives in office for political favors and support.

The surreptitious nature of intrigues for office and the loss of the bulk of the town council's minute books make it very difficult to uncover all the scheming and infighting behind city politics. However, local diarists, annalists, and pamphleteers of the era frequently mention the "grandes brigues" and "factions" organized for political advantage by aspirants to office and sitting members of the *corps de ville*.[83] Kinship ties and family interests are common and salient features of the political machinations that left a trace in the archives.

In 1572, Jean Colin, André Rousseau, and Claude Texier, all *pairs*, were competing to be named captain of the militia unit in charge of one of the towers protecting La Rochelle's harbor. Although lower in seniority than Colin or Rousseau, Texier claimed that he had been promised the job by high-ranking members of the town council.[84] Texier did not name his allies in high places. However, Texier's cousin, Guillaume Texier, an *échevin* and

---

[83] In his chronicles, Barbot discusses the intrigues of family members, compounded by religious factionalism, to win the office of mayor in 1567, "Histoire de La Rochelle," AHSA, 17 (1889): 235-236. Barbot also notes how François Pontard, mayor in 1567, gained the post with the help of his "parent," Claude d'Angliers, *échevin*, a "personage riche, bien voulu, des plus capables et judicieux de son temps, apte pour remuer et manier de grandes affiares et de hautes entreprinses," *ibid.*, 255. Writing in 1606, the rochelais diarist Joseph Guillaudeau noted the "magnifique stratagème" by which Jacques Vachet gained the mayor's office, "Diaire," AHSA 38 (1908): 30. See also Guillaudeau's account of the "brigues" surrounding the 1612 mayoral race, *ibid.*, 44-45. In one of his daily journal entries, the pastor Jacques Merlin recorded the rumors of bribery and favoritism affecting the outcome of the 1606 mayoral election, "Diaire," BMLR, MS 161, fol. 31v. According to Merlin, the 1608 race for mayor was marked by "animosité, paroles injurieuses et lettres diffamatoires" between the antagonistic contenders. Merlin attributed the final outcome to a flagrant "brigue" of unprecedented dimensions perpetated by one of the contestants, *ibid.*, fol. 25r-v.

[84] BMLR, MS 97, fol. 135r.

second vice-mayor in 1572, was probably looking out for his kinsman and trying to advance Claude's career.[85]

Every year, the first and second runners-up in the mayoral race were named vice-mayors (*co-élus*). Competition for the mayor's office was usually fierce and frequently left the *co-élus* frustrated, embittered, and persistent rivals. When the post Claude Texier had been promised went to André Rousseau (whose eldest son's godfather happened to be Jean Blandin, senior *co-élu* in 1572), Texier became enraged and repeatedly interrupted a town council meeting with mockery of his opponent.[86] Texier's charges that Rousseau was underage and inexperienced for the job were seconded by François Bouhereau and his brother-in-law, René Speau, both *pairs*. François Bouhereau and Claude Texier were kinsmen through matrimonial ties linking the Bouhereau, Guybert, and Texier families. Although his ambition was checked in 1572, Claude Texier stayed in the fray of city politics, challenging the legitimacy of other council elections, and gaining the captaincy of the St. Nicolas tower in 1576.

On 23 October 1592, Jean Bergier, a *pair*, noted in his diary that an intense competition between seven men had begun for the late Pierre Girault's office of *pair*. Girault had died without designating a successor to his office. For Bergier, the most vital information about this contest included not merely the names of the seven competitors, but also their family connections. Thus, Bergier listed the contenders as: "Berandin, son-in-law of the mayor; the son of the *sieur* de Courailles; Bouhereau, son-in-law of Beaupereau; monsieur Mousnereau; Estienne Gauvain, my son-in-law; the younger Cochon; and monsieur de la Vet.[87] Jacques Mousnereau eventually captured the post, joining his brother-in-law and a cousin by marriage on the town council.[88] In La Rochelle, contests over high civic offices were family affairs often

---

[85] *Ibid.*, fol. 153r. Michel Bigot, a senior *pair* in 1572, was another likely ally of Claude Texier. On 13 September 1573, Michel Bigot became the godfather of Claude Texier's daughter, Sara, ADCM, I 8, fol. 13r. Michel Bigot was also a close friend and confidant of Guillaume Texier. Guillaume became the legal guardian of Bigot's two daughters, ADCM, 3 E 154, fol. 51r.

[86] Claude Texier's outrageous behavior ("irreverences") earned him a hefty twenty *livre* fine for obstructing the work of the *corps de ville*, BMLR, MS 97, fol. 153r.

[87] BMLR, MS 80, fol. 111v.

[88] ADCM, I 14, fol. 42r; BMLR, MS 97, fol. 53r.

decided by the number, status, and influence of a competitor's kin.

Wealth was another common attribute of the men who made it to the top of La Rochelle's town council. Although not decisive in competitions for office, a family fortune certainly enhanced a man's stature in a mercantile community like La Rochelle and could be tapped for the large bribes occasionally exchanged to sway municipal elections.[89] Notarial archives in La Rochelle are a rich source of information about the family wealth of senior town council members. For example, notarized wedding contracts stipulate the size of dowries exchanged between families and these sums can be used as one index of a household's economic status. The utility of large dowries in attracting influential spouses to and strengthening alliances between the families of town council members imbued these "gifts" with great political significance. On 16 June 1578, Jean Blandin's daughter, Janette, married Louis Benureau, *sieur* de Haulteroche. Blandin, an *échevin*, furnished Janette with a dowry of 3,000 *livres*.[90] This amount was equal to the price of a large rochelais town house and was about three times larger than dowries typically exchanged between merchant families in the city.

Jacques Guyton, an *échevin*, was an enterprising member of the town council. The landlord for a variety of properties in St. Sauveur parish, Guyton was also a financial backer of long-distance commercial fishing ventures. When Guyton's daughter, Marie, married Mathieu Bretin, a *marchand-bourgeois* of La Rochelle, in 1595, Guyton provided a dowry of 10,000 *livres*, one of the largest recorded in town archives.[91]

---

[89] The rochelais historian Pierre Mervault contends that Jacques Vachet, who received the fewest votes in the 1606 mayoral election, was chosen to be mayor that year by the king's *sénéchal* thanks to a bribe of several thousand *livres* Vachet paid to the king's man, BMLR, MS 58, fol. 141v. According to Mervault, the 1607 mayor's race was also "fixed" with a bribe. The town council debated whether Jean Sarragan, the new mayor, should be made to swear that he paid no money for the post. Rumor had it that Sarragan gave the *sénéchal* 1,200 *pistoles d'Espange* (approximately 8,400 *livres*) to get the office. Sarragan was not compelled to swear and served out his term unmolested, BMLR, MS 58, fols. 142r-v. Mervault also states that the 1611 mayoral election was decided in favor of Martin Berrandy due to a bribe of approximately 2,100 *livres* Berrandy slipped to the *sénéchal*, *ibid.*, fol. 144v.

[90] ADCM, 3 E 154, fols. 205r-206v.

[91] ADCM, 3 E 196, fols. 107r-108v. One of the few dowries comparable to Marie

A cache of Barbot family papers preserved in the registers of
the rochelais notary David Bion reveals the economic status of the
*échevin* Jacques Barbot and his family. Besides being a town council member, Barbot was a prosperous merchant able to collect
high fees from the families of apprentices he took into his trading business.[92] Barbot's eldest son, Daniel, married the daughter
of Nicolas Benureau, the *lieutenant général* of the presidial court
in La Rochelle. The Benureaus paid out a dowry of 6,000 *livres*
to win a Barbot groom.[93]

In 1591, Jacques Barbot died. His widow, Marie Bissault, soon
remarried Nicolas Benureau, the father-in-law of Bissault's son.
For her dowry, Bissault offered Nicolas Benureau her inheritance
rights to all the moveable property ( *droits mobilièrs*) derived from
her former marriage, these rights had a cash value of 33,000 *livres*.
The rich estate now controlled by the Benureau-Bissault household easily supplied large dowries for Bissault's daughters by
Jacques Barbot. In 1593, when Sara Barbot married Jacques de
Superville, La Rochelle's chief physician, she came with a dowry
of 7,500 *livres*. Sara's sister, Elizabeth, married Pierre de la Noue,
a prominent rochelais merchant, in 1599. Elizabeth's dowry
included 4,000 *livres* from her stepfather and 2,000 *livres* from her
mother. Through his family connections with the Barbots, Pierre
de la Noue also became a *pair* in 1604, assuming the office vacated by his brother-in-law, Abel Barbot.[94]

Economic resources of this magnitude typified the patrician
families ensconced in the highest offices of La Rochelle's municipal government and tended to keep male family members close
to home. Civic diplomatic missions rather than trading excursions
most commonly took politically active patricians outside of the
region. Regular income from a variety of sources afforded prominent *pairs* and *échevins* the leisure to engage in town politics and
the means to expand their political influence through adroit
investment of their patrimony.

---

Guyton's was that which Renée Thevenin, daughter of the *échevin* Jacques
Thevenin, brought to her match with the *échevin* Jean Rochelle. Renée Thevenin's
dowry and associated inheritance rights amounted to 9,000 *livres*. See ADCM, 3
E 200, fols. 369v-370r, 7 October 1599.

[92] Barbot was charging a steep 100 *livres* a year for new apprentices in 1591,
see ADCM, 3 E 192, fol. 200r.

[93] ADCM, 3 E 192, fols. 208r-209r.

[94] BMLR, MS 97, fol. 84r.

Early adherence to La Rochelle's Calvinist Reformation was a third common denominator among prominent families represented on the town council. Although "Lutheran" ideas were circulating amongst the citizenry as early as 1530, Protestant congregations only dared to emerge from clandestine meetings late in 1561. In 1561, before public sites large enough to accommodate regular prayer meetings could be found, Jean Thevenin, an *échevin*, made his own town house available for assemblies of the faithful. Members of the Blandin, Choisy, Guyton, Pierres, and Thevenin families are repeatedly named in the earliest surviving register of Protestant baptisms in La Rochelle.[95] Shared devotion to an outlawed faith and common experience in the semi-secret organization of its ceremonies enhanced the stature of some of the chief families engaged in town politics, providing them with congruent if not identical religious values. With their residences largely concentrated in the northwest quadrant of the city (parishes of St. Barthélémy and St. Sauveur), the Blandins, Choisys, Guytons, Pierres, and Thevenins dominated the neighborhood congregation that met in the *salle* Gargoulleau, an old indoor tennis court.[96] The physical location of households and their churchgoing habits contributed to the ensemble of relations, solemn and convivial, which tied together the notable family men who rose to positions of broad authority in rochelais town government.

A man's political performance cannot be appreciated apart from the dense matrix of urban solidarities in which he lived. Outstanding political careers were made by officeholders whose intertwined family connections, profitable business activities, and devotional practices vouchsafed their trustworthiness. However, as

---

[95] ADCM, I 1, see for examples, fols. 6r, 6v, 16r, 19r, 20v, and 23r. By the mid 1560's, each of these families was closely identified with the rapidly expanding Calvinist congregation in La Rochelle.

[96] Surviving early records of baptisms, marriages, and conversions for the Gargoulleau congregation record the active participation of these families in the life of the church at its inception. As noted in Chapter 3, this high degree of patrician engagement was not sustained over the long term in all rochelais Reformed churches. For example, Jean Blandin, *sieur* des Herbiers, often stood before the baptismal font at Gargoulleau as godfather to the children of his neighbors, see ADCM, I 3, fols. 6v, 8r, *et. seq.* Blandin's own son was baptised at Gargoulleau with a minister of the church as godfather, ADCM, I 3, fol. 14r. Similar rites involving Barbots, Choisys, and Thevenins can be found throughout the surviving registers of the *salle* Gargoulleau, see ADCM, I 3, I 4, I 6, I 7, I 12, and I 13.

the town council's strong interest in the *parenté* of office-seekers makes clear, evaluations of a man's suitability for a place in town government were made with preponderant weight given to his kinship affiliations. Such links, often the means by which a man made it onto the town council, never lost their political significance; they were constant indicators of a man's real and potential political influence and governing ability.

Facilitating the day-to-day operations of municipal government, underpinning the machinations of competing clans to gain new offices, and advancing the careers of La Rochelle's most noted magistrates, family ties long formed an integral component of urban politics. The numerous cousins by marriage, cousins by blood, uncles, brothers-in-law, half-brothers, brothers, and nephews who contrived to put or keep kinsmen on the town council each testify to the persistent competitive engagement of extended Protestant families in the administration and police of La Rochelle. My findings, when compared with the work of Barbara Diefendorf and Sharon Kettering on families and politics in Catholic urban communities, suggest that the French extended family, regardless of religious affiliation, had a long and commanding presence in town government of the *ancien régime*.[97]

The solicitude town councilmen showed for building kin alliances in the political sphere had a profound effect on the broader social behavior and urban culture of La Rochelle's citizenry. The annals and diaries which give a running commentary on rochelais mores throughout the period under study show us that crimes against the integrity of the family broadly conceived warranted exemplary punishment at least by civic authorities. In 1601, for example, Catherine Paullette, convicted by the mayor's court of pimping, prostitution, and "autres debauches," was shut in an iron cage, repeatedly dunked in the sea to the point of drowning, and then chased from the city.[98] On 24 May 1603, the

---

[97] See Barbara Diefendorf, *Paris City Councillors in the Sixteenth Century: The Politics of Patrimony*, (Princeton, 1983) and Sharon Kettering, *Judicial Politics and Urban Revolt in Seventeenth-Century France*, (Princeton, 1978).

[98] BMLR, MS 40, fol. 98r. The frequency with which the mayor's court investigated and punished citizens for moral lapses suggests that municipal magistrates never seriously considered turning over full responsibility for such police to the consistory of the Reformed Church. City judges probably looked upon this ecclesiastical body as an unreliable and popularly disregarded agency of social control.

mayor's court convicted Daniel Rissant, a tailor, of adultery. On three different days, Rissant was whipped through the streets and, finally, with a noose around his neck and a candle in hand, was compelled to beg God's forgiveness before the front door of the household his act defiled.[99] The same day, another convicted prostitute was beaten through the streets. According to Jacques Merlin, in 1606, a prostitute who murdered her illegitimate child was publicly tortured to death by the municipal hangman. A distraught women who hanged herself in 1607 had her body dragged through the streets by the town executioner. Her degraded corpse was then strung up by its heels and left to rot on La Rochelle's largest square.[100]

The mayoral court's attempts to regulate strictly citizens' sexuality and townswomen's reproductive capacity were vital judicial manifestations of the community's habitual regard for the conservation of family groups. As shown earlier, decisions rendered by La Rochelle's presidial court in 1565 consistently favored the preservation of patriarchal families and upheld fateful decisions made by kinsmen close and distant on behalf of other family members. In early modern La Rochelle, the extended family had the law on its side.

Gaps in the archival record of rochelais government and the inherently secretive nature of family machinations employed by townspeople to gain municipal offices make it difficult to assess whether the power of a few city clans to dominate urban politics increased over the period under study. Comparison of local intrigues over civic offices in 1550, 1572, and 1592 reveals the persistent importance of family men and family interests in the workings of these plots. The form of urban politics in La Rochelle seems unchanged.

However, as noted above, from 1606 on, rochelais diarists and historians recorded more rumors and grievances circulating among the citizenry about the ruling oligarchy's abuse of its governing privileges. For example, blatant family favoritism and bribery were widely suspected as decisive factors in the mayoral elections of 1606, 1607, 1608, and 1611. Popular criticism of the ruling regime over these accusations of corruption reached its

---

[99] BMLR, MS 40, fol. 100r.
[100] Merlin, "Diaire," fols. 11r and 185v-186r.

apogee in 1614 when reform-minded members of La Rochelle's bourgeoisie, frustrated by their ineligibility for civic office, rebelled against the oligarchic town council, sought to break its control of municipal politics, and justified their armed insurrection in a manifesto condemning the pernicious influence of kinship on the equitable government of the city. These actions strongly suggest that numerous inhabitants of La Rochelle were convinced (or at least inclined to believe) that the power of a few irresponsible family men over town government had indeed increased, creating a decadent administration detrimental to the welfare of the entire urban community.

Examining rochelais kinship networks within the context of municipal politics reveals the broad effective and affective dimensions of urban family life. In the chapter to follow, I will explore how similar networks among the middle ranks of rochelais society facilitated a bloody rebellion and worked a revolution in the city's ancient political system.

# CHAPTER FIVE

# TRANSFORMING CIVIC AUTHORITY: BOURGEOIS POLITICAL REBELLION, DESTRUCTION OF OLIGARCHICAL TOWN GOVERNMENT, AND POPULAR ASSAULT ON THE PASTORATE IN LA ROCHELLE, CIRCA 1580–CIRCA 1614

La Rochelle's tenacious opposition to police by external agents of crown and church made this place a hotbed of political and religious intrigue throughout the early modern era. As the French Religious Wars guttered out, the city recovered its economic prosperity and stood down from a nearly constant state of high alert inaugurated by the Protestant coup of 1568 and subsequent fighting against Catholic forces. The ascension of Henry IV, slow defeat of the *Ligue*, and promulgation of the Edict of Nantes restored a tenuous equilibrium to the kingdom from which La Rochelle profited. Yet, no matter how much rochelais patricians desired a return to the old status quo in town government, a restive bourgeoisie, politicized through active service in civil defense during the last wars, now demanded a greater permanent presence within the *corps de ville*. Efforts by town councillors to roll back recently acquired bourgeois rights of participation in civic administration further antagonized the two camps. When Calvinist ministers sided too openly with kindred members of the ruling oligarchy against the political aspirations of unenfranchised citizens, full-scale civil war erupted inside La Rochelle. Traditional forms of town government did not survive this conflict. In 1614, heavily armed bourgeois militiamen demanding electoral access to the *corps de ville* rose up and defeated partisans of the old town council in bloody street fighting. Calvinist clergymen became prime targets for public vilification and felt themselves so threatened by popular abuse that they contemplated mass flight from the city. One man, the *marchand-bourgeois* Jean Tharay emerged from the protestors to take a commanding role in the rebellion.

The course of the 1614 uprising has been ignored by most mod-

ern historians of La Rochelle.[1] Analysts of rebellions in early modern western France have also given no attention to the event.[2]
Fortunately, the perpetrators, victims, and witnesses of this combat have left us multiple descriptions of how it was organized,
fought, and justified.[3] My investigation of a violent and neglect-

---

[1] No mention of the 1614 uprising is made in G. Rodrigues, *Nobles et bourgeois
en Aunis et Saintonge* (Jonzac, 1989). In the recent *Histoire de La Rochelle* (Toulouse,
1985), edited by Marcel Delafosse, dean of modern rochelais historians, only two
pages (103-104) are devoted to a brief summary of the 1614 revolt. No information is given on the chief actors or victims of this event. No investigation of the
1614 rebellion is conducted in J.N. Cue, ed., *La Charente-Maritime, L'Aunis et
Saintonge des origines à nos jours,* (Saint-Jean-d'Angély, 1981). David Parker men-
tions the 1614 events only in passing and offers no detailed analysis of the social
origins and course of the revolt, see his *La Rochelle and the French Monarchy: Conflict
and Order in Seventeenth-Century France,* (London, 1980) 40-41, 44-47, and 49-50. F.
De Vaux de Foletier, *Histoire d'Aunis et Saintonge* (Paris, 1929), ignores the 1614
rebellion entirely. A reliable though picturesque and celebratory account of the
uprising is given by the antiquarian J. Ratinaud, "La Rochelle de 1610 à 1616,
Histoire de querelles municipales qui eclatent entre 'les arts majeurs' et 'les arts
mineurs' et se dénouent par le succés des arts mineurs," *Bulletin Amical des Anciens
Elèves de l'Ecole Normale Supérièure de St. Cloud* (June 1913): 27-55. No investigation
is made here of the revolt's sociology. Leopold Delayant, *Histoire des Rochelais,* 2
vols., (La Rochelle, 1870), 1: 358-375, narrates the course of the revolt but does
not explore the rebels' leadership. M. Massiou, *Histoire politique, civile et religieuse
de la Saintonge et Aunis,* 6 vols., (Paris, 1836-1838) does not discuss the political
events of 1614 in La Rochelle. M. Dupont, *Histoire de La Rochelle* (La Rochelle,
1830), 303, devotes a page to the uprising and simply notes that the leader of
the insurrection, Jean Tharay, "tenait ceux de la commune dans une terreur con-
tinuelle."

[2] For example, no mention of the 1614 rochelais rebellion is in Y.M. Bercé,
*Révolte et révolution dans l'Europe moderne,* (Paris, 1980), despite the author's extensive knowledge of early modern French west country rebellions. No reference is
made to the 1614 revolt in Bercé's *Histoire des Croquants: Etude des soulèvements
populaires au XVIIe siècle dans le sud-ouest de la France,* (Geneva, 1974). M. Bois-
sonnade, "L'Administration royale et les soulèvements populaires en Angoumois,
Saintonge et en Poitou pendant le ministère de Richelieu," *Bulletin et mémoires de
la Société des Antiquaires de l'Ouest,* 26 (1902): xix-lii, pays no attention to contemporary insurrectionary activity in La Rochelle.

[3] Contemporary sources describing the origins, course, and outcome of the
1614 rebellion include the diary of Jacques Merlin, senior pastor of La Rochelle's
Calvinist church, who gives a minutely detailed account, "Diaire de Jacques Merlin
ou recueil des choses les plus mémorables qui se sont passés en ceste ville," BMLR,
MS 161; the diary of Joseph Guillaudeau, an *avocat* before La Rochelle's presidial
court whose family became dangerously caught up in the struggle, "Diaire de
Joseph Guillaudeau," AHSA 38 (1908): 1-415; a printed manifesto produced by
the rebels in 1614 outlining their grievances against the town council, *Brève déclaration des justes motifs qui ont porté les bourgeois jurez de commune, manans et habitants de La Rochelle à supplier leurs majestez et nos seigneurs de leur conseil de remedier
par l'octroy de leurs très humbles requestes à la domination tyrannique des maire, échevins
et pairs de ladite ville,* BMLR, Rés. 897c; compendia of the twenty-eight articles

ed episode in La Rochelle's history relies on the diaries of eyewitnesses, contemporary chronicles penned by local historians, and documents from the rochelais notarial archives illuminating the daily lives of the revolt's principal instigators. This analysis of a heretofore neglected rebellion and its most forceful proponent elaborates on the means of inciting, coordinating, and directing political violence available to residents of a large, early modern French seaport.

This chapter will first track a deterioration in the political entente between the rochelais patriciate and the city's bourgeoisie resulting in starker polarizations within the urban community by 1614. The deeper social mechanisms of the ensuing rebellion will then be examined revealing how a band of insurrectionary merchants obtained sufficient popular support to achieve the single most successful urban political uprising in seventeenth-century France. The shifting topography of rochelais power politics will be mapped in urban space. By focusing in detail on the socioeconomic traits of the Tharay family, I will show the long-term genesis of a remarkable French bourgeois rebel leader. La Rochelle's oligarchical town council and its subordinate bureaucracy were only two components of a broader urban political system animated by a variety of special interests and corporate bodies including merchant associations, craft guilds, and neighborhood militia companies. The spectacular and unusually well-documented 1614 political battles give us a unique opportunity to study the roles of urban family connections and patronage networks in the creation of a rebel faction outside the traditional institutions of civic government.

---

codifying the rebels' reform program tentatively accepted by the town council in March 1614, "Titres de la Ville de La Rochelle," BMLR, MS 81, fols. 48r-59v and Jean Chenu, *Recueil des antiquitez et privileges de la ville de Bourges et de plusieurs autres villes capitales du Royaume* (Paris, 1621), 224-233, extracted directly from the register of deliberations of La Rochelle's *corps de ville* for 28 March 1614; notarized minutes of neighborhood meetings in La Rochelle at which rebels organized their protests, ADCM, Series 3 E (Notaires) 2161 (1613) fols. 131v-132r, 229r-v, and (1614) fols. 152r-155v; and the history of rochelais civic affairs written before 1616 by Jean Bruneau, a *conseiller* of La Rochelle's presidial court well acquainted with proponents and opponents of reform in municipal government, "Histoire de La Rochelle," BMLR, MS 50.

A later history of the rebellion is given by the local *érudit* Pierre Mervault, *Recueil de la naissance, progrez, accroissement et decadence de la ville de La Rochelle* (1669), BMLR, MS 58, fols. 147v-160r.

The events of 1614 established a new regime of municipal government with a significantly expanded electorate reshaping the
town council. This system emplaced violently endured for another fourteen years carrying La Rochelle toward a final, cataclysmic
confrontation with the Bourbon monarchy in 1628.

### 1. *The Breakdown of Rochelais Communal Government After 1580*

A diminishing state of war in the west country surrounding La
Rochelle permitted the densely intermarried members of the city's
governing elite to resume their sparring for political advantage
within the municipality. The arrival of senior parliamentarians
from Paris in 1584 on a mission to reform the customary law code
of Aunis caused vitriolic disputes between La Rochelle's town
council and presidial court over which body would take precedence in receiving and counselling the judicial inspectors. This
mean squabble between local magistrates became so obstructive
that no progress whatsoever could be made in legal codification
and the reform project had to be abandoned.[4] Feuding urban dignitaries now endeavored to protect their power bases by collectively purchasing (or re-purchasing) subordinate bureaucratic
offices previously farmed out or sold to private individuals. Flush
with higher tax revenues, largely generated by recovering port
traffic, the town council in 1587 reacquired the secretariat of the
city's accounting office, buying out three private investors for a
total of 4,000 *livres*.[5] The *corps de ville* also set about repaying old,
outstanding war loans received from non-members in an effort to
diminish outsiders' financial leverage within the institution. Both
tactics hardened the boundaries of power defining the oligarchy
in charge of town government.

La Rochelle's antipathy toward the *Ligue* made the city a target
for escalating emergency loan requests from both Henry III and
Henry de Navarre. Sharp quarrels among townspeople over who
would be required to contribute the sums demanded retarded this
fund raising and immediately sapped whatever unity of purpose

---

[4] Louis-Etienne Arcère, *Histoire de la ville de La Rochelle et du pays d'Aunis*, 2
vols., (La Rochelle, 1756; reprint Marseille: 1975), 2: 54.
[5] BMLR, MS 46, fol. 1159.

the Rochelais derived from their new, unexpected status as royalists.

In June of 1588, Henry III, through his west country agent Dupin, attempted to impose excise taxes for military purposes on staples like wine, spices, and fish traded through La Rochelle's harbor. The mayor acquiesced to these new charges and instructed the city's herald to post notices of higher duty rates on the walls of the customs house next day at noon when most businessmen would be off the streets enjoying a long lunch. As soon as the imposts became common knowledge, outraged merchants, including several town councilmen, summoned up a crowd of over 600 angry artisans, shopkeepers, and traders who chased down the sly herald and tossed him into the port. A sergeant of the admiralty court also responsible for surreptitious announcement of the new duties suffered a similar fate. Workingmen readily joined merchants in these protests because increased customs rates would raise prices for many essential building supplies and other raw materials passing through the port. Rumors circulated that the mayor and senior town councilmen had accepted enormous bribes from Dupin in exchange for authorization of the war levies. The crowd ripped down and burned all notices of the royal charges while publicly denouncing the mayor and threatening Dupin with death. The king's agent barely made it out of town alive.[6] Fearing assassination, the mayor wisely let the matter drop. Henry III never received the full amount of financial aid he expected.

In 1590, desperately seeking to fund his own military campaigns, the King of Navarre sought 20,000 *écus* from the Rochelais. Staggered by the size of the subsidy demanded but unwilling to snub a Protestant battling for the French throne, the *corps de ville* resolved to make all town residents, including ministers, contribute. Now the pastors, led by the influential Odet de Nort, proved unwilling to pay. From his pulpit, de Nort vehemently preached against this plan, asserting the Reformed clergy's complete exemption from all war taxation even if the proceeds went to help a Protestant prince.[7] City officials grudgingly accepted this

---

[6] Dupont, *Histoire de La Rochelle*, 278-280; Delayant, *Histoire des Rochelais*, 1: 323-24.

[7] Arcère, *Histoire de la ville de La Rochelle*, 2: 73-74.

argument. Given popular adulation of Henry de Navarre in La Rochelle and the conspicuous size of de Nort's personal fortune, the minister's claim of immunity from payment could not have endeared him to his humbler congregants now left to foot a bigger portion of Henry's bill. The financial demands of warriors against the *Ligue* fissured the loyal Protestant communities like La Rochelle they importuned for logistical support.

Anxious to repair and upgrade La Rochelle's war-damaged defenses, the town council now rigorously exercised its ancient presumed right to call in at set intervals unpaid work gangs (*corvées*) from villages within the city's *banlieue*. These summonses starkly demonstrated the extensive police powers of the *corps de ville* and their frequent use after 1589 can be seen as one tactic by which town councilmen sought to reassert their supreme governing authority against all challengers outside and inside the city. In November 1593, when village elders in the adjacent hamlet of Thairé refused to organize a work party as demanded by the city, La Rochelle's mayor mobilized the municipal militia, broke out the city's field artillery, and prepared to march on the obstreperous rustics. Presidial court magistrates seeking to embarrass rival town councilmen and to deny them even the modicum of glory a descent on Thairé might yield, sided with the villagers and ordered the mobilization to be stopped. Royal judges and town councillors nearly came to blows in this confrontation before the consistory managed a reconciliation of all parties involved.[8]

Faltering local harvests in the 1590's aggravated by the town council's inept administration of urban provisioning further riled the citizenry. To ward off famine in town, the mayor ordered the seizure of all laden foreign grain freighters calling at the port and sale of their cargos at controlled prices. These tactics initially brought some cereals onto the market but backfired when forewarned ship captains began bypassing La Rochelle entirely. The city could not be adequately supplied by the small fleet of cargo ships based there. In 1594, food riots broke out in La Rochelle. Hungry city women with families to feed tried to stone the mayor. His contingent of bodyguards had to be doubled to cope with mounting death threats.

Growing pacification of France under the ascendant Henry IV

---

[8] *Ibid.*, 75-76.

seems to have fueled rather than allayed political tensions within La Rochelle. Freed from pressing concerns over communal defense against outside aggression, the Rochelais intensified their internal battles over local power and privileges. City councilmen aggressively asserted the preeminence of the *corps de ville* in all matters of civic administration. Greater surveillance and control of the municipal militia were prime objectives of the town councillors. In 1597, city magistrates created the new post of *chevalier du guet* and handpicked its first occupant. The duties of this functionary, who was only answerable to the town council and served at its discretion, included supervising the town watch, identifying householders who refused to man neighborhood patrols, and inventorying all civic arsenals.[9]

In the next year, La Rochelle's *échevins* altered the command structure for all city militia companies to the advantage of town councilmen. They decreed that henceforward only members of the *corps de ville* would be eligible for selection as militia company commanders and lieutenants. This move eliminated militia commissions previously accorded to members of the bourgeoisie. In an effort to mollify displaced bourgeois, town councillors reserved for them the new rank of company ensign. However, this novel post was a largely ceremonial one endowed with no substantive powers of command. *Echevins* thanked and dismissed all current militia officers, some having served continuously since the last restructuring of the town's armed forces in 1572. A new group of sixteen *échevins* and *pairs* formed the officer corps (captains and lieutenants) heading the eight main companies of the civic militia. A ninth company remained under the mayor's personal direction.[10] Another path of privilege toward greater civic stature and political influence became closed to Rochelais of middling social rank. Unenfranchised citizens, including frustrated militiamen, watching well-born neighbors employ gifts of heavy artillery to the city in competitions for a seat on the *corps de ville*, now acerbicly joked that pistols as well as cannons might be used for breaking into civic government.

The town council also showed an increasing determination to cut representatives of La Rochelle's bourgeoisie out of an advi-

---

[9] BMLR, MS 62, Jaillot, "Annales de La Rochelle," fol. 317.
[10] *Ibid.*, fols. 319-20.

sory role in the conduct of municipal government and diplomacy. In preparation for delicate negotiations with the royal governor of Poitou over acceptance of the Edict of Nantes in La
Rochelle and its *banlieue*, local burghers named fifteen deputies
to present their views.[11] Town councilmen ready to parley with
the king's envoy called the size of the middle class delegation pre-
sumptuous and detrimental to efficient bargaining. When the fifteen delegates presented themselves before the council chambers
to begin negotiations, *échevins* slammed the door in their faces.[12]
Only quick intervention by city pastors kept this quarrel from
degenerating into armed confrontation. Seconded by Calvinist
clerics, city councillors convinced assembled members of the bourgeoisie that only two of their elected representatives needed to
participate in the peace conference. Bourgeois leaders accepted
this reduction in exchange for the mayor's promise not to conclude any peace without submitting the proposed pact to public
scrutiny and approval. The reputable *marchand-bourgeois* Pierre
Bernardeau was chosen to be one of the two remaining bourgeois
delegates. Despite significant public opposition, civic leaders
accepted all provisions of the Edict of Nantes, including reestablishment of the Catholic Mass in La Rochelle. Diehard Calvinist
opponents of the treaty, incited by at least one pastor, ransacked
the only local church slated for reconversion to Catholic use.

Ominous protests did not deter the town council from expansion of its prerogatives at the expense of bourgeois political ambitions. In May 1608, the *corps de ville* spent 20,000 *livres* purchasing back from a concessionaire the right to collect a tax on all
goods handled through the royal weigh station near the harbor.[13]
Merchants denounced this transaction because absorption by the
town council of another office regulating trade gave municipal
magistrates added potential to manipulate port fees and profit at
the expense of businessmen. Promises from city officials to veri-
fy poundage account books annually and publicize the results
reduced but did not eliminate the bourgeoisie's fears of patrician
malfeasance.

Simmering popular discontent with oligarchical town govern-

---

[11] Three unenfranchised householders from each of La Rochelle's five urban
parishes were named to this delegation. See Massiou, *Histoire politique*, 5: 169-70.
[12] BMLR, MS 62, Jaillot, "Annales de La Rochelle," fol. 324.
[13] Delayant, *Histoire des Rochelais*, 1: 333.

ment boiled over as city councillors competed ever more unscrupulously to win the mayor's office and titular authority over expanding civic patronage networks. Diarists and amateur historians in La Rochelle kept a close eye on town politics. After 1600, they recorded growing public complaints over abuses in the selection of town councilmen by cooptation and over the corrupted election of mayors.

The local annalist Pierre Mervault noted popular suspicions about the bribery of voting town councilmen allegedly committed by successful candidates for mayor in 1606, 1607, and 1611.[14] The Calvinist pastor Jacques Merlin recorded in his diary that "grandes plaintes" were heard throughout the city in 1607 over the "notable somme de deniers" accepted by the king's *sénéchal* from the wealthy Jean Sarragan just before the *sénéchal* chose Sarragan to be mayor that year.[15] Merlin remarked that the 1608 mayoral election saw a vituperative, defamatory contest between the *échevins* Isaac Blandin and François Prevost. According to Merlin, Prevost and Blandin went after the mayor's office "relentlessly, because each man was determined to prevent the other from winning. Since my arrival in this city [1589], I have never seen such a dirty campaign. It was thrashed out with hatred, calumnies, and scurrilous letters, in short, by every means available to debase a fellow man. These events gave the pastors ample cause for making long and solemn public denunciations of such behavior."[16] Increasingly flagrant graft, feuding, and abuse of public confidence by town councillors undermined the old political regime of La Rochelle and, according to local ministers, threat-

---

[14] Pierre Mervault, "Recueil de la naissance, progrez, accroissement et decadence de la ville de La Rochelle," BMLR, MS 58, fols. 141v, 142r, and 144v.

[15] Merlin "Diaire," BMLR, MS 161, fols. 419r-420r. Sarragan had previously aroused public indignation when he gained admittance to the town council as a *pair* in part because he donated a powerful, costly cannon to the city's arsenal.

[16] "Sur cette nouvelle mairie est à remarquer que la recherche d'icelle s'est fait de la part desdites sieurs de Fief Mignon [Blandin] et Prevost avecques une instance extreme, d'autant qu'ils se vouloyent empescher l'un l'autre d'entrer en l'election; et puis bien dire n'avoir point remarqué une semblable brigue depuis que je suis en cette ville, que celle-la. Car elle s'est démenée par animosité, par paroles injurieuses, par lettres déffamatoires...bref, par tous les moyens desquels on s'est peu adviser pour débouter son compagnon, ce qui a donné matière aux pasteurs de faire en public des grandes et sérieuses remonstrancess, afin de reprendre telles procedures, ce qu'aussi ils ont fait," Merlin, "Diaire," fols. 25r-26r.

ened the welfare of a Christian municipality. City fathers completely ignored ministerial criticism of corrupt electioneering.

Local and national political intrigues combined to make the
1612 mayoral election in La Rochelle particularly venomous.
Ravillac's assassination of Henry IV in May 1610 hit the Rochelais
hard. Subsequent dismissal of the duc de Sully, foremost
Protestant minister of state, by the queen regent, Marie de Medici,
intensified alarm in the Protestant communities of the west country. The Rochelais had been particularly attached to both men. It
was a newly converted Calvinist minister in the entourage of
Jeanne d'Albret, Queen of Navarre and mother of Henry IV, who
first openly preached the Reformed religion in La Rochelle. In
1555, Henry IV's father, Antoine, duc de Bourbon, King of
Navarre, won the respect of the Rochelais as the French
monarch's capable lieutenant and governor for the city and
region of La Rochelle.[17] The young Henry's absent-minded tum-
ble into La Rochelle's port and rescue by a hardy rochelais sailor
was an endearing tale retold countless times in the city.

Numerous members of La Rochelle's *haute bourgeoisie* and *corps
de ville* had become financially obligated to the duc de Sully, formerly the king's *lieutenant général* in upper and lower Poitou. Since
1610, Sully's agents had been buying up first and second mort-
gages on the urban and rural properties of rochelais merchants
and town councilmen. *Rentes* between Sully and wealthier
Rochelais were drawn up whereby, after advancing the property
owners large sums of cash, the duke became the beneficiary of
what amounted to loan repayments with interest from the townsmen. The real estate in La Rochelle on which the *rentes* were established served as collateral for the money advanced. These mone-
tary transactions, largely handled by the rochelais notary Pierre
Masset and attracting numerous local participants among the city's
governing elite, multiplied economic and political ties between
La Rochelle's citizenry and royal financiers.[18] Sully's fall thus

---

[17] See Amos Barbot, "Histoire de La Rochelle," AHSA, 17 (1889): 130-133.

[18] For examples of the *rentes* created between Sully and rochelais property owners, see ADCM, 3 E 2160 (1612), fols. 180r, 184v, 204r-v, 223r, 224v, 226r-v, and
230r. The deal between Sully and Jean Gaultier, *marchand-bourgeois* of La Rochelle,
is typical of this kind of transaction. Gaultier ceded and transported to Sully a
*rente hypothèquaire* in the amount of 200 *livres* on a house Gaultier owned in La
Rochelle. Sully's agent then, on the spot, paid Gaultier 3,200 *livres* in cash, a sum

endangered not only the security of French Reformed communities, but also the personal finances of his notable rochelais allies.

In an effort to divide her Reformed opposition and deny great Protestant nobles the logistical support of strategic Calvinist towns, Marie de Medici tried to sway the outcome of mayoral elections in several west country towns. The regent bungled an attempt to remove the Calvinist grandee Henry, duc de Rohan, from his governorship of Saint-Jean-d'Angély, a Protestant town only fifty kilometers from La Rochelle. This royal meddling greatly troubled the Rochelais.[19]

Marie also tried unsuccessfully to manipulate the 1612 mayoral election in La Rochelle. Operating through her local agent, the *échevin* Jean Rochelle, the queen regent first attempted to disqualify one of the mayoral candidates suspected of allegiance to Rohan. Failing at this, Rochelle encouraged the newly elected mayor, Jean Salbert, to become a protégé of the queen. Before returning to Paris where he also served as a member of the Parlement, Jean Rochelle met with Salbert, inquiring whether Salbert would care to send the queen an ingratiating letter or to avail himself of Rochelle's talents as an influential intermediary with the court. Rochelle personally offered to carry any kind words from Salbert to the queen and, mentioning Salbert's numerous children and kinsmen, insinuated that his pliant service to the crown as mayor might win royal favors for the entire family.[20] Salbert coldly replied that he had never met the queen, that he had nothing to write to her about, no need whatsoever to send her an oral message, and that his only concern was to fulfill loy-

---

Gaultier obligated himself to repay in annual installments due on the first of January until retirement of the debt, see ADCM, 3 E, 2160, fol. 223r. Sometimes such deals fell through. The *rente hypothèquaire* of 1,125 *livres* jointly established with Sully by the *pair* Pierre Guibert, the *avocat du roi* Daniel de la Goutte, and the merchant Jacques Pronis was abrogated on 26 December 1612 because Sully's man could not come up with the 18,000 *livre* purchase price, see ADCM, 3 E 2160, fols. 226r-v. *Rentes* were legal interest-bearing investments from which Sully no doubt profited handsomely.

[19] The town council of La Rochelle had allied itself with the governor of Saint-Jean-d'Angély and met regularly with Rohan's agents who controlled the town. For a closer description of the regent's intrigues see J.A. Clarke, *Huguenot Warrior: The Life and Times of Henri de Rohan, 1579-1638*, (The Hague, 1966), 40-43. On contemporaneous local political machinations see M. Saudu, "Saint-Jean-d'Angély en 1612," AHSA 4 (1877): 231-260.

[20] Merlin, "Diaire," BMLR, MS 161, fols. 152v-153r.

ally his obligation to guard the city for the king of France and his male heirs.

Unable to control local politics through the *corps de ville*, the council of state gave Jean Rochelle a new commission as intendant of justice and police for his home town. He returned to the west country on this dangerous mission in August 1612. Rumors quickly spread through the city about the scope and purpose of Rochelle's charge. The town council met in special session and a majority of members voted to demand written assurances from Rochelle that he would never attempt to exercise such an office. Rochelle refused to comply. Citizens now surreptitiously affixed placards to Rochelle's front door denouncing him as a traitor to town and church.

On 5 September 1612, a large group of merchants, artisans, and laborers ("bourgeois et habitants" according to pastor Merlin) invaded the courtyard of the town hall, demanding that the *corps de ville* immediately exile Jean Rochelle and anyone else factionalizing the city. The mayor hesitated to act. Those assembled now directed their threats of violence at town councilmen as the confrontation grew angrier. When a gouty *échevin* and ally of Rochelle brandished his cane at the crowd, a cry of "To Arms!" went up as the mob in the courtyard streamed out to grab weapons, barricade streets, and hold the city until Rochelle was put out.[21]

A second alarm brought over 700 townspeople, men, women, and children, into the street before Rochelle's house. Armed bourgeois militiamen mingled with a crowd of "menu peuple."[22] Fearing for his life, Rochelle begged the mayor for his personal escort out of the city. Under a hail of insults and paving stones launched by porters, sailors, and workingmen, Rochelle made it to the closest town gate under the mayor's protection. Several of Rochelle's kinsmen and cohorts were seriously wounded. A sniper, firing from the city wall, tried to kill Rochelle as he galloped out of town.

---

[21] *Ibid.*, fols. 153r-154v.

[22] *Ibid.*, fol. 155r. The *procès verbal* later drawn up by the president of La Rochelle's presidial court to initiate legal proceedings against the perpetrators of this attack identified a majority of the insurgents as "portefaix, matelots, et autres de vile condition," see the "Procés verbal du tumulte de La Rochelle le 5 septembre 1612 faict par le president de ladite ville," BN, Manuscrits Français, Anciens Fonds 23339, fols. 36r-39r.

A dual threat in the person of Rochelle to the communal institutions and religious alliances of the city had been decisively met
and thwarted by popular action. Royal efforts to influence the
course of politics in La Rochelle failed dismally. However, Rochelle's sympathizers within the *corps de ville* and the mayor's temporizing discredited the town council as principal guarantor of
civic traditions, religious solidarity, and community police. Clumsy
royal intervention in the city's internal affairs accelerated a general loss of confidence amongst townspeople in the propriety and
utility of the established system of urban government, Already
undermined by the bribery and corruption scandals surrounding
the mayoral elections of 1606, 1607, 1608, and 1611, popular
acquiescence to the oligarchic rule of intensely competitive family men on the town council did not survive the events of 1612.
A politics of open confrontation between governors and governed
ensued, dramatically altering the municipal administration of La
Rochelle.

### 2. *From Bourgeois Political Dissent to Bourgeois Political Rebellion*

Restive members of the citizenry used the Rochelle affair as a pretext to press their demands for reform of recruitment to the town
council. In early October 1612, only weeks after Rochelle's igno-
minious escape, groups of disgruntled townsmen, primarily merchants with bourgeois status, began to meet clandestinely and to
discuss methods for challenging the oligarchs of the *corps de ville*.
The protestors had two initial objectives. First, they intended to
prohibit town councilmen from handpicking their successors
through resignations of office. Second, they wished to compel
local royal magistrates who also sat on the town council to choose
between their charges and serve either the king or the commune,
but not both at once. If each objective could be achieved, offices
on the town council would be freed up for which La Rochelle's
bourgeoisie could then elect candidates. Success could also better insulate the town council against crown influence by diminishing the number of royal jurists on it. By April 1613, a committee of eight bourgeois representatives had been formed to
foment opposition against the old *corps de ville*.

Who were the early leaders of this opposition? The spokesmen

of the movement were Pierre Bernardeau, Jean Brussard, Zacherie
Chatton, Jacques Grenot, Simon Papin, Bernard Philbert, Jean
Tharay, and Israel Torterue. My research has uncovered no background information on Brussard. Philbert may have been a
rochelais ship captain.[23] Pierre Bernardeau can be positively identified as a successful merchant draper and major urban landlord
in the St. Sauveur quarter. He possessed a large town house and
more than 30,000 *livres* in investment capital. Although active in
international commerce, Bernardeau also enriched himself by the
sale of grain in small quantities to artisans, laborers, and peasants.[24] As co-agent since 1589 for urban properties owned by the
ancient *commanderie* of the Knights Templar in La Rochelle,
Bernardeau was also the administrator and beneficiary of rents in
cash and kind (including grain) generated by houses and wind-
mills concentrated in his home parish of St. Sauveur. Between
1593 and 1598, Bernardeau and his partner, the *pair* François
Piguenit, paid the Knights of Jerusalem, heirs of the Templars,
1,740 *livres* a year for the right to collect these rents.[25] Aged about
70 in 1613, the father of four children by his first wife, guardian
of his second wife's two sons, and godfather for ten neighborhood
children, Pierre Bernardeau was a man of considerable repute in
the social and economic life of his quarter.[26] Finally, Bernardeau

---

[23] Merlin, "Diaire," fol. 199r. On 9 December 1614, Merlin referred to Philbert
as "capitaine Philbert." This honorific may have denoted Philbert's maritime service or possibly his office in a civic militia company.

[24] The economic activity of Pierre Bernardeau can be analyzed through contracts and other notarized documents conserved in the ADCM, series 3 E, registers of local notaries. For example, on 21 June 1594, Pierre Bernardeau invested 20,000 *livres* in a trading partnership with his brother Abraham and Pierre
Milleray, a merchant living near St. Etienne in Poitou. The partners intended to
deal in "draps, toilles et merciers," ADCM, 3 E 204 (1594) fols. 31r-33r. In
February of 1596, more than twenty artisans and rural laborers living in villages
around La Rochelle owed Bernardeau between ten and fifty *livres* for flour, wine,
and salt he had sold to them, see for examples ADCM, 3 E 205 (1596), fols. 40v-
41r, 44r, 49r, 50r, 51r, 56v, 57r, 70v, 71r, and 73r. Bernardeau was still profiting
from this trade in 1599, see ADCM, 3 E 208, fol. 5r. Bernardeau also built his
fortune by loaning money to ship captains, ship chandlers, and merchants pressed
for cash, see ADCM, 3 E 205 (1596), fol. 221v. For Bernardeau's dealings with
English merchants based in London, see ADCM, 3 E 2042 (1596), fol. 173r.

[25] ADCM, 3 E 192, fols. 161r-v. Bernardeau and Piguenit also collected rental
fees on a number of farms, fields, and vineyards outside La Rochelle owned by
the *commanderie*. See for examples, ADCM, 3 E 204 (1593) fols. 116r and 225r-v,
and 3 E 204 (1594) fols. 235v-236r.

[26] For information on Pierre Bernardeau's family life see ADCM, 3 E 204, fols.

was a seasoned representative of bourgeois interests, having served as one of the delegates from this community in negotiations with royal officials over local enforcement of the Edict of Nantes.

Zacherie Chatton, thirty-seven years old, was also a merchant and property owner in the St. Sauveur parish. His father had been a sergeant of the local royal presidial court and Chatton started out in life as a clerk apprenticed to a rochelais notary.[27] Through his marriage to the daughter and sole heiress of a recently deceased rochelais wine merchant, Chatton became deeply involved in one of the most important staple trades of the French west country.

Jacques Grenot, about sixty years old in 1613, was a prosperous *marchand-bourgeois* trafficking principally in wine and renting out small properties to a wide variety of lodgers in his home parish of St. Nicolas.[28] Simon Papin, thirty-five in 1613, was a very wealthy merchant-draper residing in the St. Sauveur neighborhood. He adroitly managed international commercial ventures and a diversified portfolio of local real estate investments.[29]

Jean Tharay, thirty-six in 1613, was a *marchand-bourgeois* engaged in diverse business ventures and urban property rentals centered in the port district of Perrot. Tharay and his kinsmen had long been involved in provisioning the city with grain, flour, breads of all kinds, wine, and other essential commodities. Tharay's lodgers included large numbers of artisans and dockyard laborers. By 1613, Tharay was both the stepson and son-in-law of his fellow conspirator Jacques Grenot.[30] The intricacies of this family connection were vital to the genesis and scope of the 1614 revolt.

The last leading dissident was Israel Torterue, thirty-nine in 1613, an enterprising rochelais spice merchant married to the daughter of a deceased town councilmen. Israel Torterue's business interests included the sale and barter of exotic spices and medicines. In May 1599, he swapped 400 *livres* worth of ginger for an equivalent value of drugs and medicinal oils provided by

---

245v-248r (his second marriage contract); ADCM, 3 E 208, fol. 5r; ADCM, Series I (*Etat civil protestant*) I 10, fol. 44r, I 12, fol. 98r, I 14, fols. 17v, 20r, 34r, 65v, 115v, 133v, and 160r, I 15, fol. 38r, I 16, fols. 5r and 93r, and I 17 fols. 22v, 71r, 79v, and 100v.

[27] ADCM, 3 E 202, fol. 114r and 3 E 207, fols. 215r-v.
[28] For an example of these activities see ADCM, 3 E 2161, fol. 152r.
[29] See for example, ADCM, 3 E 199, fol. 424r.
[30] ADCM, 3 E 2043 (1599), fols. 78v-79r.

a merchant of Montpellier.[31] Torterue also profited on the acquisition and sale of debts owed by the merchants of other cities (notably Angers) and through real estate transactions. In January of 1614, Torterue rented out a substantial portion of the commercial and domestic space of his own commodious house to a fellow merchant for 180 *livres* per year.[32] Torterue carefully stipulated in the rental agreement that he was to retain free access to the cellar for storage and sampling of his wines.

The diarist Merlin refers to these eight men as "procureurs" empowered by other members of the bourgeoisie to parley on their behalf with the town council.[33] (Figure 10 gives a map showing the arrangement of La Rochelle's neighborhoods and landmarks helpful in tracking the protestors' actions.) Although well-known to their fellow citizens, the leaders of the incipient bourgeois campaign of political protest escaped the attention of royal spies reporting back to Paris on rochelais affairs. In January 1613, Pontchartrain, a *conseiller du roi* charged with intelligence gathering from the west country, received a long report from an anonymous source describing severe factional conflicts among the citizenry of La Rochelle.[34] Although ostensibly concerned with the "principaux seditieux" of the city, this transmission makes no mention whatsoever of the *procureurs* for the bourgeoisie demanding major changes in the governance and external diplomacy of the city. The anonymous source devoted almost all of his attention to the partisans of the duc de Rohan and sympathetic members of La Rochelle's ruling oligarchy. As restive members of the bourgeoisie in La Rochelle moved toward rebellion, the king's men found themselves with little or no information about their most dangerous, locally ascendant opponents.

Determining the proximate causes of the bourgeois protest campaign inaugurated in 1612 is not difficult. The list of popular grievances against the corruption of the *corps de ville* and the

---

[31] ADCM, 3 E 200, fol. 258. Torterue may have obtained his rare spices with the help of his brother, Jean, who regularly sent ships to the Low Countries, Spain, and the Barbary coast of Africa, see ADCM, 3 E 216, fols. 21v, 93r, 97r, and 103r; also 3 E 218, fols. 1r-v and 117v-118v.

[32] ADCM, 3 E 2161 (1614), fols. 1r-2r. Torterue's house fronted on the *canton* nearest the town hall in the parish of St. Sauveur.

[33] Merlin, "Diaire," fols. 187r and 192v.

[34] BN, Collection Clairambault, 362, fols. 210r-212r. Message to Pontchartrain transmitted from La Rochelle by "un personnage" unknown.

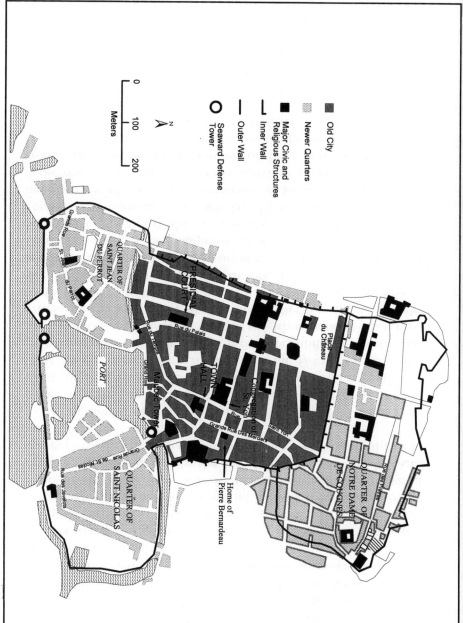

Figure 10. Neighborhoods of La Rochelle Circa 1614

imperiled military security of the city plainly states the motives
that prompted many merchants and bourgeois to call for reform
of the old oligarchy dominating municipal self-government. Fat-
homing the motives which led Bernardeau, Chatton, Grenot,
Papin, Tharay, and Torterue to become the outspoken and audacious leaders of that reform movement is more complicated. They
were certainly not goaded to act by empty stomachs or progressive impoverishment under the old regime of civic rule. Some of
these men easily ranked among the wealthiest merchants of La
Rochelle. Fortunes like those of Bernardeau and Papin rivaled
even the estates amassed by the wealthiest *pairs* and *échevins*. And
therein may lie one explanation of the *procureurs'* political behavior.

To resourceful men like Bernardeau, Papin, and Tharay, little
could be denied in La Rochelle except that extra sheen of prestige conferred by admission to the centuries-old town council. The
mercantile success of Bernardeau, Chatton, Grenot and the other *procureurs* invested each man with self-confidence, pride, and
high social status in their respective neighborhoods. Wealth, cleverness, perspicacity, and ambition won richer bourgeois the right
to do business with patricians, rent houses from them, flatter them
with invitations to become godparents, witness their weddings,
become the guardians of their orphaned children, and on occasion, even marry their daughters. However, the one thing such
respectable qualities could never assure was a place on the town
council for the *procureurs* or their kin. Under such conditions, the
familiarity of *procureurs* and patricians could only aggravate bourgeois discontent. Even the most convivial events joining town
councilmen and wealthier members of the bourgeoisie must have
contained subtle but firm reminders of the one privilege that
would ever set them apart and divide their loyalties. An incomplete camaraderie could not satisfy merchants who considered
themselves the equals of their patrician acquaintances and worthy of a crowning achievement to an honorable career: a place
on the town council through which to serve their city, protect
their religious freedoms, and further advance the reputation of
their families. The urgency of this final attainment in the minds
of its seekers could only be magnified by deteriorating relations
after 1610 between Protestant and Catholic communities in all of
France, by increasingly brazen royal efforts to subvert traditional

forms of municipal government, and by the growing evidence of corrupt electoral practices in mayoral races popularly perceived as sapping the town council's capacity to protect the city in troubled times. Bernardeau, Chatton, Grenot, and their cohorts championed the opposition to a town council on which they knew their families deserved an influential place.

Initial meetings of the procurers were held in the home of Pierre Bernardeau and at the residence of Gilles Bardonin, an *avocat* before the royal presidial court in La Rochelle. Merlin noted that rumors now circulating in town accused Gabriel de Bourdigalle, the king's prosecutor of the presidial court, of aiding the protest movement. At least five other attorneys accredited to plead before the presidial can be identified as allies of the protestors.[35]

La Rochelle's presidial court had been established by Henry II in 1552 with a staff of twenty. By 1612, the court's personnel had doubled and sixty-eight local attorneys were sanctioned to represent clients before the tribunal. At any one time, sixteen presidial court officers had royal authorization to serve simultaneously on La Rochelle's town council. To reduce this number, representatives of the rochelais bourgeoisie initiated a law suit before the *Conseil d'Etat* in late 1612, claiming that older royal statutes prohibited such dual service.

Mounted concurrently with their challenge to the town council, the deputies' legal proceeding before the crown was a bold stratagem to factionalize the presidial court in La Rochelle by fanning the personal animosities and professional ambitions of its officers. Success for the deputies in this suit would force five of the most senior presidial officers to choose between their legal posts and their positions on the town council. Five of the top ten *avocats* serving the presidial and six other jurists would face a similar choice. Such an outcome could significantly alter the rank-

---

[35] Guillaudeau, "Diaire," 95. Two other *avocats* of the presidial court met convivially with leading dissidents and may have been supporters of their attack on the town council. See the wedding contract of F. Regnault, witnessed by several leaders of the bourgeoisie's protest movement and two presidial jurists, ADCM, 3 E 219, 4 May 1614. In the 1613 report to Pontchartrain on subversive political activity in La Rochelle, only one member of the presidial court, the king's *avocat* named La Goutte, is listed among seditious agitators operating in La Rochelle, a clear understatement of the problem. See BN, Collection Clairambault, 362, fol. 210v.

ing of presidial court officers, allowing less senior legists to ascend to higher, more prestigious positions within the court. For instance, the suit might force two of Gabriel de Bourdigalle's immediate superiors to leave the court, enabling him to move up in rank and increase his opportunities to profit from his judicial office. For dissident *avocats* in a crowded legal confraternity like Bardonin, a suit resulting in fewer senior competitors for clients and fees would be a boon to their own careers. De Bourdigalle's support for the bourgeois protestors is thus highly plausible and the proven support of lesser presidial magistrates for the bourgeois deputies intelligible.

Predictably, presidial court officers also holding seats on the town council became outraged by the bourgeoisie's challenges to both institutions. Joseph Guillaudeau, an *avocat* to the presidial and a *pair* on the town council since 1574, peppered his diary with denunciations of the protestors.[36] Guillaudeau's brother, Pierre, also an *avocat* and *pair*, became a prime target of the 1614 rebellion, much to Joseph's chagrin. This information strongly suggests that the members of La Rochelle's royal presidial court divided over support for the rebels. Factions within the court enabled the rebels to gather force and prevented the court from effectively impeding their progress toward revolt.

Joseph Guillaudeau's diary provides another important clue about the consolidation of rebel forces and their leadership. As noted above, the deputies chosen to articulate the grievances of the rochelais bourgeoisie worked primarily as merchants. Although the deputies shared the status of *marchand-bourgeois*, their ages, social origins, and fortunes varied considerably. Some were richer, some were much poorer than the oligarchs they challenged on the town council. Yet, important similarities do connect leading protestors. For example, Bernardeau, Grenot, and Tharay were important urban landlords and shared business practices that regularly brought them into close contact with consumers from all ranks of rochelais society.

Joseph Guillaudeau alerts us to another similarity associating

---

[36] Guillaudeau criticized Simon Papin's defiance of the mayor's orders for members of the bourgeoisie to cease their protest meetings. The diarist castigated the protestors for acting solely on their "autorité privée" and mocked Pierre Bernardeau as a "soi-disant procureur;" see Guillaudeau's "Diaire," 51, 54, and 56.

the bourgeoisie's representatives. In early 1614, Guillaudeau referred in his diary to the deputies as "non-originaires."[37] This term, an epithet really, was subsequently used by councilmen to denigrate their bourgeois opponents as newcomers to town without a deep attachment to civic institutions and thus unfit to serve in them.

Compared to many men on the town council who could trace their family's presence in La Rochelle back over more than a century, the deputies and their supporters were, indeed, more recent arrivals. Jean Tharay's lineal ascendants had settled in the port district of Perrot in the 1550's. Jacques Grenot's presence in the quarter of St. Nicolas dates from the early 1570's. Bernardeaus are first mentioned in the registers of the Protestant état civil for La Rochelle in 1564.[38] The family of Gilles Bardonin, the presidial jurist apparently most sympathetic to the deputies, is first cited among Calvinist church records in 1599.[39] Coordinators of the protest against the old town council were mostly established residents of La Rochelle but without a long native pedigree. The bourgeoisie's challenge to the town council can thus be explained, in part, as a bid by a new cadre of citizens for admission to municipal offices previously monopolized by older, native town families.

The deputies' earliest demands call for thorough reform in the electioneering of the town council. The unenfranchised merchants, intent on controlling nepotism and graft in municipal politics, first sought abolition of all sales of office on the town council, repression of the bribery rich men used in contests for mayor, wider access to municipal offices for members of the bourgeoisie, the right to elect five *syndics* admissible to meetings of the town council, and the right of bourgeois representatives to hold a passkey for every town gate, making it impossible for the mayor to open any portal without their consent.[40]

---

[37] Guillaudeau, "Diaire," 54.

[38] See the lists of rochelais families and the first dates of their citation in the Protestant *état civil* for the city in L. M. Mechinet de Richemond, *Origine et progrès de la Réforme à La Rochelle* (Paris, 1872): 111-120.

[39] ADCM, I 18, Church Admissions, 15 August 1599.

[40] Merlin, "Diaire," fol. 160r. The rebels' dissatisfaction with both the personnel and the structure of town government and their proposals for changing both suggest that the 1614 unrest in La Rochelle rapidly became the type of constitutional crisis Christopher Friedrichs has identified as the most dangerous and destabilizing in the political history of early modern German towns; see Friedrichs,

Inter- and intra-family resignations of office were singled out by the deputies for special criticism, especially when such practices brought very young patrician men onto the council. Merlin reports that in their meetings during the summer and fall of 1613, angry bourgeois contended that: "with regard to resignations from father to son, uncle to nephew, and brother to brother, communal town government has been turned into a private patrimony and hereditary possession closed to worthy citizens...it is unreasonable that a father can resign his office in favor of a son who is still a child, who often possesses neither sound judgement nor practical business experience."[41]

To remedy this situation, bourgeois representatives proposed that, whenever an office of *pair* fell vacant, the rochelais militia companies would be assembled and elect three candidates for the position. The entire *corps de ville* would then choose one of the three candidates to fill the vacancy. For this system to work, the deputies insisted that town councilmen renounce in perpetuity all use of resignations for staffing municipal offices. These popular demands attacking the prerogatives of current councilmen elicited stubborn resistance from civic magistrates. Rumors circulated that over ninety per cent of town councilmen had sworn on the Bible to oppose the suggested changes in council formation.[42]

Members of the town council flatly refused to negotiate with their opponents. The unwillingness of civic magistrates to parley with their adversaries only heightened bourgeois fears of official malfeasance and government conspiracies against themselves and the union of French Protestant congregations.[43] A widening con-

---

"Urban Politics and Urban Social Structure in Seventeenth-Century Germany," *European History Quarterly* 22 (1992): 187-216.

[41] Merlin recorded the protestors' contention that "d'une maison de ville commune on en fait un patrimoine et une herédité particulière et en forclosant les gens de bien...n'estant pas raisonnable que le père résigne son état à son fils, qui ne sera qu'un enfant, qui n'aura le plus souvent ne jugement ni experience aux affaires," "Diaire," fol. 160v.

[42] *Ibid.*, fol. 192r.

[43] Since 12 November 1612, Protestant deputies from church councils in the provinces of Anjou, Brittany, Poitou, Saintonge, and lower Guyenne had been meeting illegally at La Rochelle, in the presence of the duc de Rohan, to review policy and formulate a response to diplomatic overtures from the crown. Dissension between the provincial delegations and local political tensions were exacerbated when the representatives of Anjou walked out of the assembly and the rochelais town council, meeting in special session, requested that the remaining envoys quit the city. Many citizens of La Rochelle were outraged by the vote

viction among the Rochelais of the town council's perfidy emboldened bourgeois demands for transcripts of council meetings,
copies of documents from municipal archives, and public readings of all correspondence written and received by the *corps de
ville*.

Councilmen at first had denied the right of deputies like Jean
Tharay to speak on behalf of other bourgeois. Confronted with
deepening opposition, civic magistrates then demanded, as a prelude to possible talks, that the deputies recall their confederates
in Paris seeking an injunction from the *Conseil d'Etat* against current methods of staffing the town council. Representatives of the
bourgeoisie would not back down. In response, the mayor
attempted to arrest Bernard de Marsan, a rochelais merchant cor-
responding with the bourgeoisie's envoys in Paris. Leading Marsan
to jail, the mayor encountered a thick crowd of merchants and
artisans who blocked his path, threatened him with death, and
compelled him to free his captive.[44]

Frightened by this insubordination, the *corps de ville* sent an
express courier to court, seeking royal edicts outlawing bourgeois
assemblies and punishing rebel leaders for subversion of municipal police. The opposition replied with new demands for complete access to town council archives and the right to read all official council correspondence. The consistory of La Rochelle's
Reformed church, ordered by the town council to shame the
rebels into submission, lost popular support in November 1613
when it criticized the new demands of the bourgeoisie as "unreasonable."[45] In February 1614, the *échevin* Jean de Mirande and the
*pair* Jean Prou went off to Paris seeking the crown's condemnation of all proposals for alterations to La Rochelle's town council. Making no progress toward peaceful resolution of their differences, both sides began to stockpile weapons.

Rebellious members of the bourgeoisie struck first in the early
morning hours of Ash Wednesday (13 February 1614). After a
final all-night strategy session in the house of Pierre Bernardeau,

---

and their anger nearly exploded into armed conflict. The mayor, in a show of
force, posted armed guards throughout the city and finally persuaded Rohan and
the deputies to leave peacefully. See Merlin, "Diaire," fols. 174v-175r. See also,
Parker, *La Rochelle and the French Monarchy*, 24-25.

[44] Guillaudeau, "Diaire," 51.

[45] Merlin, "Diaire," fol. 198v.

armed agitators moved before dawn and overpowered municipal guards in charge of two towers vital to the city's defense. The rebels first occupied the Maubec tower gate lying between the bourgeois strongholds of St. Nicolas and St. Sauveur parishes. This fortification housed one of the largest of all civic arsenals. In the port district of Perrot, where Jean Tharay's family wielded considerable influence, protestors under Tharay's command seized the tour de la chaîne containing the mechanism by which a massive chain could be raised blocking the entrance to La Rochelle's harbor. The rebels then destroyed the old locks in these gateways (an offense normally punishable by death), and installed new padlocks for which they kept the only keys. Spokesmen for the rebels informed the mayor that they were now prepared to defend the new locks with deadly force if necessary.

These insurrectionary acts were committed by bourgeois protestors to protect their customary right to keep passkeys without which none of the city's gates could be opened. Combative members of the bourgeoisie claimed they were acting in legitimate self-defense to prevent town councilmen from surreptitiously bringing armed forces into the city for an attack on merchants demanding political reforms. Leading protestors could count on backing from the militia's rank and file since, for unenfranchised householders like shopkeepers and wealthier artisans with political ambitions, the rebels' demands opened a path for them toward greater participation in municipal government.

Uncertain of the militia's loyalty to him, the mayor made no effort to challenge the rebels militarily. Instead, he turned to the local presidial court in hopes of obtaining a summary injunction forcing the dissenters to remove the locks. The royal magistrate responsible for the issuance of such an order was the *procureur du roi*, Gabriel de Bourdigalle, a confirmed ally of the rebels. According to a senior magistrate on the presidial, de Bourdigalle refused to intervene, first demanding proof that the bourgeois had indeed affixed the new locks and then suggesting to the mayor that such acts might be exonerated by the bourgeoisie's ancient privilege to keep passkeys for all town gates. Finally, de Bourdigalle reminded the mayor of the law suit involving these rights which the bourgeoisie was pursuing against the town council before the *Conseil d'Etat*. De Bourdigalle stated that he preferred to await the outcome of this litigation before drawing up any new indictments.[46] Exasperated, the mayor sent another courier to Paris to aid Mirande and Prou in seeking a royal edict against the protestors' latest move.[47] With the connivance of key local royal magistrates, the rebels stayed put.

Confronted by the fait accompli of the padlocks, the mayor attempted to negotiate with his adversaries while awaiting word from Paris. On 19 February 1614, disgruntled townsmen named thirteen negotiators: seven of the *procureurs* previously selected by the militia companies (including Bernardeau, Grenot, Papin, Tharay, and Torterue); their attorney, François Bardonin; and five other bourgeois representing the five parishes of the city (among whom were the merchants Mardochée Georget and Isaac du Querny).[48] The negotiators initially demanded more access for *marchand-bourgeois* to the posts of company captain in the municipal militia now reserved for *échevins*, more responsibility to the militia for nightly police patrols, and a better economic administration of the city. Spokesmen for the protestors soon enlarged these demands with a call for the election of previously unenfranchised bourgeois, including local merchants, shopkeepers, and master artisans, to the town council. Commercial representatives of this coalition then reminded the mayor of their general resolution to defend the occupied city towers with force, if necessary. The town council also named thirteen representatives. The two groups then agreed to go over a long list of twenty-eight grievances drawn up by the restive bourgeoisie. A week passed before even the method of reading and amending the list could be decided. The arrival of letters from the crown demanding information on the state of political affairs in La Rochelle interrupted the work of the negotiating committees and further disagreements impeding their work arose over the text of the reply to be sent to Paris.

On 16 March 1614, a crown messenger arrived in La Rochelle with an *arrêt* from the council of state ordering the removal of the new locks and submission of the bourgeoisie to town council authority. Meeting in special session, the *corps de ville* advised the mayor not to attempt enforcement of the edict "for fear of sedi-

---

[46] Bruneau, "Histoire," BMLR, MS 50, fol. 712.
[47] Guillaudeau, "Diaire," 54.
[48] Merlin, "Diaire," fol. 205r.

tion and tumult."[49] Speaking before the town council, a presidial attorney representing the bourgeoisie warned his listeners, "you
will see a fine mess in no time, for whomsoever tries to serve the
edict will be laid out cold in the street."[50]

Not to be intimidated, the mayor, on the morning of 22 March,
sent one of his sergeants to enforce the edict against the directors of the uprising, Pierre Bernardeau, Jacques Grenot, and Jean
Tharay.[51] Almost instantaneously, rebel leaders rallied sympathetic neighborhood militia companies and seized all the main street
intersections of the city, throwing up barricades and surrounding
the town hall with musketeers. This *émeute* lasted seven hours.
Towards evening, during a tour of the city with de Bourdigalle to
appease the protestors, the mayor narrowly escaped assassination
when a militiaman bent on killing him misfired his weapon.
Furious residents of the Perrot neighborhood, under Jean
Tharay's personal command, refused to lay down their weapons
and demanded that the mayor hand over the hapless sergeant for
punishment. In lieu of his servant, the mayor offered up the text
of the royal edict he had carried. De Bourdigalle publicly tore up
the king's letters to the cheers of the protestors.[52]

The next morning, a Sunday, Jean Tharay, leading a troop of
his armed followers from Perrot, invaded a Calvinist church in
the city, interrupted the prayer service in progress, dragged the
traitorous sergeant outside, and nearly beat him to death in the
street.[53] The same day, in a desperate attempt to punish this violence and arrest bourgeois leaders, the mayor and his patrician
followers sounded the tocsin alarm and tried to seize the city
before ·their adversaries could react. The mayor's men had to
retreat before superior numbers of enemy militiamen who quickly assembled against this show of force. This failed coup attempt
caused the collapse of the town council's stubborn resistance to
all political reforms proposed by the deputies of the bourgeoisie.

Contemporaneously with their showdown against the mayor's

---

[49] *Ibid.*, fols. 207r-v.
[50] *Ibid.*, fol. 208v. Merlin records the threat as follows: "dans une heure vous
verres beau jeu, car quiconque se présentera pour exécuter ledit arrêst sera esten-
du sur le carreau."
[51] *Ibid.*, fols. 209v-210r.
[52] Guillaudeau, "Diaire," 59.
[53] Bruneau, "Histoire," fols. 723-24.

forces, bourgeois dissenters hired a local printer to publish a manifesto justifying their violent protests to a wider audience.[54] In this tract, the rebels asserted that their chief goal was opening municipal government to more trustworthy householders familiar with the lives and concerns of average citizens. They compared the ancient town council—composed of "men not less venerable for their age than laudable for their meritorious regard for the public welfare"—with the current magistrates, "not less ridiculous for their youth than contemptible for what little they have done to improve the lot of the citizenry."[55] The pamphlet's author or authors condemned the "brigues licentieuses" and bribes dispensed by candidates for mayor and censured how town councilmen frequently resolved litigation by "gifts" to magistrates vitiating enforcement of traditional communal statutes. Rampant graft, bourgeois protestors alleged, diminished the stature of municipal officials, endangering effective government while keeping more humble but more reliable men from office.

According to the rebels, civic administration should not become the preserve of an hereditary caste of officeholders. Nor should urban government necessarily be construed as a closed corporation or profession. Rather, it was a worldly duty amenable to and best served by the participation of amateurs.[56] Corruption detached the *corps de ville* from the city's body politic, rendering it incapable of arbitrating or defending the essential interests of citizens. The rebels wished "not to govern ourselves inso-

---

[54] *Brève déclaration*, 1-11.

[55] *Ibid.*, 6.

[56] Evidence from La Rochelle on the conduct and justification of the 1614 rebellion suggests that "professionalism" in civic administration did not figure prominently in popular conceptions or requirements of how town government should operate. Rebel action seems predicated on the assumption that respectable householders already possessed sufficient governing skills to warrant their inclusion in the town council. This attitude, and its successful assertion in armed conflict by rebels in 1614, sharply contrast with "une professionalisation de plus en plus importante" Claire Dolan has discerned from the end of the sixteenth century in the organization of municipal administration in Aix-en-Provence, Dolan, "Des images en action: cité, pouvoir municipal et crises pendant les guerres de religion à Aix-en Provence," in L. Turgeon, ed., *Les productions symboliques de pouvoir XVIe-XXe siècle*, (Sillery, Quebec, 1990), 65-86. The "esprit communautaire" Dolan finds waning in town government at Aix well before 1600 seems quite vibrant in La Rochelle until 1628 if not later. Royal efforts to manipulate civic politics in west country towns undoubtedly contributed to this resurgence of communal values.

lently, but to be governed equitably" and thus fought for reform.[57]

Although exculpatory in conception and thus suspect as an honest declaration of rebel motives, the 1614 manifesto is notable for proposing reform of municipal government from within the urban community and by the enfranchisement of middle-ranking merchants, professional men, and skilled master craftsmen. No external actors or correctives are endorsed or invited for the task. Nor is the dispute characterized in any way as religious in origin or interpreted in religious terms. The rebels put themselves forth as citizens with the requisite skills, contacts, and sympathies essential to restoring the proper operation of municipal government in accord with older norms of communal guardianship. Critical to their qualifications was their own empowering service to the community as militiamen, neighbors, householders, and masters shouldering the many responsibilities each status entailed. Long performance of these duties confirmed their status as political amateurs. Reiterating this status in their pronouncements allowed the rebels to rouse the bulk of La Rochelle's population against the old town council and present themselves as a clear alternative to the established civic regime.

On 28 March 1614, the *corps de ville* provisionally accepted twenty-eight articles for thorough reform of town government drawn up by the leaders of the opposition. These articles established the electoral procedures for the town council advocated during the preceding months by the coalition formed against the patricians. The new articles permanently prohibited resignations of office by members of the town council. Offices of *pair* falling vacant would be filled by one of three candidates nominated by the militia companies and selected by the *corps de ville*. Militiamen also gained the right to nominate three candidates for other subordinate administrative positions in the municipal bureaucracy. A minimum age requirement of thirty was instituted for all incoming city council members. Five *procureurs* elected annually from within the militia would henceforward be permitted to observe all council meetings. The bourgeoisie, voting by militia companies, selected Zacherie Chatton, Jacques Grenot, Simon Papin, Jean Tharay, and Israel Torterue to serve as the five new *procureurs* in town council

---

[57] *Brève déclaration*, 10.

sessions. These men consolidated their leadership within the popular protest movement.

From the outset, this innovative system of government only provoked greater animosities between the contending factions. The five *procureurs* perpetually quarreled with disaffected town councilmen. Fist fights in the *hôtel de ville* had been narrowly averted. Jean Tharay pulled a knife and nearly murdered a council opponent during a vain reconciliation meeting in the mayor's own house.[58] From April to June 1614, deliberations of the *corps de ville* became increasingly impeded by the failure of outraged town councilmen to attend meetings, by voting strikes organized by opponents of the bourgeoisie, and by the refusal of old councilmen to carry out reform duties assigned to them.

Frustrated by this impasse in town government, members of the bourgeoisie reconvened and decided to reorganize their opposition movement by creating their own general council of forty-eight representatives, a shadow government to the *corps de ville*. Between April 5 and 7, elections were held within the city's militia units as each company selected six representatives to sit on the new popular council. Staffed by elected members with annual terms of office, the Council of Forty-Eight endured until 1628 as a key component in the new regime of civic government. As will be shown with greater detail in Chapter 6, local merchants, jurists, and skilled craftsmen all gained election to the Forty-Eight. Members of the bourgeoisie, voting by militia companies, also reconfirmed Chatton, Grenot, Papin, Tharay, and Torterue as their official spokesmen.[59]

On 13 July 1614, the town councilmen Jean de Mirande and Jean Prou, envoys of city government at court instrumental in obtaining royal censures of the rebels, returned to their tense and divided home town. The same evening, the bourgeois *procureurs* Tharay and Chatton, while promenading around La Rochelle's main square, denounced Mirande and Prou as royalists conspiring to destroy the new institutions of civic government. A member of the town council, coming to the defense of his colleagues, was beaten to the ground and stabbed by assailants from a crowd of Tharay's supporters including sailors, dock workers, and arti-

---

[58] Merlin, "Diaire," fol. 222v.
[59] Guillaudeau, "Diaire," 61-63.

sans.[60] Merlin repeatedly noted that Tharay moved about the city surrounded by a bodyguard of menacing stevedores from his port neighborhood.

Rumors quickly spread that Mirande and Prou carried from Paris emergency orders to quash changes in municipal government and hang the reformers. At nightfall, a large crowd of merchants, artisans, sailors, and laborers, whipped up by Tharay and Chatton to defend their city and its new political institutions, proceeded toward the envoys' houses, smashed down the doors with sledgehammers, ransacked the places, dragged Mirande and Prou from their beds, and threw them out of town clad only in their nightshirts and slippers.[61] Summoned by the mayor to intervene and stop this popular attack on town councilmen, the *procureur du roi*, de Bourdigalle, loudly endorsed the removal of Prou and Mirande as the best means of maintaining public order. These episodes of successful housebreaking deeply humiliated the victims, shocked members of the Calvinist consistory, and stiffened the town council's resolve to hit back at its opponents.

The next morning, the consistory met and denounced this "insolent and furious riot." Senior Protestant churchmen drew up a declaration reproving the "unlawful acts" of the impassioned bourgeois protestors.[62] All pastors received orders to read out this censure after every daily prayer service. Outraged by this insult, Tharay and his fellow *procureurs* immediately confronted pastor Merlin and abusively demanded that the ministers' condemnation of the "just" expulsion be publicly retracted. In response to public sentiment, leading protestors now insisted that two pastors be summarily expelled from the church for the vehemence of the anti-bourgeois remarks they had extemporaneously added to readings of the consistory's official denunciation of the riot. Representatives of the rebels loudly warned all clergymen not to dictate ("regenter") over temporal civic affairs transpiring far outside their competence and authority.[63]

---

[60] Guillaudeau, "Diaire," 63-64 and Merlin, "Diaire," fols. 220r-221v.

[61] Guillaudeau recorded in his diary that Tharay and Chatton "assembled such a large number of people and inspired them in such a manner that like wild animals they fell on Mirande's house," "Diaire," 64. According to Merlin, "Diaire," fol. 222r, Mirande was dragged from his bed "n'ayant que ses pantoufles aux pieds."

[62] Merlin, "Diaire," fol. 222v.

[63] *Ibid.*, fol. 222v.

Menaced by the insurgents' repeated threats of new violence directed at every opponent of civic reform, the *consistoire* quickly suspended all readings of the article chastising rebellious merchants and their followers. Verbally harassed by Bernardeau, Chatton, and Tharay, members of the consistory agreed to open negotiations with the *procureurs* over due punishment for the outspoken pastors. Rebel leaders affirmed the principle that ordinary congregants should have the right to discipline their ministers for offensive speech. The 1614 uprising gained strength from and reinvigorated the popular congregationalism typical of rochelais Calvinists.

In fact, two of the Protestant churches in La Rochelle served as rallying points and hallowed ground of negotiation for the rebels. Between February and August 1614, protestors compelled the mayor and members of the *consistoire* to visit the Church of St. Yon for parleys over the reform of municipal government.[64] This congregation met in a structure on the rue St. Yon near the heart of La Rochelle's commercial district. Nearly all of the merchants active in the rebellion regularly celebrated family baptisms and marriages at St. Yon. Pierre Bernardeau stood nine times before the baptismal font of St. Yon as godfather to the children of his neighbors.[65] The parents of the rebel captain Jean Tharay married in the Church of St. Yon. They baptized their son there. When, in turn, Jean Tharay became a father, he baptized eight of his own children at St. Yon.[66] Tharay's service as a godfather to the children of several neighbors was formally acknowledged at christenings in St. Yon. Since 1577, the families of Simon Papin and Israel Torterue went to St. Yon for diverse family ceremonies including the baptisms of Simon and Israel.[67] The leaders of the rebellion chose "their" congregation, rich in familial associations and empowering personal ties, as a proper spot for the affirmation of their political demands for a more democratic town government. According to pastor Merlin, the rebels also used the Church of St. Michel as a meeting place and debating hall.[68]

---

[64] *Ibid.*, fols. 206v-207r and 227r.
[65] See the archival sources cited in note 26 for this chapter.
[66] ADCM, I 8, fol. 2r, I 10, fol. 2v, I 19, fols. 5v and 55v, I 20, fols. 23r and 66v, I 21, fol. 36r, I 23, fol. 62r, and I 27, fols. 4r and 55r.
[67] ADCM, I 8, fol. 46r, I 10, fol. 70v, I 21, fols. 48v and 73r, and I 27, fol. 93v.
[68] Merlin, "Diaire," fol. 231r.

Located at the intersection of three recruitment zones for adjacent neighborhood militia companies, St. Michel was a strategic assembly point close to the Maubec tower gate giving access to the heart of the commercial quarter.

On 9 August 1614, during raucous public debates over suitable punishment for the ministers who had spoken out against rebel protesters, the town council drew up a tract reproducing the original condemnation issued by the consistory. Town councilmen then circulated this document throughout the city to obtain signatures from all critics of the bourgeoisie. Alarmed by the multiplication of signatories and the resurgence of their enemies, rebel captains ordered their followers to arm themselves and prepare for civil war.

Months of growing rancor between the adversaries culminated on the night of 9 August when the mayor and councilmen loyal to him attempted one final military crackdown.[69] Pitched street fighting with the heavily armed militia companies ensued. Pistol and musket shots were exchanged by the adversaries throughout the city and several combatants fell seriously wounded. Alarm bells rang in every quarter. Militia companies from the neighborhoods of Perrot, St. Nicolas, and Notre Dame de Cougnes took the lead in battling and pursuing armed town councilmen. In hand-to-hand combat, many supporters of the *corps de ville* were beaten unconscious. Eyewitnesses report that Jean Tharay, wearing a battle helmet and "covered with cutlasses," directed a three-pronged attack on council forces barricaded in the town hall. He moved on to coordinate the militia units' dragnet of the city to arrest fugitive patricians. Over three days, Tharay led a troop of more than one hundred rebels in house-to-house searches across the city, finally hunting down, rounding up, and imprisoning more than sixty notable opponents. The captured included four senior *échevins*, eight *pairs*, five presidial court officers still holding seats on the town council and opposed to reform of municipal government, five royal notaries, and a tax collector for the king. Numerous close kinsmen of current town council members were also summarily arrested and harshly confined.[70]

---

[69] Isaac Blandin, a reactionary *échevin* and militia company captain descended from the old apostate Amateur Blandin, led one contingent of patrician forces against the rebels. The Rochelais tended to abide by family traditions of political activity.

[70] Merlin, "Diaire," fols. 229r-233r. See also Guillaudeau, "Diaire," 69-89, and

At a critical moment in the fighting, advancing militiamen from the St. Nicolas quarter, emboldened by their killing of a council supporter, threatened to execute all captured members of the town council. Jean Tharay, seconded by his stepfather, Jacques Grenot, and other close kinsmen from the St. Nicolas neighborhood, negotiated in the street with the vengeful insurgents, persuading them to desist and to entrust Grenot with protective custody of all the prisoners. These notable captives would languish in city dungeons and jails for the next nine months. Decimated by the arrests, fighters for the town council capitulated on 12 August. Jean Tharay organized the council's public surrender, accompanying the mayor as he performed humiliating acts of contrition before companies of jeering militiamen sitting atop the barricades they had built. At the close of battle, Jean Tharay was the undisputed master of La Rochelle. As pastor Merlin ruefully noted, Tharay now "held the lives of his fellow citizens in his hands."[71]

The uprising of 1614 ended with the August street fighting. In prolonged negotiations with a rump town council for the prisoners' release, rebel captors incited by Tharay spurned every mediation effort of the Calvinist consistory and repeatedly threatened to execute their hostages. The rebels' violent rout of established civic authorities and tough bargaining for their captives' release produced a new regime of town government. A broadly expanded electorate of militiamen using legally guaranteed mechanisms of polling advanced combative merchants and artisans to powerful posts on the reconstituted town council, displacing royal jurists and patricians. Residents of neighborhoods peripheral to the old city center, previously under-represented in the highest offices of civic administration, now steadily gained seats on the town council. Given the ephemeral institutional and political changes worked by most early modern French rebels, the perpetrators of La Rochelle's 1614 uprising managed an astonishingly successful insurrection resulting in great modifications to communal government that endured for another fourteen years.

---

Bruneau, "Histoire," fols. 723-724. Guillaudeau gives the most complete lists of the prisoners taken by the rebels. All contemporary chroniclers of the *coup d'état* agree that this strike targeted the town council and its most influential supporters and succeeded in crippling their opposition to reform of municipal government.

[71] Merlin, "Diaire," fol. 236r.

### 3. *The Social Dynamics of Urban Rebellion*

Multiple surviving eyewitness accounts of the 1614 revolt in La Rochelle permit us to identify the ringleaders of this politically motivated urban violence and to follow their actions throughout the city. When complemented with information drawn from the city's notarial archives and registry of Protestant vital statistics (*état civil*), this material allows us to observe the deeper social mechanisms and spatial attributes of this struggle for the control of town government.

As noted earlier, merchants and jurists conspiring against the *corps de ville* frequented the residence of Pierre Bernardeau. Between February and August 1614, representatives of the bourgeoisie convened at least six times under Bernardeau's roof to debate tactics, gain a consensus on negotiating positions, and draft responses to deals proffered by the town council. The house of Pierre Bernardeau served as one command post for the merchants engaged in the confrontation with the council. However, if we take the word "house" in a larger sense, that of the ensemble of relations between a patriarch, his kinfolk, and his clients, we see that the house of Pierre Bernardeau was one of the most important domiciles of the rebellion.

Among the other *procureurs* of the bourgeoisie were Simon Papin, the international cloth merchant, and Israel Torterue, the spice dealer. The aunt of Simon Papin, Marie Cochet, was Pierre Bernardeau's second wife.[72] When Pierre Bernardeau's eldest son, Samuel, married on 3 August 1614, the *procureur* Simon Papin joined the wedding party along with his two cousins, the sons of Marie Cochet, now listed as stepbrothers to the groom.[73] The *procureur* Israel Torterue was also a cousin by marriage of Samuel Bernardeau. Israel's brother, Jean, and other kinsmen of the Torterue family added their signatures to Samuel Bernardeau's wedding contract.

Family ties interlinked several leaders of the rebellion and con-

---

[72] Pierre Bernardeau married Marie Cochet, widow of René Papin, on 31 July 1593, see ADCM, 3 E 204 (1593), fols. 245v-248r. By January of 1600, Pierre Bernardeau had become the tutor and trustee of Cochet's sons by her first husband. Bernardeau's charges were cousins to the *procureur* Simon Papin, see ADCM, 3 E 208 (1600), fols. 5r-v.

[73] ADCM, 3 E 219, fols 106r-107r.

stituted a vital source of solidarity among the *procureurs* and their followers. The *procureur* Simon Papin was the brother-in-law of Abraham and Gedeon d'Hinsse, merchant rebels and sworn enemies of the town council.[74] The audacious *procureur* Jean Tharay was both the stepson and son-in-law of the *procureur* Jacques Grenot. The *procureur* Zacherie Chatton, Jean Tharay's closest friend and right-hand man, was the brother-in-law of the merchants Pierre and Moise Hotton, who kept the armory of the rue du Temple militia company in their own home and put its weapons at Tharay's disposal when street fighting with the town council broke out.[75] Among the bourgeois chosen to represent the parishes of the city, Mardochée Georget, owner of a large tannery in the parish of Cougnes, and Isaac du Querny, a grain merchant and customs official living in the parish of St. Nicolas, were kinsmen by ties of marriage and godparentage between their families.[76]

Family ties and common political interests among the merchants were reinforced by proximity between the homes, shops, and other properties they owned. The main workshop and a house of Simon Papin stood in the rue des Merciers very near the house of Pierre Bernardeau. Zacherie Chatton's town house could also be found on the same street.[77] Barely 150 meters separated the properties of Bernardeau, Chatton, and Papin from the residence of Israel Torterue fronting on the canton de la caille.[78]

The stature of mature men like Bernardeau, Chatton, and Papin in their quarters and their neighborhood connections were important in the street battles of 1614 because the companies of

---

[74] ADCM, 3 E 2161, fol. 177v.

[75] ADCM, 3 E 198, fol. 401r and 3 E 199, fols. 392r-393r. The Hottons were rochelais wine merchants exporting the white wines and cognacs of the region to the French Channel ports, the Low Countries, and the Baltic, see for example, ADCM, 3 E 2159 (1610) fol. 118v.

[76] ADCM, I 17, fol. 83r, 3 E 211 (1602) fols. 15r-v, and 3 E 199, fol. 274r. Isaac du Querny shipped grain, wines, and other comestibles in and out of La Rochelle from and to all points of the compass. In June of 1605, he was transporting rye flour to Lisbon, see ADCM, 3 E 2158 (1605), fol. 168v. Du Querny also long served as the "compteur de poisson," a municipal customs official responsible for supervising and assessing the stocks of fish for human consumption imported through La Rochelle's harbor, see BMLR, MS 763, fol. 81r. Du Querny's various alimentary vocations made him a reputed provisioner of the urban community supported in his rebellion by the many clients he nourished.

[77] ADCM, 3 E 208, fols. 122v-123r.

[78] ADCM, 3 E 2161, fol. 1r.

the municipal militia, the only organized armed force in the city, were composed of all family heads living in a given street of network of intersecting streets.[79] Although officered solely by *échevins* since 1599, militia units rallied to the cause of the rebel merchants and provided the armed might indispensable to bourgeois victory in the struggle over the form of municipal government.

To give but two pertinent examples, the recruitment zone for the militia company of the rue des Merciers encompassed the residences of Zacherie Chatton, Simon Papin, Pierre Bernardeau and his children, and several other adversaries of the town council. Bernardeau's influence ran deep in another neighborhood militia unit. From one of Bernardeau's rent receipt rolls he kept as agent for the houses and other urban properties belonging to the Knights Templar, we know that at least ten active partisans of the rebels were tenants of Bernardeau living closely together in the rue du Temple. These clients all belonged to the same militia company recruited up and down both sides of the street.[80] Urban landlords possessing interparochial business and clientage networks proved themselves equally adept at coordinating violent political protest. The eyewitnesses, Merlin and Bruneau, noted the principal role of the militia companies in the street fighting against the town council and in defense of merchants' expanded political opportunities.[81]

The demands of the merchants for greater access to the office of militia company captain and for more extensive use of the companies in the city's police show the importance of the companies in the organization and articulation of rebel politics. Particularly sensible to the influence of neighborhood headmen and their kin whose homes tended to cluster together, the militia companies became the powerful instrument of a rebellion perpetrated for

---

[79] BMLR, MS 764, fols. 106r-107v. This document, excerpted from the town council minutes of 1622, concerns a reorganization of municipal militia recruitment zones in the city. A basic understanding and brief history of militia organization in La Rochelle can be gleaned from its details. On the role of town councilmen as officers in these companies see BMLR, MSS 61/62, fols. 319r-323r.

[80] BMLR, MS 116, "Censif de la Commanderie du Temple." Among the residents of the rue du Temple who aided and abetted the rebellion of 1614 were Estienne Mignot, elected to the first Council of Forty-Eight in April 1614, Jeremie Dourneau, who led neighborhood support for the rebels, and Jacques de Cuillard, also a representative for his street and quarter on the city-wide council established by the elected delegates of the bourgeoisie.

[81] Bruneau, "Histoire," BMLR, MS 50, fol. 723v and Merlin, "Diaire," fol. 229r.

the protection of the city according to the means and the values of a familial community of merchants. At no time did these neighborhood chieftains acknowledge or endorse the Calvinist consistory as an effective instrument of communal police.

Yet, as pastor Merlin ruefully acknowledged, the greatest instigator of the 1614 uprising was Jean Tharay, the townsman who also emerged from the fighting as the most powerful man in the city. What enabled Tharay to become the audacious and redoubtable leader of the prolonged rebellion transforming civic government?

Jean Tharay did not become a rebel leader overnight. He helped to keep political tensions high in La Rochelle for seven months leading up to the paroxysm of August 1614 and before that can be identified as a participant in the clandestine meetings of disaffected townsmen increasing in frequency since 1612.[82] Tharay's signal role in the 1614 uprising invites deeper investigation of the human and material resources the Tharay family accumulated in La Rochelle over generations which Jean cleverly exploited to make himself a successful rebel chief. Tracing long-term accretions of family prestige and personal reputation for rebels connects their protests to fundamental social structures and practices of everyday life that conferred status while enabling, ordering, and amplifying dissent. As Charles Tilly has argued in his search for the "repertoires" of collective action in France, "the more closely we look at...contention, the more we discover order. We discover order created by the rooting of collective action in the routines and organization of everyday social life and by its involvement in a continuous process of signaling, negotiation, and struggle with other parties whose interests the collective action touches."[83] This method of analysis gives added scope and weight to older studies of popular protest emphasizing the evanescent conjuncture of factors precipitating rebellions and the identity of faces in transient crowds.[84] This approach also favors a better

---

[82] Merlin, "Diaire," fols. 160v and 195r-v. See also Guillaudeau, "Diaire," 61-63.

[83] Charles Tilly, *The Contentious French*, (Cambridge, Mass., 1986), 4.

[84] George Rudé's innovative studies of collective action focused primarily on demarcating types, rationales, and periods for crowd activity without investigating in depth rioters' sociabilities and patronage networks contributing to the solidarity and organization of their movements. The elucidation of these comport-

understanding of the social mechanics underlying the emergence
of rebel leaders and the articulation of their influence, subjects
poorly explained in earlier studies of collective action.

Tharay's inspiration of fellow dissidents was instrumental to the
rebellion's success. The history of his notoriety transcends the
uprising itself. As Clifford Geertz has argued, "charisma does not
appear only in extravagant forms and fleeting moments but is an
abiding, if combustible, aspect of social life that occasionally
bursts into open flame."[85] Tharay's aptitude for rebel leadership
and the logic of the popular protest he directed both emanate
from the regular human interactions animating an urban polity.

In La Rochelle, rich notarial archives permit extensive reconstruction of the family alliances, economic engagements, residence patterns, clientage networks, and habits of sociability shaping the daily lives of Jean Tharay and his kin. Taken over time,
combined, and plotted in urban space, this information depicts
the sociogenesis of a rebel captain, his ordinary behaviors that
ultimately made his extraordinary acts possible.[86] Here, I wish to
show how Jean Tharay's leadership of the 1614 rebellion was facilitated by his participation in sets of interlocking urban social relationships contributing a history and a rationale to a violent process of sedition.

---

ments was also marginalized in the debate between Boris Porchnev and Roland
Mousnier and his students over the significance of French popular uprisings of
the seventeenth century. Porchnev's Marxist view of miserable plebeians desperately fomenting most uprisings could not accommodate analysis of politically significant patronage systems operating within and between a multiplicity of social
groups implicated in rebellion. Likewise, efforts of Mousnier and his protégés to
show frequent direction of "popular" uprisings by great notables and the prevalence of brief, highly localized, and uncoordinated revolts constricted explanation of how the social mechanisms of rebellion functioned and developed over
time. See George Rudé, *The Crowd in History 1730-1848*, (New York, 1964); H.J.
Kaye, ed., *The Face of the Crowd, Studies in Revolution, Ideology and Popular Protest,
Selected Essays of George Rudé*, (Atlantic Highlands, New Jersey, 1988); R.S. Holton,
"The Crowd in History: Some Problems of Theory and Method," *Social History* 3
(1978): 219-233; B. Prochnev, *Les soulèvements populaires en France de 1623 à 1648*
(Paris, 1963); R. Mousnier, "Recherches sur les soulèvements populaires en
France avant la Fronde," *Revue d'histoire moderne et contemporaine* 4 (1958): 81-113;
M. Fosil, *La révolte des nu-pieds et les révoltes normandes de 1639* (Paris, 1970); and
the essays collected in Y. Durand, ed., *Hommage à Roland Mousnier, Clientèles et
fidelités en Europe à l'époque moderne* (Paris, 1981).

[85] Geertz, "Centers, Kings, and Charisma: Reflections on the Symbolics of
Power," in his *Local Knowledge*, (New York, 1983), 123.

[86] As Roberta Senechal argues, the sociogenetic analysis of collective action—

The Tharay family was present in La Rochelle from at least 1550 when Guyon Tharay, our man's uncle, bought a house in the district of Saint Jean du Perrot and carried on his father's trade as a baker.[87] (Figure 11 presents a simplified Tharay family genealogical chart.) Guyon Tharay expanded the business by provisioning merchant ships at the nearby docks and soon established himself as a major neighborhood grain dealer.

Among Guyon's five siblings were two brothers, Jean and Nicolas, and a sister, Marie. Guyon's brother, Jean, an uncle to the rebel, became a merchant, marrying exogamously into the Javalleau family, an influential kin group holding properties on the main street of the Saint Nicolas quarter to the southeast of the city center.[88] The sister, Marie, married in the neighborhood of Perrot. Her first husband was a ship's carpenter to whom she brought a small dowry of 200 *livres*.[89] Her second marriage was to Pierre Chappron, an illiterate ship captain and small-time merchant of Perrot with many affiliates among the district's dockside artisans. A child of this union, Jacques Chappron, a cousin of the dissident Jean Tharay, was an ardent supporter of the 1614 rebellion in the Perrot quarter and helped rally his neighbors to Tharay's cause. A literate ship chandler and merchant, Jacques Chappron shared humble origins and upward social mobility with his rebellious cousin.

Guyon Tharay's other brother, Nicolas Tharay, the rebel Jean Tharay's father, also became a merchant, adding to the family's repute through lucrative local and European commerce directed

---

in her case the Springfield, Illinois race riot of August 1908—can sharpen our focus on the motivations and mechanisms of apparently anarchic public disturbances. Senechal's reconstruction of a race riot's "ecology" involves identification of perpetrators and victims, their localization in urban space, charting the riot's course through that space, and scrutiny of antagonists' working environments for evidence of social solidarities and cleavages configuring mass violence, R. Senechal, *The Sociogenesis of a Race Riot* (Chicago, 1990). Senechal's methods evoke the pioneering work of Norbert Elias who probed the sociogenesis of etiquette and ceremony in early modern Europe, a process revealing "the *order* underlying historical changes, their mechanics and concrete mechanisms." See Elias, *The Civilizing Process*, vol. 1, *The History of Manners*, (New York, 1982), xv, (italics in the original).

[87] ADCM, 3 E 2047 (1612), fols. 2v-4v.

[88] ADCM, 3 E 183, fols. 179r-180r.

[89] ADCM, 3 E 170, August 1580. The small amount of this dowry and the socioeconomic status of the groom indicate that at least a part of the Tharay family was firmly rooted in the lower middle strata of rochelais society.

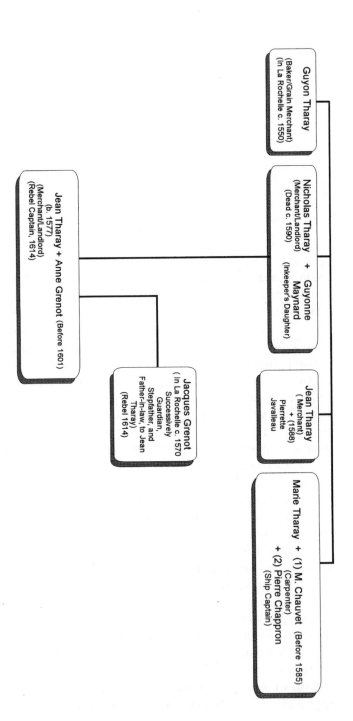

Figure 11. Tharay Family Genealogical Chart

Guyon Tharay
(Baker/Grain Merchant)
(In La Rochelle c. 1550)

Nicholas Tharay    +    Guyonne
(Merchant/Landlord)      Maynard
(Dead c. 1590)        (Innkeeper's Daughter)

Jean Tharay + Anne Grenot (Before 1601)
(b. 1577)
(Merchant/Landlord)
(Rebel Captain, 1614)

Jacques Grenot
( In La Rochelle c. 1570
Successively
Guardian,
Stepfather, and
Father-in-law, to Jean
Tharay)
(Rebel 1614)

Jean Tharay
( Merchant)
+ (1588)
Pierrette
Javalleau

Marie Tharay  +  (1) M. Chauvet (Before 1585)
                   (Carpenter)
             + (2) Pierre Chappron
                   (Ship Captain)

from a house near his brother's on the main street of the Perrot quarter, near the port and directly south of the city center.[90] Nicolas Tharay was a *bourgeois-juré de commune* and became an adjutant officer in the Perrot district militia company. In 1576, Nicolas Tharay. extended the family's important cross-quarter marriage ties by exogamously wedding Guyonne Maynard, daughter of Pierre Maynard, an innkeeper whose establishment, the Swan, fronted on the busiest commercial street in La Rochelle's northern artisanal district of Notre Dame de Cougnes.[91] Nicolas Tharay and Guyonne Maynard had eight children. Their eldest son, Jean Tharay, the future rebel captain, was baptized in August 1577. His godmother was his maternal grandmother, wife to the innkeeper at the Swan.[92] By the late sixteenth century, Tharay family networks extended widely throughout rochelais society forming a kin group composed of skilled artisans, food service workers, mariners, and merchants of middling rank.

While Jean Tharay was still a minor, his father died. For dual guardians of Jean, Nicolas Tharay had chosen his brother Guyon and Jacques Grenot, the wine merchant of the St. Nicolas quarter sharing with the Tharays close commercial and matrimonial links to the Javalleaus.[93] Jacques Grenot lived just up the street from the Javalleaus in the grande rue Saint Nicolas. Grenot soon married the widow Guyonne Maynard, becoming Jean Tharay's stepfather. In 1601, Grenot also became Tharay's father-in-law when Jean married Anne Grenot, daughter of Jacques by his first wife.[94] These marriages reinforced a multigenerational, geographically extensive, economically diversified, and politically potent consortium of three rochelais families: the Tharays, Grenots, and Javalleaus.

Over thirty years, two generations of the Tharay family embedded themselves in the social and economic life of several city neighborhoods. They did so, in part, by building up with allied

---

[90] ADCM, 3 E 2043 (1599), fols. 178v-179r and 3 E 2047 (1612), fols. 22r-24r.

[91] ADCM, I 8, fol. 2r and ADCM 3 E 187 (1586), fols. 454v-456r.

[92] ADCM, I 10, fol. 2v.

[93] ADCM, 3 E 2043 (1599), fols. 78v-79r and 178r-179r; ADCM, 3 E 2044 (1600), fols. 84r-v; ADCM, 3 E 2046, fols. 67v-68r; ADCM, 3 E 1171, 27 Nov. 1602; and ADCM, 3 E 1173, 22 March 1609.

[94] ADCM, 3 E 2043 (1599), fols. 78v-79r. For Baptisms of children born to Jean Tharay and Anne Grenot see ADCM, I 19, fols. 5v and 55v, I 20, fols. 23r and 66v, and I 21, fol. 36r (with Jacques Grenot as godfather).

families compounds of personal dwellings, shops, and rental properties.[95] In the district of Saint Jean du Perrot, one Tharay family compound of residential and commercial space centered on
the intersection of the grande rue du Perrot and the rue de la
Vache Noire.[96] (See Figure 12.) Here, between 1550 and 1617, we
can locate at least eight Tharay properties. A block of three adjacent structures, anchored by the households, granaries, and ovens
of Guyon Tharay and his niece, faced three adjoining residences
of Guyon's siblings and in-laws directly across the narrow rue de
la Vache Noire. These buildings opened for trade onto the grande
rue du Perrot close by Nicolas Tharay's main house. A brother-
in-law of the rebel Jean Tharay owned an eighth town house just
to the north in the contiguous rue de la Verdiere.

In the 1580's, Guyon Tharay bought up his sisters' shares in
their two commonly inherited properties, protecting the integrity of this familial investment from threats of dissolution posed by
the women's dowry requirements and the partible inheritance regulations of La Rochelle's customary law.[97] Guyon Tharay also profited from renting out ovens in the family compound to other bakers of the neighborhood.[98]

To the north, in the artisanal district of Notre Dame de
Cougnes, Nicolas Tharay was assembling a second family compound with the aid of his in-laws. (See Figure 13.) In 1592, we
find Nicolas owning at least two adjacent houses in the rue des
Prêtres. He used the first house for headquarters of his leather
supply business, servicing the tanners and shoemakers concentrated in the vicinity. He rented out the second house to a long-

---

[95] Like Italian medieval and renaissance urban families, the Tharays constructed a strong neighborhood base of economic and political operations. Unlike
the Italians, the Tharays established important family enclaves in more than just
one town district. Compare J. Heers, "Urbanisme et structure sociale à Gênes au
moyen âge," in *Studi in Onore di A. Fanfani*, vol. 1, "Antichita e Alto Medioèvo,"
(Milan, 1962), 371-412; D. Hughes, "Urban Growth and Family Structure in
Medieval Genoa," *Past and Present* 66 (February 1975): 3-28; *idem*, "Kinsmen and
Neighbors in Medieval Genoa," in H. Miskimin, ed., *The Medieval City*, (New
Haven, 1977), 95-111; D.V. and F.W. Kent, *Neighbors and Neighborhood in Renaissance
Florence: The District of the Red Lion in the Fifteenth Century*, (Locust Valley, New
York, 1982); and F.W. Kent, "Palaces, Politics, and Society in Fifteenth-Century
Florence," *I Tatti Studies* 2 (1987): 41-70.
[96] ADCM, 3 E 2036 (1585), fols. 179v and 226v-227v; and 3 E 2047, fols. 2v-4v
and 22r-24r.
[97] See sources cited in the preceding note.
[98] ADCM, 3 E 161 (12 June 1566).

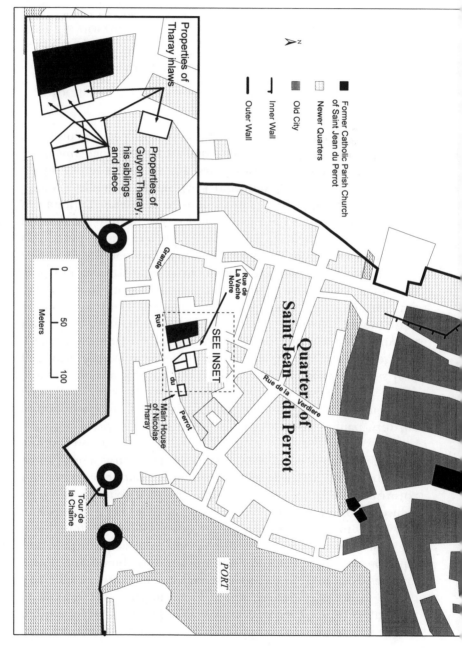

Figure 12. Tharay Family Properties in Perrot Quarter

time partner in trade. The rental adjoined the house of Tharay's mother-in-law, who had been selling Nicolas her own contiguous properties and garden plots in the same street since 1587.[99] Through his wife, Nicolas Tharay held one-third of the Swan Inn, a structure dominating the rue des Prêtres and located near the principal northeastern gate of the city. In conjunction with his shareholding in-laws, Tharay rented out this family property to a neighbor and later married his own daughter Judith to a kinsman of the new innkeeper.[100] At his death, Nicolas Tharay entrusted the ensemble of these properties to his eldest son, the future rebel Jean Tharay, who maintained and expanded them for at least another twenty years.[101]

In the parish of St. Nicolas, the Tharays were allied with the intermarried Grenot and Javalleau families. The guardian of the rebel Jean Tharay, Jacques Grenot, had a sister, Anne. Anne Grenot was the wife of the neighboring *marchand-bourgeois* Jean Javalleau. A daughter from this marriage became the wife of Jean Tharay's uncle. Jean Javalleau's brothers, Jacques and François, were close business associates of Nicolas Tharay.[102] Although the Javalleau brothers pursued diversified mercantile ventures, the family was of modest means and, in the first decades of the seventeenth century, included members by blood and marriage who worked as a shoemaker, a stocking maker, a cooper, a candle maker, and a humble notary.[103] The notary, Jean Joslain, a son-in-law of Jacques Javalleau, was a resident of the Perrot quarter. Joslain was another organizer of support in the neighborhood for Jean Tharay's captaincy of the 1614 rebellion.[104]

The Grenot clan fit the same socioeconomic profile as the Javalleaus. Jacques Grenot was active in maritime trade but was also a small scale landlord in the St. Nicolas quarter, renting cheap

---

[99] ADCM, 3 E 2039 (1592), fols. 69v-70r, 73r-v, and 152r.

[100] ADCM, 3 E 1172, fols. 89v-91r.

[101] ADCM, 3 E 223 (1619), fols. 74r-75v.

[102] ADCM, 3 E 2044 (1600), fols. 84r-v.

[103] See for examples of Javalleau family ties ADCM, 3 E 1222 (4 November 1605), 3 E 2160 (1612), fol. 117r, and 3 E 2049 (1619), fols. 48v-49r.

[104] Guillaudeau, "Diaire," 61, notes that Joslain was among the first residents of the Perrot district to be elected by the neighborhood militia company to serve on the bourgeoisie's city-wide council of forty-eight. Contemporaneously, Jean Tharay was elected to serve as a *procureur* for the same assembly. Political contacts between the two men were frequent during and after the rebellion of 1614.

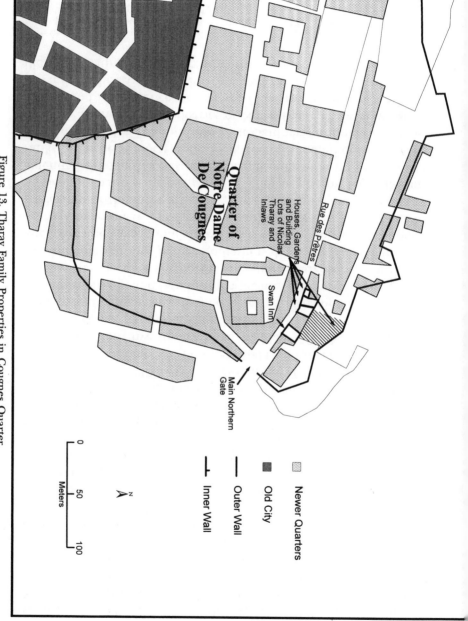

Figure 13. Tharay Family Properties in Cougnes Quarter

Quarter of Notre Dame De Cougnes

Houses, Gardens and Building Lots of Nicolas Tharay and Inlaws

Swan Inn

Rue des Prêtres

Main Northern Gate

0    50    100
Meters

N

Newer Quarters

Old City

Outer Wall

Inner Wall

rooms to barrel makers and other artisans in houses adjacent to his own.[105] Grenot also contributed to the sustenance of his neighbors by renting shops and ovens to bakers supplying the quarter.[106] The headmen of the Grenot and Javalleau kin groups were prominent members of the militia company mustered from residents of the main street in the St. Nicolas district. These regular contacts meant that Grenots and Javalleaus, like the Tharays, were personally known by an exceptionally wide cross-section of neighborhood residents.

Nicolas Tharay and his son shared other habits making their family a fixture of rochelais neighborhoods. In the baptismal registers of the Tharays' Calvinist congregation before 1614, Nicolas and Jean are remarkable as men who frequently obliged their neighbors and co-religionists by standing as godfathers to their children. Between 1576 and 1589, Nicolas Tharay served in this capacity eleven times.[107] Between 1603 and 1611, Jean Tharay went to the font five times.[108] On 21 May 1588, Nicolas Tharay obliged his new brother-in-law, Pierre Chappron I, by becoming godfather to Chappron's first-born son, also named Pierre. This boy was soon followed by a brother, Jacques Chappron. Over twenty years later, Jacques Chappron's new-born daughter was brought to the baptismal font by her godfather, the rebel Jean Tharay.[109] Such sustained interfamilial favors lie behind the strong support Pierre Chappron II and Jacques Chappron gave to Jean Tharay's leadership of the 1614 uprising.

Nicolas Tharay's own choices of godparents for his children extended the family's ties of reciprocal obligation into the lower ranks of rochelais society. In 1583, for the godfather of his son Estienne, Nicolas Tharay chose Jean Gaultier, an illiterate butcher living in the artisanal district of Notre Dame.[110] By contrast, I have found no evidence whatsoever in all the baptismal registers of La Rochelle's Calvinist churches that the members of old families dominating the oligarchical town council ever chose god-

---

[105] For examples, see ADCM, 3 E 1170, and 3 E 1171, 13 Jan. 1600.

[106] ADCM, 3 E 180, fols. 130v-131r

[107] ADCM, I 9, fols. 46v, 55r, 58r, and 113r; I 10, fol. 12r; I 11, fol. 59v; I 14, fol. 22r; and I 16, fols. 45v, 55v, 87v, and 91r.

[108] ADCM, I 19, fols. 125v, 143r, and 145r; I 21, fol. 169r; and I 25, fol. 16r.

[109] ADCM, I 25, fol. 16r.

[110] ADCM, I 16, fol. 86r.

parents for their children from among citizens of markedly lower social status. None of Tharay's rebel cohorts whose family lives I have examined in detail chose godparents so far beneath them in status. When street fighting erupted over the future configuration of town government, proponents of reform, like the Tharays, could appeal for popular support in part by evoking long-standing familial attachments to poorer members of the urban community. No such appeal could be made by the patrician family men opposing reform of municipal government.

For the Tharays, ties of godparentage helped to construct a powerful urban political faction comprised of men from different home parishes and with diverse occupational affiliations. The presidial court attorney Hercules Roy, a resident of the St. Barthélémy parish, abetted the protest Jean Tharay led against the town council. Roy was not helping a man unknown to him or without a prior claim on his allegiance. Since 1603, Jean Tharay had been serving as the godfather of a child born to one of Roy's kinswomen.[111] Roy's colleague, the renegade jurist Gilles Bardonin, another St. Barthélémy resident, also unhesitatingly backed the merchant Jean Tharay as the guide of the 1614 revolt. The interreliance of these two men stemmed in part from Bardonin's service since 1608 as godfather to Jean Tharay's nephew.[112] Among Jean Tharay's staunchest partisans in the Perrot quarter was Pierre Regnault, a baker. In 1603, Regnault's daughter became the godmother of a cousin to Jean Tharay. In 1604, Regnault himself was pleased to serve as a godparent at a Javalleau family christening. In this case, multigenerational ties of fictive kinship associated the agitator Regnault with the Tharays and their allied families.[113]

The Tharays' commercial and social contacts familiarized them with Rochelais from many strata of urban society. In the port district of Perrot, the bakeries of Guyon Tharay and his sons fed hungry consumers rich and poor. Nicolas and Jean Tharay both loaned money and sold small quantities of wheat and barley flour to a diverse clientele of seafarers, dockers, artisans, laborers, and field workers.[114] Nicolas Tharay regularly hired and made loans

---

[111] ADCM, I 19, fol. 125v (23 September 1603).

[112] ADCM, I 20, fol. 127r (8 June 1608).

[113] ADCM, I 20, fols. 17r and 22r.

[114] See, for examples, ADCM, 3 E 2038 (1590), fols. 302v-303r; ADCM, 3 E 2039 (1592), fols. 69v-70v, 73r-v, 152r, and 188v-189r; and 3 E 2061, fol. 209r.

to a work gang of roofers employed for the upkeep of Tharay's numerous rental properties.[115] Working people of the Perrot district from the same socioeconomic groups enthusiastically followed Jean Tharay on his armed forays uptown against civic authorities during the months of unrest.

Holding contiguous vineyards outside the city with the Maynards (probably to stock the cellars of the Swan Inn) and trading with Jacques Grenot, the Tharays participated extensively in the local and regional wholesale and retail wine trade.[116] Nicolas Tharay's bulk importation of hides from Ireland also made him known to tanners and makers of leather goods throughout the city.[117]

Commercial contacts with these clienteles fostered more intimate associations. In January 1611, Jean Tharay and Pierre Chappron the younger helped to celebrate the marriage of a local shoemaker, both men prominently signed the new couple's wedding contract as witnesses to the match. For another cobbler, Jean Tharay guaranteed a loan.[118] Jean also dealt regularly with literate and illiterate carpenters, shipwrights, and other workingmen as tenants in the small rental properties he and his father amassed in the neighborhoods of Perrot and Notre Dame. For example, in February 1610, a printer and a woodworker were renting rooms, shops, and storage space located in one of Tharay's Perrot houses. In November 1613, Tharay rented a small house in the neighborhood of Notre Dame to a journeyman weaver.[119] By supplying housing, foodstuffs, primary raw materials for clothing, and favors, the Tharays made themselves known to a wide public well represented in the rank and file of the rebel militia companies. The socioeconomic heterogeneity of the Tharays' commercial clients stands in striking contrast to the much more socially homogeneous patterns of business investment and partnership characteristic of the old mercantile families dominating the town council. I have found no evidence in the files of rochelais notaries that any patrician town councilman involved himself or his family as

---

[115] ADCM, 3 E 2038 (1592), fols. 73r-v.

[116] See for example ADCM, 3 E 4 April 1601.

[117] ADCM, 3 E 2038, fols. 302v-303r.

[118] ADCM, 3 E 2160, fol. 23r and 3 E 2161, fols. 112r-v.

[119] ADCM, 3 E 2159 (1610), fols. 24r-25r and 42v; 3 E 2161 (1613), fols. 265r-v.

deeply in the daily lives of the city's laboring population as did the Tharays.

Other members of the Tharay clan also acted in a solicitous manner gaining them the regard of tradesmen and domestic servants in the middle and lower ranks of rochelais society. On 1 September 1612, Jean Tharay's sister, Judith, and her husband made a generous dowry gift of 150 *livres* to one of their serving women. This attractive sum, a present and not merely the accumulation of the woman's wages, helped her to wed a master stone mason and thus gain a more secure place in the urban social hierarchy.[120] Jean Tharay's evident influence among the lower orders of rochelais society can partially be ascribed to the adroit management of family affairs conducted by his kinfolk, men and women, living and dead, ingratiating the clan with many of the humble people who formed the bulk of city residents.

The organization of La Rochelle's citizen militia into companies comprised of all members of the bourgeoisie residing in a single street or network of contiguous streets magnified the influence of reputable neighborhood family men over these units, especially when popular discontent with town council policies discredited the senior councilmen normally appointed to officer the companies. Disaffected, intermarried, impressively domiciled urban families contributing and knowing numerous militiamen could then provide the alternative channels of command and control essential to coordinate opposition against a town council widely perceived as irresponsible or impotent. The densely interconnected Tharay, Grenot, and Javalleau families entrenched in the neighborhoods of Perrot, St. Nicolas, and Notre Dame provided the rebels of 1614 with such a subversive network.

In the early 1590's, Nicolas Tharay had served as a subaltern officer in the Perrot district militia company. The multiple weapons Jean Tharay carried into the 1614 street fighting were inherited from his father and signified to rebel confederates the Tharays' long participation in communal defense. In 1614, Jean Tharay wielded these weapons in part to recapture the right of rochelais bourgeois to serve as militia officers. As Robert Descimon has argued in a recent study of the Parisian bourgeois militia, participation in such companies gave citizens from the lower

---

[120] ADCM, 3 E 2160 (1612), fol. 142r.

and middling ranks of the bourgeoisie opportunities to enhance their social stature and assert their inclusion in the civic polity. At La Rochelle, rebellious members of the extended Tharay kin group seized similar opportunities, relying in part on their militia membership to effect and legitimate an attack on the town council enlarging the bourgeoisie's participation in municipal government. This challenge was made possible not simply by the esprit de corps of the militia units (as Descimon emphasizes), but essentially by the personal and familial connections rebel leaders like Bernardeau and Tharay could call upon within and between the companies.[121]

However, as eyewitnesses to the 1614 uprising report, Jean Tharay's influence extended beyond the best-armed members of the rochelais militia companies. Pastor Merlin's diary entries during the rebellion show that he was alarmed and intrigued by the easy familiarity of relations between rebel leaders, especially Tharay, and their lowlier followers. Tharay's loyal escort of dockers from Perrot never seems to have escaped Merlin's notice and comment.[122] Tharay's joking with the rough jailers of the prisoners and the turnkeys' absolute refusal to execute the commands of anyone other than Tharay even many weeks after the fighting had ended incensed the pastor.[123] According to Merlin, the majority of these guards were artisans from the districts of Perrot and Notre Dame. When Merlin and a fellow pastor, clad in their clerical vestments, went to comfort patrician prisoners rounded up in the August coup, dungeon guards under Tharay's orders refused to admit the clergymen, mocking them and threatening them with jail time if they persisted in their visit. Tharay's unusual leadership, effective even in the heat of battle, was felt as a personal affront by Merlin and shook his conviction that artisans and laborers were a fickle lot, "hardly inclined to obey the town council or the bourgeois."[124] Merlin's consternation over his opponent's influence (perhaps tinged with envy) attests to the depth and comprehensiveness of Tharay's captaincy, characteristics indicating its long gestation.

---

[121] R. Descimon, "Milice Bourgeoise et Identité Citadine à Paris au temps de la Ligue," *Annales E.S.C.*, 48 (1993): 885-906.

[122] Merlin, "Diaire," fols. 234r-241v.

[123] *Ibid.*, fol. 242r.

[124] *Ibid.*, fol. 242r.

The formation and diffusion of Jean Tharay's influence among the lower orders of rochelais society can also be attributed to the notoriety with which a family history of work endowed him. La Rochelle's 1614 uprising was successfully led by a man whose family was popularly and even positively identified with at least four staple commodities: bread, wine, leather, and housing. Pierre Bernardeau and at least three other leading proponents of the 1614 rebellion were also widely known as landlords, mill owners, and victuallers of the city at the wholesale and retail levels. The popular rebel Isaac du Querny gained a politically potent reputation as both a wine merchant libating the community and as a customs inspector supervising vital supplies of fish in the port city. A review of the literature on European urban revolts of the medieval and early modern eras suggests that bakers, grain dealers, and landlords, although frequently the victims of collective action enforcing a just price, may also have been particularly adept at coordinating and directing other popular protests.[125]

Not only did provisioners amass diverse clienteles, their feeding and sheltering of town folk day in and day out gave them numerous occasions to claim a responsibility for and a voice in the fundamental preservation of the community they served. Feeders of the public were best situated to derive political benefit from the passions food, particularly bread, evoked. As Roy Porter has noted in his introduction to Piero Camporesi's *Bread of Dreams*, in early modern times "bread marked the divide between life and death...[m]aking, breaking, and distributing bread carried profound connotations of friendship, communion, giving, sharing, justice—indeed, literally, *companionship*."[126] A

---

[125] On the importance of innkeepers, bakers, and other artisans of the provisioning trades in fomenting rebellions see Rhiman Rotz, "Investigating Urban Uprisings With Examples from Hanseatic Towns, 1374-1416," in W.C. Jordan, B. McNab, and T. Ruiz, eds., *Order and Innovation in the Middle Ages*, (Princeton, 1976), 215-233; *idem*, "The Lubeck Uprising of 1408 and the Decline of the Hanseatic League," *Proceedings of the American Philosophical Society* 121 (February 1977): 1-45; M. Degarne, "Etudes sur les soulèvements provinciaux en France avant la Fronde," *XVIIe Siècle* (1962): 3-18; M. Foisil, *Les révoltes des nu-pieds*, 227-230; and S. Westrich, *The Ormée of Bordeaux*, (Baltimore, 1972), 40-59. For a cross-cultural comparison, juxtapose these works with Senechal, *Sociogenesis of a Race Riot*, who finds that the 1908 crowd violence in Springfield, Illinois was capably incited and led by grocers, itinerant produce vendors, saloonkeepers, and boarding house proprietors.

[126] See Piero Camporesi, *Bread of Dreams: Food and Fantasy in Early Modern Europe*, (Chicago, 1989), 10 (italics in the original).

grandfather, uncle, and two cousins of Jean Tharay were bakers. Tharay's father and Tharay himself sold bulk cereals and flours in many different quantities. So did Pierre Bernardeau. The rebel leader Jacques Grenot put his bread ovens at the disposal of his neighbors.

During the rebellion of 1614, Jean Tharay's popular following was largest and most loyal in the neighborhood of Perrot where his family, relations by marriage, and friends had been engaged in baking and selling bread for the longest time. Additional support for Tharay came from the neighborhoods of St. Nicolas and Notre Dame where his kin had long provided food, wine, hospitality, and shelter to residents. Recall that the rebels of 1614, generously identified with nourishing the city, confronted a town council notorious for its inability to cope with recurrent subsistence crises dating back to the 1590's.

Rochelais who witnessed the 1614 uprising and its aftermath recorded that ordinary townspeople gave special devotion to leading dissidents. One measure of the depth of popular reverence toward key actors in the 1614 rebellion is given by the diarist Joseph Guillaudeau. Following the release of the patrician prisoners in April 1615, further violent confrontations occurred between bourgeois representatives and members of the town council. In one heated moment, Jacques Tallemant, an old *pair* on the council, struck Isaac du Querny, now a *procureur* of the bourgeois, over the head with his walking stick. Du Querny, the wholesale wine dealer and customs broker, was a close friend of Jean Tharay. Word quickly spread through town of this assault and an angry crowd forced Tallemant to flee for his life and barricade himself inside his house. Only the mayor's pleading intervention saved Tallemant from being lynched by the 300 to 400 vengeful townspeople who surrounded his house. Commenting to his diary on this fracas, Guillaudeau reported that very humble townspeople hastened to punish Tallemant for his attack on du Querny "because, as they say, he struck a sacred individual" ("une personne sacrée").[127] Jean Tharay, no doubt, was the recipient of similar and probably stronger popular adulation for his evident devotion to communal welfare. Tharay's work in the shop and in the street encourages us to move beyond narrow socioeconomic typ-

---

[127] Guillaudeau, "Diaire," 113.

ing of rebels to explore how their performance in daily labor and commodity exchanges informed their planning and practice of rebellion.[128]

What made Jean Tharay a successful rebel chief? His command was facilitated by an extended family holding prime real estate and long identified with nourishing the residents and economies of several urban neighborhoods. That family's tradition of service to community and congregation through reciprocal obligations of godparentage, bearing witness, and standing surety added to Jean Tharay's stature. Multiple ties of real and fictive kinship extending horizontally from Tharay's own family across neighborhood boundaries to prominently placed clans in other quarters gave latitude to his ambition. So did vertical channels of favor and friendship linking Tharay and his family to richer and poorer men and women from many different parts of town.

Tharay's combat experience calls our attention to the extended bourgeois family as a catalyst and moderator of collective action at the middle and lower levels of the urban social hierarchy. Hot spots of armed opposition to the town council correlate precisely with the location of Tharay family properties and the territory of close Tharay kin. These structures anchored and amplified rebel protest within multiple city neighborhoods. The Tharays also had ingratiated themselves with disaffected members of La Rochelle's presidial court. These contacts gave the rebel leadership advance warning of their opponents' judicial machinations and emboldened the protestors since an internally factionalized court reduced the likelihood that outlaws would be prosecuted. Confident of their good repute and armed support within rochelais militia companies, the Tharays and their allies could also run the risk that their escalating protest against the town council might lead to violence.

Having made a name for themselves by supplying one French town with elemental goods and services, the Tharays could also

---

[128] As H-C. Rublack argues, norms defining urban moral economies derive essentially from citizens' common, reiterated physical acts and material exchanges. Such activities can be scrutinized for tangible markers of how moral economies coalesce and change over time, influencing the conditions and course of collective action. See Rublack, "Political and Social Norms in Urban Communities in the Holy Roman Empire," in K. Von Greyerz, ed., *Religion, Politics, and Social Protest* (London, 1984), 24-60.

reasonably expect to garner public support outside the militia companies should open war with the town council begin. The commercial contacts and clienteles they gained through these provisions were also potential weapons of rebellion Jean Tharay could wield in 1614. The accumulation of such opportunities for sedition distinguishes the Tharays from all other rebel confederates and enabled Jean Tharay, an impetuous family man, to take the lead in destroying the old regime of civic government in La Rochelle.

The 1614 rochelais rebellion shows that moderately wealthy townsmen like Jean Tharay, with dense interparochial familial, commercial, and social contacts conferring a supraparochial perspective and reputation, were well positioned to coordinate and compound volatile animosities within the urban community.[129] This was a dangerous game that could quickly veer out of control; it nearly did so when Tharay and his kinsmen had to face down angry rebels in the streets of the St. Nicolas quarter. But the socially heterogeneous factions men like Tharay could field, undergirded by family connections, food distribution networks, business obligations, shared paramilitary service, and religious affiliations were also susceptible to varieties of discipline a clever leader could juxtapose and strengthen. Uncovering the social mechanics of urban rebellions thus requires historians' balanced attention to the intra- and interparochial solidarities town dwellers proved remarkably adept at nurturing over time.

Jean Tharay captained a successful bourgeois political uprising in one of the largest pre-industrial French towns. He and his Protestant confederates employed the tangible and intangible assets honorable townsmen accrued to defeat the old *corps de ville*, to curtail the influence of Calvinist clergymen in town government,

---

[129] Figures like Tharay were thus instrumental in working the subtle changes in town dwellers' political identities Christopher Friedrichs finds essential to the outbreak of violent protests against town councils in early modern German cities. Friedrichs argues that once a third stage constitutional crisis had been reached in a German town, "a citizen's previous affiliation with family, parish, or guild tended to recede in importance...[i]nstead each citizen was pressured by the force of events to identify himself primarily as being for or against the council," "Urban Politics and Urban Social Structure," 204. Men like Tharay, Bernardeau, and du Querny, whose social responsibilities frequently allowed them to rise above parochial attachments, were ideally situated to embody and encourage such relocations of allegiance.

and to check royal efforts to control civic affairs. Jurists, merchants, and artisans fighting together against more patrician opponents shrewdly assessed and exploited their adversaries' political interests, weakening elite resistance to reform of municipal government. Such accomplishments undercut royal police of La Rochelle and surely inspired new efforts by the crown to reduce French civic and religious liberties after 1614. Tharay family socioeconomic connections were logistically vital to all phases of rebel victory. Evidence from La Rochelle suggests that the formation and decay of such networks ultimately determined the balance of power between townspeople and higher authorities in early modern France.

Successful opponents of oligarchical town government actively encouraged the largest possible number of citizens to support their energetic protests. For example, pastor Merlin grudgingly admired merchants' astute use of the printing press to publicize the motives of their rebellion. He sharply criticized the *corps de ville* for its negligence in not promptly printing a response to the widely disseminated grievances of the bourgeoisie.[130] The innovative Council of Forty-Eight, staffed through polling the militiamen, also showed the rebels' willingness to enlarge the number of citizens taking part in urban politics. This council significantly expanded the municipal electorate giving protest leaders a power base in the community unmatched by town councilmen.

Rebel captains frequently rallied their diverse supporters through strategy sessions held in the meeting halls of La Rochelle's Calvinist congregations. The siting and inclusive nature of these assemblies enabled insurrectionary members of the bourgeoisie to capitalize on popular religious solidarities already formed, in part, to counterbalance the moral pretensions of the city's patrician ministers. While they did not seek to justify their seizure of power in religious terms, La Rochelle's victorious bourgeois rebels cleverly appealed to the citizenry's more democratic, "congregationalist" sympathies for their own political gain, garnering broad support for a decisive attack on the power prerogatives of councilmen and pastors.

However, these relatively popular aspects of the 1614 uprising were counterweighted by the hierarchical arrangement of its pro-

---

[130] Merlin, "Diaire," fol. 230r.

ponents and the conservative nature of the reforms it engendered. The headmen of bourgeois families and their male kin managed to coordinate and control the violence employed to destroy the old civic regime. The town council was conquered by a rebellion both popular and familial, animated by opposition leaders united through bonds of marriage, godparentage, churchgoing, and neighborliness. These ties, fundamental to the daily life of each quarter, were reinforced by the social structure of the rochelais municipal militia charged with defense of the city's districts. Householders and artisans of middling social rank reputed within and across neighborhoods comprised the militia's rank and file. Such protestors were determined to break the power of the old oligarchy without giving free rein to the vengeance or rapacity of the city's propertyless residents.

The rebels took to the streets not to reform town government radically, but rather to refurbish a tested system of municipal administration abused by its current trustees. The decadence of that old ruling elite, its failure to abide by all the unwritten rules of government by patriarchs, especially prohibition of office to the young, served as a key pretext for the political uprising of 1614 led by merchants who expressly legitimated their seizure of power as necessary to prevent further misrule by the immature, undisciplined offspring of indulgent city fathers. Among the reciprocal obligations between governors and governed that constituted the moral economy of early modern politics in La Rochelle should be counted a respect for the protocols of behavior enshrined in respectable middle class households and the defense of those norms in the conduct of civic government.

The dramatic events of 1612-1614 that transformed La Rochelle's municipal government should make us more attentive to the importance of the extended bourgeois family as a catalyst and regulator of urban political violence and the remaking of public institutions of the *ancien régime*. In La Rochelle, the ensemble of relations between the members and allies of Pierre Bernardeau's and Jean Tharay's lineages certainly favored the successful outcome of the 1614 rebellion. Looking for kinsmen and *voisins* in the ranks of rebels is no mere antiquarian's game. The search for family and clientage networks underlying the leadership and directing the course of violent uprisings can cast new light on the origins, character, and propagation of political dissent in post-feudal France. In conjunction with standard methods of analyzing insurrectionary groups, heavily weighted toward the primary occupational affiliations and socioeconomic status of members, the study of kith and kin in politics can flesh out our knowledge of how and why such groups formed. Ultimately, this approach will permit us to recover more fully the political culture of the era, a culture in which the ethics and experience of consanguinity, congregational affiliation, and neighborliness conditioned human efforts to sustain, subvert, and amend the government of cities.

Reforms instituted by the rebellion of 1614 opened a channel into civic government for the members of bourgeois families previously excluded from municipal officeholding. The following chapter will trace the political careers of the new townsmen who joined the *corps de ville* via this route and then examine how this process influenced the daily administration of the city in a period of heightened political tension leading to open warfare between city and crown.

# CHAPTER SIX

# THE ADVENT OF A NEW CIVIC REGIME: URBAN POLITICS, RELIGIOUS DISSENT, AND DEFIANCE OF THE CROWN, 1614–1628

## 1. *The Repercussions of Bourgeois Political Violence*

The 1614 rebellion led by bourgeois kinsmen reordered but did not destroy La Rochelle's established political system. The mass arrest of town council members by the insurgents debilitated the *corps de ville,* but the newly powerful neighborhood chieftains and their followers neither demanded the old institution's destruction nor, once in power, attempted to dismantle it. Such action would certainly have gone unopposed locally given the rebels' numerical superiority and crushing military advantage over the defenders of the old civic regime still at liberty. And although rebel leaders harshly denounced city churchmen to their faces as false prophets and craven allies of the old town council, pastor Merlin and his cohorts were never physically harmed nor brutally exiled. The rebels also made no effort to destroy the Calvinist consistory. Largely indifferent to its official teachings, they did not bother to reconstruct the institution. However, the growing estrangement between Protestant churchmen and new participants in town politics indicates that the established doctrines of the French Reformed Church did not constitute a central ideological element in rochelais communal affairs after 1614. The citizens who took up arms against the oligarchic *corps de ville* and its ministerial allies aimed at substantive but not sweeping changes in municipal government. How they achieved that goal while contending with their opponents and with one another in a climate of intermittent local and national political crises from 1614 to 1628 forms the main subject of this chapter. Subsidiary arguments concern the interplay between innovative civic government and local religious dissent and the impact of this conjuncture on La Rochelle's increasingly problematic relations with the Bourbon monarchy.

The progressive *embourgeoisement* of municipal government put well-armed, charismatic, and ambitious townsmen in control of civic offices vital to communal defense and to the projection of rochelais power far beyond the city walls. Unlike the prior, more cautious ruling oligarchy, this new cadre of community leaders, when threatened by warring external authorities, tended to react with greater belligerence. As more former rebels ascended to positions of command in town government, diplomatic overtures toward a resurgent, combative monarchy became increasingly problematic and sterile. Misunderstandings between the veteran adversaries multiplied because royal intelligence networks operating feebly in the west country proved incapable of accurately determining the identity and interests of the formerly obscure men now being elected to civic offices. Even the spymaster Richelieu, who quit the neighboring west country bishopric of Luçon first in 1614 and then definitively in 1618, could not always gather reliable information from La Rochelle to guide his political manoeuvering.

The bourgeois *coup d'état* of August 9 to 12 1614, accomplished with broad popular support from the city's artisans, sailors, and laborers, at a stroke neutralized the governing power of the town council while simultaneously admitting a traditionally unruly segment of rochelais society into the fray of town politics. Pastor Merlin, like many other privileged inhabitants of the city, feared the consequences of this violent conjuncture. On 19 August 1614, Merlin noted in his diary that a royal envoy, carrying *lettres patentes* from the king denying any rochelais court jurisdiction to try the patrician prisoners of the August coup, was persuaded by senior members of the presidial court not to publicize his commission for fear that "the people would take up arms and hasten to murder the prisoners in their confinement."[1]

Merlin worried over the harsh treatment low-born jailers meted out to their notable captives. On 1 September 1614, one prominent prisoner refused to confront his accusers or make any deposition, contending that the representatives of the bourgeoisie had

---

[1] Jacques Merlin, "Diaire ou recueil des choses les plus mémorables qui se sont passées en ceste ville," BMLR, MS 161, fols. 230v-231r. Presidial jurists worried that "s'il [the royal messenger] exposoit sa charge principale, le peuple prendroit les armes et iroit couper la gorge aux prisonniers."

no right to hold or try him. It horrified Merlin to learn that the *procureurs*, without any magistrate's authorization, "took vengeance" on the uncooperative prisoner by throwing him into solitary confinement inside a deep, stinking dungeon pit.[2]

The *avocat* Joseph Guillaudeau, whose brother, Pierre, a *conseiller* of the presidial court, was among the prisoners, confided to his diary that the prisoners, after their capture, were subjected to a regimen "of such severity and cruelty that for nearly a day they went without food or water and then spent nearly two weeks sleeping on the bare stone floors" of the dungeons and cellars that held them.[3] Guillaudeau reported that the prisoners were so wary of their jailers that they long refused to eat the food that finally arrived for fear of being poisoned.[4]

Pastor Merlin recorded with alarm that an order of the *procureurs* to release one prisoner into exile riled up the lowlier inhabitants of the city. Angry workingmen, especially from the humbler neighborhood of Perrot, determined to recapture the fugitive, broke into patrician houses throughout the city while vainly searching for the escapee.[5] The fact that bourgeois leaders, like the hot-tempered merchant Jean Tharay, often spent time in the company of artisans and day laborers never escaped Merlin's observation. The uneasy pastor considered this an ominous familiarity capable of destroying the city.[6] Factional strife, Merlin

---

[2] *Ibid.*, fols. 233v-234r, "les procureurs pour se venger ont mis par force, sans ordonnance du juge ni réquisitoire du procureur du roy, ledit sieur de Prince en une basse fossé sans air ni garderobbe." After pleas from de Prince's wife and kinsmen for lenience to be shown to him, the *procureurs* ordered that he be held in a more salubrious cell under constant guard by three armed militiamen.

[3] "Diaire de Joseph Guillaudeau," AHSA 38 (1908): 1-415. See in particular 69-70.

[4] *Ibid.*, 70. These fears may not have been unfounded given the fact that poison had been the weapon of choice used in prior rochelais political assassinations.

[5] Merlin, "Diaire," fol. 232r: "...fut mis hors de prison M. de l'Isleau...le murmure à cause de cela a esté grand entre le peuple, notamment au Perrot, qui mesne le recherche en quelques maisons pour le remettre en prison."

[6] Merlin was quick to note Tharay's convivial relations with the artisans guarding the prisoners in the tour de Moureilles, see "Diaire," fol. 234r. Merlin characterized the conflict between the *corps de ville* and the militant bourgeoisie as a "funeste différent," a "disastrous quarrel" stoked by the "paroles calomnieuses et insolentes" of Tharay and others, *ibid.*, fol. 241r. Given Merlin's general contempt for the humblest residents of the city, he (and other members of the rochelais governing elite) could only view with the greatest alarm artisans' and laborers' common participation in the seizures of 1614.

averred to his diary, threatened to shatter the church comprising the city. His entire rochelais congregation was "bien malade" and risked chastisement by the Lord.[7]

Merlin's fear of divine retribution against his dissenting city brethren was perhaps heightened by the inability of the pastors or *consistoire* to impose a Christian peace upon the town. Bourgeois leaders berated the ministers as frauds and agents of the oligarchic town council, repeatedly refusing the church hierarchy any role in the pacification of the urban community. On 12 September 1614, Merlin, in full clerical garb, attempted to make a pastoral call on the prisoners held in the tour du Garrot. The jailers refused him admittance and kept him waiting for two hours in a drafty anteroom before Jean Tharay, Zacherie Chatton, and their lieutenants arrived. Merlin set down in his diary that Tharay became incensed at the pastor's visit and warned him that "the people are scandalized by your willingness to deal with traitors." Brushing aside Merlin's protests that he came only as a man of the Lord, Tharay swore "By God!, the prisoners are traitors, I know of no one who would stop me if I were to kill them."[8] Merlin's rebuff that Tharay "did not speak like a true Christian" only further aggravated Tharay, who, in concert with Chatton, refused to recognize Merlin and his cohorts as pastors, denounced the preachers as conspirators beholden to the old town council, attacked the *consistoire* as a propagator of false doctrines, condemned the synodal arrangement of government inside the Reformed church, and demanded the mass resignation of all Protestant churchmen in the city. La Rochelle, Tharay maintained, would be better off without half the current number of clerics. The rebel captain then denied the ministers any visits to the captives.

Tharay effectively repeated his orders in October 1614 when jailhouse guardians, following his lead, again denied city pastors all access to the prisoners. During this second confrontation

---

[7] *Ibid.*, fols. 234r and 245r-246v. Merlin's fear of the malefic forces generated by political conflict was compounded by his wife's death on 19 November 1615, an event he directly attributed to the "grand frayeur" provoked in the poor woman by the street battles of 1614 and the subsequent "tristesse sévère" which overcame her as the conflict continued to be fought within the sacred and secular institutions of the city, see *ibid.*, fols. 311v-312r.

[8] *Ibid.*, fol. 235r.

between ministers and rebel jailers, pastor Jean Salbert, a member of one of La Rochelle's oldest patrician families, was refused entry to the dungeons of the town hall and "audaciously insulted" by a militiaman in charge of the guards.[9] When Salbert complained to the mayor, Jean Tharay quickly showed up, verbally abused the minister, and shouted that "the pastors do not preach the word of God, they are our enemies."[10] Intensifying his attack, Tharay alleged that several pastors had obtained their offices unjustly, through the machinations of other clerics rather than by popular endorsement. Minister Samuel Loumeau stole into the rochelais church like a thief, Tharay declared, entering the institution "not by the door, but by the window," that is without congregational approval and thanks mainly to the scheming of senior church officials.[11] Tharay also accused the ministers of secretly aiding the town council in the dissemination of anti-bourgeois tracts and in stirring up opposition to the bourgeoisie's political reform movement.[12]

Growing outrage among the pastors at the "insolences" and "indignities" they were now being forced to endure prompted four of them to demand immediate dispensation from the consistory to leave La Rochelle. Pastors Louis Le Cercler, Jerôme Colomiez, Samuel Loumeau, and Jean Salbert, "seeing the diminishment of their ministries," sought to quit La Rochelle as soon as possible.[13] Apparently, the most patrician members of the city's Reformed clergy bore the brunt of popular vilification and attempted to escape this sharp embarrassment. Louis Le Cercler, *sieur* de la Chapellière, was married to the daughter of a *pair* on the old town council. Pastor Colomiez's local kinsmen held important offices in La Rochelle's mint. Samuel Loumeau was the brother-in-law of another notable Rochelais holding large landed estates. Jean Salbert was the scion of a wealthy native family long identified with the city's old ruling oligarchy. Salbert's Genevan theological training undoubtedly reinforced his unsympathetic attitude toward restive congregants and contributed to his unpopularity

---

[9] *Ibid.*, fol. 237r.

[10] *Ibid.*, fol. 237v.

[11] *Ibid.*, fol. 237v-238r.

[12] For further information on the specific points of Tharay's and Chatton's rebuke to the pastors see BMLR, MS 58, fols. 158r-v.

[13] Merlin, "Diaire," fol. 236r.

among them. This cohort of Calvinist clerics felt especially threatened and demeaned by the insurrection of their parishioners in 1614.

Pastor Merlin now felt an obligation to persuade wavering colleagues against precipitous flight. This coaxing, wearily recorded in Merlin's diary, further compromised his efforts to mediate the city's political crisis. Conflicts of opinion over the advisability of staying or leaving divided the pastors and put some of them at odds with the *consistoire*. A majority of church elders kept the disaffected ministers in town by refusing to grant them the requisite dispensations from ecclesiastical service. This policy stoked the animus of those pastors who wished to bolt.

Under these conditions, the influence of local churchmen over current civic affairs rapidly waned. By 15 November 1614, Merlin had to acknowledge the clergy's total lack of influence over rebellious bourgeois. He now begged the king's *sénéchal* in La Rochelle to intercede with rebel leaders on behalf of the *consistoire* and implore them to release the captives taken during the August coup.[14] This mission failed.

On 2 January 1615, pastor Salbert, the main target of many rebel insults, made a pointed sermon on the thirty-seventh and seventy-third Psalms followed by a public prayer for those patricians imprisoned. This was not a politic choice of scripture. Negotiations between militant members of the bourgeoisie, the *corps de ville*, and the magistrates of the presidial court over terms for the release of the prisoners had recently broken down again and kinsmen of the captives had redoubled their criticism of the rebels' arrogance and violent opposition to compromise. Partisans of the bourgeoisie took to patrolling the streets in a continuous show of force. Borrowing from Psalm 37 ("Fret not thyself because of evil doers, neither be thou envious against the workers of iniquity."), pastor Salbert warned his congregation against the politics of the insurgents and rebuked the rebels from the pulpit, asserting (from Psalm 73), "pride compasseth them about as a chain; violence covereth them as a garmet."[15] In his public prayers after the

---

[14] *Ibid.*, fol. 239r.

[15] Merlin reports that Salbert extolled his flock to be simple in combat with pride and arrogance and "dit que les simples et débonnaires ne doibvent s'étonner, s'ils voient les mechants et arrogans marcher fiérement par les rues de la ville du monde," *ibid.*, fols. 253v-254r.

sermon, Salbert contrasted the prisoners' long expectation of a just and compassionate release with the haughty and unreasonable demands of the city's new masters.

Salbert's pronouncements further undercut the Reformed church's role as a mediator in municipal politics and announced a widening rift between the official theology of the pastors and *consistoire* and the religious values informing the conduct of the rebels. The prolonged reluctance of the church hierarchy to endorse the acts of the insurgents makes it unwarranted to assume that established Calvinist dogma essentially informed the conduct of town government after 1614. Nor should one conclude that canonical Calvinist beliefs primarily drove this government into later open warfare with the French crown.

Pastor Salbert's premeditated political engagement on behalf of the prisoners and their families negated pastor Merlin's faltering effort to maintain the church as an impartial referee of urban politics. Salbert's vituperative sermon provoked an immediate protest from the rebel leaders who lodged a written complaint with the *consistoire*, and, unsatisfied with that body's temporizing, demanded disciplinary action against Salbert from regional church authorities. Jean Tharay once again loudly denounced the local pastors as "calomniateurs" and the *procureur* Simon Papin warned them that their ill-chosen words would have their fellow citizens at one another's throats in no time.[16] Under mounting pressure from representatives of the bourgeoisie, the *consistoire*, while not disavowing the propriety of Salbert's sermon on the Psalms, censured him for the use of language offensive to his congregants and to rebel leaders. This incident shows that prominent bourgeois readily and willingly challenged the city's clergymen over the daily conduct and discourse of their ministries.

The censure of pastor Salbert sought and obtained by the *procureurs* of the rebel movement is one measure of their growing influence over the exercise of both secular and sacred authority in La Rochelle. Through the audacious acts of Chatton, Papin, and Tharay, this influence rapidly widened at the expense of rochelais magistrates and churchmen. Patrician members of the

---

[16] *Ibid.*, fols. 264r-266r. "Tharay fut si audacieux de nous appeler par trois fois calomniateurs, et Papin dit que nos presches finalement feroient couper la gorge les uns aux autres."

old ruling elite lost advisory powers over municipal affairs and civic diplomacy long taken for granted. In October of 1615, pastor Merlin ruefully noted that not a single pastor was even invited to attend a "grosse assemblée" of councilmen and bourgeois called to debate whether La Rochelle should financially and materially aid Protestant communities that had taken up arms in Guyenne.[17]

The capture and prolonged imprisonment (nine months) of more than fifty patricians by the rebels also underscores the impotency of local royal magistrates to resolve the crisis or to impose the king's arbitration on the new course of municipal affairs.[18] On 19 August 1614, a representative of the crown arrived in La Rochelle with *lettres patentes* denying any local tribunal authority to judge the perpetrators or the prisoners of the uprising. Rapidly apprised of the local balance of power favoring the rebels, the king's envoy, in reading his charge to the *corps de ville* and the *procureurs* of the bourgeoisie, simply omitted any mention whatsoever of the chief injunction his master had expressly sent him to La Rochelle to announce. For fear that "the people would take up arms and hasten to murder the prisoners," the king's emissary only stated that his majesty expected a fair trial of the prisoners and was taking a special interest in the case.[19] Rochelais magistrates then proceeded to interview the prisoners, take depositions, and record confessions in preparation for local judicial proceedings against the captives.

On 26 August, the queen learned that at La Rochelle "il n'y avait plus qu'une face apparente de magistrature, et qu'en effet

---

[17] *Ibid.*, fol. 307r.

[18] Most of the prisoners rounded up between 9 to 12 August 1614 were not released until 3 April 1615. A few captives were released into exile prior to April 1615, largely due to family machinations or to influence peddling among the incarcerated and their jailers. On 3 January 1615, Merlin reports that two royal notaries, Chesneau and Cousseau, were set free, Chesneau "par commandement de M. le chancellier [Nicolas Brûlart de Sillery, chancellier de France, chief judicial officer of the crown 1607-1624]...ce fut M. Bouleau qui a l'oreille de M. le chancellier, lequel Bouleau à cause de sa femme est presque allié de Chesneau." Notary Cousseau gained his freedom "par la faveur de Mlle. de Rouaux que M. le procureur du roy recherche en mariage," *ibid.*, fols. 257r-v. The operation of such personal contacts and the human motives promoting each are notoriously difficult to document but constitute the real driving force of the political activity that can only be nominally attributed to the "institutions" of the old regime, i.e. the courts, the *parlements*, the chancelleries, etc.

[19] *Ibid.*, fol. 231r.

le peuple governait tout."[20] This prompted her to summon the *procureur du roi* of La Rochelle's presidial court to an audience at Angers on 30 August in order to explain the situation. Already a day late for his royal interview, the local king's prosecutor informed an assembly of town councilmen and bourgeois leaders on September 1 that he would be quite content ("bien aisé") if they could resolve the affair of the prisoners amongst themselves and that he would be eager to sign any mutually satisfactory accord they could present to him.

In late October, the crown suspended all prior legal injunctions regarding trial of the prisoners and, in an *arrêt* of the *Conseil Privé*, acquiesced to a fait accompli by permitting senior magistrates of La Rochelle's presidial court to prepare for adjudication of the case before the *Conseil* itself. This decision garnered no wide acceptance in La Rochelle, where substantive negotiations for release of the prisoners continued unperturbed between rebel leaders and the families of the captives. When the *Conseil d'Etat* finally ordered the release of the prisoners in an *arrêt* dated 11 March 1615, its official decision, including terms of exile and probation for the captives, almost exactly replicated conditions for their release demanded by the rebels in a written declaration of 1 January 1615.

Royal justice suffered further indignities when rebel leaders first interfered with the enforcement of the king's decree and then subjected the supposedly compelling *arrêt* to a vote of approval by the rank and file of the rochelais militia companies.[21] Senior rochelais churchmen found this popular irreverence abhorrent. According to Merlin, insurrectionary members of the bourgeoisie reasoned that "because the captives had been imprisoned by the authority of the people in arms, it was absolutely necessary that the people consent to their release."[22] Merlin confided to his diary that it was "an iniquitous procedure to make the authority of a

---

[20] As reported by Merlin, *ibid.*, fol. 232v.

[21] *Ibid.*, fols. 271v-272r. See also Mervault's, "Histoire," BMLR, MS 58, fol. 160r. Mervault related the misfortune of Joel de Lorriere, a *pair* on the town council, who voiced sharp criticism of the rebels' obstruction of justice and was then exiled from La Rochelle by order of rebel leaders. This sentence was carried out by a crowd of townspeople who broke into de Lorriere's house, finally tracked him down hiding in an attic, trussed him up with ropes, and dragged him out of the city.

[22] Merlin, "Diaire," fol. 271v.

king depend upon the consent of the people" and concluded that the entire affair of the prisoners had been treated not in accord with, but in flagrant contravention of "les formes de la justice."[23] The militia's rank and file voted to accept the *arrêt* and all patrician prisoners rounded up in the coup of August 1614 finally went free on 3 April 1615.

The course of events in La Rochelle from August 1614 to April 1615 clearly demonstrates the political powerlessness of such key governing institutions as the town council, the *consistoire*, and the royal magistracy. The armed uprising of 9-12 August 1614 shifted the locus of coercive power in the town onto the militia companies and the bourgeois family men who comprised them. The bold restructuring of municipal police authority' perpetrated by the rebels was not a transient phenomenon and exposes to detailed view the complicated inner workings of urban politics in a strategically located Atlantic frontier town at a crucial juncture in French history.

## 2. *The Embourgeoisement of Municipal Government After 1614*

Pierre Bernardeau, Zacherie Chatton, Jean Tharay, and other representatives of the defiant bourgeois amassed uncommon political influence. Pastor Merlin did not exaggerate when he publicly admonished Jean Tharay to lead his rebellious followers prudently because Tharay "had the lives of his fellow citizens in his hands."[24] Intent on representing La Rochelle's third estate at the 1614 meeting of the Estates General, Tharay bluntly demanded that the town council endorse his right to take the duty. Outraged by Tharay's plan but fearful of refusing, the *corps de ville* abandoned all traditional methods for the selection of rochelais delegates and gave Tharay the honor. This capitulation entirely thwarted carefully laid royal plans to maintain traditional modes of recruitment for deputies to the estates from towns like La Rochelle. Louis XIII had specifically ordered the city council to select a representative for La Rochelle's third estate. The king's men defended ancient

---

[23] *Ibid.*, fol. 272r.

[24] *Ibid.*, fol. 236r. "Mon. Tharay vous avez beaucoup d'authorité, vous avez la vie et la mort de vos concitoyens entre les mains: regardez de n'abuser pas de votre puissance."

electoral procedures like these in hopes of obtaining an assembly
predisposed to accept crown policies.[25]

Not satisfied with his unprecedented appointment as the deputy
for the rochelais third estate, Tharay threatened the reconstituted town council with more popular violence and imprisonment
unless the body voted to subsidize all of his travel expenses to the
assembly. Frightened councillors immediately convened and voted him the money.[26]

Pastor Merlin was particularly alarmed by the effort of men like
Zacherie Chatton, Simon Papin, Jean Tharay, and Israel Torterue
to foment further dissent through adroit use of public oratory
and networks of influence rooted in the neighborhoods where
each man's economic and social contacts were concentrated.
Merlin was strongly impressed by the willingness of Chatton,
Papin, and Tharay to thwart any quick resolution of the conflict
between the *corps de ville* and the bourgeoisie by amplifying the
suspicions of La Rochelle's humbler inhabitants. Leading rebels
then used the complaints of this volatile constituency to radical-
ize the negotiating position of bourgeois representatives, check-
ing the influence of moderates among merchant leaders.

The strength of the ties between fervent merchant leaders and
the lowliest residents of La Rochelle and the importance of these
contacts in shaping the new environment of urban politics amazed
and frightened privileged townsmen. When the bourgeois Council
of Forty-Eight and eight special twelve-member delegations drawn
from the militia companies met in January 1615 to approve stiff
conditions for release of the prisoners previously urged by Tharay
and his lieutenants, pastor Merlin denounced the severity of this
ultimatum and noted with disgust that "the plurality of votes in

[25] See the king's letter of 17 July 1614 to the rochelais *corps de ville* stipulating acceptable modes of election for all urban deputies of the third estate preparing to attend the 1614 Estates General, BN, Collection Clairambault, 364, fol.
258r. In order to protect the "bien et repos" of La Rochelle, the king later
refused to act on protests of Tharay's appointment made by obstreperous members of the town council and ordered that Tharay be admitted to the Estates
General without hindrance, see the royal letters patent dated 3 February 1615,
BN, Manuscrits Français, 18187, fols. 135v-137r.

[26] Merlin, "Diaire," fol. 242r. In January 1615, under similar threats of renewed
popular violence directed by rebel leaders, the town council also agreed to pay
all the travel expenses of Israel Torterue and Jean Guillameau, selected by the
bourgeois Council of Forty-Eight to justify its policies to royal authorities in Paris,
see Joseph Guillaudeau, "Diaire," 94-95.

favor of these harsh conditions came from bootmakers, cobblers, weavers, carpenters, and tanners."[27] Bourgeois political protestors clearly gained the active support of rochelais workingmen, a constituency equally contemptuous of the city's ruling oligarchy, more impervious to indoctrination by local churchmen, and poised to reclaim a right of consultation in civic affairs previously exercised in public assemblies during the Wars of Religion.

Popular allegiance to the insurrection of disgruntled merchants was sustained by the rebels' willingness to engage shopkeepers, master craftsmen, and workingmen in public debates over political tactics. These assemblies were animated by the militia companies and deemed vital to the collective security of the urban community. Charismatic, combative leadership from Chatton, Grenot, Tharay, and others deeply impressed their poorer partisans. Following the release of the prisoners, the redaction and implementation of twenty-eight articles drafted by the bourgeoisie's *procureurs* to restructure civic administration elicited further violent confrontations. At heated moments in the negotiations between rebel captains and representatives of the town council, rochelais workingmen scrambled out of their ateliers to escort bourgeois spokesmen and protect them from harm. Such a crowd set out with a vengeance to punish the *pair* Jacques Tallemant who had dared to strike the *procureur* Isaac du Querny, regarded among the lower orders of the community as a "sacred personage."

Popular adulation of rebel leaders can, in part, be attributed to their impassioned diatribes against abuses of privilege, election fraud, and mismanagement of city finances committed by rich town councilmen oblivious to the cares of ordinary citizens. However, to explain more fully the tactics that won militant merchants broad support among townspeople, widening influence in municipal government, and *de facto* control of the city requires analysis of their innovative political organization entrenched in La Rochelle's neighborhoods. This organization was capable of exploiting popular allegiance and renewed threats of violence to crack the closed circle of rochelais families monopolizing control of the *corps de ville*.

Shortly after their aborted *coup d'état* of 23 March 1614, mem-

---

[27] Merlin, "Diaire," fol. 254r.

bers of the town council were obliged to accept numerous merchant demands drawn up in twenty-eight articles stipulating basic
reforms in urban government and finance.[28] The first of these
articles gave the bourgeois of La Rochelle the right to elect annually five *procureurs* (one per city parish) to represent them in all
dealings with the town council and external authorities. Coupled
with this new franchise, the *procureurs* obtained complete freedom
of assembly and the prerogative to consult publicly with any number of fellow bourgeois on the orderly conduct of municipal
affairs.[29]

La Rochelle's artisans and merchants used these hard-won concessions to good advantage. First, a committee of sixteen *commis-
saires-députés*, composed of two senior members of each militia
company, met and officially selected the most outspoken bourgeois leaders—Zacherie Chatton, Jacques Grenot, Simon Papin,
Jean Tharay, and Israel Torterue—to serve as *procureurs*. This move
probably engendered broad approval among the lower ranks of
the militia companies and among the poorer inhabitants of the
urban community known for prior service and fidelity to Tharay
and his confidants.

Then, broadly interpreting the *procureurs'* right to consult with
their constituency, rebellious members of the bourgeoisie formed
a permanent advisory council of forty-eight members, comprised
of six representatives from each of the city's eight militia companies to be selected annually by the members of each company.[30]
Undergoing only slight modifications, the Council of Forty-Eight,

---

[28] See *ibid.*, fols. 212r-214v, and Guillaudeau, "Diaire," 60-61. The text of the
twenty-eight articles is given in Jean Chenu's *Recueil des Antiquitez et privileges de
la ville de Bourges et plusieurs autres villes capitales de la Royaume*, (Paris, 1621), 224-
233. See also BMLR, MS 58, fols. 152v-155v.

[29] The text of Article I reads in part: "Que les bourgeois jurez de commune,
manans et habitans de ceste ville de La Rochelle pourront eslire, choisir et nom-
mer annuellement d'entr'eux jusque au nombre de cinq procureurs, savoir de
chacun paroisse un, qui auront droict et pouvoir de s'assembler quand bon leur
semblera avecques tel nombre d'autres bourgeois et habitans que la nécessite
le requerra..." see Chenu, *Recueil*, 226.

[30] According to the diarist Joseph Guillaudeau, the first Council of Forty-Eight
was selected between 5 and 7 April 1614, barely a week after the town council's
acceptance of the rebels' political demands, see AHSA, 38 (1908): 61. Pastor
Merlin regularly referred to the five *procureurs* and the forty-eight councilmen
of the bourgeoisie as the "fifty-three," underscoring the simultaneous foundation of these political organizations and their mutual importance for articulation and defense of bourgeois interests, see Merlin, "Diaire," fols. 218r-222v.

as it became known, played an active role in rochelais urban politics until the city's capitulation to royal troops in October 1628.
This new body frequently served as a "shadow" town council, meeting to debate appropriate administrative, religious, and diplomatic
policies for the city. The Forty-Eight further served as a forum
and amplifier for grievances of the artisan and merchant communities and kept a close watch on the *corps de ville* through the
five *procureurs* who had not only the right to participate in town
council meetings, but also a new key to the municipal archives
where precious civic privileges and complete minutes of all previous town council meetings could be freely consulted.[31]

Most importantly, by Article IV of the 1614 political settlement,
militant bourgeois of La Rochelle also gained the right to nominate three candidates for each position of *pair* that fell vacant on
the town council. The town council was then empowered to select
one of the three to fill the empty office. The Council of Forty-
Eight and the five *procureurs* were given joint responsibility for
choosing bourgeois aspirants to the *corps de ville* and thus gained
the ability to influence the workings of the town council from
within and without. Composed of key members of the neighborhood militia companies, the Forty-Eight also engaged in the military defense of the city and in the maintenance of public order.
A profile of membership in the Forty-Eight shows how protestors'
well-established intra- and interparochial sociabilities shaped this
new institution. Following this course, we may also discern whose
political interests benefitted the most from the formation and
operation of the Forty-Eight.

Perhaps struck by merchant leaders' disregard for traditional
legal procedures and the precedent-setting behavior of the Forty-
Eight, the rochelais lawyer, Joseph Guillaudeau, paid special attention to the composition of his city's latest political organization.
From 1614 to 1626, Guillaudeau carefully recorded in his diary
the names and parish affiliation of every resident of La Rochelle
selected to serve as a *procureur* of the bourgeois.[32] In addition, for

---

[31] The right of the five bourgeois *procureurs* to participate in town council
meetings was confirmed by Article II of the political accord reached between
the rebels and the town council in March 1614. Article III gave the *procureurs*
the right to hold a key for opening the "tresorier" where all documents of civic
importance were stored. See Chenu, *Recueil*, 227.

[32] Guillaudeau's listing of the five *procureurs* elected annually by members of

the years 1614 to 1617, Guillaudeau noted the names and militia
company affiliation of 144 townsmen serving on the Council of
Forty-Eight.[33] Guillaudeau's list of councilmen identifies by name
76% of all the individuals who comprised the Forty-Eight between
1614 and 1617. Guillaudeau's census of politically active bourgeois
can be expanded with data drawn from notarial and church
records on the occupation, status, friendships, and family networks of *procureurs* and councilmen of the Forty-Eight. This process reveals the social factors of town life enabling a small group
of men to effect major changes in the form of civic government
and to exercise new police authority over the inhabitants of La
Rochelle.

Table 13 shows a breakdown of the occupations held by the
fifty-eight men serving as *procureurs* of the bourgeois between 1614
and 1626.

*Table 13*

Procureurs de Bourgeois 1614-1626
Classification by Occupation

| *Occupation* | *Number* | *Percentage* |
|---|---|---|
| Merchant | 32 | 55.2 |
| Lawyer | 3 | 5.2 |
| Court Officer/Clerk | 2 | 3.4 |
| Doctor/Surgeon | 3 | 5.2 |
| Apothecary | 1 | 1.7 |
| Unknown | 17 | 29.3 |
| *Totals* | 58 | 100.0 |

Rochelais merchants, most with international business connections and wholesale operations, clearly predominated in the office
of *procureur*. Over the period studied, more then 70% of the men

---

the bourgeoisie between 1614 and 1626 runs to fifty eight names and occasionally
gives the occupation of the representatives, see his "Diaire," 61, 108, 120-121,
148, 153, 160, 165, 180, 200, 235, 260, 274, and 323. Seven of the men on
Guillaudeau's list served as a *procureur* twice.

[33] *Ibid.*, 61-62, 108, 121, and 148.

who served as *procureurs* occupied the higher ranks of La Rochelle's urban economy. No master artisan or more humble workingman is specifically named by Guillaudeau as having served as a *procureur*. Although the occupations of seventeen *procureurs* are unknown to me, it seems highly unlikely that this block was composed of men much lower in the city's social hierarchy than those whose vocation is known. If master craftsmen or other artisans with the right to the *appelation* "bourgeois" did serve as *procureurs*, their numbers must have been very small in comparison to the merchants and professional men known to have occupied the position.

This supposition is reinforced by the multiple status distinctions that characterized *procureurs* serving between 1614 and 1626. At least ten *procureurs* (17.2% of the sample) were landlords of houses, shops, or taverns in La Rochelle. Ten *procureurs* either owned rural properties outright or controlled and profited from produce of farms on the outskirts of the city. At least six (10.3%) merited the titles of "honorable homme" or "sieur." At least five (8.6%) served as *anciens* or *diacres* on the *consistoire* of the Calvinist church and two held positions as farmers of various municipal tax revenues. Highly popular men like Jean Tharay, Isaac du Querny, Simon Papin, and Samuel Bernardeau, whose families had been identified with bourgeois political dissent since 1612 or before, all served as *procureurs*. However, it is doubtful that men from the lower ranks of the militia companies, who also fought bravely against partisans of the old town council, ever rose to positions of leadership in the new civic administration their risky rebellion helped to create.

Companies of La Rochelle's militia included all male heads of households residing in a given street or neighborhood of streets. From pastor Merlin's reportage, we know that master weavers, cobblers, carpenters, and other poorer tradesmen served in the companies and constituted an unruly element in the political coalition bourgeois protestors arrayed against the town council. Merlin grew alarmed by the propensity of the *menu peuple* in the militia companies to support the more extreme attacks of the rebels against the established governing institutions of the city. Merlin accused Jean Tharay and his zealous lieutenants of pandering to the emotions of the people and of using their own support among

workingmen to foment further popular dissent in an effort to rad-
icalize or subvert more moderate negotiating positions favored by
the Council of Forty-Eight in peace talks with the *corps de ville*.[34]

Was the rank and file of the militia companies better represented among the men selected to serve on the Council of Forty-
Eight between 1614 and 1617? Table 14 gives a classification by
occupation of the 144 men on the Council of Forty-Eight between
1614 and 1617.

*Table 14*

Councilmen of the Forty-Eight 1614-1617
Classification by Occupation

| Occupation | Number | Percentage |
|---|---|---|
| Merchant | 70 | 48.6 |
| Lawyer | 3 | 2.0 |
| Presidial Court Prosecutor | 5 | 3.6 |
| Royal Judge | 1 | .7 |
| Court Officer/Clerk | 3 | 2.0 |
| Notary | 2 | 1.4 |
| Civic Official | 2 | 1.4 |
| Doctor/Surgeon | 3 | 2.0 |
| Apothecary | 1 | .7 |
| Jeweller | 2 | 1.4 |
| Artisan (by type) | | |
|   a. Master Swordmaker | 1 | |
|   b. Printer | 1 | |
|   c. Master Cooper | 2 | |
|   d. Dyer | 1 | |
|   e. Blacksmith | 1 | |
|   f. Master Shoemaker | 1 | |
|   *Total* | 7 | 4.9 |
| Unknown | 45 | 31.3 |
| *Total* | 144 | 100.0 |

Here, again, merchants and professional men predominated in
representing the interests of townsmen who rebelled against the

---

[34] See Merlin, "Diaire," fols. 248v-251r and 255r-256v.

old regime of civic government. Businessmen, jurists, physicians, and dealers in luxury goods made up at least 63.8% of the councilmen serving on the Forty-Eight over the period studied. Only 4.9% of the members of the Forty-Eight can be positively identified as artisans. However, the high number of men on the Forty-Eight whose occupation can not be determined suggests that total artisan representation within that body was probably higher, perhaps approaching 10% of all members for the period. This figure, while small, still stands in stark contrast to the contemporaneous monopolization of offices in other French civic institutions by robe nobles, royal magistrates, and wealthy merchants.

Known artisans serving on the Forty-Eight tended to work in the more learned and skilled trades of La ᾽Rochelle's manufacturing economy. A printer, a sword maker, and a blacksmith joined the Council of Forty-Eight during its first years of existence. In 1616, Jean Girault, a master cooper from the grande rue militia company, served on the Forty-Eight. Girault's father had been a lowly *saunier*, working and consolidating small salt pans near La Rochelle. In 1602, Girault himself married the daughter of a rochelais ship captain who brought him a modest dowry of ninety *livres*, a sum equivalent to three years' wages for a mason or carpenter.[35] Apparently, the tradesmen who gained seats on the Council of Forty-Eight had integrated themselves in urban society and benefitted from its economic opportunities.

The relatively privileged status of many members of the Forty-Eight is attested by the fact that at least twenty-eight participants (19.4% of my sample) were landlords of urban properties.[36] At least nineteen (13.2%) owned or controlled rural estates, six held the title of "honorable homme" or "sieur," at least three were members of the *consistoire*, and at least two were municipal tax farmers. Given this status profile of members in the Forty-Eight, headstrong rebel leaders like Jean Tharay at times may well have considered these representatives of the bourgeoisie to be compromised by their own privileges, too wary of major changes in the old regime of civic government, and reluctant to impose

---

[35] ADCM, 3 E 175, marriage contract dated 16 May 1602.

[36] The percentage of landlords among councilmen of the Forty-Eight was even slightly higher than the percentage of landlords among *procureurs* of the bourgeoisie.

exemplary punishment on the routed beneficiaries of that ancient regime.

When negotiations during the winter of 1614-15 between the Forty-Eight and the *corps de ville* over just penalties for the imprisoned town councilmen approached cordial settlement, Jean Tharay and his partisans demanded and got expanded popular participation in the talks by constitution of an adjunct council of ninety-six militiamen (twelve members from each militia company) who joined the Forty-Eight in drawing up more stringent conditions for release of the prisoners. By Merlin's account, the Forty-Eight put up no resistance to the creation of the adjunct council of ninety-six and abided by the stipulations of the settlement for release of the prisoners approved through ballots cast by all 144 representatives of the militia companies.[37] But as pastor Merlin noted disdainfully, these tougher strictures were largely approved by the humbler artisans newly incorporated in the negotiations. These conditions, in slightly revised form, ultimately governed the release of all prisoners in April 1615.

The political tactics of Tharay and his followers suggest that the insurrection modifying rochelais municipal institutions was propelled by a coalition of townsmen whose differing status and comportment were played upon by ambitious neighborhood leaders, like Tharay, who sought to strengthen their own hand in the remaking of civic government. As anxious local diarists averred, this was a dangerous pursuit, but, to their relief, one that did not degenerate into continuous factional warfare, pillaging of the rich, or wholesale slaughter of political opponents or city clerics. The coalition persevered despite the inequalities of its constituents and clashes of personality among its leaders.

An incident of February 1617 highlights these tensions and their resolution among the constituents of the rebel coalition who humbled the old town council and obstructed the local operations of royal justice. On 11 February 1617, the *siège présidial* condemned Pierre Vilain, a master pastry cook, to be hanged for verbally insulting the mayor ("outragé audacieusement et insolemment Mon. le maire de paroles" according to pastor Merlin). The severity of this sentence reproving a relatively innocuous act (certainly a common one in La Rochelle) measures a high degree of

---

[37] Merlin, "Diaire," fols. 248r-252r.

patrician alarm over the general political empowerment of humbler townsmen effected by the revolt of 1614 and formation of the Forty-Eight.

The day before his execution, Vilain managed to escape with the aid of friends who spirited him out of town. Vilain's allies reported their actions to the Forty-Eight and appealed to that body to block execution of the sentence. The Forty-Eight debated the matter but hesitated to intervene.

The presidial then resolved to burn the fugitive Vilain in effigy and erected a gallows in La Rochelle's main square for this purpose. The painter hired to do the effigy was harassed in his work by townspeople and was finally threatened by the court with a fine and imprisonment if he did not swiftly complete the job. On 16 February, the gallows and freshly painted effigy were both torn down, allegedly by a master shoemaker who was taken into custody, found innocent, and scheduled for release by bailiffs of the presidial court. Before he could be freed, an assembly of artisans from the popular neighborhoods of Cougnes, St. Nicolas, and Perrot, probably including militiamen from each district, resolved to liberate the cobbler and carry off all court papers and pending indictments against Vilain, the *procureur de bourgeois* Jean Tharay, and François Bardonnin, a militant jurist and legal advisor to the Council of Forty-Eight.[38]

On the night of Friday, 17 February, fifty to sixty men, nearly all "artisans and gens de néant" according to Guillaudeau, led by Jean Demont (nicknamed "La Roze"), a member of the Forty-Eight from the parish of Perrot in 1614 and current lieutenant of the neighborhood militia company, attacked the house of the *lieutenant criminel* of the presidial court, broke down the door, rustled the prosecutor out of bed, and threatened to burn down his house if he did not order the shoemaker's immediate release. The *lieutenant criminel* quickly sent his clerk, accompanied by a large contingent of workingmen, to the city jail with an order for the cobbler's liberation at once. La Roze and his men then broke into the house of the secretary of the presidial court in a vain search for the indictments against Vilain and friendly bourgeois leaders.

---

[38] Guillaudeau, "Diaire," 142-43. The humble defenders of Vilain also spontaneously decided to use their raid on town jurists to make off with legal documentation threatening the welfare of Jean Tharay, a man of greater social status but nonetheless a trusted political ally of rochelais workingmen.

Now, the presidial court, in turn, indicted La Roze for numerous criminal acts he incited during the protests. La Roze responded by hatching a new plot with his men to capture and exile the
*lieutenant criminel* of the tribunal. Bungled execution of this
scheme caused a general alarm throughout the city, seizure of all
town squares by militiamen, and erection of barricades. Calm
returned to La Rochelle when a satisfactory settlement, negotiated by the presidial court, the *corps de ville*, and the Forty-Eight,
was read out to militiamen on their barricades dividing the city.
By the terms of this agreement, La Roze was to leave town for six
months and apologize to the individuals he outraged. In return,
all charges against Vilain, the shoemaker, Tharay, Bardonnin, and
two others were to be dropped. Militiamen guarding La Roze's
house in the district of Perrot were the last to disperse.

Although four *procureurs de bourgeois* had joined with members
of the *corps de ville* in condemning La Roze's actions and one *procureur* was nearly murdered by one of La Roze's more eager artisan followers, La Roze's conduct did not bar him from future participation in the politics of the Forty-Eight. He became a *procureur
de bourgeois* representing the parish of Perrot in 1622.[39] Clearly,
some senior members of the Forty-Eight and a majority of the *procureurs* in 1617 found La Roze's actions condemnable. Wealthier
merchants could be expected not to countenance housebreaking
by armed laborers and "gens de néant." However, the initial
appeal of Vilain's allies to the Forty-Eight, the service of La Roze
and his men to bourgeois leaders like Tharay, and La Roze's own
reincorporation into the new governing apparatus of the city indicate broad popular regard for the workings of the Forty-Eight and
a willingness—sorely tested to be sure—of senior bourgeois leaders to tolerate the militant behavior of key neighborhood leaders
and their followers among *le peuple*.[40]

---

[39] BMLR, MS 97, fol. 168 and MS 764, fols. 88r-v.

[40] Seen from this perspective, David Parker's assertion that the Vilain incident shows bourgeois leaders closing ranks with privileged members of the town
council and presidial court against the "independent interests of the *menu peuple*" and a common threat of uncontrollable popular violence seems based upon
an overly simple and misleading analysis of urban politics in La Rochelle. Since
he makes no mention of blatant popular action protecting the interests of Jean
Tharay, Parker overlooks important, lasting solidarities between protestors from
various ranks of rochelais society fighting collectively against the city's old governing elite. See Parker, *La Rochelle and the French Monarchy*, (London, 1980),

To paraphrase Benjamin Franklin, why did members of La Rochelle's rebel coalition hang together and not separately? One answer is that, through service in the militia companies, some notable artisans in each quarter of the city did gain access to the Forty-Eight and served as living testimony to the *menu peuple* that the new regime of civic government was predisposed to address their interests and thus deserved their support. A more compelling response is that the discipline of the militia companies, proven in the street battles of 1614, held up and served to shape the new political institutions that grew out of them. However, the cohesion and effectiveness of these new political organizations, like the solidarity of the militia companies themselves, must also be attributed to the fundamental social networks of family ties and personal obligations bonding together the men who comprised these institutions.

By 1614, when he assumed the post of *procureur* of the bourgeois representing the merchants, artisans, and seamen of Perrot parish, Jean Tharay had amassed a broad array of personal and professional contacts among the inhabitants of La Rochelle. Although well-established as an international merchant in La Rochelle, Jean Tharay's father, Nicolas, had also become acquainted with townsmen of lower social status and achievement. For example, in 1583, for the godfather of his son, Estienne, Nicolas Tharay chose Jean Gaultier, a butcher living in the distant artisan district of Cougnes. Gaultier could not sign the baptismal register at the christening of his godchild. Recall that shortly after reaching his majority in 1599, Jean Tharay was collecting rents and continuing to let rooms to workingmen in houses purchased by his father in the popular parish of Cougnes. Between 1603 and 1613, among other enterprises, Jean Tharay witnessed and guaranteed a real estate transaction by which a master cobbler acquired a small parcel of land. Contemporaneously, Tharay helped to celebrate the wedding of another rochelais master shoemaker and was always renting out rooms or small houses to artisans in the port quarter of Perrot. During and after the bourgeoisie's insurrection, Jean Tharay relied on these old contacts to build and maintain a base of political power in the city.

---

46-47. On the Vilain incident in general see Guillaudeau, "Diaire," 142-46 and Merlin, "Diaire," fols. 465r-472v.

Scrutiny of wedding contracts, baptismal registers, and notarized testaments reveals how intra- and interfamilial ties served
the political ambitions of men like Jean Tharay and undergirded
the operation of governing bodies like the Forty-Eight. When Jean
Tharay assumed the post of *procureur de bourgeois* in April 1614, he
did not want for kinsmen among the officers and constituents of
the Forty-Eight. Jacques Grenot, the stepfather and father-in-law
of Jean Tharay, and godfather and namesake of Tharay's son,
Jacques, also served in 1614 as a *procureur* for the parish of St.
Nicolas.[41] Heading the six-man 1614 delegation to the Council of
Forty-Eight from the militia company of St. Nicolas was François
Javalleau. Abundant evidence from the Protestant *état civil* in La
Rochelle shows ties of marriage and godparentage between the
Javalleau, Tharay, and Grenot families going as far back as 1588.[42]

François Javalleau, ranked high in the esteem of his neighbors
and fellow militiamen in St. Nicolas parish. François had not only
been chosen to represent the militia company on the Council of
Forty-Eight, but also, in November 1614, was nominated by all
members of the bourgeoisie in his home quarter to serve on a
city-wide committee responsible for choosing a single representative of La Rochelle's third estate to send to the *états généraux*. That
choice fell upon Javalleau's kinsman, the *procureur* Jean Tharay.[43]
Jacques Javalleau, brother to François, was another influential
member of the clan based in the parish of St. Nicolas. In late
March 1614, militiamen of the quarter chose Jacques to serve as
a special "commissaire-député," one of sixteen in the city (two per
militia company) empowered to select individuals worthy to serve
as *procureurs* of the bourgeoisie. Among the other Rochelais chosen for that honor in 1614 were Jean Tharay and Jacques Grenot.

In the parish of St. Nicolas, the *procureur* Jacques Grenot could
also depend on a politically valuable network of family connections. Grenot's sister, Anne, was the wife of Jean Javalleau, brother to François and Jacques.[44] In addition to being the godmother and namesake of François Javalleau's daughter, Anne, Anne
Grenot was the aunt and probable namesake of the rebel Jean

---

[41] See Guillaudeau, "Diaire," 61 and ADCM, I 21, fol. 36r.
[42] See for examples, ADCM, I 16, fols. 44v, 59r, and 93v; and I 17, fols. 17r,
43v, 51r, 53v, and 111r.
[43] ADCM, 3 E 2161 (1614), fols. 152r-v and 155v.
[44] ADCM, I 16, fol. 59r.

Tharay's wife, Anne Grenot, daughter of Jacques Grenot by his first wife. The regular practice of a generation of Javalleau siblings and their spouses from the Grenot and Tharay families to exchange service as godparents strongly reinforced interfamilial solidarities and facilitated the consolidation of powerful confraternities between brothers and brothers-in-law ideally suited to the mastery of capital-intensive maritime commerce and to the tactics of early modern urban political warfare.

Through his multiple family connections to the Grenots and Javalleaus, the *procureur* Jean Tharay was a known and influential personage in the commercial and artisanal neighborhood of St. Nicolas. When angry inhabitants of the quarter set out to murder patricians captured in the rebel coup, Tharay hailed them in the district's main street and, with the aid of his close friend and fellow *procureur*, Zacherie Chatton, persuaded them to give up their vengeful scheme and return to the defense of their neighborhood.[45] Cooler heads prevailed and the quarter settled down to representation on the Forty-Eight by six men from the local militia company, three of whom, François Javalleau, Jean Chinteau, and Samuel Fauré, can also be linked to one another through alliances of godparentage and long family friendship.[46]

Samuel Fauré's membership on the Council of Forty-Eight further clarifies the social and economic factors underpinning the operation and effectiveness of the Forty-Eight as a new urban governing body. Fauré, a prosperous master shoemaker, had also served as keeper ("portier") of the strategic St. Nicolas gate giving access to the quarter, the port, and the city from the southwest.[47] Through oversight of all traffic passing through the St.

---

[45] Merlin, "Diaire," fols. 229r-230v.

[46] On 1 November 1592, Anne Fauré, a kinswoman of Samuel Fauré, served as godmother at the baptism of Isaac Chinteau's first born son, see ADCM, I 17, fol. 86r. When Anne Javalleau, daughter of Jacques Javalleau, "commissaire-député" for St. Nicolas, was betrothed to *maître* Jean Goslain, a rochelais notary, on 7 April 1618, among the kinsmen and family friends negotiating her marriage settlement (which included a dowry of 1,000 *livres*) were her uncles Joseph and François Javalleau and her "cousins" André Javalleau and Jean Fauré, a Javalleau family confidant and kinsman to Samuel Fauré, ADCM, 3 E 2049 (1618), fols. 48v-49r.

[47] ADCM, 3 E 174, 1 October 1601. Besides his shoemaking business, run since 1594 in a large boutique on the grande rue des Merciers, Samuel Fauré was engaged in the trade of hides and woven fabrics. His business ventures put him in need of ready capital and he borrowed substantial sums from other master tradesmen living in other rochelais neighborhoods. In 1601, Fauré owed over

Nicolas gate (at which he collected fees as the farmer of municipal entry tolls and might further profit by turning a blind eye to
smuggling ventures), Fauré was well-placed to know the business
and garner the cooperation of St. Nicolas residents, rich and poor.
Fauré's local notoriety and utility on the Council of Forty-Eight
can be partially attributed to his commercial success, service to
the neighborhood, and simultaneous active presence in several
key civic institutions: guild, militia company, and municipal
administration.[48] By according membership on the Council of
Forty-Eight to successful tradesmen like Samuel Fauré from the
artisanal parishes of St. Nicolas and Notre Dame de Cougnes,
wealthier merchant leaders of the bourgeois rebellion gained
humbler yet respected allies whose own webs of family ties, clientage relations, and friendship reached deeper down into the lower ranks of urban society, reinforcing the authority of the Forty-
Eight and permitting decisive reform of municipal government
with popular support.[49]

Familial bonds between *procureurs* and members of the Forty-
Eight were not limited to those documented above. In 1617, when
Jean Tharay was serving as a *procureur* for a second time, his personal contacts among councilmen of the Forty-Eight kept him in
close touch with at least two vital constituencies. Théodore Goyer,
a rochelais physician, served among the 1615 and 1617 representatives to the Council of Forty-Eight from the Carrefour militia company formed in the wealthy parish of St. Barthélémy.[50]
Goyer was also the godfather of Jean Tharay's daughter, Magde-

---

300 *livres* to the widow of a master butcher and former creditor in the artisanal
district of Cougnes, see ADCM, 3 E 195, fols. 236v and 426v-427r. Like Jean
Tharay, Fauré profited economically and politically from dense intra- and interparochial networks of personal and professional contacts.

[48] By 1613, Samuel Fauré was certainly a notable resident of St. Nicolas parish.
At the baptism of Fauré's son, Jacques, held on 1 December 1613, the *échevin*
Jacques David served as godfather for the boy, ADCM, I 23, fol. 58r. Jean Tharay's
extensive commercial dealings with master shoemakers may also have brought
him into regular contact with Samuel Fauré, furnishing yet another basis for
political cooperation between the two rebels.

[49] Of the seven known tradesmen or artisans serving on the Council of Forty-
Eight between 1614 and 1617, three lived in the parish of Cougnes and two
resided in St. Nicolas. While, overall, the number of tradesmen on the Forty-
Eight was low, those who did serve came preponderantly from districts of the
city where merchant leaders had the greatest need of influential supporters
among the working population.

[50] Guillaudeau, "Diaire," 108 and 148.

leine, baptized on 8 March 1617.[51] The godmother and namesake of Tharay's daughter was Magdeleine Bourdigalle, a kinswoman to Gabriel, Louis, and René Bourdigalle, senior jurists and *procureurs du roi* on La Rochelle's presidial court.

After the 1614 streetfighting, Jean Tharay used his own family's natural growth to develop cordial relations with royal magistrates and wealthier residents of St. Barthélémy parish. Tharay's politically constructive use of his own godparentage choices gave the Forty-Eight important allies among La Rochelle's former ruling elite whose personal and professional support could be used to check any new efforts by vengeful town councilmen to diminish the authority of the Forty-Eight through legal or extra-legal manoeuvres. The Bourdigalles' willingness to establish ties of fictive kinship with the Tharays shows the reciprocal nature of political power relationships after the 1614 coup. Jurists also feuding with the town council and leery of popular participation in civic government found it more than merely expedient to curry favor with rebel leaders. By forging personal attachments to men like Tharay, urban notables lent their status and prestige to the rebels' cause in hopes that this engagement might also protect their own interests and estates from harm by the poorer men who rebelled under Tharay's leadership. Long animosities between royal magistrates (previously excluded from service on the town council) and members of the *corps de ville* were certainly known to townsmen on the Forty-Eight, who, like Jean Tharay, were ready to seek allies among the jurists equally prepared to humble the old town council.

Among the 1617 councilmen of the Forty-Eight from the strategic harbor parish of Perrot, long a bastion of popular support for Jean Tharay and his more radical followers, was Jacques Chappron, a merchant and ship owner engaged in the Canada trade.[52] On 2 July 1611, Chappron's newborn daughter, Suzanne, was brought to be baptized in the *salle* St. Yon by her godfather, Jean Tharay.[53] On 3 February 1613, Chappron's second daughter, Judith, was sponsored for baptism by her namesake, Judith Tharay,

---

[51] ADCM, I 27, fol. 55v.

[52] Guillaudeau, "Diaire," 108 and 148. See also ADCM, 3 E 2162 (1620) fols. 17v-18r. Jacques Chappron's younger brother, Pierre, earned a living as a highly experienced captain on one of Jacques' armed cargo vessels.

[53] ADCM, I 25, fol. 16r.

and Tharay's husband, Michel Heer, elder sister and brother-in-law to Jean Tharay.[54]

As documented in Chapter 5, exchanges of service as godparents between members of the Chappron and Tharay families can be traced back over two generations. On 21 May 1588, Nicolas Tharay (father of Jean) and his sister-in-law, Pierrette Javalleau, became the godparents to the son of Pierre Chappron I, also named "Pierre." This newborn would later become the ship captain mentioned above. On 20 December 1605, Pierre Chappron I returned the family favor when he served as godfather for Sarra Tharay, a cousin to the rebel captain. On this occasion, the baptismal register indicates that Pierre Chappron I declared he did not know how to sign his name.[55] Given the economic achievements and writing skills of Chappron's sons (Jacques Chappron confidently signed all of his own notarized business contracts), the Chapprons were clearly rising in social status and, like the Tharay's, seeking new proofs, material and political, of their accomplishments. Although no evidence survives of the voting procedures and deliberations by which militia companies chose their representatives to the Forty-Eight, Jacques Chappron's close, long-term ties to the Tharays were probably well-known to his neighbors and fellow militiamen. Appointing a man like Chappron to the Forty-Eight could thus have been seen by the militia company as a sound tactic to advance the interests of the neighborhood by advancing to a new office of local authority the trusted friend of La Rochelle's most influential political figure, the militant *procureur* Jean Tharay. Among the other noted leaders of the bourgeois rebellion who subsequently served as *procureurs*, Zacherie Chatton and Simon Papin, long-time confidants of Jean Tharay, also had kinsmen and close family friends in the ranks of councilmen on the Forty-Eight. Simon Papin, *procureur* in 1614 for the important commercial parish of St. Sauveur, could rely upon his younger brother, Jean Papin, senior representative to the Forty-Eight from the neighborhood militia company of grande rue, as a conduit of information and influence to and from his constituents.[56]

---

[54] ADCM, I 26, fol. 5r.

[55] ADCM, I 20, fol. 12r.

[56] Jean Papin succeeded his brother, Simon, as *procureur* for St. Sauveur in 1616, see Guillaudeau, "Diaire," 61 and 120-121.

Zacherie Chatton, *procureur* in 1614 for the artisanal parish of Notre Dame de Cougnes, could keep abreast of political intrigues amongst the militiamen of the company of grande rue in the adjoining parish of St. Sauveur through Isaac Desbois, one of six representatives of the neighborhood company to the Council of Forty-Eight in 1614. Desbois trusted Chatton enough to choose him as godfather for his son, Louis, baptized on 7 December 1613 in the *salle* St. Yon, where Desbois and Chatton were members of the same Calvinist congregation.[57]

In his own parish of Cougnes, Chatton was well-acquainted with the Baudier clan, one member of which was the godfather of Chatton's son, Jacques; and a second member of which served the neighborhood militia company as a representative to the Council of Forty-Eight in 1616.[58] The family wealth and commercial achievements of the Rochelais who gained high office in new bourgeois organs of town government set them apart from the rank and file members of the city's militia companies. However, the same good fortune that distinguished the *procureurs* from their fellow parishioners also made them personages of repute in each quarter, worthy of favors and flattering offers of godparentage from more humble neighbors seeking their friendship and good offices. The structure and personnel of new, more popular institutions of civic government reflect the persistent importance of such neighborhood status systems in the making of urban politics.

A closer look at the composition of the six-man delegations to the Council of Forty-Eight from the militia company of the rue du Temple in 1614, 1616, and 1617 reveals more details of how such neighborhood systems of honor, favor, and family were incorporated in the new regime of civic government.

Pierre Hotton, an international wine merchant, Estienne Mignot, a jeweller and charter-member of La Rochelle's mint and assay office, and Jacob Theroude, another wine dealer with extensive European shipping interests, were among the first six delegates the militia company of the rue du Temple sent to the Forty-Eight in 1614. The selection of Pierre Hotton was a politic move because he had been an ardent supporter of the bourgeois insur-

---

[57] ADCM, I 25, fol. 98r.
[58] ADCM, I 21, fol. 112r. See also Guillaudeau, "Diaire," 120-121.

rection since its inception, had previously represented rebel leaders in negotiations with the town council, and was known as a trusted lieutenant of Jean Tharay.[59] Hotton's younger brother, Moise, a grain merchant, who replaced his elder sibling and served the neighborhood on the Council of Forty-Eight in 1616, was also a key member of the local militia company whose large personal stock of weapons kept fightingmen of the quarter well-equipped.[60] The Hottons' ties to the Forty-Eight gave rebel leaders vital influence over a large militia company and its arsenal in the center of the city.

Jacob Theroude's presence on the 1614 delegation to the Forty-Eight from the rue du Temple neighborhood gave the numerous wine dealers of the quarter two sure representatives in the new agencies of civic administration. Jacob Theroude and Pierre Hotton were well-known to one another and faced the challenges of the international wine trade together. When in need of quick capital, Hotton sold debts owing to him to Theroude for cash. Hotton facilitated Theroude's business dealings by agreeing to purchase and consolidate debts owed by Theroude to wine merchants in other towns.[61] Both men engaged themselves in a staple trade vital to the health of the urban economy. Wine production, storage, and distribution occupied substantial numbers of city laborers and artisans, like coopers, who returned a standing favor when they joined Hotton and Theroude in fighting the old town council. Humbler participants in the local wine indus-

---

[59] Merlin, "Diaire," fol. 244r.

[60] In a family settlement of Moise Hotton's estate shortly after his death in September 1618, Pierre Hotton kept the rights to all of Moise's "armes et armures," including "picques, halebreds, mosquets, harquebuses, pistolets, espés, casques, et cuirasses," see ADCM, 3 E 2049 (1618), fols. 112r-113r. This large cache of weaponry probably comprised the main armory for the militia company of the rue du Temple and constitutes strong material proof of the Hotton clan's importance in logistical support of the rebellion and the political institutions growing out of it. Pastor Merlin noted that Moise Hotton was "fort regretté par les bourgeois pour son zèle," "Diaire," fol. 514r. The orderly transfer of Moise's arms collection to Pierre was witnessed and signed by Zacherie Chatton, *procureur* of the bourgeois in 1614, confidant of Jean Tharay, and friend to Pierre Hotton. Moise Hotton's service during the last years of his life as one of four *procureurs de police* for the town chosen by the town council suggests that the established authorities of La Rochelle also appreciated the material resources the Hottons could apply to guarding the community, see BMLR, MS 763, fol. 2r.

[61] See ADCM, 3 E 2042 (1597), fol. 207v and 3 E 2048 (1615) fol. 105v-106r.

try who joined the battle could also hope that their actions would beneficially diminish the power of the *corps de ville* to regulate the wine trade in a manner favoring the interests of patrician vineyard owners.

Estienne Mignot's presence on the Forty-Eight for the rue du Temple insured that the many jewellers and pewterers of the neighborhood had a spokesman in the new civic regime. Mignot was a colleague known to men like the Hottons who played a key role in policing the city and protecting the shops and precious commodities of its merchant community.

In 1616, besides Moise Hotton, delegates to the Forty-Eight from the rue du Temple neighborhood included Estienne Herault, a pewterer. Pierre Bernardeau's detailed rent roll for the rue du Temple, maintained between 1590 and 1609 when he farmed property rents due to the Knights of Jerusalem, reveals the close proximity of households run by key residents of the neighborhood serving on the Forty-Eight. On the north side of the street, Estienne Mignot (member of the Forty-Eight in 1614) lived four doors from the Heraults, who lived only one door up from the house Jacob Theroude (member of the Forty-Eight in 1614) rented to Jeremie Dourneau (member of the Forty-Eight in 1617). Pierre Hotton's large house sat on the south side of the rue de Temple, diagonally across from the Mignots.[62]

Estienne Herault's personal contacts with fellow militiamen from the quarter were extensive. In 1605, Herault had chosen a trusted neighbor, Jacques Pronis, a merchant draper, to be the godfather of his daughter, Esther.[63] In 1611, Herault selected another good neighbor, Pierre Morriseau, as the godfather of his second daughter, Marie.[64] In 1613, another long-time resident of the rue du Temple, Jacques Robin, a cloth merchant, became the godfather and namesake of Estienne Herault's second-born son.[65] In 1617, we find Jacques Pronis, Jacques Robin, and Paul Morriseau, the brother of Pierre Morriseau, all serving on the delegation to the Forty-Eight from the rue du Temple. Thus Estienne

---

[62] See BMLR, MS 116, fols. 245-250, "Censif de la commanderie du Temple," and ADCM, 3 E 2040 (1594), fols. 341r-4; 3 E 2042 (1597), fols 21v-23r; and 3 E 2043 (1598), fols 165v-168r.

[63] ADCM, I 19, fol. 133r.

[64] ADCM, I 23, fol. 21v.

[65] ADCM, I 25, fol. 74v.

Herault was succeeded in political service to the neighborhood by several of the godfathers to his children.

The fourth and fifth members of the rue du Temple's 1617 delegation to the Forty-Eight were Jeremie Dourneau and Samuel Audouart. Dourneau had previously rented a house in the neighborhood to Jacob Theroude, member of the Forty-Eight for their militia company in 1614. Jeremie Dourneau and Samuel Audouart were brothers-in-law. This family alliance was reinforced by ties of godparentage between the Dourneau and Audouart siblings dating back to at least 1593.[66] Through intricate and overlapping personal and professional obligations, five of the six councilmen of the Forty-Eight from the militia company of the rue du Temple in 1617 can be closely associated with councilmen from the district serving on the Forty-Eight in prior years. Evidence of similar links between the members of successive delegations to the Forty-Eight from other militia squads exists for the companies of Cougnes, grande rue, Minage, and Perrot. In five of the eight rochelais militia companies, ties between delegates to the Forty-Eight like those noted in the rue du Temple can be found.

At the level of the neighborhood, the formation and operation of the Council of Forty-Eight engaged the ambitions of influential men well-known and well-connected to one another. Service to the Forty-Eight came under the hegemony and broadened the influence of small cliques of notable neighborhood residents already accustomed to serving one another as tenants, landlords, clients, business partners, godparents, and in-laws. Previously excluded from any role in town politics, these powerful consortia of leading bourgeois families cleverly exploited their solid emplacement in the economic, social, and para-military affairs of their quarters to defeat the old town council and to install a new regime of civic administration more representative of La Rochelle's ordinary citizens.

From this perspective, the hybrid form of the municipal political organization established by the rebels of 1614—*procureurs* representing the five ancient parishes of the city, councilmen of the Forty-Eight as proxies for the newly important militia companies—becomes more comprehensible. The five *procureurs*, each endowed with the prestige of representing an entire urban district, could

---

[66] ADCM, I 17, fol. 99v and I 19, fols. 70r and 115v.

face members of the old *corps de ville*, men with no discernable
constituencies except their own clans, as more than political
equals. The office of *procureur* was well-tailored to fit the skills and
channel the ambitions of Rochelais like Pierre Bernardeau, Zacherie Chatton, and Jean Tharay who aspired to reform the old town
council and make their personal mark on city-wide politics.

The Council of Forty-Eight, by contrast, consolidated and acknowledged the collective authority of interconnected, notable
bourgeois families in each neighborhood of the city. This innovative two-tiered system and its fifty-three political activists worked
to minimize factional strife among its proponents and succeeded
in creating a durable coalition of townsmen capable of violently
reordering city government.

The urban political system established by the 1614 coup aimed
at keeping municipal offices open to respectable householders
and enterprising citizens of middling social rank. This bold strategy protected the city against patrician misrule and prevented the
domination of town government by royal magistrates, a process
well advanced in other French provincial towns of the era. La
Rochelle's new system of civic administration, annually empowering ordinary householders as elected members of the Forty-Eight
and sending veterans of the Forty-Eight onto the *corps de ville*, also
forestalled any local "professionalization" of town government.

After 1614, La Rochelle became even more anomalous among
French provincial cities, combining a majority of religious schismatics with a substantial, influential number of innovative political actors drawn from the middle ranks of urban society. This citizenry, manifestly threatening to oligarchs and to monarchs,
ultimately became the target of the early Bourbons' costliest and
most spectacular show of repressive military power. The ultimate
objective of the merchant-led insurrection of March to August
1614 was the reform of elections and recruitment to the town
council (*corps de ville*) of La Rochelle. By Article IV of the political settlement the rebels imposed on the *corps*, *échevins* and *pairs*
were barred from resigning their offices to any successor, vacant
positions of *échevin* were to go to senior *pairs*, and bourgeois of
the city were permitted to nominate three of their own candidates
to vie for every position of *pair* falling vacant. One of the three
candidates was to be selected for the empty post by the town coun-

cil voting in full session.[67] By Article XIII of the same accord, *pro-cureurs* of the bourgeoisie also gained the right to nominate three candidates for each of three key municipal posts: *contrôleur* of urban buildings and construction, *contrôleur* of municipal fortifications, and *contrôleur* of the city's artillery. The mayor got the right to choose the winner of each post from among the candidates proposed to him.

On 10 April 1614, the unwillingness of the town council and the new mayor, Louis Berne, to abide by the provisions of Article XIII led representatives of the bourgeoisie to quit the town council chamber crying "To Arms!" and directing their partisans to seize the city's strongholds.[68] Within hours, mayor Berne had dismissed the town council's nominee for *contrôleur* of buildings and accepted Gedeon d'Hinnse for the post. D'Hinnse was one of the three nominees previously proposed by the *procureurs* of the bourgeois.[69]

The three candidates for *contrôleur* of buildings nominated by the *procureurs* of 1614 (Zacherie Chatton, Jacques Grenot, Simon Papin, Israel Torterue, and Jean Tharay) were David Blais, Jean Guignard, and Gedeon d'Hinnse. Blais and Guignard are both identified by pastor Merlin as close followers of Jean Tharay and radicals among the supporters of the bourgeois insurrection. According to Merlin, Blais belonged to the violent "passionnées" determined to wreck the old town council. Guignard, quick to join Tharay in berating La Rochelle's Calvinist clergymen, defended Tharay to Merlin as innocent of all charges of abuse of authority because Tharay considered himself answerable for his actions only to "le peuple" of La Rochelle.[70] Gedeon d'Hinnse had supported the bourgeois insurrection from its beginning and was well-known to its leadership since he was the brother-in-law of Simon Papin, godfather of Papin's daughter, Marie, and had served with Papin as a witness to the marriages through which the men of the d'Hinnse clan advanced the economic and political fortunes of their family.[71]

---

[67] Chenu, *Recueil des Antiquitez*, 226.
[68] Merlin, "Diaire," fols. 212r-213v.
[69] *Ibid.*, fol. 213v. See also Guillaudeau, "Diaire," 62.
[70] Merlin, "Diaire," fols. 234v-235v and 255v-258r.
[71] See ADCM, 3 E 216 (1610) fols. 182v-183v; 3 E 2161 (1613) fol. 177r; 3 E

This evidence strongly indicates that *procureurs* of the bourgeois like Tharay and Papin used their power to nominate candidates for key municipal offices as a means of political patronage to advance their kinsmen and favorites, further integrating them in the networks of fidelity and obligation underpinning the new urban politics in La Rochelle. In this case, the mayor's and town council's animosity toward Jean Tharay, expressed in their refusal of "his man" for the position of *contrôleur* of buildings only succeeded in placing one of Simon Papin's kinsmen and political allies in the job. This check to Tharay's designs for David Blais was only temporary. In September 1615, probably with Tharay's help, Blais replaced the late Luc Perier as *procureur de bourgeois* for the parish of St. Barthélémy and served óut Perier's term in office.[72] In October of 1618, David Blais, Zacherie Chatton, and Jean Tharay were nominated by the Council of Forty-Eight to compete for the office of *pair* vacated by the death of Leonard Sauvignon. Blais' friendship with Tharay kept him actively involved in the new political regime of the city.

On 13 April 1614, the *pair* and *échevin*, Georges Maynard, died. Immediately following his funeral, the Council of Forty-Eight nominated three bourgeois to compete for the late Maynard's seat as *pair*. Within a week, the town council, incapable of opposing this procedure by force, met and accepted one of the nominees, the merchant Daniel Gaultron, to be the newest *pair* of La Rochelle and the first from outside the circle of old town families previously dominating access to the *corps de ville*.[73]

From diaries of the era, municipal documents, and surviving original minutes of town council meetings held between 1618 and 1628, one can chart the growing presence of former rebel merchants and other previously unenfranchised bourgeois on La Rochelle's town council. Table 15 shows both the number of new men who gained an office of *pair* each year between 1614 and 1628 through nomination by the Forty-Eight and the cumulative total of all new *pairs* nominated by the Forty-Eight on the town

---

2161 (1614), fol. 47r; and ADCM, I 18, fol. 135v; I 19, fol. 126v; and I 21, fols. 67v-68r.

[72] Guillaudeau, "Diaire," 114.

[73] Merlin, "Diaire," fol. 213r. See also Guillaudeau, "Diaire," 62 and the original minutes of town council meetings for the era, BMLR, MS 763, fols. 3r and 8v.

council. This second figure can also be taken as the percentage of new men on the council since the entire *corps de ville* numbered 100.

*Table 15*

Bourgeois Pairs on Town Council Through Nomination
By the Council of Forty-Eight 1614-1628

| Year | New Pairs per Year | Total New Pairs |
|------|--------------------|-----------------|
| 1614 | 4 | 4 |
| 1615 | 4 | 8 |
| 1616 | 4 | 12 |
| 1617 | 4 | 16 |
| 1618 | 0 | 16 |
| 1619 | 1 | 17 |
| 1620 | 5 | 22 |
| 1621 | 7 | 29 |
| 1622 | 9 | 38 |
| 1623 | 0 | 38 |
| 1624 | 6 | 44 |
| 1625 | 7 | 51 |
| 1626 | 5 | 56 |
| 1627 | 6 | 62 |
| 1628 | 6 | 68 |

By the time royal troops began the last great siege of La Rochelle, 62% of all sitting town councilmen were bourgeois formerly excluded from municipal office whose service on the *corps de ville* was conditioned by their long engagement in the complex politics of the militia companies, the Council of Forty-Eight, and the *procureurs* of the bourgeois.

The growing influence of new men in the deliberations of La Rochelle's town council was abetted by the typical working methods of that body. Extensive original minutes of town council meetings also recording attendance by members are available for periods from April 1618 to April 1619, February 1622 to June 1623, April 1624 to April 1625, and April 1627 to April 1628.[74] These

---

[74] BMLR, MSS 763, 764, 765 and 768.

documents show that attendance at meetings of the town council was never complete and rarely exceeded three-fifths of all serving town councilmen. Average attendance was even lower: thirty-five councilmen per meeting in 1618-19, thirty-eight councilmen per session in 1624-25, and rising to only forty-five councilmen per meeting in the troubled times of 1627-28.

New bourgeois on the town council, who had personally fought for reform of this body and consequently took a special interest in its operation, attended council meetings much more regularly than did the majority of their colleagues from old city families previously dominating that body. Attendance lists for town council members regularly precede the surviving minutes of council sessions. The steadily growing block of new *pairs* nominated by the Council of Forty-Eight is notable for its consistently high rate of attendance. Unlike the majority of patrician members, who tended to show up only at ceremonial occasions and important diplomatic debates, new men, like the *procureur* Jean Tharay, would go for months without missing a single session.

Under these conditions, newcomers to the town council could exert a collective influence on civic government disproportionate to their actual numbers. For example, of the fifty-two town councilmen meeting on 28 April 1618 to select municipal police officials and new captains of the militia companies, eleven (21%) were nominees of the bourgeois who made up only 16% of all town councilmen sitting at this time.[75]

Election to the Council of Forty-Eight and service as a *procureur de bourgeois* were important conduits feeding new men onto the *corps de ville*. Of the seventy-six *marchands et bourgeois* admitted to the town council between March 1614 and September 1628, at least thirty-four (44%) can be positively identified as having served previously either as a councilmen of the Forty-Eight (13) or as a *procureur de bourgeois* (21).[76] Relations between old town councilmen and bourgeois leaders aspiring to office on the *corps de ville*

---

[75] BMLR, MS 763, fol. 1r.

[76] It is highly probable that a larger percentage of new *pairs* on the town council had previously served on the Forty-Eight. Since we possess only Joseph Guillaudeau's incomplete listing of members of the Forty-Eight for the years 1614 to 1617, no certain count of Forty-Eight members in subsequent years going onto the town council is possible. However, all available evidence shows that members of the Forty-Eight were most advantageously placed to gain a new seat as a *pair* on the town council after 1614.

long remained embittered, recall how in 1615 the *pair* Jacques
Tallemant assaulted the *procureur* Isaac du Querny with his walking stick. However, such stark animosities could not long prevent
the ascension to the town council of bourgeois leaders repeatedly nominated by the Forty-Eight in groups of three for acceptance
by the *corps de ville*. The *procureur* Israel Torterue was made a *pair*
on 4 September 1615.[77] The *procureur* Simon Papin became a new
*pair* on 28 March 1616.[78] The gun collector Moise Hotton won a
seat as *pair* on 3 October 1616.[79] The outspoken *procureur* Zacherie
Chatton made it onto the *corps de ville* on 24 October 1618. In
this election, many old town councilmen faced an unpalatable
choice between Chatton, the firebrand Jean Tharay, or Tharay's
protégé, David Blais.[80] They chose the lesser of three evils, yet still
had to seat one of their most determined opponents, Chatton.

Even the notorious Jean Tharay, after having stood for election
to the *corps de ville* at least once before, joined the town council
of La Rochelle as a new *pair* on 22 December 1621.[81] Jean Tharay
is thus among the few seventeenth-century French rebel captains
to gain and hold high municipal office by ballot. His ascendance
shows the longevity of his political powers and the exceptional
endurance of the civic regime he championed. The new cadre of
urban magistrates he joined became the preponderant force in
rochelais politics after 1614. This cohort of leading townsmen,
devoted to communal defense and the liberties of Calvinist congregations, stood ready to oppose a monarchy growing more
intent on abridging such freedoms.

---

[77] Guillaudeau, "Diaire," 114.

[78] *Ibid.*, 120.

[79] *Ibid.*, 120.

[80] *Ibid.*, 155. See also BMLR, MS 763, fol. 66v. Faced with disagreeable choices among candidates proposed by the Forty-Eight, embattled senior members of
the town council occasionally reverted to their old ways. On 2 March 1617, when
forced to choose between the militant bourgeois Jean Torterue, a former member of the Forty-Eight; Mardochée Georget, a rebel leader in the artisanal district of Cougnes; or Pierre Maulay, who also resided in the quarter of Cougnes,
town councilmen chose Maulay, who, as pastor Merlin noted, was at least a relative by marriage of the man he replaced. See Merlin, "Diaire," fols. 465v-66r.

[81] Guillaudeau, "Diaire," 195-196.

### 3. *Disavowals of Mayoral Authority and Provocations of the Crown Committed by the New Masters of Rochelais Politics 1615–1628*

The progressive *embourgeoisement* of La Rochelle's town council was accompanied by repeated interventions in the conduct of civic affairs by the Forty-Eight and by widening rebel control over key posts in the municipal bureaucracy. Indeed, apparently despairing of sufficient authority to exercise vital offices of urban police and fiscal control, members of the old oligarchical town council simply turned these charges over to their erstwhile opponents among insurrectionary merchants and militiamen. Former rebels now stood a better chance of winning cooperation in these complicated matters from the citizenry.

The increasing control exercised by militant bourgeois over vital posts in municipal government abandoned by disaffected senior town councilmen greatly augmented rebel influence over the internal and external affairs of La Rochelle. By Article XIII of the 1614 political settlement, the bourgeoisie of La Rochelle won the right to nominate its own candidates for the offices of municipal building inspector, supervisor of urban fortifications, and captain of the city's artillery. Occupation of these offices complemented and expanded the bourgeoisie's surveillance over the internal security and military preparedness of the town. However, surviving city council minutes and staff records of the municipal bureaucracy indicate that proponents of the 1614 rebellion soon gained wide access to other vital posts in town government, giving them more power to appropriate La Rochelle's economic and military resources for defense of their politics and unorthodox religious values.

By 1617, all four municipal *procureurs de police*, charged with maintaining order in the city, were senior members of the 1614 rebellion's leadership.[82] In April of 1622, the *procureurs de police* for the coming administrative year were Jean Berchault, Estienne

---

[82] *Procureurs de police* for 1617 were Benjamin de la Salle, a rebel merchant from St. Sauveur parish, and Simon Papin, a determined opponent of the town council for over five years. In 1618, during the second year of their two-year appointment, de la Salle and Papin were joined by Jean Fauré, former *procureur de bourgeois* for St. Sauveur parish, and Moise Hotton, former member of the Forty-Eight from the rue du Temple, senior member of the neighborhood militia company, and owner of a small arsenal of weapons for the company's service, see BMLR, MS 763, fol. 2r.

d'Harriette, Jean Tharay, and Jean Torterue, all men well-known
to one another after long service leading irreverent members of
the bourgeoisie against the old town council.[83] In 1624, and again
in 1627, all four *procureurs de police* were bourgeois known for their
advocacy of the 1614 insurrection and dedicated work in the new
institutions of town government that rebellion created.

In surviving records, the complete absence of *procureurs de police*
drawn from patrician town families comprising the old oligarchic
town council suggests that these families relinquished all administration of urban police at the neighborhood level to merchants
and wealthier artisans more apt to accomplish the task. As militant members of the bourgeoisie took over policing La Rochelle,
rose to supervise its defenses, and ascended to the captaincy of
militia companies (formerly reserved to *échevins*), the old elite of
town government lost its capacity to oppose by force further transformations of civic administration and diplomacy proposed by the
Forty-Eight and its agents who became new *pairs*.

Sometime after 1617, two new militia companies were formed
in La Rochelle by dividing older units in the populous parishes
of Cougnes and St. Sauveur. Ten militia companies now existed
in the city. In 1622, three of the ten rochelais militia companies
were captained by merchant rebels. In 1624, nine of the ten had
bourgeois commanders with only the company of Carrefour, rooted in the wealthy parish of St. Barthélémy, still under the orders
of an *échevin*. In 1624, Jean Tharay commanded the company of
grande rue. In 1627, nine of the ten rochelais militia units opposing the royal siege army got their orders from former bourgeois
rebels. Besides militia service, merchant leaders like Simon Papin,
Martin d'Harriette, and others improved the city's artillery and
conducted regular inventories of all munitions available for urban
defense.[84]

At a town council session on 16 May 1618, the mayor, as commander-in-chief of the city's militia, was shocked to learn that the
former captain of the militia company of Minage and his lieutenants had spent the exorbitant sum of fifty-seven *livres* eighteen
*sols* on a remarkable flag for the company. At the same session,

---

[83] BMLR, MS 764, fol. 88v.
[84] See BMLR, MS 763, fols. 106v-115r; MS 764, fols. 88v-89r; MS 765, fol. 9v;
and MS 768, fol. 11r.

the mayor asked the council's advice on what he should do about insubordinate members of the militia company of grande rue who deliberately disobeyed his orders to diminish the company's elaborate banner.[85] Now in friendly competition to acquire potent symbols of their recently won political importance, La Rochelle's militia companies became engaged in a form of conspicuous spending highly insulting to the mayor and town council whose protests of this behavior went unheeded.[86] After 1614, more aggressive interference by the Forty-Eight and their partisans in city politics compounded official displeasure over the martial displays of the militia companies.

Louis XIII's growing assertiveness in governing his dominions and his incipient determination to curb misrule in the west country gave the Rochelais ample new pretexts for armed resistance to royal plans. Louis especially desired to fulfill his coronation oath as defender of the Catholic faith. In the Treaty of Loudon (May 1616) the king announced his intention to reunite, by force if necessary, the heavily Protestant *pays* of Béarn with the Bourbon realm. Located deep in southwestern France on the Pyreneean frontier with Spain, Béarn, under the seigneurial authority of the Calvinist d'Albret family, had become a mountain redoubt of the French Reformation. In 1617, Louis XIII formally announced his determination to retake Béarn and reestablish the Catholic church throughout the region.

This royal saber rattling did not intimidate the Rochelais. At a reunion of Calvinist clergymen representing western French provinces convened in La Rochelle in November 1616, *procureurs* of the rochelais bourgeoisie and members of the Forty-Eight harangued the assembly on the necessity of preventing the installation of royal garrisons in west country towns on the routes leading to Béarn. Bourgeois spokesmen recommended an audacious

---

[85] BMLR, MS 763, fols. 10v-11r. According to the town council's secretary, the mayor was incensed at the militiamen's refusal to "assister à la réduction de l'enseigne de ladite compagnie."

[86] The town council timidly advised the mayor to pursue by all legal means his efforts at fining the disobedient militiamen for their inaction; if, upon reflection, he found any of their excuses unsatisfactory, BMLR, MS 763, fol. 11r. The Forty-Eight, naturally, refused to take any part in the matter. On the importance of flags as vital forces in the shaping of radical urban political parties see Richard Trexler, "Follow the Flag. The Ciompi Revolt Seen from the Streets," *Bibliothèque de l'humanisme et renaissance*, 46 (1984), 178-196.

course of action, including surprise attacks on royalist bourgs and
demolition of fortifications in suspect towns, far bolder and more
insubordinate than any proposal put forth by old town councilmen who also addressed the assembled clerics.[87] Disquieted by
these exhortations to armed conflict with the king in defense of
endangered Calvinist congregations, a majority of the clergymen
resolved to follow the lead of senior town councilmen and pursue negotiations with the crown in hopes of saving west country
Protestants from renewed royal attacks. Thwarted in their suit,
restive members of La Rochelle's bourgeoisie decided to combat
their sovereign by other means.

In May 1618, several merchants of La Rochelle complained to
the mayor that Jean Tharay was now notorious for issuing commissions to rochelais ship captains and seamen authorizing them
to become pirates, arm their boats, and hunt down Catholic vessels and royal spy ships navigating just off shore. These rochelais
businessmen complained that Tharay's imprudent behavior was
"grandement prejudicable au trafficq de cette ville" and demanded that the town council put a stop to it.[88] However, the many
seamen in Tharay's harbor parish of Perrot appreciated his special "congés" as valuable licenses to commit piracy, offering humble men a chance of riches in tough economic times. The city
council immediately voted to do nothing about these complaints
(certainly for fear of antagonizing Tharay and his dockside partisans even more) and only recommended that the mayor arrange
to visit Tharay at his house and ask him if the allegations were
true. In the absence of any standing royal fleet, Tharay's encouragement of sea raiders threatened both Catholic maritime commerce and vital royal communications by sea with loyal field commanders in the south preparing for the assault on Béarn.

The king repeatedly ordered the town council to stop recruitment of Protestant corsairs in La Rochelle. These commands did
nothing because the council's powers of persuasion were out-

---

[87] See the "Extraict des actes de l'assemblée des conseils des six provinces
convocqués à La Rochelle le 16 novembre 1616," BN, Manuscrits Français, 15818,
fols. 404r-410r. This assembly continued to meet in La Rochelle until the spring
of 1617 and was repeatedly addressed by *procureurs* of the rochelais bourgeoisie,
including Jean Papin, and by representatives of the Forty-Eight. Individually and
collectively, these spokesmen urged the assembly to fight for the security of La
Rochelle and other "oppressed towns and churches."

[88] BMLR, MS 763, fols. 17r-v.

matched by the capacity of influential rebel leaders like Tharay to encourage seditious acts by their followers at all levels of the urban social hierarchy. In a royal summons to the *corps de ville* dated 28 October 1616, the king demanded immediate action against a local pirate captain named "Chaperon" operating out of La Rochelle's harbor.[89] It is highly likely that this outlaw was none other that Pierre Chappron, a local master mariner commanding one of his family's armed merchant vessels (appropriately christened "La Brave"). Pierre Chappron and his brother Jacques, sole proprietor of the "La Brave," were residents of the Perrot quarter and cousins of Jean Tharay, kinsmen advantageously placed to benefit from Tharay's pirate licensing.[90] Jacques Chappron was one of Tharay's strongest supporters in the harbor parishes and became a member of the Council of Forty-Eight for the Perrot district in 1617. More imperative royal commands issued in 1618 for the suppression of rochelais piracy could not dismantle entrenched networks of armed dissent developed by politically ascendent bourgeois townsmen.[91]

The arrival in La Rochelle on 29 July 1618 of letters from the king, requesting immediate supply of information about all outstanding disputes between the *corps de ville* and the bourgeoisie, engendered new conflicts among townsmen. The Forty-Eight strongly opposed the king's suggestion that envoys from the town council and the Forty-Eight come to Paris and explain the political situation in La Rochelle. Sensing a threat to the twenty-eight articles of the 1614 political settlement, deeply suspicious of royal motives for the inquiry, and alarmed by senior town councilmen's willingness to comply with the king's request, leaders of the bourgeoisie—Jean Tharay in particular—threatened to assemble the militia companies and run out of town any member of the *corps de ville* who took up the commission to go to Paris.[92]

---

[89] BN, Collection Dupuy, 323, fols. 246r-v.

[90] ADCM, 3 E 2159 (1610), fol. 101r and 3 E 2162, fols. 17v-18r. Pierre Chappron's well-known acts of piracy and angry disputes with the town council over his share of the prize money from vessels he captured are documented for example in BMLR, MS 763, fol. 135r.

[91] See BN, Collection Dupuy, 323, fols 247r-248r.

[92] Pastor Merlin identifies Jean Tharay as the leading opponent of all compromise with the *corps de ville* and as a man entirely contemptuous of royal requests for information about the political situation in La Rochelle. According to Merlin, bourgeois threats of fomenting a popular uprising against the town

After 1614, leaders of La Rochelle's dissident bourgeoisie increasingly disregarded the old town council's preferences to avoid open confrontation with French monarchs and to achieve mutually beneficial rapprochements through negotiations with royal envoys. The town council temporized in the face of renewed popular agitation and suggested that representatives of each side prepare drafts of a mutually satisfactory written reply to the king.

The *procureurs* of La Rochelle's militant bourgeoisie intended to send their own letter to the king explaining their reasons for disobeying the sovereign's direct orders. Having obtained a copy of this inflammatory communication, the town council voted to condemn it as impolitic and insulting to the monarch.[93] Speaking for La Rochelle's Calvinist clergy, pastor Merlin also criticized the *procureurs'* declaration to the king as "rude, impolite, and couched in disrespectful terms."[94] Merlin confided to his diary that senior town councilmen strongly objected to the wording of this dispatch, but, like the ministers, were constrained to accept it under threat of force by the bourgeoisie.

The next day, bourgeois *procureurs* informed the town council that its vote was deeply offensive to their constituents. The *procureurs* then announced their intention to assemble all of the city's militia companies, read out the city council's condemnation verbatim, and then poll the militiamen to determine a suitable reaction to the affront. As the scribe of the *corps de ville* recorded, a majority of town councilmen considered these plans so "greatly prejudicial to public peace," that they quickly voted to make whatever concessions necessary to forestall the impending assemblies. In a new vote, preserving the "bien public et tranquilité" of the city, councilmen not only endorsed the content of the *procureurs'* letter, but also moved that it be sent to the king signed "under the general and common name of the mayor, *échevins, pairs,* bourgeois, and residents of this city."[95] The new regime of communal government suppressed older town councilmen's pacific overtures toward the monarchy, conveying to the king's men a false mea-

---

council greatly intimidated *échevins* and *pairs* prepared to cooperate with the king's requests. See Merlin, "Diaire," fols. 509r-514r.

[93] BMLR, MS 763, fol. 49v.

[94] Merlin, "Diaire," fols. 513v-514r.

[95] *Ibid.*, fols 49v-50r.

sure of support for confrontation with the crown among all segments of rochelais society.

Royal secretaries fruitlessly petitioned all members of the
rochelais town council to make the king aware of their differences
and to rely upon the sovereign as an arbiter of their disputes.
*Procueurs* of the bourgeoisie used reiterated threats of violence to
quash any official replies to these mediating royal inquiries.[96]

On 26 September 1618, new letters from the king arrived in
the city and immediately provoked further confrontations
between merchant leaders and the town council. Again, the Forty-
Eight opposed any reply to Louis XIII, and, on 20 October, *procureurs* of the bourgeoisie and bourgeois members of the town
council joined forces to inform the mayor that they would not
consent to any meeting with senior town councilmen to draft a
response.[97] Worried that further delay might provoke even more
unwanted royal attention, already aroused by an impending illegal national assembly of Protestant churchmen in La Rochelle,
long-time members of the *corps de ville* made a draft reply to the
king's letters and urged the *procureurs* to circulate the proposed
response among members of the Forty-Eight. On 31 October
1618, the *procureurs* repeated the Forty-Eight's objection to the dispatch of any letter, asserted that the town council's draft was
unworthy to be sent, and advised the senior councilmen to
appoint representatives to meet with envoys of the Forty-Eight to
discuss the necessity and possible content of any reply. Failure to
agree to these demands would force the *procureurs* to assemble
"tous le peuple de cette ville" in their militia companies and read
to them the offensive letter of the unfriendly town councilmen.
The secretary of the town council noted that "to avoid any such
convocation of the people," *échevins* and *pairs* immediately named
six representatives to meet with the Forty-Eight. Desultory negotiations continued on for weeks and, by late November, no
response had yet gone to the king.[98]

While rochelais patricians still held nominal control of the *corps
de ville*, their influence over the bulk of the urban population was

---

[96] See for examples, *ibid.*, fols. 60r and 63v.

[97] BMLR, MS 763, fols. 60r and 63v-65v.

[98] Joseph Guillaudeau noted that dissident bourgeois successfully prevented
any response from ever being made to the king, see Guillaudeau, "Diaire," 153-
154.

much smaller than that wielded by disgruntled members of the bourgeoisie. Rebellious townsmen convincingly demonstrated their powers of command over humbler citizens and effectively used threats of controlled popular violence to stifle their opponents and alter the course of urban politics toward outright contempt for kingly powers and a looming military showdown with royal armies.

With prompting from the Forty-Eight, the town council became very concerned about the content of all official correspondence leaving the city addressed to agents of the crown. In the spring of 1619, as Louis XIII battled his mother for complete control of monarchical government, royal agents upped their demands for information about political and religious affairs transpiring in the French west country. La Rochelle's royal presidial court magistrates received orders to report on an illegal assembly of delegates from French Calvinist churches meeting in La Rochelle since December 1618. On 5 February 1619, La Rochelle's town council, worried over the contents of this report and menaced by the Forty-Eight, ordered royal judges to submit a copy of their memorandum for review by representatives of the *corps de ville* and the militia companies. This action was necessary to protect "la tranquilité publique" and to insure that the dispatch contained nothing "prejudicial to the majority of townspeople."[99]

By February 1619, the town council was turning over even correspondence from its own ambassadors in Paris to members of the Forty-Eight so that joint instructions satisfactory to all parties could be sent back to representatives of the city in Paris.[100] By March 1622, conflation of authority between the town council and the Forty-Eight reached the point where militia companies were issuing the titles of office on the town council to new *pairs*, receiving new town councilmen's sworn, ceremonial promises of loyal service to the city, and even collecting their thirty *livre* initiation fee. These rights had previously belonged exclusively to the town council.[101]

---

[99] BMLR, MS 763, fol. 103r.

[100] Upon their receipt, letters to the town council from the *échevin* Simon Thevenin, serving in Paris as envoy of the *corps de ville*, went directly to the Forty-Eight for review, see BMLR, MS 763, fols. 116v-117r (27 February 1619).

[101] The secretary of the town council recorded that councilmen were shocked to discover that "les 48 s'emancipoient en leurs compagnies de donner lettres

La Rochelle's increasingly dissident municipal government soon confronted large royal armies moving southwestward to suppress heresy and bring traditionally rebellious provinces under greater monarchical control. In a swift pacification campaign from July to October 1620, Louis XIII personally led an armed force, numbering more than 10,000 troops, southward from Caen toward Pau. En route, this army put an end to Marie de Medici's political intrigues by easily defeating her ragged soldiery at Ponts-de-Cé. The king installed new royal garrisons in the many west country bourgs whose governors contritely opened town gates to salute the sovereign. Pushing deep into Protestant Béarn, Louis XIII quickly succeeded in annexing the province, reorganizing its customary courts into a single *parlement*, reestablishing the Catholic Mass throughout the region, and emplacing loyal troops in its key mountain fortresses. Before leaving the province, Louis inaugurated a local Counter-Reformation by enhancing the police authority of the bishops serving at Oloron and Lascar. Louis' fidelity to his role as "the most Christian king" defending the Catholic faith largely inspired this crusade.

To counter this new peril menacing the French Reformed churches, deputies from nearly all the Huguenot provinces assembled at La Rochelle in December 1620. The king immediately declared this reunion illegal and commanded its participants to disperse at once. Great Protestant nobles like Rohan and La Tremouille steered clear of this conclave, endeavoring to close it as quickly as possible. Direction of the assembly fell to rash, unscrupulous, and self-aggrandizing adventurers like Jean de Favas, Viscount of Castets.

Ignoring royal orders to disband and fearing that a renewal of civil war was imminent, the Protestant assembly of La Rochelle took a fateful step and resolved to organize armed defense of the faith without delay. Provincial Protestants responded in force to the religiously inspired, punitive campaigns of a more bellicose Catholic monarchy. Deputies divided the regions of France most thickly populated by Calvinists into eight "circles," each under the command of a Protestant grandee and expected to field an army

---

et provisions de pair à ceux qui sur leur nomination estoyent esleus à cette charge par ce corps et leur faisoient prester des serments qui ne peuvent apartenir qu'au droit et autorité de cette compagnie," BMLR, MS 764, fols. 57v-58r (18 March 1622).

of proportionate size. The assembly authorized the military governors of these departments to levy war loans, organize troops,
appoint subordinate officers, and join battle at their discretion
with royalist forces.

These provocative arrangements for armed opposition to the
crown occurred almost simultaneously with Louis XIII's departure
on a greater west country military campaign intended to destroy
the capacity of French Protestants to make war in the region.
Proceeding down the Loire valley from Orléans, the king's army
turned due south to invest Huguenot towns in Brittany, Poitou,
Saintonge, and Aunis. In late May 1621, a royal army growing in
excess of 20,000 men began to draw up outside the walls of Saint-
Jean-d'Angély, a stalwart Protestant town less than a day's ride
from La Rochelle. Outnumbered by more than ten to one, the
besieged Protestant garrison, commanded by Benjamin de Rohan,
duc de Soubise, put up a heroic but ultimately futile resistance.
By mid-June, the old town's masonry ramparts crumbled to pieces
under the pounding of royal cannonades. The king's heralds
repeatedly summoned Soubise to capitulate.[102]

On 25 June, Soubise surrendered the town, marching his decimated forces out with all the gallant honors of war obtained in
a general amnesty from the king. Louis vented his spleen against
the rebel town by ordering its walls razed to the ground, by revok-
ing all of its civic privileges, by disbanding all organs of communal government, and by obliterating even its name, rechristening
the place "Bourg Louis," a title that never stuck. The king's eradi-
cation of Saint-Jean-d'Angély, his utter decivilizing of the place
(comparable to the imposed derogation of a wayward nobleman),
shocked the neighboring Rochelais and stoked new town governors' resolution to defend their municipality. Although menaced
by the duc d'Epernon and 5,000 men detached from the king's
main army, La Rochelle's inhabitants redoubled their preparations for war, encouraged by news of Montauban's tenacious resistance against the bulk of Louis' troops. Royal gendarmes within
sight of La Rochelle's walls now built up a fortified camp, soon
known as "Fort Louis," to maintain constant surveillance over the

---

[102] For the text of these orders see AAE, Mém. & Doc., France, 1475, fols.
12-13, "Procés verbal d'un herault de France portant sommation à Benjamin de
Rohan," 3 June 1621.

rebel town. This redoubt became a thorn in the Rochelais' side they never managed to dislodge, reminding them at every sunrise how close the enemy had come.

Fierce resistance by the besieged residents of Montauban, inadequate· supplies, and inclement weather forced the king reluctantly to abandon his assault on the town in November 1621. Buoyed up by this providential news, La Rochelle's civic leaders fervently organized communal defense. Their efforts were also inspired by a decisive naval victory won in October by a rochelais fleet over a larger royal squadron cruising just off shore.

The new men in rochelais town government had long ago taken over key fiscal posts in municipal administration and used their business skills and social contacts to raise the money essential for defending the city against increasingly threatening royal forces. In 1618, the new *pair* and militia company commander, Benjamin de la Salle, was assisting with the collection of excise taxes imposed by the Rochelais on the nearby town of Rochefort for defense of the Protestant cause.[103] In February 1622, the rochelais merchant Abraham Tessereau, a former member of the Forty-Eight and a newly made *pair*, presented the town council with an elaborate report on the best means of organizing a new "armée navalle" to combat the bloodied royalist fleet.[104] In partial recompense for his services, Tessereau would later be appointed treasurer of all city revenues.[105] Financing for this aggressive naval building program would be provided in part by Jean Papin, previously a *procureur* of the dissident bourgeoisie and now "recepveur général" of all extraordinary municipal income. Additional subsidies for rearmament would come from Jean Papin's kinsmen, Helie Papin, now the collector of all transit levies imposed on cargo vessels entering the Gironde river. Rochelais warships now patrolled the estuary with impunity enforcing this policy on all traffic.[106]

At the same town council meeting, Pierre Mestayer, merchant rebel, elder of the Calvinist church, and the second bourgeois

---

[103] BMLR, MS 763, fol. 19v.

[104] BMLR, MS 764, fol. 60v.

[105] Tessereau was chosen by the town council to become its chief treasurer in April 1625, see BMLR, MS 765, fol. 207v.

[106] BMLR, MS 767, fol. 4r.

nominated by the Forty-Eight to be accepted as a new *pair* on the town council, was put in charge of collecting new tolls on all ships entering the river Sèvre. Funds amassed here were also to be used for strengthening La Rochelle's military forces on land and sea.[107] In 1622, Samuel Bernardeau, Jacob Theroude, and Jean Guerineau, all merchants of political repute, were appointed to collect similar levies the Rochelais imposed on commerce in the port of Royan. Jean Tharay was already busy spending—in advance—the sums to be raised at Royan for the acquisition and shipment of food supplies to Protestant infantrymen and marines, under rochelais command, billeted there.[108] Notable leaders of the 1614 rebellion now handling the logistics of armed rochelais resistance to the crown often ventured far outside the city. Their distance from supervision by the *corps de ville* permitted them a wide latitude of action, a license in matters of great military and political consequence easily exploited by determined men like Jean Tharay.

Also in the spring of 1622, as royal troops gathered ominously in Nantes for new punitive forays southward, the full town council ordered the Forty-Eight and the *procureurs* to cease and desist from commissioning former members of the Forty-Eight to harvest timber illegally on the strategic island of Oléron. Old and new members of the Forty-Eight went after the trees in order to erect better fortifications against the king's men and to feed the blazing furnaces of La Rochelle's cannon foundry, now also under the control of superintendents chosen by the Forty-Eight.[109] At its next session, under pressure from the militia companies, the town council empowered the new *pair* Jean Tharay and another representative of the bourgeoisie to negotiate with the Protestant Deputy General, the Vicomte de Favas, over rochelais logistical

---

[107] BMLR, MS 764, fol. 60v.

[108] *Ibid.*, fols. 5v and 73r. As La Rochelle's need for money to finance military preparedness increased, neighborhood chieftains like Jean Tharay were also appointed by the town council to organize the collection of special levies imposed upon all residents of each parish in the city to pay for the cost of lodging and feeding troops arriving in ever greater numbers, *ibid.*, fol. 144r. When the town, in September 1622, needed to come up with 36,000 *livres* to pay the wages of sailors and captains serving in its fleet of warships, Samuel Bernardeau, Zacherie Chatton's widow, Pierre Hotton, and Jean Tharay were all listed by the town council among the wealthy and influential bourgeois whose financial and moral support should be tapped, *ibid.*, fols. 258v-259r.

[109] BMLR, MS 764, fols. 17v-18r.

support for Calvinist armies in the field. Tharay pursued the task with his usual alacrity.[110]

On 9 March 1622, the bellicose *procureurs de bourgeois* further complicated local military organization and logistics by informing the full town council of the Forty-Eight's decision to name one of their partisans, André Brunet, "procureur de la cause" on the island of Oléron. Brunet would be responsible for boosting the morale of Protestant soldiers and preparing the isle's defenders to repulse any landing by royal troops.[111] Past and present members of the Forty-Eight became instrumental in gearing up La Rochelle for a final military showdown with the Bourbon monarchy.

In May of 1625, as religious war in the French west intensified, the Forty-Eight engineered the compact by which La Rochelle joined forces with Benjamin de Rohan, one of the last great Protestant aristocrats to do battle with Louis XIII. The Forty-Eight and its allies within the town council ordered the entire *corps de ville* to accept this alliance. Members of the Forty-Eight, patrolling the city in armed squads, threatened to exile all town councillors and their families who opposed the accord.[112] The Forty-Eight compelled the mayor to call a public assembly at which all citizens could voice their opinion about the proposed treaty. The patrician jurist, Joseph Guillaudeau, noted disdainfully that only about a third of the population turned out, mostly artisans, stevedores, and day laborers whose opinions ranked equally in the debate with the advice given by "responsible men of quality."[113] The general assembly endorsed alliance with Soubise and support for his armed resistance against the king's forces. Such decisions made individually and collectively by the Rochelais at the instigation of the Forty-Eight gave the French crown multiple justifications for ever harsher punitive campaigns against the city.

In September 1625, a rearmed royal fleet inflicted a severe check to rochelais military ambitions when it hunted down and destroyed most of the city's capital warships in three days of running battle. This defeat enabled the ascendant Richelieu to tempt

---

[110] *Ibid.*, fols. 19r-v.

[111] *Ibid.*, fols. 50r-v. André Brunet was a kinsman to one of the *procureurs de bourgeois* representing the parish of St. Barthélémy in 1622.

[112] Guillaudeau, "Diaire," 278.

[113] *Ibid.*, 281.

and divide the Rochelais with offers of peace negotiations. The terms he set for cessation of all hostilities reveal precisely what the great lords of state found most threatening in La Rochelle's new constitution. In late November 1625, Richelieu informed the king that as a prelude to peace with La Rochelle he should demand that "the government of the city will no longer be in the hands of the people but only vested in magistrates."[114] This prime ultimatum became incorporated in the first article of the draft treaty Richelieu proposed to the Rochelais. The king would call off further attacks on the city provided that: "Firstly, the council and government of the city will be replaced and reestablished in the hands of those who formed the *corps de ville* as it was constituted in the year 1610."[115]

This primary condition required abandonment of the twenty-eight articles regulating town government imposed after the coup of 1614, dismantlement of the Council of Forty-Eight, discharge of the bourgeoisie's *procureurs*, and removal of all town councilmen emplaced by new electoral procedures since 1614. Richelieu's principal worry seems to have been the new politics, not the new religion of the Rochelais. However, his peace terms are also notable for the implicit compromise he sought with the old organs of municipal government. It is the conservation, not the abolishment of ancient civic ruling bodies that Richelieu proposes. At this juncture, crown diplomacy does not conform to any "absolutist" agenda of centralized territorial administration at the expense of intermediate agencies of government.

Temporarily at a loss in the fortunes of war, the Rochelais elected to accept in February 1626 the crown's proffered treaty, an accord they had no real intention of honoring. In fact, they never abided by the strictures of its initial clause. The Council of Forty-Eight, although cosmetically reduced in size, continued to function and continued to nominate its own candidates for offices

---

[114] See the diplomatic instruction from Richelieu to the king dated 25 November 1625, AAE, Mém. & Doc., France, 246, fols. 32-39, reprinted in P. Grillon, ed., *Les papiers de Richelieu*, 6 vols., (Paris, 1975-85), 1 (1624-1626): 226-233.

[115] See the "Articles de la paix donnez par Sa Majesté à ses subjetz de la religion prétendu réformée. Paris 5 fevrier 1626," AAE, Mém. & Doc., France, 782, fols. 48-50, reprinted in Grillon, *Papiers de Richelieu*, 1: 287-88: "Premièrement, Que le Conseil et gouvernement de la ville sera remis et restabli ez mains de ceux qui sont du corps d'icelle en la forme qu'il estoit en l'année 1610."

of *pair* falling vacant on the town council. None of the new bourgeois members of the town council elected after 1614 resigned. Surviving minute books of town council meetings and elections for 1627-1628 make this continuity indisputably clear.[116]

Richelieu's apparent expectation that the old regime of rochelais town politics could be restored proved illusory and signals his misapprehension of how thoroughly La Rochelle's civic institutions had been infiltrated by a new cadre of local political actors. The ignorance of the king's chief minister in this matter can be attributed to the incomplete and misleading intelligence he received from his agents trying to penetrate rochelais affairs. Reports he got back from this center of intrigue kept him well informed of plots hatched by highly visible opponents like the duc de Rohan but this precision evaporated when his contacts tried to describe the deeper machinations of town politics. Here, gross generalities are the rule. Richelieu's secret correspondents speak of a civic regime influenced by "the mob," ("la canaille") without identifying its real animators.[117]

Even the envoys Richelieu sent into La Rochelle relayed back inaccurate information about rochelais compliance with the 1626 peace accord. Claude Le Doulx, named "commissaire royal" to La Rochelle's *corps de ville* in 1626, misleadingly informed his master that the reconversion of town government to its state in 1610 had indeed occurred and then vaingloriously took personal credit for taming the "grandes constestations" and "esmotions populaires" this supposed reconfiguration engendered.[118] Contemporaneous

---

[116] See for examples, BMLR, MS 768, fols. 15v and 17v. The rochelais jurist Guillaudeau also noted in his diary that the twenty representatives of the bourgeoisie who replaced the Forty-Eight in March 1626 exercised exactly the same political powers and prerogatives as their predecessors, see Guillaudeau, "Diaire," 320. This reduction was a minor concession to the crown leaving bellicose town politics essentially unchanged.

[117] See for example the dispatch dated 27 March 1626 from Pontchier du Lilon to Richelieu, AAE, Mém. & Doc., France, 1475, fols. 32-33, in which the prime minister's agent, posted at Marans, 20 kilometers northeast of La Rochelle, speculates on how "la canaille" controlling rochelais affairs will react to recent political developments. Such details would naturally escape an observer so far away. This piece of correspondence is not included in Grillon's recent edition of Richelieu's papers. Communiqués from Pontchier du Lilon cited by Grillon (see for example *Les papiers de Richelieu*, 1: 302) often do not give place of composition and convey a false impression of how well Richelieu's west country contacts understood the events on which they reported.

[118] See the letter of Le Doulx to Richelieu, 2 July 1626, AAE, Mém. & Doc.,

personnel lists for La Rochelle's town council show no changes
whatsoever in the composition of communal government.[119]
These discrepancies suggest that Richelieu's secret service was
afflicted by all the foibles of modern intelligence agencies, specifically the deformation of information policy makers receive by the
personal ambitions and bureaucratic infighting of subordinates.
Grappling with an opponent his own *créatures* helped him to mis-
understand, Richelieu only succeeded in further antagonizing the
Rochelais, accelerating the renewal of civil war.

As the cost of prolonged sparring with royal armies and fleets
rose, the town council of La Rochelle became increasingly dependent on veterans of the Forty-Eight and on notable militia leaders to raise money for local defense of the Protestant cause. In
1625, 1626, and 1627, key men in each militia company were
empowered by the town council to obtain long-term loans and
gifts of cash from the rank and file of each militia unit. All monies
collected went to acquire lodging, food, and equipment for Protestant troops in service to the city.[120] In 1627, the crown sent the
largest royal army ever assembled in the religious wars southward
to destroy this concentration of militant dissidents. When the time
came for the besieged Rochelais to husband their dwindling
resources of food, militia company commanders, their lieutenants,
ensigns, and officers, along with new *pairs* and other notable bourgeois from each neighborhood, got the tough job of rounding up
the "bouches inutiles"—the useless mouths—to be driven out of
the city.[121]

When the town council of La Rochelle met on 30 March 1628
to approve a last, desperate defensive alliance with the king of
England, an act of high treason and *lèse-majesté*, sixty-three councilmen were present and endorsed the treaty without dissent. Of
the sixty-three councilmen approving the compact, forty (63.5%)

---

France, 1475, fol. 36, in which he deceptively claims that the remaking of municipal government has been accomplished. Nine days later, Le Doulx informed
his master that, although the current form of rochelais civic administration was
"not entirely in conformity with that of 1610," changes effected would certainly
suffice to prevent any further disturbances, letter dated 11 July 1626, AAE, Mém.
& Doc., France, 781, fol. 185. These lies seriously misled the Cardinal by grossly understating the real extent of continuing disobedience by the Rochelais.

[119] See for example, BMLR, MS 768, fol. 6r.

[120] BMLR, MS 768, fols. 19v-21v and 53r.

[121] *Ibid.*, fol. 115r.

were new *pairs* previously nominated to the town council by the Forty-Eight.[122] From the inception to the conclusion of La Rochelle's open war with the crown of France, the merchant rebels of 1614 and their sympathizers did their utmost to manage the political, diplomatic, economic, and military affairs of their Protestant city. They led La Rochelle to its destruction. As a privileged, strategically located frontier town and a peculiar center of the Reformation in France, La Rochelle was certain to become a target for royal armies once Louis XIII came of age and began to assert his Catholic dominion over the fractious west country. However, the king's necessity of making war upon the city can only be fully appreciated in the context of the dramatic local events shaping the internal and external politics of the town from 1614 to 1628.

From evidence presented above, it is clear that this period witnessed the eclipse of the old, oligarchic town council as the preeminent governing institution of La Rochelle. Under continual pressure from the Council of Forty-Eight and infiltrated by new *pairs* loyal to the Forty-Eight and to the militia companies, the old town council could not survive. The former ruling oligarchy in La Rochelle was supplanted by a political regime more effective in civic administration, more conscious of its obligation to defend the unique form of rochelais town government, more solicitous of Calvinist congregational liberties underpinning its rule, and thus more bellicose in its confrontations with the encircling agents of royal authority. Contemptuous of the old oligarchs irresponsibly inclined to accommodation with the crown, the new bourgeois city fathers were inherently suspicious of political compromise as a threat to the government they and their kinsmen felt paternally obligated to protect. They had not inherited a town government, they had made one, deftly joining new agencies of police to older administrative institutions guaranteed by the city's ancient privileges. Partisans of this movement widely accepted recourse to the force of arms as a just means to accomplish their ends and to guarantee the survival of the government they created and the church they peopled.

The willing participation of *anciens* and *diacres* from La Rochelle's *consistoire* in the new regime of civic administration

---

[122] *Ibid.*, fol. 195r.

underscores the fact that protection of religious liberties was a
duty integral to the tasks of government assumed by rebellious
bourgeois in 1614. But religious values, especially a militant congregationalism, were not the sole motivation for their actions nor
the exclusive reason why the town of La Rochelle posed such a
threat to the crown of France. The operations of the Forty-Eight
left no room at all for the participation of local royal officers in
the governance of the city. The combative ideology embodied in
new agencies of civic administration grafted onto the ancient stock
of La Rochelle's privileged municipal institutions made the city
an even more dangerous hybrid, setting an example for similar
political experiments elsewhere and threatening to stymie all royal efforts to assert more control over great towns throughout the
realm.

Before printing his latest work on the traditions and privileges
of French civic government, the assiduous jurist and legal schol-
ar, Jean Chenu, gained special permission from La Rochelle's
town council to consult and copy various documents in the municipal archives. Chenu showed greatest interest in records relating
the details of the innovative and legally binding political settlement between the bourgeois Council of Forty-Eight and the town
council that ended the rebellion of 1614, a settlement imparting
democratic characteristics to civic administration. Chenu published annotated versions of the twenty-eight articles and other
accords effecting the bourgeois reconfiguration of La Rochelle's
government in his noted compendium of typical French urban
statutes (*Recueil des Antiquitez et privileges de la ville de Bourges et
plusieurs autres villes capitales de la royaume*, Paris, 1622). This publication gave the rebel city of La Rochelle a legal notoriety especially threatening to the king and to his claims of just Catholic
sovereignty at a time when the loyalty of many French urban communities remained in grave doubt. The audacity of La Rochelle's
bourgeois governors and the recognition they won in legal circles
made them doubly dangerous adversaries of the crown, capable
of fighting and inciting others to fight, legally and militarily, royal efforts to police more stringently the Protestant communities
and "bonnes villes" of France.

Thus La Rochelle could not be left unmolested. Impregnable
behind its towering, well-maintained defenses, the city could only

be reduced—as Richelieu so wisely decided—by starving out its determined, enterprising defenders.

After another sally by a royal army deep into western France, the long and final siege of La Rochelle began in the summer of 1627. It continued to strangle the city for another fifteen months. The discipline of the communal militia companies never broke and capitulation came only after all hope of relief from England was abandoned and hunger had reduced the number of Protestant fighting men to fewer than 200. More than 15,000 of the 21,000 inhabitants and refugees trapped by the siege died of wounds, disease, or starvation. The price in human lives of confrontational politics with the crown became catastrophically high for the Rochelais. To learn the causes and the effects of that conflict requires close attention be given to the social structures underpinning the political behavior and values for which rochelais combatants were prepared to die miserably.

The following chapter will track changes in the form and content of rochelais politics brought about by royal victory in the siege of 1627-28. Examination of whether the siege altered the fundamental sociology of urban politics in La Rochelle is my objective and, in my opinion, the best test of that event's long-term historical significance.

# COUNTER-REFORMING LA ROCHELLE: FEUDALIZING THE TOWNSCAPE, CATHOLICIZING MUNICIPAL GOVERNMENT, AND TRANSFORMING AGENCIES OF POLICE WITHIN URBAN SOCIETY, CIRCA 1628–1650

## 1. *Introduction*

The great siege of La Rochelle lasted from July of 1627 until November 1628. Wary of the city's high walls bristling with cannon, royal troops and sappers, under the personal command of the duc de Richelieu, avoided a direct assault and instead constructed a thick ring of trenchworks around the city. This noose closed, in a spectacular feat of military engineering, with the completion of a long, fortified dike across the channel separating La Rochelle from the open ocean. This massive barrier against naval assistance sealed the city's fate. Cut off from aid by land or sea, the Rochelais became prisoners behind their own stout battlements and many slowly began to starve to death.

From September 1627, the local diarist, Joseph Guillaudeau, began recording the deadly trajectories of cannon balls falling on the city at a murderous rate from royal batteries on every side.[1] Guillaudeau's private chronicle of war includes quotations of steadily rising prices for basic foodstuffs growing ever scarcer within the strangled city. By September 1628, a single cow was worth the incredible price of 1,200 *livres*, a donkey 200 *livres*, and a chicken seven *livres*.[2] Only the richest citizens could afford to buy nourishment on the open market. In late October 1628, Guillaudeau sadly estimated that 18,000 of his fellow townspeople had died of

---

[1] "Diaire de Joseph Guillaudeau," AHSA 38 (1908): 1-415. See in particular 344, 354, and 360-361.

[2] *Ibid.*, 377. Royal propagandists capitalized on the misery of La Rochelle's inhabitants and sent a warning to other obstreperous Protestant towns by publicizing the terrible inflation in food prices in the besieged city. See the anonymous *Mémoire très particulier de la despense qui a esté faicte dans la ville de La Rochelle avec le prix et qualité des viandes qui ont esté vendues en ladite ville depuis le commencement du mois d'octobre jusque à sa réduction*, (Paris, 1628), BMLR, 2581c.

wounds, disease, and starvation since the siege began.[3] With all food supplies exhausted, desiccated cadavers littering the streets, and barely 200 soldiers left in any condition to fight, the town council of La Rochelle capitulated to Louis XIII on 28 October 1628. The king, resplendent in shining armor, personally led his disciplined troops into the famished city on All Saints' Day 1628.[4]

Louis XIII's victory over his rebel city was manifold. By terms of the surrender, La Rochelle's massive walls were to be razed, its many cannons forfeited, the ancient *corps de ville* and bourgeois political organizations abolished, the city militia disbanded, the town hall's meeting bell melted down, all civic privileges revoked, an annual *taille* of 4,000 *livres* imposed on the community, settlement in the city by Protestant immigrants forbidden, and all Catholic religious institutions reestablished.[5] As the city's last bourgeois defenders had feared, La Rochelle underwent the same process of decivilization inflicted on its west country neighbor, Saint-Jean-d'Angély, in 1621.

By destroying La Rochelle's capacity to defend the French mid-Atlantic coast, the crown also eliminated a fundamental justification of the community's existence vital to residents' own sense of self-worth. Seen from this perspective, seventeenth-century royal campaigns to fortify the mid-Atlantic littoral with massive citadels by Vauban and costly new naval bases may have had as their principal target the *amour-propre* of the Rochelais.[6]

---

[3] Guillaudeau, "Diaire," 379. Guillaudeau's estimation of total deaths in La Rochelle due to the siege falls between minimum and maximum mortality rates established for the event and may be fairly accurate. Louis Pérouas, an expert on rochelais demography, puts the death toll at between 12,000 and 15,000, see Pérouas, "Sur la démographie rochelaise," *Annales E.S.C.*, 16 (1961): 1131-1140. The medical historian, Etienne Guibert, places the total of dead Rochelais at 19,800, see his "La Rochelle en 1628, état sanitaire des Rochelais et des assiégeants, mortalité, morbidité," (Ph.D. diss., University of Bordeaux II, 1979), 52.

[4] Detailed histories of the siege of La Rochelle and its principal actors include: F. de Vaux de Foletier, *Le siège de La Rochelle*, (Paris, 1931) and P.S. Callot, *Jean Guiton maire de La Rochelle et le siège de 1628*, (1840; reprint, La Rochelle, 1967).

[5] *Déclaration du Roy sur la réduction de la ville de La Rochelle en son obéissance contenant l'ordre et police que sa majesté veut y estre establie*, (Le Mans, 1628), BMLR, 2745c.

[6] Considerations of military logistics alone, for example, did not dictate the nearly ruinous choice of Rochefort as the main arsenal of the French Atlantic fleet. Masters of this port, thirty-five kilometers south of La Rochelle, had to dredge the estuary of the Charente river perpetually in order to keep a chan-

To check any possible organization of popular resistance to the pacification of La Rochelle, the king imposed six-month sentences of banishment on notable and obstreperous Protestant political leaders who survived the siege, including the former rebel captains Jean Tharay, Israel Torterue, and Abraham Tessereau. The king also exiled Jean Guiton, the last mayor of the city, and seven other surviving civic dignitaries.[7] Royal force of arms destroyed both the system of civic administration established in La Rochelle by the bourgeois rebellion of 1614 and the ancient accretion of municipal privileges and compacts that guaranteed the working and reworking of rochelais town government free from significant interference by the crown. An important episode of contentious and independent urban politics in La Rochelle was over.

The capitulation of La Rochelle in 1628 ingloriously ended one chapter of the city's history and seems to have given later scholars few incentives to study its short-, medium-, or long-term aftermath. Indeed, the period from 1628 to 1650 remains one of the least studied and least understood periods of rochelais history. How Louis XIII won his victory over the city is well-known. How that conquest affected the fortunes of important religious communities in the city has also been investigated.[8] What remains unknown is how, and to what extent the rebel city was reincorporated in the apparatus of royal government. How did the king and his ministers capitalize on La Rochelle's submission? Once

---

nel open for heavy warships and to prevent complete blockage of the harbor by thick deposits of silt. These were the continual expenses the crown was willing to pay in support of a broader campaign bringing greater religious discipline and political order to the fractious west country. See Daniel Dessert, *La Royale: vaisseaux et marins du roi-soleil,* (Paris, 1996), and Nathalie Moreau, *Vauban et la côte atlantique entre Loire et Gironde,* (Saint-Leger-Vauban, 1993).

[7] Callot, *Jean Guiton,* 53 and n. 68. See also the contemporary account by the Rochelais Raphael Colin, "Annales de La Rochelle," BMLR, MS 153, fol. 119; and Guillaudeau, "Diaire," 380, n. 1.

[8] See François Moisy, "Le rétablissement des structures catholiques à La Rochelle (1628-1648), un épisode de la Contre-Réforme en France," *La revue du Bas-Poitou et des provinces de l'ouest,* 82, No. 5 (1971): 343-373; 83, No. 1 (1972): 45-61; and 83, No. 2: 117-145. Moisy examines in detail the reemplacement, organization, work, and material holdings of regular and secular Catholic clergy in La Rochelle during this period. Jean Soumagne also presents a careful urban mapping and census of Catholic orders reestablished in the city after 1628, see his article "La place des anciennes communautés religieuses dans la structure urbaine de La Rochelle," in *Etudes géographiques offertes à Louis Papy,* (Bordeaux, 1978), 383-391.

the ancient *corps de ville* and the political organizations of the bourgeoisie had been abolished, what new institutions of civic government did the crown invent to replace these powerful bodies? Who ruled La Rochelle on a daily basis after the famous siege? Where did the king turn to find his new local agents and how well did they serve their master? How did the siege and the new institutions of urban administration it engendered affect the traditional familial arrangement of civic affairs in which important, interconnected kin groups shaped the politics and sociology of municipal government? And how important were the latest secular institutions of city government in the religious reeducation of La Rochelle's citizenry mandated by the Counter-Reformation? Answers to these questions will not only illuminate one of the most obscure segments of La Rochelle's history, but also strike me as the best test of the great siege's long-term historical significance.[9]

Capitulation of a withered La Rochelle was a transient sign of the king's ability to muster and concentrate military force sufficient to enforce his will. The real battle for control over the place began after the gates of the starving city were thrown open to the king's men and the royal army had been disbanded. Nor did this struggle end with redaction of the royal edicts defining the new components of municipal government. As William Beik and James Collins remind us, a new political history of the *ancien régime* requires recognition of French absolutism as a social construct, coopting and engaging, not destroying, local elites.[10] How the

---

[9] A chronicle of events in La Rochelle, written by several authors and issued in the series devoted to French urban history by the publishing house Privat, contains no account of La Rochelle's history between 1628 and the local resurgence of maritime commerce in the latter seventeenth century, see M. Delafosse, ed., *Histoire de la Rochelle*, (Toulouse, 1985). Louis Pérouas' detailed study of the Counter-Reformation in and around La Rochelle begins in 1648 and most of Pérouas' documentation and analysis apply to the last decades of the seventeenth century and the first decades of the eighteenth century; see his *Le diocèse de La Rochelle de 1648 à 1724, sociologie et pastorale*, (Paris, 1964). David Parker's *La Rochelle and the French Monarchy, Conflict and Order in Seventeenth-Century France*, (London, 1980), succinctly describes fundamental values motivating each side in the growing conflict between crown and city and elucidates the national significance of the siege and its outcome. However, Parker's work does not address the local political and sociological ramifications of the king's victory after 1628.

[10] William Beik, *Absolutism and Society in Seventeenth-Century France*, (Cambridge, 1985), 10-15. James Collins, *The State in Early Modern France*, (Cambridge, 1995), 79-124.

consolidation of royal government over the French west country affected the politics and politicians of La Rochelle now becomes my topic. What did and did not change in the strategy and tactics of rochelais urban government in the decades after 1628 will be the main subject of this chapter.

According to the articles of surrender negotiated and approved by representatives of La Rochelle and the king on 28 October 1628, the Rochelais were pardoned for all their acts of rebellion against the crown, the free exercise of the Protestant religion was guaranteed in the city (to the astonishment of natives), and the surviving inhabitants were spared from pillage by royal troops.[11] Although decimated by the siege, townspeople salvaged their goods and their religion, essential supports for rebuilding the Protestant community and potential bulwarks against complete domination by the crown. Quick remarriage of men and women left single by the siege and rapidly rising numbers of Catholic migrants to the town sparked a demographic resurgence that pushed annual baptism rates steeply upward after 1628 and brought La Rochelle's total population to approximately 18,000 by 1635.[12]

The professional papers of rochelais notaries for the years immediately following the siege show a quick resumption of national and international commerce by both Catholics and Protestants residing in the city. For example, by 1630, consortia of local Catholic merchants were outfitting large ships, loading them with grain, and sending them to Italian, Portuguese, and Spanish markets.[13] Back from his banishment, the merchant, Jean Tharay, quickly began dealing with the widow of his old friend, Zacherie Chatton, settling multiple business obligations in September 1631 worth over 1,500 *livres*.[14] Although less prosperous than before the siege, La Rochelle was briskly recovering from its defeat, presenting the crown and its agents with a sizeable task of municipal administration and police.

---

[11] See the transcript of "Articles accordés à la ville de La Rochelle par Louis XIII le 28 Octobre 1628," (Rouen, 1628), reprinted in Callot, *Jean Guiton*, Appendix II, 131-134.

[12] Pérouas, "Démographie rochelaise," 1133-1134.

[13] ADCM, 3 E 225 (1630), fols. 155v, 159v-160r, and 179r.

[14] ADCM, 3 E 253 (1631), fols. 126v-127r.

## 2. Subjecting the Rochelais to the Fief St. Louis, An Ineffaceable Punishment of Their Rebellion

At his siege camp before La Rochelle, Louis XIII had been attended by a distinguished array of noble cavaliers and courtiers. Claude de Rouvroy, *Sieur* de Saint-Simon, figured prominently in this company. After the disgrace of François de Baradet in 1626, Saint-Simon became the male favorite of the king. Bonding with the sovereign through their mutual delight in exploits of horsemanship and arduous hunting expeditions, Saint-Simon received a wealth of presents and preferments from the smitten monarch. Beginning in 1627, Saint-Simon became *prémier écuyer* of the royal stables, captain of the châteaux at Saint-Germain and Versailles, *grand louvetier*, first gentleman of the king's chamber, commander of the royal fortresses at Meulan (Yvelines) and Blaye (Gironde), and a *chevalier des ordres du roi* (1633). This meteoric rise through the offices of a jealous court culminated in January 1635 when Louis made Saint-Simon a duke and peer of the realm.[15]

In recompense for Saint-Simon's valiant personal service at the siege of La Rochelle, the king, in early November 1628, indulgently gave his favorite all of the land around La Rochelle on which the city's condemned fortifications stood.[16] This gift, soon to be known as the fief St. Louis, comprised a great swath of property nearly encircling the city and stretching from the inside base of the town wall outward beyond the earthen berms of the primary battlements to the farthest lip of the moats on the defensive perimeter. The total area of this tract now under Saint-Simon's complete control exceeded 130 acres.[17] To the east, this

---

[15] For details on the life, court career, and correspondence of the first duke de Saint-Simon, see Johel Coutura, "Claude de Rouvroy, prémier duc de Saint-Simon (1606-1693)," *Cahiers St. Simon* 8 (1980): 75-87, and *idem*, "Correspondence de Claude de Saint-Simon," *Cahiers St. Simon* 15 (1987): 3-81. Saint-Simon's son, the renowned memorialist of the court of Louis XIV, describes his father's ascension under royal favor alone, his subsequent disgrace, and life-long devotion to Louis XIII, see Louis de Saint-Simon, *Mémoires*, 2 vols., (Paris, La Pléiade: 1953), 1: 52-85.

[16] This gift was ratified in a royal edict dated 30 December 1628, see the text of this declaration included in a large dossier of printed matter relevant to the duke de Saint-Simon's landholdings, AN, Q1 120. The *Chambre des Comptes* in Paris and the *cour* of the Parisian Parlement received news of the king's gift and instructions for honoring it in a supplementary edict of January 1629.

[17] AN, Q1 120, see the "arpentage" of Saint-Simon's rochelais property carried out by royal surveyors on 5 October 1633.

royal gift encompassed the entire faubourg of the *ville neuve* on which most of La Rochelle's seventeenth-century urban development would occur. To the south, the king's present to Saint-Simon included valuable commercial real estate on the stone quays of the city's fortified harbor (Figure 14 presents a map of the royal land grant of the fief St. Louis to Claude de Saint-Simon).

Within this new domain, Saint-Simon also received rights to the material of "all towers, walls, gates, bridges, pavements, houses, warehouses, guard houses, arsenals, sheds, and mills." Now the vassals of a great, ascendent aristocrat, all residents and property holders within the boundaries of the king's territorial grant became liable for payment of seigneurial rents and dues including the *accapte, banalités, cens,* and *lods et ventes.* Although monetarily small, the *cens,* for example, was an irredeemable and imprescriptible signifier of a commoner's subservience to a noble lord. By the customary law of Aunis, now fully applicable to La Rochelle, *lods et ventes* obligated vassals to pay their lord a tax on all transfers of property within a demesne amounting to one-twelfth of the value of the entities exchanged.[18] The king's revocation of La Rochelle's chartered freedoms and gratification of his favorite doubly annulled all of the municipal franchises formerly exempting the Rochelais from the obligations of *roturier* tenancy.

Probably misreading the political intent of his patron's largesse, Saint-Simon immediately sold his rochelais estate for a quick cash gain to *maître* Louis Martin, a wealthy tax farmer from Nevers. For all rights to the king's gift, Martin agreed to pay Saint-Simon 21,000 *livres* in two equal installments one year apart.[19] Because *maître* Martin's bourgeois status made him ineligible to collect the seigneurial dues now affixed to the rochelais properties he swiftly acquired, confirmations of the sale between Saint-Simon and Martin issued by the *Chambre des Comptes* in Paris stipulated that

---

[18] See Réné Valin, *Nouveau commentaire sur le coutoume de La Rochelle et du pays d'Aunis,* 2 vols., (La Rochelle, 1756), 1: 111-113.

[19] See the contract of sale between Saint-Simon and Martin redacted in Paris and dated 18 November 1628, AN Q1 120. The sum Martin agreed to pay for the rochelais land only amounted to approximately one-quarter of the total value of all real estate, ground rents, and buildings Saint-Simon acquired through Louis' gift. See the assessment of Saint-Simon's entire rochelais estate dated 5 October 1633, AN, Q1 120. Local assessors estimated the net worth of this domain at 84,452 *livres.*

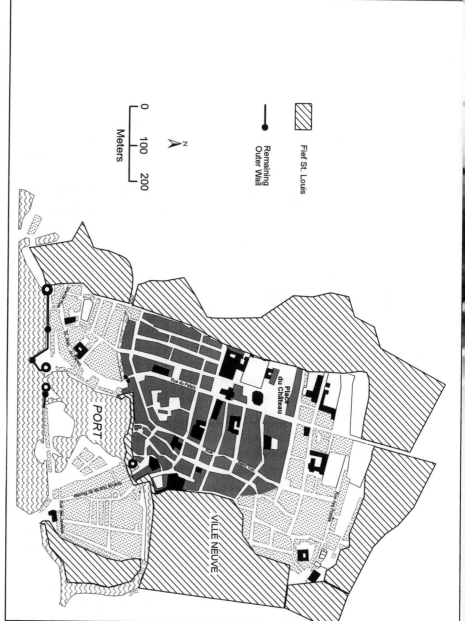

Figure 14. Dimensions of the Fief St. Louis Surrounding La Rochelle

all present and future purchasers of the real estate in question would be required to pay their charges of vassalage directly into the coffers of the royal domain.[20]

This arrangement, caused unexpectedly by a bourgeois interloper sullying a delegation of suzerainty between monarch and noble lord, greatly angered the king. By another edict dated 29 November 1629 addressed to the councillors and financial officers of the Paris Parlement, Louis censured their earlier confirmations of *maître* Martin's purchase, calling these arrangements "tout contraires à nostre intention." The king felt cheated because successive sales of the property originally transferred to Saint-Simon would produce a welter of new owners, including many Rochelais, whose real estate speculations would ultimately dissipate any real sense of the lordship the king wished to impose on La Rochelle as clear chastisement for the city's revolt. Louis protested that Martin's enterprise would allow the Rochelais "to efface and extinguish insensibly the mark of punishment for their rebellion."[21]

To counter potential commercial obliteration of the tangible discipline Louis XIII intended for La Rochelle, the king, by his November decree, reverted to a more medieval strategy of statecraft. Sweeping aside convoluted accountancy for reception of seigneurial dues from new city tenants, Louis simply redefined his rochelais land grant as the creation of a new fiefdom, a direct dependency of the crown.[22] Resurrecting ancestral dominion inside the city by virtue of the long-vanished royal château once lowering over the townscape, the monarch made the new fief and manor of St. Louis coterminous with the property previously awarded to Saint-Simon.

To fashion an authentic demesne, Louis improvised a manor house, expropriating the city's old cannon foundry in the *ville neuve* and dressing it up as the "manoir du fief St. Louis."[23] Crown agents tore the city's arms off the facade of the building and

---

[20] Printed edict of the *Chambre des Comptes* dated 6 April 1629, 5-7, AN, Q1 120.

[21] See AN, Q1 120, printed royal edict dated 29 November 1629, page 6.

[22] *Ibid.*, 6-7.

[23] See the detailed description of this rather dilapidated structure included in the inspection report of the fief St. Louis completed on 6 April 1630 by La Rochelle's new royal intendant of justice, police, and finance, Gaspard Coignet, AN, Q1 120.

replaced them by the king's crest. They affixed a sculpted figure of St. Louis above this armorial device and capped off the entire display by deeply incising the motto "MANOIR DU FIEF S. LOUIS" high on the main wall. Royal surveyors set to work installing stone boundary markers clearly delimiting the fief in all sectors of the city. These enduring mementos were inscribed "ST. L." so that "in the future anyone may understand that they were emplaced to conserve the dependencies of the said fief St. Louis."[24]

Louis XIII completed his erection of the fief St. Louis by instructing *maître* Martin that henceforward all annual rents, seigneurial dues, and fees generated by estate property were to be paid by tenants in perpetuity only at the manòr house on the feast day of St. Louis (25 August).[25] By this invention, residents of the chastened city would continually pay a dual homage to the saintly medieval patron of the French royal house and to the latest, homonymic crusader of that line. In a final gesture of investment, the king commanded Louis Martin to swear a solemn oath of fidelity to him as the new *Sieur* de St. Louis.

Although Martin fully complied with his orders and successfully asserted his rights to the *droits seigneuriaux* of the fief St. Louis in a series of lawsuits against delinquent tenants, new land grabs by jealous neighbors, including Catholic religious orders returning in force to La Rochelle, disrupted Martin's exploitation of the properties sold to him by Saint-Simon. Mounting legal costs also ate into Martin's expected profits from real estate speculation within his seigneurie. Complaining that full, free use of his acquisition was being denied to him, Martin now sued the duc de Saint-Simon for abrogation of the deal and restitution of the purchase price. Through the intermediary Parisian Parlement, the contending parties reached an accord whereby Martin's full investment was refunded and the duke recovered all rights and seigneurial entitlements to the fief St. Louis.[26] Departure of the

---

[24] *Ibid.*, 3.

[25] For evidence of compliance with this command by holders of the fief and their tenants see the land rental contracts redacted in the office of the rochelais notary Jean Juppin, ADCM, 3 E 1772, fols. 248v, 250v, and 256r.

[26] This recourse was confirmed in an *arrêt* of the Paris Parlement dated 26 May 1636. See the collection of printed royal edicts and parliamentary rulings relative to this matter entitled "Establissement du Fief St. Louis à La Rochelle," AN, Q1 120.

vexing commoner undoubtedly pleased Louis XIII, a punctilious
observer of aristocratic etiquette, who now with satisfaction reconfirmed Saint-Simon's lordship over the fief enveloping rochelais
urban space. In June 1636, Saint-Simon formally swore his homage
to Louis as a fiefholder of the crown.

Beginning in 1636, the duc de Saint-Simon settled down to
exploit as rigorously as possible his real estate interests in La
Rochelle. The duke's attentiveness to his domains in southwestern France increased after his precipitous disgrace at court in
October 1636 and banishment to his garrison command at Blaye
on the Gironde estuary.[27] Although the duke fruitlessly petitioned
Richelieu for readmission to Louis' charmed circle at court, neither the king nor his predatory first minister ever moved to strip
Saint-Simon of his offices and prerogatives in the French west
country.

To aid him in the administration of the fief St. Louis, Saint-
Simon retained two deputies. *Messire* Hierosme Dangenoust, *Abbé
Commendataire* of the monastery of St. Nicolas des Prez became
Saint-Simon's general *procureur* for manorial affairs.[28] Dangenoust,
in turn, with the duke's permission, hired *maître* Josué Berchaud,
collector for income from the royal domains in La Rochelle,
Aunis, and Saintonge, as the local estate agent overseeing daily
administration of the duke's rochelais holdings. The status of all
parties to this delegation of authority made manifest the conflu-
ence of royal, ecclesiastical, and seigneurial power by which La
Rochelle was to be subdued.

Among Berchaud's many supervisory duties, he handled the
redaction of annual rental contracts between the duke and his
tenants leasing commercial and domestic properties within the
boundaries of the fief. Surviving registers of the rochelais royal

---

[27] Saint-Simon lost the king's favor by defending too vehemently his kinsman
Estienne de Rouvroy de Saint-Simon, Baron de Saint-Leger, commander of
French forces at Catalet in Picardy, who abandoned this outpost to advancing
Spanish troops in July 1636. The duke defended his uncle's retreat as inevitable
given Saint-Leger's cruel want of supplies and munitions. This argument, implic-
itly criticizing Louis' and Richelieu's misconduct of the border war with Spanish
forces, lost Saint-Simon the favor of both men. This discord, compounded by
the machinations of other jealous courtiers against Saint-Simon, led to the duke's
eclipse and removal to Guyenne at royal command. See Louis de Saint-Simon,
*Mémoires*, 1: 88-71, and Johel Coutura, "Claude de Rouvroy," 84-86.

[28] See the edict of the Parisian *Chambre des Comptes* dated 27 September 1636,
AN, Q1 120.

notary Jean Juppin, Berchaud's preferred local scribe in these matters, are full of such agreements, always growing more numerous in the weeks preceding the feast day of St. Louis when rentals and renewals came due.[29]

Since the bulk of Saint-Simon's rochelais demesne was comprised of open ground yielded by the demolition of the city's fortifications, he could not charge exorbitant rents for undeveloped lots. Existing shops on the port, however, fetched far higher rental fees. The average value of twenty-one varied rental contracts drawn up by the duke's agents through the notary Juppin between July and December 1640 was sixteen *livres*. The total annual value of these allotments, forming only a portion of the duke's entire income from the estate, was 337.5 *livres*. Individual contracts ranged from a low of half a *livre* for a garden plot to 100 *livres* for two adjacent boutiques on the "grande rive," the busiest stone quay of La Rochelle's harbor.

To increase his rental return over the medium- and long-term, Saint-Simon shrewdly required leaseholders for vacant ground to pledge a certain minimum investment in their properties as a condition of the contract. These investment obligations for renters went as high as 2,000 *livres* over the course of one lease.[30] Investors regularly committed themselves to outlays of 200 *livres* or more to enhance the value of Saint-Simon's holdings in La Rochelle. Renters obeyed ducal orders to present documentation of their building expenses at all renewals of their lease. In some cases, leaseholders performed these duties in the presence of the duke himself. On at least two documented occasions, Claude de Saint-Simon, duke and peer of the realm, sat in Jean Juppin's spartan notary office, personally concluding rental deals with his plebeian tenants.[31]

---

[29] See for examples, ADCM, 3 E 1772, fols. 247v, 248v, 250v, 256v, and 268v; and ADCM, 3 E 1773, fols. 37r-v, 128r-v, and 161v. In 1640 and 1641, between July and December, Saint-Simon's agents, at a minimum, drew up a rental contract every week. Often, five or six would be concluded simultaneously.

[30] See AN, P 2907, records of the Parisian *Chambre des Comptes* relevant to the fief St. Louis. These records include a lease dated 19 September 1640 drawn up by the rochelais notary Juppin between Saint-Simon and Pierre Burtet, a rochelais merchant. This agreement for the lease of vacant building ground in the parish of St. Nicolas obligates Burtet to invest 2,000 *livres* "afin que la rente et cens soyent plus assurez."

[31] See, for examples, ADCM, 3 E 1773, fols. 189r-190v for rentals organized in 1646 between Saint-Simon and a local innkeeper and between the duke and the poor widow of a local sword maker.

By these tactics, the duke de Saint-Simon became a driving force in the urban redevelopment of La Rochelle. An aristocrat, fiercely loyal to the reigning sovereign despite his exile to the provinces, exercised decisive control over the enfeoffment of rochelais civic space. The *ville neuve* quarter, site of the manor for Saint-Simon's fief, rapidly became an important locus of the city's Counter-Reformation.

At the end of the 1628 siege, the king evicted local Protestants from all of their temples inside the city and donated these structures to returning Catholic orders. The king accorded surviving Calvinist ministers and congregants the right to erect one new church and cemetery but stipulated that this complex must be sited in the *ville neuve* quarter within the confines of the land grant made to Saint-Simon. This royal instruction denied rochelais Protestants permanent ownership of any land for church or burial ground and confined them to the status of temporary leaseholders at the pleasure of the crown and its immediate vassals. In September 1636, the royal fiscal officer charged with the local investiture of the duc de Saint-Simon as seigneur of the fief St. Louis, duly instructed senior pastors representing La Rochelle's surviving Protestants that their congregation would be fully liable for paying Saint-Simon an annual rent of thirty *livres* for their church and cemetery property plus all "droits feodaulx" customarily owed by tenants on noble estates in Aunis.[32] This judgment overrode the penurious Calvinists' vehement protests that the king's "gift" of this tract to the congregation exempted them from payment of such dues.

The vulnerability of the last Protestant temple in La Rochelle sensed by its defenders in 1636 was borne out in the persecution of Huguenots preceding revocation of the Edict of Nantes. Saint-Simon's agents made no attempts to stop repeated vandalism of the Protestant temple, presumably committed by vindictive local Catholics, and allowed the entire structure to be razed to the ground by a Catholic wrecking crew in 1686. The king installed La Rochelle's new general hospital on the former site of the Calvinists' temple. This asylum centralized local poor relief, med-

---

[32] AN, TT 263B, fols. 17-22. Sentence of 22 September 1636 rendered in La Rochelle by Nicholas Mandat, "conseiller du Roi, maître ordinaire en sa Chambre des Comptes."

ical care, and police of the vagrant under the aegis of Catholic townsmen and Catholic religious orders. These authorities working concertedly later implanted the convent of the Dames Blanches for penitent prostitutes in the *ville neuve* neighborhood. Barracks for troops of the king's rochelais garrison also occupied the new quarter. The embellishment of this permanent military camp with standardized, multi-story neo-classical buildings and a large paved parade ground made it one of the grandest landmarks in early modern La Rochelle.

Saint-Simon's strict estate management paid off handsomely allowing his son and heir to command high fees at auction for the privilege of collecting rents and seigneurial dues from the property. Eager bidders paid more than 6,000 *livres* per year for these fee farms between 1700 and 1717.[33] As late as 1742, the descendants of the first duke Saint-Simon, led by his son, Louis, successfully defended their preeminent right to collect vassalage fees from residents on ancestral lands encircling La Rochelle granted to the family by Louis XIII 114 years earlier.[34] For more than a century, noble feudatories of the French king meticulously supervised punitive alterations in the topography of power at La Rochelle mandated by the crown. From the ground up, grids of aristocratic privilege now encumbered the civic space of the last free French town.

## 3. *The Catholicizing of Municipal Government After 1628*

Louis XIII defined key institutions of new civic administration for La Rochelle in a royal edict delivered to the city in November 1628.[35] A new royal *intendant de justice* with a standard three-year term of office and jurisdiction over La Rochelle and the provinces of Saintonge and Aunis from the Loire to the Gironde was created.[36] The king preserved the royal presidial court in La Rochelle

---

[33] See AN, M 536, "Titres généalogiques de Saint-Simon," Dossier 2, Nos. 79-85, "Baux de Fief St. Louis."

[34] AN, M 536, Dossier 2, *arrêt* of the *conseil d'état* dated 14 August 1742 confirming *lods et ventes* from rochelais properties owing to Louis de Saint-Simon.

[35] BMLR, 2745c, "Déclaration du Roy sur la réduction de la ville de La Rochelle en son obéissance."

[36] The king's intendant was ordered to "avoir l'oeil à l'observation de nos

and ordered it to supervise the administration of municipal justice previously handled independently by committees of town
councilmen. The new intendant was charged with effecting this
transfer of judicial power. Major criminal cases previously heard
in the mayor's court, and now potentially subversive of renewed
royal authority, were henceforward to be tried before the presidial. To handle the extra work, the king created six new judge-
ships on the presidial court and appointed loyal Catholics to fill
them.[37]

Despite the presidial's expanded legal purview over the city, the
old mayoral court was retained and reorganized by the crown.
The king's edict of pacification provided for a new municipal
police court modeled upon the older urban magistracy. Like its
predecessor, the new civic tribunal had primary jurisdiction over
ordinary civil and criminal cases involving the citizenry to include
disturbances of the peace, domestic disputes, and violations of
municipal ordinances. Law enforcement at this level now became
the responsibility of the royal intendant's subordinates: two magistrates of the presidial appointed annually with the crown's
endorsement as *commissaires de police*, aided by four *conseillers de
police* chosen by royal agents from among the Catholic bourgeoisie
of the city, and four *procureurs de police* also selected by the king's
men from among trustworthy Catholic residents. *Commissaires* and
*conseillers de police* had the independent authority to judge cases
brought before them and to sentence offenders. The new municipal police court swiftly became operational in 1629 with a full
slate of officers and a meeting schedule of two sessions per week.[38]

---

ordonnances, exercice de la justice en toutes functions, soulagement de notre
peuple, et à tout ce qui concerne notre service et l'execution de nos ordonnances, suivant les commissions que nous leur ferons expedier," *ibid.*, 16.

[37] The names and terms of office for La Rochelle's new police authorities are
listed in the post-1628 registers of municipal judicial administration now conserved in the municipal archives of La Rochelle. See AMLR, *Recueil* 360, E Suppl.
292 (FF 17), E Suppl. 293 (FF 18), E Suppl. 294 (FF 19), E Suppl. 295 (FF 20),
E Suppl. 296 (FF 21), E Suppl. 297 (FF 22), E Suppl. 303 (FF 28), E Suppl. 305
(FF 30), E Suppl. 306 (FF 31), and E Suppl. 307 (FF 32). Information from
these sources can be augmented with data drawn from various civic histories of
the era, see, in particular the "Annales de La Rochelle," written by Raphael
Colin, a Protestant member of La Rochelle's presidial court (BMLR, MS 153).
This chronicle is a rich source of information about the offices and careers of
local police officials after 1628.

[38] AMLR, *Recueil* 360, "Ordonnances et proclamations 1629-1633."

However, by 1634, the press of business was so great that the court frequently met daily.[39]

The *conseillers* initially served staggered, two-year terms of office with two of the four men being replaced annually, assuring some continuity of personnel in municipal police work. After 1632, *conseillers* began to be appointed for a single one-year term. Veterans of the office occasionally served longer to familiarize new men with the duties of office. Among the *procureurs de police*, who made two rounds of the city every week, much longer service was the norm. For example, one of the first *procureurs* appointed in 1629 completed twelve annual terms of service. A colleague, first appointed in 1632, served for another eleven years. Other *procureurs* from local Catholic families amassed four to six years of experience, gaining a knowledge of the city essential to police it effectively.

Recognizing La Rochelle's undamaged economic potential, the king chose to preserve the old commercial tribunal designed to expedite adjudication of disputes between merchants trading in the city. However, all past members of this vital mercantile court were turned out of office and the king reserved the right to appoint new magistrates for the next three years. This court was to be composed of a senior judge, two *consuls*, and eight *conseillers* drawn from among local Catholic businessmen and jurists acceptable to the crown.[40]

By his edict of November 1628, the king also reserved the right to establish any other administrative or judicial institutions in La Rochelle that circumstances or the advice of his agents warranted.[41] Among these bodies should be counted a board of eleven *syndics* and *commissaires* handling the more mundane tasks of municipal administration. The five *syndics* were apparently selected annually by the Catholic residents of each parish. The six *commissaires* were elected at a public assembly in the presidial court's chambers where townsmen voted in a manner to insure that one *commissaire* was always chosen from among the magistrates of the presidial court, one *commissaire* from the royal *élus* supervising col-

---

[39] See AMLR, E Suppl. 292 (FF 17), fols. 10v-31v, where a "multitude d'affaires" causes municipal jurists to hold court sessions every day.

[40] BMLR, MS 98, fols. 165r-v, "Matricule generalle des juges, consuls et conseillers...extraict du livre des nominations."

[41] "Déclaration du Roi sur la réduction de la ville de La Rochelle," 12.

lection of the *taille* newly imposed on the city, one from the *avo-cats* and one from the *procureurs* accredited to plead in the presidial court, and two from among the merchants of the city.[42] This convoluted system did occasionally allow a surviving Protestant from the presidial or merchant community to serve as a *commissaire*, but was clearly designed to produce a consistent Catholic majority, dominated by royal jurists and lay Catholic parish headmen, for handling all the routine business of civic administration.[43]

In the weeks immediately following La Rochelle's capitulation, the king created a new, multi-tiered system of municipal government and law enforcement intended to "excise the sources of evil and range the city and its inhabitants under our obedience in such a manner that the troubles which proceeded from them will never again have a means of rebirth."[44] Who did the king choose to fill these new offices and carry out the ambitious task he assigned to them?

Since only a small and dwindling number of Protestants were active in post-siege town government, pursuit of an answer to this question requires investigation of the long-ignored social and political history of the Catholic community of La Rochelle.[45] During the era of Calvinist hegemony in La Rochelle, local Catho-

---

[42] The "Annales" of Raphael Colin remain the best source of information about the electoral system by which *commissaires* were chosen, see fols. 123-124, 134, and 142. The election and work of the *syndics* are poorly documented. Surviving legal papers generated by lawsuits in which the *syndics* were involved suggest that *syndics* were all Catholic parish officers collecting church rents, overseeing repairs to church buildings, and reporting breaches of municipal ordinances, see BMLR, MS 308, fols. 37r-38v. This cadre of new civic officials helped to advance the confessionalization of town government desired by the crown.

[43] The wealthy Protestant merchant, Antoine Allaire, was among the *commissaires* elected in 1630. The Protestant Helie Mocquay represented *procureurs* of the presidial on the board of *syndics* and *commissaires* in 1631. Also serving as a *commissaire* in 1631 was Raphael Colin, Protestant representative from among the officers of the presidial, see Colin, "Annales," fol. 123. The presence of Allaire, Colin, and Mocquay on the board of *syndics* and *commissaires* shows that rochelais Protestants were not uniformly excluded from municipal and judicial office after the siege of 1628.

[44] "Déclaration du Roi sur la réduction de la ville de La Rochelle," 2.

[45] There currently exists no in-depth study of the Catholics of La Rochelle who assumed control of the city after 1628. The social and political histories of local Catholic families in the years immediately before and after the 1628 siege remain completely unknown despite abundant sources of documentary evidence in La Rochelle.

lics were beleaguered and distrusted members of the urban community. Truce accords punctuating the French Wars of Religion gave Catholics the right to live and exercise their religion even in strongholds of Protestantism like La Rochelle. Despite the destruction of nearly all the city's Catholic churches in the early 1560's, the Catholic cult was openly practiced in La Rochelle from January 1571 to September 1572, from September to December 1576, from 1577 to 1585, from August 1599 to May 1621, from January 1624 to April 1625, and from the spring of 1627 until the end of September 1627. According to pastor Merlin, reestablishment of the Catholic mass in the parish Church of St. Marguerite in the summer of 1599 caused grumbling amongst the city's Protestants but local "Papists" were allowed to continue their services relatively unmolested.[46]

From the surviving parish records of St. Marguerite, Louis Pérouas has fixed local Catholic baptisms at over 100 per year during the two decades preceding the siege of 1628.[47] Pérouas estimates that, by 1610, approximately 5,000 Catholics inhabited La Rochelle. The bulk of this community comprised artisans and laborers living in the popular quarter of Notre Dame de Cougnes. However, Catholic families residing in La Rochelle around 1600 could also claim at least three *conseillers* of the presidial court, three *élus* charged with administration of the *taille* in the surrounding countryside, several *avocats* and *procureurs* to the presidial, and a number of wealthy merchants engaged in international commerce. Pérouas notes that rochelais Catholics quickly recovered from the siege of 1628. Pushed upward by substantial Catholic immigration to the conquered city, the number of Catholic baptisms per year finally surpassed the Protestant figure in 1630 and increased steadily as the total Catholic population of La Rochelle climbed to over 10,000 by 1635.[48] A resurgent Catholic

---

[46] BMLR, MS 161, Jacques Merlin, "Diaire ou recueil des choses plus mémorables qui se sont passées en ceste ville," fols. 380r-382v.

[47] Pérouas, "Sur la démographie rochelaise," 1132-1133.

[48] *Ibid.*, 1133-1134. My own investigation of marriages recorded in the parish registers of rochelais Catholic churches shows an average of over sixty per year from 1603 to 1620. In 1629, total Catholic marriages increased to 309, spurred by the conversion and remarriage of Protestant widows with Catholic newcomers to the city. Although Catholic marriage rates dropped off slightly from this peak, the average annual number of marriages remained well above pre-siege figures. See the marriage registers for the Church of St. Marguerite and affiliated parishes, BMLR, MSS 251, 254, and 255.

population, dominated economically and socially by old Catholic families long resident in the city, offered the crown ready candidates, untainted by prior municipal political activity, for the new offices of civic administration.

Before leaving La Rochelle on 18 November 1628, Louis XIII appointed *maître* Gaspard Cougnet, *Sieur* de la Thuillerie, as his *intendant de justice* for the city.[49] Cougnet, in turn, appointed two senior Catholic members of La Rochelle's presidial court, Jacques Fouchier, *Sieur* de Sauzay, *lieutenant particulier* and *assesseur civil* of the court, and Nicolas Bertinaud, a *conseiller* of that tribunal, to serve as *commissaires de justice* on the municipal police court, overseeing the daily governance of La Rochelle with the aid of the four new *conseillers* and four new *procureurs de police* also chosen by the crown.

How the process of selecting new town officers actually worked from year to year after the inception of the new civic regime remains obscure. Few surviving documents in La Rochelle pertain to this operation and I have been unable to track down records of explicit deliberations on this subject between councillors of the king in Paris. The best rochelais source of information on this topic remains Raphael Colin, the Protestant *lieutenant particulier criminel* of the presidial court, who recorded in his "Annales de La Rochelle" for 1629 the intendant Cougnet's appointment of the *commissaires de justice*.[50] In 1630, Colin noted the delivery of a "billet" from the king containing the "nominations" of two other presidial members selected to serve new terms as *commissaires de justice*.[51] In late 1632, Colin remarked the departure to Paris of La Rochelle's new intendant, François de Villemontée. In January of 1633, de Villemontée returned to his post in La Rochelle carrying the king's "billet" naming the new *commissaires*.[52] In December 1635, according to Colin, Villemontée himself named the new *commissaires* for the coming year. The local royal intendant evidently became a key figure acting to select and recommend to the king townsmen suitable for the new posts of civic adminis-

---

[49] "Déclaration du Roi sur la réduction de la ville de La Rochelle," 16. See also Guillaudeau, "Diaire," 381. The *Sieur* de la Thuillerie was a member of the *conseil d'état* and a *maître des requêtes* of the king's household.

[50] Colin, "Annales," fol. 120.

[51] *Ibid.*, fol. 122.

[52] *Ibid.*, fols. 130-132.

tration. Who did the intendants and their agents advance to fill these positions?

Appendix 1 lists the names of all Rochelais known to have served as *commissaires, conseillers,* and *procureurs* for the municipal police court between 1629 and 1649. The local merchants' tribunal retained by Louis XIII but swiftly restaffed at royal insistence with local Catholics became a second key legal institution dispensing justice in the urban community after 1628. Appendix 2 gives annual lists of all *juges, consuls,* and *conseillers* of the commercial court chosen between 1629 and 1650. Careful comparison of Appendices 1 and 2, especially for the decade 1629-1638, shows that many new offices of town government were recurrently filled by the same men or by townsmen sharing the same surname from among a small coterie of families. Appendix 1 reveals interesting patterns of recruitment among the *commissaires, conseillers,* and *procureurs de police* charged with municipal law enforcement after 1628. During the fourteen years for which information survives on the personnel of the new town police court, a total of 140 offices had to be filled. The occupants of 123 of these offices are known to me by name. A total of only fifty-nine individuals held the 123 offices whose occupants are known, indicating that repeated service by the same police officials was common.

The new royal intendant, Gaspard Cougnet, carefully exercised his authority to choose the *commissaires de police* by initially appointing Catholic jurists like Jacques Fouchier and Nicolas Bertinaud, notable for long prior service on La Rochelle's presidial court.[53] Bertinaud's reappointment in 1630 reinforced this practice and subsequent *intendants de justice* continued to select experienced Catholic members of the presidial as *commissaires.* From 1629 to 1634, at least one of the *commissaires* was always an established resident of the city and well-known member of its judicial community. Beginning in 1634, Catholic *conseillers* of the presidial court, newly appointed by the king in November 1628, were chosen more regularly to fill both offices of *commissaire de police.*

This influx of new men unfamiliar with La Rochelle and its inhabitants, a factor potentially threatening effective royal admin-

---

[53] Cougnet's 1629 appointment of Fouchier and Bertinaud, probably at royal behest, as *commissaires* insured some continuity in the police of La Rochelle. Both men had been influential members of the *siège présidial* for over a decade, see Colin, "Annales," fol. 120.

istration of the city, was counterbalanced by the presence of established Catholic townsmen who continued to dominate the offices
of *conseiller de police* and *procureur de police* long into the 1640's.
Among the *conseillers*, members of old rochelais Catholic families
like the Auboyneaus, Bigotteaus, and Gaigneurs served repeatedly. As Appendix 1 makes clear, the offices of *procureur de police*
changed hands even less frequently. *Procureurs* were usually long-
time residents of the city holding other minor judicial posts and
sinecures in the local bureaucracy of royal administration, men
like Jacques Alleaume, *huissier* of the presidial court, *huissier-audi-
encier* of the *taille* collection court, and the king's inspector of
roads for Aunis and Saintonge (who apparently served continuously as a *procureur* from 1631 to 1649), the royal notary François
Apurillaud (eleven years of service), and Michel Maigre, *sergent
du roi* and *archer de la marine* (six years service).[54]

Apurillaud solidified his ties to the new ruling regime of La
Rochelle by becoming one of the duke de Saint-Simon's most
important tenants within the fief St. Louis, renting large tracts of
open ground and committing himself to heavy investments here
enhancing the net worth of the duke's estate.[55] While outsiders
gained senior offices in La Rochelle's bureaucracy of justice, small
numbers of established residents, through their domination of the
municipal police court, continued to play a crucial role in the
day-to-day interpretation and application of the law. These local
agents of civic justice contributed vital, experienced manpower to
the remaking of La Rochelle in accord with the dictates of crown,
church, and aristocracy.

Townsmen belonging to a small group of old local Catholic families also dominated La Rochelle's newly reconstituted merchants'
tribunal. Between 1629 and 1650, a total of 242 offices had to be
filled on the merchants' court. Archival sources identify the men
who held 219 (90%) of these posts.[56] As illustrated in Appendix
2, a total of only seventy-nine individuals filled the 219 offices
whose occupants are known, showing that a small cohort of preponderantly Catholic townsmen also controlled this tribunal
through recurrent service. Scrutiny of Appendix 2 indicates that

---

[54] AMLR, E 293 (FF 18), fol. 1r and E 303 (FF 28), fol. 1r.
[55] For examples of these rental contracts see ADCM, 3 E 1772, fols. 256v and
275r.
[56] BMLR, MS 98, fols. 165r-v and 166r-v.

members of the Auboyneau, Barreau, Bigotteau, Feniou, Gaigneur, Labourier, Mondot, Picaudeau, Thibault, and Venette families frequently became officers of the court. Indeed, from 1629
to 1650, members of these ten intermarried Catholic families held
places on the court seventy-seven times, controlling by themselves
at least a third of all offices available on this tribunal over the
period examined.

Surveying the rosters of officeholders in the new regime of
rochelais town government, one repeatedly encounters members
of the same prominent Catholic families serving interchangeably
as parish *syndics, commissaires* representing urban corporations in
the daily administration of the city, judges of the merchants' court,
and municipal police agents. In the years immediately following
La Rochelle's capitulation, the crown relied heavily on the city's
old Catholic clans as a source of new and trustworthy civic officials. This policy effectively marginalized surviving Protestant
magistrates, but also favored the quick reestablishment of dense
networks of kinsmen embedded in the apparatus of town government.

When juxtaposed with specific family information from notarial and church records, the lists of municipal officeholders after
1628 reveal complex networks of kinfolk extending throughout
the new administration of the city. These webs of kinsmen radi-
ated outward from only five major Catholic families interlinked
by ties of marriage, godparentage, guardianship, and common
commercial enterprise. Present in La Rochelle for generations,
the Auboyneaus, Bigotteaus, Gaigneurs, Mondots, and Thibaults
proceeded to supplant their old Protestant rivals, exercise multiple public offices under a rigorously Catholic regime of town government, and remake urban politics with the support of an appre-
ciative and indulgent hierarchy of local royal officers.

Complete citation of the myriad documents demonstrating the
longevity and multiplicity of the personal and professional ties
connecting the new authorities of La Rochelle would only tire and
confuse the reader. As illustrative examples, Figures 15, 16, and
17 present simplified schematic views of crucial family ties linking the Catholic occupants of powerful royal and municipal offices
in La Rochelle after 1628. Figure 15 profiles Bigotteau family
members and their emplacement in the social and political world

of Catholic La Rochelle.[57] Figure 16 shows political connections radiating out from two lines of the Catholic Gaigneur family.[58] Figure 17 presents a partial reconstruction of the personal and political connections linking one generation of Mondot brothers to other key Catholic clans governing the city after 1628.[59]

Comparison of these figures shows the control over vital offices of post-siege municipal government exercised by several generations of three intricately linked rochelais Catholic clans. The political influence of the Bigotteaus, Gaigneurs, and Mondots was amplified by the variety of offices held by intermarried members of these families. Important personal and professional links had long existed between newly influential Catholic jurists of the presidial court, the Catholic merchants now regularly staffing the city's commercial tribunal and the Catholic townsmen now responsible for urban police work. The entire governing bureaucracy created in the city by royal command was permeated by officeholders known and accustomed to working with one another as blood relations, fictive kin, and commercial partners.

Concerted economic activity was common among the new Catholic officeholders linked by blood and marriage. For example, Jean Mondot became the primary investor in a consortium of Catholic merchants, operating since the late sixteenth century, that shipped grain to Italy, Portugal, and Spain. Other partners in this enterprise included René Mondot, Pierre Bouildron, Pierre Feniou, and Mathurin Gaigneur.[60] Sales and trades of highly valued land near La Rochelle occupied kinsmen of the inter-

---

[57] Sources for Figure 15 include: ADCM, 3 E 256, fols. 138v-140v, 3 E 1287, (1637) 20 June 1637, and 3 E 1720, fols. 489v-490v; BMLR, MS 251, 27 July 1591 and fol. 27r; MS 252, fols. 173r and 216r; and MS 254, fols. 10r and 43v.

[58] Sources for Figure 16: ADCM, 3 E 217, fols. 115r and 187r. See also the detailed family wedding contracts recorded by the notary Combaud, 3 E 1251 21 May 1615, 12 December 1617, 21 April 1618, and 13 July 1619; and 3 E 1252, 30 January 1633. See also BMLR, MS 251 (1600), fols. 28v and 42r, (1602), fols. 74r, 75r, 76v, and 77r, (1603), fol. 84r, (1604), fol. 114r, (1607), fols. 145r, 149r, 152r, 156r, and 157r; Ms. 252, (1605) fol. 18r, (1612), fols. 111r and 143r, (1614), fol. 187r, (1615), fol. 268r, and (1616), fol. 224r; MS 354, fols. 1v and 7r;, and MS 255, 31 January 1632.

[59] Sources for Figure 17 include: ADCM, 3 E 187, fols. 415v-416r; 3 E 195, fols. 363v-364r; 3 E 216, fol. 22v;, 3 E 217, fol. 219r; and 3 E 1290, fols. 48r-49r; BMLR, MS 251 (1606), fol. 135v, (1607), fols. 150v and 152r, and (1608), fol. 175r: MS 252, fols. 18r, 37r, 66r, and 143r; and MS 254, fol. 1v.

[60] See ADCM, 3 E 203, fol. 122v and 3 E 216 (1610) fols. 16r, 36r, 49v, and 163r. The operating capital of this group exceeded 20,000 *livres* in 1610.

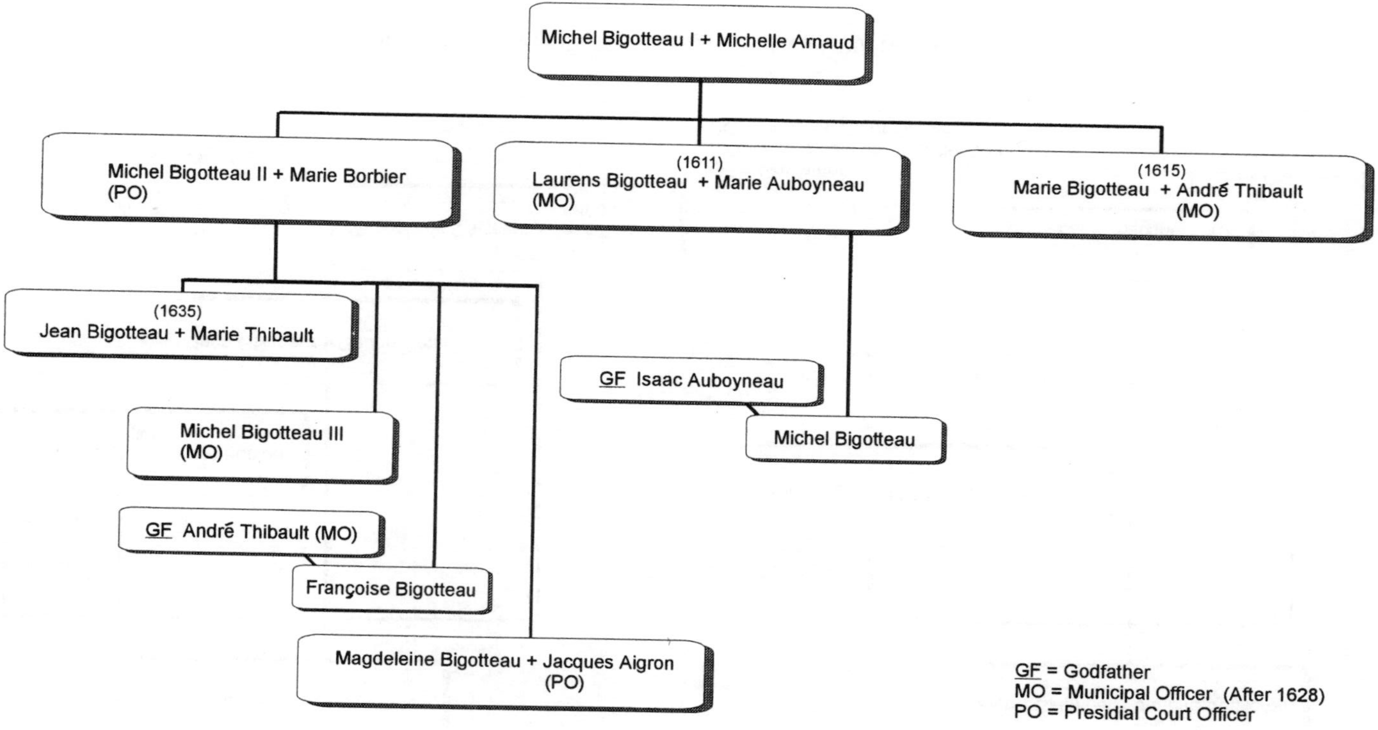

Figure 15. Sociopolitical Connections of Catholic Bigotteau Family

GF = Godfather
MO = Municipal Officer (After 1628)
PO = Presidial Court Officer

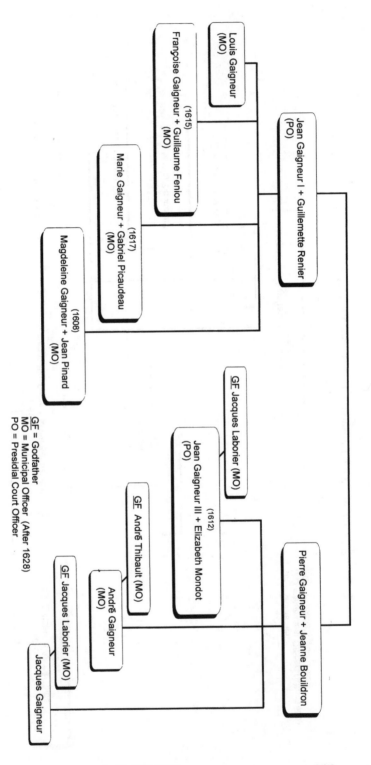

Figure 16. Sociopolitical Connections of Catholic Gaigneur Family

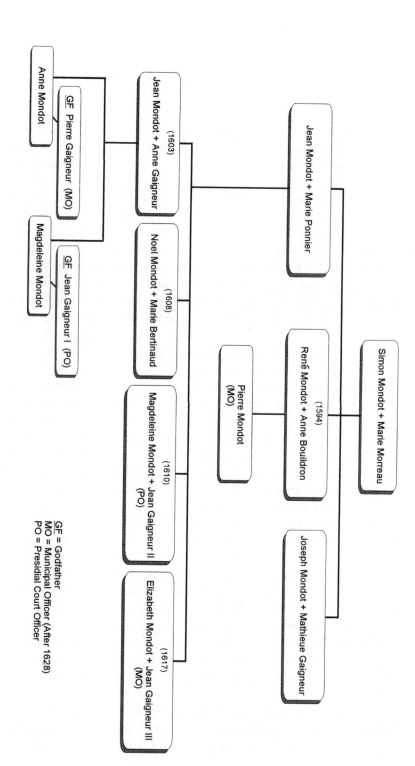

Figure 17. Sociopolitical Connections of Catholic Mondot Family

GF = Godfather
MO = Municipal Officer (After 1628)
PO = Presidial Court Officer

married Gaigneur and Laborier families throughout the fall of
1615.[61] In 1630, Isaac Auboyneau and Gabriel Picaudeau put up
4,000 *livres* to buy the right to collect for three years all ground
rents in La Rochelle and rural fees due to the ancient *commanderie* of the Knights Templar.[62] In this transaction, the Catholics
Auboyneau and Picaudeau acquired the exact property rights previously exploited for economic and political profit by the notable
Protestant rebel leader Pierre Bernardeau. However, among new
Catholic municipal officials, only Auboyneau and Picaudeau attempted to amass the diverse commercial interests in multiple
urban neighborhoods by which earlier Calvinist political leaders
decisively influenced civic affairs.

The presence of senior members of the presidial court among
the *commissaires de justice* and magistrates of the commercial tribunal appointed after 1628 indicates that royal intendants, alien
to the city, sought to retain and promote experienced, trustworthy jurists thoroughly familiar with the community and capable
of aiding outsiders to govern the place effectively in the king's
name. A smoothly functioning municipal bureaucracy, staffed by
cooperative townsmen who knew the city, its neighborhoods, and
its inhabitants, was necessary to enforce royal edicts and bring to
light violations of civil and religious laws more easily hidden from
outsiders. This was a situation especially favorable to the emplacement of local, established Catholic kin groups in the new administration of the city.

Evidence available in Catholic parish registers, in the professional papers of rochelais notaries serving the Catholic community, in the rosters of post-siege officeholders, and in chronicles
of city government written by contemporaries suggests that royal
agents accepted family solidarities as conducive to the work of
town government and requisite for a vital *esprit de corps* among the
new municipal administrators. Royal victory in the siege of 1628
did not make the importance of kinsmen in rochelais town government a thing of the past. At the level of day-to-day control of
the community, a familial system for the exercise of police authority nearly identical to that operating under prior regimes of town
government remained in place, only the names and religious affil-

[61] ADCM, 3 E 1251, 28 October 1615.
[62] ADCM, 3 E 1723, 17 April 1630.

iation of its related actors had changed. Accidents of birth rather than proven administrative skills largely determined the personnel of rochelais civic government for decades after 1628.

In his personal history of La Rochelle, Raphael Colin, a member of the presidial court until 1647, noted how frequently royal *intendants de justice* relied on experienced Catholic members of the presidial to fill important posts in the new regime of civic administration. Presidial members selected for such service worked diligently to place their kinsmen in subordinate positions of authority, maintaining the familial quality of rochelais town government well into the seventeenth century. Indeed, candidates known to royal officials specifically for the number of their immediate relations capable of filling key positions of town government advanced to civic officeholding in greater numbers than less well-connected aspirants.

The expanded responsibilities of the presidial ensured that this institution and its personnel received special attention from the royal intendant of justice. By taking advantage of that attention to recommend and promote kinsmen, Catholic jurists of the presidial controlled a vital avenue for the advancement of their own interests and relations while in service to the crown.

The political "system" as outlined above existed in La Rochelle from the outset of the new civic regime. In 1629, the first members of the presidial court to become *commissaires de justice* were Jacques Fouchier and Nicolas Bertinaud, senior Catholic magistrates of the presidial court. In 1630, Bertinaud again won appointment as a *commissaire*. Serving under Bertinaud as *conseillers de police* in 1630 were Louis Gaigneur, a *procureur* to the presidial court and one of Nicolas Bertinaud's oldest Catholic colleagues in the local judicial bureaucracy, and Gabriel Barreau, a merchant. Nicolas Bertinaud was well-acquainted with the Gaigneurs both professionally and personally. The Gaigneur family had not only supplied Bertinaud with some of his oldest colleagues in the rochelais judicial community, but also was related to him through intermarriage with the Catholic Mondot family. On 16 November 1608, Noel Mondot married *dame* Marie Bertinaud, daughter of Nicolas Bertinaud.[63] Mathurin Gaigneur, uncle by marriage to Noel Mondot, joined the wedding festivities as a member of the

---

[63] BMLR, MS 254, fol. 1v.

groom's company. In 1610, Mathurin Gaigneur's own son, the *pro-cureur* to the presidial Jean Gaigneur II, married Magdeleine Mondot, sister to Noel Mondot.[64] Nicolas Bertinaud's legally trained and experienced close kinsmen among the Gaigneurs provided him with ideal candidates to staff key judicial offices in the new town government. The Gaigneurs' own relations could also be tapped to fill subordinate positions in municipal administration. In 1629 and 1630, Jacques Laborier served as the chief magistrate of the merchants' tribunal in La Rochelle. Laborier was the husband of Marie Gaigneur.[65] Laborier's own sister was the wife of Mathurin Gaigneur, and Laborier himself became the godfather for two children of his brother-in-law, Pierre Gaigneur.[66]

*Conseillers* to the merchants' tribunal in 1629 and 1630 included: Thomas Gaigneur; Thomas' cousin, Louis Gaigneur; Jean Pinard; Gabriel Picaudeau; and Guillaume Feniou.[67] Pinard, Picaudau, and Feniou all had previously married sisters of Louis Gaigneur and were thus brothers-in-law and kinsmen to the Gaigneur men on the court. Gabriel Barreau, *conseiller* on the merchants' tribunal in 1629, joined Louis Gaigneur as a *conseiller de police* in 1630. Barreau had long been a neighbor of Louis Gaigneur in the parish of Perrot, owned a large financial interest in the house next door to Gaigneur's, and later served with Gaigneur as a *syndic* of Perrot's parish church.[68]

From a group of Catholic kinsmen dominated by the Gaigneurs, the crown obtained an initial cadre of officeholders recurrently employed in policing the city and adjudicating cases tried before the municipal and commercial courts. Even after the Catholic population of La Rochelle had expanded to more than twice its pre-siege level, the king's men continued to call upon members of the same limited number of wealthy Catholic kin groups for help in running La Rochelle.

Like most of the Protestant political leaders they supplanted, Catholic officeholders in the municipal bureaucracy were also

---

[64] *Ibid.*, fol. 7r.

[65] ADCM, 3 E 1251, 17 May 1615.

[66] BMLR, MS 251, (1604) fol. 114 and (1608) fol. 145r; and MS 254, fol. 7r. Jacques Laborier also exchanged services as a godparent with his brothers-in-law, see BMLR, MS 251 (1607) fol. 149r and MS 252, (1614) fol. 187r.

[67] BMLR, MS 98, fols. 165r-v. See also ADCM, 3 E 1251, 10 May 1615, 12 December 1617, and 21 April 1618.

[68] BMLR, 3 E 1252 (15 August 1633) and 3 E 1292, fols. 26r-v.

respected chieftains in their city parishes. As long ago as 1564, Simon Mondot, patriarch of the Mondot clan, had served as chief administrator of the All Saints lay Catholic confraternity of La Rochelle.[69] In June of 1616, Jacques Laborier, Noel Mondot, and six others served together as *fabriqueurs* of the five ancient Catholic parish churches in La Rochelle. These lay parochial officers had responsibility for the maintenance of all ecclesiastical property and collection of ground rents and other obligations owed to each Catholic congregation. That month, the *fabriqueurs* met with Isaac Auboyneau, Louis Bigotteau, Nicolas Bertinaud, Mathurin Gaigneur, Thomas Gaigneur, André Thibault, and Jacques Thibault, senior representatives of each parish, to discuss collection of rents owed to Catholic religious institutions in the city and to agree on proper disbursement of monies received.[70]

In August of 1634, Jean de l'Escalle, *lieutenant criminel* of the presidial court and now co-commander of the new Catholic city militia, boosted Isaac Auboyneau's local notoriety by choosing him to be lieutenant of the militia company assembled in the parish of St. Nicolas.[71] Michel Maigre, a *procureur de police* for the city between 1633 and 1639, also became known to fellow residents of the Perrot quarter as one of the 1636 *fabriqueurs* for the parish Church of St. Jean. In 1638, Isaac Auboyneau used his neighborhood influence to help raise a special levy of 6,000 *livres* from the Rochelais for subsidizing the operation of the king's armies.[72] As late as 1644, Louis Gaigneur, son of Jean Gaigneur I, was carrying on the family tradition of superintending the finances and real estate of the parish Church of St. Jean du Perrot as a *fabriqueur* of the congregation.[73]

One contrast, however, should be drawn between the new Catholic masters of town government and the Protestant notables like Jean Tharay they supplanted. As noted in Chapters 5 and 6, key Calvinist leaders in rochelais urban politics managed to establish supraparochial reputations and popular followings in multiple urban neighborhoods simultaneously. Judging by their family papers preserved in rochelais notarial archives, very few Catholic

---

[69] BMLR, MS 250, fol. 16v.
[70] ADCM, 3 E 1251, 22 June 1616.
[71] Colin, "Annales," fol. 137.
[72] ADCM, 3 E 1288, 3 April 1638.
[73] ADCM, 3 E 1293, fols. 298v-299r.

political actors after 1628 ever amassed similarly extensive interparochial ties of clientage and influence. Catholic town councillors were primarily notables within specific quarters whose long
devotion to the neighborhood parish church neatly delimits the
effective range of their political personae. This stature made them
valuable royal servants but safer, more reliable subordinates. Their
highly endogamous patterns of marrying, godparenting, and business dealing (developed over decades of Protestant persecution)
prevented them from acquiring elaborate networks of personal
influence transcending the borders of urban neighborhoods and
social status groups.

La Rochelle's Catholic leaders lacked the intimate, city-wide
contacts obstreperous Protestant rochelais politicians cultivated
and relied upon to bulwark their collective opposition to outside
authorities. Without such support to fall back on, La Rochelle's
Catholic rulers could hardly play any other role than minions of
the crown. In its exclusiveness, at least, La Rochelle's post-siege
town government resembled more closely the oligarchical *corps de
ville* in place prior to the coup of 1614, a disposition entirely complementing the retrospective methods of governance employed by
the crown to police the old rebel city.

The wives and kinswomen of politically active Catholic townsmen also tried to strengthen their local religious communities.
Records of conversions to Catholicism after 1628 show that Magdeleine Bigotteau, Magdeleine Mondot, and Mondot's daughters,
Magdeleine and Marie Gaigneur, occasionally stood as witnesses
for new converts at ceremonies marking their reception into the
Catholic church.[74] Such work allowed these women to form their
own small clienteles of spiritual godchildren that might be
employed to advance the administrative work and political careers
of their husbands.

The long involvement of male and female Auboyneaus, Bar-
reaus, Bigotteaus, Gaigneurs, Mondots, and Thibaults in conservation and surveillance of neighborhood Catholic communities
augmented the utility of these families to magistrates of the presidial court on whom the crown depended for staffing and operating La Rochelle's post-siege administration. From among these

---

[74] See BMLR, MS 779, "Papier des conversions," fols. 9r, 29r-31v, 35r, 38r-v,
40v, and 41r-v.

interconnected families came the experienced parish vestrymen, jurymen of the merchants' tribunal, competent police inspectors, judges of the municipal police court, and presidial officers who could work in concert to make La Rochelle a pious and obedient town in keeping with the king's expressed wishes. Containment and reduction of the local Protestant community were tasks integral to completion of this mission. How did the new governors of La Rochelle handle this spiritual combat?

## 4. Prosecuting the Counter-Reformation in La Rochelle

Despite the fact that Bourbon monarchs persistently and effectively combated Protestantism in their realm, historical scholarship on the French Counter-Reformation remains sparse. Few investigations have been mounted to explore in detail the effects of this campaign for Catholic orthodoxy on the politics and culture of French towns.[75] This is especially incongruous for at least two reasons. First, because a leading specialist on the French Counter-Reformation has concluded that "French reforming catholicism was essentially a "bourgeois religion" employing "legalistic definitions" of the sacred and profane and "invoking authority to support a highly ascetic and demanding conception of true religion."[76] And second, because one of the most spectacular and

---

[75] Among the rare studies of the French urban Counter-Reformation are Robert Sauzet, *Contre-Réforme et réforme catholique en Bas-Languedoc au XVIIe siècle: le diocèse de Nîmes de 1598 à 1694*, (Brussels, 1979); Louis Châtellier, *Tradition chrétienne et renouveau catholique dans le cadre de l'ancien diocèse de Strasbourg 1650-1770*, (Paris, 1981); Philip T. Hoffman, *Church and Community in the Diocese of Lyon 1500-1789*, (New Haven, 1984); Alain Lottin, *Lille, citadelle de la Contre-Réforme? (1598-1668)*, (Lille, 1984); and Robert A. Schneider, *Public Life in Toulouse 1463-1789*, (Ithaca, New York, 1989). Châtellier gives no analysis of how any urban judicial institutions figured in the prosecution of religious reform. Although Sauzet, Hoffman, and Schneider do investigate the participation of urban jurists in the local Counter-Reformation, their focus is primarily on the officers of higher royal courts and their participation in lay confraternities practicing post-Tridentine devotions. The role of municipal courts as agents of the *Contre-Réforme* is not explored. Only Lottin has checked the records of Lille's municipal magistracy to measure this institution's participation in the Counter-Reformation. Unfortunately, the bulk of his information here antedates Lille's annexation by France (1668).

[76] Robin Briggs, *Communities of Belief, Cultural and Social Tension in Early Modern France*, (Oxford, 1989). See in particular chapter 9, "*Idées* and *mentalités*. The case of the catholic reform movement in France," 364-65, 370, and 372.

sustained episodes of the Counter-Reformation in seventeenth-century Europe was a French urban event: the 1628 siege, reduction, and subsequent police by Catholic forces of La Rochelle, formerly the freest city in the kingdom.

Rich contemporary documentation of this struggle permits concerted investigation of the human actors and civic institutions, secular and sacred, responsible for the implementation of the local Counter-Reformation. These sources show us how town Catholics used multiple agencies of town government, integral to La Rochelle's civic identity, in efforts to break their fellow citizens' Calvinist allegiance. Comparison of the day-to-day operation of these institutions under Protestant and Catholic regimes of municipal administration allows us to track changes in the conduct and ethos of communal police brought about by the French Counter-Reformation. The parallel transformations this movement for doctrinal orthodoxy wrought in civic life were as important as—and perhaps more enduring than—the alterations it fostered in the spiritual life of French urbanites. These transformations, emphasizing the individual's sinfulness and personal duty of atonement, undercut the communal and congregational solidarities structuring the old rochelais polity.

At the king's invitation and through the victory of his siege army, Catholic religious orders returned in force to La Rochelle after 1628. Eleven major companies of the regular clergy reestablished themselves within the city at sites granted by the crown or donated in perpetuity by feudatories like the duke de Saint-Simon.[77] In the provisions of the peace treaty by which the king "reduced La Rochelle to his obedience," the crown confiscated the Protestants' great temple on the city's main square. In anticipation of the structure's conversion to the Catholic cathedral church of the community, the king entrusted the Oratorians with use of the building. As early as 12 July 1628, while the siege still dragged on, the Capuchins, supported by the influential *père* Joseph, received a royal *brevet* entitling them to future use of a large rochelais town house for their base of operations. When this site proved to be too small for the growing company, the duc de

---

[77] The best brief history of this return by regular Catholic clerics to La Rochelle remains the series of articles by François Moisy, see his "Le rétablissement des structures catholiques à La Rochelle, (1628-1648)."

Saint-Simon stepped in and gave the monks more than four acres of property from his rochelais land grant on which to build a new religious house including a large chapel, sacristy, and cloister. The duke exempted the Capuchins from any rents or seigneurial fees on this property forever.[78]

Also by terms of the peace treaty imposed on the city, the Frères de la Charité and the Religieuses Hospitalières gained complete supervisory powers over the male and female inmates of La Rochelle's old municipal hospital, an institution previously under the directorship of Protestant town councilmen like Jean Tharay. Another order of nuns, the Minimes, also benefitted from the king's treaty, receiving more than eight acres of ground just outside the city on which to construct a convent from whence they were continually to watch over the cemetery implanted there for royal troops killed during the siege.

In addition to these grants written into the text of La Rochelle's capitulation, the crown abetted the resettlement in the city by the Recollets, who occupied the old rebel assembly hall of Saint Michel in December 1629; by the Augustins, who reclaimed their *salle* St. Yon previously housing the most politically subversive Calvinist congregation in the city; and by the Jesuits, who through royal letters patent dated December 1629, received free use of La Rochelle's old municipal *collège* and Calvinist seminary. This gift put the Jesuits at odds with the returning Cordeliers whose original convent had been expropriated by the Reformed municipality in 1565 to make room for the Protestant school. Here, again, Saint-Simon worked to mollify feuding religious orders by giving the Cordeliers a large tract of land within his urban seigneurie for the emplacement of their new house.[79] Establishment of a convent for Ursuline nuns in La Rochelle, by the same royal letters of December 1629, reinforced the local influence of their male counterparts, the Jesuits. This sequence of foundations put five post-Tridentine missionary orders of the regular clergy in La Rochelle, organizations committed to articulation and enforcement of the Counter-Reformation.

The reestablishment of Catholic missions in La Rochelle, aptly described by one historian of this process as an "encadrement reli-

---

[78] See AN Q1 120, royal edict of January 1629 ratifying transferral of all rochelais fortification sites to Saint-Simon with the exception of a large plot given by the duke to the Capuchins.

[79] See Moisy, "Le rétablissement," 365.

gieux" of the old rebel commune, had important material consequences reminding citizens of their new subservience to representatives of the first and second estates.[80] By terms of the city's
capitulation, the king permanently assigned 540 *livres* from all
municipal revenues to subsidize the reemplacement of *curés* in the
refurbished parishes in and around La Rochelle.[81] The local chapter of the Oratorians assiduously administered its right to collect
the *dîme* due at a rate of 2.5% on all grains, wines, and salt produced on urban territory. The fee farm for collecting the proceeds of the *dîme* from just the extramural sector of the parish of
Notre Dame de Cougnes brought the Oratorians over 400 *livres*
per year by 1645.[82]

Orders of the regular clergy now in charge of La Rochelle's
civic hospital also became responsible for the collection of all
rents on properties once owned or donated to the institution. The
pursuit of delinquent tenants became complicated because the
vestrymen for every reactivated Catholic parish church in the city
now dusted off ancient rent rolls and demanded that the current
inhabitants of all properties once constituting the church fabric
pay off arrears accumulated over decades of Protestant ascendancy
and repudiation of these debts. The enterprising François Lebre-
ton, one of the Catholic *commissaires de police* in 1634, turned this
treasure hunt into a lucrative business, selling his legal talents and
title search skills to church *fabriqueurs* for one-third of all rents
recovered.[83] The Protestant owners and occupiers of properties
liable for rents due to the parish churches could expect no sympathy from the Catholic magistrates now dominating the local
courts where such cases were argued. The municipal police court
regularly issued orders for massive repayments, threatening recalcitrant Protestant property holders with imprisonment for refusal
to pay. Calvinist merchants using the port now also found themselves obligated to pay small but vexing duties on vegetable oils
and building materials long ago assigned by the crown to the benefit of Catholic parochial institutions.

---

    [80] *Ibid.*, 359.
    [81] "Declaration du roi sur la réduction," 3-4.
    [82] ADCM, 3 E 1294, notarized sales contract for the fee farm dated 21 January
1645.
    [83] ADCM, 3 E 1275 (*liasses* of the notary Combaud, 7 March 1632). See also
Combaud's *registres* for the year 1633, ADCM, 3 E 1253.

John Bosher has recently, and I think rightly, argued for the existence of an important religious connection between the history of La Rochelle after 1628 and the contemporary development of French colonial possessions in North America.[84] Bosher attributes La Rochelle's importance as the main staging area for seventeenth-century French communication and trade with Canada to the fact that the subjection of the rebel city and the French bid for domination of North America were simultaneous, complementary, and intertwined "religious missions" organized and funded primarily by regular Catholic orders like the Jesuits under the direct supervision of devout and powerful courtiers. Increased rochelais Atlantic commerce in the seventeenth century is thus not attributable to indigenous maritime adventurers, but rather to the presence of wealthy, evangelizing outsiders. Bosher contends that La Rochelle was "deliberately and systematically catholicized" in a process beginning even before the city's capitulation in October 1628.[85] To substantiate his assertions, Bosher primarily emphasizes the swelling numbers of regular clergy who flocked to La Rochelle after 1628 and the significant physical expansion of their landholdings within the city. As we have seen, these trends profoundly altered the topographical and material characteristics of La Rochelle's urban environment.

But the impressive success of powerful Catholics in remaking the rochelais townscape was not matched by commensurate transformations worked on the citizenry's attachment to Protestantism. At least judging by the rate at which local Calvinists converted to Catholicism after 1628, advocates of the Roman church had little success in breaking established habits of worship among rochelais dissenters. The "papier des conversions" maintained by Catholic church authorities in La Rochelle shows a total of 532 abjurations of Protestantism by townspeople between November 1628 and December 1648.[86] Conversions peaked early at 198 in 1629, but rapidly fell away to fewer than twenty annually after 1634. All

---

[84] See John Bosher, "The Political and Religious Origins of La Rochelle's Primacy in Trade with New France 1627-1685," *French History*, 7 (1993): 286-312.

[85] *Ibid.*, 299-301. This religiously inspired assault was later perpetuated by the implantation of Vauban's west country citadels and the creation of the royal naval base at Rochefort.

[86] BMLR, MS 779 (Abjurations à St. Marguerite, 1628-32 and 1640-1) and

tolled, fewer than 10% of surviving rochelais Protestants abandoned their faith. And scrutiny of abjuration lists reveals that widows, humble artisans, and laborers comprised the bulk of converts, indicating that Catholic proselytizing was largely ineffective
against wealthier, more literate, and more influential members of
La Rochelle's surviving Calvinist congregation.[87]

Referring to these numbers, François Moisy emphasizes the limited spiritual achievements of the early *Contre-Réforme* in La Rochelle. Louis Pérouas, author of the most comprehensive religious
history of La Rochelle in the later seventeenth century, also qual-
ifies early Catholic campaigns for religious orthodoxy as irresolute
and unrewarding.[88]

Despite their contrasting interpretations of La Rochelle's confessionalization, Bosher, Moisy, and Pérouas commonly focus their
attention on the activities of major Catholic religious institutions
(the monastic orders, the secular clergy, the parish churches, and
the lay confraternities) to judge the intensity of the local Counter-
Reformation. While these authors mention the catholicizing of La
Rochelle's civic government, none explores in detail the reorganization of the municipal judicial system by the crown or the role
of this system in the propagation of religious reform.[89] Such
research methods strike me as parochial and ill-suited to reconstructing the interconnected religious, political, and cultural histories of La Rochelle, especially in a period when royal courts of
law were assuming a more prominent role in the prosecution of

---

ADCM, C 134 bis, (Abjurations à Notre Dame de Cougnes, St. Marguerite, chez
les Recollets, les Minimes, et les Jesuites 1633-1668). See also Moisy, "Le rétablissement," Annexe II.

[87] Of 532 converts to Catholicism registered between 1628 and 1648, 408
(77%) were women, mainly Protestant widows converting in order to marry new
Catholic husbands. The precarious physical existence of unmarried women in
an early modern town, a condition impelling quick remarriage on almost any
terms, probably outweighed true crises of religious conscience as a motive
prompting these women to abjure their old beliefs.

[88] Pérouas, *Le diocèse de La Rochelle*, 220-231. Pérouas' choice of inclusive dates
for his study of the urban and rural Counter-Reformation in the region of La
Rochelle is indicative of his belief that the work of Catholic churchmen was
insubstantial before the creation of a bishopric in La Rochelle in 1648. "Le
catholicisme demurait timide, attendant qu'on installât à La Rochelle l'évêché
promis par Louis XIII," *ibid.*, 129.

[89] See for examples Bosher, "La Rochelle's Primacy," 302 and Moisy, "Le rétablissement," 45-46.

heretics and in the police of Catholic doctrine.[90]

To what extent were the nominally secular institutions of La Rochelle's new municipal government after 1628 engaged in promoting the Counter-Reformation? What effects did the religious sanctions of civic tribunals have on the character of urban life in La Rochelle? And how do the operations of municipal justice in La Rochelle after 1628 compare to civic legal procedures in other French towns of the era? Answers to these questions may help to settle the new controversy over the nature of the Counter-Reformation in La Rochelle and the French west country.

The civic archives of La Rochelle hold numerous registers of the cases heard and sentences rendered in both the mayor's court, existing before 1628, and in the new municipal police court established after the siege by royal command.[91] This tribunal, long exercising extensive jurisdiction over citizens' lives and property, became the most important agency of town government appropriated by advocates of the Counter-Reformation in La Rochelle. Its operations have never been systematically investigated before. Nearly complete transcripts of all cases adjudicated in this court during the years 1618, 1620, 1634, 1640, 1646, and 1649 provide the raw data on case types underpinning my analysis of trends in the operation of rochelais municipal justice. Sampling dates bracket the great siege of 1628 by which La Rochelle was transformed from a preponderantly Reformed community with Calvinist magistrates into a religiously divided town with Catholic governing officers confronting a substantial Protestant minority. As will be shown below, a refurbished municipal court staffed by

---

[90] Standard French legal histories document how royal tribunals, especially *parlements*, superseded ecclesiastical courts at the diocesan level in the prosecution of iconoclasts, public blasphemers, and dealers in sacrilegious books. Senior royal magistrates obtained jurisdiction over these criminals and other Protestant heretics by official reclassification of their actions as a *cas privilégié* attacking the public order upheld by the crown, see J. Declareuil, *Histoire générale du droit français des origines à 1789*, (Paris, 1925), 682-684 and 997-1004, and F. Olivier-Martin, *Histoire du droit français des origines à la Révolution*, (Paris, 1951), 493-494. In the realm of early modern French legal theory, note David Parker's sound insistence on "the continued primacy of religious teleology as the fundamental determinant of contemporary conceptions of justice," "Sovereignty, Absolutism, and the Function of the Law in Seventeenth-Century France," *Past and Present*, 122 (1989): 36-74.

[91] AMLR, E Suppl. 286 (FF 9), E Suppl. 287 (FF 10), E Suppl. 288 (FF 12), E Suppl. 292 (FF 17), E Suppl. 296 (FF 21), E Suppl. 297 (FF 22), E Suppl. 304 (FF 29), and E Suppl. 307 (FF 32).

Catholics became a vital instrument of the Counter-Reformation
in La Rochelle. Scrutinizing the daily operations of this town court
also demonstrates the great utility of voluminous, neglected civic
legal archives for historians intent on deciphering seventeenth-
century religious conflicts and the development of urban cultures
in early modern Europe.

The right of La Rochelle's sworn citizens to establish and maintain a court of municipal justice was among the fundamental civic
privileges English and French kings generously bestowed on the
community. Charters from Jean II and Edward III in 1360 invested the mayor and town council of La Rochelle with primary civil and criminal justice over all sworn citizens and the population
of the city's hinterland. The town hall court was the institution
through which these legal powers were exercised. The mayor in
person served as the court's presiding judge aided up to the last
quarter of the sixteenth century by two *co-adjuteurs* chosen annually from within the assembly of *échevins*. Sometime before 1618,
the number of *co-adjuteurs* was doubled to four, producing a five-
judge civic tribunal. Four *procureurs de la police*, responsible for surveillance of different urban quarters, drew up indictments and
presented cases to the court. Twelve municipal sergeants were
yearly empowered by the *corps de ville* to identify miscreants, summon defendants, arrest criminals, and enforce sentences handed
down. Before the siege of 1628, the town hall court convened at
least weekly but pressing business, such as the conferment of civic
tax farms and cases involving interpretation of the municipal tax
code could keep it in continuous daily sessions.

*Co-adjuteurs* were normally recruited from among the most
senior *échevins* of the town council, men with long and varied
experience in municipal government whose judicial authority was
reinforced by their proven probity in civic affairs.[92] *Procureurs de
la police* were usually chosen from among the *pairs* on the town
council. Staffing the town court bureaucracy also gave town councilmen an extensive patronage distribution network useful in
strengthening the city's internal government and consolidating
popular support for civic government.

The town council's complete control over selection of all munic-

---

[92] In 1622, for example, the four *co-adjuteurs*, the *échevins* Martin de Berrandy,
Jacques David, Pierre Guillaudeau, and Jean Guiton had served an average of
thirty-four years on the town council before election to their judicial posts.

ipal court officials down to the lowliest clerk protected the tribunal from infiltration and manipulation by royal jurists. Civic magistrates vigilantly protected their legal prerogatives against encroachment from below by the king's *prévôt* who held judicial authority over ordinary residents of the commune. La Rochelle was not the seat of a bishopric before 1648. Up to the mid-seventeenth century, no ecclesiastical court was headquartered in the city. The closest church tribunal was the episcopal court attached to the bishopric of Saintes, sixty kilometers to the south. Infrequent disciplinary proceedings against rochelais clerics were conducted there but La Rochelle's town hall court and resident royal officials also took active (and at times conflicting) roles in the police of local religious affairs.

The formation of a royal presidial court in La Rochelle in 1552 confronted the town court with a more potent legal rival. Civic magistrates aggressively defended their judicial turf against the new tribunal. Royal letters patent obtained by city fathers in July 1553 confirmed civic magistrates' primary civil and criminal jurisdiction over all rochelais bourgeois and their powers of criminal prosecution against non-bourgeois and foreigners.[93] In 1558, the mayor of La Rochelle obtained two edicts from the Parlement of Paris reiterating his tribunal's exclusive jurisdiction over all civil and criminal cases in the first instance involving bourgeois of the city or members of their households. By letters of 6 March 1576, Henry III confirmed that the "entière jurisdiction et police" of La Rochelle's bourgeoisie belonged by right to the mayor, *échevins*, and *pairs* of La Rochelle and was to be exercised through the established municipal tribunal.[94]

As outlined above, in the aftermath of the 1628 siege, the crown salvaged the old mayoral court, renaming it the "municipal police court." All Protestant members of the former tribunal were dismissed and rochelais Catholics exclusively empaneled as civic magistrates. How important was the new civic police court imposed by the crown in fostering the religious reeducation of La Rochelle's citizenry mandated by the Counter-Reformation?

Here, a comparison of cases heard and sentences rendered in both the town hall court, existing before 1628, and in the new

---

[93] BMLR, MS 81, "Titres de la ville de La Rochelle," fol. 162r.
[94] BMLR, MS 82, fol. 157v.

municipal police court established after the siege can clarify the local Counter-Reformation's effects on the conduct of municipal justice.[95] The jurisdictions of both tribunals (civil suits, petty crimes, violations of municipal ordinances, disturbances of the peace, and lewd behavior contrary to religious norms) were similar, allowing one to track changes in typical case loads under Protestant and Catholic regimes of town government. I have done a census of both the number and type of cases adjudicated by these courts during the years 1618, 1620, 1634, 1637, 1640, 1646, and 1649. Both before and after the 1628 siege, the work of these tribunals can be divided into six categories: 1) cases involving private disputes between townspeople over debts, breaches of contract, inheritance disputes, etc., 2) violations of food retailing and market laws, 3) conflicts over the letter and application of guild statutes regulating the various *métiers* of the urban economy, 4) infringements of city ordinances maintaining the cleanliness, health, and safety of the urban community, 5) cases arising from transgressions of religious laws deemed appropriate for municipal enforcement, and 6) miscellaneous proceedings (mainly reviews of prior sentences, determinations of whether preliminary inquiries should be made in new cases, and decisions on court procedure). Table 16 shows the number and types of cases adjudicated in the sample years. In Table 17, the raw numbers of cases in each category presented in Table 16 are expressed as a percentage of all cases heard during each sample year.

Comparison of these figures over time reveals several interesting patterns in the work of La Rochelle's municipal courts under Protestant and then Catholic domination. First, and most importantly, a steep decline is evident in the annual number and percentage of private disputes city tribunals adjudicated before and after 1628. This decline was accompanied by significant increases in the volume and proportion of cases involving enforcement of guild statutes, municipal health and safety ordinances, and religious codes. The increase in cases involving breaches of religious strictures (from three in 1618 to 187 in 1649) is particularly striking. As explained below, the municipal court's role as a defend-

---

[95] These case histories and sentences are now conserved in the following sources: AMLR, E Suppl. 286 (FF 9), E Suppl. 287 (FF 10), E Suppl. 288 (FF 12), E Suppl. 292 (FF 17), E Suppl. 296 (FF 21), E Suppl. 297 (FF 22), E Suppl. 304 (FF 29), and E Suppl. 307 (FF 32).

*Table 16*

Typical Cases Heard by Town Hall Court (1618 and 1620) and
Municipal Police Court (1634, 1637, 1640, 1646, and 1649)

*Types of Cases*

| Year | P.D. | F.M. | G.S. | M.O. | R.L. | Misc. | Total |
|------|------|------|------|------|------|-------|-------|
| 1618 | 663 | 251 | 96 | 61 | 3 | 43 | 1,117 |
| 1620 | 605 | 191 | 100 | 110 | 29 | 25 | 1,060 |
| 1634 | 728 | 258 | 170 | 132 | 108 | 39 | 1,435 |
| 1637 | 197 | 149 | 153 | 152 | 95 | 71 | 817 |
| 1640 | 394 | 244 | 199 | 581 | 95 | 73 | 1,586 |
| 1646 | 328 | 349 | 288 | 441 | 141 | 78 | 1,625 |
| 1649 | 329 | 383 | 194 | 156 | 187 | 7 | 1,256 |

(Abbreviations used for case types are as follows: Private Disputes: P.D.,
Food and Market violations: F.M., Guild Statute disputes: G.S., Municipal
Ordinance compliance: M.O., Religious Law enforcement: R.L., and
Miscellaneous: Misc.)

*Table 17*

Typical Cases Heard by Town Hall Court (1618 and 1620) and
Municipal Police Court (1634, 1637, 1640, 1646, and 1649)
as Percentages of All Cases Tried in Sample Years

*Types of Cases*

| Year | P.D. | F.M. | G.S. | M.O. | R.L. | Misc. | Total |
|------|------|------|------|------|------|-------|-------|
| 1618 | 59.35% | 22.48% | 8.59% | 5.47% | 0.26% | 3.85% | 100% |
| 1620 | 57.0% | 18.0% | 9.4% | 10.5% | 2.7% | 2.4% | 100% |
| 1634 | 50.7% | 18.1% | 11.8% | 9.2% | 7.5% | 2.7% | 100% |
| 1637 | 24.1% | 18.2% | 18.7% | 18.6% | 11.6% | 8.8% | 100% |
| 1640 | 24.8% | 15.4% | 12.6% | 36.6% | 6.0% | 4.6% | 100% |
| 1646 | 20.2% | 21.4% | 17.8% | 27.1% | 8.7% | 4.8% | 100% |
| 1649 | 26.1% | 30.6% | 15.5% | 12.4% | 14.8% | 0.6% | 100% |

er of Catholic orthodoxy after 1628 expanded even more rapidly
than these numbers would suggest. Regulation of victualling and
market activity also increased in the 1640's after an initial decline.
Considered in their entirety, these figures show that, after 1634,
La Rochelle's municipal court lost its importance as a referee set-

tling disputes between private citizens and became much more active as an enforcer of official edicts, civic and sacred.

Prior to 1628, nearly two-thirds of the cases adjudicated by the town hall court while dominated by Protestants involved legal disputes between private citizens. Handling over 1,000 lawsuits annually, La Rochelle's active municipal tribunal functioned primarily to resolve the feuds of highly litigious townspeople and to foster more equitable relations between the many different ranks of rochelais society. The court regularly served as an intermediary between litigants of disproportionate socioeconomic resources and continually prosecuted outsiders accused of violating the civic privileges by which the urban commune securely defined itself.

Case registers for 1618 and 1620 show that many different members of the rochelais bourgeoisie relied on the court for redress of their grievances against irresponsible business partners or cheating customers. Innkeepers, numerous in a heavily trafficked port town, petitioned the court for permission to seize the goods or bills of exchange of travelling merchants who stole away without paying their lodging expenses.[96] Tradesmen, tailors in particular, used the court like a collection agency to recover payment for services rendered or loans made to insolvent clients.[97] In such cases, the plaintiffs were frequently of a humbler social status than the defendants. Regardless of pedigree, parties judged guilty by the court were subject to imprisonment or confiscation of property for settlement of their obligations. But the court could also serve as a guardian for the households of poorer men who ran afoul of the law. When the destitute weaver André Belanger was jailed for debt in 1618 for example, city magistrates granted him a conditional release provided that he work to support his family and pay off his creditors according to a schedule they worked out with the judges.[98]

The mayoral court further defended the commune's integrity by regularly prosecuting foreign merchants who attempted to participate illegally in market activities reserved to native businessmen by town charters.[99] The court also instructed town sergeants to ensure that outsiders trading commodities in the city abided

---

[96] AMLR, E. Suppl. 287 (FF 10), fol. 59v.
[97] See for examples, AMLR, E Suppl. 287 (FF 10), fols. 61v and 72r.
[98] AMLR, E. Suppl. 287 (FF 10), fols. 189r-v.
[99] See for example AMLR, E. Suppl. 287 (FF 10), fol. 148r for the case of a

by the local weights and measures prescribed in municipal code books. Although quick to prosecute violations of commercial statutes, town judges were more reticent about enforcing the religious precepts of Calvinism. In the two sample years before 1628, less than three percent of all mayoral court cases involved public infringements of Protestant doctrine. It can be surmised that in this area of police the municipal court almost entirely deferred to the *consistoire* of the Calvinist church, the institution established by the discipline of French Reformed churches for the surveillance and rebuke of wayward communicants.[100] The small number of such cases before the court makes generalization hazardous; however, they suggest that the court intervened in church affairs only when foreigners or notorious town dwellers repeatedly broke religious injunctions or willfully ignored the sanctions of the consistory.

Before 1628, the town hall court was also the agency through which the important and lucrative rights to collect various municipal levies were sold at auction to tax farmers.[101] Contemporaneously, the court was the primary legal venue where disputes arising over civic tax assessments and immunities were adjudi-

---

merchant for Limoges fined by the court for attempting to sell grain in town without first delivering it to the municipal grain market for inspection, tax, and future sale by the city's licensed dealers.

[100] Unfortunately, nearly all the records of La Rochelle's Calvinist church bureaucracy have been lost. In the absence of such documentation, it can only be presumed that the city's consistory tried like *consistoires* elsewhere to combat the ethical failings of Reformed church members. In 1618 and 1620, at least, the mayoral court showed little inclination to sanction such transgressions. For the extensive moral and police authority claimed by Calvinist consistories within other French urban communities see Solange Bertheau, "Le consistoire dans les églises réformées du Moyen-Poitou au XVII siècle," BHSPF 116 (1970): 332-359 and 513-549; Henry Heller, *The Conquest of Poverty: The Calvinist Revolt in Sixteenth-Century France*, (Leiden, 1986), 176-203; and R.A. Mentzer, "*Disciplina nervus ecclesiae*: the Calvinist Reform of Morals at Nimes," *Sixteenth Century Journal*, 18 (1987): 89-115. Although a Calvinist consistory had been functioning in La Rochelle since 1558, good evidence suggests that its ability to discipline a bustling port city was minimal and that its interventions in the lives of the citizenry may have been less pervasive than the work of consistories in other, more stable Protestant towns. The Protestant pastor Jacques Merlin, resident in La Rochelle from 1589 to 1620, frequently confided to his diary that all ranks of rochelais society, but especially the lower orders, were unmindful and contemptuous of the Reformed church's admonishments. See for examples Merlin's "Diaire," fols. 30r-31r, 217r, 232v-233r, and 260r-262v.

[101] For the 1620 bidding sessions on the tax farms see AMLR, E. Suppl. 288 (FF 12), fols. 33v-35v.

cated. Both procedures accounted for a significant portion of the court's time and labor. The extensive fiscal and commercial liberties town charters conferred on rochelais citizens made the determination of their local tax liabilities extremely complicated. In 1620, for example, one-sixth of the private disputes argued before the mayor's tribunal involved the municipal tax farmers as plaintiffs or defendants.

Here, again, the mayor's tribunal tended to rule impartially, evaluating each case on its merits, frequently requesting documentation of fiscal status from all parties engaged, and never uniformly approving or disallowing tax farmers' impositions. The municipality's interest in facilitating taxation at the highest legal limits (inducing the farmers to bid up the city's fee for collection rights) was counterbalanced by the urban magistracy's fear of popular tax revolt and determination to conserve inviolate all communal liberties as a defense against unwanted royal meddling in town government. Higher tax revenues would not compensate for either public riot or a diminution in local political freedoms. Operating in accord with this axiom, the mayoral court did not treat the tax farmers indulgently. Since the farms were usually bought up by the wealthiest local merchants who collected from the poorer residents in town, the judges' evenhandedness worked to moderate social tensions within the urban community and guard its integrity.

The siege of 1627-28 smashed this delicate mechanics of justice and police in La Rochelle. The treaty of surrender dissolved the old town council, converted council property into royal domain owing taxes directly to the crown, and reorganized the municipal court. The capacity of civic jurists to reconcile the competing interests of their fellow citizens diminished greatly. Under the new regime of town government, forthright enforcement of royal edicts shaping political and religious affairs took complete precedence over the judicious use of legal force. This transition supports John Bosher's assertion of a vigorous Counter-Reformation in La Rochelle from late 1628 onward.

After 1628, the police court's *procureurs* intensified their watch on the city's retailers in a dogged campaign to stop the adulteration of foodstuffs and other subterfuges perpetrated by unscrupulous merchants to cheat consumers. In the spring of 1634, many of La Rochelle's *boulangers* were fined for selling standard loaves of bread weighing less than municipal statutes specified.[102] In February of 1640, another forty-six rochelais bakers were fined by the court for "light bread."[103]

Little in the urban environment fell outside the purview of the new police court. In 1646, for example, municipal judges fined an innkeeper for building an unauthorized addition to his premises, slapped a shoemaker with a fine for erecting an illegally large shop sign, ordered one townsman to expel the pigs he was keeping in his house, and fined a tripe-seller for the impudent behavior of his children toward neighbors.[104]

Dereliction of fatherly duty, especially by townsmen who failed to discipline their wives and children, allowing them to "faire des insolences," was repeatedly censured as a serious infraction of private mores and public order by the Catholic family men who served as judges on the police court after 1628. They regularly lectured and fined negligent parents, especially fathers, for the misbehavior of their children. In April 1646 for example, three such cases were prosecuted in a single week.[105] At La Rochelle, verdicts of the municipal police court after 1628 promulgated an all-encompassing paternalism characteristic of Counter-Reformation theology.[106]

The labor, leisure, and home life of townspeople were all subject to stricter police court regulation, especially during divine services, on Fridays and Sundays, and throughout Lent. In January of 1634, the widow Chauvet was fined for serving bread and wine in her *auberge* while mass was being said, an offense "contrary to the statutes, regulations, and ordinances of the city."[107] Several other food-sellers and widows running *auberges* in the city were fined on the same day for similar offenses. Frequent court sanctions against widows for a variety of market infractions and reli-

---

[102] AMLR, E Suppl. 292 (FF 17), fol. 32v.
[103] AMLR, E Suppl. 297 (FF 22), fols. 60v and 81r-84v.
[104] AMLR, E Suppl. 304 (FF 29), fols. 25r, 43r, and 59r.
[105] *Ibid.*, fols. 59r-v.
[106] On the Counter-Reformation's institutional empowerment of the *paterfamilias* see Albano Biondi, "Aspetti della cultura cattolica post-tridentina. Religione e controllo sociale," in Corrado Vivanti, ed., *Storia d'Italia*, Annali 4, "Intellettuali e potere," (Turin, 1981), 253-302, especially section 2, "Il quatro comandamento. Una società sotto l'occhio del Padre." I thank my colleague, Wietse de Boer for bringing this essay to my attention.
[107] AMLR, E Suppl. 292 (FF 17), fol. 5r.

gious code violations suggest that this subgroup of the urban population, existing outside the normal structures of family life, warranted special surveillance and reproach by the Catholic directors
of the new municipal police tribunal.

Humble workingmen also regularly ran afoul of the new police
court. On 13 June 1634, a stevedore was found to be too poor to
fine for working on Pentecost.[108] "Selling meat during the sacred
time of Lent," was the charge in February 1635 against several
local butchers who were fined for doing so without a special dispensation from the court.[109] Selling meat on a Friday got another butcher into serious trouble in 1646.[110] In January of 1649, fifteen tavern keepers and tennis court owners were fined by the
police tribunal for allowing various kinds of gaming on Sunday.[111]
New Catholic magistrates in La Rochelle kept victualers and pub-
licans, key actors in earlier episodes of urban political rebellion,
under tight surveillance.

The court's defense of post-Tridentine Catholic doctrine took
many forms. In March 1631, the tribunal forbade begging in the
streets and commanded all citizens to cease giving alms at their
doors, before churches, or in any public place.[112] Neither would
the court tolerate poor men, beggars, and vagrants being sheltered in the private homes of townsfolk. The "shameful poor"
(*pauvres honteux*) were instructed to register with Catholic parish
vestrymen, curés, assessors of the *taille*, or other royal officials for
a check on their places of origin and confinement under church
supervision where appropriate.[113] Civic magistrates and their subordinate constables enacted and enforced legal sanctions popu-

---

[108] *Ibid.*, fol. 125v.

[109] AMLR, E Suppl. 293 (FF 18), fols. 44r-46r.

[110] AMLR, E Suppl. 304 (FF 29), fol. 3r.

[111] AMLR, E Suppl. 307 (FF 32), fols. 9r-v.

[112] This legislation was in keeping with prevailing Catholic and Protestant
opinions about the greater efficacy of institutional care for relief of the poor.
See Robert Jutte, *Poverty and Deviance in Early Modern Europe*, (Cambridge, 1994),
100-125.

[113] AMLR, *Recueil* 360, declaration of 5 March 1631. The rochelais diarist
Joseph Guillaudeau reports that during the hard winter of 1631-32, nosey *procureurs de police* concealed themselves in houses near La Rochelle's Protestant
church and sprang out to arrest several members of the congregation they spied
giving alms to beggars on the church porch, Guillaudeau, "Diaire," 382. The
almsgivers were later heavily fined by the magistrates of the police court. In
March 1637, judges of this tribunal were again fining townspeople for having
given food, lodging, and coins to "persons of abject condition," AMLR, E Suppl.

lating the city's expanding charity hospitals. The king's 1628 edict of pacification had turned these institutions over to male and female monastic orders. Town judges later took the lead in founding La Rochelle's first *hôpital général* and workhouse, the *hôpital* St. Louis.[114] In La Rochelle, the municipal police court was instrumental in effecting the *grand renfermement* characteristic of the Counter-Reformation's response to the ubiquity of the poor. This sequestration under the watchful eyes of clerics disempowered individual citizens, especially Calvinists, as patrons and redeemers of the poor.

The police court also intervened to prevent more intimate violations of church teaching. In January 1634, the *procureurs* brought in a tradesman and his wife who, after marrying in the Catholic church, were found to have abjured their religion and turned to practicing Calvinism. City judges fined the pair twenty *livres* and gave them a week to leave town.[115] On 20 May 1634, the *procureurs* brought suit against Marin Mantel, a Catholic Rochelais and innkeeper of wavering faith, who had allowed his child to be baptized as a Protestant. Shocked at this father's neglect of his child's spiritual and moral welfare, the court first stiffly fined the Protestant pastor and both godparents involved in the baptism and then ordered Mantel to raise his child as a Catholic. Mantel was additionally required to inform the court regularly of his son's progress in Catholic catechism or "be struck from the roster of legal residents of La Rochelle, be whipped through the streets, and then be driven from the city."[116] Such interventions by civic magistrates and the financial penalties and corporal punishments they could mete out (strictures unavailable to church courts) helped to reduce the number of Protestants in La Rochelle and disrupted the proselytizing efforts of a shrinking religious minority.

The previously self-governing guilds of La Rochelle now also found themselves subject to greater control by the municipal judi-

---

296 (FF 21), 4 March 1637. Heightened surveillance over almsgiving as noted by Guillaudeau was also probably intended by civic officials as another check on illegal Protestant immigration to the city.

[114] Arcère, *Histoire de la ville de La Rochelle*, 2: 517-519; and Pérouas, *Le diocèse de La Rochelle*, 291.

[115] AMLR, E Suppl. 292 (FF 17), fols. 9v-10r.

[116] *Ibid.*, fols. 109v-111r.

cial system, particularly when their internal politics worked to the advantage of the remaining local Calvinists. In January 1635, the court quickly invalidated the election of two Protestant chief masters by the guild of tailors and ordered that this confraternity only select Catholics to fill supervisory offices of the organization.[117] In May 1637, the *procureurs de police* summoned officers of the shoemakers' guild and legally compelled them to enlist no new members without consultation and approval of all masters. This tactic was intended to ensure that a minority of Protestant masters did not meet surreptitiously to admit fellow Huguenots to the ranks of cobblers.[118] Verdicts of this kind undercut the material resources of rochelais Protestants and diminished their authority within artisanal organizations. After 1628, Catholic civic magistrates attacked corporatist solidarities they perceived as inimical to advancement of the Counter-Reformation.

Among the most recurrent operations of the new court, accounting for both a steep rise in cases involving municipal codes and religious law, were orders to homeowners to clean the street before their door on Wednesdays and on Saturdays and to decorate their house fronts for regular Sunday religious processions and parades of the Holy Sacrament through the town on major Catholic holidays. Numerous residents from every neighborhood of the city were repeatedly fined for failure to reverence the urban pathways of Catholic rituals. New municipal judges ordered the heads of local Protestant households to lay out tapestries, clean linens, and other appropriate decorations honoring the passing Host during Catholic festivals and processions.[119]

Dereliction of Saturday street cleanings was punished more often and more severely by the magistrates of the municipal police court. It was not uncommon for twenty or thirty miscreants to be tried and sentenced all at once. It seems that Saturday street cleaning was considered by the court as a necessary part of preparations for Sunday churchgoing and processions by Catholics.

---

[117] AMLR, E Suppl. 293 (FF 18) fols. 5r-12r. The tailors, a large number of whom were Protestants, appealed this decision to the Parlement of Paris. The result of their appeal is unknown to me. However, in May of 1635, La Rochelle's police court ordered the guild to expedite admission of two more certified Catholics to mastership. The guild complied.

[118] AMLR, E Suppl. 296 (FF 21), 11 May 1637.

[119] See for example, AMLR, E Suppl. 296 (FF 21), 10 January 1637, E Suppl. 297 (FF 22), fol. 58r, and E Suppl. 304 (FF 29), fols. 3r-4r.

Strong Protestant opposition to this mundane task suggests that the Catholic masters of the city infused it with religious significance. In Tables 16 and 17, I have counted court actions against homeowners who refused to sweep the streets in the category of municipal ordinance enforcement (nominally, it was the civic health code that was being broken). However, the sharp rise in such prosecutions in the 1640's should also be appreciated for its religious implications as part of a renewed Catholic campaign to police the rites of the Counter-Reformation throughout the city. In the tables above, if municipal court prosecutions for failure to sweep were counted in the category of religious law enforcement, as Catholic judges probably intended, this category would comprise progressively more than ten percent of all court cases in each year after 1634, rising to nearly twenty percent of all cases in 1649.

Wealthier Protestants clustered in the St. Sauveur quarter, which was frequently circumnavigated by major Catholic processions, protested legal decisions constraining them to dress their houses.[120] A 1638 letter from the king to François de Villemontée, royal intendant of justice in La Rochelle, instructed local authorities that Protestant householders should not be held personally responsible for decoration of their facades and could be allowed to employ surrogates to do the necessary work. After reading this letter into the minutes of the police court, officers of the tribunal reiterated their ordinances on procession etiquette with the new provision that Protestant home owners and renters could buy court dispensations allowing them to hire decorators.[121]

After 1628, the magistrates of La Rochelle's new police court worked continuously to enforce respect among the citizenry for Catholic ceremonies and institutions, prosecuting the Counter-Reformation in every street of the city. By multiplying injunctions, summonses, and fines, particularly against Calvinists, this civic institution under Catholic control hammered away at La Rochelle's old Reformed neighborhoods, intending to humiliate surviving Protestant notables, to diminish the socioeconomic resources of the Calvinist community, and to thin the ranks of

---

[120] On Catholic procession routes in La Rochelle, see AMLR, *Recueil* 360, ordinances of 10 and 25 June 1631 and 16 June and 31 October 1632.

[121] AMLR, E Suppl. 295 (FF 20) entries of 28 April and 14 May 1638.

heretics. Catholic patriarchs among the laity, long covetous of greater influence within the refurbished urban parishes, stood to gain the most from these endeavors. The work of police court magistrates was facilitated by their kinsmen and confidants holding sinecures above them on the royal presidial court.

The premeditated religious activism of the new regime of civic administration surpassed that of previous Protestant town governments which had allowed separate mediating institutions, like the Calvinist *consistoire*, the guilds, and the city's militia companies, to retain some control over discipline of the faithful. Evidence from La Rochelle indicates that within the Calvinist town a plurality of urban police agencies, secular and sacred, interacted to shape communal justice. Within the Counter-Reformation municipality this concerted articulation of the law diminished as Catholic magistrates promoted the identity of church and court. The vigorous rochelais Counter-Reformation described by John Bosher was also advanced by a cadre of civic judicial officers allied to the religious orders and ministers of state who made the city a focal point of Catholic missionary activity.

As this profile of the municipal police court's daily operations makes clear, political service to the royal household and its church by local Catholics diminished the urban magistracy's role as an ostensibly impartial arbiter of citizens' disputes and increased the police tribunal's direct, programmatic intervention in the social, political, religious, and family life of each parish. The treatment townspeople, especially Protestants, could expect from the city's judicial institutions was fundamentally altered by the royal imperative of a tightly policed community loyal to the social, political, and religious doctrines authorized by the crown. Rochelais Protestants and Catholics both faced a more authoritarian, a more paternal civic regime, less charitable, more suspicious of the individual existing outside the bonds of family life, and more censorious of moral lapses than prior administrations of the city.

As Andrew Barnes has recently argued, changes in the rituals of the Counter-Reformation Catholic church can be construed as an assault on *communitas*, the epitome of late-medieval Catholicism in which the individual's faith was continually renewed in rites celebrating the church as a sacred collectivity of believers responding to their shared needs.[122] By contrast, the post-Tridentine church emphasized priestly direction of lay devotions and, through its widely circulated, printed catechisms, an intensely personal, introspective soul-searching antithetical to the exciting communal rites of earlier times.[123]

Evidence distilled from the municipal legal archives of La Rochelle suggests that the transformation Barnes has tracked within Catholic ritual practice had a contemporaneous judicial complement at least at the level of civic tribunals controlled by Catholic patriarchs.[124] Here, the older norms of communal justice by which courts operated to balance and reconcile the disparate interests of citizens in the name of a quasi-sacred and independent urban polity to which all litigants belonged were replaced by legal procedures designed to isolate and humiliate lawbreakers. The law's power to dissuade the citizen from crime, originally derived from the integrity of the urban commune and its corporate institutions, now descended from individuals' more acutely felt senses of personal inadequacy, guilt, and shame, components of conscience it was the urban magistracy's new duty to intensify and refine. Seen from this perspective, bourgeois respectability, contributing to the elaboration and pathology of French urban culture, gained newly compelling force from the Counter-Reformation's enactment of municipal justice.[125]

How do the operations of civic courts in La Rochelle after 1628 compare to the functioning of municipal judicial systems in other French cities of the age? Answering this question is extremely difficult because so few details are currently known about the

---

[122] Andrew E. Barnes, "*Ces Sortes de Pénitence Imaginaires*: The Counter-Reformation Assault on Communitas," in Andrew Barnes and Peter Stearns, eds., *Social History and Issues in Human Consciousness: Some Interdisciplinary Connections*, (New York, 1989), 67-84. See also Barnes, "From Ritual to Meditative Piety: Devotional Change in French Penitential Confraternities From the 16th to the 18th Centuries," in *Journal of Ritual Studies*, 1 (1987): 1-26.

[123] Barnes, "Counter-Reformation Assault on Communitas," 75-80. For post-Tridentine attacks by Catholic curés against older communal institutions and neighborhood solidarities in Lyon, see Hoffman, *Church and Community*, 141-142.

[124] On the commitment of high French royal magistrates to the doctrines of the Counter-Reformation see C. Kaiser, "Les cours souveraines au XVI siècle: morale et Contre-Réforme," *Annales E.S.C.*, 37 (1982): 17-31.

[125] Robin Briggs' characterization of French reforming Catholicism as "bourgeois" and "legalistic" thus finds firm institutional grounding in La Rochelle at least. See Briggs, *Communities of Belief*, 199-200, 261, and 370-372.

operation over time of civic tribunals in other French towns.[126]
While little or no evidence is available elsewhere on the role of
city magistrates in advancing the French Counter-Reformation,
several works make clear a contrary reality. The Counter-Reformation was appreciably slowed in those towns where municipal
magistracies continued to be occupied by Protestants. At Nîmes,
the researches of Robert Sauzet show that Calvinists' tenacious
hold on civic administrative offices until the mid-seventeenth century acted as a brake on the prosecution of the local *Contre-
Réforme*.[127] At Montpellier in 1624, the bishop Fenouillet led the
effort of local Catholics in petitioning the crown to purge municipal government of all Calvinists. The local Counter-Reformation
gathered speed after this dismissal of Protestant magistrates was
effected by royal order in 1630.[128]

Also instructive here is Alain Lottin's detailed study of Lille
(annexed to France in 1668).[129] Lottin finds that in this Catholic
town municipal judges, despite recurrent jurisdictional disputes
with regional and episcopal courts, did work with the church hierarchy to prosecute religious heretics endangering the peace, piety,
and good repute of the city. Although inclined to toleration in
their jurisprudence, city fathers nonetheless used their legal
powers to defend the Catholic faith against scandal and punish
those who repudiated the discipline of the church. Civic magistrates here definitely took part in the local Counter-Reformation.

While these examples do not prove my arguments concerning
La Rochelle, they do clearly indicate that municipal legal institutions were elsewhere embroiled in the religious conflicts of the
era and that instances of cooperation between Catholic prelates
and civic officials were observable in the French borderlands. The

---

[126] Older studies such as Jacques Maillard's *Le pouvoir municipal à Angers de
1657 à 1789*, (Angers, 1984), 55-94, document the existence of civic courts but
focus almost exclusively on their arcane jurisdictional disputes with royal tribunals. The actual dockets and judicial work of municipal magistracies, religious
or otherwise, are rarely investigated. Even such a recent and meticulous urban
study as Wolfgang Kaiser's *Marseille au temps des troubles 1559-1596* (Paris, 1992)
gives no information on the existence or operation of judicial institutions at the
level of the municipality.

[127] Sauzet, *Contre-Réforme et réforme catholique*, 311-324, 381-382, and 397.

[128] Jean Baumel, *Histoire d'une seigneurie du Midi de la France*, 4, "Montpellier
au cours des XVIe et XVIIe siècles," (Montpellier, 1976), 204-205. Unfortunately,
Baumel presents no analysis of how this confessional cleansing of town government affected the dispensation of civic justice.

[129] Lottin, *Lille, citadelle de la Contre-Réforme?*, 147-163.

history of La Rochelle after 1628 is marked by a more aggressive manifestation of this contemporary partnership in religious reform between churchmen and urban magistrates. By thoroughly reorganizing local justice at the civic level, the French crown appropriated the legal institutions endowed with the broadest purview over citizens' lives and least encumbered by Protestant functionaries who owned their offices (as was the case in the presidial courts and parlements). At La Rochelle, the new municipal police court became an auxiliary of state and church, concentrating doctrinal police while advancing the missionary work through which the old rebel city was steadily subdued and catholicized.

Royal victory in the siege of 1628 reconsolidated the actors and objectives of urban government in La Rochelle. By abolishing the *corps de ville*, the Council of Forty-Eight, and the Protestant-dominated militia companies that fed them members, Louis XIII snuffed out the only regime of rochelais government that might have legitimately claimed to function through approval by and recruitment from a large proportion of the city's male inhabitants. La Rochelle's post-siege administration was drawn from a far narrower social base, recalling the oligarchic configuration of pre-1614 civic government. The king's reactionary intervention in rochelais politics also eliminated prior limitations on the service of presidial magistrates in municipal government, stoutly defended by past town councilmen. Reversing the destabilizing *embourgeoisement* of urban politics by putting trained royal jurists in town offices, Louis XIII left La Rochelle with a government composed of local Catholics anxious to profit materially and socially from identification with the crown's interests and thus more inclined to obedient enforcement of the law than to dangerous experimentation with the forms and precedents of civic administration.

Retention by the king of institutions like the merchants' tribunal and the municipal police court, bodies contending with one another and with the presidial court over jurisdictions under prior civic regimes, suggests that the crown was unwilling to invest the presidial with absolute authority over La Rochelle after 1628. This tactic in La Rochelle would seem to conform with a general ruling strategy of the French monarchy that called for conservation and manipulation of lesser administrative institutions to keep members of local ruling elites quarreling with one another and incapable of concerted action against the interests of the royal household.[130] While such a policy was perhaps essential in controlling cities home to the great parlements and religious bureaucracies of France, in La Rochelle, the absence of such power blocks lessened the threat of an entente between municipal institutions of police. The presidial court was not given entirely free reign by the crown, but royal agents also did nothing to discourage a proliferation of family ties bonding together local royal jurists and the holders of civic offices. This inaction ran the risk of permitting the local sympathies of townsmen to impede the prompt and obedient enforcement of edicts from Paris. However, keeping consortia of kinsmen at the controls of local police agencies promoted a continuity of personnel in town government and the staffing of key positions by family men likely to think twice before acting in an official manner prejudicial to the distinctions their clan owed to royal service. Evidence from La Rochelle suggests that the French crown employed a wide range of tactics in dealing with local authorities and was capable of striking a variety of mutually beneficial bargains with urban ruling elites.

Efficient rule by interconnected family men had been retained in La Rochelle. Certain forms of urban politics endured, but the character of the government kinsmen dispensed was changing. Catholics supplanted Protestants in a familial system of urban police the king could not do without and no transient show of force could displace. Incorporation of that system under the direction of Catholic royal jurists reduced its capacity to challenge royal authority while making uncontested imposition of the law its primary social and political function. La Rochelle's unstinting loyalty to the crown throughout the period of the *Fronde* is one measure of that program's success. Local Protestants' prolonged resistance to Catholic proselytization through private practice of their

---

[130] As Robert Schneider has argued in an article on relations between the French monarchy and the municipal government of Toulouse, it is inaccurate to characterize these two institutions as inveterate enemies. In Toulouse, the ruling policy of the emerging absolutist monarchy did not entail the destruction of municipal administration, but rather its conservation as a counter-weight to and potential ally against the regional parlement also headquartered in the city. The manipulation, not the destruction, of contentious local institutions of police was the objective of the crown's ruling tactics. See Schneider, "Crown and Capitoulat, Municipal Government in Toulouse 1500-1789," in P. Benedict, ed., *Cities and Social Change in Early Modern France*, (London, 1989), 195-220.

faith is an indication of that initiative's limitations. A dense network of interrelated municipal policemen ordering the urban environment, regulating the city's economy, busting older communal solidarities, stifling dissent, and prosecuting law breakers of every description was among that policy's institutional legacies with which subsequent generations of townspeople would have to contend. Only the revolution of 1789 would finally challenge and modify the structures of municipal governance the crown managed to establish in La Rochelle with the aid of notable local Catholic kinsmen in the weeks immediately following the capitulation of 1628.

# CONCLUSION

The tale I have told about La Rochelle is, at best, only a rough approximation of what happened in the city between 1530 and 1650. The ravages of time have taken a heavy toll on the documents through which the city's tumultuous history can best be reconstructed. Given the relative paucity of studies devoted to the cities and culture of the French west country, any conclusions regarding the history of La Rochelle and its region in the early modern era must, perforce, remain tentative and solicitous of revision by other scholars determined to explore the urban cultures of early modern France.

Surveying the history of La Rochelle recoverable in its neglected archives, a sequence of interconnected summations can be made which may complement the current understanding of post-feudal France. First, La Rochelle's rise to greatness as one of the freest, self-governing urban communes in the realm must be appreciated within the enduring geopolitical realities of the French Atlantic littoral. This was a landscape manifestly inhospitable to sustained human settlement and to the implantation of the wealthy ecclesiastical and aristocratic governing institutions framing the lives and political aspirations of most other French people during the era. The thickly mured, distantly spaced towns of this environment sheltered hardy urbanites ruthlessly devoted to communal defense and to the subjugation of an alien hinterland. A chronically penurious, still itinerant French monarchy whose administrative powers declined precipitously over any distance toward the kingdom's frontiers, quickly learned the value of coopting peripheral townspeople with indulgent gifts of civic liberties and commercial advantages. No town in France benefitted more from such royal largesses as did La Rochelle up until the outbreak of the Wars of Religion. Even this trauma and the wholesale conversion of the Rochelais to Calvinism could not break an old entente between the densely fortified urban outpost and courting monarchs. At least until the early seventeenth century, the French crown needed the loyalty of frontier communities like La Rochelle so desperately that successive monarchs found it a bargain to buy their cooperation with lavish privileges.

Indulgences from the crown enabled the Rochelais to surround their city with an impregnable circuit of the most modern defenses. Before 1628, the crown placed absolutely no limits on the size and drill of the rochelais civic militia. Consequently, this big, well-equipped force, entirely under local command and supported by the largest park of heavy artillery amassed in any French town of the age, became a vital instrument of civic authority and a catalyst of urban politics engaging ordinary householders. Gallic monarchs from François I to Henry IV relied heavily on the Rochelais as capable defenders of a coastal province dangerously exposed within the striking distances of inveterate enemies such as Spain and England. This mutually beneficial correspondence brought a semblance of delegated royal administration to a wild corner of the kingdom infrequently traversed by lieutenants of the crown or by French kings themselves. Louis XIII's three punitive military campaigns through the west country in nine years (1619, 1621, and 1627) put an end to this isolation and confounded the wayward Rochelais whose ancestors were lucky to see a sovereign once in a generation. Consolidation of French monarchical authority after the perilous furor of the Religious Wars made the cherishing of strategically sited municipalities an outmoded method of territorial governance. Aggressive royal fortification of the Atlantic facade after 1650, spurred by Catholic confessionalization campaigns in the region, steadily reduced royal dependence on the armed forces of the region's fractious towns.

Agents of Catholicism were also scattered thinly across this uncharitable landscape. Local inhabitants lived largely outside what few circuits of predication small, poor bishoprics afforded. Isolated regional churches built before 1700 are remarkable for their resemblance to fortresses, crenellations not crucifixes dominate their architecture. These structures more often served as practical havens in a threatening environment rather than as anchors of orthodox spirituality for marine communities. Local vigilantes kept watch atop them, on occasion venturing out to destroy other sanctuaries captured by gangs of highwaymen or thieving curés. Many natives, rural and urban, persistently regarded all men of the cloth with deep suspicion as potent magicians especially adept at diabolically sabotaging the procreative powers of the laity by robbing male parishioners of their virility. On a dangerous frontier, popular anxiety over threats to communal reproductive security ran high for centuries, frequently operating to the great detriment and affront of churchmen, Catholic and Protestant alike. Even in west country towns, where the clergy of both faiths tended to concentrate, prelates only chipped away at a deep, hard substrate of irreverent folk belief intact until the end of the nineteenth century. In 1591, nearly a century after the onset of the French Reformation, a learned Calvinist pastor publishing in La Rochelle testified to the endurance and socially widespread character of a strong, regional anticlericalism. Paradoxically, he endorsed these convictions of westerners by exhorting his brethren to practice their new faith in an exemplary fashion as a means of protecting themselves against malevolent, venereal wizards probably operating even among the Protestant clergy and within Reformed congregations.

The rochelais bibliography of controversial Protestant books published in the sixteenth and seventeenth centuries incensed the more doctrinaire members of the city's pastorate, ministers appalled at (and occasionally sharing) the avid heterodoxy of their congregants' spiritualism. Pastor Odet de Nort (ministry 1563-1593) preached against many rochelais imprints, denouncing these heretical publications at regional and national synods of the French Reformed Church, but securing official, hierarchical condemnation of these best sellers only well after their subversive distribution throughout an urban readership. A key instance of documented local ministerial censorship of a text printed in La Rochelle (La Popelinière's scandalous *Histoire de France* of 1581) shows patrician pastors determined to suppress one noted author's repeated endorsements of popular debate over church teachings within Reformed congregations. Such encouragements of a fractious laity vexed rochelais clerics already confronted by many superstitious, quarrelsome, and intractable urban parishioners. La Rochelle's inhabitants adhered with varying degrees of rigor to the fundamental tenants of Calvinism and long competed amongst themselves for spiritual guidance of this community.

Between 1589 and 1621, de Nort's colleague, pastor Jacques Merlin confided to a private diary not only his own fears of attack by evil wraiths infesting the seaboard, but also a mounting disdain for middling and humbler townspeople disinclined to heed the admonishments of La Rochelle's Calvinist ministers. Merlin's real bête noire was Jean Tharay, the supremely irreverent leader of the 1614 urban political rebellion that brought down La Rochelle's old town council while directly challenging the moral authority of the city's pastors. In Tharay's profane tirades against Merlin and his ministerial cohorts, castigating them for siding with oligarchical civic magistrates and opposing popularly demanded alterations in town government, one can see a deep current of egalitarian, congregationalist sympathy among ordinary Rochelais rise to the surface of municipal affairs, crash against established governing institutions, and push them toward more democratic modes of operation. The municipal militia companies fostered this movement that also gained inspiration from Protestantism's empowerment of the laity. Political and religious innovations were profoundly intertwined in the history of La Rochelle, accelerating beyond the control of traditional urban ruling elites over the two decades before the great royal siege of 1628 arrested these developments.

Select serial sources gleaned from rochelais archives, such as wills redacted by a cross-section of Protestant residents in the sixteenth and seventeenth centuries, bear out pastor Merlin's doubts about his congregants' fidelity to all the precepts of Calvinist church doctrine. While most inhabitants of the city renounced Catholicism, forsaking its locally moribund institutions and sincerely turning to Protestantism as a more comforting, practical bulwark against worldly dangers, they did so without excessive zeal, electing to practice their new faith in different manners complementing rather than effacing older personal and communal devotions. Surviving records indicate that Calvinist teachings informed but did not dominate the civic polity. In general, rochelais Protestants did not bother to heed ministerial injunctions about posthumous benevolence with the attentiveness observed among the laity in other French Reformed towns. Rates of Protestant testamentary charity among all ranks of La Rochelle's population fall far below those found in other Calvinist communities. Calvinist testators in La Rochelle dealt more and more parsimoniously with their own ministers, preferring final donations to the poor of their own congregations and to collectivities like the local collège and the city's hospitals. A small but growing number of congregants over time flouted ministerial preaching entirely and wished for their executors to put coins directly into the hands of beggars attracted to the funeral cortege. Such good works are of a more Catholic inspiration and point up additional local limits to Protestant indoctrination among the citizenry. A steep decline in Protestant posthumous giving to ministers is coincident with the diminution of the pastorate's political influence inflicted by bourgeois rebels during the 1614 battle for control of town government. The pastors' unequivocal support for the oligarchical corps de ville in this struggle led to their further estrangement from a majority of townspeople and to a clear reduction in the material support local Calvinists were prepared to offer their clergymen.

The loss of all records kept by La Rochelle's Calvinist consistory makes it impossible to test rigorously my assessment of faltering rochelais church discipline against the operations of the one sacred body specifically charged with enforcing that discipline. However, pastor Merlin's persistent laments about popular irreverence toward church strictures coupled with blatant judicial evidence that wealthier Rochelais used local and Parisian courts to challenge the disciplinary operations of the consistory strongly suggest that this organ of ecclesiastical government was significantly less effective here than elsewhere in establishing its regulatory powers.

The extreme reluctance of west country church officials to employ excommunication as punishment for the persistently disobedient, a sanction the free use of which Jean Calvin demanded as the sine qua non of securing his ministry in Geneva, further limited the tutelage La Rochelle's consistory could impose. And while the very small number of religious disputes adjudicated by the city's mayoral court in the early seventeenth century suggests that municipal magistrates may have largely deferred to the consistory in these matters, the Reformed tribunal was never without formal and informal competitors in moral police of the community. Indeed, the mayoral court's heavy annual case loads, exceeding 1,000 judicial actions per year in the early seventeenth century, do not suggest that La Rochelle's consistory was especially effective at engendering the amicable reconciliations among feuding brethren such pious corporations were intended to achieve.

Among the consistoire's less formal competitors, Jean Chantre, the "good Christian king of the Bazoche," was a ribald carnival constable proudly defending his traditional jurisdictions against encroachment by humorless churchmen. Recall that La Rochelle's royal presidial court theatrically exonerated Chantre for his arrest of two suspected prostitutes and mockery of the consistory's failure to remove such miscreants from the streets prior to Lent. Long after the Reformation began in La Rochelle, ordinary townspeople like the law clerk Chantre denied ecclesiastical officials any monopoly over the articulation and defense of communal mores.

Although two of La Rochelle's most prestigious institutions, the ancient town council and the consistory of the Reformed church, joined forces in 1614 to oppose insurrectionary members of the bourgeoisie demanding access to town government, this alliance was no match for the rebels who broke the municipal oligarchy and repudiated instruction in civic affairs from the clergy. Rebel leaders like Pierre Bernardeau, Jean Grenot, and Jean Tharay, men with supraparochial reputations and personal contacts reaching deep into the city's restive laboring populations, engaged supportive family and friends in a campaign of mounting intimidation and political violence against established civic and church authorities.

Shrewdly insisting that communal militia companies should gain the right to elect all new town councilmen, bourgeois challengers decisively turned these units against the old corps de ville, precipitating one of the rarest events in the annals of early modern French urban history, a highly successful, middle-class coup d'état violently installing a new, more egalitarian regime of civic administration that endured through elections for over a decade. Rebels' neighborhood affiliations, militia company camaraderies, and old congregational solidarities all informed and undergirded this novel urban government, contributing to its strength and longevity. The new masters of rochelais politics openly criticized senior Calvinist clergymen not only for their meddling in communal affairs, but also for their rule of the church in contempt of the laity's opinions about proper ecclesiastical organization.

At precisely the moment when the control of other French cities was shrinking into the hands of royal appointees and venal robe nobles, the Rochelais, to the astonishment of contemporary legal scholars, took a step in the opposite direction, moving toward greater public participation in civic politics. Representatives of the victorious bourgeoisie and the defeated town council drew up a new charter of municipal government enacting an expanded electorate of militiamen, revised office eligibility requirements favoring burghers, and rigorous standards for more open conduct of civic administration. Swearing to uphold this new covenant of town government, its authors ordered all citizens to acknowledge its constitutional power and pledge themselves by sacred oath to its defense. Entire neighborhoods and whole militia companies subscribed at once.

This was the exceptional governing regime operating within La Rochelle when Louis XIII made west country towns the first targets of a pacification campaign intended to break the capacity of French Protestant grandees and assemblies of the Reformed church to foment armed opposition against the crown's ruling policies. Although the new craftsmen of rochelais politics were by no means the natural allies of aristocrats or synodal officials, they cautiously joined forces with fellow dissenters under the intensifying pressure of threatened royal attack in defense of Catholic institutions. The king's destruction of Saint-Jean-d'Angély and reduction of Béarnese municipalities demonstrated clearly what could happen to Calvinist civic regimes at the mercy of royal armies.

Ultimatums from the crown in the 1620's making restoration of the old corps de ville at La Rochelle a precondition of peace with the city could never be honored by a new majority of civic officeholders who had fought bravely in the rebellion of 1614 for access to the positions they now held. Having solemnly vowed to defend the innovative system of communal government they constituted, leaders of La Rochelle's third estate adamantly rejected noble commands to abandon politics. The duc de Richelieu may have sincerely preferred to reinstate and negotiate with locally discredited patricians (historically more compromising interlocutors), but by insisting on this restoration of an antique status quo he assured that there could be no peaceful resolution of the conflict opposing La Rochelle and the crown of France. This may have been the cardinal's ultimate aim anyway, but his diplomatic correspondence here for once shows him poorly informed about the real adversaries he faced in rochelais town government.

Through premeditation or ignorance, both sides missed opportunities for reconciliation. And here the sources suggest that it was not Richelieu's quest to establish absolutist modes of royal government which led inevitably to botched negotiations.

As an enormous royal siege army mustered against them, a new cadre of rochelais civic leaders found they could not count on aid from many of their town's former aristocratic and ecclesiastical allies. Among the great Calvinist seigneurial families of the west country, only the Rohans kept until the end their defensive compact with the region's most important, partially Reformed municipality. Cavaliers and clerics supervising the military circles formed in other Huguenot provinces made no concerted effort to help a beleaguered La Rochelle. The alacrity with which former rebels and current town councilmen like Jean Tharay and Zachery Chatton turned to logistical preparations for battle could not have flattered all those personnages who now needed extra coaxing to join the fray. For distinguished outsiders, any personal sacrifices on behalf of the Rochelais after 1614 more noticeably benefitted a municipal governing regime controlled by impolite and ignoble militiamen.

Bereft of significant domestic support, the Rochelais turned to the king of England, treasonably dealing with a foreign monarch and committing one final, irremediably fatal act of lèse-majesté. Thus the major reconfiguration men like Jean Tharay worked in rochelais town government after 1614 should definitely be included among the factors eventually disrupting that old coalition of dissenting seigneurs, pastors, jurists, patricians, and skilled citizens upon which the security of French Protestantism ultimately depended. Failure of the French Reformation can be attributed in part to the powerful centrifugal forces peripheral townspeople like the vexatious Rochelais generated among Gallic Calvinists.

La Rochelle's unconditional surrender to the royal siege army in 1628 gave Louis XIII an unprecedented opportunity to remake and re-catholicize a frontier town too important to raze entirely. This chance was all the rarer because no regional estates or provincial parlements ever had jurisdiction over La Rochelle and thus could not now interfere in royal rebuilding plans. Louis' reconstruction of the entire community gives singularly clear insights into the modes of statecraft he preferred when spared the meddling of subordinate legislatures.

Among these methods, the expansion of seigneurial authority, the curtailment of most municipal liberties, and the strengthening of royal justice were paramount. Through the creation of the fief St. Louis, a lordship the king personally wished to establish, a vast tract of formerly civic space around La Rochelle was ceremoniously handed over to a member of the French peerage. Louis advocated direct and imprescriptible experience of vassalage as the most reliable means of bringing fractious urbanites to heel. The dukes of the Saint-Simon family repaid a generous sovereign by rigorously administering his gift of suzerainty over the Rochelais for decades.

By the edict through which Louis reduced La Rochelle, all of the community's civic privileges were revoked and the walls physically defining urban space obliterated. Over the nucleus of city streets left standing the king's justice prevailed. An intendant responsible for supervising police of the community in accord with crown directives was established and given the authority to employ the jurists of the refurbished royal presidial court in La Rochelle as subordinates. From this body of the king's judges, further delegations were made to assure that the redesigned municipal police court operated formally and informally as an auxiliary of the presidial.

Tracking cases handled and sentences rendered by new judges on the municipal police court after 1628 shows that royal appropriation of this tribunal dramatically altered the dispensation of justice within the urban community. The court ceased to be a steward of arbitration in defense of collectively held civic values and became a more dictatorial agency of town government enforcing the administrative decisions and religious opinions of the king and his retainers. The police court, through the domination of a narrow coterie of native Catholic family men, took the lead in prosecuting the local Counter-Reformation, subjecting all residents of the city to censorious enforcement of official church doctrine. The rigor of this initiative, reflected in police court sentences, altered the balance of coercive power between custom and statute, consensus and compulsion in the internal governance of the urban community. This transformation was part of a calculated and sustained royal assault on the corporative foundations of La Rochelle's civil society, a communal ethos fostered by the old urban institutions targeted either for destruction or for more constrictive regulation by the crown: the town council, bourgeois political bodies like the Council of Forty-Eight, the civic militia companies open to all householders, the organs of municipal justice, the independent craft guilds, and the multiple Calvinist congregations inside the city. In the aftermath of the 1627-28 siege, agents of the crown diminished the corporative structures of La Rochelle's third estate, while endeavoring to supplant them with the sodalities of the first and second estates dominant elsewhere. The banality of rochelais politics after 1650 registers the success of this campaign. Post-siege La Rochelle became a proving ground for the tactics of urban administration by which successive monarchs in the Bourbon line ultimately managed to stunt the development of municipal government and civic culture within their dominions.

However, the triumph of this initiative in La Rochelle should not blind us to other, more enduring features of the local urban culture it either left relatively undisturbed or positively reinforced. Throughout this book, I have tried to study municipal government not as an extraneous imposition upon, but rather as an integral part of urban society in La Rochelle. Central to this task was adoption of an analytical framework allowing investigation of rochelais town politics without recourse to modern, anachronistic distinctions between the "public" and "private" spheres of citizens' lives. Instead, the basic format of this inquiry has been shaped by the vocabulary of sixteenth- and seventeenth-century rochelais documents telling the story of civic affairs as witnessed and understood by contemporaries. Their commentary on how and why town government worked or failed emphasizes the perennial influence of kinship and its obligations on the political activities of La Rochelle's governors, Protestant and Catholic. Diverse documents drawn from La Rochelle's surviving archives attest that the world of the household and the world of the town hall were long and thickly interconnected.

Modifications in the form and changes in the personnel of rochelais civic institutions allow one to speak of three governing regimes in the city from 1548 to 1650. The first, running from reestablishment of the full corps de ville in 1548 to the defeat of this body in the rebellion of 1614, can be typified as a closed oligarchy of wealthy, Calvinist bourgeois families long resident in the city and competing for control of all major posts in municipal government. Local royal officials had little direct or indirect influence over this civic administration.

The second regime, inaugurated by the 1614 insurrection of unenfranchised citizens and running until the royal siege of 1628, can be classified as a hybrid, outwardly retaining the institutions of the first but introducing new, unique electoral procedures giving a wider cross-section of Protestant townsmen access to positions of governing authority and rendering important decisions of civic officials subject to approval by all members of the city's militia companies voting in referendums. Agents of the king were even more unwelcome in the deliberations of these new governing bodies, further reducing the monarchy's control over city politics and heightening royal suspicions of citizens' fidelity to the administrative, diplomatic, and religious priorities of the crown. As a legally constituted, precedent-setting municipal administration committed to its own interpretation of the Protestant cause in France, this regime was destined to provoke a Catholic ruling dynasty increasingly intolerant of religious and political dissent. This conflict repeatedly flared into open warfare and La Rochelle's second administration was finally dismembered after its capitulation to besieging royal armies in 1628.

The third civic regime, established after the debacle of 1628, was dominated by a small number of Catholic townsmen and royal jurists serving at the pleasure of the king. These royal agents were largely recruited from a few densely intermarried Catholic kin groups established in La Rochelle since before the middle of the sixteenth century. Reduction of the city's surviving Calvinist community and enforcement of the Counter-Reformation's mandates were among the principal tasks the king expected his new local vassals to undertake.

The transitions outlined above show that La Rochelle ultimately got caught up in two general trends promoted by the crown to the detriment of early modern French cities: progressive infiltration and capture of town governments by royal officers, particularly judicial officials, and a consequent, epoch-making loss of political autonomy by the *bonnes villes* of the Bourbon kingdom. Yet, proof of these transformations in La Rochelle should not obscure the common and enduring social structure of successive city governments the crown was never able nor really disposed to alter. Integral to that structure was a familial system for the definition, distribution, and exercise of governing authority. The persistent local operation of that system from 1530 to 1650 suggests that the three regimes of rochelais civic administration discernable over this period are best understood as variations on an archetypical familial form of French urban government exploited by Huguenots and Catholics, and do not, of themselves, mark profound breaks in the social history of town and country.

In La Rochelle during the latter sixteenth century we have witnessed contention over municipal offices among ruling oligarchs regularly engaging their entire, extensive networks of kinsmen. The decadence of that ruling elite, its failure to abide by all the unwritten rules of government by patriarchs, served as a valid pretext for the political uprising of 1614 led by thickly interrelated bourgeois rebels who expressly justified their violent seizure of power as necessary to prevent further misrule by the immature, undisciplined offspring of irresponsible city fathers. Among the reciprocal obligations between governors and governed that shaped the moral economy of early modern rochelais politics must be counted a respect for the protocols of behavior enshrined in well-managed households and defense of those norms in the conduct of civic government.

After 1628, the crown restaffed rochelais city government with more trustworthy Catholic townsmen and encouraged, or at least quietly acquiesced to, the emplacement of a new civic regime dominated by densely intermarried Catholic kin groups and their confidants. Under their aegis, the institutions of municipal police were engaged in a strict, city-wide campaign to enforce respect for paternal authority and for the good government of families, popular mores appropriated and judicially intensified by the local agents of the French Counter-Reformation to win the hearts and minds of town dwellers.

Seen from this perspective, the "family-state compact" historians like Sarah Hanley identify as a statutory product of seventeenth-century French royal jurists, possesses a far longer, less overt history integral to the politics of early modern French towns. However, after 1628, La Rochelle became a renowned demonstration site for the elaboration and enforcement of this traditional compact by Catholic patriarchs, part of Louis XIII's triumph over the city (an improved domestic economy) celebrated in innumerable pamphlets, poems, patriotic songs, engravings, and medals. Weaker members of the old urban community, Protestants, women, children, widows, and the homeless poor now bore the brunt of the social discipline the male elders of Catholic clans instructively dispensed with royal approval. The inclination of the chronically overburdened and under-financed French monarchy to cut the material costs of rulership by accommodation with local governing elites and the serviceable systems of police they controlled perpetuated the old sociology of urban politics in La Rochelle. Here, bonds of Catholic kinship sustained and strengthened the networks of authority the crown accepted and turned to its own short-term advantage.

Over the long century covered by this study, I have searched for alterations in the form and content of La Rochelle's government. Important reconfigurations and confessional reorientations of municipal institutions did occur and can be traced in the archives. Yet, fundamental continuities in the political life of the city should not be overlooked. Among these are a high degree of independent decision making for rochelais magistrates in the day-to-day governance of the town that was never fully subject to control from Paris. Reinstatement of a rochelais citizens' militia strictly limited to Catholics in 1634, six years after the great siege ended, demonstrates how the royal bureaucracy persistently expected local civic leaders to take responsibility for the traditional, onerous, and costly tasks of urban police and defense. Conservation of La Rochelle's commercial and municipal tribunals by royal order after 1628 also gave Catholic townsmen and neighborhood chieftains powerful means to assert their own patriarchal values in the surveillance and regulation of the community.

At a more fundamental level of society and politics, it is the persistent importance of extended, multi-generational bourgeois kin groups in the staffing and operation of municipal government that stands out against the dramatic events of La Rochelle's history from 1530 to 1650. Supplementing the ties of consanguinity and affinity that linked municipal officials and shaped their conception and practice of civic office were the enduring reciprocal obligations of godparentage regularly exchanged by governors of La Rochelle during this period. The subtext of rochelais politics communicated to us by contemporary agents and observers of city government throughout this era is dominated by the terms *famille, parenté, alliance,* and *parrainage.* Kinsmen and the confidants they convinced to accept the duties of godparents are ubiquitous in the ranks of officeholders who formed, challenged, and operated successive regimes of rochelais town government. Intrigues among townsmen for the conquest and control of municipal offices persistently tended to follow lines of blood, marriage, and godparentage major kin groups always negotiated and competed to maintain. The habits of mind and comportment these practices required of successful aspirants to municipal posts, including deference to the authority of elders, regard for the fidelity of in-laws, and care for the well-being of neighbors, were also elemental components of the political culture townsmen shared. Contests for civic offices in La Rochelle played out in accord with the rules of that culture which varied little over the time span of my study.

Restoring the public and political history of the extended urban family broadens our knowledge of the principles that informed urban government and the nature of the social groups engaged in the making and unmaking of municipal police. This approach is most useful in the search for the factors imparting cohesiveness to both the institutions of early modern French government and the movements of political and religious dissent common to the era. Archival evidence in La Rochelle suggests to me that historians confronted by the nagging anonymity of seventeenth-century rebel crowds, the paucity of first-person accounts by contemporary political actors stating their objectives, and the difficulty of avoiding reductive judgements about which calculations of morality and economy influenced the behavior of governors and governed, can better meet these challenges through new efforts at reconstructing the social context in which political events, broadly and narrowly defined, occurred.

In early modern France, the kin group was a fundamental component of rural and urban society. The rich histories such groups left behind in parish church records, in the papers of notaries, and in quickly recorded courtroom transcripts situate their members in the community, recount the obligations they assumed, and evoke the values they espoused. It is this corpus of information that provides the most ample means of interpreting the traces of political activity townspeople also left in the archives.

Of course, recapturing the public and political histories of extended families will not alone suffice to explain the function and dysfunction of government under the ancien régime. Attention must also be given to economic trends and ideological conflicts as precipitants of the political crises family men and magistrates faced throughout the era. However, the approach to politics I have followed can lead to the recognition of similarities in the form and spirit of the institutions serving to police the early modern world. Such resemblances were not hidden to the political actors of the epoch and transcend the narrow fields we have created to study the period. Understanding families in politics and politics in families can only help us to see more clearly how the social fabric of the time was stitched together.

Reconstructing the sociology of urban politics can also cast new light on old historical problems generated by the troubled relationship of the French crown and its *bonnes villes*. In La Rochelle, as in other provincial urban centers, the French monarchy preferred the manipulation of local authorities over the cost and chaos their complete destruction would have entailed. Even after the great siege of 1628, the crown was willing to conserve some key civic institutions and to tolerate the operation of a traditional system for the recruitment of their officers dominated by established urban kin groups. In La Rochelle, this process of cooptation should not be construed as a simple mortal combat between royal absolutism and municipal corporatism. As my research suggests, the ideological dimensions of rochelais urban politics encompassed not only corporative principles, but also the mores of disciplined and respected kin groups which municipal officeholders could flaunt only at the peril of their political careers. This was a combination of values that would continually shape town dwellers' reactions to royal initiatives of government and which the crown, too, could not disregard with impunity. Investigation of how royal agents responded to the sociology of urban politics in the towns of provincial France (employing local power brokers in Aix, putting men with powerful connections at court in charge in Toulouse, and giving local Catholic patriarchs decision-making powers in La Rochelle) advances our understanding of the wide repertoire of opportunistic governing tactics by which the kings of France sought to police their realm. Where, how, and why opposition to these royal stratagems took root also becomes clearer.

Over the course of the seventeenth century, the French crown managed to form uneasy alliances with urban ruling elites through enlistment of those authorities and their familial systems of police in royal projects of government. This practice was expedient but also continually jeopardized by the monarchy's favorite method of raising money. Venality of office posed a direct threat to the tenure of kinsmen in municipal posts and worked to subvert the advancement of local *chefs de famille* to positions of influence in town government. The vehement criticism venality inspired among governors and governed in early modern France, loudly expressed for example in the *cahiers de doléances* drawn up for the *états généraux* of 1614, can, in part, be explained by the threat sales of sinecures posed to established systems for recruitment of officeholders subordinating a candidate's wealth to his status, reputation, and kinship ties in the community he aspired to govern. City fathers could not be expected to tolerate for long a new system that might put a stranger in their midst. To eliminate that possibility, consortia of townsmen were willing to buy up the venal posts the king added to their municipal bureaucracies, diverting funds to royal coffers that might otherwise have been used for local investment or municipal improvements. This was a grudging investment, incapable of endearing buyer to seller, but indicative of the lengths to which civic authorities were prepared to go in defense of a traditional nepotism deeply satisfying to the moral and political values they respected. The cost of these transactions by family men to the towns and kingdom of France, in terms of long-term productive investments lost, was surely very great. Analyzing their motives adds further social and cultural vantage points on the economic troubles that would dog the country for decades to come.

The well-stocked and partly explored archives of French provincial towns like La Rochelle offer historians a wealth of sources permitting reassessment of the social and ideological dimensions of sixteenth- and seventeenth-century French urban politics. In La Rochelle, investigation of these topics has yielded both a better understanding of how civic government functioned on a daily basis and a more accurate chronology of what did and did not change in the governance of the city between 1530 and 1650. Getting at what politics meant to the townspeople of early modern France requires a multiplication of perspectives on the social organizations charged formally and informally with the police of urban communities. Looking at town governments from above, behind, and beneath, from the standpoints of the families that ruled, staffed, and obeyed them, works to accomplish this goal. In the process, we can more accurately measure the political weight of these institutions and the strength of the power relationships they formed.

# APPENDIX ONE

Commissaires, Conseillers, and Procureurs de Justice in La Rochelle's Municipal Police Court 1629-1638 and 1645-1649

| | 1629 | 1630 | 1631 | 1632 | 1633 |
|---|---|---|---|---|---|
| *Commissaires* | Jacques Fouchier | Nicolas Bertinaud | Jean de l'Escalle | Jean de l'Escalle | Zenis Remigoux |
| | Nicolas Bertinaud | Pierre Baudry | Pierre Herbert | Julien Robin | Julien Robin |
| *Conseillers* | Louis Gaigneur | Isaac Auboyneau | Jacques Alleaume | Jacques Alleaume | Jacques Alleaume |
| | Gabriel Barreau | Jean Tharay | André David | André David | André David |
| | ? | Louis Gaigneur | Gabriel Picaudeau | Jean Pinard | F. Apurillaud |
| | ? | Gabriel Barreau | Jean Pinard | F. Apurillaud | Michel Maigre |
| *Procureurs* | ? | ? | Jacques Thibault | Jacques Thibault | Jean Ollivier |
| | ? | ? | Jean Tharay | Laurens Bigotteau | Jacques Thibault |
| | ? | ? | Isaac Auboyneau | Isaac Auboyneau | Thomas Venette |
| | ? | ? | Jean Tharay | Jean Tharay | Gaspard Cabesse |

| | 1634 | 1635 | 1636 | 1637 | 1638 |
|---|---|---|---|---|---|
| *Commissaires* | Jacques Aigron | Jacques Foucher | Pierre Moriceau | Jean de l'Escalle | Olliver Nicolas |
| | Jacques Gattet | Jean Rogier | Jean Grisseau | Louis Durand | Pierre Maupronge |
| *Conseillers* | B. Barbier | B. Meurguier | Jacques François | Jacques Bigotteau | Jean Soucy |
| | Jean Bertinaud | Jean Macquand | ? | Jacques François | Jacques François |

| 1634 | 1635 | 1636 | 1637 | 1638 |
|---|---|---|---|---|
| *Conseillers* | | | | |
| Louis Gaigneur | Jean Tuffet | ? | Isaac Auboyneau | Antoine Prieur |
| François Lebreton | Jacques François | ? | Jean Gaigneur | Jean Macquand |
| *Procureurs* | | | | |
| Jacques Alleaume | Jacques Alleaume | Jacques Alleaume | Jacques Alleaume | Jacques Alleaume |
| André David | F. Apurillaud | F. Apurillaud | F. Apurillaud | F. Apurillaud |
| F. Apurillaud | Michel Maigre | Michel Maigre | Michel Maigre | Michel Maigre |
| Michel Maigre | Pierre Aubin | Pierre Aubin | Michel Portay | Michel Portay |

| 1645 | 1646 | 1647 | 1648 | 1649 |
|---|---|---|---|---|
| *Commissaires* | | | | |
| Louis Voyneau | Alexandre Landez | Pierre Baudry | Henri Chappet | Jean Rougier |
| François Guibert | Michel Brunet | Jean Corue | Jean Corue | Jacques Tuffet |
| *Conseillers* | | | | |
| B. Meurguier | Jacques Bigotteau | B. Meurguier | Jacques Bigotteau | Simon Guerry |
| Emanuel Leborgne | Jean Droualt | Gabriel Barreau | Isaac Auboyneau | Pierre Groyer |
| Isaac Auboyneau | Jean Roy | Jean Bernier | J. Suger | Nicolas Denis |
| François Billon | Helie Fond | Antoine Prieur | Pierre Nerve | Augier de Chavin |
| *Procureurs* | | | | |
| Jacques Alleaume | Jacques Alleaume | Jacques Alleaume | Jacques Alleaume | Jacques Alleaume |
| F. Apurillaud | F. Apurillaud | F. Apurillaud | F. Apurillaud | F. Apurillaud |
| Michel Portay | Michel Portay | Michel Portay | Michel Portay | Michel Portay |
| François Persony | Abraham Buffard | Abraham Buffard | Abraham Buffard | Abraham Buffard |

Juges, Consuls, and Conseillers of La Rochelle's Merchants' Tribunal, 1629–1650

|  | 1629 | 1630 | 1631 | 1632 | 1633 |
|---|---|---|---|---|---|
| *Juge* | Jacques Laborier | Jacques Laborier | Thomas Vinette | Jacques François | Jacques Thibault |
| *Consuls* | Michel Bigotteau | Isaac Auboyneau | Jacques François | Jacques Thibault | Gaspard Cabesse |
|  | Jacques Chauvet | Louis Gaigneur | Thomas Gaigneur | Laurens Bigotteau | Gabriel Barreau |
| *Conseillers* | Isaac Auboyneau | Thomas Gaigneur | Jean Mondot | Jean Mascault | André Thibault |
|  | Louis Gaigneur | Jacques Thibault | André Thibault | Guillaume Feniou | Jean Mondot |
|  | Gaspard Cabesse | André Thibault | Pierre Le Barthe | Pierre Le Barthe | Guyon Rabret |
|  | Gabriel Barreau | Laurens Bigotteau | Laurens Bigotteau | Antoine Prieur | Pierre Gaigneur |
|  | Jean Pinard | Jean Mondot | Jean Mascault | Guyon Rabret | Nicolas Venette |
|  | Gabriel Picaudeau | Pierre François | Pierre Naudin | Pierre Gaigneur | André La Fasque |
|  | Laurens Bigotteau | Guillaume Feniou | Gabriel Barreau | Nicolas Venette | Gilles La Gorse |
|  | Jean Marchais | André La Fasque | ? | Jacques Viole | Gabriel Picaudeau |

|  | 1634 | 1635 | 1636 | 1637 | 1638 |
|---|---|---|---|---|---|
| *Juge* | Isaac Auboyneau | Jean Tuffet | Jacques Laborier | Jacques Thibault | Jean Tuffet |
| *Consuls* | Gabriel Barreau | Jean Mascault | André Thibault | Emanuel Leborgne | Louis Gaigneur |
|  | Jean Mascault | Antoine Prieur | Emanuel Leborgne | Gilles La Gorse | André La Fasque |

| | 1634 | 1635 | 1636 | 1637 | 1638 |
|---|---|---|---|---|---|
| *Conseillers* | André Thibault | Jean Mondot | André La Fasque | Guillaume Feniou | André Cornut |
| | Guillaume Feniou | André La Fasque | Gabriel Picaudeau | André Cornut | Jean Donnage |
| | Gabriel Picaudeau | Guyon Rabret | Gilles La Gorse | Pierre Gaigneur | Jean Savin |
| | Antoine Prieur | André Cornut | Nicolas Venette | Louis Gandin | Mathieu Giraud |
| | Gilles La Gorse | Jean Bigotteau | Jean Roy | Jacques Mousnier | Jean Chanson |
| | André Cornut | Pierre Desnier | François Blanchard | Jean Donnage | André Gaigneur |
| | Emanuel Leborgne | Jean Roy | Jacques Viole | André Gaigneur | Jean Neau |
| | F. Apurillaud | Louis Gandin | Jean Forion | Jean Neau | Louis Auboyneau |
| | | | | Louis Auboyneau | |

| | 1639 | 1640 | 1641 | 1642 | 1643 |
|---|---|---|---|---|---|
| *Juge* | Isaac Auboyneau | Thomas Venette | Jean Mascault | Louis Gaigneur | Antoine Prieur |
| *Consuls* | Antoine Prieur | Gabriel Barreau | Emanuel Leborgne | Gaspard Cabesse | Jean Roy |
| | Jean Le Roy | Gabriel Picaudeau | Jacques Viole | Jean Savin | André Cornut |
| *Conseillers* | Jean Mondot | Jean Pinard | ? | André Cornut | Jacques Mousnier |
| | Guillaume Feniou | Jean Savin | ? | Jean Chanson | Jean Chauvet |
| | Gabriel Picaudeau | Jean Chanson | ? | Pierre Gaigneur | ? |
| | Jacques Viole | Guy Gertin | ? | Pierre Mondot | Pierre Chapeau |

*Conseillers (Cont.)*

| 1639 | 1640 | 1641 | 1642 | 1643 |
|---|---|---|---|---|
| Jacques Mousnier | Jacques Pillard | ? | Louis Gandin | Augier de Chavin |
| Louis Gandin | Jean Chauvet | ? | Martin Poirier | Pierre Robert |
| Jean Masse | ? | ? | Dominique de | Dominique de |
| Chuerry | ? |  | Jean Lucquot |  |
| Bernard Bouvin | ? |  |  |  |

| | 1644 | 1645 | 1646 | 1647 | 1648 |
|---|---|---|---|---|---|
| *Juge* | Emanuel Leborgne | Thomas Venette | Gabriel Barreau | Emanuel Leborgne | Antoine Prieur |
| *Consuls* | Jacques Viole | Jean Savin | Jean Roy | Jean Drouault | Jacques Mousnier |
| | Jean Drousult | Jacques Mousnier | Augier de Chauvin | Jean Meau | Nicolas Venette |
| *Conseillers* | ? | Jean Mondot | Guillaume Feniou | Jean Chanson | Jean Chauvet |
| | ? | Jean Chauvet | Nicolas Venette | ? | Pierre Robert |
| | ? | Pierre Robert | Isaac Auboyneau | Simon de Vaucousin | ? |
| | ? | Simon de Vaucousin | Edmond Desprez | Jean Gaigneur | Estienne de Mourron |
| | Jean Gaigneur | Jean Gaigneur | Estienne de Mourron | Antoine Sugier | Bernard Bouvin |
| | Antoine Lucas | Antoine Lucas | Louis Gaigneur | Jacques Nadau | Claude Dandet |
| | Claude Dandet | Claude Dandet | Germain Girard | Pierre Votas | Claude Chaumet |
| | Jean Roy | Jean Roy | Antoine Chauvet | Gabriel Cabesse | Philippe Rozet |

| 1649 | | 1650 | |
|------|---|------|---|
| *Juge* | | | |
| Thomas Venette | | Jean Roy | |
| | | | |
| *Consuls* | | | |
| Jean Savin | | Augier de Chauvin | |
| Jean Chauvet | | Isaac Auboyneau | |
| | | | |
| *Conseillers* | | | |
| Jean Mondot | | Guillaume Feniou | |
| Simon de Vaucousin | | Pierre Robert | |
| Jean Gaigneur | | Antoine Lucas | |
| Edmond Desprez | | Louis Gaigneur | |
| Antoine Sugier | | Antoine Chauvet | |
| Pierre Votas | | Mathurin Eyquem | |
| Gabriel Cabesse | | Jean Fleury | |
| Jacques Bonitton | | Christoffle Piqueray | |

# SELECT BIBLIOGRAPHY

## I. *Manuscript Sources*

### *Archives Départmentales de la Charente-Maritime, La Rochelle*

| Series B: | Presidial Court of La Rochelle | | |
|---|---|---|---|
| B 1338 | Registre de la cour du governement 1579 | | |
| B 1339-B 1357 | Audiences ordinaires du présidial 1609-1646 | | |
| B 1466 | Audiences extraordinaires du présidial 1614 | | |
| B 1469 | Audiences extraordinaries du présidial 1617 | | |
| B 1473 | Audiences extraordinaires du présidial 1633 | | |
| B 1522-B 1523 | Sentences civiles 1609-1617 | | |

| Series E: | Notaries | | |
|---|---|---|---|
| 3 E 10-11 | Joslain: | Registres | 1584-1629 |
| 3 E 132-137 | Lecourt: | " | 1549-1560 |
| 3 E 138-141 | Barrault: | " | 1555-1559 |
| 3 E 142 | Coultret: | " | 1556-1558 |
| 3 E 143-161 | Tharazon: | " | 1563-1588 |
| 3 E 164-175 | Boutet: | " | 1564-1602 |
| 3 E 176-178 | Baulouet: | " | 1565-1572 |
| 3 E 180-183 | Verdelet: | " | 1569-1588 |
| 3 E 184-185 | Bomyer: | " | 1576-1580 |
| 3 E 186-201 | Bion: | " | 1585-1600 |
| 3 E 202-210 | Bigeard: | " | 1589-1602 |
| 3 E 211-231 | Cousseau: | " | 1603-1650 |
| 3 E 245-259 | Chesneau: | " | 1616-1646 |
| 3 E 267-270 | Cherbonnier: | " | 1637-1649 |
| 3 E 1171-1194 | Combaud: | Liasses | 1600-1610 |
| 3 E 1219-1222 | Pierre: | Registres | 1603-1606 |
| 3 E 1226-1244 | Conay: | " | 1605-1628 |
| 3 E 1245-1250 | Conay: | Liasses | 1614-1628 |
| 3 E 1251-1254 | Combaud: | " | 1615-1640 |
| 3 E 1255-1283 | Combaud: | " | 1612-1640 |
| 3 E 1284-1296 | Teuleron: | Registres | 1631-1650 |
| 3 E 1720 | Savarit: | " | 1587-1611 |
| 3 E 1767-1774 | Juppin: | " | 1620-1650 |
| 3 E 1777-1779 | Tongrelou: | Liasses | 1629-1650 |
| 3 E 1780-1783 | Tongrelou: | Registres | 1629-1650 |
| 3 E 2025-2027 | Pancereau: | " | 1563-1570 |
| 3 E 2033-2044 | Bonnyn (père): | " | 1578-1602 |
| 3 E 2045-2050 | Bonnyn (fils): | " | 1603-1627 |
| 3 E 2147-2157 | Naudin: | " | 1561-1589 |
| 3 E 2158-2162 | Masset: | " | 1603-1624 |

| *Series I:* | *Protestant Etat Civil* | |
|---|---|---|
| I 1-I 38 | Baptisms/Marriages/Burials | 1561-1658 |

### Archives Municipales, La Rochelle

| | | |
|---|---|---|
| DD 44 | Voierie   c.1634-c.1638 | |
| E Suppl. 280 (FF 4) | Police Municipale | 1590-1591 |
| E Suppl. 281 (FF 5) | Cour de la mairie | 1600-1602 |
| E Suppl. 282 (FF 6) | "     "   "     " | 1603-1605 |
| E Suppl. 286 (FF 9) | "     "   "     " | 1617-1618 |
| E Suppl. 287 (FF 10) | "     "   "     " | 1618 |
| E Suppl. 288 (FF 12) | "     "   "     " | 1620 |
| E Suppl. 292 (FF 17) | Police Cour Municipale | 1634 |
| E Suppl. 293 (FF 18) | "          "          " | 1635-1636 |
| E Suppl. 294 (FF 19) | "          "          " | 1636 |
| E Suppl. 295 (FF 20) | "          "          " | 1638 |
| E Suppl. 296 (FF 21) | "          "          " | 1637 |
| E Suppl. 297 (FF 22) | "          "          " | 1640 |
| E Suppl. 298 (FF 23) | "          "          " | 1641 |
| E Suppl. 299 (FF 24) | "          "          " | 1642 |
| E Suppl. 300 (FF 25) | "          "          " | 1642 |
| E Suppl. 301 (FF 26) | "          "          " | 1642 |
| E Suppl. 302 (FF 27) | "          "          " | 1643-1644 |
| E Suppl. 303 (FF 28) | "          "          " | 1645 |
| E Suppl. 304 (FF 29) | "          "          " | 1646 |
| E Suppl. 305 (FF 30) | "          "          " | 1647 |
| E Suppl. 306 (FF 31) | "          "          " | 1648 |
| Recueil 360 | Ordonnances et proclamations | 1622-1633 |

### Bibliothèque Municipale, La Rochelle

| | |
|---|---|
| MS 40 | "Livre de la Poterne," f. 1-103. |
| MSS 45/46 | "Baudouin Ms." Chronicle of La Rochelle. |
| MS 50 | Bruneau, "Histoire de La Rochelle." |
| MS 58 | Mervault, "Histoire de La Rochelle." |
| MS 61-62 | Jaillot, "Annales de La Rochelle," 1563-1620. |
| MS 80 | "Diaire de Bergier," 1570-1596, fols. 92r-153r. |
| | "Diaire de Pierre Guillaudeau," fols. 155r-208v. |
| MS 81 | "Titres de la Ville de La Rochelle." |
| MS 82 | "Recueil," collection of municipal privileges. |
| MS 97 | Lists of civic officeholders c.1574-c.1622. |
| MS 98 | "Matricule des juges, consuls, et conseillers." |
| MS 99 | Lists of civic officeholders c.1629-c.1748. |
| MS 127 | Municipal economic affairs. |
| MS 116 | "Censif de la commanderie du Temple," 1590-1615. |
| MS 131 | "Analects de l'égilse de St. Jean du Perrot." |
| MSS 150-151 | "Recueil," includes P. Vincent, "Recherches sur la réformation en la ville de La Rochelle," fols. 3-20. |
| MS 139 | "Confrairies en les églises de La Rochelle." |
| MS 153 | Colin, "Annales de La Rochelle," c.1560-c.1720. |
| MS 161 | "Diaire" of pastor Jacques Merlin. |

| | |
|---|---|
| MS 209 | "Registre de la cour du governement," 1551-1556. |
| MSS 211-213 | "Registres: Audiences de la cour du gouvernement," 1564-1565. |
| MSS 217-222 | "Registres: Audiences de la cour du gouvernement," 1565-1566. |
| MSS 235-236 | "Insinuations, cour de la ville," c.1564-c.1580. |
| MS 250 | "Registre des confrairies," c.1564-c.1567. |
| MS 251 | "Registres," Church of St. Marguerite, Catholic baptisms, marriages, burials, c.1598-c.1608. |
| MS 252 | Baptisms, St. Marguerite, 1608-1619. |
| MS 254 | Marriages, St. Marguerite, c.1608-c.1618. |
| MS 255 | Marriages, St. Marguerite, c.1619-c.1636. |
| MS 308 | "Recueil," municipal ordinances. |
| MS 346 | Jaillot, notes on major town families. |
| MS 350-354 | Jourdan, family biographies. |
| MS 761 | Lettres sur les affaires de La Rochelle. |
| MSS 763-765 | "Conseils du corps de ville," 1618-1619, 1622-1623, and 1624-1625. |
| MS 768 | "Conseils du corps de ville," 1627-1628. |
| MS 773 | Registre des resultats des affaires de la ville. |
| MS 779 | "Papier des conversions," abjurations of Calvinism, c.1628-c.1692. |
| MSS 1787-92 | Registres of Notary Busseau 1579-1602. |
| MSS 1809-13 | Registres of Notary Dubet 1600-1606. |
| MSS 1824-40 | Registres of Notary Moreau 1632-1650. |
| MS 1862 | Registres of Notary Paillu, 1582-1600. |
| MSS 1863-68 | Registres of Notary Papin, 1617-1627. |
| MSS 1873-75 | Registres of Notary Servant 1608-1614. |
| MS 2667 | Correspondence of Guy Chabot de Jarnac. |
| MS 2935 | Correspondence of Guy Chabot de Jarnac. |

*Archives des Affaires Etrangères*
*Quay d'Orsay, Paris*

Mémoires et Documents, France, 49, 246, 250, 781-785, 787-789, 795, 800, 828, 1475, and 1696.

*Archives Nationales, Paris*

| | |
|---|---|
| E 42a/b | Registre, Conseil d'état de des finances, 1613. |
| 43a/b | 1614 |
| 44-45 | 1614 |
| 46a/b | 1614 |
| 47a/b | 1614 |
| 48a/b | 1615 |
| E 1684-1696 | Arrêts, Religion Réformée. |
| K 1222/1223 | Provinces, Saintonge/Aunis 1199-1778. |
| K 1251 | La Rochelle. |
| M 536 | "Titres généalogiques de Saint-Simon." |
| P 2907 | Paris, *Chambre des Comptes*, edicts relative to |

Fief St. Louis of La Rochelle.

Q1 116-120      Titres des arrondissements de La Rochelle.
                Dukes de Saint-Simon, Property Transactions.
TT 263B         Affaires et biens des protestants. Généralité
                de La Rochelle 1559-1663.
TT 264          Protestants, La Rochelle.
V5              Grand Conseil
                1228-1230
V6              Conseil Privé
                20-30, 69-72, 1196-1198, 1224, 1230, 1232


*Bibliothèque Nationale, Paris*

Collection Clairambault 354, 357, 361, 362, 364, 379, 579, and 963.
Collection Dupuy 100, 187, 323, 427, and 588.
MSS fr.   3795      La Rochelle, Corps de Ville.
MSS fr.   3805      Rochelais correspondence.
MSS fr.   15588     Peace Negotiations 1626.
MSS fr.   15818     "Extraict des actes de l'assemblée."
MSS fr.   15880     "Lettres et depeches originales."
MSS fr.   18183-18188 Conseil d'Etat, Registres 1613-1616.
MSS fr.   18256     Etats Généraux, 1614.
MSS fr.   (Anciens Fonds) 23339 La Rochelle, Sédition.
Pièces Originales 803 (Coignet Family.)
Pièces Originales 3008 (Villemontée Family.)


II. *Printed Primary Sources*

*Articles accordez par le Roy à ses subjets de la ville de La Rochelle.* Rouen: Imprimerie
    du Petit Val, 1628.
Barbot, Amos. "Histoire de La Rochelle." Edited by Denys d'Aussy.
    *Archives historiques de la Saintonge et de l'Aunis,* 14, 17, and 18 (1886, 1889, and
    1890).
Bégon, Michel. *Mémoire sur la généralité de La Rochelle. Archives historiques de la
    Saintonge et Aunis,* 2 (1875): 9-148.
Bèze, Theodore. *Histoire ecclésiastique des églises réformées au royaume de France.* Edited
    by G. Baume and E Cunitz, 3 vols. Paris: Fischbacher, 1883-1889.
*Brève declaration des justes motifs qui ont porté les bourgeois jurez de commun, manans
    et habitans de La Rochelle à supplier leurs majestez...de remedier par octroy de leurs
    resquestes à la domination tyrannique des maire, echevins et pairs.* n.p. n.d.
Chandieu, Antoine. *La confirmation de la discipline ecclésiastique observée en églises
    réformées du royaume de France.* Geneva: 1566.
Chenu, Jean. *Recueil des antiquitez et privileges de la ville de Bourges et de plusieurs
    autres villes capitales du royaume.* Paris: 1621.
*Le coustumier général du pays, ville et gouvernement de La Rochelle.* La Rochelle: 1613.
Guillaudeau, Joseph. "Diaire." *Archives Historiques de la Saintonge et de l'Aunis,* 38
    (1908).
Haize, Jean de la. *Discours brief et veritable de ce qui s'est passe en la ville et gou-
    vernement de La Rochelle, depuis l'an 1567, jusques en l'année 1568.*

Hesnard, Louis. *Traité de l'enchantement qu'on appelle vulgairement le nouement de l'Esguillette.* La Rochelle: 1591.

La Popelinière, Lancelot du Voisin de. *Histoire de France.* 3 vols. La Rochelle: 1581.

*Lettre d'un avocat de La Rochelle escrite à un amis de la R.P.R. de present à Paris,* La Rochelle: 1622.

*Manifeste ou déclaration des églises réformées de France et souveraineté de Béarn de l'injuste persecution qui leur est faicte par les ennemis de l'estat et de leur religion.* La Rochelle: 1621.

Mornay, Philippe. *Traicté de l'église.* London: 1579.

Napier, John. *Ouverture de tous les secrets de l'Apocalypse ou revelation de S. Jean.* La Rochelle: 1603.

Quick, John. *Synodicon in Gallia Reformata.* London: 1692.

*La reduction de la ville de La Rochelle à l'obéissance du Roy ensemble les articles accordées par sa majesté aux capitaines, soldats, et habitans de ladite ville.* Rouen: Ferrand et Mallard, n.d.

Valin, R. *Nouveau commentaire sur le coutoume de La Rochelle et du pays d'Aunis.* 2 vols. La Rochelle: 1756.

Vigier, Jean. *Les coustumes du pais et duché d'Angoumois, Aunis et gouvernement de La Rochelle.* Paris: 1650.


III. *Secondary Sources*


Abray, Lorna J. *The People's Reformation, Magistrates, Clergy, and Commons in Strasbourg 1500-1598.* Ithaca: Cornell University Press, 1985.

Anderson, Michael. *Approaches to the History of the Western Family 1500-1914.* London: Macmillan Press, 1980.

Arcère, Louis-Estienne. *Histoire de la ville de La Rochelle et du pays d'Aulnis.* 2 vols. La Rochelle: R-J. Desbordes, 1756-1757.

Archer, Ian. *The Pursuit of Stability: Social Relations in Elizabethan London.* Cambridge: Cambridge University Press, 1991.

Ariès, Philippe. *L'Enfant et la vie familiale sous l'ancien régime.* Paris: Editions du Seuil, 1973.

Arnaud, Emile. *Synode général de Poitiers 1557.* Paris: Grassart, 1872.

Audiat, Louis. *Essai sur l'imprimerie en Saintonge et Aunis.* Pons: N. Texier, 1879.

Babelon, Jean-Pierre. *Henri IV.* Paris: Fayard, 1982.

Barnavi, Elie. *Le Parti de Dieu.* Louvain: Nauwelaerts, 1980.

Baumel, Jean. *Histoire d'une seigneurie du Midi de la France,* 4, "Montpellier au cours des XVIe et XVII siècles." Montpellier: Editions Causse, 1976.

Baumgartner, F.J. *Henry II King of France 1547-1559.* Durham, North Carolina: Duke University Press, 1988.

Beik, William. *Absolutism and Society in Seventeenth-Century France.* Cambridge: Cambridge University Press, 1985.

Benedict, Philip. *The Huguenot Population of France, 1600-1685.* Philadelphia: Transactions of the American Philosophical Society (Vol. 81, pt. 5), 1991. *Rouen during the Wars of Religion.* Cambridge: Cambridge University Press, 1981.

Benedict, Philip, ed. *Cities and Social Change in Early Modern France.* London: Unwin Hyman, 1989.

Bergin, Joseph. *The Rise of Richelieu.* New Haven, Conn.: Yale University Press, 1991.

Bonald, L.G.A. *Demonstration philosophique du principe constitutif de la société*. 1875; rpt. Paris: J. Vrin, 1985.

Bonney, Richard. *Political Change in France Under Richelieu and Mazarin 1624-1661*. Oxford: Oxford University Press, 1978.

Bornert, Réné. *La Réforme protestante du culte à Strasbourg au XVIe siècle (1523-1598)*. Leiden: E. J. Brill, 1981. (Vol. 28 in *Studies in Medieval and Reformation Thought*.)

Bosher, John. "The Political and Religious Origins of La Rochelle's Primacy in Trade with New France, 1627-1685." *French History* 7 (1993): 286-312.

Brady, Thomas A., Jr. *Ruling Class, Regime, and Reformation in Strasbourg*. Leiden: E.J. Brill, 1978. (Vol. 22 in *Studies in Medieval and Reformation Thought*.)

Briggs, Robin. *Communities of Belief: Cultural and Social Tension in Early Modern France*. Oxford: Oxford University Press, 1989.

Cabantous, Alain. *Le ciel dans la mer: Christianisme et civilisation maritime XVIe-XIXe siècle*. Paris: Fayard, 1990. *Les côtes barbares: Pilleurs d'épaves et sociétés littorales en France 1680-1830*. Paris: Fayard, 1993. "Espace Maritime et Mentalités Religieuses en France Aux XVIIe et XVIII Siècles." *Mentalities/Mentalités* 1 (1982): 4-12.

Callot, P.-S. *Jean Guiton Maire de La Rochelle et le siège de 1628*. La Rochelle: Quartier Latin, 1967.

Camporesi, Piero. *Bread of Dreams: Food and Fantasy in Early Modern Europe*. Chicago: University of Chicago Press, 1989.

Chevalier, Bernard. *Les bonnes villes de France du XIVe au XVIe siècle*. Paris: Aubier Montaigne, 1982.

Chevalier, Bernard and R. Sauzet, eds. *Les réformes: enracinement socio-culturel*. Paris: Editions de la Maisnie, 1985.

Clarke, Jack. *Huguenot Warrior: The Life and Times of Henri de Rohan, 1579-1638*. The Hague: M. Nijhoff, 1966.

Colle, Robert. *Saintonge Mystérieuse Aunis Insolite*. La Rochelle: Editons Rupella, 1976.

Collins, James. *The State in Early Modern France*. Cambridge: Cambridge University Press, 1995.

Collomp, Alain. *La Maison du père. Famille et village en Haute-Provence aux XVIIe et XVIIIe siècles*. Paris: Presses Universitaires de France, 1983.

Corbin, Alain. *The Foul and the Fragrant*. Cambridge, Mass.: Harvard University Press, 1986. *The Lure of the Sea*. Cambridge: Polity Press, 1994. *The Village of Cannibals*. Cambridge, Mass.: Harvard University Press, 1992.

Coutant, Bernard. *La Rochelle essais sur la naissance d'un quartier 1628-1689*. La Rochelle: Quartier Latin, n.d. *La Rochelle le vieux marché, la fontaine du pilori, les rues du Minage et Gargoulleau*. n.p.n.d. *La Rochelle le quartier Saint Nicolas*, La Rochelle: Imprimeur Père Coutant, 1981.

Croix, Alain. *La Bretagne aux 16e et 17e siècles: la vie, la mort, la foi*. 2 vols. Paris: Maloine, 1981

Crouzet, Denis. *Les guerriers de Dieu: la violence au temps des troubles de religion*. 2 vols. Seyssel: Champ Vallon, 1990.

Crozet, Réné. *Villes d'entre Loire et Gironde*. Paris: Presses Universitaires de France, 1949.

Delafosse, Marcel, ed. *Histoire de La Rochelle*. Toulouse: Privat, 1985.

Delayant, L. *Histoire du département de la Charente-Inférieure*. La Rochelle: H. Petit, 1872. *Histoire des Rochelais*. 2 vols. La Rochelle: A. Siret, 1870.

Delumeau, Jean. *Naissance et affirmation de la Réforme*. Paris: Presses Universitaires de France, 1965. *La peur en occident*. Paris: Fayard, 1978.

Denis, Philippe and Jean Rott. *Jean Morély et l'utopie d'une démocratie dans l'église*. Geneva: Droz, 1993.

Desgraves, Louis. "Aspects des controverses entre catholiques et protestants dans le Sud-Ouest entre 1580 et 1630." *Annales du Midi* 75 (1964): 153-187. *L'imprimerie à La Rochelle*. vol. 2, *Les Haultin 1571-1623*. Geneva: Droz, 1960.

Devlin, Judith. *The Superstitious Mind: French Peasants and the Supernatural in the Nineteenth Century*. New Haven, Conn.: Yale University Press, 1987.

Dez, Pierre. *Histoire des protestants et des églises réformées du Poitou*. La Rochelle: Imprimerie de l'Ouest, 1936.

D'Huisseau, J. *La discipline des églises réformées de France*. Geneva: 1666.

Diefendorf, Barbara. *Beneath the Cross: Catholics and Huguenots in Sixteenth-Century Paris*. Oxford: Oxford University Press, 1991. *The Politics of Patrimony: Paris City Councillors in the Sixteenth Century*. Princeton: Princeton University Press, 1983.

Diefendorf, Barbara and Carla Hesse, eds. *Culture and Identity in Early Modern Europe 1500-1800*. Ann Arbor, Mich.: University of Michigan Press, 1993.

Donzelot, Jacques. *La Police des familles*. Paris: Editions de Minuit, 1977.

Doucet, R. *Les institutions de France au XVIe siècle*. 2 vols. Paris: Editions A. et J. Picard et Cie., 1948.

Doussinet, Raymond. *Les travaux et les jeux en veille Saintonge*. La Rochelle: Editions Rupella, 1967.

Droz, E. *L'imprimerie à La Rochelle*, vol. 1, *Barthélémy Berton 1563-1573*. Geneva: Droz, 1960. *L'imprimerie à La Rochelle*, vol. 3, *La veuve Berton et Jean Portau 1573-1589*. Geneva: Droz, 1960.

Dubourg, Jacques. *Les guerres de religion dans le sud-ouest*. Bordeaux: Editions de Sud-Ouest, 1992.

Duby, Georges and Jacques Le Goff, eds. *Famille et parenté dans l'occident médiéval*. Rome: Ecole Française de Rome, 1977.

Duke, Alastair. "The Face of Popular Religious Dissent in the Low Countries, 1520-1530." *Journal of Ecclesiastical History* 36 (1975): 41-67.

Dupont, M. *Histoire de La Rochelle*. La Rochelle: Mareschal, 1830.

Durand, Yves, ed., *Hommage à Roland Mousnier, clientèles et fidélités en europe à l'époque moderne*. Paris: Presses Universitaires de France, 1981.

Durston, Christopher. *The Family in the English Revolution*. London: Basil Blackwell, 1989.

Dyvorne, Paul. *Folklore Saintongeais*. Bordeaux: Editions Delmas, 1935.

Estèbe, J. and B. Volger. "La genèse d'une société protestante: étude comparée de quelques registres consistoriaux Languedociens et Palatins vers 1600." *Annales E.S.C.* 31 (1976): 362-388. Fatio, Olivier, ed., *Confessions et catéchismes de la foi réformée*. Geneva: Labor et Fides, 1986.

Faust, Katherine. "A Beleagured Society: Protestant Families in La Rochelle, 1628-1685." Ph.D. Diss. Northwestern University, 1980.

Favre, L. *Glossaire du Poitou de la Saintonge et de l'Aunis*. Niort: Robin et Favre, 1867.

Ferraro, Joanne. "Oligarchs, Protestors, and the Republic of Venice: The `Revolution of the Discontents' in Brescia, 1644-1645," *Journal of Modern History*, 60 (1988): 627-653.

Flandrin, Jean-Louis. *Familles, parenté, maison, sexualité dans l'ancienne société*. 1976; rpt. Paris: Editions du Seuil, 1984.

Foisil, Madeleine. *La révolte des nu-pieds et les révoltes Normandes de 1639*. Paris: Presses Universitaires de France, 1970.

Forster, Robert. *Merchants, Landlords, Magistrates, The Depont Family in Eighteenth-Century France.* Baltimore: Johns Hopkins University Press, 1980.

Fracard, M.-L. *La Fin de l'ancien régime à Niort.* Paris: Desclée de Brouwer, 1956.

Frigo, Daniela. *Il padre di famiglia governo della casa e governo civile nella tradizione dell'"economica" tra cinque e seicento.* Rome: Bulzoni, 1985

Fumagalli, Vito. *Landscapes of Fear: Perceptions of Nature and The City in the Middle Ages.* Cambridge: Polity Press, 1994.

Gallimard, K. "Quelques exemples régionaux du vocabulaire maritime à La Rochelle," *Aguiaine* 22 (1990): 433-440.

Gambrelle, Fabienne and M. Trebitsch, eds., *Révolte et société.* Paris: Publications de la Sorbonne, 1989.

Garrison, Janine. *L'Homme protestant.* Paris: Hachette, 1980. *Les protestants au XVIe siècle.* Paris: Fayard, 1988. *Protestants du Midi 1559-1598.* Toulouse: Privat, 1980.

Gigon, S.-C. *La révolte de la gabelle en Guyenne 1548-1549.* Paris: Champion, 1906.

Giry, A. *Les établissements de Rouen, études sur l'histoire des institutions municipales.* Vol. 1. Paris: F. Vieweg, 1883.

Goubert, Pierre. "Les officiers royaux des présidiaux, bailliages et élections dans la société française du XVIIe siècle." *XVIIe siècle,* 42-43 (1959): 54-75.

Graham, W.F., ed. *Later Calvinism International Perspectives* Kirksville, Missouri: Sixteenth Century Journal Publishers, 1994.

Grenédan, J. du Plessis de. *Histoire de l'autorité paternelle dans l'ancien droit français.* Paris: A. Rousseau, 1900.

Greyerz, Kaspar von. *The Late City Reformation in Germany, the Case of Colmar 1552-1628.* Wiesbaden: F. Steiner Verlag, 1980.

Greyerz, Kaspar von, ed., *Religion, Politics, and Social Protest.* London: George Allen & Unwin, 1984.

Grillon, P. *Les papiers de Richelieu.* 6 vols. Paris: Pedrone, 1975-1985.

Grinberg, Martine. "Carnival et société urbaine XIVe-XVIe siècles: le royaume dans la ville." *Ethnologie française* 4 (1974): 215-245.

Guenée, Bernard. *Tribunaux et gens de justice dans le bailliage de Senlis à la fin du moyen age.* Strasbourg: Publications de la Faculté des Lettres, 1963.

Hanlon, Gregory. *Confession and Community in Seventeenth-Century France.* Philadelphia: University of Pennsylvania Press, 1993.

Hareven, T.K., ed. *Family and Kin in Urban Communities 1700-1930.* New York: New Viewpoints, 1977.

Heller, Henry. *The Conquest of Poverty, the Calvinist Revolt in Sixteenth-Century France.* Leiden: E.J. Brill, 1986. (Vol. 35 in *Studies in Medieval and Reformation Thought*) *Iron and Blood: Civil Wars in Sixteenth-Century France.* Montreal: McGill-Queen's University Press, 1991.

Hoffman, Philip. *Church and Community in the Diocese of Lyon.* New Haven, Conn.: Yale University Press, 1984.

Holt, Mack. *The French Wars of Religion.* Cambridge: Cambridge University Press, 1995 "Wine, Community and Reformation in Sixteenth-Century Burgundy." *Past and Present,* 138 (1993): 58-93.

Holt, Mack, ed. *Society and Institutions in Early Modern France.* Athens, Gerorgia: University of Georgia Press, 1991.

Hunt, David. *Parents and Children in History. The Psychology of Family Life in Early Modern France.* New York: Basic Books, 1970.

Huppert, George. *Les Bourgeois Gentilhommes, an Essay on the Definition of Elites in Renaissance France.* Chicago: University of Chicago Press, 1977.

Jacquin, Dominique and Philippe Jacquin, eds. *Récits et contes populaires d'Aunis et Saintonge*. Malesherbes: Editions Gallimard, 1979.

James, Mervyn. *Family, Lineage, and Civil Society, A Study of Society, Politics, and Mentality in the Durham Region 1500-1640*. Oxford: Clarendon Press, 1974.

Juline-Labruyère, François. *Paysans charentais*. 2 vols. La Rochelle: Editions Rupella, 1982

Kaplan, Steven L., ed. *Understanding Popular Culture*. Berlin: Mouton, 1984.

Kelley, Donald R. *The Beginning of Ideology, Consciousness and Society in the French Reformation*. Cambridge: Cambridge University Press, 1981.

Kent, D.V. and F.W. *Neighbours and Neighbourhood in Renaissance Florence*. Locust Valley, New York: J. Augustin, 1982.

Kettering, Sharon. *Judicial Politics and Urban Revolt in Seventeenth-Century France. The Parlement of Aix 1629- 1659*. Princeton: Princeton University Press, 1978. *Patrons, Brokers, and Clients in Seventeenth-Century France*. Oxford: Oxford University Press, 1986.

Kingdon, Robert M. *Geneva and the Coming of the Wars 'of Religion in France 1555-1563*. Geneva: Droz, 1956. (*Travaux d'humanisme et renaissance*, vol. 22) *Geneva and the Consolidation of the French Protestant Movement 1564-1572*. Geneva: Droz, 1967. (*Travaux d'humanisme et renaissance*, vol. 92) "The Political Resistence of the Calvinists in France and the Low Countries." *Church History*, 27 (1958): 220-233.

Kintz, Jean-Pierre. *La société Strasbourgeoise 1560-1650*. Paris: Editions Ophrys, 1984.

Knecht, R.J. *Francis I*. Cambridge: Cambridge University Press, 1984.

Kselman, Thomas, ed. *Belief in History*. Notre Dame, Indiana: University of Notre Dame Press, 1991.

Lebigre, Arlette. *Les grands jours d'Auvergne, désordres et répression au XVIIe siècle*. Paris: Hachette, 1976.

Léonard, Emile. *Histoire générale du protestantisme*. 2 vols. Paris: Presses Universitaires de France, 1961. *Le protestant français*. Paris: Presses Universitaires de France, 1953.

Leproux, Marc. *Du berceau à la tombe: contributions au folklore charentais*. Paris: Presses Universitaires de France, 1959.

Lestocquoy, J. *Etudes d'histoire urbaine, villes et abbayes, Arras au moyen age*. Arras: Memoires de la Commission Départmentale des monuments historiques du Pas de Calais, 1966. *Les villes de Flandre et d'Italie sous le gouvernement des patriciens*. Paris: Presses Universitaires de France, 1952.

Lièvre, Auguste. *Histoire des protestants et des églises réformées du Poitou*. 2 vols. Paris: Grassart, 1856.

Ligou, D. *Le protestantisme en France de 1598 à 1715*. Paris: Société d'Edition d'Enseignement Supérieur, 1968.

Livet, Georges and B. Vogler, eds. *Pouvoir, ville et société en Europe 1650-1750*. Paris: Editions Ophrys, 1983.

Luc, Jean-Noel. *La Charente-Maritime: L'Aunis et la Saintonge des origines à nos jours*. Saint-Jean-d'Angély: Editions Bordessoules, 1981.

Manot, S. *Folklore vivant en Aunis, Saintonge et Angoumois*. Niort: Imprimerie Nicolas-Imbert, 1970.

Marion, M. *Dictionnaire des institutions de la France XVIIe- XVIIIe siècles*. 1923; rpt. Paris: A. et J. Picard, 1989.

Massiou, M.D. *Histoire politique, civile et religieuse de la Saintonge et de l'Aunis*. 6 vols. Paris: E. Pannier, 1836- 1838.

McNeill, John T. *The History and Character of Calvinism.* New York: Oxford University Press, 1954.

Mehl, Roger. *Explication de la confession de foi de La Rochelle.* Cahors: A. Coueslant, 1959.

Méjan, F. *Discipline de l'église réformée de France.* Paris: Editions "Je Sers," 1947.

Mentzer, Raymond. "*Disciplina nervus ecclesiae:* The Calvinist Reform of Morals at Nîmes." *The Sixteenth Century Journal* 18 (1987): 89-115.

Mentzer, Raymond, ed. *Sin and the Calvinists: Morals Control and the Consistory in the Reformed Tradition.* Kirksville, Missouri: Sixteenth Century Journal Publishers, 1994.

Mettam, Roger. *Power and Faction in Louis XIV's France.* New York: Basil Blackwell, 1988.

Meyer, Judith. *Reformation in La Rochelle: Tradition and Change in Early Modern Europe 1500-1568.* Geneva: Droz, 1996. (*Travaux d'humanisme et renaissance,* vol. 298.)

Moote, A. Lloyd. *Louis XIII, The Just.* Berkeley: University of California Press, 1989.

Mours, Samuel. *Le protestantisme en France au XVIe siècle.* Paris: Librairie Protestante, 1959.

Mousnier, Roland. *Les Institutions de la France sous la monarchie absolue.* 2 vols. Paris: Presses Universitiares de France, 1974.

Nichols, David. "The Nature of Popular Heresy in France, 1520- 1542." *The Historical Journal* 26 (1983): 261-275. "Social Change and Early Protestantism in France: Normandy, 1520-1562." *European Studies Review* 10 (1980): 279-308.

Noguès, J.-L.-M. *Les moeurs d'autrefois en Saintonge et en Aunis.* Saintes: Secretariat de la Commission des Arts, 1891.

Nussdorfer, Laurie. "The Vacant See: Ritual and Protest in Early Modern Rome," *Sixteenth Century Journal,* 18 (1987): 173-189.

Ozment, Steven E. *The Reformation in the Cities.* New Haven: Yale University Press, 1975. *When Fathers Ruled, Family Life in Reformation Europe.* Cambridge, Mass.: Harvard University Press, 1983.

Papy, Louis. *La côte Atlantique de la Loire à la Gironde.* Bordeaux: Editions Delmas, 1941.

Pannier, Jacques. *Les origines de la confession de foi et la discipline des églises réformées de France.* Paris: Félix Alcan, 1936.

Pardailhé-Galabrun, Annik. *La Naissance de l'intime.* Paris: Presses Universitaires de France, 1988.

Parker, David. *La Rochelle and the French Monarchy, Conflict and Order in Seventeenth-Century France.* London: Royal Historical Society, 1980.

Pérouas, Louis. *Le diocèse de La Rochelle de 1648 à 1724.* Paris: S.E.V.P.E.N., 1964.

Pettegree, Andrew, ed., *The Reformation of the Parishes.* Manchester: Manchester University Press, 1993.

Pillorget, René. *Les mouvements insurrectionnels de Provence entre 1596 et 1715.* Paris: Editions A. Pedone, 1975.

Po-Chia Hsia, R. *Society and Religion in Munster 1535-1618.* New Haven: Yale University Press, 1984.

Po-Chia Hsia, R., ed. *The German People and the Reformation.* Ithaca: Cornell University Press, 1988.

Prestwich, Menna, ed. *International Calvinism 1541-1715.* Oxford: Clarendon Press, 1985.

Pugh, Wilma. "Catholics, Protestants, and Testamentary Charity in Seventeenth-Century Lyon and Nîmes." *French Historical Studies* 11 (1980): 479-504.

Rézeau, Pierre. *Dictionnaire du français régional de Poitou-Charentes et de Vendée.* Paris: Editions Bonneton, 1990.

Richet, Denis. *De la Réforme à la Révolution: Etudes sur la France moderne.* Paris: Aubier, 1991.

Rizzi, Franco, and Gérard Delille, eds. *Le modèle familial européen, normes, déviances, contrôle du pouvoir.* Rome: Ecole française de Rome, 1986.

Rublack, Hans-Christophe. *Eine burgerliche Reformation: Nordlingen.* Gutersloh: Gutersloher Verlagshaus Mohn, 1982.

Sauzet, Robert. *Contre-réforme et réforme catholique en bas Languedoc le diocèse de Nîmes au XVIIe siècle.* Louvain: Nauwelaerts, 1979.

Savatier, Michel. *Contes et légendes de l'île d'Oléron.* Paris: Temps Présent, 1964.

Schneider, Robert A. *Public Life in Toulouse 1463-1789.* Ithaca, Cornell University Press, 1989.

Schnucker, Robert, ed. *Calviniana: Ideas and Influence of Jean Calvin.* Kirksville, Missouri: Sixteenth Century Journal Publishers, 1988.

Schilling, Heinz. *Civic Calvinism in Northwestern Germany and the Netherlands.* Kirksville, Missouri: Sixteenth Century Journal Publishers, 1991. *Religion, Political Culture and the Emergence of Early Modern Society.* Leiden: E.J. Brill, 1992. (Vol. 50 in *Studies in Medieval and Reformation Thought.*)

Sébillot, Paul. *Le folklore de France.* 4 vols. Paris: Librairie Orientale, 1904-1907. *Légendes, croyances et superstitions de la mer.* 2 vols. Paris: Bibliothèque Charpentier, 1886.

Sée, Henri. *Les idées politiques en France au XVIIe siècle.* Paris: M. Girard, 1923.

Senechal, Roberta. *The Sociogenesis of a Race Riot.* Chicago: University of Illinois Press, 1990.

Serr, Georges. "Henry de Rohan: Son rôle dans le parti protestant de 1617 à 1622," in J. Allier, ed., *Divers aspects de la Réforme aux XVIe et XVIIe siècles.* Paris: Société de l'Histoire du Protestantisme Français, 1975.

Sutherland, N.M. *The Huguenot Struggle for Recognition.* New Haven, Conn.: Yale University Press, 1980.

Strauss, Gerald. "Protestant Dogma and City Government: The Case of Nuremberg." *Past and Present* 36 (1967): 38-58.

Talbert, Jean and R. Crozet. *Petite Histoire du Poitou, Angoumois, Aunis et Saintonge.* Paris: Delalain, 1936.

TeBrake, William. *Medieval Frontier: Culture and Ecology in Rijnland.* College Station, Texas: Texas A & M University Press, 1985.

Thompson, J.W. *The Wars of Religion in France 1559-1576.* New York: F. Ungar, 1957.

Tolley, Bruce. *Pastors and Parishioners in Wurttemberg During The Late Reformation 1581-1621.* Stanford: Stanford University Press, 1995.

Toulgouat, Pierre. *Voisinage et solidarité dans l'Europe du moyen âge.* Paris: Maisonneuve, 1981.

*La Tradition en Poitou et Charentes.* Sociéte d'ethnographie nationale et d'art popularie. Paris: Tradition Nationale, 1897.

Trocmé, Etienne. "La Rochelle de 1560 à 1628. Tableau d'une société réformée du temps de guerres de religion." Thèse, Bachelier en Théologie. Faculté libre de théologie protestante, Paris: 1950. "L'Eglise reformée de La Rochelle jusqu'en 1628." *Bulletin Société de l'histoire du protestantisme français,* 99 (1952): 133-199. "Reflexions sur le séparatisme rochelais 1568-1628." *Bulletin Société de l'histoire du protestantisme français,* 122 (1976): 203-210.

Trocmé, Etienne and M. Delafosse. *Le commerce rochelais de la fin du XVe siècle au début du XVIIe.* Paris: Armand Colin, 1952.

Vaux de Foletier, F. de. *Histoire d'Aunis et de Saintonge.* Paris: Boivin, 1929.

Veillot, Thierry. *La ville blanche.* La Rochelle: Editions Rupella, 1992.

Wall, Richard, *et. al.*, eds. *Family Forms in Historic Europe.* Cambridge: Cambridge University Press, 1983.

Westrich, Sal A. *The Ormée of Bordeaux, A Revolution during the Fronde.* Baltimore: Johns Hopins University Press, 1972.

Wheaton, Robert, and Tamara Hareven, eds. *Family and Sexuality in French History.* Philadelphia: University of Pennsylvania Press, 1980.

Williams, Peter. "Constituting Class and Gender: A Social History of the Home 1700-1901." In *Class and Space The Making of Urban Society,* edited by Nigel Thrift and Peter Williams. London: Routledge & Kegan Paul, 1987, 154-206.

Wood, James. *The Army of the King: Warfare, Soldiers, and Society during the Wars of Religion in France, 1562-1576.* Cambridge: Cambridge University Press, 1996.

Zeller, Gaston. *Les institutions de la France au XVIe siècle.* Paris: Presses Universitaires de France, 1948.

# INDEXES

# 1. INDEX OF PERSONAL NAMES

# 2. INDEX OF PLACE NAMES

# 3. INDEX OF SUBJECTS

*Ligue*, Catholic, 244
*Ligue* wars, impact on La Rochelle, 241, 246

Marine commerce, scope of rochelais trade, 22-23
Marshes, impact on rochelais mentalities, 10-18
Mayoralty, in La Rochelle, administrative duties of mayors, 31; elections of mayors, 31; legal powers of, 32; mayor's court, 64-66; purview of mayor's court, 41-42, 42n; restoration of mayor's court by Louis XIII, 368-369, 393; service of court as agency of local Counter-Reformation, 391-410

Militia, civic, in La Rochelle, arsenals for, 64-65; battles against forces of royal governor, 85-86; bourgeois participation in as political act, 289-290; company commanders, 66-67, 336-337; key role in support of 1614 bourgeois revolt, 272-273; mayor's role in, 64; organization, 37, 64, 208, 247, 275-276; recruitment, 67; size, 32; under Catholic control after 1628, 383; used to intimidate residents of rochelais hinterland, 246
Minimes, female religious order of, in La Rochelle, 387
Moral economies, formation and structure of, 141, 292-293, 293n, 296

Nobles, absence of in La Rochelle, 29-30
Nuns, scandalous behavior of in La Rochelle, 111-112

Oratorians, in La Rochelle, 386, 388

Parlement of Paris, 33, 71-72, 120, 144-145, 303-304
Passion plays, in La Rochelle, 109
Peace of Amboise, 194
Peace of Beaulieu, effects in La Rochelle, 219
Peace of Longjumeau, effects in La Rochelle, 205
Peace of Saint Germain, effects in La Rochelle, 208
Poor relief, in La Rochelle, 136-137; under strictures of Counter-Reformation, 400-401
Presidial court of La Rochelle, challenges to consistory, 137-146; dissident members back 1614 bourgeois revolt, 259-260; *insinuations* before as local legal custom, 105-106; political infighting among members, 260, 264; reconfigured and restaffed by Louis XIII after siege of 1628, 367-368; repression of religious dissent by, 120; structure and operations of, 59, 102; types of cases heard annually (1565), 103-105
Printing, in La Rochelle, 131-132; and rochelais religious politics, 173-183
Psalms, importance in spiritual life of Rochelais, 116-117

Rebellions, popular and urban, methods for study of, 277-278
Recollets, religious order of, in La Rochelle, 387
Reformation, French, 4; in La Rochelle, origins of 109-120; clerical advocates of, 121-132; disciplinary institutions created by 132-146; factors promoting local spread of, 185-186; impact on civic politics, 185-210, 335-353; unpopular in rochelais hinterland and among *vignerons*, 40-41
Religieuses Hospitalières, religious order of, in La Rochelle, 387
Royal governor of La Rochelle, functions and entourage of, 32-33

Salt harvesting, impact on local economies and mentalities, 17-18; working conditions for *sauniers*, 17, 42-43, 84
Scotsmen, in La Rochelle, 6, 131-132, 181-182

# STUDIES IN MEDIEVAL
# AND REFORMATION THOUGHT

EDITED BY HEIKO A. OBERMAN

1. DOUGLASS, E. J. D. *Justification in Late Medieval Preaching.* 2nd ed. 1989
2. WILLIS, E. D. *Calvin's Catholic Christology.* 1966 *out of print*
3. POST, R. R. *The Modern Devotion.* 1968 *out of print*
4. STEINMETZ, D. C. *Misericordia Dei.* The Theology of Johannes von Staupitz. 1968 *out of print*
5. O'MALLEY, J. W. *Giles of Viterbo on Church and Reform.* 1968 *out of print*
6. OZMENT, S. E. *Homo Spiritualis.* The Anthropology of Tauler, Gerson and Luther. 1969
7. PASCOE, L. B. *Jean Gerson: Principles of Church Reform.* 1973 *out of print*
8. HENDRIX, S. H. *Ecclesia in Via.* Medieval Psalms Exegesis and the *Dictata super Psalterium* (1513-1515) of Martin Luther. 1974
9. TREXLER, R. C. *The Spiritual Power.* Republican Florence under Interdict. 1974
10. TRINKAUS, Ch. with OBERMAN, H. A. (eds.). *The Pursuit of Holiness.* 1974 *out of print*
11. SIDER, R. J. *Andreas Bodenstein von Karlstadt.* 1974
12. HAGEN, K. *A Theology of Testament in the Young Luther.* 1974
13. MOORE, Jr., W. L. *Annotatiunculae D. Iohanne Eckio Praelectore.* 1976
14. OBERMAN, H. A. with BRADY, Jr., Th. A. (eds.). *Itinerarium Italicum.* Dedicated to Paul Oskar Kristeller. 1975
15. KEMPFF, D. *A Bibliography of Calviniana.* 1959-1974. 1975 *out of print*
16. WINDHORST, C. *Täuferisches Taufverständnis.* 1976
17. KITTELSON, J. M. *Wolfgang Capito.* 1975
18. DONNELLY, J. P. *Calvinism and Scholasticism in Vermigli's Doctrine of Man and Grace.* 1976
19. LAMPING, A. J. *Ulrichus Velenus (Oldřich Velenský) and his Treatise against the Papacy.* 1976
20. BAYLOR, M. G. *Action and Person.* Conscience in Late Scholasticism and the Young Luther. 1977
21. COURTENAY, W. J. *Adam Wodeham.* 1978
22. BRADY, Jr., Th. A. *Ruling Class, Regime and Reformation at Strasbourg, 1520-1555.* 1978
23. KLAASSEN, W. *Michael Gaismair.* 1978
24. BERNSTEIN, A. E. *Pierre d'Ailly and the Blanchard Affair.* 1978
25. BUCER, Martin. *Correspondance.* Tome I (Jusqu'en 1524). Publié par J. Rott. 1979
26. POSTHUMUS MEYJES, G. H. M. *Jean Gerson et l'Assemblée de Vincennes (1329).* 1978
27. VIVES, Juan Luis. *In Pseudodialecticos.* Ed. by Ch. Fantazzi. 1979
28. BORNERT, R. *La Réforme Protestante du Culte à Strasbourg au XVIᵉ siècle (1523-1598).* 1981
29. SEBASTIAN CASTELLIO. *De Arte Dubitandi.* Ed. by E. Feist Hirsch. 1981
30. BUCER, Martin. *Opera Latina.* Vol I. Publié par C. Augustijn, P. Fraenkel, M. Lienhard. 1982
31. BÜSSER, F. *Wurzeln der Reformation in Zürich.* 1985 *out of print*
32. FARGE, J. K. *Orthodoxy and Reform in Early Reformation France.* 1985
33, 34. BUCER, Martin. *Etudes sur les relations de Bucer avec les Pays-Bas.* I. Etudes; II. Documents. Par J. V. Pollet. 1985
35. HELLER, H. *The Conquest of Poverty.* The Calvinist Revolt in Sixteenth Century France. 1986

36. MEERHOFF, K. *Rhétorique et poétique au XVI<sup>e</sup> siècle en France.* 1986
37. GERRITS, G. H. *Inter timorem et spem.* Gerard Zerbolt of Zutphen. 1986
38. ANGELO POLIZIANO. *Lamia.* Ed. by A. Wesseling. 1986
39. BRAW, C. *Bücher im Staube.* Die Theologie Johann Arndts in ihrem Verhältnis zur Mystik. 1986
40. BUCER, Martin. *Opera Latina.* Vol. II. Enarratio in Evangelion Iohannis (1528, 1530, 1536). Publié par I. Backus. 1988
41. BUCER, Martin. *Opera Latina.* Vol. III. Martin Bucer and Matthew Parker: Florilegium Patristicum. Edition critique. Publié par P. Fraenkel. 1988
42. BUCER, Martin. *Opera Latina.* Vol. IV. Consilium Theologicum Privatim Conscriptum. Publié par P. Fraenkel. 1988
43. BUCER, Martin. *Correspondance.* Tome II (1524-1526). Publié par J. Rott. 1989
44. RASMUSSEN, T. *Inimici Ecclesiae.* Das ekklesiologische Feindbild in Luthers "Dictata super Psalterium" (1513-1515) im Horizont der theologischen Tradition. 1989
45. POLLET, J. *Julius Pflug et la crise religieuse dans l'Allemagne du XVI<sup>e</sup> siècle.* Essai de synthèse biographique et théologique. 1990
46. BUBENHEIMER, U. *Thomas Müntzer.* Herkunft und Bildung. 1989
47. BAUMAN, C. *The Spiritual Legacy of Hans Denck.* Interpretation and Translation of Key Texts. 1991
48. OBERMAN, H. A. and JAMES, F. A., III (eds.). in cooperation with SAAK, E. L. *Via Augustini.* Augustine in the Later Middle Ages, Renaissance and Reformation: Essays in Honor of Damasus Trapp. 1991 *out of print*
49. SEIDEL MENCHI, S. *Erasmus als Ketzer.* Reformation und Inquisition im Italien des 16. Jahrhunderts. 1993
50. SCHILLING, H. *Religion, Political Culture, and the Emergence of Early Modern Society.* Essays in German and Dutch History. 1992
51. DYKEMA, P. A. and OBERMAN, H. A. (eds.). *Anticlericalism in Late Medieval and Early Modern Europe.* 2nd ed. 1994
52, 53. KRIEGER, Chr. and LIENHARD, M. (eds.). *Martin Bucer and Sixteenth Century Europe.* Actes du colloque de Strasbourg (28-31 août 1991). 1993
54. SCREECH, M. A. *Clément Marot: A Renaissance Poet discovers the World.* Lutheranism, Fabrism and Calvinism in the Royal Courts of France and of Navarre and in the Ducal Court of Ferrara. 1994
55. GOW, A. C. *The Red Jews: Antisemitism in an Apocalyptic Age, 1200-1600.* 1995
56. BUCER, Martin. *Correspondance.* Tome III (1527-1529). Publié par Chr. Krieger et J. Rott. 1989
57. SPIJKER, W. VAN 'T. *The Ecclesiastical Offices in the Thought of Martin Bucer.* Translated by J. Vriend (text) and L.D. Bierma (notes). 1996
58. GRAHAM, M.F. *The Uses of Reform.* 'Godly Discipline' and Popular Behavior in Scotland and Beyond, 1560-1610. 1996
59. AUGUSTIJN, C. *Erasmus. Der Humanist als Theologe und Kirchenreformer.* 1996
60. McCOOG SJ, T. M. *The Society of Jesus in Ireland, Scotland, and England 1541-1588.* 'Our Way of Proceeding?' 1996
61. FISCHER, N. und KOBELT-GROCH, M. (Hrsg.). *Außenseiter zwischen Mittelalter und Neuzeit.* Festschrift für Hans-Jürgen Goertz zum 60. Geburtstag. 1997
62. NIEDEN, M. *Organum Deitatis.* Die Christologie des Thomas de Vio Cajetan. 1997
63. BAST, R.J. *Honor Your Fathers.* Catechisms and the Emergence of a Patriarchal Ideology in Germany, c. 1400-1600. 1997
64. ROBBINS, K.C. *City on the Ocean Sea: La Rochelle, 1530-1650.* Urban Society, Religion, and Politics on the French Atlantic Frontier. 1997

Prospectus available on request

**KONINKLIJKE BRILL — P.O.B. 9000 — 2300 PA LEIDEN — THE NETHERLANDS**